ALSO BY MICHAEL KAZIN

*Barons of Labor: The San Francisco Building
Trades and Union Power in the Progressive Era*

The Populist Persuasion: An American History

America Divided: The Civil War of the 1960s
(with Maurice Isserman)

A GODLY HERO

A Godly Hero

THE LIFE OF
WILLIAM JENNINGS BRYAN

Michael Kazin

ALFRED A. KNOPF   NEW YORK

THIS IS A BORZOI BOOK
PUBLISHED BY ALFRED A. KNOPF

Copyright © 2006 by Michael Kazin
All rights reserved. Published in the United States by Alfred A. Knopf,
a division of Random House, Inc., New York, and in Canada by
Random House of Canada Limited, Toronto.

Knopf, Borzoi Books, and the colophon are
registered trademarks of Random House, Inc.

ISBN 0-375-41135-6

Manufactured in the United States of America

For Beth, of course

CONTENTS

ACKNOWLEDGMENTS

In the mid-1990s, when this book was just an idea, I asked a distinguished Washington journalist what he thought of it. "People will not understand," he responded with pitch-perfect disdain. Fortunately, I found a number of people and institutions who did grasp what I was trying to write and made it possible for me to write it.

The Woodrow Wilson International Center for Scholars—particularly Michael Lacey, its former grand impresario of United States studies—funded a year of research and sublime scholarly fellowship. Georgetown University provided a generous grant that helped me complete the leisurely crawl through the archives. My colleagues at the GU history department first welcomed me and then reminded me how much I had left to learn. The John Simon Guggenheim Memorial Foundation awarded the fellowship that enabled me to complete the first draft of the manuscript.

Other historians, archivists, and authors supplied hints, details, and wisdom. Richard John planted the idea in my mind during the first Gulf War, when our adjoining offices looked out on Colonial Williamsburg. Neil Basen sent along key Populist documents, Andy Rieser tutored me about the mysteries of Chautauqua, and David Brion Davis told me a few things about his Bryan-loving grandfather. Karl Moore of the Illinois State Archives and Harold Boyles of the Marion County Genealogical and Historical Society helped me understand the history of Salem during Bryan's youth. Barbara Sommer shared her work about Mary Baird Bryan, and Arva Parks sent me a thick bundle of clippings about the couple's life in Miami. Nick Hollis introduced me to several descendants of the Commoner and kept the flame of Bryan's memory flickering. Jack Randorff explained the mysteries of acoustics to a nonscientist. I am also grateful for the work and advice of the people at the Nebraska State Historical Society, the Special Collections division of the library at the University of Tennessee, Knoxville, and to Jovanna Frazier, at Georgetown's Lauinger Library. The expert and witty archivists at the Manuscript Division of the Library of Congress tolerated my presence at their tables month after month, and year after year.

This is the first book for which I had research assistants. But the resourcefulness and good humor of Siobhan McNeil, Kate Delimitros, Sarah Snyder, and Laura Wacker made me regret that I took so long to seek help.

Audiences at the University of Delaware, the University of California at Santa Barbara, Brown University, Hokkaido University, and the Georgetown University Law Center invited me to spout off about Bryan and his times. As the book began to take shape, I was able to seek correction from some of America's more gifted historians: Victoria Bissell Brown, Tony Fels, Richard Fox, Robert Johnston, Lawrence Levine, Joseph McCartin, and Katherine Kish Sklar. Jun Furuya, one of Japan's leading Americanists, offered his own critique; he also invited me to participate in several wonderful conferences.

Steve Fraser and Julie Greene made acute, encouraging comments on big chunks of the manuscript. Eric Alterman, Nick Salvatore, and Grant Wacker accepted the burden of reading the whole thing. This cliché is on the mark: their help was invaluable. I am particularly grateful to Grant for his knowledge and enthusiasm—and for welcoming a political junkie into his fellowship of religious historians.

Serious biographers of Mr. Bryan belong to a tiny, endangered species. But four were willing to inform and inspire me. No one knows more about Gilded Age Nebraska and Bryan historiography than does Robert Cherny, my old colleague from San Francisco days. Paolo Coletta, the founding father of Bryan studies and author of the fullest work about the man, drove me around Annapolis one foggy day, dropping anecdotes faster than I could jot them down. During a long Pasadena afternoon, Rudd Brown told stories about her famous grandfather and once-famous mother I could have learned nowhere else. I eagerly await her biography-memoir of her family. Larry Levine—whose first book is the smartest study of WJB ever written—is the most generous of scholars.

My agent, Sandy Dijkstra, guided me through the shoals and rapids of trade publishing with a rare combination of passion and good sense. The first piece of advice she gave me ought to be pasted above every writer's desk: "One cannot assume interest."

At Knopf, Ash Green quietly demonstrated how a great editor can bring coherence to an author's mind and thus to his work. Luba Ostashevsky responded warmly and skillfully to every anxious question and request.

Kathleen Fridella was a splendid production editor, Robert Olsson produced an elegant design, and Abby Weintraub created an arresting cover.

A few months before he died, my father bought me all three volumes of Coletta's biography and even offered to do a little research, if that would help. Stern, curious, and loving, he is with me whenever I sit down to struggle at the keyboard. My mother may not read this book, but she has always supported me in every possible way.

Danny and Maia keep me thinking and laughing at myself—and try to keep me humble. Sure, winning isn't everything, they acknowledge. But did you have to write about a guy who lost *three* times? Beth Horowitz is the wisest, most compassionate, and most seductive woman I know. Yet despite all that, she's still married to me.

❧✝❧

The Romance of Jefferson and Jesus

Next to each religion is a political opinion that is joined to it by affinity.

—Alexis de Tocqueville[1]

I fear the plutocracy of wealth, I respect the aristocracy of learning, but I thank God for the democracy of the heart that makes it possible for every human being to do something to make life worth living while he lives and the world better for his existence in it.

—William Jennings Bryan[2]

THE DAY BEFORE the election of 1896, twenty-three married couples from central Pennsylvania sent a letter of tribute to their candidate for president. They gave thanks that "divine Providence" had allowed Bryan "in splendid health and form" to wage a campaign in which he had "pilloried plutocracy . . . and revealed to the people the privileged class, in all its revolting nakedness." They praised his wife, Mary, for "risking health and life" to make "the cause of her husband, the people, her cause." Assuming he would win, they looked forward to "the redemption of a monopoly cursed people" from "the power of mammon."[3]

Bryan lost the election, as he did two subsequent campaigns for the White House. Yet this letter, one of hundreds of thousands he received that fall, suggests why we should care about him—a man who was elected to no office higher than that of congressman from Nebraska and who is best known today for prosecuting a young teacher in Tennessee who taught evolution to his students.

For many of his correspondents, Bryan was not merely a favorite politician. They believed him to be a godly hero who preached that the duty of a true Christian was to transform a nation and world plagued by the arrogance of wealth and the pain of inequality. That could only mean a radically progressive interpretation of the Gospels, so that, as the Pennsylvanians phrased it, "our gaping social wounds may be healed ... and class distinction leveled." Bryan's creed drove his three campaigns for the White House, his work for a dazzling variety of causes both secular and religious, and thirty continuous years of theatrical speechmaking throughout the nation and the world.

His energetic performances and relentless good cheer made him a wealthy celebrity whose face and voice were as familiar as anyone's in the nation. After his death, a reporter remarked that the press should build a memorial to him "because he was to the world of news what Babe Ruth is to baseball—the real drawing card."[4]

Mass appeal lifted Bryan to the top rank of American leaders, despite his failures at the ballot box. Only Theodore Roosevelt and Woodrow Wilson had a greater impact on politics and political culture during the era of reform that began in the mid-1890s and lasted until the early 1920s. Bryan wooed a following as large as that of either man, and usually more ardent. And the affection was always mutual. The historian Richard Hofstadter wrote that other leading progressives only "sensed popular feelings; Bryan embodied them."[5]

Remarkably, few loyalists abandoned him after he failed to win the presidency. Some were even glad that, without the responsibilities of state power, the man they called, oxymoronically, the Great Commoner would be free to thunder against corporate "predators" and to champion the unalloyed demands of small farmers and wage earners. In their eyes, Bryan was spiritual kin to the patriarchs and prophets who, according to Hebrews 11, "subdued kingdoms, wrought righteousness, obtained promises, [and] stopped the mouths of lions." His fame and influence depended on his adherence to a worldly faith shared by millions of citizens, one that resisted the compromises endemic to policy making.

THAT CREED married democracy and pietism in a romantic gospel that borrowed equally from Jefferson and Jesus. A leveling faith had dominated the nation's religious life since the Second Great Awakening of the early nineteenth century, which spawned thousands of new Protestant churches and made the passion of evangelicalism the common discourse of most Americans. The idea that anyone, regardless of learning or social background, could "come to Christ" dovetailed with the belief in equal rights emblazoned in the Declaration of Independence. This synthesis of evangelical Protestantism and republicanism was found in no other nation—at least not with such passionate conviction nor for such a long period of time.[6]

All Democrats honored the author of the Declaration as the founder of their party. But no one in politics could match Bryan's unstinting devotion. "Jefferson trusted the people and believed that they were the source of power and authority," he wrote to an admirer. "Jefferson's motto of equal rights to all and privileges to none is the fundamental law that governs legislation and the administration of government." Bryan yoked the legitimacy of nearly every major reform for which he campaigned to "Jeffersonian principles."[7] In a practical sense, Jefferson was more important to him than Jesus. After all, the Son of God had never uttered an opinion about the protective tariff, the gold standard, or corporate power. But Jefferson was a fierce partisan warrior and thus left an inexhaustible legacy of opinions and principles for those of a similar ideological persuasion.

Bryan gained a reputation as an agrarian rebel, and it is natural to assume that this explains his affinity for Jefferson. The squire of Monticello had famously intoned that "those who labor in the earth are the chosen people of God," and described "great cities as pestilential to the morals, the health, and the liberties of man." But Bryan's own speeches and writings contain no such references to his idol's views. Instead, he applauded Jefferson in universal terms—as a militant defender of popular democracy and the scourge of privilege, whether it stemmed from an accident of birth or the favoritism of public and private authorities. Nothing was said about the Virginian's ownership of slaves or his elaborate apologies for an institution that mocked his egalitarian principles and those of every other nineteenth-century Democrat. Bryan's favorite gift to other public figures was a hefty reference book, *The Jeffersonian Cyclopedia,* which served up the great man's opinions in short paragraphs, organized alphabetically by topic. When asked in the 1920s to name ten books that "affected my life and influenced my conduct," Bryan placed only the Bible ahead of it.[8]

He never had to choose between them. During the late nineteenth century, when Bryan was a young man, evangelical rhetoric saturated nearly every mass movement in America. Spokesmen for the Knights of Labor, which had over a million members in the 1880s, cursed "the money power" as the "anti-Christ" that only a "new Pentecost" could humble. Father Edward Glynn, a charismatic labor priest excommunicated for his vigorous defense of the Knights, portrayed Christ as "an evicted peasant" who "came to preach a gospel of liberty to the slave, of justice to the poor, of paying the full hire to the workman." The Woman's Christian Temperance Union (WCTU), the largest women's group in the nation, claimed that its work to close down saloons, improve prison conditions, shelter prostitutes, and support labor unions for women were all examples of "God in politics." The altruistic sisterhood, wrote one member, "continually opens its windows toward Jerusalem and prays the government to make it easy for the people to do right and hard for them to do wrong." The two-million-strong Farmers' Alliance held mass encampments identical in form to the revival meetings common in the South and Great Plains. From Colorado to the Carolinas, rebel lecturers told their audiences, "God has promised to hear the cry of the oppressed," and preached that "no man in this nation can live a consistent Christian life" unless he threw himself into the agrarian insurgency.[9]

This was a social gospel from below, and it produced its own breed of prophets. The journalist Henry George predicted that the enactment of his Single Tax on unimproved land, proposed in his popular 1879 tome *Progress and Poverty,* would bring about "the culmination of Christianity—the City of God on earth, with its walls of jasper and its gates of pearl!"[10] His writings and speeches evangelized a religiously diverse mass of followers, many of whom persevered in their singular mission years after George's death. Edward Bellamy's best-selling 1888 novel, *Looking Backward,* described a future egalitarian utopia that had come about when Americans of all classes rejected the cutthroat immorality of capitalism and embraced instead a "gospel of solidarity." Disciples of Bellamy flocked to new Nationalist Clubs as if to church, while the author pondered "what part I am to play in the great deliverance...daily more convinced that it is at hand." All the mass protests of the era called on the language of the Bible because, like the Declaration of Independence and the Constitution, it was the common property of Americans and thus needed no explanation or apology.[11]

Celebrity preachers were just as vital to shaping the world of Bryan and his followers as were such godly insurgencies. During the Gilded Age, crowds of the reverent and the curious flocked to hear both itinerant revivalists and "princes of the pulpit," eloquent ministers of the largest urban churches. Both types of preachers built their reputations, as did Bryan later, by defining a moral code through performances that were at once didactic and pleasurable.[12]

Henry Ward Beecher, pastor of Brooklyn's Plymouth Church, was a gifted apostle of Christianity as good news. The former abolitionist refused to dwell on original sin, divine punishment, or the need for moral discipline. "I am apt to look at the bright side of things and take a cheerful view of life," he admitted.[13] A man of furious energy—he once told a close friend that "he had more health than he knew what to do with"—Beecher thought it his mission to install a "gospel of love" in place of the grim doctrines on which his own Congregational (originally Puritan) denomination had been founded. Beecher gave most of his sermons while seated—"in the midst of the people, raised above them that all might see him, yet still among them and one of them," as one admirer put it.[14]

Intimacy was also a hallmark of mass revivals, although the leaders of such events were quite eager to preach against sin. Certain evangelists who yearned to rescue Americans from the fleshpots of modern urban culture were as entertaining and sentimental as any actor on the vaudeville stage. Samuel P. Jones, a Georgia Methodist, traveled around the South during the Gilded Age, wisecracking his case for prohibition and the inerrancy of Scripture. He called his backsliding listeners "flop-eared hounds, beer kegs, and whisky soaks" and dismissed his inability to grasp all "the mysteries of the Bible" by declaring, "I believe the whale swallowed Jonah. I would have believed it just the same if it had said that Jonah had swallowed the whale." Jones, nicknamed the Sledge Hammer, candidly admitted that he fashioned his tough, humorous patter to attract crowds. "I give you what you want first," Jones told a reporter, "and I give you what you need second."[15]

The leading revivalist of the period was the Sledge Hammer's rhetorical opposite. Dwight L. Moody, his 280 pounds wreathed in a full beard and encased in a dark suit, looked like a conservative businessman or politician—a teetotaling, cigar-abstaining Ulysses S. Grant. In a strong if nasal voice, Moody, a former shoe salesman, linked simple Bible narratives to the spiritual fears of men and women living, many for the first time, in a grasping, wicked metropolis. His rhetoric, like Beecher's, was optimistic and inclusive. "When we search for God," he assured audiences, "we are sure to find Him." The evangelist and his music director—the slim, handsome Ira Sankey—led thousands in song: "Go tell it to Jesus / He knoweth thy grief; / Go tell it to Jesus, / He'll send thee relief."[16]

Beecher and Moody had their theological differences, but they fashioned a common style—relaxed, sentimental, open to all—that resembled that of a barnstorming politician.

There was a marked decrease in conflicts between the major evangelical denominations during the Gilded Age, and such preachers contributed to and benefited from the new ecumenism. Beecher and Moody could transcend sectarian rivalries by speaking simply as "Christians" eager to point out the path to a joyful life and eventual salvation to anyone who would listen. Which church an individual belonged to seemed of little significance— as long as it was a Protestant one.[17]

The tolerant nature of their preaching fit the adoption by many churches of a more accepting view of mass leisure. In antebellum America, Protestant ministers had denounced "amusements" of all kinds as immoral diversions from a life of productivity and prayer. But by the last decades of

the nineteenth century, pastors from both "liberal" and "conservative" congregations called for *improving* forms of mass entertainment, rather than
prohibiting them altogether. YMCAs offered concerts, game rooms, and
stereopticon lectures on foreign lands and peoples. Amusements, wrote
Washington Gladden, a pioneer of the Social Gospel, should not be dominated by those with "mercenary" motives; "the intelligence, the conscience,
and the benevolence of the community ought to recognize this realm...as
belonging to them, and ought to enter in and take possession."[18]

This new culture of popular religion skirted the grand controversy
between faith and science and had little to say about the Second Coming.
While Darwinism led theologians to either shudder at or guardedly welcome what one historian calls "the breakup of an intellectual system that
had endured from the beginning of European civilization," most Protestants
seemed comfortable both with a supernatural faith and with the rigors and
pleasures of modern America.[19] They prayed every day and went to the theater on Saturday, agreed that one could not serve both God and Mammon
yet consumed at least as lavishly as their incomes allowed, fretted about the
afterlife and fought for their rights in the present. Bathing their faith in sentimental hues, ordinary Americans ignored what appeared to seminarians
and philosophers as glaring contradictions. William James once tried to
explain the motivations of religious Americans to an audience of university-
trained skeptics: "As a rule we disbelieve all facts and theories for which we
have no use."[20] Outside the lecture hall, few Christians doubted the utility
of their own convictions.

From such sources grew a romantic gospel for the common American,
which Bryan would echo repeatedly throughout his career. He and millions
of his fellow citizens embraced a democratic bargain—whether they preferred the deathless phrases of Jefferson and his disciples, the messianic
rage of labor and farmer activists, the ministerial salvation of a troubled
mass public, or a combination of all three. The injunction *vox populi, vox
dei*—the voice of the people is the voice of God—worked equally well in
both directions.

I WROTE THIS BOOK, in part, to gain a measure of respect for Bryan and
his people. I would like to help "rescue" them what from E. P. Thompson,
the great historian and activist, called "the enormous condescension of pos-
terity."[21] Bryan was the first leader of a major party to argue for perma-
nently expanding the power of the federal government to serve the welfare
of ordinary Americans from the working and middle classes. With the back-

ing of his followers, he preached that the national state should counter the overweening power of banks and industrial corporations by legalizing strikes, subsidizing farmers, taxing the rich, banning private campaign spending, and outlawing the "liquor trust." He did more than any other man—between the fall of Grover Cleveland and the election of Woodrow Wilson—to transform his party from a bulwark of laissez-faire into the citadel of liberalism we identify with Franklin D. Roosevelt and his ideological descendants. His one great flaw was to support, with a studied lack of reflection, the abusive system of Jim Crow—a view that was shared, until the late 1930s, by nearly every white Democrat. Herbert Hoover once snapped that the New Deal was "Bryanism under new words and methods," which proves that bitterness need not impair one's historical judgment.

But after Bryan's death in 1925, most intellectuals and activists on the broad left rejected the amalgam that had inspired him: a strict, populist morality based on a close reading of Scripture. The only barriers to a just society, he believed, were man-made; God was always on the side of common men and women. Liberals and radicals from the age of FDR to the present have tended to scorn that credo as naive and bigoted, a remnant of an era of white Protestant supremacy that has, or should have, passed.

One result is that the notion of Bryan as a creative forerunner will be quite different from the portrait familiar to most contemporary readers. Below that hazy image runs a caption that reads "old-fashioned." Bryan is easy to portray as a tribune of lost causes. Since the Civil War, no other major-party nominee has been defeated three times for the presidency. Bryan railed against financiers, saloonkeepers, and evolutionists—all of whom have prospered quite nicely despite his best efforts. For decades after his death, influential scholars and journalists depicted him as a self-righteous simpleton who longed to preserve an age that had already passed. "It is probably true that in the modern climate of opinion no man who can genuinely understand Bryan will be capable of writing his biography," wrote a respected historian at the end of the 1950s.[22]

Indeed, anyone who probes into his personal life meets with frustration. Bryan probably received over a million pieces of correspondence during his career, but only 2 or 3 percent of that vast outpouring has been preserved. Few letters between Bryan and his wife, Mary, survive, and almost none between him and his three children or his parents still exist. He was also a poor autobiographer. Thus, speculations about his intimate life must take the place of a detailed interpretation.[23]

Fortunately, Bryan was a man who lived most of his adult life in public and away from home. Although his marriage was both cooperative and loving, he seemed happiest when on the road, performing for thousands of strangers. Bryan's "public life was virtually his entire life," writes an earlier biographer. "The people were his family, the platform his study, crusading his relaxation." From all evidence, Bryan acted in private much as he did in public—with kindness and optimism, yet stiff-necked toward anyone who violated his sense of ethics or belittled his ideas.[24]

The private Bryan we can learn about was a rather simple man. He showed little interest in literature, art, or philosophy and borrowed many of his political ideas and proposals from others. Like a veteran Shakespearean actor, he gladly delivered many of the same speeches, year after year, to a variety of audiences. But Bryan was also a clever political strategist who retained a formidable degree of influence long after he stopped running for office. Thus, his career was not a simple story, and the effect he had on Americans during his era was quite profound. Like Eugene V. Debs then and Martin Luther King Jr. later, he had the ability to articulate widely held grievances in original phrases that delighted his listeners and persuaded many to join or support movements from the bottom up that altered American society.

As a secular liberal, I confess to a certain ambivalence about both Bryan and his many admirers, who swore that a supernatural force was guiding him. When asked, "Do you like him?" I have no short or easy answer to give. But empathy is essential to the writing of good history, and I have tried to avoid judging either Bryan or his loyalists and enemies by the standards of the present, whose own blinders sit quite firmly in place.[25]

A hero, as understood by the ancient Greeks, is not a man whose life is free of errors and contradictions. He is instead, as the classicist Moses Hadas has written, "a man whose career has somehow enlarged the horizons of what is possible for humanity and who has therefore, after his death, been deemed worthy of religious commemoration." A man without flaws, adds Hadas, "is not apt to possess the determined energy heroism requires."[26]

William Jennings Bryan became a hero to people who believed that politics should be a moral enterprise and that religion should purify the political world. In many ways, he does belong to an age we have lost—when few Americans could vote if they weren't male and white, when farmers were a pivotal interest group, and when traveling lecturers and other performers offered thrilling diversion to millions of people who otherwise might have gone without.

Yet in some ways, Bryan's time is not unlike our own. Large corporations still dominate our economy, bankroll our politicians, and frame our mass culture. Pious, if often intemperate, voices still denounce the corrosive impact of modern society and look to a spiritual awakening to cleanse the body politic. But we lack politicians, filled with conviction and blessed with charisma, who are willing to lead a charge against secular forces whose power is both mightier and more subtly deployed than a century ago. Perhaps the story of an earnest and eloquent, if not godly, hero can help.

A GODLY HERO

CHAPTER ONE

Education of a Hero, 1860–1890

He borrows from the philosopher his principles, from the poet his language, from the warrior his courage, and mingling with these his own enthusiasms, leads his hearers according to his will.

—William Jennings Bryan on oratory, 1877[1]

SALEM MAY NEVER be more than a pleasant stop along the interstate highway that slices through the verdant prairie of south-central Illinois. Stretched out beyond the sign listing a population of eight thousand is the usual array of chain hotels and restaurants, gaudy gas stations and car washes, and tiny convenience stores. An imposing Caterpillar rental and repair place suggests that the local economy is thriving, while twenty-six local churches compete to fill a set of loftier needs. Yet one can stroll down the main street of Salem in the middle of a weekday in summer without encountering more than a handful of residents. The nearest movie theater is down in Centralia, sixteen miles away.[2]

A different fate seemed possible in the 1850s, when Silas Bryan moved to town. The Ohio and Mississippi Railroad had just run tracks down Main Street, which made it possible to reach St. Louis in only ninety minutes—the same time it takes to drive the distance today. A Methodist women's college with two faculty members had recently opened its doors, and freshly built churches dotted the dirt streets of the newly incorporated town, the seat of Marion County. A few miles outside town, there lay ample deposits of bituminous coal, and three flour mills were unable to keep up with the demand of a growing population. "Salem is rapidly improving," boasted the local weekly in 1854, "and its elements of wealth and prosperity are now being rapidly developed." Soon it would be "a commanding point...where industry, sobriety, and honesty will surely thrive; where good health may be found, where long life may be enjoyed and where all the concomitants of competence and oppulence [*sic*] are inevitable."[3]

3

Silas Bryan's own ambitions dovetailed with those of his town. He was born in 1822, the eighth child of a farm family from Point Pleasant, a village that then lay inside Virginia's western border with Ohio. At the age of eighteen, he left a crowded log cabin to move westward in search of an education and, perhaps, a fortune. Harvesting crops and chopping wood, he slowly amassed enough credits to graduate, at the age of twenty-seven, from McKendree College, a Baptist institution in southern Illinois. He then followed a career path common to educated men in rural America during the middle of the nineteenth century: a few years of teaching school followed by reading law books and passing a bar examination.[4] In 1851, Silas moved to Salem and opened a legal practice. A year later, he married Mariah Jennings—a reverent, resourceful, lovely young woman who was one of his former pupils. They built a small two-story frame house on Broadway Street—a five-minute walk from the county courthouse, which still marks the epicenter of Salem.

Silas matured into a man of substance and an indispensable father of his town. He was a pioneering member of the provincial legal elite that did much to establish genteel society in the hinterland of midcentury America. Townspeople admired his legal skills and compensated him well—so well that in 1866 he was able to buy a 520-acre farm a mile outside of town with a deer park alongside it. Area voters, most of whom were Democrats, also elected him to a series of public offices. Over a twenty-year span, Silas served in the state senate, as a circuit court judge, and as a leading member of the committee that drafted a new Illinois constitution.[5]

And he never wavered from the gospel of the Democratic Party. It was a potent mixture of egalitarian principle and racist fear. Democrats in the nineteenth century often spoke as class warriors, American style. They preached that every small farmer and wage earner was equal to the rich and the well-born, and that the "producers" who fed, built, and clothed the nation deserved access to every opportunity society could offer. Yet Democrats also vowed to defend the livelihood, moral values, and families of the white majority against black Americans who refused to accept their servile destiny. As late as the 1870s, the party filled its campaign broadsides with images of "popeyed, electric-haired and slack-jawed" black men straight from the minstrel shows that were the most popular form of theater in nineteenth-century America.[6]

These ugly stereotypes served a populist purpose. Updating and hardening Jefferson's anti-elitist suspicions, Democrats accused their political enemies of shedding tears for unworthy blacks but sneering at the language and manners of the productive white majority. In the party's demonology,

New England divines and schoolmarms mocked the Irish-born men and women who built and cleaned their houses, while speculators made quick fortunes manipulating markets instead of gaining a just reward after "years of patient industry."[7] Good Democrats believed their task was to uphold the libertarian principles of the early republic. The Democracy—as the party was commonly known—stood tall, a pillar of resistance against well-born zealots who wanted to shut off immigration, prohibit drinking and other private amusements, and increase the powers of the federal government to enrich their friends.[8]

Silas Bryan dated his own loyalty to the Democracy to boyhood memories of the 1828 election of Andrew Jackson, a stalwart defender of slavery. Later, as a Democratic partisan in Illinois, Silas Bryan endorsed the views of Stephen Douglas, who in his famous debate with Lincoln declared, "Our people are white people, our state is a white state, and we mean to preserve the race pure without any mixture with the negro."[9]

In the spirit of Old Hickory, Silas mingled a plebeian ethic with a fealty to racist assumptions. In 1856, he ran for the Illinois Senate against a opponent friendly to abolition. At one rally, Salem's "hardy yeomanry" filled the county courthouse to hear Bryan blast "the Black Republican press" for saying that he was friendly to Mormonism. In 1872, Silas ran for Congress on a platform that advocated inflating the money supply to rescue farmers and wage earners from the burden of debt. But a former general in the Union army narrowly defeated him and ended Silas Bryan's office-chasing career. The judge remained a prominent Democrat in southern Illinois and one of the richest men in town.[10]

However, Silas was never content with the trappings of material success. By all accounts, he embodied the virtues that nineteenth-century Americans summed up as "character." He was loyal and honest, industrious and pious—qualities prized by moral philosophers from the Hebrew prophets to Cotton Mather. And Silas attempted to apply these virtues to the life of his local community and state. When he died of a diabetic stroke in 1880, thousands filed by his casket as it lay in the county courthouse, and every business and school in Salem closed down for the afternoon. Obituary writers praised him for never wavering from his beliefs, for routinely feeding hobos who came to his door, and for kneeling in prayer three times a day, wherever he happened to be. Silas had specified the hymns to be sung and the Bible passages to be read at his funeral. Among the most memorable were verses from Paul's Second Epistle to Timothy: "For I am now ready to be offered, and the time of my departure is at hand. I have fought a good fight, I have finished *my* course, I have kept the faith."[11]

A year after his father's death, Will Bryan paid a florid tribute to character in the valedictory he gave at his college graduation: "If each day we...plant ourselves more firmly upon principles which are eternal, guard every thought and action, that it may be pure, and conform our lives more nearly to that Perfect Model, we shall form a character that...will bring success in this life and form the best preparation for that which is beyond."[12] Others may have mouthed such nostrums without taking them too seriously; one biographer comments that the talk "was more suitable for an eighth-grade exercise than a college commencement."[13] Yet like most Americans in the Gilded Age, both father and son were convinced that character underlay good governance as well as sound religion.[14]

WILL BRYAN spent his childhood in social tranquility, if not utter innocence. He was born on March 19, 1860, a year before the onset of the Civil War. More than fifteen hundred residents of Marion County served in the Union army; one out of every six succumbed from either wounds or disease. But no battles took place in the area, and the bloodshed left only a mild impression on local history—perhaps because many residents, like Silas Bryan, had migrated from the South and didn't favor the end of slavery and the rule of the Republican Party, which were prime consequences of the war. Neither Will's memoirs nor the little early correspondence of his that survives mentions the conflict that ruptured the nation.[15]

As a child, he was also unfamiliar with the afflictions and joys of an increasingly polyglot and industrial society. In Salem, Will probably met few people of a religion or ethnic group different from his. In 1860, a large majority of the thirteen thousand inhabitants of Marion County were native-born white Protestants of British or Irish heritage who farmed modest plots of corn and raised pigs and cattle. A few small mills finished lumber or ground cereals; by 1870, one lone shop in Salem turned out wooden plows and carriages. Schoolteachers and store clerks outnumbered day laborers and servants.[16] Will could always find abundant rabbits and squirrels to hunt in the woods near his house. The Ohio and Mississippi Railroad was the only real sign that the machine age, with its yawning if mutable class divisions, had arrived on the prairies of southern Illinois.

A biracial society and a religiously diverse one also lay off in the future. Although the slave state of Missouri began just seventy miles west of town, across the broad Mississippi, Silas Bryan and his neighbors seldom needed to police a color line. The antebellum Illinois constitution barred blacks from entering the state, and subsequent laws prescribed stiff penalties for hiring them. The year Abraham Lincoln was elected president, census takers found only nine black people living in all of Marion County.[17]

European immigrants were almost as rare. In the crowded port cities of the East, Know-Nothings raged against an influx of "Papist hordes." But Salem had just one small Catholic church, serving a few score of Irish and German residents. Tolerance toward whites from abroad seems to have come rather easily to town notables. Salem Democrats published campaign literature in German as well as English, and the town's religious life was relatively free of rancor. As a child, Will witnessed regular visits to his home by ministers of every denomination; Silas reserved a guest room for traveling divines, as well as politicians, and annually donated a load of hay to every local church, including the Catholic one.[18]

Mariah Bryan, at least in her son's eyes, was no less ethical and open-minded. Twelve years younger than Silas, she was his equal in character. "Mother was a very competent woman," recalled Will, "of rare native ability, of lofty ideals, and as devout as my father."[19] She educated him at home until the age of ten, drawing lessons from the Bible, the McGuffey's Readers, and a geography text. She also held him responsible for feeding the farm animals and cutting the wood that heated their brick mansion. After he became famous, Will credited "this drudgery" for giving him the strength "to endure fatigue and withstand disease" during long periods on the road.[20]

The few surviving photos of Mariah Bryan, grimly posed in high collar and tight bun, betray no hint of her independent spirit. Raised as a Methodist, she refused for twenty years after marriage to "take her letter" to the local Baptist congregation in which Silas was a leading elder. Mariah was active in the local chapter of the WCTU and the Royal Templars, another temperance group, though the precise nature of her work is unknown. But her membership alone suggests she welcomed the state as a moral guardian—a notion that made most good Democrats cringe.[21]

Neither did Mariah confuse piety with prudishness. She played the piano often and well, and liked to tell stories about acquaintances who took their religion a bit too seriously. When Will asked his mother's opinion of his first political speech, a long-winded plea in 1880 to support the local Democratic congressman, she responded, "Well there were a few good places in it—where you might have stopped!"[22]

Mariah's relaxed attitude may have influenced her son's choice of a church. Instead of becoming a Baptist like Silas or a Methodist like Mariah, Will embraced an option of his own. At the age of thirteen, he attended a revival led by a traveling minister from the Cumberland Presbyterian Church and then helped establish a small congregation with about seventy

other teenagers. Cumberland Presbyterians—who took their name from
the Kentucky town where the sect was founded in 1813—discarded the
Calvinist idea that God "elected" a minority at birth and left all others to
face the prospect of hell. Although the Cumberland way prohibited drinking, dancing, gambling, and other enticements to evil, it brimmed with hope
for the salvation of all Americans and, following that, the world. As an adult,
Will often attended services of other denominations, and most Cumberland
congregations, including that in Salem, joined the larger Presbyterian
Church in the U.S. in 1906. Still, he clung to the expansive vision of his first
spiritual home for the rest of his life.[23]

Yet long shadows chilled his family in the middle of the Midwest. Will
was his parents' fourth child; a girl and a boy born earlier had both died of
whooping cough before reaching their first birthdays. The next boy also
filled an infant's grave; another brother died at sixteen. Following the first
two deaths, Silas dolefully wrote in the family Bible that he thought his own
end was near.[24] In the mid-nineteenth century, with only the crudest of
pediatric medical treatment available, it was not unusual for even wealthy
Americans to lose a child in infancy. But only a bare majority of the Bryans'
nine offspring lived to adulthood. Grief beyond the norm may have bolstered Will's parents in their resolve that at least one son would do the family proud.

WHEN HE TURNED fifteen, Will was sent off to private school in Jacksonville, a city of ten thousand in the central part of the state. He stayed
there for six years, attending and graduating from Whipple Academy and
then from Illinois College. In contrast to his hometown, Jacksonville looked
more like what America was becoming. It boasted a three-story textile factory and a state mental hospital, and the local elite of bankers and landown-
ers wielded influence at the state capital in nearby Springfield. About 40
percent of Jacksonville residents were foreign-born—housemaids and
laborers from Portugal, railroad hands from Ireland, craftsmen and shopkeepers from Germany, and a scattering of immigrants from other lands.
The black population, some five hundred, was large enough to be confined
to a tiny ghetto, known as "Africa." Local political campaigns bristled with
debates over emancipation, prohibition, and law and order. To the chagrin
of town boosters, Jacksonville had recently lost out to Champaign-Urbana
as the site of the new state university, and it lagged behind the industrial
growth of Peoria and Decatur. But it was still large enough to acquaint Will
Bryan with the rudiments of a modernizing America.[25]

The slim, muscular teenager came to town, in the words of one teacher, as "a typical farmer lad with all the crudities that are characteristic of the species." He left it equipped to make his mark on the world.[26] During his years in Jacksonville, Bryan lived with Dr. Hiram K. Jones and his family. Jones was a distant cousin of Bryan's father, but he and his wife, Elizabeth, moved in an intellectual world Silas had never known. Jones was a transplanted New Englander who was as learned in philosophy as in his own profession of medicine. He had taught classes on Plato and Hegel at an academy near Boston and was friends with Ralph Waldo Emerson and the educational reformer Bronson Alcott.[27] Although the Joneses regularly attended the local Congregational church, Darwin's theories fascinated them, as they did most liberal Protestants of the era.

Illinois College further tested the bucolic verities of Salem. Courses in geology and biology raised doubts in Will's mind about the truth of Genesis and even led Bryan to write to the great agnostic Robert Ingersoll for advice (he dismissed the young man with a form letter). Julian Sturtevant, a prominent economist and the college's second president, argued that a society in which most workers "live in disgusting squalor and rudeness" frustrated "the beneficent designs of the Creator." Before the Civil War, the school had been known as a haven for "red hot abolitionists"; for many years, Edward Beecher, Henry's older brother, was its president.[28]

The college's reputation may have been the reason Wendell Phillips, the aging radical firebrand, came to address the student body. The event so stimulated Will that he quickly read through the entire corpus of speeches by the eloquent opponent of slavery, war, intemperance, and the exploitation of labor. In 1879, the college senior, sounding a bit like Phillips, wrote an anguished letter to a cousin who seemed bent on a military career: "I rejoice that in a few years it will not be necessary to shoot a man to convince him that you are right and to blot out a nation to prove to them that their principles are false."[29]

Yet none of these men or experiences did much to shake Bryan's faith in his cultural patrimony. He remained a loyal Democrat, and his affair with religious skepticism was brief. Will was a regular congregant at the local Presbyterian church, whose pastor later praised him for "bringing many [young men] into the church and starting them on the right road."[30] He also joined the YMCA and was several times elected chaplain of Sigma Pi, a campus "literary society" that doubled as a fraternity. The boy from downstate never touched alcohol or played cards and was often seen with a Bible tucked under his arm. Affable talk about character came as easily to him as breathing. "He was very good," a classmate remembered, "but for some reason Bryan's goodness was not the kind that rubbed against you and turned the fur the wrong way."[31]

Will did best in Greek and Latin, the backbone of his college's curriculum, as it was in eastern colleges. He seems to have read little in any subject beyond the assigned textbooks. This may not have been by choice. Although several of its professors were learned figures, the college kept its library open for only an hour a day, perhaps to safeguard its fragile volumes. Will became valedictorian of his class of eleven men by scoring just a few points higher than the average. "On the face of the record," writes a historian about his college days, "Bryan's place . . . was won by consistent industry and uniform application rather than exceptional brilliance."[32]

HE RESERVED his zeal for oratory. It had been a remarkably early passion. At the age of four, according to the family's doctor and neighbor, Will began giving "little talks" to his playmates from the steps of the house on Broadway Street. Some of the boy's speeches were sheer nonsense; others borrowed such lines as "Eternal hope, in yonder sphere sublime / Tuned the first note in the march of time," from a justly forgotten poem.[33] As Will grew up, the oratory of adults was a constant companion: he heard his father give dozens of campaign talks and addresses in court, sat through innumerable sermons at local churches, and attended the occasional revival that swept into town.

For an American coming of age in the last third of the nineteenth century, one of the surest ways to gain prominence or to secure it was to become a fine public speaker. Oratory was an indispensable element in both politics and religion, on every public holiday and anniversary, at every unveiling of a statue or laying of a cornerstone, and at the banquets obligatory for any group able to hire a cook and rent a hall. Dozens of lecture circuits had sprung up by midcentury, enabling farmers as well as city dwellers to hear the best-known politicians, writers, actors, and preachers in the land.[34]

Frequent speaking contests provided young men and an increasing number of young women with opportunities to display their poise in the public arena. Only a minority of citizens was able to postpone a life of labor by attending school through adolescence. But that only encouraged the link between the ability to give a fluent address and the achievement of middle-class status and a degree of social power. In the 1870s, after a long day spent rolling cigars, Samuel Gompers attended the free elocution courses offered at Cooper Union in New York. His refined platform manner facilitated his climb a decade later to the leadership of the American labor movement.[35] As Mr. Dooley—the Irish-born saloonkeeper invented by a wry Chicago journalist—commented at the turn of the century, "Ivry thrue-born American regards himsilf as a gr-reat orator."[36]

Like Will Bryan, nearly every adult had been able to witness a variety of oratorical performances. They thus evaluated public speaking with much the same mix of canny criticism and admiration we now apply to professional athletes and movie stars. Newspapers routinely published the full or nearly full transcripts of major political speeches and sermons by celebrated ministers; editorial "impressions" accompanied the texts.

The explosive growth of print media helped spur the democratization of speechmaking. Between 1870 and 1900, the number of daily newspapers increased twice as fast as the U.S. population, and their average circulation zoomed up at an even faster clip. Readers in big cities had a lavish variety of morning and evening papers to choose from—in several foreign languages as well as English—and, thanks to rural free delivery and the advertising budgets of large firms, most farm families could also afford a daily paper. Local weeklies, many aligned with social movements, were everywhere. Magazine editors caught the same fever, slashing their prices and marketing their periodicals far beyond the erudite easterners who had long been their main readers.[37]

This created a huge appetite for details about personalities who captivated a mass public through their words and stagecraft. Reporters were sent out to ask popular orators about their family life, their eating habits, and how they prepared to face an audience. Of course, such interviews only boosted the speakers' allure and the demand for their performances. Most newspapers were unabashed advocates of a political party; the creed of "objectivity" made few converts until the twentieth century. But, in the battle for the pennies of a diverse readership, any campaigner or officeholder who drew big crowds could expect respectful coverage—at least outside the editorial pages.[38]

That nearly every American in the Gilded Age could imagine him- or herself a speechmaker does not mean that most speeches were models of reason and clarity. Indeed, sentimentality was the hallmark of Gilded Age rhetoric. Few orators dispensed with the mawkish mode, although it regularly invited derision from the unsmitten. After quoting a speaker who rambled on about "th' most gloryous people that iver infested th' noblest counthry that th' sun iver shone upon," Mr. Dooley snapped, "I guess a man niver becomes an orator if he has anything to say."[39]

Sentimentalism was so prevalent in American oratory during the late nineteenth century because it was so common in American culture. Millions hung chromolithographs of pink-cheeked toddlers and luxuriant bouquets in their homes, read novels and advice literature that equated sincerity with an overflow of emotions, and flocked to hear preachers who spoke more to the passions than to the intellect. Rhetoric textbooks counseled budding speakers to gratify the public's appetite for gush.[40]

By the time he got to Jacksonville, Bryan yearned to excel at the craft. Nothing in his memoirs is more poignant or precisely rendered than the story of his struggle to win a top prize in elocution. He heard lectures by three acknowledged masters—Ingersoll and Henry Ward Beecher as well as Phillips. He became a competent debater, grappling with such controversial subjects as temperance, race relations, and the tariff. He took to Latin and Greek "because of the training they give one in the choice of words" and participated in every speaking contest sponsored by his prep school and college. "In my first year in the academy...I entered the declamation [recitation] contest.... The judges did not seem to regard me as especially promising." The next year, he tried again and finished third. "Dr. Jones thought that my failure may have been due to indistinctness of articulation," which "spurred me up on that particular subject" and "became a controlling passion for me."[41]

Bryan found the college's speaking instructor to be a didactic bore. His classes taught only that "it is hard to be graceful in gesticulation when one is thinking about the movements to be made, just as it is difficult for one to speak naturally when he is engaged in an artificial effort." So he practiced by himself, occasionally in the woods. "I left nothing undone that would contribute towards success." Finally, in his junior year, Bryan came in first. The topic of his prize-winning oration was "Individual Power."[42]

The content of these talks dripped with the bathos that Gilded Age audiences expected from public speakers. "Character," said Bryan, could only be grasped as an "entity, the individuality of the person, shining from every window of the soul." The Democratic Party kept losing presidential elections. But, like Samson with his arms around the "mighty columns" of principle, "it will die only when this governmental fabric shall fall, involving parties, freedom, and human hopes in one common ruin."[43]

Bryan put his reading of the classics to good use; references to such worthies as Ulysses, Cicero, Demosthenes, and Philip of Macedon are sprinkled through every youthful talk. He had a particular fondness for ancient sages for whom sincerity was not just a rhetorical device. "Earnestness is a requisite of no mean importance," he wrote in a schoolboy essay. "Virgil well says, 'If you would bid the tears of others flow, yourself the signs of grief must show.' "[44] A lifelong romantic, Bryan could not imagine that inauthentic motives could lead to moral behavior.

HE PURSUED his future wife with the same heartfelt diligence he brought to public speaking. Mary Elizabeth Baird was a student at Jacksonville Female Academy, a tiny school local men dubbed "the Jail for Angels." They met in the autumn of 1879 at a tea-and-cookie reception, and Bryan fell instantly in love with the attractive, quick-witted young woman of eighteen who hailed from the nearby town of Perry, Illinois. From all existing evidence, he stayed that way until his death forty-six years later. Mary Baird was not so impulsive. The sole child of the keeper of a general store who owned the only two-story house in town, she shrewdly assayed Bryan's looks and bearing. "His face was pale and thin;...his nose was prominent— too large to look well, I thought...I noted particularly his hair and his smile. The former, black in color, fine in quality, and parted with distressing straightness; the latter, expansive and expressive."[45] She wondered if, over time, she'd be able to bear his unceasing goodness.

But Will's smiling ardor overcame her doubts and even his own scruples. For months, he ingeniously violated the Female Academy's rules against gentleman callers. The wife of his Latin professor allowed regular trysts in her parlor; he made sure to visit Mary's ailing mother in a local sanatorium whenever her daughter was present; and he drove his beloved out to the country in a rented buggy. A year after meeting, the couple had endured the mild sanctions imposed by Mary's principal (who forbade more than a weekly exchange of letters), and Bryan was ready to ask for her father's approval.

He couldn't take it for granted. Mr. Baird was a practical man, and he knew Will's prospects had recently darkened. Silas Bryan had died the previous March at the age of fifty-eight. Shock soon followed mourning when creditors demanded payment on $15,000 worth of loans the judge had generously countersigned for delinquent friends. His wife and children were left with the house, the farm, and a deskful of creditor's notes. Bryan's father, it seems, had had too much character for his family's own good.

But Will parried Baird's doubts with a clever display of biblical knowledge. "I have been reading Proverbs a good deal lately," he told Mary's father, "and find that Solomon says, 'Who findeth a wife findeth a good thing and obtaineth favor of the Lord.'" That was true, admitted Baird, "yet Paul suggests that 'he that giveth her in marriage doeth well; but he that giveth her not in marriage doeth better.'" Bryan thought for a moment. Then he replied, "Solomon would be the best authority upon this point because Paul was never married while Solomon had a number of wives." The grocer beamed at the answer and agreed to the match. He was evidently untroubled by Bryan's praise for a monarch who, according to the Book of Kings, kept seven hundred wives and three hundred concubines.[46]

Mary proved to be a formidable partner. She lacked the desire to emulate such contemporaries as Jane Addams and Florence Kelley, who challenged all manner of social evils and held powerful men responsible for them. She turned down most interview requests and began giving speeches only after her husband stopped running for office. But Willa Cather and other contemporary writers considered Mary Baird Bryan a "New Woman," engaged with ideas and issues rather than with dressing well and entertaining guests. It is easy to understand why.[47]

Will Bryan's long, peripatetic career would have been impossible without Mary's continuous and varied labors. She managed his correspondence, helped prepare his speeches, edited his articles, and on occasion even negotiated with his fellow politicians. After he died, she quickly completed his memoirs. At the same time, she performed the duties expected of a middle-class wife at the turn of the last century—raising the children, running sequential households in three different cities, and guarding the health of a husband who was particularly fond of fried meats and heavy desserts. After giving birth to her first child, Ruth, in 1885, Mary found time to study law and pass the bar exam, the better to help Will in his office. Later, she acquired a reading knowledge of German in order to alert him to influential writings on political economy published in that language. For many years, Mary and Will shared a large double desk that allowed them to work across from each other. It was a fitting symbol of the enterprise they built together.

But she entirely lacked his rosy ebullience. In 1896, a female reporter for the *New York World* noted Mary's "silent aggressiveness" and mentioned that she was "rather studious and very reserved." William Allen White, the famous journalist, met her four years later and remembered "an introvert who surveyed me, and I think everyone around her husband, with a fishy eye of distrust." Reversing the gender stereotypes of the day, Mary was the pragmatic skeptic, her husband the didactic visionary. Will insisted the young should have a moral education; Mary scoffed that "children must to a great extent work out their own character."[48]

At times, her unsentimental gaze turned hard and cynical. Recalling a childhood trip to the St. Louis waterfront, Mary disdained the "negro deckhands, droning their monotonous songs, and hurrying up and down the gangplanks like busy ants." After she died, her younger daughter, Grace, observed, "*In her heart* she was always a bit more of a plutocrat than a democrat." But when has one's top political aide needed to empathize with the powerless? Mary's sangfroid was a key weapon in Bryan's cause. As she aged, he was often anxious about her health; he seldom worried about the rigor of her mind or spirit.[49]

THERE WAS NEVER much question that Will Bryan would enter the law. In the 1880s, it remained the ideal profession for a man who spoke well and had political aspirations—and it could make an energetic, quick-thinking individual a comfortable income. At the age of six, Will had mused about becoming a Baptist minister. But his father's career and his own ambitions dissuaded him from that path long before he got to Jacksonville. "Law will be his profession," Will wrote to Mary in 1880, referring to himself in the oracular third person, "his aim, to mete out justice to every creature, whether he be rich or poor, bond or free. His great desire is to honor God and please mankind." He also confessed a desire "to stand with Webster and Clay."[50] As it had been for those giants of the antebellum Senate, the rhetoric of American ideals would be his ticket to immortality.

In the fall of 1881, Bryan began his quest for moral and political renown with a two-year course at Union Law College in downtown Chicago. He chose the school on the recommendation of a cousin who had attended it and because, unlike more elite institutions, it allowed students to work at a law office while taking classes. Mariah Bryan was still paying off her late husband's debts; she could afford her son's tuition but nothing more. So, sporting a full beard for the big city, Will rented a small, windowless apartment. Each morning, he walked the four miles to the campus near the shore of Lake Michigan. He fed himself on a portion of the $5 a week he earned working for Lyman Trumbull—a former U.S. attorney who, thirty years before, had examined Silas Bryan for the bar.

Either by design or accident, Bryan left few records of his sojourn in the metropolis of middle America, whose population had doubled to over six hundred thousand since the terrible fire of 1871. His letters to Mary, now lost, evidently portrayed Chicago as a vast den of inequality and sleaze. He complained to his fiancée about manufacturing trusts that crushed their small competitors and impoverished workers, a Democratic machine that cared only about staying in power, and a justice system plagued by careless police and selfish residents.[51]

Bryan's indictment echoed that of such Social Gospelers as Washington Gladden and W. T. Stead, who were fashioning a new theology of protest and healing for industrial cities. But these activist voices—and more secular ones such as Jane Addams and Henry Demarest Lloyd—were intensely attracted to the drama and color of Chicago, its ethnic neighborhoods, and its narratives of ingenuity as well as exploitation. Bryan just seemed disgusted and homesick. "There is no place so lonely to a young man," Clarence Darrow recalled about the Chicago he moved to later that same decade, "as a great city where he has no intimates or companions. When I walked along the street I scanned every face I met to see if I could not perchance discover some one from Ohio."[52]

Bryan's aversion to Chicago prevented him from exploring the contentious, creative world of labor politics that thrived there in the early 1880s. Thousands of socialists and anarchists, most of them immigrants from Central Europe, organized unions where they worked and squabbled at radical meetings and in the press over whether the proletariat ought to abolish the state or take it over. The Knights of Labor ran a cooperative grocery store, and the cigar makers' union operated a factory that employed four hundred of its members. Irish nationalists demanded the freedom of their homeland and inspired boycotts by laborers of every political tendency and both genders.[53]

Such activists could have taught the pious young man from downstate that big-city workers were not merely victims of the new corporate order. To win their hearts, one had to spend less time preaching about "character" and more time appreciating their deep awareness of class and their need to organize for economic self-defense. Although Bryan sympathized with anyone bruised by the big money, he never quite learned that lesson—and it probably cost him votes and sympathy in the years to come.

Will felt more at home during the afternoons he spent at Trumbull's firm. Trumbull, who turned seventy while Bryan was copying his pleadings and filling his inkwells, was a rare politician who cherished social reforms over the demands of any party. He had started his career as a Jacksonian Democrat but jumped to the Republicans during the crisis of the 1850s and got elected to the U.S. Senate. There he spearheaded passage of both the Thirteenth Amendment banning slavery and the bill that established the Freedmen's Bureau. Disgusted at the venality of the Grant administration, Trumbull returned to his old party in the early 1870s. He died in 1896, soon after writing a bravura declaration of principles for the People's Party of Chicago. Trumbull remembered that Silas Bryan had encouraged him to run for president in 1872, and the distinguished attorney took a liking to Silas's son, whose ideals matched his own. After Will graduated from law school, the two men remained friends and became political allies.[54]

Bryan left Chicago eager, as he wrote to Mary, to "develop powers that exert a great influence for good."[55] But first he had to make a living. Jacksonville seemed an appealing place to start. The paternal Dr. Jones secured him a place in one of the leading firms in town, and Will, beardless once again, looked forward to using the local knowledge he had gained during his six years of schooling in the city. He was also prepared to bend his moral preferences to build a clientele.

One of his first clients was a saloonkeeper named John Sheehan. During Will's college days, the man had done odd jobs around the Jones house and grown fond of the boy. Now he promised "to bring" Bryan "all the business that he could." Would the young lawyer mind first collecting some unpaid bills? Bryan didn't hesitate. "I told him that I did not drink myself nor advise drinking, but that I thought those who bought liquor ought to pay for it." Instead of a necessary compromise, the Sheehan story became, for Bryan, a quasi-spiritual lesson in the value of tolerance. He recalled, "This was one of the earliest instances—they have been numerous since—where I saw the return of bread cast upon the waters."[56] As any politician knows, one can never have too many friends.

The quotidian business of lawyering in Jacksonville yielded few such edifying moments. Bryan spent four years tracking down debtors for insurance companies and his alma mater, Illinois College. He also sold real estate and located relatives' wills for out-of-town clients. After the Democrats captured the White House in 1884, he sought a patronage job as assistant district attorney for southern Illinois but lost out to a man with better connections. By 1886, Bryan was earning a respectable $1,500 a year and had time to practice his oratory and to preside over the local YMCA. Attentive and cheerful, he became close to Congressman William Springer, for whom he'd campaigned as a college student. But Bryan had soured on the city's potential to bring him either wealth or political opportunity. Jacksonville's economy was stagnating, and the GOP held a secure grip on the local government. It was time to move.

Like his father half a century before, Will was drawn to the West. Returning from a routine business trip to Kansas in the summer of 1887, Bryan decided to stop in Lincoln, Nebraska, to visit Adolphus "Dolph" Talbot, a friend from law school and a Republican. After two days, he "caught a vision" of future triumphs and returned home to persuade Mary to leave for "a new country."[57] She quickly assented.

Lincoln was well suited to Will's ambitions and personality. It had a population of forty thousand, twice that of 1885 (and four times greater than Jacksonville's). It was the capital of a state that grew faster than any other that decade—from 450,000 to over a million—but where raw prairie still dominated the landscape.[58] Lincoln was also home to the University of Nebraska, which pleased Mary's intellectual side, and to flourishing Presbyterian and Methodist churches and thirteen temperance societies, which gratified the pious new parents. True, Republicans ruled both city and state, with a leadership of Union army veterans. But Nebraska's mushrooming variety of immigrants—from Ireland and Germany, Bohemia and Scandinavia—might give a friendly, tolerant Democrat a chance. On October 1, his third wedding anniversary, Bryan moved to Lincoln and began a partnership with Talbot that would last almost a decade. Mary and Ruth arrived the next summer, after Will had overseen construction of a frame house just a few blocks from the imposing new capitol.

Bryan and Talbot made a successful team—in part because of their differences. Active in competing parties, they welcomed clients of both persuasions. Before Bryan arrived in town, Talbot had spent most of his time representing the Missouri Pacific, one of the smaller of the fourteen railroads that crisscrossed the state in wood and iron.[59] Will always mistrusted corporations and refused to accept money from a railroad company. So principle compelled him to seek out other business if the partnership was to flourish. A cluster of new creditors soon furnished the firm with a round of steady, if often dreary, work.

Bryan did attract a number of cases with political import. He argued that it was illegal for a small town to issue bonds for the construction of a privately owned factory to process sugar beets. He took the side of a local Democratic newspaper editor who had been badly beaten by police and wanted to sue. The constable in charge refused to serve the papers unless the editor first paid a large fee. Bryan maintained that "a remedy in a criminal case could not depend upon the financial ability of the party injured," and he won the day.[60]

Both cases allowed Bryan, with Talbot's aid, to apply Jefferson's hatred of "special privilege" to rather mundane events. Both times, the partners argued successfully before the Nebraska Supreme Court, where they appeared as frequently as any attorneys in the state.[61] By the end of the 1880s, Bryan was consistently earning larger fees than he had in Jacksonville and could look forward to even more profitable times ahead. And prosperity gave him the freedom to engage in politics.

ALTHOUGH THE DEMOCRATS had won just one presidential election since the Civil War, they were not without power. Bryan's party was well entrenched in the commercial metropolises of New York, Chicago, and San Francisco as well as in the South and most border locales, such as Bryan's home county. The swelling of immigration from Catholic Europe to the urban North and fear of "Negro domination" in Dixie strengthened the party's appeal in those regions. One consequence was that the Democrats controlled the House of Representatives through much of the 1870s and 1880s and kept the GOP's majority in the Senate to a handful of seats. The party was also competitive in such key industrial states as New York and Illinois, where it fought back efforts by well-born, old-stock Republicans such as Francis Parkman and E. L. Godkin to strip the franchise from new immigrants and men without property.[62]

And the Democracy was a lively party indeed. Urban machines, while they made their bosses rich, also bestowed jobs and charity on working-class residents at a time when federal welfare payments went mainly to veterans of the Union army and their nearest kin. Tammany Hall, largest and most notorious of the breed, was a prodigious fount of municipal jobs and contracts; in the late 1870s, one of every twelve family men in New York held a position with the city.[63] For every campaign, Tammany and its counterparts in Indianapolis and Chicago, Buffalo and Baltimore, New Haven and Omaha mounted massive street parades, fireworks displays, and free banquets. In southern locales where the GOP still had a fighting chance (as long as black men were able to exercise the franchise), Democratic orators stretched the vernacular with florid denunciations of Yankee-Negro plots, while party stalwarts beat the towns and countryside to ensure that every white loyalist made it to the polls. "Let me know if it is lawful," one registrar asked a Democratic official in North Carolina, "for anyone who has partly lost his mind to register and vote."[64]

To be a Democrat (or a Republican) during the Gilded Age was to indulge in a set of male rituals that offered both mass entertainment and the chance to demonstrate one's civic vigor. Party spirit reached its zenith at state and national party conventions, accounts of which top reporters drenched with details on everything from the language of the platform to thermometer readings inside the hall. In 1876, at the age of sixteen, Bryan had, with the help of a friendly policeman, climbed through the window of a St. Louis auditorium to hear speeches for and against the nomination of Samuel Tilden at that year's Democratic gathering. The party's rule that a candidate had to gain two-thirds of the delegates to win (a sop to the South) almost guaranteed a multiballot contest, with tactics and allegiances shifting on each call of the roll. The sticky summer temperatures and lack of amplification inside packed convention halls only added to the tension.[65]

After his election in 1884, President Grover Cleveland managed to keep his party united by taking stands that pleased each of its major constituencies. The white South cheered him for naming former Confederate officers to his cabinet, northern workers and merchants shared his anti-trust fervor, and state and city bosses loved his willingness to replace thousands of Republican postmasters—even if the president did try to avoid giving the jobs to obvious hacks. After Cleveland was defeated for reelection in 1888, Bryan wrote him a letter declaring, "We would rather fall with you fighting on and for a principal [*sic*] than to succeed with the party representing nothing but an organized appetite." Why not move to Nebraska? asked the young lawyer. "As a Western man with friends you have in the East, we can elect you [in 1892]."[66]

But beneath such gestures of harmony simmered a clash of views and interests that would tear the Democracy apart over the next decade. Bryan's vow of support for Cleveland was an ephemeral oddity, signifying a hope for future partisan triumphs more than a true commitment to the fallen leader. At the end of the 1880s, two species of Democrats—conservatives and reformers—were emerging from a shared ancestry of Jeffersonian ideals and a resentment of Republican rule.

Dominant on the party's right were men from the North and certain border states who were skillful at making money and holding on to their local bailiwicks. For them, Jefferson's old passion for "equal rights" had cooled into the boilerplate of banquet speeches. There was William Collins Whitney, scion of New England gentry, astute New York lawyer, street-railway magnate, and owner of several forests and prize racehorses. There was Arthur Pue Gorman, the smooth, cautious chieftain of the Maryland party, who loathed the civil service law that he thought prevented the Democracy from ever gaining sway over the federal government. There was Henry Watterson, the acerbic editor of the *Louisville Courier-Journal,* who stood on guard against any Democrat he suspected of favoring anything but "a tariff for revenue only" (a phrase he invented).[67] In photos, their stiff moustaches and belligerent gazes bespoke a regard for timeless principles and nostalgia for the awful, glorious war many had fought as young men.[68]

"Bourbons," they got branded by contemporary critics fond of metaphors from European history, and subsequent historians have echoed the term. Certainly no one could match the ardor of these men for safeguarding the powers of individual states, curbing federal finances, and opposing agitators for such moral causes as prohibition and the redistribution of wealth. In Dixie, their partners were ex-Confederates who had erected a "redeemed" social order that terrorized black voters it could not control and eviscerated funding for education and medical care. Yet the conservatives had learned how to translate traditional principles into a governing philosophy. And their tactical alliances with Irish Catholic urban bosses demonstrated a respect for cultural pluralism that many on the left of the party did not yet share.

A growing corps of insurgent Democrats accused the Bourbons of peddling a flawed analysis of the nation's ills and having too little sympathy for citizens in trouble. Most of these rebels were legislators, state and federal, who came from areas peripheral to the metropolitan East and the industrial Midwest. In their districts, it was impossible to ignore the anguish of farmers who couldn't pay their mortgages or afford to transport their goods to market, of railroad workers fired for union organizing, and of small-town merchants shackled by high interest rates. Mushrooming insurgencies such as the Knights of Labor and the Farmers' Alliance gave a degree of collective voice and muscle to the protests.

On the floor of the House of Representatives in 1882, Congressman John Reagan of Texas thundered, "How long will it be until... a few railroad magnates shall own most of the property of the country, while the masses of the people must be reduced to a condition of serfdom, poverty and vassalage?" Several times, the House passed a Reagan-authored bill that aimed to stop railroads from charging small shippers higher rates than large ones and imposed on violators a stiff fine and possible time in prison. But the Senate, filled with wealthy conservatives from both parties, refused to go along.[69]

Although slow to acknowledge it, Reagan, a former member of the Confederate cabinet, and like-minded Democrats were beginning to revise the party's gospel of hostility to federal intervention. The swiftness and novelty of corporate manipulation of the economy and national politics demanded a modest break with tradition. One's political survival might also be at stake. Across the South and West, agrarian and labor movements were spawning a welter of third parties that made such radical demands as protection for union organizers, public jobs for the unemployed, and a financial plan that would allow farmers to use their own staple crops for collateral, thus bypassing banks altogether. While still small, these independent parties could tip the balance in close elections. For most Democrats outside the Northeast, the Bourbon way seemed both economically callous and electorally idiotic.

BRYAN TOOK HIS time deciding which faction to support in the gathering conflict. Soon after moving to Lincoln, he had introduced himself to every Democratic leader in the state.[70] The most significant was J. Sterling Morton. The stern-jawed gentleman farmer had settled in Nebraska before the Civil War and had been aggressively promoting both the state's Democracy and its agricultural bounty ever since.

As an advocate for the latter, he was a great success. With subsidies from railroad companies, Morton toured the country armed with bushels of home-grown apples and corn to advertise Nebraska's cheap land and easy transport. In 1872, he came up with the clever idea of devoting an annual spring holiday to the cultivation of shade and fruit trees on the open prairies. Within two decades, schoolchildren in nearly every state were planting saplings on the same day in late April—which just happened to be Morton's birthday. Arbor Day caught on as a symbolic stake in the future and a nostalgic bow to America's agrarian origins.

But in Nebraska, the father of the holiday was continually frustrated by the power of the state GOP and squabbles among his fellow Democrats. Morton failed to get elected to any of the offices—congressman, senator, governor—for which he ran. When, in 1888, he met the newcomer from Illinois and heard him speak, Morton was overcome with hope. This fresh talent might at last bring the state party out of the wilderness. "Bryan...is a remarkably promising young man," Morton wrote in his private journal. "He has gifts. He will be, with good habits and right direction, a benefactor to good government."[71]

The paternal tone was a harbinger of future conflict. Bryan was grateful for the older man's support and returned it handsomely that fall with numerous speeches for Morton's campaign for a seat in Congress—which ended in defeat, like all the others. But Will had never taken political direction from anyone but his father and had no reason to do so now. Morton was a principled conservative, dedicated to keeping government out of the marketplace, whether for whiskey or textiles. Like most Bourbons, he was a devotee of free trade and viewed high tariffs as a "diabolic" tax on American consumers as well as a violation of the natural laws of the economy.[72] Bryan also despised the tariff, but his vision of reform was larger than that. And he was beginning to see that the Bourbon gospel offered no remedy for the problems of ordinary Nebraskans.

At the close of the 1880s, a nasty mix of calamities, natural and man-made, put an end to good times. A massive blizzard in January 1888 killed stock animals across the northern plains, ruining Nebraskans who had invested nearly everything they had in pigs and cattle. Two years later, the worst drought since the Civil War destroyed millions of acres of corn, wheat, and oats. The health of Nebraska's urban economy depended upon the bounty of its farms. Bankrupt businesses and unfinished buildings scarred the streets of Lincoln and Omaha.[73]

A growing number of rural Nebraskans had begun to rail at a human scourge as deadly as the elements. They called it by a variety of names— "monopoly," "the money power," "Wall Street," or "organized wealth." But the indictment was simple enough: a powerful conspiracy was robbing small farmers of the fruits of their labors. They accused the railroads of imposing sharp and unfair hikes in freight rates, bankers of committing a legal form of usury, and the political establishment of serving the rich and the cities at the expense of productive families in the countryside. Men and women who had broken the prairie sod, expecting it to yield them an independent life, if not always a comfortable one, were forced to mortgage their farms and sometimes even their plows and animals to stay in business.[74]

Since 1880, a state branch of the Farmers' Alliance had been trying to mobilize these discontents. Like its counterparts in states to the north and south, the Nebraska branch of the alliance did not begin as a political insurgency. Organizers launched cooperative stores and sold hail and life insurance at rates lower than commercial firms were offering. For most of the decade, good crop prices and the rush of optimistic newcomers kept its membership in the low thousands.

Then in 1889, a bumper harvest of corn—Nebraska's biggest crop— resulted in the lowest prices in memory. Some farmers resorted to burning their corn for fuel instead of selling it to buy coal. City newspapers blamed the crisis on too many ears chasing too few buyers and blandly predicted the market would readjust itself in time. But a hundred weekly papers from the rural counties told a more dramatic story, and skilled lecturers from the alliance helped drive it home. Children who scented their parents' anger began to sing:

> *When brokers are freed from all their harm*
> *And lobbyists are dead*

The banker'll bow unto the farm
And come to us for bread.[75]

Bryan did not immediately join the agrarian rebellion. In his law practice, he was more engaged with collecting debts for suppliers than with
serving as an advocate for farmers struggling to escape them. And, as a neo-
phyte politician, he originally thought to expand his party's core electorate
instead of courting a new one. Immigrants from Ireland, Germany, and the
Slavic lands—most of whom were Catholic—formed the base of the
Nebraska Democracy. They viewed the party as a wall of defense against
native-born moralists who wanted to shut down saloons and require that
only English be spoken in public schools. Occasional support for the state's
small, hard-pressed labor unions and swipes at railroad "monopoly" had
gained the Democrats few votes. This left jousts at the tariff and what Morton called the "radical pulpit-hangers" of the GOP as the Democrats' sole
rhetorical strategy.[76]

Bryan spent the 1888 campaign giving hard-hitting speeches on conventional themes. He stumped his district for Morton and the state for Grover
Cleveland, refreshing party doctrine with such vivid metaphors as the tariff
as a cow fed by western farmers but milked by eastern factory owners.[77]
Bryan had quickly learned to decipher the party loyalties of ethnic voters.
When he spoke to Irish or German audiences, Bryan assumed he was among
friends. Some confused his name as "O'Brien," and he laughed instead of
objecting.[78]

At one stop, Bryan correctly guessed the affiliation of several men in the
crowd. He joked that he could tell a Democrat from a Republican: members
of his party were simply "better looking." Then, according to a witness, "he
saw a man with a Swedish face looking at him with a hostile eye" and
"thought he would have a little fun with him." "You're a Democrat, aren't
you, my good man?" The Swede responded, "Naw, I ban no Democrat. I ban
sick 'bout six weeks, makes me look like one."[79]

In college, Will's oratory had been marred by a baroque style and a tendency to strain his voice for effect. But he had gradually learned to relax his
manner and simplify his language, and now he spoke fluently without either
text or notes. His voice rang out with a clarity and sonority that pleased
everyone who heard it, whatever they thought of his views. "His style is so
different from that of any other public speaker," commented a local paper.
Bryan used no "high-sounding phrases, demagogic appeals to passion or
prejudice or . . . tragic gestures. . . . He thoroughly believes what he says and
his entire lack of artfulness makes him invincible." A fellow Lincoln attor-

ney enthused, "By your personal magnetism you won all the hearts and by the force of your eloquence and the irresistible character of your logic and argument you *vanquished* the enemy." Nebraska Democrats took to calling him "Bryan the invincible."[80]

Early one morning, he returned from a trip to the northwestern corner of the state and woke up his wife. "Last night I found that I had power over the audience," he told Mary. "I could move them as I chose. I have more than usual power as a speaker.... God grant that I may use it wisely." Then he knelt by the bed and prayed.[81]

His performance in 1888, when Nebraska Democrats went down to yet another defeat, lifted Bryan to a status no other young activist in his forlorn party enjoyed. He was so proud of his effort that he approached a major New York publishing house about issuing his tariff "essays" as a book.[82] Bryan's political elders encouraged him to run for various state offices. But he declined, perhaps because of the GOP's historic domination of the far-flung rural counties or because administrative tasks held no appeal. Instead, he decided to run for Congress in 1890—from the same district in the southeast corner of the state that, by a healthy margin, had just elected a genial Republican named William Connell over J. Sterling Morton.

Bryan could not have chosen a more fortuitous time to wage his first political campaign. Across the Great Plains, 1890 was a terrible year to be a Republican. Farmers' Alliances set aside their self-help schemes and leaped into the contest for state power. In Colorado, agrarian radicals joined with miners and railroad workers to form the Independent Party. In Kansas and the Dakotas, the same men who had been promoting cooperative grain silos and general stores shifted to organizing third parties. The Nebraska Farmers' Alliance didn't launch a new party until the end of July. But the People's Independent Party then grew with a speed and ferocity that startled observers described as a "revolution."

In Nebraska and neighboring states, the GOP had always claimed the votes of most small farmers and of wage earners who were native-born and Protestant. On Election Day, their support for prohibition and memories of the Civil War usually trumped any grievances of class. But the Independent Party appealed most strongly to those same citizens who were now determined to save themselves. With their crops withering from the drought, agrarian families had time and more than enough energy to drive their wagons into town to attend rallies, parades, and picnics. They sang protest lyrics penned by Luna Kellie, a militant "hayseed" from central Nebraska who had lost her homestead to a bank. And they cheered the Independent candidate for governor, John Powers, a Presbyterian evangelist who lived in a simple sod house. One Nebraska conservative wrote with a shudder that Powers's campaign resembled "a composite of Hugo's pictures of the French Revolution and a western religious revival. The popular emotion more nearly approached obsession than…seemed possible for the American temperament."[83]

Bryan tried to make himself the symbolic leader of the prairie insurgency. Alongside attacks on the tariff, his congressional platform thundered with calls to "supress" the trusts, to aid debtors by coining silver "on equal terms" with gold, and to ban land speculation by "non-resident aliens"—all demands he shared with the agrarian rebels. Nationalization of railroads was the only major Independent plank on which Bryan was silent. He also reached out to angry farmers for whom the Bible was a primary political text. In his first campaign speech, Bryan vowed, "I shall go forth to the conflict as David went to meet the giant of the Philistines, not relying upon my own strength, but trusting to the righteousness of my cause." This was not enough to dissuade Independents in the district from running their own candidate. But it did mark him as a Democrat who sympathized with their grievances and, if elected, might advance their solutions.[84]

At the same time, Bryan was careful not to alienate the base of his own party. The Republican legislature had placed a prohibition amendment on the fall ballot. Omaha, the biggest city in the state, lay in his district, as did the third largest distillery in the nation. Fear of the dry army drove a good many of its residents to vote Democratic. The party's candidate for governor, the wealthy Irish-born meatpacker James E. Boyd, came from Omaha. And Boyd was "a sopping wet" who could count on the backing of whiskey makers and saloon owners organized in the Personal Rights League.

As a strict Presbyterian and the son of a temperance worker, Bryan loathed the "liquor traffic." In precampaign speeches at the Lincoln YMCA and the chapel of the state prison, he had called for its eventual abolition. But when he stumped through the immigrant wards of Omaha, he stopped by saloons and had an aide buy beer for all the customers—while he quaffed a glass of soda water. Somehow, his adversary failed to exploit the contradiction.[85]

In fact, William Connell proved to be a remarkably inept opponent. He accepted Bryan's challenge to a series of eleven debates in venues throughout the district, despite the Democrat's oratorical renown. With a possible upset in the air, the events drew overflow crowds. Connell was mostly content to repeat the gospel of tariff protection and moral order that had served the GOP so well in the past. The Republican press sneered that Bryan was just another "calamity howler" impeding the return of economic confidence

But the challenger honed his attacks and rebuttals with great care and won every encounter. Bryan spoke in a clear, vigorous timbre and, as a regular reader of Proverbs, had acquired the knack of coining couplets that summed up an issue in memorable moral phrases. Advocating tariff relief, he remarked that most Americans "are interested, not in getting their hands into other people's pockets, but in keeping the hands of other people out of their pockets." As the campaign concluded, local Democrats bristled with glee. One pugnacious editorial cartoonist drew "David" Bryan felling his opponent with a rock labeled "facts," then portrayed him as a razor-sharp sawmill blade shearing off Connell's fingers. The challenger's rhetorical mastery made up for his lack of cash. Bryan spent less than $200 on the race.[86]

On Election Day, he became just the second Democratic congressman in Nebraska history. Bryan outpolled Connell by over sixty-seven hundred votes, a margin of 10 percent. He swept Omaha with the help of some ballot stuffing by Boyd's supporters and held his own elsewhere in the district. The Independent candidate drew 18 percent of the tally, which deprived the young Democrat of a majority. A decade after the death of Silas Bryan, his son had realized the political goal that had eluded the father. "Oh it makes me feel good to hear of your successes Will," wrote John Sheehan, the one-time saloonkeeper who had been one of the young lawyer's first clients and had switched to selling shoes instead of whiskey. "I was just thinking that you mite [*sic*] live in Jacksonville a long time before you would be given a chance to get to go to congress."[87]

The Democracy had many heroes that fall. James Boyd squeaked into the governor's office past John Powers by a margin of eleven hundred ballots. Accounting for fraud, this was no wider than the head on a pint of fresh lager.[88] Independents swept Nebraska's two other congressional districts and took control of the state legislature. Nationwide, Democrats gained seventy-six seats in the House, enough for an ample majority. Their campaign harped on grievances held by whites in different regions—GOP reliance on black voters in the South and border states; temperance, high tariffs, and English-only schools in the East and Midwest.[89] Across the Plains, the agrarian rebels, who were beginning to call themselves "Populists," had split the normal Republican constituency and elected nine congressmen and two senators of their own.

Something unusual did occur in Nebraska's First District, however. In a year of Democratic triumph, Bryan had begun to attract the kind of passionate followers who would soon lift him to national prominence. That fall, a Democratic pharmacist met a Republican traveling salesman who, after hearing Bryan speak, vowed he was going to vote for him "if he had to go a hundred miles to reach Lincoln." Another druggist and his wife praised God for the victory and confessed, "Language fails us when we try to express ourselves." A third correspondent, a county clerk, believed that Bryan would inspire other young men to clean up politics by "representing the Masses and not a Select few."[90]

Bryan's skill on the stump was largely responsible for his appeal to people he'd never met. Even the general counsel of the Union Pacific Railroad—a political foe—praised him for "possess[ing] the happy faculty of making the worst appear the better reason to a degree which was a surprise to your adversaries."[91] The rhetorically gifted did not always sweep to victory, particularly in an era saturated with oratory. But Bryan was using his talent to signal, to a growing number of young professionals and shopkeepers as well as small farmers, the arrival of a new era—one devoted to harnessing mass discontent to the nation's oldest political party. "He is enamored with his cause," commented the *Omaha World-Herald,* the leading Democratic daily in the state, "and believing fully in it, forces his listeners to do the same." The same paper predicted that Bryan had "the physical and mental qualities to make him a remarkable man in the history of this nation."[92] It was a prophecy the congressman-elect was quite confident of fulfilling.

CHAPTER TWO

Speaker in the House, 1891–1894

For the men in the furrows have paused to say
That a Moses has come, to lead on the fray
For the hour has come, and the place, and the man,
And the right will triumph as right only can.
And now our oppressors may clamor and rave,
For we march on to victory with Bryan the Brave.

—An anonymous Nebraska poet, 1892[1]

MEMBERS OF THE august chamber Bryan entered in the fall of 1891 displayed little of the efficiency that was increasingly being practiced at the heights of American business. In session, the House of Representatives often resembled market day in a crossroads town graced with unusually ornate architecture. During floor debates, many congressmen were deep in conversation, and the Speaker frequently had to bang his gavel to enforce a modicum of order. "The members are seated, are standing or walking," wrote one observer, in and around "long rows of desks crowded closely together and with very narrow aisles" between them. "They appear like a swarm of bees, just settling."[2]

Then as now, most of the work of the House took place in a variety of standing committees—from Ways and Means, where tax laws were written, to the bureaucratic sinecure of Public Buildings and Grounds. But the committees were slow to reach decisions, and the diffusion of power made it hard to enforce party discipline. So did the notorious "short session," in which Congress met for several months after the biannual election that usually reduced scores of them to lame-duck status. The frequent turnover of members made for a House short of expertise in the intricate affairs of a culturally diverse, economically vibrant nation of sixty-five million. Almost half of Bryan's colleagues were freshmen like him. Whether newcomers or veterans, most congressmen were lawyers and thus accustomed to lengthy, unresolved disputes.[3]

In frustration, House leaders had begun to exert a degree of authority over the place. Elected Speaker in 1889, Thomas Reed of Maine quickly persuaded his fellow Republicans to give him new powers to curb delaying tactics by the minority party. At first, Democrats protested the "Reed rules." But they preserved most of them when they took control of the House two years later. As a result, sharp contests for partisan and regional gain were gradually replacing the chaos of inaction. The new rules, created to ensure that a disciplined majority would get its way, ironically boosted the value of an individual congressman such as Bryan—a budding crusader with an eloquent tongue.[4]

Before he could start orating, he needed a place to live. The size of Bryan's family had kept pace with his political fortunes. Mary gave birth to a son, William Junior, in 1889, and then a second daughter, Grace, in the winter of 1891. In a city filled with transients who wanted to live within walking distance of the Capitol, not many landlords were willing to rent to a couple with three small children. After searching for months, Will found a suite of rooms at First and B Streets, across from the construction site of the Library of Congress. They quickly became friends with their landlord, Cotter Bride, who lived in the house with his wife and nephew. The modest rent and Bryan's frugal habits allowed him to save much of his $5,000 congressional salary; whatever the weather, he dressed in a long black Prince Albert jacket, with tie and trousers to match.

Will enjoyed doing favors for young people, and the new residence gave him another occasion to display his generosity. His landlord's nephew was a recent immigrant from Ireland, Dan Bride, an uneducated boy who had run a chronic fever since moving to Washington. Dan Bride frequently had dinner with the Bryans, and between legislative sessions they often put him up at their house in Lincoln, where he regained his health. Each morning, the reverent Catholic from County Cork kneeled in prayer next to the faithful Presbyterians from Nebraska. For the rest of his life, Dan Bride was devoted to the man he had met at the dawn of a celebrated political career. He believed Bryan possessed "some Supernatural power" that enabled him to fight off a legion of "contemptable" foes.[5]

In the early 1890s, the nation's capital was a growing city of 230,000 that still had the ambience and racial pecking order of a southern courthouse town. Most of the government clerks who clustered in boardinghouses and small apartments near Capitol Hill drew adequate pay and had plenty of time to gossip and dream. Their workday began at nine, was punctuated with a proper lunch hour, and ended at four, when public buildings closed for the night. Higher up the social ladder, Republican cabinet officials, senators, and their wives entertained one another and a small number of resident diplomats, none of whose duties required them to give up many evenings. In Washington, only laborers, craftsmen, and domestics toiled the long hours familiar to workers in other metropolises. Black people made up one-third of D.C. residents but a majority of its servants, fixers, and haulers. Thousands lived in tiny alley houses, tucked behind the broad avenues of the capital city.[6]

By conviction and temperament, Bryan could never join a leisured class—although racial barriers seldom troubled him. During his first week in Congress, he put in long days promoting his old Illinois representative, William Springer, for Speaker of the House. Springer lost the race to Charles Crisp of Georgia but gained the chairmanship of Ways and Means and secured a place on the committee for his young supporter from Nebraska. Bryan also quickly introduced a flurry of bills to aid his constituents—requests for federal pensions, funds for new public buildings in Lincoln and South Omaha, and the like. He demonstrated his Jeffersonian convictions in proposing the direct election of U.S. senators, a perpetual cause that inevitably died in the upper chamber. Robert La Follette, then a lame-duck GOP congressman, remembered his colleague from Nebraska as "a tall, slender, handsome fellow who looked like a young divine."[7]

In mid-January, Bryan delivered his first speech on the House floor. It lasted only a few minutes but made a strong impression. Ignoring the caution expected of new members, Bryan spoke out sharply against spending $100,000 to charter a ship to bring relief supplies to Russia, where millions were suffering from famine. Why, he asked, had Congress not responded to Nebraska's plea for help during the "unparalleled drought" of 1890? Bryan urged private citizens to donate crops and currency to "those subjects of the Czar who bear the double burden of want and persecution." But he objected to setting a precedent for public aid abroad while neglecting the misery of Americans at home.[8]

The brief address gave Bryan's home-state allies and critics an immediate cause to wrangle. The two Populist congressmen from Nebraska backed his stand, as did the state's Democratic press, which claimed that "ninety percent" of local voters agreed. But the Republican governor, John Thayer— who had temporarily unseated James Boyd on a legal technicality—called the talk "weak, puny, and contemptible." Thayer predicted it would doom "O'Bryan, our Billy," to a single term. Bryan returned the governor's fire with a droll restatement of Democratic doctrine: "He has so long been sup-

ported by taxation that no other method of relieving distress really occurs
to him."[9] If nothing else, the speech indicated that the freshman congressman was a skillful partisan, eager for frontline duty.

During the next four years, Bryan made the most of his opportunities.
He undertook an exhaustive study of the key economic issues of the day—
taxes and the coinage of silver. Then he anticipated climactic moments in a
major floor debate and volunteered to sum up the case for his side. Each of
these occasions generated a flood of newspaper reports and boosted his
stock among like-minded Democrats. They also demonstrated a growing
mastery of the rhetorical method he had prized since his schoolboy days:
ethical content garbed in stirring, melodramatic prose.

The first of these performances was dedicated to the tariff, that perennial bugaboo of most Democrats. In the winter of 1892, the majority on the
Ways and Means Committee proposed to amend the high duties that
Republicans had instituted two years earlier, under the leadership of Congressman William McKinley, who hailed from a manufacturing district in
Ohio. With the GOP still in charge of the White House and Senate, Bryan
and his colleagues had no hope of abolishing the long, arcane schedule of
import taxes. So they decided to focus on a handful of raw materials used by
ordinary people, particularly those who toiled on the land: wool, twine,
barbed wire, iron fence posts, salt, and lumber. Bryan would argue for liberating the first two commodities from the protectionists' grip.[10]

It did not appear a propitious way to launch a national reputation. On
March 16, the day of Bryan's speech, the House whiled away several hours
debating a bureaucratic triviality: whether to double the number of workers
hired to fold the estimated ten million copies of speeches and reports generated by its members. Some Democrats complained about wasting "the
people's money" on an additional dozen clerks; Jerry Simpson, a flamboyant
Populist from Kansas, accused unnamed House officers of using current
"folders" to do their personal errands.[11] As the discussion droned on,
bunches of congressmen strolled out of the chamber, leaving just over half
the total membership to vote on the bill, which passed by a wide margin.
Bryan nervously waited. With his wife's help, he had spent a good deal of
time revising and rehearsing what he would say on this particular afternoon.
Mary, watching from the gallery, feared a postponement would sap his confidence.

When he finally did take the floor at about three o'clock, Bryan began
slowly and a bit apologetically, as if clearing away the political brush.
He acknowledged that he'd prefer "to attack the tariff in detail" but averred

that any progress from "a vicious to a correct system" was better than none at all.[12]

Then he went on the offensive. From memory, Bryan cited statistics showing that Americans consumed far more wool than they grew and that the tariff on twine made inordinate profits for a small number of domestic corporations. He quoted Alexander Hamilton and Henry Clay—fathers of the high tariff—who believed that "the protected arts" would eventually have to compete with foreign manufactures. He mocked the Republican minority for claiming, at the same time, that protection didn't raise prices and that removing the tariff would flood the nation with cheap goods from abroad.

Democrats had been making similar arguments since the GOP took power in the 1860s. But Bryan gave them a class-conscious twist that made the Bourbon leaders of his party uneasy. "These men tell us that they can not live without the collections they make," he said of the "protected interests." Yet they supped magnificently "at $10 per plate, when within a stone's throw of their banquet hall" in New York City "were people to whom a 10-cent meal would be a luxury." He insisted that a graduated income tax should be the main source of federal revenues, which underscored his main point. The tariff was nothing more than a massive subsidy to some of the wealthiest, best politically connected men in America. It was an outrage, in dire need of reform, if not outright abolition.

Bryan's vigorous stand raised the moral stakes in a debate that had grown stale over the years as advocates brought up the same self-interested points in predictable language—while many congressmen used the time to catch up on their correspondence. He also showed a flair for gentle ridicule. Bryan jibed that a leading Republican had "stated to us seriously that the tariff on wool had made more pounds of wool grow on a sheep's back." After noting how a policy of free trade had benefited England, he quipped, "Someone has said that the onion is a vegetable that makes the man sick who does not eat it. It would seem that protection does the greatest good to the country that does not have it." To drive home his argument, Bryan made ironic use of various texts—from Genesis to *Robinson Crusoe* to contemporary doggerel. Many of these jests came in response to GOP critics who interrupted, hoping to trip him up on the reliability of a statistic or the consistency of a statement. According to the official transcript, Bryan's remarks were interrupted fifty times by laughter.

As word of his performance spread through the Capitol, congressmen and senators rushed to the chamber, and curious spectators filled the gallery. When he'd held the floor for an hour, as scheduled, a bedazzled GOP representative, Julius Burrows of Michigan, moved to give him more time. Almost two hours later, Bryan, his voice unflagging, denounced the Republicans, who were unaccustomed to minority status: "You rioted in power, you mocked the supplication of the people, you denied their petitions, and now you have felt their wrath." Then he concluded with the sainted Jefferson's admonition that government "shall not take from the mouth of labor the bread it has earned." Burrows pronounced it the best speech for tariff reform he'd ever heard.[13]

Reporters across the political spectrum agreed. Ignoring Bryan's barbs at the wealthy, they focused almost exclusively on his oratorical prowess. The *New York Times*, a leading organ of conservative Democrats, remarked, "His voice is clear and strong, his language plain, but not lacking in grace. He uses illustrations effectively and he employs humor and sarcasm with admirable facility." The hometown *Lincoln Sun* considered its own high-tariff position irrelevant, at least for the moment: "Where is the Nebraskan with soul so dwarfed by what he falsely imagines to be politics that he cannot rejoice in the merited popularity . . . of our young congressman? Bryan is worth more to us than an advertising train."[14]

Less than five months after he'd arrived in Washington, Will had become one of his party's most popular orators. Invitations to speak flooded in from civic and political groups all over the country. As the Lincoln paper suggested, his appeal transcended the rugged bounds of partisanship. Jaded reporters and politicians were glad to have a new personality to liven up their dispatches and freshen their store of gossip. Some thought he resembled Samuel Randall, a former Democratic Speaker of the House; "he has the same poise of the head, and the same firm lines of the jaw," observed one writer. Others compared the Nebraskan's eloquence to that of William McKinley, the Republicans' rising star from Ohio.[15] Bryan's muscular good looks, his informal manner, his string tie and inexpensive boots, and his broad smile all seemed emblems of the rising West—its entrepreneurs as well as its angry Populists. A decade before Theodore Roosevelt praised "the strenuous life," the freshman legislator from Nebraska was embodying it on the floor of Congress.

The tariff speech ensured Bryan a wide audience for whatever he chose to say. He made the fateful decision to speak out for the free coinage of silver. No issue carried so strong a charge in the politics of the time. High material stakes and fervent symbolic ones made for a combustible mix. Through the 1860s, both gold and silver had been recognized as legal tender, with the white metal pegged at one-sixteenth the value of its more valuable counterpart. But gold dollars circulated far more widely than ones based on the alternative specie. During the Civil War, a cash-poor federal government had issued greenbacks based on nothing more than faith in a Union victory.

In 1873, a solidly Republican Congress retired the old silver dollars and placed the nation exclusively on the gold standard. When the economy fell into depression soon after, critics blamed the act for constricting the nation's money supply—stabilizing prices and exchange rates, which made creditors happy. Debt-ridden farmers and anyone else who felt the rules of the financial system were rigged to deny affordable capital to hardworking "producers" on the land and in the factory believed they were the creators of all tangible wealth. "The Crime of '73" became a rallying cry for a disparate congeries of outsiders—labor unionists, Populists, self-taught economists, and romantic pamphleteers. "The money monopoly is the parent of all monopolies—the very root and essence of slavery," charged Andrew Cameron, editor of a national labor paper.[16]

By the time Bryan got to Washington, few politicians could avoid taking a stand on the matter. Unlike the tariff, the money debate split each of the parties along regional lines: within the northeast quadrant, hub of the nation's industry and commerce, gold sentiment reigned supreme, but everywhere else, most politicians backed a currency based on both precious metals. In 1890, Congress had passed the Sherman Silver Purchase Act, which required the Treasury to purchase several million ounces of silver every month. This did not fully reinstate a policy of bimetallism, but it was enough to convince nervous investors at home and abroad to convert their greenbacks into gold, lest they be stuck with wads of inflated silver certificates. Conservatives fretted as the gold reserve fell below $100 million, the legal minimum set a decade before. But advocates of silver urged advancing toward the "free" or unlimited coinage of silver rather than retreating back to the gold standard.

Bryan had begun to make forceful arguments for free silver during the year between his election to the House and the opening of the new Congress. In April 1891, he promoted silver with the same crowd-pleasing trope he had unleashed against the high tariff just a few months before. "We simply say to the East," he told a Commercial Congress in Kansas City, "take your hands out of our pockets and keep them out." He stumped for pro-silver Democrats in Iowa and Ohio and debated a prominent banker in Omaha. These addresses drew praise from monetary reformers incensed at "the gold trust" and even gained the admiration of critics more impressed with his "noble" eloquence than with his economic reasoning.[17]

But they also signaled that Bryan was no longer the darling of a united

Nebraska Democracy. J. Sterling Morton condemned his support for "a cheap and nasty" dollar and accused him of forsaking the party's conservative principles for radical Populist ones.[18] There was good reason to be concerned. The boom of the 1880s had gained Nebraska three additional congressional seats, and the state legislature graced Omaha with a district of its own. Bryan would have to run for election in a district with the fewest foreign-born voters in the state—and where Democrats were the minority. To win, he would have to convert most of the eight thousand residents who had voted Independent two years before.[19] And their gospel was free silver.

So in 1892, Bryan ran, in all but name, as a Populist. He confessed to having "strong Alliance tendencies" and secretly dispatched his campaign manager to solicit donations from silver mine owners in the mountain West.[20] For president, Bryan actually backed the People's Party candidate—James Weaver, a former officer in the Union army—instead of Grover Cleveland, whom everyone knew would finish a poor third in the state. The Populist nominee visited the First District to return the favor. Morton was not amused. Running a thankless race for governor (and hoping for appointment to a future Democratic cabinet), he made sure his fellow conservatives gave Bryan the most tepid of endorsements—and nothing more.

But Bryan had attracted an energetic group of young lawyers who would form the backbone of his campaigns in Nebraska for several years to come. As in his first race, he stumped through nearly every town in his revamped district. In a series of debates, he bested his GOP opponent, Allen Field, a judge from Lincoln. He was not able, however, to lure William McKinley to debate with him when the GOP's tribune of high tariffs made a brief campaign trip to Nebraska that fall. In an election so close it took four days to decide, Bryan won reelection by a mere 140 votes.[21]

Across the nation, the campaign of 1892 marked the end of an era. Each major party nominated for president a respected but colorless figure—Cleveland and the incumbent, Benjamin Harrison—who abstained from campaigning for himself. As in every national election over the previous two decades, the task of turning out voters fell to party machines. They responded with torchlight parades, oceans of printed propaganda, and bombastic talk about issues—particularly the tariff and white supremacy—that had been partisan staples since Lee's surrender. On Election Day, Cleveland recaptured the White House, and the Democrats narrowly won the Senate and held their majority in the lower chamber. But the once and future president had done nothing ambitious during his first term in office, and few expected him to try to change anything now—except, perhaps, the tariff rates. As if to announce the modesty of his intentions, Cleveland stuffed his cabinet with laissez-faire stalwarts—including J. Sterling Morton as secretary of agriculture.[22]

James Weaver ran a courageous campaign, braving rocks and rotten eggs in the South and a blackout of coverage by GOP papers in the Midwest. Despite the animus of the old parties, he gained over a million ballots—almost 9 percent of the total—and twenty-two electoral votes in the Plains and Rockies. Although they failed to win over many eastern voters, the joyful insurgents expected greater successes in the years to come.[23]

It was not to be. The People's Party's first presidential campaign was its last as a serious contender. The Populists inherited a rich legacy of Gilded Age protest against immoral "monopolists" and financiers that had fueled earlier campaigns by Greenbackers, Union Laborites, and the Prohibition Party. However, the major parties grew increasingly adept at absorbing mass insurgencies before they could harden into competitors. In the future, every alternative national ticket of significance would feature either an ideologue on the left (Eugene Debs, Robert La Follette, Henry Wallace, Ralph Nader) or a protestor from the right (George Wallace, Ross Perot, Pat Buchanan).

Grover Cleveland had no time to savor his return to power. In February, weeks before the inauguration, the Philadelphia and Reading Railroad went bankrupt, triggering a sharp decline on Wall Street. After a brief rebound, panic hit the stock market on May 5, when brokers learned that the National Cordage Company, the country's leading rope maker, was also going into receivership. "The floor might have passed for a morning in Bedlam," commented the *New York Times*.[24] In a sickening if inevitable sequence, five hundred banks closed their doors, hundreds of additional railroads (including the once mighty Union Pacific) declared bankruptcy, thousands of factories slashed production and jobs, and many farmers could find no wholesaler to buy their grain and cotton, even at deflated prices. It was the worst economic crisis since the birth of the republic.

In many big cities, private charities ran short of bread and clothing, and sympathetic local and state officials could muster more creativity than cash. Detroit's mayor, Hazen Pingree, a Republican reformer, invited the hungry to grow potatoes on vacant city land. By late fall, thousands of immigrant workers were sleeping under bridges and in city parks. Others tramped along highways and railroad tracks and listened to speakers such as Jacob Coxey, a wealthy Ohioan with a social conscience, who vowed to lead them on a march to Washington, "a petition with boots on," to demand federal jobs and an eight-hour day.

True to its convictions, the administration offered only the remedy of bankers. "Though the people support the government," Cleveland had once intoned, "the government should not support the people."[25] The culprit must be silver. Repeal the Sherman Silver Purchase Act, urged the president, and newly confident businessmen would renew the health of the economy. In June, Cleveland called Congress into an extraordinary special session for just that purpose. Then he left the city to undergo an operation in New York to remove part of his jaw, grown cancerous after years of gripping and chewing cigars. Physicians operated in secret on a yacht sailing up the East River. "My God, Olney," Cleveland blurted out to the attorney general, a good friend, after the ordeal was over, "they nearly killed me."[26] Only much later did Americans learn how close Vice President Adlai Stevenson, a free-silver man, had come to taking power.

Bryan quickly emerged as a leader of the opposition to Cleveland when the House convened in August. His closeness to Populists and his break with Morton had gained him a reputation as a rebel, and his oratorical renown had grown steadily since the tariff speech seventeen months before. An admirer from Delaware hailed him as a "true friend of the people" and wondered why other Democrats were "willing to become cowardly slaves" to gold. From Hastings, Nebraska, came a petition urging him to wield "the sword of Justice and truth" and "send conviction to your hearers."[27]

Few doubted that Cleveland would win repeal of the Silver Purchase Act. The phalanx on his side was simply too powerful and well connected. As Henry Adams, that wise cynic from the old elite, observed, "All one's friends, all one's best citizens, reformers, churches, colleges, educated classes, had joined the banks to force submission to capitalism."[28]

The president mobilized his entire cabinet and the Democratic leadership of Congress behind what he saw as a test of loyalty and resolve. He could also count on nearly every Republican from the East and Midwest. In the final vote, repeal carried by more than a two-to-one margin.

So debaters on the House floor were aiming more to impress reporters and gain future advantage than to convert their colleagues. On the morning of August 16, a few hours before his scheduled speech, Bryan wrote to Mary at home in Lincoln that he was praying to be able to serve as "an instrument in the hands of Providence of doing some good for my country."[29]

He delivered a call to moral combat, liberally sprinkled with the particulars of monetary history. Standing in a packed House chamber, Bryan began by invoking a historic Christian triumph: Charles Martel's defeat of Muslim invaders at Tours in 732. This battle, "historians tell us ... [,] determined the history of all Europe for centuries." Bryan went on, "A [battle] greater than Tours is here! In my humble judgment the vote of this House ... may bring to the people of the West and South, to the people of the United States, and to all mankind, weal or woe beyond the power of language to describe or imagination to conceive."[30] It was a grandiose opening. How would the young crusader back up his claim?

For the next three hours, Bryan portrayed the cause of free silver as a defense of hardworking Americans and the sovereignty of the nation itself. Except when quoting others, he spoke entirely from memory. With jabs of irony, Bryan punched away at creditors who demanded an "honest dollar" based on gold but seemed unconcerned that banks were closing because they had too few dollars to lend. "Will a repeal of the Sherman law cure these evils?" he asked rhetorically. "Can you cure hunger by a famine?" With biting couplets inspired by the Book of Proverbs, Bryan scored the hypocrisy of the powerful: "The poor man is called a socialist if he believes that the wealth of the rich should be divided among the poor, but the rich man is called a financier if he devises a plan by which the pittance of the poor can be converted to his use."

So far, Bryan had avoided venting the regional hostility that infected the writings of many silver advocates. He realized he could not win over the country by demonizing the large and growing population of the urban Northeast. But then he let fly a memorable blast at eastern elitists, for which his targets would repay him in the future by muddling the distinction between the interests of their class and of their region. Referring to lawmakers who favored bimetallism only if the British government agreed, Bryan asked, "Are we an English colony or an independent people? If there be some living along the Eastern coast—better acquainted with the beauties of the Alps than with the grandeur of the Rockies, more accustomed to the sunny skies of Italy than to the invigorating breezes of the Mississippi Valley—who are not willing to trust their fortunes and their destinies to American citizens, let them learn that the people living between the Alleghanies and the Golden Gate are not afraid to cast their all upon the Republic and rise or fall with it." Holding up a silver dollar minted in 1795, Bryan demanded "the restoration of the money of the fathers."[31]

It was a riveting performance—and a blatantly demagogic one. In his attack on the McKinley tariff a year before, Bryan had mingled affability with high purpose. He wanted to display the full range of his oratorical talents for an audience that barely knew his name. But now, before a full gallery and the entire Washington press corps, he was in deadly earnest, pausing only five times for laughter after comments that were derisive rather than humorous. The economic woes of common people—and Grover Cleveland's alleged tilt toward the rich—had concentrated his mind on national salvation. For public officials, there was no longer any neutral ground, no room for compromise: "Just as long as there are people here who would chain this country to a single gold standard, there is war—eternal war; and it might as well be known now!" Bryan then evoked the "immortal Jefferson" and took his seat as "cries of 'Vote!' 'Vote!' " and an explosive ovation rang through the chamber.[32]

Few journalists from newspapers that favored the gold standard echoed the applause. The *Chicago Tribune* acknowledged that Bryan's "flowers of speech" had "pleased the galleries and the girls," but the paper argued that his oratory had obscured the flimsiness of his brief for "a short dollar" that would cheat the very masses he wanted to help. The *Omaha Bee* dubbed him an "infant phenomenon" who foolishly supposed his theatrical bravado a match for Cleveland's integrity under pressure. For their part, pro-silver papers strained to find language worthy of what their young hero had accomplished. In Mexico, Missouri, a weekly journal stammered, "That was one of the most wonderful speeches that ever emanated from a human brain that ever passed the lips of man."[33]

The money issue was too vital to allow Bryan's opponents to appreciate the performance and downplay his message, as they had after his tariff address. Now they scorned him as too *much* the performer, a matchless voice in a facile mind. "I am Bill, Bill the Metaphor manipulator," began a satirical poem published in the conservative press. "When I talk the universe listens / And the little stars stand on their heads in ecstasy / All the silver in the bowels of / The earth rolls over on its side and yearns to be discovered." A pro-Cleveland Democrat from Nebraska scorned the thirty-three-year-old congressman as "this Solon in swaddling clothes, this Demosthenes in diapers."[34]

For the rest of his life, the image of a man in love with his words but heedless of rigorous argument would dog Bryan's campaigns for president and for a variety of causes, political and religious. Oratory, the only endeavor in which he routinely excelled, also became one of his greatest obstacles to gaining power.

Repeal of the Silver Purchase Act improved neither the American economy nor Cleveland's political standing. Unemployment and business failures only increased as investors hurried to exchange their silver certificates for gold coins. Then, in the summer of 1894, the president sent two thousand troops and five thousand federal marshals to break a national railroad strike that had begun as a conflict between the makers of Pullman sleeping cars and their autocratic employer. This angered many wage earners and reformers and made railway union leader Eugene V. Debs a working-class hero. In the fall, the administration took the humiliating step of asking J. P.

Morgan and a handful of other Wall Street bankers to shed some of their excess bullion for $50 million in government bonds. This was a logical act, given Cleveland's fealty to gold. But it further inflamed Populists and rebel Democrats, who already suspected the president of being a lackey of the "money power."

Bryan spent the year after his big silver speech preparing to do combat in a larger arena. Inside and outside Nebraska, political allies were comparing him to a David who had bravely challenged Grover the Goliath without yet being able to hurl the decisive shot. Perhaps a seat in the Senate would give Bryan that opportunity, as well as free him from the need to raise funds for biannual campaigns in a fiercely competitive district. In May 1894, he announced he would not run for reelection; early in August, he declared his candidacy for the higher office.

Encouraged by public regard, Bryan added to the roster of reforms for which he was willing to fight. The depression was increasing class feeling among ordinary Americans, making it feasible, even popular, to stand up for causes that only agrarian radicals and urban socialists had advocated before. Free silver was only the most prominent issue that separated the Bourbons, in their shaky dominance of the party, from the growing army of insurgent Democrats who sounded more and more like Populists. Through the remainder of his term in the House, Bryan spoke out for a graduated income tax and federal insurance for bank deposits. He denounced the court injunction that had allowed Cleveland to intervene in the Pullman dispute and endorsed, perhaps for the first time, the freedom of workers to join a union and go on strike.[35]

In order to keep his views before Nebraska voters, Bryan also dipped a toe into the ancillary career of journalism. In the summer of 1894, after Congress adjourned, he became editor in chief of the *Omaha World-Herald,* the state's most popular daily and a loyal friend of the Democratic Party.[36] The post was more a tribute to his name than a guide to his duties. Most editorials that carried Bryan's byline were actually written by Richard L. Metcalfe, who, as the paper's Washington correspondent, had been tirelessly promoting the young congressman's deeds to the folks back home and thus was quite familiar with his ideas and rhetoric. Quotations from Jefferson and the Bible studded the ghostwritten efforts.

The real editor of the *World-Herald* was its publisher, Gilbert Hitchcock, an ambitious Democrat exactly Bryan's age whose family had been in Nebraska since its founding. Hitchcock saw his new colleague as possibly a future president and certainly a booster of circulation. Now he could afford to buy new typesetting machines.[37]

For Bryan that fall, running for the Senate was all-consuming. In his habitual mode of campaigning, he charged through Nebraska delivering more than eighty talks that assailed the goldbugs and lauded the producing masses. Audiences who knew his reputation but had never heard him speak cheered his attacks on GOP candidate John Thurston, who happened to be chief counsel of the Union Pacific, that icon of arrogant capitalism. Pro-silver politicians from elsewhere in the nation asked for copies of his speeches to use in their own campaigns, and James Weaver sang his praises all over the Plains. Even from within Grover Cleveland's Interior Department came words of adulation. "So deep is my interest in your election," wrote chief clerk Josephus Daniels, "that I would like to be a resident of Nebraska long enough to lend a helping hand."[38]

Soaring on the gale of change, Bryan persuaded a majority of Democrats at their state convention to take a daring step—to endorse the Populist candidate for governor and two of his brethren running for Congress. The People's Party returned the favor by nominating nobody for Senate. Outraged by Bryan's perfidy, conservative Democrats, led by J. Sterling Morton, bolted the convention and nominated their own splinter ticket of men loyal to Grover Cleveland and the gold standard. They seemed not to care that in 1894 the president was about as popular in Nebraska as a corn virus.

Unfortunately for Bryan, the Founding Fathers had not considered public esteem a sufficient qualification for the U.S. Senate. He needed a majority in the Nebraska legislature to elect him to the office and could only hope that enough Democrats and Populists would win seats that fall to put him over the top. But the father of Arbor Day was hardly the only powerful Nebraskan determined to shoot down Bryan's star before it rose any higher. The Republican campaign fund swelled with thousands of dollars from major railroad firms, the anti-Catholic American Protective Association, and banks all over the state. Some of the latter may have warned debt-plagued customers that their loans would come due immediately if the GOP did not triumph. Even as Bryan was drawing applause and laughter at Thurston's expense before thousands of spectators, his campaign chairman reported, "We are without a cent in the Treasury," adding he'd have to pay the costs of the next senatorial debate out of his own pocket.[39]

On Election Day, Bryan demonstrated that he was probably the people's choice. In lieu of direct elections for the Senate, Nebraska allowed voters to cast a nonbinding preference vote. In this tally, Bryan crushed his opponent by a margin of 73 percent. The ridiculously large spread indicated that the GOP advised its loyalists not to participate, knowing what the result would be. In the only contest that counted, Republicans elected a majority of state legislators—who crowned their victory by naming John Thurston the new senator from Nebraska.

Across the nation, the Republican Party was celebrating a historic triumph. From the cities of the Northeast to the shores of the Pacific, voters punished the Democrats for stumbling and squabbling in Washington as wages declined, jobs disappeared, and the currency contracted. Republicans gained 121 seats in the House, the largest increase ever, and wrested back the majority they had lost the year Bryan was first elected to Congress. The tide swept over pro-silver Democrats in Nebraska as well as stalwarts of Grover Cleveland, who still held the reins of most state parties. Throughout the Midwest, apex of partisan conflict, the GOP elected eighty-six out of eighty-nine representatives, almost doubling their numbers in the region. The sole Democratic victor in all of New England was John "Honey Fitz" Fitzgerald, the Boston Irishman whose future grandson was John F. Kennedy. Champ Clark, a Bryan admirer who lost his own seat in Missouri, described the 1894 election as the greatest slaughter of innocents since Herod. Only in the South did the party of Jefferson—and of Jim Crow—remain supreme.[40]

The debacle did little to dampen Bryan's natural optimism. To readers of the *World-Herald,* he (or his ghostwriter) paraphrased the Book of Job: "The people gave and the people have taken away, blessed be the name of the people." He rejoiced that the alliance of Nebraska Democrats and Populists had elected a governor and saw fusion as the only way to defeat "the enemies of good government" who "act as one man, with unlimited means at their disposal."[41] With Cleveland's forces thoroughly discredited, the way was now clear to capture the national party. James Dahlman, an ally from Omaha, declared, "We want to march right ahead, and I have begun to talk you for President—and I mean it. No gift in the hands of the people is too high for you in my judgment."[42]

And why not? Seven years after arriving in Nebraska, Bryan had become a hero to a widening circle of people who seemed hungry for a voice to follow and a politician to respect. His frequent references to the Bible and to Christian history dovetailed effortlessly with his condemnations of worldly evils. Bryan had not always been a paragon of public character; those saloon visits in 1890 revealed the dross of pure ambition that lay beneath the glint of ethical rhetoric. But to a growing number of admirers, there was no one who spoke more clearly, more vigorously, or more often about the reasons why the country was in trouble than the young orator from Lincoln.

"You are the first man in politics whom I have fully and completely trusted," wrote an Omaha lawyer three days after the election of 1894. "I would stake my life on your honor, sincerity and love of our country." The former Republican added, "I know you for the large warm-hearted man you are. I know how you love your country and the poorer and weaker people." That kind of adulation would have been hard for any politician to ignore. For Bryan, who since adolescence had dreamed of becoming great by doing good, it was undoubtedly proof that he was on the side of the angels.[43]

THE NIGHT Mary Bryan learned her husband would not be going to the Senate, she allowed herself a rare moment of doubt about their future. Dan Bride was staying with the Bryans at the time. As he mounted the stairs to bed, he overheard husband and wife in their sitting room, discussing what should come next. A quarter-century later, Bride recalled that Mary asked Will "to grant me one request." Bryan agreed, "unless you ask me the impossible." Then Mary confessed that "it is anything but pleasant for me to be left alone" with three children "and bring them up as they should be brought up." Couldn't Will "settle down" to his law practice and his writing? It was a dramatic example of her assertive nature, as well as a glimpse of the quiet desperation a politician's wife had to endure.

In her concern, Mary foretold the defeats that lay ahead. But she was asking her husband to change his personality, to become an ordinary man—shorn of an ambition intertwined with the creed of character. "It would seem to me," Bryan answered, "as if I was born for this life and I must continue to fight the battles of the people for what I think is right and just"—even if he had to wage them alone and without an official position. Bride remembered "the ring of his voice" as Bryan committed himself to "such a sacrifice, pledging his life to the cause of humanity."[44] It was an utterly melodramatic moment—but also an authentic one, in the vision expressed if not in the precise words that were spoken. A career of thrilling "sacrifices" had only just begun.

CHAPTER THREE

In the Armor of a Righteous Cause, 1895–1896

Take sentiment from life and there is nothing left. When our opponents tell us we are running a sentimental campaign and that they are running a business campaign, we reply to them that we are simply placing the heart of the masses against the pocketbooks of a few.

—William Jennings Bryan, September 1896[1]

A Word fitly spoken is like apples of gold in pictures of silver.

—Proverbs 25:11

THE SOUND AND FURY of most American presidential campaigns between the end of the Civil War and the start of the Great Depression signified far less than their partisans imagined. Major party activists routinely predicted that the country would hurtle into a calamitous descent—social, economic, moral—should their adversaries win the race. But once in office, chief executives neglected to consider radical changes in any area of national life. A shared desire to gain the goodwill of business and to promote class and regional harmony in a large, growing, and quick-tempered republic inclined most presidents toward conservative policies that made the rhetoric of the previous campaign sound rather silly. But then, most adult Americans did not take the language of politicians at face value.

The contest of 1896 was different. In his campaign, Bryan was challenging more than a man and an opposing party. Speaking to and for a legion of admirers, he voiced a romantic, class-aware protest against an order increasingly being governed by the intellectual assumptions and material might of big corporations, in both finance and manufacturing. More inchoately, he proposed an alternative regime of Christian decency, one that would consider the well-being of farmers and wage earners before the anxieties of big investors. His campaign endeared him to countless Americans who came to regard him as a godly hero. And in his advocacy of a stronger, more interventionist state, Bryan calmed his party's ancestral dread of federal power. Every Democratic president from Woodrow Wilson to Lyndon Johnson would reap the benefits of his apostasy.

For their part, Bryan's lavishly funded opponents believed his victory would deliver the country to a mob of anarchists and fools. Free silver would undoubtedly ruin the economy for years to come. "This issue has forced itself to the foreground in spite of the efforts of the most influential politicians to hold it back," lamented *Harper's Weekly*. "In the face of it all the old watchwords and battle-cries of the two great political parties lose their significance and power."[2] Both campaigns, drawing support across traditional party lines, were convinced that they were battling for the fate of the nation. But tens of thousands of Bryan voters adored their candidate and told him so—loudly cheering at his speeches and writing him letters of encouragement and worship. Many would remember the campaign that turned a politician from a rural state into a national leader as the most gripping public event of their lives.

TO WIN THE NOMINATION, their hero had to overcome a daunting set of obstacles. He was a decade younger than any other serious candidate; at the close of his congressional service on March 3, 1895, Bryan remained two weeks shy of the minimum age for the presidency. In addition to holding no public office, he hailed from a small western state that had never voted Democratic in a national election, and he was still unknown to most Americans who did not live in Nebraska or belong to the clique of professional politicians. He had no funds to contribute to his own campaign and had incurred the antagonism of Grover Cleveland and his still-powerful loyalists. A prudent man would have sat out the next election or, from his visible perch at the *Omaha World-Herald,* sought to recapture his old seat in the House.

But Bryan, as he told his wife, was on a mission, and no true missionary diverts his mind from the task of conversion, no matter how high the barriers to achieving it may appear. In the sixteen months that remained before the Democratic convention, he undertook a speaking tour for free silver and the transformation of his party that made him an acknowledged leader of a national insurgency. Bryan also took less publicized steps to dissuade prominent Populists and pro-silver Republicans from running independent tickets that would dilute the strength of their common cause. As in his Nebraska races, he combined a grand vision with the search for a winning election strategy, aware the latter would require fusion with the Populists and, perhaps, a degree of ideological compromise. He proved to be as adept at the intrigues of Gilded Age politics as he was committed to the evangelical dream of a nation cleansed of cupidity and economic inequality.

Bryan spoke both widely and wisely, choosing locations that would do his presidential ambitions the most good. On several occasions, he repeated resonant lines from the final speech he had given in Congress at the end of December 1894: "The money centers present this insolent demand for further legislation in favor of a universal gold standard. I, for one, will not yield to that demand. I will not help to crucify mankind upon a cross of gold. I will not aid them to press down upon the bleeding brow of labor this crown of thorns."[3]

In May 1895, Bryan traveled to Memphis to counter a plea for "sound money" by John Carlisle, the articulate secretary of the Treasury. In June, he attended a gathering of silver Democrats in Springfield, Illinois, where delegates, led by Governor John Peter Altgeld, cheered his call to defeat "a conspiracy greater than that attacked by [Andrew] Jackson, one international in extent and destined . . . to produce more misery than war, pestilence and famine." In November, Bryan spoke at the Texas State Fair in Dallas and met privately with such Lone Star party notables as ex-governor James Hogg and the current governor, Charles Culberson, who were enchanted by his eloquence and zeal. Each state was critical to a Democrat's chances for the presidency, and a separate Populist ticket would almost guarantee victory for the GOP. Bryan's combination of stump thunder and backroom sweetness might nudge mistrustful partisans of the two pro-silver camps into a tactical embrace.

He also stopped practicing law, realizing that skillful oratory was more lucrative than prairie litigation. By the end of Bryan's time in Congress, managers of several lecture firms had begun to capitalize on his way with an audience. In the spring and summer of 1895, he gave paid talks in states from Pennsylvania to Missouri to Oregon. Some of these were planned as debates with an advocate for the gold standard. Others were less confrontational efforts, aimed to soothe a crowd instead of provoke it. For twenty-five cents, friendly periodicals offered a self-published collection, entitled simply *Speeches of Congressman Bryan.*[4]

The peripatetic whirl was making Bryan many new friends; "I perhaps was personally acquainted with more delegates than any man who was mentioned as a [presidential] candidate," he later wrote. It was also beginning to make him famous. One admirer wrote in May that before he met Bryan at a free-silver convention, he'd known him "by reputation, like every other person on the continent." Bryan's correspondence glinted with rapturous reviews. "Your visit to our little city marked an epoch," wrote the manager of a lyceum agency in Greenville, Ohio; "your effort gave more satisfaction than anything enjoyed here for years, or probably ever." A court clerk from Jackson, Tennessee, swore, "No man can draw a larger crowd in the South than you." Within a few months, Bryan was commanding $100 per talk, about what he'd earned for two long weeks of legal work before his election to Congress.[5]

How did he do it? One born too late to hear Bryan on the stump or in a convention hall can only gather up reminiscences and marvel that, in an era satiated with oratory, he could lead so many people, foes as well as allies, to describe him as the most compelling speaker they'd ever heard. The technology to capture a speech on location did not yet exist, and the first studio recording of Bryan's voice that has survived, primitive as it is, dates from 1908.[6]

Nearly every recollection begins by describing the quality of that voice. "Sonorous and melodious," "deep and powerfully musical," "soothing but penetrating," "free, bold, picturesque," "clear as a cathedral bell," "sometimes familiar as if in personal conversation, at other times ringing out like a trumpet"—these are terms more suited to a stage actor than to a politician.[7] Indeed, Bryan modulated his tone and varied the rhythm of his lines in the manner of an Edwin Booth or a Lawrence Barrett, great actors whose performances he had probably never witnessed.[8] Like them, the Nebraskan could project his voice a remarkable distance. Mary Bryan recalled one day in 1898 when, from inside a hotel room in Corpus Christi, she could hear her husband perfectly "three long blocks" away.[9] At national conventions, before the introduction of amplified sound in the early 1920s, Bryan's was often the only voice that could reach every seat in the house. And his diction—clear, precise, and rendered with a slight prairie twang that passed for no accent at all—ensured that listeners could understand every word.

In the mid-1890s, his look was almost as appealing as his sound. Although he was approaching middle age, Bryan seemed as strong and vigorous as a college man. His muscular chest, thick arms, and well-defined jaw made a sharp contrast with the many politicians who sported beards, bushy moustaches, and ample bellies. Only his receding hairline betrayed his true age. Supporters saw his youthfulness as a sign of resolve. "His stalwart, broad-shouldered presence fills and satisfies the eye," reported the New York Journal; "his face, with its black eyebrows and strong features, shows the expression afar off." Opponents inevitably suggested that "boy Bryan" was too immature to wield national power. In a series of 1896 cartoons for Judge magazine, Grant Hamilton portrayed him as a lad in sailor suit, with straw hat and fishing pole, and stark naked as he futilely chased a butterfly.[10]

Unlike most actors, Bryan wrote his own scripts, and they unfailingly conveyed the attitudes listeners either admired or satirized. Notwithstanding his thorough preparations, he tried to say just what he believed and to say it as directly as he could. His frequent allusions to distant historical events and to Scripture did not compromise his purpose; Bryan usually had one big point to make in a given address, and references to the Battle of Tours or Proverbs only drove it home with a certain elegance. His dry wit diluted whatever turgidity crept into such passages.

Nearly every observer agreed that Bryan was a "magnetic" speaker. The allusion to a power of nature is instructive. He appeared to be free from all doubt, ambivalence, and insincerity. Whether talking to Mary in their sitting room or to thousands of people in a park or metropolitan arena, he uttered the same sentiments in a mode of unapologetic sentimentality. William Allen White, a lifelong Republican, mused that Bryan "seemed as one apart from practical life.... His magnificent earnestness was hypnotic, first of all self-hypnotic, because he lost no force of eloquence in convincing himself." A less illustrious GOP partisan named Ira Smith first heard Bryan in 1896. Half a century later, he recalled: "I listened to his speech as if every word and every gesture were a revelation. It is not my nature to be awed by a famous name, but I felt that Bryan was the first politician I had ever heard speak the truth and nothing but the truth." The next day, Smith read the same speech in a newspaper and "disagreed with almost all of it." He was glad, in retrospect, that "the most remarkable orator of the century" had passed his prime before the onset of radio. Otherwise, Smith, who ran the White House mailroom for five decades, believed the Nebraskan would certainly have been elected president.[11]

Bryan's magnetism lifted him above the ranks of the typical Gilded Age politician whose florid words smacked of artifice and insincerity. In his widely read book about heroes, Thomas Carlyle wrote that "a deep, great, genuine sincerity is the first characteristic of all men in any way heroic."[12] Bryan's ability to give carefully rehearsed addresses that seemed to come from his heart won him the affection of audiences, even when some in the crowd took exception to his positions or his reasoning. Listeners enjoyed being in his presence and often felt inspired by a guileless orator who seemed an authentic representative of the producing classes. A politics of character thus blended into a politics of celebrity as Bryan's voice became known throughout the land.

But one does not gain political power through rhetorical wizardry alone. Bryan's stock rose in tandem with the rise of insurgents within the three main parties who saw the next election as their best opportunity to punish the establishment for forcing the gold standard on an unwilling populace. On the first day of March 1895, thirty-one congressional Democrats issued a manifesto calling on "the rank and file of the party" to unite behind a demand for free silver.[13] Throughout the spring and summer, various bimetallic "leagues," "congresses," and "unions" held meetings, where sympathetic politicians from all camps came to orate and talk strategy. In the South and West, insurgent Democrats fought to take their state parties away from the likes of Henry Watterson and J. Sterling Morton. Some Populists began warming to the idea of fusion on pro-silver grounds. They feared, however, that the Democrats would nominate for president someone such as Ben Tillman of South Carolina, who had attacked the third party in his state as vehemently as he had blasted the Cleveland administration. Meanwhile, many GOP officeholders in the Rocky Mountain states vowed to challenge the goldbug domination of their national party or go it alone.

Today, the passion for free silver—or the gold standard—seems bizarre and naive, akin to a faith that apricot pits can cure cancer. Few citizens of advanced capitalist nations fret that they can't convert their paper money into a tidy amount of precious metal. We may mistrust bankers and currency traders, but we are usually comfortable enough with abstract monetary values not to blame those who manage them for causing depressions. Over the past century, economics has become a highly specialized profession that repels those who question its authority.

But in the mid-1890s, most Americans assumed that wealth consisted largely of products that were tangible and visible—crops, livestock, iron, coal, textiles, real estate. When calamity struck, they naturally fell to arguing whether the fault lay in a surplus or shortage of the shiny commodities, or specie, on which their dollars were based. Because creditors, industrialists, and the Bank of England favored gold, ordinary Americans who resented their power, and often found it mystifying, rallied to the promise of free silver. They were groping for a flexible currency, tailored for a fast-growing economy, but they trafficked in the argot of conspiracy.[14]

For intellectual ammunition, silver advocates relied on the oratory of quick studies such as Bryan and on self-taught monetary experts such as William Hope Harvey, whose 1894 tract, *Coin's Financial School,* sold at least half a million copies in its first year of publication. Harvey crowded most of his pages with a point-by-point refutation of the case for gold. He delighted in tarring academic economists. Harvey accused one scholar of being "endowed with the money of bankers, his mental faculties…trained with his salary," and charged that bankers themselves were "controlled by a central influence in London and New York."[15]

Gold advocates held no less fervently to their own position and were no more restrained in their attacks. "A sound currency is to the affairs of this life what a pure religion and a sound system of morals are to the affairs of the spiritual life," intoned Republican senator George Frisbie Hoar of Massachusetts in 1893. Silver was "an inferior metal" that encouraged inflation, speculation, and a lackadasical attitude toward debt.[16] To its propagandists, the battle of standards became an elemental struggle between right and left, and both sides wrapped themselves in the mantle of tradition. Harvey saw the fight for free silver as a battle to restore economic democracy in America. Hoar viewed it as a tumult of cranks and anarchists who would destroy the character and economy of the republic. The argument had reached such an emotional pitch that no compromise was possible. Only political warfare could resolve it.

Gold versus silver was not the only issue driving the battalions into combat readiness. In 1894, when the Democrats still controlled Congress, they had passed the first peacetime income tax as an amendment to the lengthy Wilson-Gorman bill, which lowered tariff rates across the board. Bryan drafted the amendment, which provided for a flat levy of 2 percent on incomes over $4,000, and debated its merits with his customary vigor and sensitivity to class differences. Those citizens who get the most from government, he argued, should pay for it: "Who demands a standing army?" he asked. "Is it the poor man as he goes about his work, or is it the capitalist who wants that army to supplement the local government in protecting his property when he enters into a contest with his employes?"

Since fewer than a hundred thousand Americans earned enough to qualify, the tax, which Cleveland signed into law, was largely a symbolic swipe at the wealthy. Bryan himself would have preferred a graduated income tax that would replace the tariff entirely. But a year later, the Supreme Court, in its *Pollock* decision, struck down the law; Justice Stephen Field called it a "stepping stone" toward "a war of the poor against the rich."[17] The Court rarely overturned acts of Congress, and the decision angered social reformers in general and Populists and like-minded Democrats in particular.

Most of the same people had already been denouncing the justices for openly siding with the big money. That January, the Court gutted the Sherman Anti-Trust Act with an argument that seemed to violate the spirit of the first serious federal attempt to regulate corporate power. Even though the American Sugar Refining Company produced 98 percent of all the sugar refined in the United States, all but one justice ruled for the firm and against the government. Chief Justice Melville Fuller, writing for the majority, patiently explained that Congress had only sought "to protect trade and commerce against unlawful restraints and monopolies." As a manufacturing firm, the sugar giant was exempt. The decision irked even Grover Cleveland, who echoed the aversion that Jefferson and Jackson had felt toward meddling judges.[18]

But the president had kinder thoughts about the Court a few months later. In May, the justices voted unanimously to uphold the injunction Attorney General Richard Olney had used to crush the Pullman strike, the act that landed Eugene Debs and his fellow railway union leaders in jail. According to the justices, these dangerous "rioters" had conspired to throttle the nation's commerce, which was a clear violation of the Sherman Anti-Trust Act. Whether Cleveland appreciated the irony is not recorded. At the age of eighty-two, Lyman Trumbull, Bryan's old mentor, helped Clarence Darrow argue Debs's defense before the Court.

By the spring of 1896, with business still stagnant, the accumulated grievances of money, taxes, and labor had convinced a variety of insurgents to break with the old political order. But no one yet had a common strategy capable of toppling the goldbugs and monopolists. Growing numbers of Republicans in the mountain states favored joining a new silver party if the GOP didn't endorse their position; a handful, including Senator John Jones of Nevada, left to join the People's Party. The Populists, at the behest of James Weaver and other top leaders, decided to delay their national convention until the major parties had held theirs—the better to scoop up disgruntled renegades or assemble a fusion ticket. In February, Bryan declared in the *World-Herald*, "The Democratic party cannot serve God and Mammon; it cannot serve plutocracy and at the same time defend the rights of the masses."[19] Most Democratic delegates from the West and South agreed. They would either rescue the party from the grasp of Cleveland and his ilk or organize a militant alternative.

Bryan believed he could resolve and direct this yeasty confusion if he ran for president. In Nebraska, he had campaigned as a fusionist in all but name, and the influential Weaver remained a friend and close ally. A number of home-state Populists and rank-and-file Democrats told him he was their first choice for the White House. Insurgents from every party applauded his efforts to focus on a broad platform of social and economic reforms instead of on the tariff, that hardy perennial of partisan conflict.[20]

To boost his chances and those of the pro-silver forces, Bryan spent most of the spring on the road. He lobbied hard at state Democratic conventions, where scattered numbers of delegates talked up his chances for the presidential nomination. He also found time to cover the Republicans' national convention in St. Louis as a correspondent for the *World-Herald*, a journalistic exercise he would repeat in subsequent election years.

The whirl kept Bryan away from Salem, where his mother, sick and confined to her room for almost a year, was failing rapidly. On June 27, Mariah Bryan died at the age of sixty-two, before either of her sons could reach her bedside. Will did return to his hometown in time for her funeral, held in a packed Baptist church. Together with the congregation, he recited the same verses from 2 Timothy that had been read at the services for his father, sixteen years before: "I have fought a good fight, I have finished my course, I have kept the faith."[21]

Bryan had unlimited faith in himself, but he had to confront the reality that, in a time of depression, millions of Americans sought reassurance more than soaring rhetoric. For all his new friends, he had only half a decade of experience in national politics, none in an executive position, and currently held no office at all. He knew that a veteran Democrat from the West—such as Congressman Richard Bland of Missouri, a champion of silver in the House since the 1870s, or Horace Boies, governor of the GOP bastion of Iowa, or even Vice President Adlai Stevenson of Illinois—seemed a surer, if less exciting, choice to lead his badly divided party.

As Democrats began to arrive in Chicago for their nominating convention in the first week of July, Bland was gaining strength. He had the strong support of the Illinois delegation—led by Governor John Peter Altgeld, a champion of urban labor—as well as that of the sizeable contingents from Texas and his own state. Bland, obeying the ritual of favorites past, stayed away from Chicago and invited reporters to watch him work on his large farm near Lebanon, Missouri. There, "knee-deep in the red clover among his young apple trees," he feigned disinterest: "I hope they will not nominate me...if they can find a stronger man." Actually, Bland spent most of the week at his law office in Lebanon, waiting anxiously for news to arrive over the telegraph.[22]

BUT THIS WOULD be a rare convention, one that clashed more over principles than personalities. A clear majority of delegates came to Chicago pledged to ratify a free-silver platform; they could hardly wait to snatch the party away from the Bourbon minority. A month before, the Republicans had nominated William McKinley for president on a platform of high tariffs and "sound money." GOP delegates jeered, "Go to Chicago!" at twenty-three pro-silver delegates from the West who tearfully walked out in protest. The conservative *Nation* smirked, "Silver is, we think, the first raw material that has ever been wept over."[23] There was no longer much doubt that the fall campaign would be fought over the issue of money, with all its encrusted emotions and symbols.

The rebel Democrats were a mixed lot. Leading the charge for silver were prominent men from the South and West—senators, congressmen, and governors who had been at odds with Cleveland and his faction over economic policy for the past four years or more. As on the eve of previous conventions, insiders spent most of their time in caucuses and committee meetings, attempting to secure an outcome that would give the Democracy a chance for victory that fall. Not all these politicians were as zealous about silver as were Bryan and Bland. But, as practical men, they knew voters would punish their party if it didn't make a clean break with the administration.

Around them in the streets and hotel lobbies of downtown Chicago gathered advocates for causes that reached beyond a change in the currency. Henry George, eloquent prophet of the Single Tax on land, came to file his impressions for Hearst's *New York Journal*. Also on hand were crusaders for woman suffrage, prohibition, socialism (both secular and Christian), civil rights for Chinese immigrants, and many Populists—including James Weaver and Ignatius Donnelly, the party's best-known orator. The Sunday before the convention, a prominent Baptist minister warned his congregation, "The Populist and the anarchist... have planned deliberately to use this opportunity to press their dangerous doctrines as far as they may be able."[24] Newspapers all over the country reported his genteel shudder.

Even before the first gavel fell at the Chicago Coliseum, the convention was turning into a disorderly, quarrelsome affair. At Cleveland's request, the dapper William Whitney, former secretary of the navy, sped to Chicago on a private train stocked with gourmet food and wine to rally the forces of sound money and conservative government. But silverites spat on his aides and disrupted his first public meeting with loud cheers for Altgeld, who had been the Bourbons' favorite bogeyman since he protested the smashing of the Pullman strike. "For the first time," exclaimed a goldbug Democrat, "I can understand the scenes of the French Revolution!"[25]

The two factions battled over the identity of every convention official—temporary chairman, permanent chairman, chairman of the resolutions (platform) committee, keynote speaker—and the makeup of several state delegations, including that of Nebraska. The silverites won every vote and seemed eager to humiliate their rivals. After Bryan and his friends replaced their goldbug opponents, they hounded them off their seats on the floor and up to the galleries. In a rare burst of vengefulness, Bryan expressed his joy at being able "to walk down the aisle and put the gold standard delegation on the tip of my toe as they are being kicked out of the Convention."[26]

The platform was suffused with the same spirit. Unlike the typical document of the era, which concealed internal party differences under a blanket of downy clichés, it shouted defiance at Cleveland and his futile policies. As the "paramount" issue, the money plank came first. One of three sections that Bryan helped draft, it charged that the act of 1873, passed "without the knowledge or approval of the American people," had resulted in deflation and higher taxes, "the enrichment of the money-lending class," and the "impoverishment of the people." It stated flatly that the gold standard was "not only un-American but anti-American" because it placed the nation's economy under England's heel. Without mentioning the president's name, the next plank, against issuing government bonds during peacetime, condemned "trafficking with banking syndicates"—Cleveland's deals with J. P. Morgan and friends that had shored up the gold reserve. For that matter, the federal government ought to issue each note of currency, instead of allowing banks to share the task, "in derogation of the Constitution."[27]

The rebellion against authority didn't stop there. Of course, the platform acknowledged, the Republicans would try to restore McKinley's tariff if they took back the White House. However, "until the money question is settled," all "agitation" on that issue ought to cease. But Congress should "use all the Constitutional power" it could muster to reverse the Supreme Court's nullification of the income tax. The judicial branch, in other words, should not be the final arbiter of the public welfare.

Neither could federal judges, after the Supreme Court's outrageous intervention in the Pullman strike, be trusted to protect the rights of labor. Bowing to the tradition of states' rights, the platform called this "arbitrary interference...in local affairs," but its intent was clear. "Government by injunction" was condemned as a "highly dangerous form of oppression" that elected lawmakers must halt. And by the way, the document concluded, "no man should be eligible for a third term" as president. Grover Cleveland, the only man alive who could be affected by that plank, spent the convention week fishing off Cape Cod and wondering, no doubt, what demons had possessed his old Democracy.[28]

The Chicago platform was an act of protest and transformation. Never during seven previous decades of nominating conventions had a majority of delegates thoroughly repudiated the incumbent president of their own party. And the issues for which they chose to fight in 1896 set the Democrats on a course that led away from their laissez-faire past and toward the liberalism of the New Freedom, the New Deal, and the Great Society. To demand that the government control the money supply, tax the rich, and defend the right to strike was not quite a blueprint for a regulatory state. But the platform officially declared that Democrats were in favor of beginning to redistribute wealth and power in America. In rhetoric at least, the party has never gone back.

The old guard was not going to yield without a struggle. Supporters of the gold standard wrote a minority report on the platform and insisted on debating the main issues on the floor of the convention. The majority, preening in triumph, welcomed the opportunity to show the country that the Democratic Party was not afraid to air its differences and assert its principles. Each side put together a roster of speakers for July 9, the third day of the convention. The majority would lead off the debate and complete it, sandwiching two of its best orators—Ben Tillman of South Carolina and William Jennings Bryan—around a trio of worthies from the opposing faction. Anticipating a climactic event, ticket brokers charged as much as $50 for a seat in the gallery. In comparison, a skilled worker in the city considered himself fortunate if he took home $3 a day.[29]

The setting was as grandiose as the subject. The Chicago Coliseum occupied an entire city block at 1513 South Wabash Avenue, a short walk from Lake Michigan. The largest exhibition building in the world, it could hold as many as twenty thousand people and had hosted such outsized features as Buffalo Bill's Wild West Show. The three-story, wood-and-glass structure was a bit larger than a football field (305 by 172 feet); frequently renovated, it would later be the venue for ice hockey games, roller derby matches, the first presidential nominations of both Theodore Roosevelt and his distant cousin Franklin, and the last convention, in 1969, of the radical Students for a Democratic Society.[30]

In 1896, the Coliseum offered a good test of oratorical talent in the era before amplified sound. The space was as large as that of many a Gothic cathedral, albeit with a ceiling only about sixty-five feet high. Beyond the front rows, a speaker could be heard but not clearly understood, as his words echoed down the aisles and off the walls. To compete with the chatter of a packed audience, a man had to use every trick he knew to increase the volume of his voice—spreading and raising his arms to expand the diaphragm and lungs and moving around the podium to project his words to the rear and corners of the hall. The sole advantage of this reverberatory cavern was that it increased the volume of applause.[31]

The first speaker who mounted the twenty-foot-high rostrum late that morning struck up an incendiary overture. Senator Ben Tillman was already loathed or admired as a demagogue with a violent nature. Two decades before, the one-eyed politician with an unruly shock of hair had led terrorist onslaughts against black Carolinians who dared to exercise their right to vote for GOP candidates, and he remained an unapologetic supporter of disenfranchisement. Tillman hated "plutocrats" with an equal passion. Earlier in 1896, he had threatened to "tickle Cleveland's fat ribs with [a] pitchfork" for siding with financiers against the people. Now he was aching to express the naked truth about the new civil conflict.

Tillman was unable to separate his ire against the Bourbons from his hatred of their region, home to Wall Street and erstwhile foe of the Confederacy. "I am from South Carolina, which was the home of secession," he announced, drawing loud hisses from conservatives and easterners in the crowd. Tillman inflamed them further when he vowed to divide the Democratic Party again, as in 1860, but this time "to accomplish the emancipation of the white slaves" from the tyranny of New York, Connecticut, and New Jersey. "I want to say to you here that we have at last recognized in the South that we are mere hewers of wood and drawers of water, while the great states I have named have eaten up our substance." With his fists in the air and his clothing a sweaty jumble, Tillman appeared to one unfriendly reporter to be "the incarnation of the mob." A biographer later marveled, "He made the ghost of secession walk!"[32] Such future southern demagogues as Eugene Talmadge, Theodore Bilbo, and Lester Maddox would follow in his footsteps, winning acclaim within their region and scorn nearly everywhere else.

At this time and place, Tillman's speech was a disaster. It exposed the clumsiness of pro-silver leaders who had let their animosity overwhelm their political common sense. He left the podium to shouts of "You're no Democrat!" Senator James K. Jones, the white-goateed Confederate veteran from Arkansas who chaired the resolutions committee, rushed to calm the proceedings. In a courtly tone, he insisted that a man from the South must still "love the whole of this country." He "repudiate[d] the charge that this question is sectional." Then he gave way to speakers for the minority, who now appeared to hold a winning hand, at least dramatically.[33]

Their first orator was David Bennett Hill, a senator from New York and the leading Democrat in the most populous state in the nation. Hill owed Cleveland no loyalty; the president had blocked his path to the nomination in 1892. But the silverite platform filled the balding, expensively dressed career politician with contempt. "It smacks of Populism and Communism," Hill had written in that morning's *New York World*. Now he coolly told the

big crowd that was still buzzing over Tillman's tirade, "I am a Democrat; but
I am not a revolutionist." Did the delegates really want to force longtime
stalwarts out of the party "to make room for a lot of Republicans and Populists and political nondescripts who will not vote your ticket at the polls"?
No Democrat, Hill suggested, could be elected president without carrying
New York; only one ever had. This year, defeat would surely come if bimetallism became "a question of patriotism" or "bravery" instead of "a question
of business" and "economics."[34]

As Hill rolled out his logical if bloodless phrases, Bryan received a note
from a journalistic ally, Clark Howell of the *Atlanta Constitution.* "You have
now the opportunity of your life," wrote Howell. "Make a big, broad, patriotic speech that will leave no taste of sectionalism in the mouth and which
will give a sentiment that will touch a responsive chord in the heart of the
whole country. You can make the hit of your life." Bryan scribbled a reply:
"You will not be disappointed.... I will speak the sentiment of my heart and
I think you will be satisfied."[35]

Behind his optimism lay the cleverness of an experienced performer. To
preserve the uniqueness of the moment, Bryan had turned down several
offers to speak earlier in the convention. He had persuaded Tillman, who
craved more time, to let him give the shorter but final speech for the silver
forces. Bryan's work on the platform and his rout of the Nebraska conservatives had kept his name on the lips of delegates. With his many contacts
around the floor, he knew that neither Bland nor anyone else could yet
claim the votes of a majority. Democrats now possessed a Decalogue of
reform, but they lacked a Moses to lead them to the White House.
Reporters, perhaps to promote a better contest, had been steadily ranking
Bryan higher on their roster of favorites. By July 9, according to the *Chicago
Tribune* and several other papers, he'd emerged from the pack of dark horses
to compete with the front-runners, Bland and Boies. "I have never had such
an opportunity before in my life," Bryan wrote in his *Memoirs,* "and never
expect to have again."[36]

Now, from his seat in the middle of the arena, he watched the two goldbugs who followed Hill to the podium fumble and sputter. Senator William
Vilas of Wisconsin offered a dull, lengthy defense of Cleveland's financial
policy, drawing cheers only when his voice gave out and he left the stage.
William Russell, a former governor of Massachusetts whom some Bourbons
regarded as a possible nominee, predicted that future Democrats would
honor the minority "when the dark clouds of passion and prejudice have
rolled away." But few delegates could make out his hoarse words; the frail
Russell, it turned out, had only a week to live. After two hours of debate,

many spectators muttered their disappointment; they had anticipated a livelier exchange. Several voices called out for Bryan.[37]

He sprang from his seat in the Nebraska delegation and almost leaped up the twenty-odd steps to the stage. He had felt acutely anxious at the start of the day's session, as he always did before giving a major speech. Later, he confessed to "a feeling of weakness at the pit of my stomach" and had to gulp down a sandwich and a cup of coffee to steady himself. But the crowd inside the Coliseum applauded him for several minutes before he could say a word. So, dressed in his customary black alpaca suit and baggy pants, Bryan suddenly "felt as composed as if I had been speaking to a small audience on an unimportant occasion."[38]

He began with a disarming gesture. "I would be presumptuous, indeed, to present myself against the distinguished gentlemen to whom you have listened if this were a mere measuring of abilities."[39] False modesty, perhaps, but it made a pleasing contrast with Tillman's rant. Bryan quickly added, "But this is not a contest between persons. The humblest citizen in all the land, when clad in the armor of a righteous cause, is stronger than all the hosts of error. I come to speak to you in defense of a cause as holy as the cause of liberty—the cause of humanity."

In three elegant sentences, Bryan had summarized the argument of his speech—and, as it happened, the theme of the ensuing campaign. Free silver may have been the "paramount issue," but that is because of who advocated it and who opposed it. The issue was thus not really the issue.

Bryan and his fellow insurgents believed they were battling over nothing less than the fate of democracy and the welfare of "humanity." Bryan felt he was serving his part in a grander conflict that began with Christ and showed no sign of approaching its end. With evangelical phrases, several of which he'd used before, he seized the audience's attention. Thereafter, it followed his every cue, "like a trained choir."[40]

But he was still engaged in a debate. No matter how deft his phrases or captivating his voice, he would not have kept the big crowd enthralled if he'd given them nothing but moral platitudes. True to the occasion, the heart of his speech was a series of thrusts and counterthrusts that came naturally to a man who'd been participating in debates for half his life and who had been responding to charges such as Hill's and Russell's since the onset of the depression. As Bryan wrote later, "No new argument had been advanced and therefore no new answers were required."[41]

So he vigorously rebutted the charge of sectionalism, defended the income tax, and ridiculed those who swore they would support bimetallism if it was ever secured by an international treaty. He refrained from attacking

Cleveland or any other Democrat. A few sparks of wit kept the audience smiling as they cheered: William McKinley had once mused that he resembled Napoleon. Well, remarked Bryan, "he was nominated on the anniversary of the battle of Waterloo" and now "can hear with ever-increasing distinctness the sound of the waves as they beat upon the lonely shores of St. Helena."

Bryan never forgot that he was speaking to a gathering dominated by people, both on the floor and up in the gallery, who agreed with him. What they craved was a memorable statement of what they already believed—one they could wave over their heads in battle against the mighty "hosts of error." His voice—clear, robust, and sincere—gave it to them, in rhythmic phrases that countered the arguments of the arrogant with the sentiments of the masses.

In counterpoint, Bryan mocked, "You come before us and tell us that we are about to disturb your business interests.... We say to you that you have made the definition of a business man too limited in its application." This began as stirring a defense of "the common man" as had ever been uttered in American politics. But it was a Jeffersonian's plea for moral equity, not a radical's demand for power:

> The man who is employed for wages is as much a business man as his employer, the attorney in a country town is as much a business man as the corporation counsel in a great metropolis; the merchant at the crossroads store is as much a business man as the merchant of New York; the farmer who goes forth in the morning and toils all day ... and who by the application of brain and muscle to the natural resources of the country creates wealth, is as much a business man as the man who goes upon the board of trade and bets upon the price of grain; the miners who go down a thousand feet into the earth, or climb two thousand feet upon the cliffs, and bring forth from their hiding places the precious metals to be poured into the channels of trade are as much business men as the few financial magnates who, in a back room, corner the money of the world.

No other passage in the speech, until the famous peroration, drew more applause. From the gallery came shouts of "Go after them, Willie" and "Give it to them, Bill."[42]

To redress a linguistic injustice made it easier to imagine winning more tangible victories. But Bryan lavished his words of praise entirely on rural and small-town Americans. The only wage earners he singled out were miners, most of whom toiled in company towns quite dissimilar from the swelling metropolises where factory hands and building tradesmen lived and worked. This silence highlighted, unintentionally, a major weakness of the insurgents' cause. Bryan exacerbated it several minutes later when he said, "You come to us and tell us that the great cities are in favor of the gold standard; we reply that the great cities rest upon our broad and fertile prairies. Burn down your cities and leave our farms, and your cities will spring up again as if by magic; but destroy our farms and the grass will grow in the streets of every city in the country." Like most pledges of defiance, it probably made few converts.

As the speaker moved toward his conclusion, the audience inside the Coliseum quieted down for a moment, savoring his language and preserving their energy for the climax. In the last of his twenty paragraphs, Bryan repeated the anti-British claim he had made for free silver on the floor of Congress and at countless meetings in Nebraska and across the nation: "It is the issue of 1776 over again." If "our ancestors" who numbered only three million could "declare their political independence of every other nation," could not a nation of seventy million do the same?

Bryan then stepped forward a few inches and straight into the headlines of American history. "Having behind us the producing masses of this nation and the world, supported by the commercial interests, the laboring interests, and the toilers everywhere," he declared, before raising his hands to his temples and stretching his fingers out along his forehead for the penultimate phrase, "we will answer their demand for a gold standard by saying to them: You shall not press down upon the brow of labor this crown of thorns, you shall not crucify mankind upon a cross of gold." As he spoke the final words, Bryan stunned the crowd with an inspired gesture of melodrama. He stepped back from the podium, pulled his hands away from his brow, and extended them straight out from his body—and held the Christlike pose for perhaps five seconds.[43]

For several "painful" moments, the Coliseum was silent, as if thousands of people were all holding their breath. Bryan left the stage and walked slowly toward his delegation. Then it exploded. "The floor of the convention seemed to heave up," marveled the *New York World*. "Everybody seemed to go mad at once...the whole face of the convention was broken by the tumult—hills and valleys of shrieking men and women."[44]

The joyful riot produced a wealth of distinct memories. Willis J. Abbot, a pro-Bryan reporter from New York City, saw two southern delegates "of advanced years" embrace while "crying bitterly, great tears rolling from their eyes into their bearded cheeks." A young editor from Nebraska recalled that both women and men stood on their chairs and flung off their hats, "never caring where they should come down." A farmer in the gallery who before the speech had called Bryan "that crazy Populist" banged his coat against a gallery seat and yelled, "My God! My God! My God!" John Peter Altgeld kept his composure, telling journalists he'd rather make an address like the one he'd just heard than be elected president.[45]

Bryan had spoken for about twenty minutes, but the celebration lasted almost twice as long. Several Texas delegates picked up their state standard and ran across two aisles to plant it by the Nebraska contingent. Men bearing the guidons of thirty other states joined them there; New York's delegation, the largest in the hall, remained silent and seated. As a band played "For He's a Jolly Good Fellow," the pro-silver throng marched around the Coliseum in time to the music, brandishing their blue-poled standards, a variety of umbrellas, and portraits of Bryan torn out of daily newspapers. Future conventioneers would copy this procession well into the next century to boost their favorite candidates. But only at its origin was the object of affection carried on the shoulders of the crowd and driven to exhaustion by the press of his admirers. Bryan's theatrical tour de force had made him an instant hero.

Yet, contrary to historical legend, the speech did not ensure him the presidential nomination. The following morning, thirteen other candidates were on the first ballot, and the New York delegation sullenly refused to cast any votes at all. Richard Bland initially led the pack with 235 votes, almost a hundred more than Bryan had in second place. Altgeld kept his Illinois delegation solidly behind "silver Dick," as did leading Democrats in Texas and Kansas, where the Populists were strong. They knew their party was the underdog in the fall campaign and feared going to the country behind a young orator whom millions of voters had just become acquainted with on the front page of their morning paper.[46]

However, the rank and file inside the hall could not long be denied. For over a year, Bryan had assiduously wooed Democrats in states outside the Northeast, and since no other candidate was able to gain momentum in the early balloting, his speech's wild reception convinced many that his time had come. On the next two ballots, he peeled away votes from favorite sons and chipped away at Bland's support in the South. On the fourth ballot, Bryan pulled away from the aging Missourian; on the fifth ballot, he easily gained the two-thirds margin required to win the party's nomination. The next day, in a hasty attempt to balance the ticket regionally and secure funds for the campaign, Arthur Sewall—a wealthy shipbuilder from Maine who favored both free silver and the income tax—was chosen for vice president.

Before the convention adjourned, Altgeld finally accepted the inevitability of Bryan. But he would not abandon his suspicion, or envy, of his party's new leader. "It takes more than speeches to win real victories," he told Clarence Darrow, his friend and close ally. "Applause lasts but a little while. I have been thinking over Bryan's speech. What did he say, anyhow?"[47]

COMPARED TO THE FURY of party conservatives, Altgeld's diffidence was a mild thing indeed. Many Cleveland supporters responded to Bryan's scorn by declaring him a fanatic and a socialist, no true follower of Jefferson. The revivalistic quality of his rhetoric filled them with particular contempt. The *New York World* likened the Chicago convention to a camp meeting "where religious exhorters work upon the sensibilities of their hearers until hysterical women fall into a state resembling catalepsy." The *New York Times* headlined a front-page story about the proceedings "The Silver Fanatics Are Invincible: Wild, Raging, Irresistible Mob Which Nothing Can Turn from Its Abominable Foolishness." Grover Cleveland was grateful to them and hoped the bolters would aid McKinley. But as "president of all the people" he refrained from taking part in the campaign.[48] Throughout the Northeast and upper Midwest, Democrats who couldn't stomach their party's new platform and the rhetoric of its new leader made plans to defeat them. In early September, they convened, as the National Democratic Party, to nominate a ticket committed to the gold standard and a last-ditch defense of the incumbent administration.

In the days following Bryan's nomination, scores of urban newspapers that had backed every Democratic candidate for a generation announced that this year they would urge their readers to vote against him. The bolters included the *World,* whose circulation of nearly eight hundred thousand was the largest in the country, and the most popular dailies in Brooklyn, Philadelphia, Baltimore, Louisville, Detroit, Boston, and Washington, D.C. The great majority of the German-language *Zeitungen*—serving a large and politically engaged constituency—joined the exodus, afraid that free silver would lead to higher prices and a breakdown of the social order that sheltered old-stock immigrants.[49] Few southern papers deserted Bryan, but this was often due more to expedience than to conviction. For white voters in Dixie, the GOP still conjured up fears of "Negro rule." Thus, at a time when most journalists relished taking sides, Democrats began the campaign knowing the urban press outside the solid South would be overwhelmingly arrayed against them.

Bryan could, however, take some comfort in the prospect of fusion with the agrarian left. The Populists gathered for their convention in St. Louis during the last week of July and faced a dilemma endemic to third parties in the United States. If they insisted on running their own national ticket, as in 1892, they might educate Americans about the virtue of such ideas as government ownership of the railroads and the telegraph, which were absent from the Democratic platform. But they would certainly take votes away from Bryan and probably ensure his defeat. On the other hand, if they decided to join the Democratic campaign, they would divide their own movement and perhaps lose their radical soul. The choice of isolation or co-optation was particularly painful for Populists in the cotton South, where in previous campaigns local Democrats had disrupted their rallies, destroyed their ballots, and maligned their character. "Do you expect us to run now with the creatures who heaped these insults on us?" one Texas Populist demanded of his fusionist comrades. "So help me God, I will never march with you into ... that cesspool of hell."[50]

Yet third-party leaders also knew that "Bryan and free silver" had become an irresistible battle cry for many of the small farmers and miners on whom their hopes for a social transformation depended. Across the Great Plains and Rocky Mountains, the Democratic nominee was already the choice of most Populist voters. In late July, twenty-two men from Helena, Montana—where the Democrats had finished a poor third in 1894—sent him a rabbit's foot for use in his campaign and lauded him as "a Moses to lead the flock of wandering American husbandmen out of the darkness of selfishness and corruption and into the light of equality of man and honest government." Even southern Populist stalwarts exempted the Nebraskan from their aversion toward his party. Opponents of fusion wanted to name Eugene Debs the third party's nominee. But the hero of the Pullman strike doused their plans. He wrote to Bryan, "You are at this hour the hope of the Republic—the central figure of the civilized world."[51]

So after four days of passionate, agonized debate, the People's Party voted overwhelmingly to endorse a Democrat for president. In his nominating speech, James Weaver predicted that the election of Bryan, "that matchless champion of the people," would usher in "a new Pentecost" of democratic abundance. After the 1894 campaign, Weaver and a number of other Populists had begun to downplay such radical planks in their platform as the public ownership of railroads to focus on free silver, which they knew a majority of voters in the South and West already favored. They trusted Bryan, with whom they had forged a warm alliance in Nebraska, as much any figure in either major party. But the anti-fusionists proved correct: once their independent movement had descended from the heights of radical virtue, it could never climb up again. "We will not crucify the People's Party on the cross of Democracy!" vowed an elderly Texas delegate. He had tears in his eyes when he said it.[52]

To demonstrate at least a shred of autonomy, the Populists named their own candidate for vice president, Tom Watson of Georgia, and asked the Democrats to embrace him as their own. Bryan quickly telegraphed his refusal to dump Sewall from the ticket, and the snub made little difference in the delegates' decision. Asserting there was "no middle ground" between "the allied hosts of monopolies, the money power" and "all others who produce wealth," the Populists vowed to help put Bryan in the White House.[53]

It would be a formidable task. Voters who had humiliated the Democrats in the last midterm election needed to be convinced that the fusion ticket could revive the economy and not inflame civil conflict. What is more, neither silver Democrats nor Populists had much contact with immigrant workers in cities, where the press was condemning Bryan and his allies as dangerous men whose pet idea would cause rampant inflation. Party bosses in New York City and Chicago saw nothing for them in free silver and planned to give only tepid support or none at all to the hothead from the prairies.

Bryan's emotional appeal to Americans disgusted with the nation's political and economic establishment also earned him the staunch opposition of anyone who identified with elite rule. "There are two ideas of government," he had told the Chicago convention. "There are those who believe that, if you will only legislate to make the well-to-do prosperous, their prosperity will leak through on those below. The Democratic idea, however, has been that if you legislate to make the masses prosperous, their prosperity will find its way up through every class which rests upon them." Moved by self-interest and conviction, millions of voters viewed this idea as a threat of upheaval instead of the promise of justice it was meant to be.

And they were blessed with two clever, resourceful leaders. For years, William McKinley had thoroughly schooled himself in the art of inoffensiveness. A Civil War major who never led a charge or fired a shot, he made his name as a champion of the protective tariff, which he always draped in patriotic bunting. He avoided other controversial issues whenever possible and only declared his support for the gold standard just before the convention that nominated him for president. Thomas Reed, the acerbic House Speaker and an intraparty rival, remarked, "McKinley isn't a silver-bug, McKinley isn't a gold-bug, McKinley is a straddle-bug."[54] A Methodist elder and Sunday-school teacher, the major guarded his incorruptible image and spoke in a plain, patient manner that put listeners at ease but seldom inspired them.[55]

Soon after the 1896 campaign began, McKinley shrewdly decided, against the advice of some of his managers, not to try to match Bryan's oratory. "I might just as well put up a trapeze on my front lawn and compete with some professional athlete as go out speaking against Bryan. I have to think when I speak."[56] So he stayed at home in Canton, Ohio, bestowing a smile and brief remarks on each entry in a two-month-long parade of visiting ethnic societies, trade unions, women's clubs, business associations, veterans' and fraternal lodges, and religious denominations—most of whose members were loyal Republicans. The ever dignified McKinley campaigned from his front porch like a man who had already been elected.[57]

His best friend in politics was also the gifted impresario of his campaign. Marcus (Mark) Alonzo Hanna, a wealthy, cynical businessman from Cleveland, adored McKinley's personality and political intelligence and had helped to bankroll his electoral career. The two men had expected the Democrats to name a colorless figure such as Bland, whom they could easily chain to the ongoing depression. The choice of the charismatic Bryan forced them to make a swift change in strategy.[58]

Hanna organized the most sophisticated campaign to that point in U.S. history, one that became a model for the selling of future presidents-to-be. From dual headquarters in Chicago and New York, he hired some fourteen hundred speakers to stump in doubtful states and oversaw the printing of more than 120 million pieces of literature. The party distributed pamphlets in nine European languages—which encouraged immigrants in key midwestern states to forget the GOP's past support for prohibition and English-only schools. The campaign even hired two pioneer cameramen to film McKinley strolling and chatting in front of his porch in Canton. The production, less than a minute long, was shown only once in public during the campaign, but friendly papers touted the existence of what was both a technological novelty and a vignette of small-town bliss.[59]

The campaign's message—echoed by leading newspapers, such influential magazines as *The Nation* and *Harper's Weekly*, and many college professors—mingled alarm with self-confidence. Republicans derided their opponents as "Popocrats" who would repudiate the Supreme Court, wreck the economy, and, in an echo from the 1860s, tear the nation apart by class and region. At the same time, they promised that "a full dinner pail" awaited voters who chose McKinley, "the advance agent of prosperity" and of social harmony. To symbolize both themes, the GOP distributed millions of American flags and flag buttons and organized hundreds of marches to display them, in cities large and small.

The cost was beyond all precedent. Businessmen who feared that Bryan and free silver meant confiscation and class war were quite willing to pay the fare, and no law limited or regulated their giving. Hanna "wanted to place the corporations in the saddle and make them pay in advance for the ride," as one historian put it. Wall Street warmed to his pleas for cash, and Hanna already knew many industrialists from his own region, such as John D. Rockefeller, who contributed $250,000 of his profits from Standard Oil. In the end, the Republican National Committee raised at least $3.5 million (which would be about $50 million today) and didn't even spend it all.[60]

Against this juggernaut, the primary weapon that Democrats and Populists possessed was the voice of one man. The two parties together could match only about a tenth of the GOP's war chest, which left practically nothing to pay the expenses of auxiliary orators.[61] Fortunately, Bryan approached the presidential race the same way he had run for Congress and the Senate. Candidates favored by wealthy "interests" had always outspent him in Nebraska, and he had always countered them with an ability to speak widely and eloquently for his principles. Thus, mingling egotism with character, Bryan welcomed the opportunity to place his stamina against Mark Hanna's "plutocratic" machine. After his nomination, the John Henry of the producing classes even turned down a railway executive's offer of a private sleeping car to transport him back to Lincoln in style. "You are the great Commoner," journalist Willis Abbot advised him, "and it would not do to accept favors from the great railroad corporations." Bryan wore the title with pride for the rest of his career; he had already created the image.[62]

Before the campaign of 1896, it was thought rather unseemly for a nominee to crisscross the nation, proclaiming his ideas and burnishing his reputation. With George Washington as their model, civic moralists insisted that "the office should seek the man" and considered major-party nominees who stumped for votes to be demagogic panderers. Two men who violated the canon—Horace Greeley in 1872 and James G. Blaine in 1884—got branded as desperate figures, and both were defeated. Third-party candidates felt less restraint, since their main reason for running was to promote an alternative agenda. Both in 1880 and 1892, James Weaver took his campaigns—the first as the Greenback-Labor nominee, the second for the People's Party— to the roads and rails. His stumping exposed him to a vituperative barrage in person and in the press that went beyond a mere attack on his ideas. But he would surely have won fewer votes if he'd stayed at home.[63]

Bryan was determined to turn necessity into a virtue. With little help from the Democratic National Committee or its inept chairman, Senator James Jones, he organized a tour by rail that lasted, save a few days of rest, from the first week of August until November 2, the eve of Election Day.

Bryan and the reporters who traveled with him toted up the miles he covered—just over eighteen thousand—and tried to count the number of
speeches he gave. Because the candidate often gave brief, impromptu talks
from the back of his train, that was an impossible chore. He made some 250
scheduled stops in twenty-six states, averaged about eighty thousand words
a day, and spoke to as many as five million people.[64] Mary was able to
accompany him for about half the voyage.

To critics who scoffed that his marathon style "lacked dignity," Bryan
acknowledged that "it might be more dignified for me to stay at home and
have people come to see me." But, he quipped, "our people do not have
money to spare...if they could come all the way to Nebraska to see me, it
might show that they have money enough now." Theodore Roosevelt
famously observed that "Hanna advertised McKinley as if he were a patent
medicine"; Bryan gladly took up the task of selling himself.[65]

Although he campaigned from Maine to Nebraska, Bryan spent the
majority of his time in the region of the Great Lakes. Here lay a cluster of
adjoining states from Wisconsin to Ohio that held one-fifth of all electoral
votes. The region had swung from the GOP to the Democrats in the two
previous presidential elections, and the triumph of free-silver forces over
the Bourbons in these states gave Bryan hope. As a midwesterner, he felt
comfortable speaking to the huge crowds of native-born and immigrant
whites who gathered in country villages, industrial towns, and large cities
to glimpse his face and bask in his oratory. It is quite possible that a majority of the men who voted for Bryan in November had heard him speak that
fall.

In September, he began a speech to ten thousand in Springfield, Ohio—
home to a major farm machinery factory—with a warning that he would be
brief, "because a large portion of my voice has been left along the line of
travel, where it is still calling sinners to repentance." Then he urged the
wage earners in the crowd to "recognize their dependence upon the farmers...who convert the natural resources of this country into money."[66]

Despite his affection for agrarian America, Bryan knew his chance for
victory depended upon winning over urban workers. In Springfield, as elsewhere in the Midwest, he struggled to create an alliance between small farmers and labor that could trump the cross-class partnership the GOP had built
between industrial wage earners and their employers, grounded in the protective tariff. The bottom-up coalition of the "producing classes" that Bryan
envisioned had never been forged in national politics; its very prospect gave
conservatives nightmares about armed barricades and pitchfork-wielding
madmen. The Populists preached that "the interests of rural and civic labor

are the same; their enemies are identical."[67] But outside the silver-mining states in the Rockies, they were unable to explain why hard-pressed urban wage earners should embrace a third-party program designed to serve the inflationary needs of cotton and wheat farmers. Perhaps an eloquent Democrat who had spent most of his life in midsized midwestern cities could do better.

On Labor Day, Bryan traveled to Chicago to address a huge picnic sponsored by the powerful Building Trades Council. Unionists in the city had traditionally voted Democratic, and working-class radicals were among the leaders of the local People's Party. Yet the American Federation of Labor, led by Samuel Gompers, had abstained from making any endorsement, which left Eugene Debs the only unionist of national significance to come out for Bryan. So the Chicago event was an opportunity to tell a large and friendly audience, with a sizeable press corps on hand, why wage earners should back the fusion ticket.[68]

Bryan flattered the crowd of fifteen thousand; he quoted Lincoln, King Solomon, and Jesus, all of whom evidently had a high regard for the laboring masses. But his main thrust was a critique of politicians who favored the corporate rich. Bryan mentioned that on a recent visit to Iowa, he'd seen "a number of hogs rooting in a field and tearing up the ground." During his youth, he had kept the Bryan swine tethered so they would not tear up the family estate. "And then it occurred to me that one of the most important duties of government is to put rings in the noses of hogs.... We submit to restraint upon ourselves in order that others may be restrained from injuring us."[69] He concluded with a ringing call to resist any boss who tried to dictate how his employees should vote.

It was a telling occasion. Bryan eschewed any mention of bimetallism and never directly criticized his Republican opponent. His hour-long address was a brief for regulating private wealth, one Franklin Roosevelt could easily have delivered forty years later, albeit without the porcine metaphor. But Bryan's appeal to principle underlined an uncomfortable reality of his campaign: labor had nothing concrete to gain from free silver and would only suffer if a change in the currency drove up prices for food and other necessities. His hope that urban wage earners would unite with his agrarian supporters depended almost entirely on his ability to persuade them to vote their ideals and their consciences rather than their fears and their wallets.

That summer, the opposition thought he might well succeed. Bryan's instant celebrity was galvanizing white workers, including many who had taken little interest in politics before. In August, a Republican editor from

New York reported that ninety-eight of the one hundred printers at his newspaper—"drunken, worthless fellow[s]"—were planning to vote for Bryan. Around the country, most local unions, whatever their views on free silver, were supporting the Democratic nominee. Labor organizations only had half a million members, but Hanna was still worried. Perhaps wage earners, buffeted by the depression, would accept the notion that "the money power" had conspired to drive them into poverty.[70]

Corporations responded with a blast of economic realism. In September, railroads in the Midwest told employees they would go bankrupt if forced to pay bondholders in inflated silver dollars; other businesses in the region warned that layoffs would be inevitable if Bryan won. Meanwhile, Hanna hired several union officials to stump for McKinley, and the Republican candidate repeatedly tied joblessness to Democratic policies, reminding laboring men that the protective tariff was their friend.

By the final month of the campaign, the two experienced politicos became increasingly confident that, come Election Day, most workers would make the practical choice.[71]

Meanwhile, Bryan continued to dream about a populist future. On October 3, he told a meeting of Democratic clubs that even if he lost the election, "the day will come when the money of the Constitution will again be ours;...the day will come when corporations will cease to consider themselves greater than the Government which created them; the day will come when the people of this country will be content to walk side by side, each one satisfied to enjoy life and liberty and the pursuit of happiness, without attempting to deprive his neighbor of equal opportunities and equal rights."[72]

The main source of such rhythmic prophecies was clear. Rarely did Bryan give a campaign speech devoid of biblical invocations and metaphors. While he didn't repeat the stagecraft of the Cross of Gold speech, he persisted in describing the race as a battle for the nation's soul. Bryan told a crowd in Hornellsville, New York, "The Bible speaks of certain persons who love darkness rather than light...because their deeds are evil." At a meeting of Jewish Democrats in Chicago, he likened the Republicans to a pharaoh who "lives on the toil of others and always wants to silence complaint by making the load heavier." Before an audience of women in Grand Rapids, he justified bimetallism with the claim that "the Almighty Himself" had created both precious metals "to meet the needs of man."[73]

To ministers and devout laymen who disliked Bryan's politics, such statements reeked of blasphemy. Their Christianity was a religion of individual salvation and moral order; it required deference to legitimate authorities and the quelling of mobs. How dare Bryan posture as Jesus and cite the Bible to glorify his repudiation of debt and defiance of the Supreme Court? Thousands of clergy returned the "Popocrat's" rhetorical fire with spiritual grapeshot of their own, surpassing their partisan involvement in past campaigns. In mid-September, the Reverend Cortland Myers of Brooklyn's Baptist Temple announced that "the blood-stained banner of the cross" was endangered by the "anarchist" Chicago platform—a document "made in hell." Scores of clergymen in other eastern cities agreed, although usually in cooler terms.[74]

The furor left Bryan unperturbed. Like other evangelical reformers, ordained or not, he was not surprised that conservative churchmen turned their backs on "the clamorings of the people." He knew that many of his supporters viewed Christ, in the words of one North Carolina Populist, as "the great emancipator and the great equalizer" and that they shared his contempt for haughty backsliders in clerical collars. The goldbugs might "buy the ministers," a young woman from upstate New York wrote to Bryan, but "they cannot buy the congregations."[75]

In response, Bryan sought to emulate the spirit of apostolic Christianity. Like St. Paul and every itinerant preacher in his wake, he took to the road, speaking "unto men to edification, and exhortation, and comfort." The great evangelist Dwight Moody, while endorsing McKinley, marveled at Bryan's "crusade" and compared it to that of Peter the Hermit, the peasant inciter of medieval Europe. Indeed, the Democrat seldom missed a chance to stump for Jesus as well as free silver. At one stop in Fredericksburg, Virginia, an admirer shouted, "I am not a Christian, but I am praying for you." Bryan adroitly responded that the outburst gave the "community an additional reason for desiring my election, because, if they could convince the gentleman of the efficacy of prayer, they might make a Christian out of him."[76]

The campaign made compelling news. Most papers outside the Deep South and the Rockies supported McKinley, but his front-porch campaign lacked drama and spontaneity. In contrast, nearly every day with Bryan supplied an occasion either to ridicule the statements and habits of the "boy Orator," to marvel at his skill and endurance, or both. Reporters gleefully disclosed that the candidate ate as many as six meals a day and refreshed himself with an alcohol rub on hot afternoons, which made the lifelong teetotaler smell as if he had spent the night in a saloon.

The giddy reporting in the *New York World* often clashed with the disapproving tone of its editorials. On the front page of Pulitzer's flagship daily, Bryan spoke to ecstatic crowds in Cleveland, jousted with heckling Yale students "dressed in golf outfits" on the New Haven green, and sang along with an adoring choir at a church service back in Jacksonville, Illinois. The *World,* like most urban papers, also printed large helpings of the Democrat's speeches. All this free publicity helped offset the GOP's huge advantage in funds. "It used to be the newspapers educated the people," Bryan told a crowd in Des Moines, "but now the people educate the newspapers." His frankness with and fondness for journalists, a fraternity he had joined two years before when he became editor of the *Omaha World-Herald,* no doubt sweetened the coverage. Bryan was probably the only presidential nominee of his era to praise by name each "of the newspapermen [a few of whom were female] with whom I was thrown."[77]

The few big-city papers that endorsed him returned the compliment in vigorous and often creative ways. On their front pages, the *St. Louis Post-Dispatch* and Denver's *Rocky Mountain News* frequently ran multicolumn cartoons depicting Bryan as Lincoln, Paul Revere, a champion pugilist whipping goldbug bullies, and David hurling a fatal rock at the forehead of a top-hatted, monopoly-girded Goliath. In New York City, William Randolph Hearst directed the staff of his *Journal* to exploit every positive angle. He sent Winifred Black, his star woman reporter, to cover Mary Bryan's travels, writing at length about her couture and child-rearing techniques. Cartoonists drew both candidate and wife looking fit, handsome, and visionary, while memorably depicting Mark Hanna as a fat, pompous ass in a tight suit checkered with dollar signs. At one point, the *Journal's* search for fresh political copy even led it to the Central Park Zoo, where twin pumas had just been born. Keepers named the elder cat Bryan because "it possessed a pleasant voice and agreeable manners...and had crawled to every part of its cage." His younger brother got dubbed McKinley after he "showed a strong aversion to moving about, and persisted in not uttering a sound."[78]

THE MARATHON CAMPAIGN and the deluge of writing about it made Bryan appear a most uncommon kind of politician. He had emerged from his dismembered party a figure of great energy and even greater empathy. "It was the first time in my life and in the life of a generation," remembered William Allen White, "in which any man large enough to lead a national party had boldly and unashamedly made his cause that of the poor and the oppressed." White, editor of a Republican daily in Emporia, Kansas, added that Bryan also seemed "the incarnation of demagogy" and "the apotheosis of riot." Both images generated a torrent of sentiment, on a scale no national candidate since Lincoln had elicited. One writer who traveled with Bryan saw "the weak, the humble, the aged, the infirm rush forward by the hundreds" after his speeches "and hold up hard and wrinkled hands with crooked fingers and cracked knuckles... as if he were in very truth their promised redeemer from bondage."[79] From such spectacles sprouted a popular culture of Bryanism that would endure as long as the man himself.

The poet Vachel Lindsay, who witnessed the campaign of 1896 as a teenage boy in Springfield, Illinois, later wrote a tribute to his childhood hero. "When Bryan speaks, the sky is wide / The people are a tossing tide, / And all good men the world around / With our own heart-strings seem allied / When Bryan speaks."[80] Lindsay had become famous by the time he wrote the poem. But at the age of sixteen, he was no different from the multitude of Americans of all ages and both sexes who jammed Bryan's appearances, devoured reports about his campaign and his personality, and wrote him a massive number of letters and telegrams. Some of these correspondents included a token of fortune or gratitude: a self-composed poem or song lyric, such gifts as a silver charm, a broom ("for a clean sweep"), a set of china, a four-leaf clover, and two live eagles. A few sent small checks.[81]

The volume of mail was astonishing. According to Mary Bryan, her husband routinely received about two thousand letters a day during the campaign; a much smaller number—usually from women—were addressed to Mary herself. On several days just before and after the election, the quotidian number reached over three thousand. If these estimates are accurate (and Mary was not given to exaggeration), then roughly a quarter of a million people wrote to the Bryans between his nomination on July 10 and the aftermath of his defeat in early November. As early as August 4, the candidate had begun replying to most of these missives with a form letter: "My Dear Sir—I thank you for your kind expressions of good will. Yours truly, W. J. Bryan." Regretfully, the candidate and his wife seem to have harbored an unconscious desire to torture future historians and biographers: they burned or threw away about 98 percent of the campaign correspondence they received.[82]

No other political leader in Bryan's era was graced, or burdened, with such a flood of mail. As candidates, Grover Cleveland and William McKinley received only a trickle of letters from anyone other than businessmen and fellow politicians, and this pattern continued during their stints in the White House. As president, McKinley's correspondence averaged about one hundred pieces a day, rising briefly to ten times that amount in 1898, on the eve of the war with Spain. Theodore Roosevelt's mailbag was somewhat fuller, particularly when he ran as a Progressive in 1912. But not until the 1930s, when FDR's warm, confident voice came to symbolize federal largesse, for good and ill, did the mail of any presidential nominee or chief executive surpass the total Bryan received during the 1896 campaign.[83]

The approximately five thousand pieces of correspondence sent that summer and fall that did make their way into Bryan's posthumous papers offer an intriguing glimpse into the social psychology and worldview of his admirers.[84] If there was a matching surge of critical mail, it has not survived. At a time when adult men of comfortable means tended to monopolize the writing of letters to public figures, Bryan's correspondents were a rather egalitarian bunch. Just under 10 percent were women, and about the same number were adolescents or children, some younger than six years old. Handwritten notes, often submitted on cheap notebook paper, outnumbered ones created on a typewriter. Only a minority of writers mentioned their occupation—or lack of one. The disclosers were mostly self-employed businessmen, professionals, or skilled wage earners on the railroads or in the construction trades. Few admirers stated their denomination, but those who did were invariably Catholics or Jews—a sign that members of religious minorities wanted to make themselves visible to so popular a Protestant.

What stands out from these letters is a great longing to believe in one man's desire and will to battle the evils of the world. "I have felt the pangs of hunger," wrote a thirty-six-year-old railroad brakeman from Elkhart, Indiana, "and if humanity in the United States were as deeply interested in the welfare of this nation as I am you would be elected by the largest majority that any man ever received for any office." He concluded his letter, "May the God of the widow and the fatherless—the God of the poor and the oppressed—be with you and guide you." Other workers cursed intimidating employers or warned about "dark, deep well-laid plots against the toilers of this nation."[85]

But many correspondents' admiration of their man seemed independent of their own economic status or woes. A physician and drug manufacturer from Dallas praised the candidate as a "Patriarch," a "Statesman," and "a pure and spotless Christian Gentleman"—and boasted that he'd beaten up a local Republican who called the Democrat nominee "a lunatic and a liar." A vaudevillian from New York City wrote a poem of twenty lines, each beginning with an initial in Bryan's name: "We hail thee a leader of whom we are proud, / In whom we have hopes, fondly cherished; / Let your words and your actions be chosen with care, / Lest our hopes be like others, long perished." A druggist from a small town in Iowa confessed, "I have not only learned to revere you but to love you and during the campaign I have wished many times to see you." Like several other correspondents, the man reported he'd been "on the stump" since July, not for any personal ambition but "in the name of God and humanity without money and without price."[86]

Such references to the divine were not mere flattery or perfunctory bows to convention. Most Americans in the 1890s were indeed religious people, but when a letter writer from Missouri called the candidate "the saviour of our nation" and swore "in god and Bryan I put my trust," he undoubtedly meant it.[87] Bryan had tapped into a deep well of spiritual longing. Many admirers embraced him because he so publicly campaigned in the name of Christian principles and was never known to have transgressed them. This image enabled him to avoid the reputation of most politicians as opportunistic hypocrites, which even blemished William McKinley, an exemplar of piety in his private life.

The view of Bryan as a solitary fighter for justice inevitably encouraged many admirers to view him as a prophet, guided by divine will. From a Colorado mining camp, D. D. Hatfield claimed, "In all times of great peril to the people God has raised up a leader to save them from their errors and lead them up to a higher plane of hight [*sic*] and to a knowledge of their rights and duties." From Baltimore, Mary Martin assured Mary Bryan that "the hand of the Almighty is in this election" and hoped "our Dear Lord" would protect her husband from powerful foes who wished him dead. From Pittsburgh, a furniture salesman wrote, "God has brought you forth, and ordaind [*sic*] you, to lead the people out of this state of oppression and despondency into the Canaan of peace and prosperity."[88] Hundreds of correspondents, adults and children of both sexes, told Bryan and his wife they prayed every night for his election.

Of course, the Almighty could have no objection to a hard-fought contest. Thousands of letter writers thought Bryan a godly hero, a tribune of exploited producers, or both. But others saw him primarily as a happy warrior and were thrilled to fight on his side. Children took a particular delight in the political game, which in 1896 was played with unusual tenacity and verve. Girls organized their own Bryan Clubs and Bryan Quartettes and complained that they couldn't vote for him even if they'd been adults. In Paterson, New Jersey, the third-graders in a parochial school class all changed their middle names, informally, to Bryan, as did their teacher, a nun. A five-year-old from Denver complained that her Sunday-school teacher "hadn't anything to say but Solomon, Solomon, Solomon, all the time, and not one word for Mr. Bryan." And a four-year-old from rural Michigan wrote, "When I am a man I want to be like you a grand big man making speeches."[89]

AS ELECTION DAY approached, both camps anxiously prepared for a close outcome. Since 1872, no winning nominee had won a majority of the popular vote, and only the fiercest partisans expected that the climax of the current drama would break the pattern. Across the country, innumerable wagers were made, ranging from the lighthearted (a Chicago merchant who vowed to drink nothing but ginger ale for a year) to the grim (two Milwaukee men on opposing sides agreed to sell all their property and leave the country forever if their candidate lost). On Halloween afternoon, Republicans staged huge, flag-bedecked rallies for McKinley in New York, Chicago, San Francisco, and several other big cities. Many businessmen gave their employees the day off to attend. At a Democratic counterrally in Cleveland, marchers wore masks and carried a banner reading, "We cover our faces for fear of losing our jobs."[90]

Despite the tension and angry rhetoric of the campaign, there was little talk of violence. A physician from Fort Smith, Arkansas, did promise Bryan that if he lost, "I would have to take the field. There are hundreds of thousands no doubt as ready as I."[91] But no other correspondent echoed his threat. Bryan ended the race by giving seven speeches in Omaha just after midnight on November 3, Election Day, and then returned home to vote. "If they elect McKinley, I will feel a great burden lifted off my shoulders," he told Dan Bride. Then he went to sleep, at six-thirty in the evening.

Perhaps he should have stayed in bed. McKinley's victory was no landslide, but it was decisive enough. He won twenty-three states with 271 electoral votes and took 51 percent of the popular tally, which defied the expectation that neither man could win a majority. Bryan carried twenty-two states, good for only 176 electoral votes. The Gold Democrats and Prohibitionists each drew about 1 percent of the total.

The enthusiasm of the campaign was reflected at the polls: almost fourteen million Americans cast ballots, 79.3 percent of the eligible voters, and two million more than in 1892. In the states of the upper Midwest, where both campaigns focused their time and resources, average turnout topped 90 percent. But Bryan's exertions along the crescent of the Great Lakes yielded him not a single electoral vote. Only in Indiana did he come within three percentage points of beating McKinley, his fellow midwesterner.

The Democrat's willingness to accept the Populist nod and to stump as a rebel proved both a boon and a handicap. With no alternative on his left, Bryan won 6,511,495 votes, a million more than Cleveland in 1892. He swept every state in the West and South (including his own) where James Weaver had run well four years before. He also came within a few thousand votes of taking all the states that lay outside the northeastern quarter of the nation. However, free-silver evangelism was a bust in most urban and manufacturing centers. Outside the Deep South, Bryan carried only one city with over a hundred thousand residents—and that was Denver, stronghold of the white metal, where Republicans hardly bothered to campaign.[92]

How did the candidate with a massive following of volunteer activists lose to a man beloved only by his family and his closest adviser? Over the decades, scholars have offered two broad answers.

One echoes the GOP's strategy in emphasizing the impact of geography and economics: McKinley won because he appealed to the most advanced and most prosperous regions of the nation, while Bryan antagonized them. Inhabitants of New York and New England, Illinois and Ohio may have admired Bryan's spirit, but they voted for the party that represented a stable dollar, high tariffs, and an emerging industrial order and national market.[93] The second answer stresses ethnic and religious factors: the GOP won over many Catholics and new immigrants with a promise of impartial treatment and silence on the divisive issue of prohibition. Bryan supposedly alienated these same voters with what a leading German-language paper called "bombastic phrases in Western Methodist camp-meeting style."[94] So the same magnetism that drew big crowds and bushels of letters repelled voters the Democrats badly needed.

As with most historical explanations, these illuminate only part of the truth. Bryan worked just as hard as McKinley to woo voters in the big manufacturing states, where he gave a majority of his speeches. He often praised organized labor, received aid from many union locals in return, and said virtually nothing about the tariff. Only in September, when his opponents—both the GOP and the Gold Democrats—mobilized the entire economic establishment in the industrial Midwest, did they stop and reverse the surge of support Bryan had enjoyed in the wake of the Chicago convention.

The ethnic interpretation certainly fits German Americans, whose votes may have put Illinois and Indiana in McKinley's column. But Irish Catholics were almost as numerous in the Great Lakes region, and they stayed loyal to the Democratic nominee (even when they learned his name was not O'Brien). Neither the lackluster efforts of urban machines nor a well-publicized endorsement of McKinley by Archbishop John Ireland, leading prelate of the Midwest, could alter the habits of Hibernian voters, the core of the working class in many big cities.[95]

What is remarkable is not that Bryan lost but that he came as close as he did to winning. He had much to overcome: a severe economic downturn that occurred with Democrats in power, a party deserted by its men of wealth and national prominence, the vehement opposition of most prominent publishers and academics and ministers, and hostility from the nation's largest employers. By necessity as much as inclination, Bryan had to run as a protest candidate, a Populist in Democratic clothing. But he couldn't conjure up a grand activist coalition from fewer than a million unionists and a People's Party that had little presence east of the Mississippi and north of the Mason-Dixon line. "He was an agitator by profession, and the agitator is always vulnerable," historian Richard Hofstadter wrote about Wendell Phillips. Despite a similar reputation, Bryan would have been elected president if he'd drawn just 19,250 additional votes, distributed across six states where the result was agonizingly close: California, Delaware, Indiana, Kentucky, Oregon, and West Virginia. But he still would have lost the popular vote overall, which would have been hard for a true democrat to swallow.[96]

For thousands of his followers, the cause of Bryan's defeat was quite simple. Factory owners imposed "a reign of terror," claimed a correspondent from Anderson, Indiana. They closed some plants and threatened to shut others if Bryan was elected. "A good many workmen toled [sic] me that they would gladly vote for you but they can't risk a year's starvation which they were sure would come," reported a young laborer from Jersey City.[97] Such reports were widespread and, when added to allegations of GOP fraud, grew into a hardened conviction that McKinley and his henchmen had stolen the election.

Over a century later, it is impossible to prove more than a handful of these charges—or to conclude that they would have altered the result. Manufacturers certainly made clear which candidate they favored, yet 1896 was not the first election in which they had urged employees to vote Republican, usually to safeguard jobs sheltered by high tariffs. Coercion, both explicit and subtle, was routine in a system where the bulk of wage earners lacked union protection and where joblessness often meant going hungry. In a few midwestern and border states in 1896, Republicans miscounted ballots and paid out small sums to friendly voters. But the fact that southern Democrats, using state laws and vigilantes, were barring many black men from the polls altogether may have balanced out such fraudulent acts. The secret ballot was widespread by 1896, and no scholar has tried to prove the election was any more corrupt than its Gilded Age predecessors.[98]

McKinley's victory did mark two transitions in American politics, neither of which became evident for several decades. The GOP's victory over the left-wing coalition of Democrats and Populists ended the most serious challenge that eastern industrialists, based in the growing cities, would face until the Great Depression. Any realistic hope for a "producer's republic," governed in the interests both of wage earners and small farmers, died in 1896. Yet Bryan's doomed campaign was also a brave departure from his party's legacy of viewing federal power as an alien beast tearing at the liberties of an otherwise free people. In 1896, the Democrats embarked on a voyage, of ideology and policy, that would remake governance in America during the Progressive Era. They would soon pull such Republicans as Theodore Roosevelt and Robert La Follette along with them.[99]

For his part, Bryan seemed, at least in public, unruffled by his loss and the controversies that trailed after it. On November 5, after making sure that uncounted rural votes could not elect him, he telegraphed McKinley: "We have submitted the issue to the American people and their will is law." Then he and Mary assembled a thick, illustrated volume containing speeches, platforms, reminiscences, and a short biography, and oversaw its publication at the end of December. Its title, *The First Battle*, succinctly proclaimed the message Bryan's admirers longed to hear. On the final page of the book appeared an unsigned poem, "Inspiration," which many readers would have recognized as the work of Ella Wheeler Wilcox, a spiritualist and feminist who wrote for a variety of popular magazines. As with Bryan's campaign, it is difficult to separate the uneven conflict with Mammon from the optimism of a born crusader. The poem's last stanza reads:

> *O man bowed down with labor!*
> *O woman young, yet old!*
> *O heart oppressed in the toiler's breast*
> *And crushed by the power of gold!*
> *Keep on with your weary battle*
> *Against triumphant might;*
> *No question is ever settled*
> *Until it is settled right.*[100]

CHAPTER FOUR

A Republic, Not an Empire, 1897–1900

The fruits of imperialism, be they bitter or sweet, must be left to the subjects of monarchy. This is the one tree of which the citizens of a republic may not partake. It is the voice of the serpent, not the voice of God, that bids us eat.

—William Jennings Bryan, 1899[1]

As for what you say of Bryan, I have fallen in love with him so, for his character, that I am willing to forget his following.

—William James, writing to a friend, 1900[2]

A FEW DAYS after the election, an unemployed printer from Des Moines wrote to Bryan on a piece of stationery lifted, with permission, from a local funeral parlor. "Don't infer from this letter head that I think you are dead," quipped W. R. Alexander. Then he turned serious. "I want to tell you of a coincidence which happened at our house yesterday.... I took off the badge (a little silk flag with 16 to 1 stamped upon it) which I had worn during the campaign and left it on the dresser." His wife and fellow printer found the badge, "burst into tears," and then quickly pressed it within the pages of the family Bible. Later that day, the Alexanders opened the Book to find that the silk insignia rested next to the Thirty-seventh Psalm. It begins, "Fret not thyself because of evil-doers, neither be thou envious against the workers of iniquity. For they shall soon be cut down like the grass, and wither as the green herb."

The couple cried together as they read the psalm; "every word in it," wrote Alexander, "is a word of comfort." Having depleted their savings and fearful of defaulting on their $800 home mortgage, the Alexanders, who belonged to a Presbyterian church, thought the import of the episode was clear: "We feel that we have lost a near and dear friend in this campaign, but thank God *he is not dead,* but more determined than ever to lead us out."[3]

Bryan received an abundance of such letters during the fall and winter after his defeat. Remarkably, the result of the election only increased the flow of his correspondence and the ardor of his followers. They wrote to console him, to brag about the part they'd played in his campaign, to condemn the powerful enemies they shared, and to promise unflagging aid in his next battle—which, given four more years to educate and inspire, he would undoubtedly win. "The 6 million of People who supported you will Let no man or no trust or monopoly stand between Their God and their Conscience," assured a candy store owner from Camden, New Jersey.[4]

Many of his admirers believed Bryan had lost not merely to McKinley and his party but to a cartel of ungodly evils. A correspondent from Latrobe, Pennsylvania, labeled the juggernaut "money, coercion, and the devil" and assumed, like nearly every other correspondent, that Bryan would challenge it again in 1900.[5]

Defeat had turned his supporters into members of a hugely extended, loving family—uncritical of his tactics and anxious only that he stick to a righteous course. Such Democratic insiders as party chairman James K. Jones grumbled that the result would have been different in 1896 if the candidate had avoided "skylarking through the East" and instead spent all his time in the upper Midwest, where free silver was popular.[6] But the Lincoln post office filled up with dispatches whose writers meant to bind themselves closer to Bryan, not to question his decisions or undermine his confidence.

The cascade of mail convinced Bryan that the next campaign had already begun. "The number of letters...made it certain that unless some change in conditions occurred, I would be renominated in 1900," he remembered with pride, "for although defeated, the six and a half millions of voters came out of the campaign of 1896 a compact and undismayed army."[7] Bryan knew that many people who had voted for him were not his fans; even a lackluster, discredited Democrat would have won millions of ballots. But by vaunting so many loyalists, he hoped to scare conservatives in the party—many of whom had deserted the ticket—from mounting a counteroffensive.

Bryan's claim to have a vast army behind him also indicated the quality that was beginning to make him an intriguing and rather novel figure in American life. Most politicians of his day tried to attract and retain a body of supporters drawn mainly from their own party; Bryan wooed a legion of followers, most of whom seemed more loyal to him and his stand on key issues than to the Democracy itself. This relationship was forged through his speaking style and populist message, voiced in an evangelical key, and perceptions of his character. Bryan consistently contrasted the bigness of God to the bigness of Mammon and had no doubt which force would be victorious in the end.

An ingenious personal organization strengthened the bond. In 1897, Charles Bryan, with help from Mary, sifted through the mountain of letters sent to his older brother in order to create a huge card file of admirers. Charles jotted down every bit of information he could find about a correspondent: party affiliation, job, religion, even income. He updated the file constantly for the next thirty years and used it to send out regular mailings to the Bryan network. The index contained some two hundred thousand names in 1897 and grew to half a million by 1912. It represented, in embryo, the type of candidate-centered machine that would become utterly routine by the last decades of the twentieth century.

The tireless Charles also kept a "politician file" stuffed with the voting records, election totals, and important speeches of thousands of figures from every region of the country. These numbers and clippings helped Will—who Mary admitted was "a poor organizer"—to plan his own presidential races and decide which Democrats to support for other offices. Charles refused to lend either file to any other politician.[8]

In the closing years of the nineteenth century, Bryan employed his popularity to become the best-known critic of American imperialism and to win a second presidential nomination. These acts secured his place as the dominant—and most controversial—figure in his party. They bolstered his image, whether celebrated or lampooned, as a Christian in politics who drew no distinction between the views of his pious followers and his own.

This was a kind of political leadership Americans had never experienced before, at least not on a national stage. Since Lincoln's death, most presidential candidates had strived to be stalwarts of their party, shrewd managers of discordant voices rather than tribunes of mass discontent and sweeping reforms. Grover Cleveland's stolid sincerity personified the role. Although William McKinley was a talented orator, he campaigned and governed as a steward of state affairs who thought carefully about every option before making a decision. But "it was Bryan," writes one historian disapprovingly, "who began the long process of creating a new political culture full of programs and crusades—with catchy names that would require for success more than simple honesty."[9] In that new setting, a candidate prized the affection of his followers as much as, if not more than, the respect of his peers.

In the year after the 1896 election, thousands of parents revealed their lofty regard for Bryan by giving their newborns his name. "I look upon you as almost a Prophet sent from God," wrote a father from Waterford, Kentucky, who prayed that his son "may make such a man as you are." An admirer from Flatrock, Indiana, named his baby after the spellbinding orator he'd driven his buggy fifteen miles through the rain to hear. In the steel town of McKeesport, Pennsylvania, a boy was given the name of the "man who had the courage to champion the cause of Justice and Humanity," while his twin sister was christened Mary, after "your beloved wife who has shared your labors in the trying ordeal wich you are now passing through."

Some namesake correspondents had a mercenary motive, at least in part. From a small town in the Ozark Mountains, a mother wrote that her William Jennings "is a fine boy with a good head on him I think you could afford to send him a calico dress." Such "begging" letters were usually scrawled in pencil and contained numerous misspellings.[10]

But they were not necessarily insincere. In the late nineteenth century, parents often named baby boys, and a scattering of girls, after deceased presidents such as Jefferson and Lincoln and generals such as Lee and Grant whose greatness seemed beyond dispute. A losing candidate ridiculed by the big-city press was a different matter. Most people who named their children for Bryan admired his personality as much as his opinions about money and other issues.

Even most "begging" correspondents mingled a display of piety with a request for help. Early in 1897, a farm woman from western Iowa wrote to Mary Bryan that "corn is so cheap we cant hardly live." Sallie Miller named a new baby, her fifth child, for the defeated candidate and hinted that "if Mr B presents my Baby with anything it will greatfully [receive it]." Yet Miller also added details that revealed her family's affinity with the Commoner's ideals. Her husband hung a portrait of Bryan in the house and refused to sell it for $20, a good week's wages. In better times, the couple had been active churchgoers, and Mr. Miller was in charge of the local Sunday school. Ashamed of their poverty, his wife ended her letter with a plea that it not be published.[11]

Bryan always encouraged voters to view his politics as a reflection of his character and his faith. From his first campaign for Congress to the great contest of 1896, he had lived frugally, spoken indefatigably, and framed nearly every position—from the tariff to the income tax—as a conflict between the venal and the moral. Bryan was not a prig, and he never brought up an opponent's personal life in a debate. For him, character revealed the soul of a public man—to adhere to one's political principles, no matter what the odds on victory, was to side with the angels.

Beyond his correspondence, there were abundant signs that Bryanism, in defiance of the election returns, was a surging persuasion. Two-thirds of a year after its publication, *The First Battle* had sold two hundred thousand copies, making it one of the best-selling books in America.[12] As a national party, the Democrats essentially closed down operations in between presidential campaigns. But at off-year state conventions, pro-Bryan politicians kept or took control of the party organization in most of the West and South and ousted the Bourbon faction in Pennsylvania and Massachusetts, states McKinley had won in a landslide.

Bryan himself was in constant demand as a speaker and writer, which earned him a tidy income and enabled him to give up his legal practice. In the summer of 1897, he made a weeklong tour of California, drawing overflow crowds at each of fifteen speeches. He donated several thousand dollars of his earnings, in $250 increments, to colleges throughout the Midwest and South that agreed to sponsor undergraduate essay contests on "the science of government." The *New York World,* keener to boost circulation than to flail a defeated foe, paid Bryan $1,000 for what an editor called an "admirable article" in its Sunday edition and promised that, when reprinted, the piece would reach "at least forty million readers."[13]

Bryan made news wherever he traveled, almost as if he *were* president. Leaving a speaking engagement in Kansas that September, his train had an accident outside the town of Emporia. Bryan, unhurt, helped to rescue victims, and his action led coverage of the event in the national press. Hearst's *New York Journal* gushed, "It is directly due to his personal efforts that many lives were saved." The Good Samaritan faltered only once, when a badly injured man he'd just pulled from the wreck looked up at him and "gasped": "I went to hear you at Burlingame to-day, Mr. Bryan. I am dying now, but I want to shake your hand and say God bless you." Such attention helped make a second nomination appear all but inevitable.[14]

But the popularity of his free-silver platform was far less secure. At the end of the 1890s, higher prices for staple crops—corn, wheat, and cotton—reduced agrarian debt, lessening the anger of farmers in the Plains and South who had formerly blamed their woes on "the money power."[15] At the same time, the discovery of vast deposits of gold in Alaska and the Yukon suddenly made the "hard" specie more plentiful. From 1897 to the end of the century, $439 million worth of the yellow metal flowed into the U.S. Treasury, reversing the pattern of the depression years. Early in 1900, the Republican Congress, with help from some eastern Democrats, passed a bill to put the United States on the gold standard for good, and President McKinley signed it.[16]

Bryan's big-city supporters had never been apostles of free silver; now they urged him instead to emphasize the growing power of trusts and the exploitation of labor. "We will win surely if we fight the fight of the poor against the rich," asserted Willis Abbot, the Hearst editor from New York

City who was a frequent Bryan adviser. "Don't press the silver issue too much."[17] With the federal government firmly opposed and many citizens seemingly indifferent, did it make sense to keep preaching the gospel of cheap money?

Bryan's response was unequivocal. He wrote back to Abbot, who was trying to soften the hearts of Democratic pols in his state, "I can say to bimetallism at sixteen to one as Ruth said to Naomi: 'Entreat me not to leave thee or to return from following after thee: for whither thou goest, I will go; and where thou lodgest, I will lodge: thy people shall be my people, and thy God, my God.' "[18] The quotation revealed how doggedly Bryan stuck to his position on any major issue once he had defined it as a moral principle. Like Ruth, the Moabite who chose to become a Jew, he had not been raised on the gospel of silver, fully embracing it only after being elected to Congress. But once converted, he never looked back.

At least in 1897 and early 1898, principle meshed with pragmatism. To shift away from silver so soon after the "first battle" would have disenchanted Bryan's political base, as well as violated his own sense of character. Some followers reported that their advocacy of sixteen to one had cost them jobs and gotten them into fights with neighbors and schoolmates.[19] The presidential campaign also left behind thousands of pro-silver clubs and dozens of local party factions that eagerly anticipated the next encounter. Bryan asked all these organizations to drop his name from their title, but a good many endorsed him for the 1900 nomination. He was, after all, the unrivaled leader of their movement. "We meet every Saturday in our little hall," wrote an eleven-year-old boy from Michigan on behalf of a youthful band that called itself the Knights of the Silver Club. "Your noble face graces the room," alongside those of Washington, Lincoln, and other icons. "Our mottoes are 'Bryan is our King,' 'Free Silver is the Thing,' and 'True to our Country.' "[20]

At home in Lincoln and while away on speaking tours, Bryan worked diligently to defend the core of the Chicago platform. Party chairman James K. Jones continued to prove inept at both raising money and rousing the faithful, which left Bryan as the only national figure who could effectively defend his cause. Bryan donated the proceeds from *The First Battle* to pro-silver groups, urged Democratic allies to purge from their state organizations anyone who had not backed his ticket in 1896, persuaded leaders of the Populists and Silver Republicans to keep their "triple alliance" intact, and scoffed that prosperity was shallow and would be short-lived since goldbugs still reigned in Washington and on Wall Street.[21]

Defeat would have taught a typical politician to alter his appeal in order to win over doubters and mobilize the uninvolved. But Bryan believed he had committed no error in 1896, either of tactics or of doctrine, and his admirers were passionate in confirming that opinion. So he resolved to persevere along the same lines, to continued admiration and, if necessary, to continued defeat.

BUT THE APPROACH of war conspired to change the subject. In the winter of 1897–98, President McKinley and his advisers gradually adopted a policy of demanding that Spain grant independence to Cuba, the last remnant (along with Puerto Rico) of an empire that had once held dominion from the Colorado River to Tierra del Fuego. Citing the Declaration of Independence and the Monroe Doctrine, Americans from all political persuasions supported the Cuban insurgency—particularly after reading gruesome reports in the daily press about Spanish prison camps under the command of General Valeriano Weyler, where tens of thousands of peasants succumbed to starvation and disease.

At first, McKinley pressured Spain only to offer the rebels a generous degree of autonomy within its crumbling imperium. But publication of a hostile private letter from Madrid's ambassador to the United States and the death of 260 sailors in an explosion on the battleship *Maine* as it lay in Havana harbor (later revealed to be an accident) inflamed opinion in Congress and forced the president's hand. Nothing but outside power, it seemed, would bring justice and stability to the island. The fact that U.S. private investment there was large and growing only bolstered the argument for war. On April 11, McKinley asked Congress to give him the authority to intervene in Cuba; two weeks later, the legislators declared war on Spain. They also unanimously passed an amendment, sponsored by the Silver Republican senator Henry Teller, promising that the United States would never acquire Cuba for itself.[22]

Bryan, like nearly all Democrats, had long sympathized with the cause of *Cuba libre;* now he endorsed intervention, claiming, "Humanity demands that we shall act." On the day war was declared, he wrote McKinley, "I hereby place my services at your command ... and assure you of my willingness to perform to the best of my ability any duty to which you ... may see fit to assign me."[23] In Bryan's view, the public's enthusiasm for the war did not contradict his deep-seated belief that militarism was an unchristian tool of the upper classes. He opposed the big increase in the standing army that top Republicans were promoting. But the Cubans were suffering to win their freedom, and for Bryan this gave them an unimpeachable moral claim. "Far from betraying his principles," wrote one historian, "he was a crusader: he had never condemned a holy war."[24] That spring, Bryan pleased lecture crowds with a fresh bit of theater: he waved a miniature U.S. flag in one hand and a small Cuban flag in the other.

The onset of war did, however, pose a political dilemma. Should Bryan, a thirty-eight-year-old with no military experience, join the armed forces, thus placing his life at the disposal of his past and probably future opponent? Or should he remain a civilian, free to criticize McKinley yet vulnerable to the charge that he was not fully committed to the nation's great cause?

Among Bryan's allies in government, there was little dispute. William V. Allen, the Populist senator from Nebraska, told him "it would be a serious mistake" to don a uniform and "place yourself in the grasp of Hanna and McKinley whom I do not doubt would be glad to expose you to every conceivable danger." Congressman Jeremiah Botkin, a Populist from Kansas and a Methodist minister, urged Bryan to preserve himself, "the servant of the people," for the "much more important war" with the evil plutocracy. Leading Democrats made similar arguments, albeit in less grandiose terms.[25]

But their warnings were overwhelmed by requests from ordinary men to serve under their chosen leader. Thousands of clerks, lawyers, miners, small-town editors, and pharmacists wrote from all over the Plains and the Midwest to tout their zeal, their physical fitness, and sometimes their military experience—in the Civil War, an Indian war, or a European army. A thirty-six-year-old Kansan named Thomas O'Toole offered both his own services and those of his teenage son and also mentioned that his wife and daughter were eager to serve in the Red Cross if "attached to the regimental corps that we are in." A sizeable minority of applicants were over fifty years old and asked to fill specific jobs—chaplain, muleteer, cook, physician— they occupied in civilian life.

Both young and old invoked the support they'd given Bryan in 1896 and viewed the war as almost an extension of that campaign. Few mentioned free silver or any other political issue. His personal allure transcended the platform for which he'd campaigned. A Methodist divine and military veteran from Friend, Nebraska, pleaded, "Give a chance to a preacher who believes he preaches the right Gospel, votes the right ticket, and can shoot in the right direction if opportunity is given." From Missouri, a fifty-four-year-old former bugler in the Union army confessed that since reading the

Cross of Gold speech "I have admired you, and, pardon me, I fear I idolize
you." Didn't his young hero need an orderly, "active as a cat and remarkably
well preserved"?[26]

If Bryan had any doubts about serving, such letters probably dispelled
them. On May 19, he enlisted in the Nebraska National Guard, after Governor Silas Holcomb, a Populist ally, asked him to recruit a new regiment
of volunteers. In a shrewd political move, Bryan filled the ranks with close
to two thousand men from each of the six congressional districts in the
state, taking pains not to choose anyone from towns that had already sent
a resident to the war. Most were farmers, laborers, or clerks—single men
in their late teens or twenties who probably viewed this as the adventure
of their lives. The faithful Dan Bride came along as an unofficial aide-
de-camp.

It was then the rule for volunteer regiments to pick their own officers. So
in mid-July, members of the Third Nebraska elected Colonel Bryan as their
chieftain. They held a parade in Lincoln, with Bryan atop what his daughter
Grace called a "beautiful prancing coal-black charger." Then the regiment
boarded a train for the long trip to Camp Cuba Libre in the piney woods of
north Florida. Large crowds greeted the volunteers at nearly every stop
along the way.[27]

For the colonel and his men, it proved to be a passive and frustrating little war. In Florida, typhoid and malaria killed several members of the regiment and sent scores of others to sick bay. The healthier men of the Third
Nebraska kept busy drilling, swimming, reading, and trying to keep a
menagerie of tropical insects and snakes out of their floorless tents. When
the regimental band ventured into Jacksonville, Florida, it apparently
neglected to play "Dixie," thereby angering the local gentry. Two weeks
after their arrival in camp, Spain sued for peace, but the Third Nebraska
stayed on in Florida for another four months. Some Bryan supporters
thought the president was deliberately keeping his rival away from combat,
with all its potential glory.[28]

Bryan wrote almost daily to his worried spouse, declaring his love and
seeking her advice. He tried to console Mary with a horoscope an admirer
had drawn up for him predicting that his "secret political enemies" would
fail and that he would survive the war. When Bryan himself came down
with a weak case of typhoid, his wife and younger daughter came to care for
him and stayed for several weeks. Neither he nor any member of the Third
Nebraska Regiment ever raised his rifle in a foreign land.[29]

Their commander's democratic ways helped soften the ordeal. Bryan
may have been the least officious officer in military history. He made him-

self available to "the humblest private" without an appointment, ate the same food as the enlisted men, and diligently inspected and improved their latrines. In September, although he was coming down with a fever, Bryan traveled to Washington to persuade McKinley to allow the regiment to return home. The president listened courteously and did nothing—which kept his rival from taking any part in that fall's midterm election campaign, in which the GOP lost fewer House seats than expected. In December, the United States signed a peace treaty with Spain, and Bryan finally resigned his commission—though as a volunteer officer, he could have done so at any time. He left his shrunken, demoralized regiment in the hands of Lieutenant Colonel Victor Vifquain, a Medal of Honor winner in the Civil War and a loyal Democrat.[30]

"I had five months of peace in the army," Bryan quipped to reporters, "and resigned to take part in a fight."[31] The issue was annexation of the Philippines, which the Spanish had surrendered for a face-saving price of $20 million. McKinley and most Republicans argued that the United States had an obligation to "Christianize" and "civilize" the seven million inhabitants of the vast archipelago and that American overlords, innately humane and generous, could be trusted not to repeat the errors of their European counterparts. Bryan, along with most Democrats and Populists, charged that colonization betrayed the noble crusade that had freed Cuba from the imperial yoke. It would rob Americans of their claim to political exceptionalism, as well as saddle the nation with a new "race problem" of unimagined proportions.

Bryan had made his position clear before he departed for Camp Cuba Libre. In June 1898, he had warned an Omaha audience that the U.S. Navy's recent victory over the Spanish fleet in Manila harbor might be the first act in a war for empire. "Is our National character so weak," he asked, "that we cannot withstand the temptation to appropriate the first piece of land that comes within our reach?" The speech was widely reported and laid down a principle all assumed would guide his postwar actions. As the Senate prepared to debate the peace treaty, journalists anticipated a resumption of the conflict between the campaigners of '96, with the nation's future as a global power at stake.[32]

Then Bryan took a step that startled both his friends and his enemies. Two days after leaving the army, he came to Washington to urge lawmakers to *approve* the treaty with Spain. This represented no change of heart about the evils of colonization. As senators jousted over the question, Bryan kept denouncing conquest as a form of grand larceny and wrote in the *World-Herald* that "preach[ing] the gospel to every creature" does not include "a

Gatling gun attachment."[33] But he thought opposition to the treaty itself would only damage the anti-imperialist cause.

His reasoning was uncharacteristically complex, awkwardly mingling principle with political strategy. Bryan argued that foes of empire had not yet persuaded most Americans of their position; they were only attempting to deny McKinley the two-thirds margin the Constitution required for treaty ratification, and they had no hope of winning a majority of legislators to their side. The more honest course would be to terminate the war officially by approving the treaty, which would allow most troops to come home, then vote to grant Filipinos their independence. "My plan cannot fail if the people are with us and we ought not to succeed unless we do have the people with us," he wrote in mid-January to Andrew Carnegie, who had donated his name and part of his massive fortune to the opposition.[34]

There would, after all, soon be another presidential campaign to wage. If a minority of senators voted down the treaty, Bryan might be unable to heal jagged divisions in his own camp over the issue. Henry Teller, the best-known Silver Republican, supported ratification, although without enthusiasm, and most Populist lawmakers planned to vote "yea" as well. The *New York Journal* roared its approval of empire, as did leading Democratic papers in the South. Perhaps a minority of Bryan's large and usually loquacious following out in the country disagreed with his position, but if so, they were remarkably quiet about it.[35]

So the once and future candidate backed the treaty, hoping an end to the war would reunite the "triple alliance" behind the demand for silver coinage and a furious attack on corporate power, both of which he believed had majority support. The trusts, he claimed in late December, were a greater scourge of liberty than General Weyler had ever been. And couldn't President Bryan do more to defeat imperialism than mere Citizen Bryan, who talked of nothing but?[36]

These dual motivations—soaring ideals and a politician's desire to change the subject—were difficult to explain, and reporters who smelled a good story about political infighting had no reason to help him do it. Most Democrats in the Senate were determined to vote against the peace treaty, and their leader was the shrewd conservative Arthur Pue Gorman, who disliked Bryan's populist views and hoped to run for president himself. The only Republican senator willing to speak out vigorously against McKinley was the aged George Frisbie Hoar, an erstwhile Free Soiler who mistrusted Democrats on principle, particularly one who opposed him on an issue he held dear. Both men labeled Bryan an opportunist hankering after a glory he had not been able to win in battle.[37]

When the treaty gained ratification by a mere two votes, 57–27, these senators and other anti-imperialists charged that Bryan had made the difference. They pointed out that two lawmakers—William V. Allen of Nebraska and John Jones of Nevada—usually followed his lead and had decided to vote yes only at the last moment. But neither man agreed with that judgment. Nor did Gorman, who would have had everything to gain from the charge.[38] It was less surprising that the president and Senator Henry Cabot Lodge, who managed the fight for the treaty, gave their unexpected Democratic ally no credit at all.

Whatever the truth about Bryan's influence, ratification certainly didn't sap his anti-colonial zeal. Days after the treaty fight ended, he took off on a six-month speaking tour devoted mainly to drawing a line in the sand between democratic principles and the arrogance of an administration bent on conquest. "The people have not voted for imperialism; no national convention has declared for it; no Congress has passed upon it," he declared on Washington's birthday. "To whom, then, has the future been revealed?"[39]

The beginning of an imperial war made the question both more urgent and more difficult to resolve. On the night of February 4, half a year of armed tension between U.S. occupiers and the Filipino Army of Liberation was broken when William Grayson, a volunteer from the First Nebraska Regiment, fired on a patrol of independence fighters who had not obeyed his order to halt. Afterward, Grayson boasted to American reporters that he had "got" two of the "niggers" and could have killed more.[40]

U.S. troops quickly gained the advantage in the ensuing combat. The Filipinos, commanded unsteadily by the young aristocrat Emilio Aguinaldo, at first tried to fight a conventional war instead of a guerrilla conflict and lost almost every battle. But the Americans had neither the forces nor the resources to occupy the villages and provincial cities they seized. In November, the *insurrectos* switched to more furtive tactics and a decentralized command structure. The rugged topography of their insular nation and support from many areas outside Manila allowed them to keep on fighting through the next U.S. presidential campaign. Aguinaldo and his fellow leaders would never forgive Bryan for his support of the peace treaty. Yet they also knew their prospects for independence were poor if the Democrat and his fellow opponents of empire could not defeat McKinley in the next election.[41]

To their misfortune, the *insurrectos* had linked their fate with perhaps the most disjointed anti-war movement in U.S. history. Its primary organization was the Anti-Imperialist League. Based in Boston, the league was led by mugwumps over the age of sixty who wrote and distributed broadsides, reports of wartime atrocities, and well-reasoned pamphlets—but were unwilling and probably unable to stage mass demonstrations or mount a concerted lobbying campaign. Their ranks did not lack for men of prominence and recent power: former presidents Cleveland and Harrison, William James, Charles Francis Adams, Carl Schurz, Andrew Carnegie, George Hoar, and Mark Twain all lent their names and some of their time to the effort. But most of these figures had vehemently opposed Bryan in 1896 and still viewed him as a dangerous, untrustworthy character with contemptible followers. Their suspicions made it difficult to forge even a temporary, tactical alliance to stop McKinley's bloody adventure.

Clashing ideas about race also sapped the movement's potential for unity. Some European immigrants—Irish and Polish Catholics, Russian Jews—who'd fled imperial dominion bridled at talk of "Anglo-Saxon" supremacy. But others viewed America as a liberating power. "Our flag flies over Manila! Hurrah for our flag!" cheered the Yiddish *Tageblatt.* Native-born foes of empire who hailed from the abolitionist tradition equated the violence of Jim Crow with the war against the *insurrectos.* In late April, Hoar told a Boston audience, "I can see no difference in the lynching of a Southern [black] postmaster and lynching a people because they think a government derives its just powers from the consent of the governed, and got those ideas from the Constitution of the United States."[42] American soldiers such as Private Grayson who routinely used racist slurs to describe their enemies made the linkage quite clear.

But most Democrats who opposed the war juggled their higher principles with their dread of annexing a distant nation populated by what one Missouri senator called "half-civilized, piratical, muck-running inhabitants." Since its creation, Bryan's party had combined a majoritarian vision with explicit avowals of white supremacy. A dread of racial mixing had always driven Democrats' opposition to seizing the lands of darker people south of the border and across the Pacific. Now, with Ben Tillman warning that imperialists were plotting to "inject this poisoned blood" of Filipinos "into the body politic," it was hard to tell which side of the Jeffersonian tradition had pride of place.[43] Torn by a racial divide older than the republic, anti-imperialists could not effectively counter the boasts of expansionists such as Theodore Roosevelt that the United States was embarked on an "Anglo-Saxon" mission to redeem the benighted throngs of Asia.

Bryan tried to steer the opposition toward an altruistic middle ground. Anglo-Saxon civilization, he told audiences, was an aggressive, warlike phenomenon that had "taught the individual to protect his own rights" and had served its historical purpose. But *American* civilization preached a superior and explicitly Christian message—"to respect the rights of others," to "excite in other races a desire for self government," and to practice the commandment "Thou shalt love they neighbor as thyself." Bryan also advocated, a decade before Roosevelt embraced it, the idea of the United States as a melting pot, at least for those peoples whose roots lay in Europe. "Great has been the Greek, the Latin, the Slav, the Celt, the Teuton, and the Anglo-Saxon, but greater than any of these is the American, in whom are blended the virtues of them all."[44]

But Bryan's flag-waving Social Gospel was blind to the parallels between domestic racism and the international variety. During and between the presidential campaigns of 1896 and 1900, he said little about the cruel and unequal treatment of black Americans, even when it was a vital matter for his audiences. Speaking before Democrats in Louisiana and North Carolina who were busy disenfranchising black voters, he avoided the issue entirely. Bryan publicly condemned lynchings and quietly courted blacks in the North who resented Booker T. Washington for chaining the political future of their race to the GOP. But he also defended his southern allies for promoting what he delicately called "suffrage qualifications" that, by design, favored most whites and excluded most blacks.[45]

When Hoar and other Republicans faithful to anti-slavery ideals challenged such hypocrisy, Bryan resorted to a lawyerly distinction. He alleged that Dixie Democrats had merely chosen, for "today," to bar people who "may qualify themselves to vote tomorrow; the condition is not hopeless." But in the colonized Philippines, "the qualification is permanent. There is no means provided whereby the subject may become a citizen."

Bryan was least convincing when he struck such a disinterested, amoral pose. And in this case, history proved him wrong. By 1907, Filipinos, while still under American rule, were allowed to elect a national assembly. In 1946, they gained their independence. But not until 1965 did the U.S. Congress finally step in to ensure that black citizens in the Deep South could exercise the franchise granted them in the Fifteenth Amendment, ratified almost a century before.[46]

Bryan's habit of ignoring the "race problem" or minimizing it with fatuous rationales followed naturally from his political philosophy. The dutiful son of a Virginia-born apostle of Stephen Douglas, he could believe in a mass of pious "commoners" in perpetual conflict with a greedy and irreligious elite only if he omitted black people from membership in either camp. At the turn of the century, Bryan's support was most fervent in the upper Mississippi Valley and the mountain states, where few of his admirers knew many black people or, given the advance of Jim Crow in nearly every region, felt the need to consider a coalition across racial lines. His party's southern base expected any Democrat who ran for the presidency to assuage its fear of a return to "black and tan" rule. Party chairman James Jones, the son of a slaveholder, spoke wistfully about his youth on the old plantation. Tillman began his political career in 1876 at the head of a "rifle club" that terrorized black voters in South Carolina and helped bring Reconstruction to a bloody end.[47]

Bryan thus felt little pressure to change a stance that excluded millions of Americans from public life. While actively chasing the presidency, he seldom articulated this position either as hostility or as paternalism. He seemed to consider the presence of nine million black citizens to have no great political significance at all.

As HE TRAVELED through friendly territory during the late winter and spring of 1899, Bryan could ignore such contradictions. He spoke mainly in the urban South and West, filling auditoriums with capacities of five thousand and more and crowding out every other story in the local press with fond anecdotes and admiring interviews. The tour was intended to scare away any contender for the presidential nomination and to set the tone for the next campaign, and it succeeded at both tasks. A year before, Henry Cabot Lodge asked Mark Hanna if the Democrats wouldn't "hesitate" before handing the loser of 1896 another chance. "Hesitate," the GOP's impresario exclaimed. "Does a dog hesitate for a marriage license?"[48]

The adulation did often smack of a love affair. The *Denver Post* began a lengthy story about the first day the Bryans, husband and wife, spent in the mountain metropolis with a description of the politician's "laughter, deep-voiced but gentle," wafting over from his breakfast table. The reporter added that military service had only made the Commoner more attractive: "It was good to just sit there and look at him and note his grand virility, his turns of the head that showed the pillar-like neck that upbore the magnificent head ... a modest, unaffected man who caressed his leg and talked and acted like anybody else." A day after hearing Bryan call for Americans to live up to the principles of Jefferson, an Irish immigrant vowed to become a citizen and "to pledge that henceforward throughout my life I should try and fulfil your wish."[49]

At one stop in the cotton-trading town of Brenham, Texas, such admiration briefly slipped into indiscretion. A sixteen-year-old girl named Ruby Gardner tried to kiss Bryan as he paused for a public greeting. Bryan grinned but refused. "I am not Hobson," he explained, referring to Richmond Hobson, a handsome naval hero of the war against Spain who had recently made himself notorious by accepting such requests on his own national tour.[50]

The incident drew attention in faraway newspapers such as the *New York World,* which led the poor girl to write Colonel Bryan a long letter of apology and rededication. Gardner vowed never to be so brazen again and to emulate the behavior of her peers in such evangelical youth groups as Christian Endeavor and the Epworth League. At the same time, she proudly reported getting letters of sympathy every day "from all over the country" and scorned "the very proper old ladies who see great wrong in my action."[51] Such was the balancing act required of a young woman who was dazzled by a virile man of character in late Victorian America.

Away from the embrace of the crowd, Bryan faced a serious dilemma—how to lead a party pessimistic about its future and divided about its course. The McKinley administration held nearly every advantage. Commodity prices, wages, and employment were on the rise in most regions, the military had just won one war and was prevailing in another, and the president and his party were earning a reputation for sensible, if undramatic, governance. Even in Ruby Gardner's hometown, a Democratic bastion, merchants were enjoying a spurt in business brought on by an increase in cotton to over $7 a pound and improvements in service provided by the Santa Fe Railroad. The editors of the Brenham newspaper were not fond of imperialism, but their suspicion of Tammany Hall and any other faction of the party cool to free silver eclipsed their dislike of McKinley. "It behooves all good democrats," wrote the editors, "to look well to their movements, for an enemy in the open is far less dangerous than a foe who is masquerading as a friend."[52]

Such quarrels persisted among Democrats as the election year of 1900 began. Among partisans, there seemed at least three excellent reasons to unseat the incumbent GOP: its war of conquest in the Philippines, its reluctance to curtail the power of big corporations, and its commitment to a financial system run for the benefit of New York and London bankers. But which one would enable Bryan to gain enough votes to topple McKinley? His broad popularity among grassroots Democrats was no guarantee that he could keep all elements of the party united during a second underdog campaign.[53]

The gleam of a silver standard still mesmerized his loyalists in the South, the Great Plains, and the Rockies. In a prosperous nation, they could no longer advance the slogan "sixteen to one" as a panacea for hard times. But a flexible currency continued to appeal to indebted farmers and small businessmen in the South and West as well as to Silver Republicans and Populists whose determination was stronger than their numbers. As often happens in politics, the continued vehemence of its foes—in this case, goldbugs who heaped ridicule on the idea of a "cheap dollar"—only strengthened the conviction of its friends that free silver was the key to preventing future calamity and restoring economic independence.

There was also the question of character. In April 1900, George Fred Williams, Bryan's leading apostle in the unfriendly precincts of Massachusetts, urged him to ensure that silver would retain a prominent place in the Democratic platform. "The people," Williams wrote, "want a man of principle in the White House...for two generations [since Lincoln], they have not had a single man in the presidential chair upon whom they could count for loyal service." To turn his back on the "true spirit" of 1896 would destroy Bryan's bond with his millions of admirers and signal that the Bourbons had been right all along.[54]

But for many Democrats, particularly in the East and urban Midwest, the growth of trusts seemed a more potent threat—and a more fruitful issue—than refighting the last campaign. From 1898 to 1900, industrialists engaged in a flurry of mergers, with a total capitalization of close to $6 billion. Determined to avoid the price wars that had been endemic during the depression of the 1890s, they boasted they were replacing chaos with efficiency. A statistician for the federal government reported that this "reorganization of the manufacturing business" roughly equaled the value of all the industrial concerns that had existed just a decade before. The new trusts dominated the market for such basic goods as glass, paper, salt, tobacco, and steel. Bryan condemned these developments with a few words about the benefits of competition, and added a Christian flourish: "There can be no good monopoly in private hands until the Almighty sends us angels to preside over the monopoly."[55]

Since the Civil War, American opinion makers who agreed about little else had warned about the dangers corporate bigness posed to the ideals of democratic government and individual opportunity. Grover Cleveland and the arch-Republican E. L. Godkin rang the same alarm, while such radical tractarians as Edward Bellamy and Ignatius Donnelly and novelists Frank Norris and Jack London beguiled a mass audience with lurid portraits of a future society where the mass of citizens had become slaves to a handful of bloated moguls.[56]

Clearly, no relief from the current wave of consolidations would be forthcoming from the federal courts—whose rulings had made the Sherman Anti-Trust Act all but unenforceable. The White House and the GOP majority in Congress tut-tutted about the need for business restraint but were unwilling to take any action that might frighten Wall Street or harm the interests of a major campaign contributor. McKinley publicly denounced any arrangement "whereby prices are unduly enhanced." In private, he remarked to his secretary that "he 'guessed' combination must necessarily control largely in the near future.... The great need in such matters was protection to the companies as well as to consult the interests of the people at large."[57]

Still, Democrats found it difficult to convert the abstract fear of bigness into political capital. GOP spokesmen managed to mollify troubled partisans by promising to investigate the problem and to consider remedies thereafter. Ordinary citizens who grumbled that trusts charged high prices and provided impersonal service still preferred a stable economy under *anyone's* direction over the unpredictable one they had known, in which small businesses floundered and investors often panicked. Trade unions grew swiftly at the turn of the century, and most of their officials followed labor leader Samuel Gompers, who tried to convince the trusts to bargain with their employees instead of denouncing their very existence.

On the left, radicals who favored public ownership of the economy were increasingly supplanting the Populists, with their vision of a smallholders' republic. An attorney from Brooklyn wrote to Bryan early in 1900 that he was abandoning the Democrats because "it seems very clear to me that the machine and the trust are given to us by an all-wise Creator to lighten and lessen our toil, and that only the stupid management of them has made them a curse rather than a blessing." For this budding socialist, "half-way reforms" were rather cowardly and even unchristian.[58]

Opposing the war for empire seemed to offer Bryan a political opening that free silver and anti-trust could not match. Many well-educated easterners who styled themselves the conscience of the nation were appalled by the conflict in the Philippines. "The republican party is fattened to kill, with its lying cant about taking of colonies to 'give them freedom,' " William James wrote to his son that March, adding, "This question is going to haunt the country till it is settled, as the slavery question did."[59] Such prominent Gold Democrats as Bourke Cockran hinted that they would return to the partisan fold if Bryan would only give up his obsession with silver and talk mainly about imperialism. So did dailies such as the *New York World* and the *Louisville Courier-Journal* and much of the German-language press that had boomed Grover Cleveland's races for the presidency.

But how many Americans would vote against a war across the Pacific that seemed to be going well? During the winter and spring of 1900, few of Bryan's correspondents, other than well-known foes of empire, even raised the issue. An informal but extensive survey conducted early that year in the swing state of Indiana found, to the relief of Republicans, that many rank-and-file Democrats backed the war and that hardly anyone from either major party thought it would sway their vote. At least in this state, William James was a hasty prophet.[60]

Other prominent men who had reviled Bryan during his last campaign now urged him to rescue the nation's honor and to reject the issues and rhetoric that had made him the leader of his party in the first place. In the august *Atlantic Monthly,* Henry Loomis Nelson, a Cleveland Democrat and a foe of empire, sniffed at the "perilous belief, held by hundreds of thousands of voters, that the owners of wealth in this country are oppressing, through the law, those who have no wealth, and especially those who till the earth and labor with their hands." Nelson predicted "an exciting political campaign over the policy of imperialism."[61] But he did not disclose how Bryan would make up for the votes he could lose if he abandoned the convictions that bound him to his most fervent supporters.

So Bryan entered the 1900 campaign season knowing there was probably no way to please all the factions vying to control his message. If he clung to the gospel of silver, he would drive away the Bourbons, with their money and power of the press. If he mounted a crusade against the trusts, he would have to make radical proposals unacceptable to many voters and to nearly every businessman, or risk sounding little different from Mark Hanna's clever and seasoned wordsmiths. If he talked about nothing but imperialism, he could drown his chances in a sea of popular apathy and mugwump hauteur.

In June, Bryan strained to articulate a common approach in a lengthy article he wrote for the popular *North American Review.* The contest, he trumpeted, was "between plutocracy and democracy." He likened the McKinley administration's "attempted overthrow of American principles" to the "last plague, the slaying of the first-born, which will end the bondage of the American people, and bring deliverance from the Pharaohs who are enthroning Mammon and debasing mankind."[62]

Reflecting on the 1900 campaign, journalist Henry Pringle observed, "For all his magnetism and despite the fact that he perceived current evils with a kind of emotional vision, William Jennings Bryan always spoke for disorganized minorities. They did not seek some common end, they disagreed violently among themselves."[63] Only a congenital optimist who believed he was on the side of the angels would have bet on Bryan's chances.

To have any hope of winning, the Democrats had to stage a spirited and unified convention. They gathered in Kansas City—an implicit tribute to the region's favorite son and a location farther west than any major party had chosen before. Most eastern Democrats would have preferred a less controversial standard-bearer, but Bryan's popularity among the rank and file intimidated anyone from mounting a serious challenge. A spring hope that Admiral George Dewey, victor over the Spanish fleet in Manila Bay, would pose an alternative soon wilted after the handsome officer blithely told reporters, "Since studying this subject I am convinced that the office of the President is not such a very difficult one to fill.... Should I be chosen for this exalted position, I would execute the laws of Congress as faithfully as I have always executed the orders of my superiors."[64]

On July 4, the Democratic convention opened with a reading of the Declaration of Independence, which a delegate from Michigan claimed was "a rebuke to the Republican Party." Then officials unveiled a plaster bust of Bryan to cheers from the twenty thousand people crowded into the sweltering amphitheater. The next evening, delegates nominated the man himself, unanimously and on the first ballot. Bryan remained in Lincoln throughout the whole affair. Perhaps fearing comparisons with the Cross of Gold speech, he decided against making what would have been a dramatic and unprecedented appearance.[65]

He did, however, manage every significant decision. Equipped with a direct telegraph line, long-distance telephone service, and regular delivery of Associated Press bulletins to his home, Bryan could respond almost instantly to his fellow Democrats meeting two hundred miles away. He was pleased that William Oldham, a loyal admirer from Omaha, nominated him with an energetic feat of bombast and that David Hill of New York, his adversary at the 1896 convention, delivered a gracious seconding address in which he declared that the Commoner's "integrity has never been questioned."[66]

Indeed, the nominee insisted—to reporters and delegates alike—that principle not be compromised on the altar of unity. The platform must explicitly "reiterate" the demand for "free and unlimited coinage of silver and gold at the present legal ratio of 16 to 1" or Bryan would decline to run at all. Such allies as James K. Jones and Ben Tillman urged him to accept a more ambiguous pledge, while opposition dailies charged he was "pursuing as dictatorial a course as the most arrogant boss ever ventured on." But he prevailed, narrowly, in the Resolutions Committee, where delegates from nearly every eastern and midwestern state voted against his stand.

Wisely, Bryan did not push his point too far. He recognized that opposition to empire was the one issue that could unite party activists and avert a second bolt by Gold Democrats—and its urgency was hard to question. So

Bryan agreed to label imperialism the "paramount issue" of the campaign, although he believed the trusts and silver should get equal billing. And he acquiesced in the vice presidential nomination of sixty-four-year-old Adlai Stevenson of Illinois, although he preferred the young firebrand Charles Towne, an eloquent former Republican from Minnesota. Having held the same post in Cleveland's second administration, Stevenson retained some appeal among the old guard and hailed from the third most populous state.[67]

The odds on Bryan's victory were long, but reporters were still fascinated by the unorthodox figure he cut in public life. Partisan journalists continued to describe him in simple terms—as spotless hero or unprincipled crowd-pleaser. On July 4, Hearst began publishing a daily paper in Chicago to provide Bryan with a high-circulation voice in that part of the country. In the small town of Anamosa, Iowa, a Democratic weekly claimed that Bryan had "held the undivided esteem of the people for four years" because "the inherent qualities of honor and genius" were "the fibre of his make-up."[68] But that summer, two gifted writers penned more critical portraits to explain why, despite holding no office, he had become, in one editor's words, "the most prominent man in the United States."[69]

For William Allen White, whose own rise to fame began during the 1896 campaign, Bryan was a naive man of limitless charms. He had a youthful smile as "clear and steadfast and cheerful as the sunrise" and "the breezy amiability of a St. Louis shoe-drummer" but never let an insincere phrase pass his lips. So Bryan was certainly not the demagogue his enemies charged.

Yet neither was he a statesman in the making. White browsed around his subject's ample home library and was amused to find a collection devoted almost solely to texts chosen for moral edification and/or display. Sets of old histories and orations abounded; novels were scarce, and ones published since the prime of Charles Dickens even rarer. Bryan seemed to read only to gain ammunition for his next debate and "lost no force of his eloquence convincing himself."[70] Thus, in the first of a series of articles he would write about national politicians, White merged opposing images of his celebrated subject. Bryan's personality had made him a popular hero, but it should warn reflective Americans to choose somebody else to govern them. "There is really no more reason for electing an orator to office than for electing a fiddler. Both talents rouse the emotions."

At the same time, White seemed confused about, and a little in awe of, his subject's political presence. Was Bryan just a big voice spouting anti-monopoly rancor unaltered since the era of Jackson, a simpleton who hadn't learned "that the present phase of industrial evolution is not a conspiracy against God and man"? Or was he a Pied Piper of socialism, who cleverly voiced "a hope to see the State lay hold of the industrial system and untangle its many snarls"? In the end, White—who, like Bryan, would spend a long career defending both "small-town" values and a government strong enough to restrain selfish corporations—resisted the urge to dismiss his subject as a man only fools could admire. "More power for good than evil," he wrote, "rests under Bryan's black slouch hat than under any other single head-piece in America."[71]

Willa Cather also tried to balance her wonder at Bryan's oratory with her lack of respect for his mind. In a piece written soon after the Kansas City convention, the writer from Nebraska recalled hearing him deliver a eulogy in the early 1890s for a fellow Democrat at her "sun-scorched, dried-up, blown-away little village" of Red Cloud: "Surely that was eloquence of the old stamp that was accounted divine.... I saw those rugged, ragged men of the soil weep like children." Yet this was the same fellow who urged everyone in Lincoln to read *Les Misérables,* which he thought was the greatest novel ever written—but cared only for "Hugo's vague hyperbolic generalizations on sociological questions."[72]

Still, Cather could not help but marvel at the man. She praised Bryan for treating Mary as an equal partner in the family business of politics: "From the outset their minds and tastes kept pace with each other, as they have done to this day." And while she disliked his earnest piety, habitually imparted with "a glance as penetrating as a searchlight," Cather, like White, was not content to condescend. "It is an interesting study in reactions," she observed, "that the most practical, and prosaic, and purely commercial people on the planet should be dazzled and half convinced by a purely picturesque figure—a knight on horseback."[73]

Bryan's critics frequently offered insights about him that his admirers ignored. White and Cather certainly captured the limits of his imagination and the myopia that attended his moralism. But they too easily dismissed his critique of the emerging corporate, imperial order. And they struggled to grasp that Bryan's followers found in him a quality lacking in the cautious organization men whom the major parties had routinely ran for high office throughout the Gilded Age. Cather wrote, "The man himself would scorn a machine.... His constituents are controlled not by a commercial syndicate or by a political trust, but by one man's personality."[74]

For a decade, Bryan's renown had depended on his ability to compose and deliver a memorable speech. To infuse his second presidential campaign with some hope and enthusiasm, he would have to do so again. In early August, Democratic chairman James Jones reported that the party was finding it hard "getting money enough to make much of a campaign." Meanwhile, apathy raged among voters throughout the Midwest, scene of intense partisan conflict and high turnout four years earlier. The People's Party split in two, with the largest faction again nominating Bryan. But, in contrast to 1896, neither group could claim many members or funds. Without a strong third party behind him, Populist voters in the Plains and Mountain states were drifting back to the GOP. Bryan's speech accepting the Democratic nomination on August 8 in Indianapolis was thus his best opportunity to reverse his waning fortunes.[75]

Only recently had the ritual of acceptance taken on much importance. Before the Civil War, candidates penned only a brief letter, politely agreeing to be the nominee of their party and touching on the major issues of the campaign. Beginning with the 1868 contest, each Democratic candidate also made a public address. Since few were eager orators or deft ones, their remarks made little stir. In 1892, Grover Cleveland broke with this precedent when he gave, before a large crowd at Madison Square Garden, a slashing speech in favor of lower tariffs.

Four years later, inside the same arena, Bryan had delivered, to a massive and expectant crowd, an acceptance speech that may have doomed his chances of winning New York State. Anxious to seem statesmanlike in the citadel of the urban East, he had read verbatim a dry, two-hour-long exposition of the case for silver. It failed to persuade skeptics and drove half his audience to the exits before he had stopped speaking.[76] In 1900, in the capital of a key swing state, he had a chance to reverse that bad impression.

On a hot, breezy afternoon, some fifty thousand people crowded into a thirty-acre expanse, ironically named Military Park, to hear Bryan read a speech that contained few of the melodramatic frills that had earned him both renown and derision. His strong, confident voice—"never more completely at his command," wrote a reporter for the *New York Times*—reached everyone in the park. What they heard was as forceful and well argued as any speech he would ever deliver.[77]

Bryan wisely decided to play to his strengths. He sought to put his opponents on the defensive with a sweeping attack on the morality of empire. After repeating his claim that the election was "a contest between democracy and plutocracy," Bryan turned to the war in the Philippines and focused solely on that issue for the remainder of his hour-long talk.[78]

Each point Bryan made that August day was animated by the spirits of Jefferson and Jesus, separate or intertwined. As in the Cross of Gold speech, he invoked his favorite Virginian and other Founding Fathers who "declared that the colonists must choose between liberty and slavery." But this time, he used Christianity not as a metaphor of justice but as its very core. Even if the Declaration of Independence had never been written, announced Bryan, "a war of conquest would still leave its legacy of perpetual hatred, for it was God Himself who placed in every human heart the love of liberty. He never made a race of people so low in the scale of civilization or intelligence that it would welcome a foreign master."

The candidate kept his audience's attention with quick thrusts of argument, keen debating points made to pierce through a GOP platform that pledged "to confer the blessings of liberty and civilization upon" the "rescued" Filipinos.[79] How did this claim, asked Bryan, differ from the one the British government had made in 1776, or that offered by the Spanish a century later? Imperialism would require a large standing army, he charged, and that would encourage more "wars of conquest" and "turn the thoughts of our young men from the arts of peace to the science of war." Republicans contended that the United States had a right to have colonies because it had the capacity to govern them well. Bryan responded, "The question is not what we can do, but what we *ought* to do. This nation can do whatever it desires to do, but it must accept responsibility for what it does."

Only at the end of his remarks did the nominee sound a romantic note—and then, in contrast to his convention speech in 1896, he did so to evoke the future. "Behold a republic," Bryan urged, one that had achieved its cherished ideals. It would be a nation "in which civil and religious liberty stimulate all to earnest endeavor and in which the law restrains every hand uplifted for a neighbor's injury—a republic in which every citizen is a sovereign, but in which no one cares to wear a crown."

During the Great Depression of the 1930s, that last image—shortened to "Every man a king"—helped the Louisiana populist Huey Long build a large and angry, if short-lived, mass movement for the redistribution of wealth. But in the summer of 1900, Bryan was speaking as a near-pacifist on a Christian mission. In his final sentence, he quoted from the Book of Proverbs, most of which he knew by heart: "Behold a republic gradually but surely becoming the supreme moral factor in the world's progress and the accepted arbiter of the world's disputes—a republic whose history, like the path of the just, 'is as the shining light that shineth more and more unto the perfect day.' "[80]

The speech did brighten his own prospects a little. What one correspondent called its "lofty spirit" helped to persuade most officers in the Anti-Imperialist League to support him, ending any possibility they would launch a third party. A few influential easterners—the financier Perry Belmont, the editor Thomas Wentworth Higginson, and the orator Bourke Cockran—now agreed that Bryan cared deeply about the issue. Several military men wrote to the candidate from the Philippines to affirm that the United States was fighting an unjust, brutal war and that islanders who favored independence viewed him as a savior. According to an army surgeon, they "pray to a watchful father asking that they may be relieved from the bondage thrust upon them by America."[81]

For the first time all year, Republicans were worried. In mid-August, Mark Hanna began, as in 1896, to ask large industrial and Wall Street firms to donate all the money they could spare. The GOP raised $2.5 million in total—almost ten times what the Democrats could muster. Meanwhile, McKinley was angered by Bryan's implicit charge that he was acting like King George III and, even worse, forsaking the Gospels. In September, the president released a lengthy acceptance letter justifying what his government was doing in the Philippines. After the exchange, William James wrote to a friend, "Say what you will, our presidential campaigns are a magnificent educational institution."[82]

Still, sharp debate on the "paramount issue" didn't alter the terms of battle. The Democrats remained sure of victory only in the white South, whose loving embrace of Jim Crow laws mocked Bryan's image as the upholder of government by the consent of the governed. Everywhere else, he had to juggle the triad of issues—silver, trusts, and empire—in hopes of snagging voters who cared enough about one of them to lay aside their misgivings about the others.

Democratic control of most big cities—New York, Chicago, Baltimore, Indianapolis, San Francisco—should have given Bryan an advantage in states he needed to win. But metropolitan papers in the East and Midwest, save those owned by Hearst, still mocked and chided him. Intraparty feuds and a shortage of money also hampered the campaign in urban states, and the candidate was sometimes maladroit in handling them.

Bryan gave more than a hundred speeches in New York, the biggest electoral prize. But he failed to rise above the long-running battle between David Hill, chief of the upstate party, and Richard Croker, the Irish-born boss of Tammany Hall, who everywhere outside the big city was regarded as a symbol of infamy. On October 16, Bryan spoke at Cooper Union in lower Manhattan. He interrupted his address to walk across the stage and stand beside the prince of municipal corruption. "Great is Tammany, and Croker is its prophet!" he announced to the roars of the partisan crowd. Bryan had sealed his bargain with the machine but had given his enemies a priceless piece of evidence that no politician, however pure his image, was immune from hypocrisy.[83]

And then he had to compete with Theodore Roosevelt. TR's combat exploits in Cuba had made him a national celebrity. The press gorged its readers with stories about his bravery in leading the Rough Riders—to which he recruited men from a variety of social classes and white ethnic groups. His toothy grin, pince-nez, and combative speaking style quickly became as recognizable as Bryan's mighty baritone, broad smile, and black fedora. In 1898, he narrowly won election as governor of New York.

A year later, Vice President Garret Hobart died, leaving the second place on the Republican ticket open for another man from the East. GOP delegates at their 1900 convention would consider no candidate except "Teddy," and their ardor overcame Mark Hanna's fear that "this madman" would not toe the party line if he ever attained the presidency. Hanna also knew he could use a candidate able to match Bryan's athletic oratory and popular appeal. As the incumbent, McKinley would remain in the White House or on his tidy front porch in northeastern Ohio.

TR reveled in the opportunity. His opinion of Bryan and his followers swung between contempt and loathing. In 1896, he had vowed to take up arms, if necessary, to stop the fusion candidate and the "semi-socialistic" movement he represented. On the stump that fall, Roosevelt didn't hesitate to label Bryan's platform "criminal," "vicious," and "fundamentally an attack on civilization." By 1900, he had softened neither his opinion of the man nor his politics. Roosevelt told crowds that Bryan was still a monetary crackpot and a purveyor of "communistic and socialistic doctrines." He wrote to a friend that behind the Democratic nominee gathered "all the lunatics, all the idiots, all the knaves, all the cowards, and all the honest people who are slow-witted."[84]

The men were probably destined to be rivals. Born just two years apart (TR in 1858), they belonged to different parties, came from mutually suspicious regions, and disagreed about the purpose of political leadership. Roosevelt was the tough-minded advocate of a new, yet essentially conservative social order. A wealthy insider with a popular touch, he sought to reconcile often hostile interests—business and labor, city and country, blacks and whites, recent immigrants and the native-born—inside a mildly regulatory state that would unify Americans with the glue of foreign expansion and war. "I am not advocating anything revolutionary," he explained. "I am advocating action to prevent anything revolutionary."[85] In contrast, Bryan viewed himself as the champion of discontented outsiders, whom he always imagined as native-born citizens with white skins. He mistrusted compromise, despised militarism, and preached a sentimental populism that irritated the intellectual Roosevelt as much as did the idea of free silver itself.

What the two had in common was their skill and joy at cultivating a mass public, on the stump and with the assistance of a small army of journalists. In 1896, Bryan had waged the most strenuous presidential campaign in U.S. history, while TR was known only as an author and a New York City police commissioner. But Roosevelt refused to allow the dangerous "radical" to repeat his performance unchallenged. Their shared status as celebrities only sharpened the rivalry, even though TR and Bryan weren't running for the same job. As a result, the 1900 campaign was the first of a new and enduring type: opposing candidates for the Republic's highest offices had never stumped against each other before.

Roosevelt determined to beat the Democratic nominee at his own oratorical game. "'Tis Tiddy alone that's running," joked Mr. Dooley about the Republican ticket, "and he ain't running, he's galloping." TR made a point of traveling more miles (21,000) and giving more speeches (673) than did Bryan (16,000 and 600). Roosevelt devoted most of his energy to western and midwestern states his party had either lost in 1896 or won by only a few thousand votes. At several stops, local GOP activists hired men to impersonate Rough Riders. In his high-pitched voice, TR denounced free silver and punched the air with a warrior's defense of empire: "The man goes out to do a man's work, to confront the difficulties and overcome them, and to train up his children to do likewise. So it is with the Nation."[86]

Bryan, after spending most of August at home in Lincoln, did his best to keep up the pace. During the final two months of the campaign, he spoke widely through the upper Midwest as well as the urban East. When crowds failed to respond enthusiastically to his attacks on the war abroad, he shifted to attacking the trusts; he seldom mentioned silver, unless a reporter asked him about it. As in 1896, Bryan urged wage earners to look past the size of their weekly pay envelope; the real evil was a corporate system that was "condemning the boys of this country to perpetual clerkship."[87] A bitter coal strike in the anthracite mines of Pennsylvania gave Bryan a chance to side with one of the most indispensable groups of workers in the country—before Mark Hanna pressured their employers to settle late in the campaign.

Roosevelt drew the most lavish coverage, although not the biggest crowds. It was novel for an articulate war hero to make a whirlwind tour for his party and himself. Despite Bryan's own tireless eloquence, urban papers—most of which were again unfriendly—could scoff that he was running a sequel of 1896, and with less hope of victory. Even the Hearst press seemed to lose its ardor for the fight. In mid-September, editors of the *New York Journal* began to shrink the amount of campaign reportage in the paper and instead filled its columns with news of the Galveston flood, the aftermath of the Boxer Rebellion in China, and other, more dramatic subjects.[88]

Some of Bryan's followers sensed the futility of his efforts. An admirer from Kenton, Ohio, predicted his man would triumph on his *third* campaign for the White House if he continued to "stand by the poor of this country." "Did you ever notice," asked J. G. Krembelbine, "that everything is done by 3 just look in the New Testament and see how often you will see three mentioned." Bryan seems to have received less mail than in 1896 and proportionally fewer messages from women and children. Correspondents in 1900 dwelled more on Bryan's image as, in the words of an elderly farmer, "a good, honest, whole souled Christian man" than on his views about any single issue. That spring, a middle-aged apostle left a durable sign of his affection and his faith in his idol's ultimate triumph. On the tombstone of B. H. Norris, address unknown, it read: "Died Apr. 9, 1900, aged 51 yrs. Kind friends I've left behind Cast your vote for Jennings Bryan."[89]

Notwithstanding such unorthodox forms of publicity, the GOP was in command. Compared to the Democrats, they had ten times the money, almost three times the local speakers, and a ferociously efficient party structure. Almost fifty million copies of McKinley's prosaic acceptance speech reached voters compared to just eight million copies of Bryan's rather masterful one. The disparity of resources made a difficult task all but impossible: the Democrats had simply failed to generate enough anger or enthusiasm to topple an incumbent from the majority party. As Mark Hanna put it with customary succinctness during a visit to Nebraska, "There's only one issue in this campaign, my friends, and that is, 'let well enough alone.' "[90]

THE RESULT surprised hardly anyone. As befit a status quo election, McKinley increased his margins in both the popular and the electoral vote—but only slightly. He defeated Bryan by more than 6 percent of the ballots (compared to less than 5 percent the first time around) and held every state he had carried in 1896, save Kentucky. What is more, he reasserted Republican dominance in the Great Plains and the West Coast and ceded only four small mountain states to the Democrat. The morning after the election, Bryan even had to stomach the loss of his own state, city, and precinct.

His exertions were not entirely in vain. With Tammany's aid, Bryan carried New York City and cut by half McKinley's previous margin in the Empire State. His positions on trusts and the Philippines—and the absence of a splinter ticket—no doubt increased his vote in other working-class cities and in New England, bastion of the anti-imperialist movement. Still, a healthy gain of fifty thousand ballots in Massachusetts (and victory in Boston) left Bryan with only 38 percent of the vote there, and he ran behind local and state candidates of his own party throughout most of the region.

Since the Civil War, Democrats had never counted on winning the Yankee Northeast, cradle of abolitionism and high tariffs. Their prospects always depended on carrying big states in the Midwest. But, despite several energetic tours through his native region, Bryan improved his performance only in Illinois, where he took almost 45 percent of the vote, three points better than in 1896. Everywhere else in the heartland of big factories and staple crops, it was McKinley who augmented his previous totals. Most German Americans, wary of free silver and grateful for prosperity, again chose the GOP. Of the major immigrant groups, only Irish Catholics stayed faithful to the Democracy. The stark truth is that Bryan's long campaign had done nothing to alter the verdict of 1896.[91]

The 1900 race also began an ominous trend, one that few party officials in either party noticed at the time. The turnout of eligible voters was only 73.6 percent, six points lower than in 1896 and the lowest since 1872, when Ulysses S. Grant won reelection in a landslide. The biggest decline was in the South, where the disenfranchisement of many black men and the virtual disappearance of the People's Party caused a drop of 14 percent. But nearly everywhere, the fierce individual competition between Roosevelt and Bryan failed to produce the rush to the polls that one might have expected from the size of their crowds and the avidity of the reportage.[92]

Since the beginning of mass politics in the 1830s, it had been the task of parties to excite, educate, and mobilize men (and not a few women, despite their legal exclusion) to regard voting as an obligatory rite of citizenship. Few presidential candidates thought it proper to campaign for themselves or even believed it was necessary. In 1896, Bryan had broken with this tradition, inspiring a host of Americans and repulsing just as many. But the decline in turnout four years later suggested that personality was still less potent than organization. The Republican Party, which possessed both TR's charisma and Mark Hanna's machine, had learned how to combine the two. The election only confirmed its reign over a nation preening with industry and empire.

CHAPTER FIVE

❧✠❧

I Have Kept the Faith,
1901–1904

He had been abused by every party leader, he had been deserted by the better democracy. . . . He was down and out, but his political deathbed was the big memory of that convention.

—*Philadelphia Press*, 1904[1]

THE 1900 RETURNS drove many of Bryan's followers to despair. After his first defeat, they had paused only briefly before resuming their praise for his sincerity, his courage, and his clear desire to resume the battle. But now their letters were filled with the metaphors of hopelessness. A college president from Ohio worried that it might take "a bloody revolution" to "extricate" Americans "from the slavery into which they have drifted." A Democrat from Nebraska compared the losing candidate to Christ beset by "the wealthy Sadducees and aristocratic Pharisees." A professional lecturer from Chicago wailed, "Our country is unworthy of you." John Peter Altgeld, who had campaigned hard among his fellow Germans, called the result a "crime" and feared "the republic is lost."[2]

But other correspondents discovered a nugget of redemption beneath the ashes of defeat. "You are a Prophet-statesman," declared the rector of an Episcopalian church in New Jersey, "and you lost the presidency because you are."[3] Several of the faithful quoted the famous lines of James Russell Lowell, written in 1844 as a hymn to the cause of anti-slavery:

> *Truth forever on the scaffold,*
> *Wrong forever on the throne,*
> *Yet that scaffold sways the future,*
> *And behind the dim unknown*
> *Standeth God within the shadow*
> *Keeping watch above His own.*[4]

The image of farseeing rectitude was easy to ridicule. Only three weeks before, Bryan had dubbed the boss of Tammany Hall a "prophet" when it served his electoral interest. For most Republicans and some Democrats, his faith in free silver and resentment of large employers bespoke a nostalgia and bitterness toward social changes that were benefiting most Americans. "What a thorough paced hypocrite and demagogue he is," snarled Theodore Roosevelt in a letter to his close friend Henry Cabot Lodge, "and what a small man."[5]

But Bryan's followers were keen to anoint him a lonely sage, and attention should be paid to their reasons. Few had believed the loss of 1896 more than a temporary setback; in fact, many thought Hanna and his corporate minions had stolen that election through vote buying and intimidation. Thus, the frustrating campaign of 1900 and its demoralizing conclusion struck loyal Bryanites as a sign that the republic was in deeper trouble than they had realized. A majority of Americans seemed content to live in an imperial nation dominated by trusts, whether or not they actively supported Republican policies.

Perhaps Bryan would still "lead us out" of this degraded state, as the Alexanders of Des Moines had prayed after the 1896 election. But until that Pentecostal day, it was a comfort to know he would continue to articulate a set of unwavering principles—in appealingly romantic and biblical prose. "Let us thank God," wrote a devotee from Michigan days after the 1900 vote, that Bryan "still survives in renewed and giant strength...the rock upon which the liberties of the people of this and coming time, will build."[6]

The notion of the unsuccessful politician as a prophetic hero was drenched in melodrama, a genre ubiquitous in American culture at the time. Men and women who wept at Dickens's novels and *Uncle Tom's Cabin* (the play as much as Stowe's book), who thrilled to the sermons of Henry Ward Beecher (whether or not they agreed with his liberal theology) and the temperance homilies of Frances Willard, and whose altruistic imagination was kindled by Bellamy's *Looking Backward* could find in Bryan a sympathetic scourge of the privileged and the greedy. "At its most ambitious," writes the critic Peter Brooks, "the melodramatic mode...may appear to be the very process of reaching a fundamental drama of the moral life and finding the terms to express it."[7]

In 1896, Bryan had riveted the nation with what his supporters perceived as a one-man crusade against cynicism and selfishness on high. Because he never rested from what Brooks calls "an active, lucid confrontation of evil," he retained that image until the curtain fell.[8] After his loss in 1900, Bryan's oppositional rigor became, for his followers, a saving virtue.

The man himself appeared as sanguine as ever. On election night, he took a nap after hearing the early returns and awoke near midnight only to please reporters facing deadlines. "So far as his outward expression went," one writer recalled, "there was nothing to indicate that he had, for the second time, lost the highest office in the world." This time, however, Bryan chose not to draft a lengthy synopsis of the disappointing campaign. He did help compile a book, *The Second Battle, or The New Declaration of Independence*. But it contained only speeches and articles that had already appeared in thousands of newspapers, and it sold poorly.[9]

Of course, he never considered retiring from the fray. Bryan knew he could continue to make a fine income on the lecture circuit and that no other Democrat could match his independent following or his ability to make news. So he decided to become a freelance political celebrity—to speak his mind on a range of issues, spiritual as well as secular, and to invite controversy within his party as well as outside it. From his base in the Lincoln suburbs where he occasionally taught a Sunday-school class at a Methodist church, Bryan spent the next four years elaborating his self-image as the independent conscience of moral, insurgent white Americans. As with every big step in Bryan's career, the personality and the politics were indistinguishable.[10]

The chief instrument of his new campaign was a weekly newspaper named, inevitably, *The Commoner*. Only days after the election, Bryan began hiring staff members and arranging for a union press to print the paper. The first issue appeared in late January 1901. "The common people do not constitute an exclusive society...," wrote Bryan in the lead editorial; "any one can become a member if he is willing to contribute by brain and muscle to the nation's strength and greatness." Surrounding that paean to the producer ethic, he gathered declarations of an evangelism tethered to worldly concerns. Paraphrasing Jeremiah 2, *The Commoner* warned Americans not to repeat the "backslidings" of ancient Israel by "turn[ing] back to the once discarded doctrine of empires." In its first issue, the paper also called for "a revival that will prevent highway robbery by monopolies and wars for the purchase of trade." Reverent readers applauded its tone. "The most important feature of the paper," wrote a mill worker from Minnesota, "is the application of the teachings of Jesus Christ to every day life and public affairs."[11]

Thousands of reform and radical periodicals glutted the post offices and newsstands in turn-of-the-century America. But *The Commoner* was the only significant one dedicated to promoting the ideas and career of a single man. Bryan's paper reprinted his major speeches as well as many of the interviews and articles he did for other publications, and it passed along commentaries that either praised him in a colorful way or damned him with a jibe of such malignancy that it discredited the author. Columns of topical humor and household advice and a slew of political cartoons provided relief from the steady diet of Bryaniana. When Bryan was away, his brother Charles edited the paper and also handled its business affairs. Assisting him was Richard Metcalfe, Will's erstwhile ghostwriter on the *Omaha World-Herald* and a close aide during his first two presidential campaigns, and Mary Bryan, when she had the time.

Such egoism could have ensured a tiny press run and a brief life. Yet by the spring of 1901, Bryan's paper had grown from eight pages to twelve; a year later, it consistently ran sixteen pages, with advertisements filling the last half of every issue. With help from admirers selling subscriptions, its circulation expanded from 18,000 at the start to 145,000 by mid-decade. Bryan invited other periodicals to reprint anything they liked for free. Even though most of its subscribers lived in the upper Mississippi Valley, *The Commoner* was frequently quoted by the major papers of eastern cities.[12]

At its zenith, the paper could claim a readership larger than all but a handful of other political weeklies in its era. If one takes account of the increase in population over the last century, *The Commoner* would have more than double the circulation of any contemporary journal of opinion, from *The Nation* to the *New Republic* to the *National Review*. Unlike the proprietors of such magazines, then or now, Bryan refused to take ads from big corporations, which he always equated with trusts. Liquor and tobacco firms were also taboo. He paid his employees—many of whom were female—union wages and required them to work no more than eight hours a day.[13]

At the same time, the Great Commoner began to live in a most uncommon fashion. In 1902, Bryan, Mary, and their three children moved into a freshly built mansion located some four miles east of downtown Lincoln. Will dubbed the house, which cost $17,000, "Fairview," because it overlooked thirty-five acres of "as beautiful a piece of farm land as can be found anywhere." He referred to the estate as "the Monticello of the West" and invited politicians and diplomats from all over the world to come for a stay. A dining room large enough to seat twenty-four, several guest bedrooms, and a full complement of servants underlined his ambition. Bryan planted corn on his adjoining acres and liked to ride into town to purchase seed and tools. Like his father, he had become a country gentleman, albeit one who frequently left the manse to promote his ideas and enlarge his fortune.[14]

But defeat in the "second battle" had cost him the leadership of his party. Conservative Democrats from the East and South blamed Bryan for tearing their cherished institution apart with intemperate rhetoric and betraying its laissez-faire traditions with his talk of taxing the rich and smashing all trusts. Such party nabobs as David Bennett Hill in New York, Henry Watterson in Kentucky, James Smith in New Jersey, Arthur Gorman in Maryland, John Daniel in Virginia, and Thomas Taggart in Indiana moved to reassert control. Pulitzer's *New York World,* the nation's only million-circulation daily, portrayed them as sturdy Jeffersonians who posed a sober alternative both to the power-mad, empire-building GOP and to Bryan's failed attempt to remake the party in the Populists' image.

A decade before, Grover Cleveland had led the Democrats to their only presidential victories since the Civil War. The "reorganizers," as the anti-Bryanites called themselves, saw no reason why a nominee who emulated his moderation and honesty couldn't do so again. Some even tried to persuade the former president himself to wage another dignified campaign for low tariffs and rigid adherence to the letter of the Constitution. Cleveland's refusal didn't discourage the conservatives. Surely, there were a number of "available" men who, in Gorman's words, would be able to "repress the Wild People" who had flocked to Bryan.[15]

Nothing in politics is so fatal as a hope rooted in nostalgia. After an unemployed anarchist murdered William McKinley in September 1901, Democrats had to compete against a new president who was equally adept at using his office to address social ills and to boost his personal renown. Theodore Roosevelt governed as fiercely and as innovatively as he had campaigned. During his first two years in the White House, he initiated an antitrust suit against a major transport company, convinced Congress to set up the Bureau of Corporations, created wildlife refuges and national parks, forced anti-union employers to accept arbitration in a major coal strike, and schemed to seize control of land in Panama for a canal to link the Atlantic and Pacific. With the aid of his adventurous, photogenic young family, TR seduced reporters into describing him with an anecdotal fondness enjoyed by none of his forerunners. And he made their task easier by regularly venturing out into the country to show his fellow Americans how much he loved being their president.[16]

Having stirred up an affair with part of the nation, Bryan could appreciate Roosevelt's allure—both as a personality and an icon of reform—and the challenge he posed. It bolstered Bryan's conviction that Democrats would also have to garb themselves in the raiments of progressivism if they wanted to compete for national power.

To that end, he began to argue for an impressive array of proposals that broadened his earlier focus on money, monopoly, and empire. Bryan revived talk of a federal income tax, endorsed the initiative and referendum process for passing state laws, called on Congress to enact pure food and drug laws, cheered municipal ownership of utilities and streetcars, demanded a ban on corporate financing of campaigns, and favored constitutional amendments to elect senators by popular vote and to restrict presidents to a single term in office. At one time or another over the previous decade, Bryan had spoken up for each of these reforms. But since he was unlikely to run in 1904, he was now freer to equip his breed of Democrats with a legislative agenda they could champion, and perhaps win, in the years to come.

He also drew a sharp line between TR's ideas and his own. Bryan accused the president of falsely advertising himself as an agent of beneficial change. The president's love of war indicated "an eagerness for bloodletting" that violated the Ten Commandments and the Sermon on the Mount. No wonder Roosevelt looked the other way when U.S. soldiers committed atrocities during the war to conquer the Philippines. And did he have any reason to invite Booker T. Washington to dine at the White House other than to secure black votes and promote the pipe dream of "social equality" between the races? *The Commoner* also charged the president with speaking loudly about the evils of trusts but rarely employing his prosecutorial stick—and never against his corporate friends. Only Republicans who emulated the tough remedies being espoused by Governor Robert La Follette of Wisconsin could "save the country from corporate domination."[17]

But the rift in Bryan's party was far more serious than any dispute among leaders of the GOP. Conservative Democrats had no desire to win him over, and he continued to blast every move they took to bring back the alleged glories of the Gilded Age. After the 1900 election, the humorist Finley Peter Dunne had his characters bemoan the state of their party: " 'I wondher,' said Mr. Hennessy, 'if us dimmy-crats will iver ilict a prisidint again.' " Responded Mr. Dooley, " 'Me frind Willum J. Bryan reads th' Commoner to them an' they pack up their bags an' lave.... No, sir, th' dimmycratic party ain't on speakin' terms with itsilf.' "[18] In 1903, banqueters at a gala Jefferson Day dinner in Manhattan hissed loudly at the very mention of Bryan's name.

The marked man was not about to surrender. In 1902 and 1903, Bryan campaigned hard in the Midwest for state and local candidates who stayed loyal to him, while *The Commoner* urged readers to set up Democratic clubs dedicated to his progressive platform. But Republicans defeated most of his favorites. Into the breach rushed William Randolph Hearst, with his fortune and his press empire. The publisher had gotten himself elected to Congress from New York City in 1902 and was spending $1.5 million on Hearst for President Clubs. He counted on an endorsement from the man his papers had backed to the hilt in the last two campaigns.[19]

But on the eve of his party's 1904 convention in St. Louis, Bryan's political stock was lower than it had been since he failed to win a Senate seat a decade before. The front-runner for the nomination was Alton Parker, an appeals judge in his early fifties, who had made his name as the only Democrat to win election to a state office in the vote-rich lode of New York. On the bench, Parker had consistently opposed an active government and had long been close to David Hill, cautious boss of the upstate party. The judge had voted for Bryan in 1896 and 1900. But his colorless demeanor, laissez-faire opinions, and indifference to public speaking made him the quintessential anti-Commoner.[20]

"There was no one to meet Mr. Bryan this morning when he came into St. Louis to head the fight against Judge Parker and a conservative platform," wrote James Creelman of the *New York World* on July 3. "Time has taken the eagle sharpness from Bryan's face and left it heavier, coarser, jollier.... The huge jaws are set as hard, but the powerful lines which gave distinction to his countenance have vanished." The description was father to the thought. Men who had been grumbling for eight long years since the "Popocrats" seized the party at the Chicago convention now exulted that Bryan, who hung on as chair of the Nebraska delegation, had become "a dwindling figure and a weakening force" whose "pathetic" statements could be dismissed, if not entirely ignored.[21]

Still, the conservatives were anxious. A day after Bryan arrived in town, he was once again getting mobbed in the streets and hallways and was huddling with allies in an effort to sway the proceedings. Would Bryan find a way to stir the delegates and hijack the platform? William Randolph Hearst came to the convention with pledges from about a quarter of the delegates. If Bryan teamed up with the wealthy publisher, they might be able to stop Parker from being chosen, if not swing the nomination to Hearst himself, whom the conservatives despised as a radical at home, an imperialist abroad, and a rake who couldn't keep his hands off pretty women. "The first duty of this convention," declared John P. Hopkins, head of the Illinois delegation, "is to kill Bryanism, root and branch." To which the intended victim replied, "I shall stand here until the last dog is dead."[22]

Bryan's enemies failed to realize they had prepared the stage for another great performance. When the convention opened on July 6, he was running a high fever and suffering from chest pains. A doctor advised him to stay in bed. If Mary had been present, she might have prevailed. But Bryan would never allow poor health to prevent him from doing his political duty. He worked all night trying to snatch delegates away from the conservatives and draft a progressive platform, especially regarding the power of trusts and the rights of labor.

Gulping glass after glass of ice water, Bryan took his fight to the floor of the convention. There he battled unsuccessfully to unseat the Parker slate from Illinois, charging that it was a creature of fraud. In a feverish tremor, he called Hopkins a "train robber" while the galleries chanted, "Bry-an! Bry-an! Bry-an!" Hill, seeking to appease the progressives, accepted planks criticizing trusts and supporting labor that were only slightly milder than ones the Democrats had adopted in 1900. In addition, the upstate boss, despite his fondness for the gold standard, agreed to omit from the platform any mention of the politics of money.

The next day, a bitter editorial in the *World* scorned "the white-livered majority" for allowing Bryan, "the prince of populists," to dictate the plat-form. If he had truly been in control, the party would have endorsed a longer, more radical set of proposals. But it had been an enervating struggle for a middle-aged man running a temperature of well over 100 degrees. When nominating speeches began on the evening of July 9, Bryan was clearly exhausted; he had not slept in two days.[23]

According to the morning papers, Parker already had enough votes to win. But twelve thousand people still crowded into the hot St. Louis Coli-seum, just to see the show. For hours, the ritualized event rolled on, speech after speech, one staged bit of hoopla following the next. There were few sparks of drama. One conservative speaker mocked Bryan for thinking "that laryngeal activity is the supreme test of statesmanship," while Clarence Darrow, in seconding Hearst, rued the fact that "men who scuttled the Democratic ship shall once more be placed in charge."

At four-thirty in the morning, Bryan finally rose to speak. He had agreed to second the nomination of Senator Francis Cockrell, a faithful silverite from Missouri who in his youth had fought for the Confederacy. Hearst never forgave what he took to be an act of cold betrayal. Yet less than three paragraphs of Bryan's forty-five minute address concerned Cockrell, a man of almost seventy and a decidedly minor figure. The two-time nominee was seeking instead to recapture the soul of his party.[24]

Bryan began almost in a whisper, murmuring about the illness and fatigue that "make it difficult for me to make myself heard." Of course, his apology ensured that the delegates and spectators, wilted from a night of indifferent oratory, would fix their attention on whatever he had to say. "Eight years ago a Democratic national convention placed in my hand the standard of the party and commissioned me its candidate," Bryan went on, his famous voice growing stronger with each phrase. "Four years later that commission was renewed." Now he had come back "to return the commission"—without the slightest regret: "You may dispute whether I have fought a good fight, you may dispute whether I have finished my course, but you cannot deny that I have kept the faith."

It was the same rhythmic verse from the Second Epistle to Timothy that had been read at his father's funeral in 1880 and then at his mother's in 1896. And it was a particularly apt, if self-aggrandizing, choice for their son. The itinerant Apostle Paul, sensing his death was near, left his sacred if perilous commission to a close friend and ally: "Preach the word," Paul urged Timothy, "be instant in season, out of season; reprove, rebuke, exhort with all longsuffering and doctrine." In St. Louis, the only death Bryan was in danger of suffering was a political one. But the itinerant evangelist of reform refused to depart without giving his party and nation a final blast of righteousness.[25]

The content of the speech itself was unoriginal. Repeating a common theme, Bryan called Roosevelt a war lover whose election would spell "a lowering of the ideals of the nation...a turning backward to the age of violence." He blamed his defeats in 1896 and 1900 on Democrats who "helped to elect my opponent," and applauded himself for helping, this time, to unite the party behind a common platform. Then he warned the delegates not to rely on raising "a great campaign fund" to defeat TR: "Under such a system the price will constantly increase, and the elections will go to the highest bidder." Win or lose, the Democrats "must appeal to the conscience of the country."[26] On the page, the address seemed neither vivid nor eloquent.

But Bryan hadn't said anything novel at the 1896 convention either; the speech he delivered there, although a superior piece of writing, depended for its success on timing and delivery. In St. Louis, on an early morning eight years to the day since he'd defiantly rejected "a cross of gold," Bryan again captured the hall, if not the country. This time, he triumphed by appearing to rise from the depths of electoral irrelevance. William Allen White, reporting for *Collier's,* noticed that Bryan's eyes, "dull" with weariness and fever, "began to glow as his voice cleared out and the passion of his soul began to come out in very sharp gestures." Believing Bryan might be delivering his epitaph, the audience stayed hushed, as if in a cathedral, applauding only at lines the speaker had designed for that purpose.[27]

The speech probably impressed his opponents more than his followers, who had never really doubted their hero's ability to rise to an occasion. One journalist observed Pennsylvania party boss James Guffey, who had recently pledged his delegation's votes to Parker, weeping openly as Bryan reached the end of his address. Henry Watterson's *Courier-Journal* confessed to a "sincere liking for the man that endures in so many hearts." August Belmont, erstwhile financier of the Gold Democrats, was overheard to say, "Now I understand how that man gets his great following. He is a giant, isn't he?" even as Bryan asked the crowd, "Must we choose between a god of war and a god of gold?"[28]

Perhaps the most surprising response came from H. L. Mencken. Just twenty-four at the time, Mencken was already a star reporter for the *Baltimore Herald* and was swiftly ripening into the brilliant skeptic whose roasting of Bryan in the 1920s "as a quack pure and unadulterated" would do much to fix his baleful image for the rest of the century. But Mencken first saw Bryan in action at the St. Louis convention, and he remembered it as perhaps the best political speech he had ever heard:

> Certainly I listened to it myself with my eyes wide open, my eyes apop and my reportorial pencil palsied. It swept up on wave after wave of sound like the *finale* of Beethoven's Eroica, and finally burst into such coruscations that the crowd first gasped and then screamed.... What a speech, my masters! What a speech! Like all really great art, it was fundamentally simple.[29]

The rest of the Democratic gathering was an anticlimax. Bryan didn't have the last word at the convention, but he uttered the only words anyone cared to remember. Parker won the nomination later that same morning on the first ballot; for all his millions, Hearst could muster only two hundred delegates.

The victorious candidate immediately riled delegates from the West and South with his first, and only, message to the gathering. If elected, telegraphed the judge from his estate along the Hudson, he would uphold "the gold standard as firmly and irrevocably established." Already his managers had persuaded the convention to nominate for vice president Henry Gassaway Davis, a coal and lumber baron from West Virginia who had fought his workers' attempts to organize unions and had never been fond of free silver. Picked for his great wealth (up to $40 million) rather than his opinions, Davis did have one distinction. At a spry eighty-one, he was the oldest candidate a major party had ever chosen for either of the top spots.[30]

Conservative Democrats had selected two "safe and sane" figures they believed would contrast favorably with Roosevelt's unpredictable bluster. It didn't bother them that Parker confessed "the gift of oratory was never mine" or that Bryan, out of party loyalty, did more speaking that fall for a ticket he abhorred than did either of the nominees.[31]

But the conservatives failed to recognize that the unintentional duo of TR and Bryan had transformed the terrain of presidential politics forever. Most voters clearly enjoyed the zest of their personalities and their furious talk of reform—even if they didn't always agree with the specifics. No longer could a man get elected president by staying close to home and restating his party's platform. In 1904, the Democratic National Committee raised more than twice as much money as it had during either of Bryan's two campaigns. But there was "nothing in Parker to campaign on," as Charles F. Murphy, the new chief of Tammany Hall, bluntly put it.

The result was the worst debacle in the history of the nation's oldest political party. Roosevelt defeated Parker by almost 20 percent of the popular vote. The first landslide since the reelection of Grant in 1872 followed a campaign so dreary that voter participation dropped another 8 percent. Democrats won not a single state outside the South and lost by double-digit margins everywhere else. As one journalist quipped, Parker had been defeated "by acclamation." His party also lost forty-two seats in the House of Representatives, which reduced its ranks to where they had been after the calamitous midterm election of 1894. Ironically, those who longed for a return to Cleveland's Democracy had been granted their wish. Not since the pit of the depression of the 1890s had their party been so unpopular.[32]

The Democrats had also kicked away a good opportunity to build on the anti-corporate foundation Bryan had laid in the previous two campaigns. Without a charismatic figure at their head and plagued by an ideological and regional division similar to that of 1896, the party could not persuasively challenge Roosevelt's reputation as the progressive leader of a nation aching for reform. Thus the 1904 election campaign, whose conclusion surprised nobody, put the Democrats firmly on the defensive at a time when a majority of voters were troubled with the inequalities of power in America.

The results did, however, vindicate Bryan. The first postelection issue of *The Commoner* featured a large editorial cartoon that presumed to teach the lesson of the party's "Crushing Defeat." A disembodied hand gestured at a blackboard where it was written: "Do not Compromise with Plutocracy."

The editor pointed out that he had received more than a million more ballots in each of *his* campaigns for president than the forlorn Parker had been
able to win in his race. The judge's gray personality and old-fashioned
views had also spurred some Bryan followers to seek out a radical alternative. In 1904, many of the 402,000 voters for Eugene Debs, the Socialist firebrand, were no doubt erstwhile supporters of the "Popocrat" from
Nebraska.[33]

"Keeping the faith" was the least of Bryan's achievements that year. He
had preached fealty to one's ideals in nearly every talk he delivered and
article he wrote about political issues. The more difficult task was to drive
away memories of the defeats that followed the "first battle"—the frustration of military service, the confusion of favoring the peace treaty but
opposing imperialism, and his followers' dismay at the second loss to
McKinley and Hanna. As Theodore Roosevelt took the oath of office in the
late winter of 1905, every American who cared about politics knew that
Bryan was once again the titular leader of the opposition—and a figure
whose talents at provocation and self-promotion could not be ignored. It
was a good time to share his singular mission with the world.

CHAPTER SIX

Prophet on the Road

When you hear a good democratic speech it is so much like a sermon that you can hardly tell the difference between them.

—William Jennings Bryan, 1904[1]

Each nation can give lessons to every other, and while our nation is in a position to make the largest contribution . . . to the education of the world, it ought to remain in the attitude of a pupil and be ever ready to profit by the experience of others.

—William Jennings Bryan, 1906[2]

ON SEPTEMBER 27, 1905, Will, Mary, and two of their children—Grace and William Junior, both teenagers—left San Francisco on the steamship *Manchuria* for a trip around the globe. They arrived back in New York City the following August after visiting eighteen nations in Asia, the Middle East, and Europe. Bryan paid for the tour by giving speeches and writing a weekly "letter"—part travelogue, part commentary on politics and religion—that was published each week in the Hearst press and several other papers (and reprinted, of course, by *The Commoner*).[3]

The publicity-soaked voyage accomplished two purposes. It bestowed a certain statesmanlike status on the twice-defeated nominee, who drew big, respectful crowds and held audiences with rulers in many of the lands he visited. It also helped him to rise above the inevitable skirmishes that broke out between Democrats seeking to recover from yet another electoral defeat at the same time as Theodore Roosevelt was boosting his stock with the public by battling corporate moguls and their allies in his own party. Unconventional as ever, Bryan managed to become the favorite for the 1908 nomination while sailing through the Philippines, strolling around the Holy Land, and conversing with the king of England and the emperor of Japan.[4]

No other American politician had ever circled the planet during the prime of his career. But hardly any of Bryan's contemporaries thought that fact worth mentioning. Since the 1896 campaign, he had already traveled twice to Mexico and once to Europe, speaking and writing articles at nearly every stop. More to the point, itinerant oratory and journalism *were* his career, one he'd combined for a decade with the quixotic pursuit of the presidency.[5]

When Bryan arrived in Bombay in the spring of 1906, a local paper commented that he "is not only a great American, he is also, by common consent, the greatest living orator in a nation of orators." The former honorific always depended upon the latter skill. Even after he was no longer a serious contender for the White House, Bryan continued to tour widely, although seldom outside North America.[6]

His feats on the road became a kind of legend to Americans in the opening decades of the twentieth century. Journalists filed a vast number of amusing, astonished stories about his stamina, his appetite, and his utter lack of pretense. Traveling through Iowa one day (in a nonelection year), Bryan gave fifteen impromptu speeches to workers, farmers, and anyone else who joined the crush around his railway car. After an early morning talk, laced with biblical allusions, he repaired to the washroom to shave. The reporter Edward Lowry observed "a half-dozen men and some dear old ladies in sunbonnets" asking Bryan, his face full of lather, to " 'stick your head out of the window and let us have a look at you.' " The celebrity immediately "pulled the towel from his neckband" and shook every hand he could reach. "Neither he nor the people outside," observed Lowry, "seemed to think there was anything unusual in the performance."[7]

During more than thirty years in the national spotlight, Bryan delivered over six thousand scheduled addresses and a myriad of spontaneous ones at a remarkable variety of venues: civic banquets, church revivals, political forums, college and high school commencements, under tent pavilions, atop wooden boxes, in city parks, and from the back of numberless trains. He appeared most frequently under the auspices of the Chautauqua circuits that erected tents in towns and small cities every summer from the turn of the century through the 1920s.[8]

Like any professional lecturer, Bryan knew that a joke or two could relax a crowd in preparation for the more serious fare ahead. He told stories about sanctimonious Sunday-school teachers, poor but jolly Irishmen, and wisecracking "colored brothers" straight from the minstrel stage. Often, he made fun of his own career, with punch lines that underlined a political message. One favorite quip featured a farmer who'd traveled scores of miles in his wagon to hear Bryan speak during one of his campaigns. After the talk, he came up to offer his praises, swearing, "If I weren't a Republican, I'd vote for you!"

Bryan also mocked his own loquaciousness. Once he warmed up an audience of railroad executives by telling them he had "speeches on almost every conceivable subject... and if you will just tell me before I get too far along what kind of audience I am addressing, I will have a speech. But this is no place for my 'Girls' boarding school speech. It is no place for a graduating commencement address. My Y.M.C.A. addresses are to be delivered elsewhere. My farmers' picnic—and heaven knows I would not think of springing a 'Labor Day Speech' on this crowd." The last sentence was greeted, according to the stenographer, by "great laughter and applause."[9]

The scribe was no doubt feeling generous. Bryan's studied inoffensiveness signaled to his listeners that he shared their good opinion of themselves, even if they differed on one political issue or another. The kind of jokes he told would soon become the stock in trade of periodicals such as *Reader's Digest* and the *Saturday Evening Post,* which seldom challenged the worldview of a mass audience anxious to claim or secure a perch in the expanding middle class.

Other national leaders of the era—Robert La Follette, Eugene Debs, Theodore Roosevelt—spoke widely and often, in distinctive styles that boosted their renown and advanced their ends. But for Bryan, tireless speechmaking was both a means *and* an end. It enabled him to express what, to his mind, were self-evident verities about morality, religion, and government. It also made him a prosperous and celebrated man who continued to make news for the rest of his life. Speaking common truths to millions of common people, he persuaded himself that he was doing God's work by defending the interests of suffering humanity.[10]

"SOMETIMES THE CHRISTIAN has sought to prepare himself for immortality by withdrawing from the world's temptations and from the world's activities," wrote Bryan a few months before he sailed on the *Manchuria;* "now he is beginning to see that he can only follow in the footsteps of the Nazarene when he goes about doing good and renders 'unto the least of these,' his brethren, the service that the Master was anxious to render unto all."[11]

One cannot miss the leitmotif of the Social Gospel in those words. For Bryan, doing God's work meant that pious democrats such as himself should dedicate their lives to reforming both their own society and the world. The progressive credo may seem out of keeping with his image as a "fundamentalist" Protestant. But he didn't acquire that label until the early 1920s. Bryan's commitment to bottom-up reform—and endorsement of a stronger role for the state in achieving it—was faithful to the nineteenth-century evangelical tradition. From antebellum abolitionists to postbellum temperance activists to millennial utopians such as Bellamy and George, the most influential dissenters had been devoted Protestants who cited Scripture to legitimize their moral aims. All that changed during the 1890s and the early twentieth century was the emergence of an aggressive, optimistic theology—rooted in the problems of cities and industrial labor—to articulate these ends.

Regrettably, the long shadow of the Scopes trial has obscured Bryan's close affinity with such activist ministers as Washington Gladden, Walter Rauschenbusch, and Charles Sheldon (author of an enormously popular novel that asked "what would Jesus do" about the plight of the urban poor), who made evangelical reform seem respectable as well as urgent. Of course, Bryan never became a liberal Protestant; he always made clear his disagreement with scholars who questioned the divine authorship of Genesis and theologians who made room for Darwinism in their doctrines. But for most of his career, he spent little time on such matters. Nor did Bryan expend much energy worrying about individual sinners and their struggles for redemption. In his view, the prime duty of pietists was to side with the common man and woman in their perpetual battle with the defenders of privilege, corruption, and big money.[12]

Bryan thus agreed, quite passionately, with leading Protestant reformers that the only authentic Christianity was "applied Christianity." The Social Gospel, according to Shailer Matthews, one of its leading exponents, sought to apply "the teaching of Jesus and the total message of the Christian salvation to society, the economic life, and social institutions ... as well as to individuals." Most progressives shared that crusading spirit, whether or not they attended church. Ministers such as Shailer, activist intellectuals such as Jane Addams, and muckrakers such as Lincoln Steffens all believed "that everyone was in some very serious sense responsible for everything," as historian Richard Hofstadter put it. "Christ is not only a guide and friend in all the work that man undertakes," Bryan told a Methodist audience in 1912, "but his name can be invoked for the correction of every abuse and the eradication of every evil, in private and public life."[13]

The biographical roots of such convictions ran deep. Silas Bryan had encouraged his son to view the producer Democracy of Jefferson and Jackson as a holy cause, and Will's college mentors taught him not to put his social conscience aside after Sunday services. In Nebraska, the budding politician had eagerly allied with Populists who equated "the money power" with the Antichrist. For Bryan, whose romance with idealism often spilled over into self-righteousness, there could be no separation between the tenets of his religion and the demands of his politics.

Most Americans first glimpsed this hard-charging faith in the final sentences of the Cross of Gold speech, which his enemies scorned as blasphemous. It was a gospel the preacher-politician would amend continuously in subsequent battles with powerful men whose personal piety often matched his own. After the heyday of free silver, Bryan blasted McKinley, a longtime Sunday-school instructor, for trying to convert the Filipinos by killing them. Next, he trained his wrath on churchgoing captains of industry whom he accused of cheating the public, abolishing competition, and exploiting their workers. Bryan argued that no private or public institution—college, YMCA, or board of missionaries—should accept donations from John D. Rockefeller. The fact that the aging baron of Standard Oil was a faithful Baptist made his lucre all the filthier. How could this multimillionaire "preach so much religion while he practices so much sin"? Bryan even temporarily turned down a request to join the board of trustees of Illinois College, until his underfunded alma mater agreed to cut its ties with Rockefeller's affluent University of Chicago. "It is not necessary," Bryan instructed, "that all Christian people shall sanction the Rockefeller method of making money merely because Rockefeller prays."[14]

Bryan's gospel of collective good works avoided debates about the particulars of his faith. Although a Presbyterian, he, like most of his contemporaries in the church, shied away from a central tenet of its Calvinist founders: the doctrine of election, which holds that God chooses which individuals He will save, independent of human will. On one occasion, Bryan reconciled himself to the doctrine by recounting a tale about "two colored preachers down in Georgia" who were debating the matter. "It's just this way," the Presbyterian said to the Methodist, "the voting is going on all the time; the Lord is voting for you and the devil is voting against you, and whichever way you vote, that's the way the election goes." Bryan seemed unconcerned that the punch line repudiated the whole point of the doctrine, and he often attended and preached at Methodist churches.[15]

What is more, he never took an explicit stand in the dispute between pre- and postmillennialists that at the time preoccupied some of the best minds in Protestant seminaries. "There are so many people who do not believe in the first coming of Christ," he told a church official in 1923, "that we ought not to worry them about the second coming until we can get them to accept the first." Both his personality and his politics made him a tacit ally of the liberal optimists for whom Jesus was a benevolent figure and hell an anachronistic abstraction. Faith in God's word, Bryan told *Commoner* readers in 1906, would allow ordinary Americans to envision "a government brought into harmony with divine will" and then to get busy realizing that lofty goal. "Applied Christianity" was as simple to understand, and as difficult to achieve, as that. It was a politician's Social Gospel—capacious enough to appeal to diverse constituencies, yet capable of inspiring pointed challenges to "entrenched interests."[16]

In defining his vision, Bryan relied on an altruistic reading of the Scriptures and on the example of a single contemporary—Leo Tolstoy. In its first year of publication, *The Commoner* lauded the Russian novelist-sage for condemning imperialism, violence, and the czar's repression of free speech and worship. Then, on a frigid day in December 1903, Bryan visited the Russian writer at Yasnaya Polyana, his estate south of Moscow. Twelve hours of uninterrupted conversation, in English, persuaded each man that he had found a kindred spirit.

Afterward, Bryan rejoiced that Tolstoy was a foe of protective tariffs, trusts, and a system where a manicured elite ruled over a sweaty mass of peasants and workers. The great writer could almost have drafted the last Democratic platform. For his part, Tolstoy was pleased that the politician was determined to "know the will of God" so that he could "fulfill" it. He praised Bryan as "remarkably intelligent and progressive" and, despite his own anarchist beliefs, later advised his American correspondents to help elect Bryan to the presidency.[17]

The two men didn't agree about everything. Tolstoy viewed governments as intrinsically evil and, following Henry George, favored no tax but a single one on unimproved land. And his pacifism was absolute. At one point during their long day of dialogue, Bryan asked the philosopher of "nonresistance" how he could abstain from using force to prevent the murder of a child. Tolstoy replied that, in his seventy-five years, he had heard of no one who actually faced such a dilemma. On the other hand, "I perpetually did and do see not one but millions of brigands using violence toward children and women and men and old people and all the labourers, in the name of a recognized right to do violence to their fellows." Bryan laughed appreciatively. Tolstoy assumed this response meant "my argument was satisfactory."[18] But Colonel Bryan never became a pacifist. While advocating nonviolence in principle, he supported every war declared by Congress and backed armed interventions in the Caribbean when he was secretary of state.

In the years before Tolstoy's death in 1910, Yasnaya Polyana was a frequent destination for foreign notables and reformist pilgrims eager to sit at the feet of the prophet of anarchism and peace. When Jane Addams visited in 1896, she mingled with people from several countries attracted by the man who "had made the one supreme personal effort... to put himself into right relations with the humblest people, with the men who tilled his soil, blacked his boots, and cleaned his stables." But Addams's fling with hero worship didn't survive her meeting with Tolstoy. The ascetic sage upbraided the founder of Hull House for not growing her own food and for wearing a garment whose ample sleeves impeded manual labor. She came away skeptical that her host's dogmatic standards would do much to uplift the poor.[19]

Bryan didn't concern himself with the fine points of Tolstoy's philosophy. It was enough that the white-bearded "apostle of love" had endorsed the American's version of the Social Gospel. This made them allies against an army of cynics and political adversaries. Both men, in the metaphor refreshed by Isaiah Berlin, were "hedgehogs" who connected "everything to a single central vision, one system, less or more coherent or articulate, in terms of which they understand, think and feel." In 1905, Bryan explained to doubtful *Commoner* readers why he regarded Tolstoy so highly, despite the Russian's fulminations against "all forms of government." "His philosophy," Bryan assured them, "rests upon the doctrine that man, being a child of God and a brother of all the other children of God, must devote himself to the service of his fellows." For two supreme moralists who believed they had transcended egoism, the aim of political activity was essentially reduced to the Golden Rule.[20]

UNLIKE TOLSTOY, Bryan could never put his stamp on the world by staying at home. Like any evangelist, he needed to immerse himself in crowds and to test his convictions in new settings. His trips abroad provided a fine opportunity to gauge the progress being made toward realizing his internationalist vision and to share it, through the press, with millions of Americans over their morning coffee. But it also gave him a chance to accumulate ideas about state-sponsored reform that might prove useful to his party and himself. On his return to the United States after the yearlong tour, he published his findings in a volume with the prosaic title *The Old World and Its Ways.*

Critics mocked its contents, as they did Bryan's every attempt at intellectual reflection. An unfriendly journalist remarked, "He could have written it without stirring from his library at Fairview. He had made his world trip without receiving a single impression."[21] Bryan was certainly not a paragon of self-discovery. Large sections of the book read like a guide writ-

ten by a middle-aged tourist more diligent at gathering details about alien
societies than truly curious about their "ways." But when he wrote about
politics, he stopped slinging platitudes and showed he was quite capable of
learning from his foreign peers.

Bryan's first tour of Europe, in 1903–04, when he was accompanied only
by his son, was a case in point. Besides making him a lifelong admirer of
Tolstoy, it gave him a salutary glimpse of welfare states in embryo. He
toured Glasgow with the labor leader John F. Burns and marveled that its
city government provided better and cheaper services than private companies did back home—and with far less corruption. In Germany, he paid a
stunning tribute to the powerful Socialist party, the SPD. "They have educated the working classes to a very high standard of political intelligence
and to a strong sense of their independence and of their social mission," he
wrote in an implied criticism of political parties back home.[22] Only the
Marxists' rejection of economic competition gave him pause.

Two years later, Bryan found even more to like and for his own nation to
emulate. He praised the progressive income and inheritance taxes adminis-
tered by Britain's new liberal government. He appreciated the many neigh-
borhood parks, filled with working-class children, that Helsinki officials had
sprinkled around the most crowded parts of the Finnish capital. He compared their policy favorably to that of city planners in the United States
who supposedly "lavished" all their park funds on outlying areas, where
working people rarely ventured. "Bryan's globe was a great, eclectically
stocked cupboard," writes historian Daniel Rodgers, "its shelves overflowing
with usable and interesting things."[23] But Bryan valued almost exclusively
the wares he found in Europe, a continent of racial compatriots whose par-
liaments and clothing, churches and cuisine any ordinary white American
would find congenial. In contrast, vast stretches of Asia and the Middle East
seemed mired in poverty and cultural backwardness.

The great exception was Japan. The bustling nation seemed to Bryan a
near-perfect blend of traditional culture and a modern society bent on self-
improvement. He admired the fervent nationalism of the Japanese and the
elegance of their tea ceremony, the efficiency of the ceramics industry and
the click of wooden sandals on railway platforms. He marveled at being told
(erroneously) that most Japanese had learned how to read only since the
Meiji Restoration, less than forty years before. He also noted happily that
the government operated most public utilities and that, despite a limited
franchise, "they have politics in Japan"; competing parties spoke out vigorously for liberal and conservative views. Bryan even found a political
soulmate, although a recently deceased one, in Fukazawa Yukichi, the pio-

neering Westernizer and orator whom some called "the Great Commoner." He told students at Waseda University, "We are very much alike," dismissing differences in height, dress, and complexion that separated the two races.[24]

At the time, other U.S. leaders tended to share his rosy perspective. When Bryan visited Japan in the fall of 1905, its military had just defeated Russia in a war U.S. officials thought was justified to block the expansion of czarist tyranny. During the climactic sea battle of that conflict, President Roosevelt "grew so excited" by telegraph reports about the success of Admiral Togo's fleet "that I myself became almost like a Japanese, and I could not attend to official duties." American journalists and politicians cheered the nation's adaptation of Western institutions and dress, albeit with some condescension. The tributes soon turned to suspicions, however, when the Japanese government protested discrimination against their compatriots in California, and Americans began to fear a potent new rival in the Far East.[25]

But Bryan's affection for Japan was more durable. This stemmed in part from a personal experience. In 1898, a Japanese youth of eighteen had arrived at his front door in Lincoln. During the presidential campaign two years earlier, Yamashita Yashichiro had written Bryan a fan letter, asking to study by his side and then apply his teachings back home. Bryan tried to dissuade the boy from making the voyage, but Yamashita came anyway.

He stayed for over five years, living with the Bryan family, incorporating Bryan's name into his own, and attending and graduating from the nearby state university. As William Jennings Bryan Jr. later explained, citing Exodus, "We could not turn away a stranger in a strange land." When the Nebraskans traveled to Japan, Yamashita served as their guide and interpreter. Warm, substantive contacts continued as long as both men lived. After World War II, Yamashita's daughter assured Bryan's son that "the true friendship of true friends" had survived the conflict. Partly in memory of that bond, she invited a group of evangelical missionaries to use her house near Tokyo for prayer meetings.[26]

Bryan's relationship with Yamashita—his Japanese "son"—clearly affected his attitude toward the emerging Asian power. When he traveled to America's East Asian colony, the biggest compliment he could pay to Filipinos was to remark that they resembled Japanese, if "a little darker" and "a little taller." Later, as secretary of state, Bryan worked hard to relax tensions between the Japanese government and his own that were inflamed by a proposed California law to ban aliens from owning land.[27]

Bryan's approach to Japan revealed the most sanguine—and, according to his own lights, the most Christian—aspect of his view of the world. Unless a nation closed itself off to moral and progressive influences, he smiled on its interests and minimized its problems. As he told a Japanese commission that visited Omaha in 1909, "Most of the conflicts between individuals and between nations grow out of misunderstandings."[28]

But he extended no handshakes to the architects of empires. Bryan's itinerary in 1905–06 led him and his family through colonies belonging to three Western powers: the United States, Great Britain, and the Netherlands. At each stop, he observed that the evils of imperial rule far outweighed its virtues. British rule in India was "as arbitrary and despotic as the government of Russia ever was"; Bryan claimed the heavy taxes the Raj piled on the peasantry caused recurrent famines. He mocked the Dutch claim to have educated their Malay subjects by quoting an "intelligent Hollander" who responded to the question, "What, then, have the Dutch taught the Javanese?" with the quip "We have taught them to pay us their money." In the Philippines, Bryan warmly greeted Emilio Aguinaldo, the former rebel leader, and commented on the "gross injustice" of American rule. In Turkey, seat of another empire, he condemned the Ottoman autocracy as "the worst on earth," because the sultan refused to allow his subjects even the most limited experiments in representative government.[29] Bryan thus traveled the world as a Social Gospeler, dispensing moral verdicts on the powerful and sympathizing with the exploited.

At the same time, he observed every land through the lens of an evangelical who could not rest until everyone shared his progressive faith. Bryan was most charitable, of course, to the Japanese. If only they would shed their "outgrown Buddhism" and embrace Christianity, the nation would become a sterling model for its backward neighbors. Hinduism in India received no such dispensation from the messianic traveler (although his daughter Grace did pose for photographs wearing a sari). Bryan scolded bathers in the sacred Ganges River for engaging in "idolatry in its grossest and most repulsive forms." And the fact that "Mohammedanism" segregated the sexes struck Bryan as a chief reason why its adherents were "sluggards in intellectual pursuits." Sadly, Muslims failed to understand that women made the best teachers.[30]

The only points of light he glimpsed in the Islamic world were lit by Protestant missionaries. About one girls' school in Istanbul he wrote, conflating secular and spiritual ideals, "It is another evidence of the far-reaching sympathy of the Christian people of the United States and adds to the feeling of pride with which an American citizen contemplates the spreading influence of his country."[31]

To Bryan's sorrow, that influence had not yet reached the kitchen. "We have enjoyed the experiences through which we have passed, but we can not say that we have fallen in love with Asiatic food," he confessed. This was a real calamity for a man who, while campaigning, had been known to eat as many as six meals a day. "We have been afraid of the raw vegetables; we have distrusted the water, unless it was boiled, and we have sometimes been skeptical about the meat." Fortunately, the staple of his normal breakfast was nearly ubiquitous: "When all else failed we could fall back upon the boiled egg with a sense of security and a feeling of satisfaction." The Commoner never felt more American than when he was hungry.[32]

ALIENATION was never a problem for Bryan when he traveled the Chautauqua route of tent meetings and local assemblies. Beginning in 1904, he spent the better part of twenty summers as the star attraction on the week-long programs that edified, titillated, and amused millions of Americans who seldom had access to a big-city theater or lecture hall. His appeal was extraordinary for both its zeal and its longevity. One entrepreneur testified that Bryan was good for "forty acres of parked Fords, anywhere, at any time of the day or night." On a rainy evening just after the end of World War I, Bryan's train derailed thirty miles from a speaking date in Sioux Falls, South Dakota. He promptly engaged a horse and wagon, which took back roads and ended up in the mud. When a car finally deposited him at the tent five hours late, the entire audience was still waiting. They listened attentively until after two in the morning.[33]

Bryan was hardly the only Chautauqua orator with a national reputation. Roosevelt, Woodrow Wilson, and William Howard Taft occasionally appeared on the circuits when they weren't running for president or serving in the White House. So did a long line of less successful politicians and tribunes of reform, from Debs to La Follette to the blind senator Thomas P. Gore, and from Jane Addams to Samuel Gompers to the suffragist Carrie Chapman Catt. Tough-talking evangelists Billy Sunday and Sam Jones pummeled sin with language and gestures that resembled a boxing match with the devil. Winston Churchill even planned a few Chautauqua appearances in the 1920s, which illness forced him to cancel. Russell Conwell repeated "Acres of Diamonds," the original get-rich motivational speech, an estimated six thousand times inside the big tents, as well as at schools and churches; most native-born Americans probably heard him recite it at least once in their lifetime.[34]

But Bryan was Chautauqua's "greatest name" and biggest draw. No other speaker routinely attracted capacity crowds, had his name attached to a special day at nearly every weekly gathering, or made as much money for his performances. His standard rate was $250 per lecture, plus half the proceeds over $500. Brother Charles handled the arrangements from the *Commoner* office in Lincoln, routinely scheduling his only client for two talks per day. During the summer, Will routinely earned at least $2,000 a week—as much as a national headliner on the urban vaudeville circuit. He invested nearly all of it in government bonds and property; speculating in the stock market was, of course, out of the question.[35]

The Chautauquas never managed to establish themselves in metropolitan centers, and Bryan's image as a virtuous celebrity appealed strongly to rural audiences. Reinhold Niebuhr, the child of an evangelical pastor, heard him speak at several summer assemblies that were a highlight of his youth in Lincoln, Illinois, a town encircled by corn and oat fields. Niebuhr's father sometimes rented a modest tent for his German-speaking parishioners. His son, the future theologian, thrilled to hear the great orator who headlined bills featuring lecturers, singers, and actors, which gave him his first taste of a wider world of ideas and culture.[36]

But Bryan's summer appearances were scarcely less popular in areas thick with factories and immigrants. Nearly every year, he embarked on a busy itinerary that included both farm towns and industrial cities that lay along the same rail lines. Delivering at least sixty talks each season in as many different locations, Bryan seemed to favor no type of venue over another. His brother and the circuit managers tried to squeeze as many talks as they could into each tour, responding to the demands of a market that seldom disappointed. During the last three weeks in August 1915, for example, Bryan spoke in forty-eight different towns from Nebraska to Illinois.[37]

Three hectic days in the summer of 1912 illustrate the diversity and enthusiasm of his public. On July 18, he opened with two speeches in and near Lansing, the capital of Michigan and thus home to throngs of office workers and their families. On the nineteenth, he gave a brief morning talk in Lansing, then an afternoon address in the Detroit suburb of Mt. Clemens, and finished with a packed evening lecture in the auto manufacturing center of Flint. On Saturday the twentieth, Bryan again spoke three times—to largely rural audiences in Angola and Goshen, Indiana, and in Niles, Michigan. In seventy-two hours, he'd traveled over four hundred miles and spoken eight times to perhaps ten thousand people.[38] The pace resembled that of his presidential campaigns, absent the spur of an opponent.

Bryan had rapidly traversed a social landscape fairly typical of the United States in that era. The octet of counties in which he spoke had an urban population of 43 percent, just below the figure for the nation as a whole. A sixth of the region's inhabitants were either immigrants or the children of immigrant parents. But Flint and the other Michigan venues on the outskirts of major industrial cities had double that number of ethnic residents, more than their proportion in the nation as a whole.[39]

The last two times Bryan ran for president, he had lost all these counties, most rather handily. But nowhere in 1912 did this dampen the hoopla or diminish the size of his audiences. "Crowd Will be Great and Holders of Tickets Should be at Tent Early," announced the *Flint Daily Journal* in a headline echoed by other papers along the route. Harry P. Harrison, Bryan's usual booking agent, accompanied his star on the swing through the upper Midwest. In Lansing, Harrison recalled, "a chorus of factory whistles and church bells announced the Democrat's arrival. Stores closed and offices hurried employees out to the street to wave flags" as Bryan's car passed by. In Charlotte, a National Guard band escorted him to the big tent where a capacity crowd was waiting. Two days later, two hundred people in fifty autos draped with flags cleared away traffic to rush him from the industrial center of South Bend, Indiana, back to his next engagement across the border in Michigan.[40] Although Bryan's base of support lay among farmers and townspeople who shared his evangelical Protestantism and middle-class status, such affection confirmed that it didn't limit his sphere of renown.

Turnout for his summer performances did decline over the years. In 1899, Bryan traveled to a Chautauqua assembly in the lumber-mill town of Marinette, Wisconsin, where he blasted imperialism and the gold standard before an audience of six thousand. A local capitalist, and Republican, swelled the numbers by distributing more than two thousand free tickets to his employees. In 1922, Bryan returned to Marinette to attack Darwin and his disciples. On that occasion, he could not quite fill the largest church in town, with a capacity of just over a thousand.[41]

But the quality of adulation was a sturdier thing. Most of that 1922 audience arrived at the church half an hour early and then cheered for Bryan and laughed along with him throughout a two-hour address. As Harrison recalled, "Babies could cry, trains roar by, thunder and rain shake the tent, but absorbed men and women still just sat and listened. The soothing voice comforted them. This simple, kindly man spoke to their hearts, never over their heads."[42]

The admiration was clearly mutual. Bryan insisted on eating midday dinner with local organizers whenever possible and hated to disappoint any group that sought to hire him. Charles usually completed the summer schedule by mid-spring, but as Will traveled, he sometimes urged his brother to squeeze in extra appearances along the route, even if sponsors couldn't pay his regular fee. And the celebrated common touch was quite genuine. Bryan often took time to get to know the workers who erected the tents, distributed the programs, and refilled his pitcher with ice water—and he was an exceedingly generous tipper. "Crews were critical," recalled Harrison. "They might think some other lecturer too standoffish, pompous or demanding. To a man they cheered Bryan."[43]

Why did Bryan and the local Chautauquas suit each other so well? Historians typically follow Harrison in citing the emotional bond between a famous moralizer and small-town innocents who longed to hear the reassuring virtues of "Mother, Home, and Heaven" delivered by an eloquent yet familiar personality. Mary Bryan struck the same chord, writing in the *Memoirs* that when her husband "stood in the Chautauqua tent at night under the electric lights and the starlight, with practically every adult and most of the children from miles around within sound of his voice...his voice would grow deep and solemn, for he knew he was speaking to the heart of America."[44]

But that answer is both too sentimental and too static. It fails to grasp the historical context for Bryan's popularity and neglects the fact that he often challenged his audiences with political talks—from recitals of the Cross of Gold speech to long critiques of World War I and arguments for prohibition and woman suffrage. Neither does it explain what he meant to these Americans—in small cities as well as crossroads villages—that other well-known speakers on moral topics did not.

Like Bryan himself, Chautauqua was a phenomenon that straddled piety and entertainment. It began in 1874 next to a beautiful lake of that name in New York's westernmost county. The founding spirits were John Vincent, a Methodist minister and editor of his church's *Sunday-School Journal,* and Lewis Miller, a layman who manufactured farm machinery and had a knack for architecture. The two shared a grand, if comfortably bourgeois, ambition. They wanted to create an institution that would imbue American Protestantism with the vivid colors of modern theology and genteel culture.

At first, their dream amounted to little more than a fortnight of sermons and hymns, a Sunday-school camp in an open-air pavilion with good hiking trails nearby. But by the 1880s, they were attracting presidents and biologists, temperance leaders and professors of modern literature to what had become a desirable, even fashionable vacation spot. Chautauqua was a temple of Christian enlightenment for middle-class Americans who embraced the notion that lectures, cooking lessons, and strenuous walks all reaped spiritual benefits. After William James lectured there in 1896, he joked to a friend, "The Chautauqua week... has been a real success. I have learned a lot, but I'm glad to get into something less blameless.... The flash of a pistol, a dagger, or a devilish eye, anything to break the unlovely level of 10,000 good people."[45]

The institution was such a success that it spawned a movement. In 1878, to bring his formula to the masses, Vincent initiated the Chautauqua Literary and Scientific Circle, a way for "busy people who left school years ago" to get the benefits of a college education without leaving their jobs or families. Those who managed to complete the four-year program (always a minority) were invited to receive their diplomas at a formal Recognition Day by the lake.

These courses helped publicize Chautauqua's good works and whetted the desire of pious self-improvers throughout the land. By 1900, over a hundred independent Chautauqua assemblies had sprung up in localities from southern California to New Hampshire. Most were scattered in such mid-sized, midwestern communities as Marinette, Wisconsin, and Crete, Nebraska, each half a day's train ride from a regional metropolis. Bryan frequently spoke in Crete, since his home was less than thirty miles away.[46]

The local assemblies first sought to mimic the qualities that had made the original lakeside development so popular. Many were founded by ministers from evangelical churches who offered families a blend of Bible study, religious music, open-air recreation, and a few "clean" diversions. But local merchants raised the funds to construct the buildings and hire the outside talent, and they depended on railroads to discount fares and schedule special trains for the big event. As businessmen with an investment at stake, they naturally wanted to offer goods that would sell.

"The best of everything in Oratory, Music and Art," guaranteed the 1905 program of the Chautauqua Assembly in Beatrice, Nebraska. "All that is good in the better class of entertainment. Attention given to the comfort of everyone." The local organizers reserved an hour each day for "study of the Word," led by the wife of a circuit manager. But most of their two-week schedule was clogged with secular delights. Speakers at the four-thousand-seat hall included Robert La Follette (then Wisconsin's crusading governor) and Richmond Hobson (who was still milking his heroism during the war of 1898). Also featured were a "Master of Magic," two comedians, an all-female saxophone "quintette," and the Nightingale Jubilee Singers, a black gospel group. The organizers proudly announced that they had paid "the highest price ever" to hire D. W. Robertson's Famous Edison Projectoscope Company to show moving pictures that "will eclipse all previous efforts." All this for only $2 per season ticket.[47]

It took little imagination to shift from holding such programs in expensive, permanent structures to presenting them inside mobile folds of brown canvas. In 1910, an Iowa entrepreneur named Keith Vawter established the first successful tent circuit, which Harry Harrison helped to run. A decade later, there were about a thousand circuits in business, reaching up to forty million people each summer. As with revivals starring Dwight Moody or Billy Sunday, town committees had to pledge to sell their quota of tickets, guarantee the fervor of the local press, and make sure that the business district looked tidy and prosperous.[48]

However, the saving of souls was only a minor aspect of the Chautauqua traveling shows. Most patrons paid to listen to world explorers, famous politicians, talented accordion players, jugglers, brass bands, even opera singers—not the same kind of sermon they could hear in church. Circuit managers soon began programming Sundays like any other day, which didn't please the local clergy. "We haven't enough religion to run a camp meeting, so we organize Chautauquas," complained the combustible evangelist Sam Jones, who nevertheless traveled the circuits on occasion.[49]

Still, none of this departed radically from the original ideals of Vincent and Miller. Sensitive to what we now call "community standards," Keith Vawter and his competitors eschewed any hint of the profane. Drama troupes performed little beyond Shakespeare and plays based on the Bible, which eased the minds of Methodists and members of several other churches who were not supposed to attend the theater at all. A musical company in Kansas staged its own version of Bizet's *Carmen* in which the title character worked in a dairy instead of a cigarette factory.[50]

Bryan always felt comfortable treading the middle ground between sober worship and commercial hedonism. Like other Social Gospelers, he wanted to offer Americans edifying ways to spend their leisure time instead of frowning on the very idea of mass amusements. "The people must have entertainment," Bryan told his 1912 audience in Goshen, Indiana, "and unless good entertainment is furnished, they are apt to find entertainment not so good." So he didn't mind sharing a bill with the likes of Bohumir Kryl's Bohemian Band. Moreover, as lawyer, journalist, and politician, Bryan had long associated with people who took a variety of moral stands—or none at all. Once on tour in Indiana, he was chatting with a group of admirers from the local chapter of the WCTU when he saw a fellow performer, the humorist Opie Read, drinking in a bar a few feet away. According to Harrison, who was there, Bryan "moved just enough to cut off the view, so the ladies would not be shocked at the sight of their other lecture-hero." He had always worked hard to excite and uplift audiences, to urge them, with a broad smile, to heed their better natures. A visceral optimist, he could never exhort listeners to renounce their spineless, sinful ways, as did Sam Jones, Billy Sunday, and other popular evangelists.[51]

Yet Bryan did not become the uncrowned king of the circuits by peddling inoffensive nostrums. The perennial message he delivered to Chautauqua crowds was a call to articulate and act upon convictions that married a faith in secular reform with the coming of the Kingdom of God. His relaxed manner and old-fashioned, habitually rumpled clothes disarmed critics who came to see him perform. Bryan spoke as a friendly adviser, nudging listeners with a smile to do the right thing. This demeanor was particularly effective because it masked the disciplined professionalism of an entertainer who delivered the same talks hundreds of times in a fluent, expertly paced voice that seldom, if ever, flagged.

He gave two particular lectures so frequently they became as famous and familiar to Americans as the Cross of Gold speech. "The Value of an Ideal" was first delivered at a Chautauqua assembly in 1901 and "The Prince of Peace" at a similar gathering three years later. Together, he repeated them over three thousand times in the United States and in nearly every foreign country he visited.

"The Value of an Ideal" began with an echo of Bryan's youthful tribute to "character." In his 1881 college valedictory, he had insisted that sticking to "eternal principles" was "the best preparation" for both a successful life and a providential afterlife. A quarter-century later, he was less concerned with the fate of individuals and more certain that altruism was the core of true character. "If...a man measures life by what others do for him, he is apt to be disappointed, but if he measures life by what he does for others, there is no time for despair."[52] If the speech had only reiterated that fine sentiment, Bryan might as well have stayed at home.

However, after a few paragraphs of abstraction, he started telling stories, and audiences warmed to the occasion. The first tale was about himself. "I have had three ambitions," Bryan confessed, "two so far back that I can scarcely remember them, and one so recent that I can hardly forget it." As a small child, he dreamed about becoming a Baptist preacher, but one frightening glimpse of total immersion made him abandon that goal. Then he briefly thought of growing pumpkins before following his father into the law. "There are doubtless a great many people," he noted with a smile, "who are glad that I now have a chance to realize my second ambition without having my agricultural pursuits interrupted by personal cares."

In contrast to such deliberate ends, Bryan claimed, less than honestly, that his entrance into politics in 1890 was a mere happenstance. Nebraska

Democrats needed someone to run in a rock-solid Republican district, so he whimsically took the plunge. It was just a "joke" to play on his law partner, he explained. Bryan then quoted an anonymous orator who "had known men to go to Congress as a result of a joke they had played upon an entire community."[53]

Abruptly he turned from that line to a spirited defense of public life: "I have no patience with those who feel that they are too good to take part in politics. When I find a person who thinks he is too good to take part in politics, I find one who is not quite good enough to deserve the blessings of a free government." For ideals to have value, they must be put to work.[54]

With a set of brisk narratives, Bryan then illustrated just what kind of work he had in mind. He described the "splendid" mission of Jane Addams's Hull House, where privileged men and women "find a delight in bringing life and light and hope into homes that are in dark." He told of Tolstoy's conversion from aristocratic novelist to apostle of the Golden Rule. Without mentioning Yamashita by name, he depicted a young man who came to learn about American government and then returned home "to be useful to his country." "You might have offered him all the money in the treasury," Bryan mused, "but it would have been no temptation to him."[55]

Woven into these paeans to selflessness was an implicit critique of the ethics of untrammeled capitalism. Addams, Tolstoy, and Yamashita were devoted to a communal ideal that refuted the credo that the free market would yield happiness to the greatest number. "We are all working for somebody," asserted Bryan midway through the 7,700-word address. There are, in reality, no "self-made men," individuals who transcend the "environment" of their class and family, make a fortune, and owe nothing to the past. One must embrace one's dependence on others, he preached, if one wishes to live "an honest life."[56]

This advice led into a searing indictment of contemporary politics. Bryan articulated, as clearly as any progressive, the faith that only a mass awakening could heal the damage done to the republic by men who thought only of their narrow interests. "Men sell their votes, councilmen sell their influence, while State legislators and federal representatives turn the government from its legitimate channels and make it a private asset in business." To stop these outrages, "we must appeal to the conscience—not to a democratic conscience or to a republican conscience, but to an American conscience and to a Christian conscience and place this awakened conscience against the onflowing tide of corruption in the United States."[57]

The best exemplar of political reform was Jesus himself. Not only did he provide "the highest ideal of human life that this world has ever known," but it was a democratic ideal, "within the comprehension of the fisherman of his day, and . . . the common people heard Him gladly." Bryan concluded with a reiteration of the need for national character that he and his fellow Presbyterian elder Woodrow Wilson would later adapt into a mission for the world. "The nations that have fallen have decayed morally before they have failed physically. If our nation is to endure, it must stand for eternal principles and clothe itself in their strength."[58]

One can only imagine how Chautauqua crowds received such lines. Reporters rarely commented on "The Value of an Ideal"; they saw nothing newsworthy in so familiar an address. The text certainly demonstrated Bryan's mastery of the orator's craft. The mounting list of grievances built up a sense of alarm, while the repetition of the word *conscience* drove home the main theme of the lecture. The glints of self-deprecating wit succeeded by bolts of moral principle set up audiences for the next change in tone, even if they had already read the words. Bryan's speeches at Democratic conventions had more emotional punch, and others contained more memorable lines. But "The Value of an Ideal" lived on and prospered, one suspects, because it expressed his political critique so confidently and pointed the way to a solution that anyone who revered both Jefferson and Jesus could understand and embrace.

At first glance, "The Prince of Peace" appears to draw its inspiration from a source outside the public realm altogether. Bryan began by stating, "I offer no apology for speaking upon a religious theme, for it is the most universal of themes," and declared that he "would rather speak on religion than on politics." Indeed, most audiences welcomed the talk as a powerful brief for orthodox Christians in their intellectual conflict with modernist skeptics. It introduced Bryan's argument with Darwinism and defended both the divinity of Christ and the existence of miracles. In so doing, he exposed himself to the unceasing ridicule of scientists. How, asked Bryan, can we explain the growth of a forty-pound watermelon from a tiny seed? "Until you can . . . do not be too sure that you can set limits to the power of the Almighty and say just what He would do or how He would do it."[59]

Bryan's apologia was, characteristically, full of hope and stirringly democratic. Behind the silly tale of the watermelon seed and other displays of ignorance (such as the statement that "every time we move a foot or lift a weight" we defy the law of gravity) lay a rather pragmatic observation. Bryan admitted that he couldn't explain "everything in the Bible" and could only "assume" there existed "a Designer back of the design" of the universe. Still, he maintained that "if we will try to live up to what we do understand, we will be kept so busy doing good" that no time would be left to ponder the rest. It was a reformer's equivalent of Blaise Pascal's famous wager for the existence of God. Once one admits the possibility of winning "an eternity of life and happiness," maintained the seventeenth-century French philosopher and scientist, "you would act stupidly" to bet against it.[60]

In fact, Bryan devoted most of the two-hour speech to elaborating a point that, ironically, required *no* belief in the hereafter. "Religion is the foundation of morality" in individuals and groups, he asserted. By trying to live up to a standard of "personal responsibility to God," men and women learn to restrain their selfish appetites and to serve the common welfare.

This gospel of good behavior brought Bryan perilously close to the position taken by Thomas Jefferson, a lifelong skeptic about the supernatural. In his own reading of the Bible, the icon of democracy had praised Christ for erecting a "system of morals" that, while incomplete, still stands as perhaps "the most perfect and sublime that has ever been taught by man." Bryan obviously didn't share his hero's doubts about the divine, but that didn't mean his own faith was any less worldly or present-minded. "What greater miracle than this," he exclaimed, "that converts a selfish, self-centered human being into a center from which good influences flow out in every direction!"[61]

"The Prince of Peace" built its case, like many a sermon, through examples drawn from contemporary life. The most telling ones had a strongly anti-elitist flavor. Bryan praised Tolstoy for scolding the "cultured crowd" who failed to realize their "finiteness amid an infinite universe." He charged that the theory of evolution was no more than *social* Darwinism, a hateful, "merciless law by which the strong crowd out and kill off the weak." And he called on his listeners to practice the commandment "to overcome evil with good" if they sincerely wanted to banish war and tyranny from the earth.[62]

Bryan had little doubt that such a future was within reach. More and more, he concluded, Christians were reading the Bible as a social document and "learning that to follow in the footsteps of the Master we must go about doing good." Like most of his fellow progressives—of either party or none at all—he believed that good politics was a thoroughly moral enterprise. He agreed with liberal Protestants such as Jane Addams and the pioneering sociologist Richard Ely that redemption could take many forms and occur through a variety of institutions, including secular ones such as settlement houses and trade unions. But, unlike these modernist intellectuals, he always insisted that one's moral compass was unreliable unless it pointed toward an absolute faith in the word of God.[63] For most of the evangelical Protestants who flocked to Bryan's lectures, that must have been comforting to hear. How could their government be purified without the guidance of the only moral tradition they knew?

The Chautauqua tours supplied Bryan with a surfeit of opportunities to refresh his fame. They kept him in the news, they extended his popularity far beyond Democratic ranks, and they made him a good deal of money— which allowed him to lecture gratis to partisan audiences on other occasions. Early in 1908, he told a crowd in Omaha, "The people of this country have made it possible for me to acquire an independent income for all time to come." When critics sniped that Bryan's repetitious lectures marked him as a barker of homilies rather than a statesman, he responded with a tribute. No other forum but Chautauqua welcomed "the presentation of those subjects which appeal to the general mass of the people without regard to party or creed."[64]

Of course, the lecture circuit also brought him less tangible rewards. The uncritical audiences and knots of admirers he met between engagements proved that the people still loved him as much as in 1896, when he steamed around the nation "in the armor of a righteous cause." Bryan cared deeply about specific policies—from the income tax to prohibition to arbitrating disputes between nations—and worked diligently to promote them. Once he learned he could gain mass adulation by preaching how to cure the ills of the world, he turned that task into a career and that career into a calling. "Both writing and speaking furnish such agreeable occupation," he scribbled, half facetiously, in *The Commoner,* "that one does not notice the loss of a little thing like the presidency."[65]

CHAPTER SEVEN

✹✙✹

The Ordeal of Reform, 1906–1908

He's like Kentucky whiskey. He can't spoil, and the longer you keep him the better he gets.

—A Bryan fan from Nebraska, 1906[1]

Mr. Bryan is an Aaron, but not a Moses; a Henry, but not a Washington; a Wendell Phillips but not an Abraham Lincoln. He is the storm of unrest which clears the atmosphere, but not the trade winds that carry to port the freighted ships of a people's hope.

—Senator Albert Beveridge (R-Ind.)[2]

AT THE END of August 1906, New York City took on all the trappings of a political convention. State delegations crowded into midtown hotels, party leaders paraded in carriages down Broadway, and the putative nominee for president spelled out his program before a capacity crowd at Madison Square Garden. It was unusual for a party to stage such an event more than two years before the next election. But the Democrats had seized a fitting occasion to break with precedent: William Jennings Bryan was returning from a trip around the world.

During his year abroad, the political environment had shifted in ways that made even his opponents within the party eager to welcome him home. Probes by muckraking journalists and crusading legislators uncovered multiple examples of corporations that had bribed and bullied their way to greater wealth and privilege. In the high-circulation *Cosmopolitan*, David Graham Phillips detailed the blatant bias of federal lawmakers toward the desires of big business. His article bore the lurid, unforgettable title "The Treason of the Senate." In New York, life insurance executives confessed to a state assembly committee that they routinely purchased the favors of the Republican majority. In Alabama, an insurgent Democrat won the governorship on a pledge to "free the people from the alien and arbitrary rule" of railroad companies. In cities from Philadelphia to San Francisco, prosecutors teamed up with reporters to crack open networks of corruption, most involving private utilities.

From the White House, Theodore Roosevelt rushed to keep in step with the march leftward. TR advocated strict federal controls on railroad rates and slaughterhouses and a flat ban on corporate funding of campaigns. Although GOP legislative leaders grumbled that such curbs on business would damage the economy, the president's popularity only seemed to soar—at least outside the high echelons of his own party. Congressman Bourke Cockran, a sometime ally of Tammany Hall, observed in May 1906, "At this moment, the only support in either House of Congress which Mr. Roosevelt can depend upon with certainty is the democratic vote."[3]

Just one Democrat had emerged from the debacle of the 1904 election with a national following and a reputation as an uncompromising reformer. So when a group of traveling salesmen who despised the trusts offered to give Bryan "a big reception" upon his return, party officials from every region roused themselves from their quarrels and agreed to take part. At least this way, they might be able to convince him to avoid taking positions that would divide his own forces and confirm the latent impression that he was too radical to be allowed to run the country.[4]

Bryan certainly didn't look like a hardened rebel. At the age of forty-six, the erstwhile "boy orator" who had once frightened half the nation could have passed for an amiable businessman with an attractive product to sell. His husky, muscular body had softened, with a slight paunch visible under the buttons of his vest. Bryan's hair, never full or thick, had receded to thatches curling around each ear and halfway down his neck. But journalists noted that his smile was as broad and his voice as strong as ever. As if to dispel any hint of physical decline, Bryan bragged about the planting and hauling he performed on his small farm adjacent to Fairview. Nearly every summer, he played baseball at the annual *Commoner* picnic and, if one can believe the in-house accounts, was usually the star of his team.[5]

The revival of Bryan's political fortunes was not solely due to a favorable shift in the political weather. During Will's year abroad, his brother Charles had expanded the size and efficiency of the Bryan machine. He took full charge of *The Commoner* and boosted its circulation to a historic high of 145,000. Augmenting the total were many readers who agreed to buy subscriptions for poorer friends and neighbors. The subscriber list helped Charles update his state-by-state roster of Bryan voters and political officials, for use in subsequent campaigns.[6]

The Commoner also mounted a drive to block conservative Democrats from foisting another Alton Parker on the party. For a year and a half, Charles regularly printed pledges by readers to vote in party primaries so that, in the flowery words of a loyalist from Minnesota, "the interests of the common people will receive such attention as will bring to naught the scheming of the few." It pleased the editor that more pledges came from subscribers in swing states than anywhere else; Missouri, West Virginia, and Indiana led the pack. Unlike most letters Bryan received before and after his first two presidential campaigns, few correspondents now lauded the once and future candidate himself. A powerful desire to alter what a Tennessee teenager called "social conditions... unbearable to a liberty loving people" apparently counted for more than did regard for the solitary hero.[7]

Not that political affinity extinguished the personal kind. One newspaper observed that thousands of New Yorkers seemed more eager to take in Bryan's broad smile and famous voice than to hear the content of his homecoming speech.[8] And a few days before his ship steamed into port, a major Manhattan publisher released *The Leader*, a novel by Mary Dillon, whose romantic hero was unmistakably modeled on the Commoner himself.

"He is certainly not of our politics, and I know none of our friends approve of him," acknowledges Margaret LeBeau, a lovely "bachelor maid" who falls for John Dalton's exemplary character long before she meets the middle-aged idol in the flesh. "But ever since that great speech four years ago that carried the convention off its feet, he has seemed to me the one interesting figure in American politics. I believe it is because he stands for something.... No one else in either party seems to have any particular interest in anything but place and power."[9] Mutual affection flowers during the party's convention, which conveniently takes place in San Carlos, Margaret's strangely bucolic hometown.

The love story in *The Leader* bulges with the clichés of its genre. Margaret and John exchange smoldering looks between gallery and convention floor, and her overprotective brother interrupts tête-à-têtes held on horseback in a forest and after a summer thunderstorm. When the incipient lovers are finally alone, Dillon writes, "The silver-tongued orator, who... knew exactly on the platform how to say the right thing in the right way, found himself awkward and halting when his only audience was a young and beautiful woman."[10]

But the novel's political melodrama is somewhat more convincing, grounded in dispatches about the events in St. Louis just two years before. John Dalton looks like Bryan, if more "lean and muscular" than the original. Like Bryan, he despises the trusts for "grinding the faces" of farmers and wage earners. He wins a platform fight on that issue but loses the presidential nomination to a colorless figure from New York who is a virtual puppet of his state's party boss. Before Dalton leaves the scene, Margaret in hand, he even offers a tribute to the unnamed Republican opponent in the coming campaign: "He is alive and full of generous impulses and if he sometimes blunders they like him the better for that—it shows them he's human." Bryan also applauded TR, although not in such empathetic terms, when the president used his "bully pulpit" to lambaste the trusts.[11]

The *New York Times* considered *The Leader* significant enough to run a full, illustrated page on it in one Sunday edition. According to the feature writer, Dillon had "selected the Nebraskan for hero not because she is keen on politics or because she knows anything about politics, but because she finds the career of the Commoner sentimentally appealing."

The dismissive tone was understandable but unfair. Notwithstanding John Dalton's plebeian roots, his character fits the image Bryan had been cultivating since his first race for Congress. That Margaret's haughty sibling considers Dalton "a political demagogue and filibuster" only strengthens *her* conviction that he is a man of character whose attacks on big business and corrupt urban machines are hitting home. To be credible, a romantic hero must give off a scent of danger.

ONLY SWEET ADULATION followed Bryan during most of his sojourn in the big city. The *World,* normally a fierce critic, reported that he was "browned by the suns of alien lands and look[ed] many years younger than in 1896." Metropolitan journalists were charmed when a few hundred whooping "Nebraska boys" met his steamship in the middle of the harbor on August 29; Mayor James Dahlman of Omaha, a former cowboy, lassoed the local hero and held him tight until he laughingly agreed to beat a prompt return to the prairies.

The next day, Bryan attended a reception at a downtown hotel where he shook a hundred hands per minute for over two hours. He managed to dodge a kiss from a young woman but not the embrace of an older widow who cried out, "God bless every hair in your head." Politicians, labor officials, and curious New Yorkers paid large sums for a handful of the ten thousand tickets to the address he would deliver in Madison Square Garden that evening. The two-day welcome may have been, in the words of a contemporary scholar, "the greatest ovation ever given to a private American citizen."[12]

But Bryan soon provided his fellow Democrats with a fresh cause to wrangle. While abroad, he had fed reporters only a morsel or two about his political views, allowing them to assume he was edging rightward for the sake of party unity. For the first hour of his talk at the Garden, the sweltering audience, relieved only with paper fans, heard an undramatic statement of his familiar positions on familiar issues. Bryan denounced colonialism in the Philippines, called for an income tax and the popular election of senators, favored arbitration to resolve quarrels among nations and those between employers and workers, and demanded that violators of the anti-trust law be thrown in jail and that corporations stop funding political campaigns. In passing, he also declared a truce in the long battle between proponents of the gold standard and a currency based on silver. With a huge expansion in supplies of the yellow metal, money was now plentiful, and all Democrats ought to be pleased.

Then, a few minutes before midnight, he dropped a little bomb. Noting that "the railroad question" was "interwoven with the trust question," Bryan proclaimed that the most powerful industry in America "must ultimately become public property and be managed by public officials in the interests of the whole community."[13]

While on his global tour, Bryan had thought carefully about the details of government ownership. He knew it would be the most controversial subject he would raise that evening—the main reason why, against Mary's advice, he read his entire lecture from a printed text. Impressed by the efficient and rapid railways of Germany, Bryan proposed that the United States emulate that nation's model of having individual states own and operate local lines while the federal government ran the trunk lines tying the country together. Such dual ownership might also assuage fears of a federal leviathan replacing the railroad barons with a new form of tyranny.

Bryan confessed that he wasn't sure if "the country was ready for this change" or even whether most Democrats endorsed it. But then he switched from prophet to politician. One didn't have to agree with his plan to appreciate its short-term advantages. "Nothing will so restrain the railroad magnates," he observed, as the fear that the government might put them out of business.[14]

Neither his doubts nor his qualifications mattered to influential Democrats in the press and Congress who had never trusted him. Once again, they warned, Bryan had revealed himself to be a dangerous man whose personality might seduce the masses into acting against their best interests. Now he wanted them to embrace socialism. The *World* asked feverishly, "Are not the

Democrats…, by their folly and stupidity, tying their own hands and closing the door of opportunity upon themselves?" The *Times* was more confident that Bryan's party would not follow him "upon this perilous adventure in radicalism and centralization." Perhaps, scoffed the conservative daily, the clever scoundrel was just trying to grab attention away from Roosevelt, who would never take up such an irresponsible doctrine. The president, not surprisingly, agreed.

In Congress, several leading southern Democrats, backbone of the party caucus, also disapproved of public ownership, albeit more quietly. Humbling the might of big corporations was a laudable aim, acknowledged Senator Joseph W. Bailey of Texas and Representative John Sharp Williams of Mississippi. But handing that same authority over to Washington bureaucrats threatened the entire tradition of local and state control over racial matters, which many a Dixie lawmaker or his father had taken up arms to preserve. Moreover, the image of black men pressing themselves against white women in crowded railroad cars struck at the core of their fears. It was no coincidence that the plaintiff in *Plessy* v. *Ferguson*, the landmark Supreme Court ruling that blessed segregation in 1896, was a light-skinned "colored" man who had been ejected from a compartment reserved for whites.

Bryan was quite aware of the problem—and of how it could frustrate his purpose. A year later, he bluntly told a group of southern lawmakers, "You…are opposed to government ownership because you are afraid your Jim Crow laws against the negroes will be abolished by the general government. As if your personal objections to riding with negroes should interfere with a great national reform." But he could not win the presidency without the "Solid South."[15]

Upon arriving in New York, Bryan told a throng of reporters that he had heard "there had been something of a revolution" in economic opinion since he'd been away. Constantly on the move, he'd mistaken the ubiquitous rhetoric about the need for sweeping change for a true sea change in attitudes. A newspaper humorist joked, "No wonder Bryan wants the Government to own the railroads—he's on them all the time."[16]

The resistance to public ownership from a hostile press and inside his own party forced Bryan to confront a dilemma familiar to many reformers, past and future. Should he promote the railroad plan as fervently and consistently as he had once advocated bimetallism and independence for the Filipinos? This would redivide the Democrats, who had been out of power for a decade, and perhaps defeat his chances for a third nomination. Or should he back away from the controversy and take a more palatable, if less honest, approach to curbing the power of the trusts—one similar to the strategy Theodore Roosevelt had already adopted?

Bryan made the safe decision, rationalizing it with a characteristic bow to the wisdom of the majority. Speaking in Louisville a few weeks later, he assured his fellow Democrats that the content of the next platform was entirely up to them. "I have spoken for myself and for myself only" in advocating government ownership, he explained. But he asked that they keep his plan in mind if regulation of the railroads failed to "secure justice to the shippers, to the traveling public, and to the taxpayers."[17]

A man who yearned for the White House had no other choice but to retreat. For the first time in his career, Bryan had leaped ahead of all but a small minority of activists in his party and in the country at large. Free silver and anti-imperialism had animated mass movements before he lent his eloquence to their causes. Yet other than the Socialist Party, which then had only twenty-seven thousand members, no constituency openly favored public ownership of any business larger than urban streetcars. Temporarily dazzled by the achievements of European states more powerful than his own, the apostle of Jefferson had forgotten how devoted most Americans were to their libertarian traditions. By retreating, Bryan preserved his status as the man to beat for the 1908 nomination. He would now campaign as a progressive in a hurry, instead of having to disprove a reputation as a Red.[18]

BUT WHAT KIND of progressive was he? Historians tend to define the breed in ways that place Bryan on the margins of the reform impulse that altered public life for good in the opening years of the twentieth century. American progressives, the scholarly wisdom goes, were urbane individuals rooted primarily in the metropolises of the East and Midwest. Sophisticated modernists, they had shed the evangelical core of their childhood Protestantism but retained the husk of a crusading spirit. Armed with the new faith of social science, they sought to diagnose and heal the multiple wounds of a polyglot nation whose future depended on mechanized industry and a state that ruled in "the public interest." Such emblematic figures as Jane Addams and W. E. B. Du Bois, Theodore Roosevelt and Woodrow Wilson, John Dewey and Herbert Croly stroll with sober majesty across the pages of recent books, "determined to transform people and create utopia," as one author puts it.[19] Bryan, by contrast, seems a die-hard Populist who somehow got caught up in a whirlwind of reform he neither generated nor understood.

Political influence, however, is never monopolized by those with the most original minds. Armed with a Christian vision of reform, Bryan became the leading figure in a group of unsung progressives who had substantial grassroots support and, in a few years, would be able to boast a strong record of legislative achievement. Southern Democrats made up the core of this tendency. That fact does much to explain its near invisibility a century later, when it is hard to imagine an officeholder who was a flagrant racist being anything else worth mentioning.

Indeed, such men as James Vardaman of Mississippi, Jeff Davis from Arkansas, Ben Tillman of South Carolina, and Josephus Daniels from North Carolina were prime culprits in ripping the franchise away from black men in their states and whipping up fears of rape and anarchy to justify the deed. Yet at the same time—from governor's chairs, U.S. Senate seats, and editorial offices—they fought to enact measures intended to help anyone who owned a small farm or worked for wages. In the 1890s, to beat back the Populist challenge to the "party of the fathers," they had learned how unconvincing the old gospel of laissez-faire was to voters who felt trapped in an order dominated by big business.

The coolness of most southern Democrats to the idea of government-run railroads did not prevent them from championing a long list of other economic and political reforms. The roster included the strict regulation of stock markets and banks as well as railroads, an income tax on corporations and wealthy individuals, protection for strikers and union organizers, federal support for highway construction and education, and a ban on the private leasing of convict labor. Most also supported devices to ensure a more direct form of democracy—the initiative, referendum, recall, and party primaries.[20]

This ambitious program gestured backward toward the legacy of Populism and forward to Woodrow Wilson's New Freedom and FDR's New Deal. Dixie reformers yearned to free their white agrarian constituents from the grip of the big money. They hoped to forge, within their own party, the "union of producers" that Gilded Age insurgents had proclaimed but never realized.

They were joined by prominent Democrats from the booming industrial cities. Mayor Tom Johnson of Cleveland made millions on shady streetcar contracts but then converted himself into a scourge of corporate privilege. Joseph Folk's ardent prosecution of St. Louis grafters and strong backing for unions propelled him into the Missouri governorship. In the Northeast, a new generation of Irish Catholic legislators such as Al Smith of New York and David Walsh of Massachusetts championed the rudiments of a welfare state yet managed to stay loyal to the machines that had groomed them. In the upper Midwest, Republican rebels such as Robert La Follette signed on to much the same agenda.[21]

But white southerners, who held the majority of Democratic seats in Congress through the first decade of the new century, anchored the anti-corporate insurgency. With the help of the National Farmers Union, a growing agrarian lobby strongest in their region, they also tried to help the American Federation of Labor (AFL) in its uphill battle against court injunctions and strikebreakers.

In this stance, they parted company with their fellow reformers in the GOP. Republican progressives, from Roosevelt on down, damned militant unions and arrogant employers with equal passion. But most southern reformers resented the economic elite of the North for keeping their region poor as well as for criticizing Jim Crow.

Such bitterness, filtered through the Jeffersonian language of producer democracy, led them to favor an alliance of white outsiders from anywhere in the nation. "I would rather be a humble private in the ranks of those who struggle for justice and equality," declared Thomas P. Gore, a Mississippi-born blind orator who became one of Oklahoma's first senators, "than to be a minion of plutocracy, although adorned with purple and gold." Most white progressives endorsed segregation of the races; many argued that black people would advance more quickly and suffer less violence if they did so apart. So racism—whether aggressive or paternalist—posed no barrier to the potential bond between rural Dixie and the blue-collar North.[22]

Bryan was the inevitable standard-bearer of this embryonic coalition. For over a decade, he had blazed against trusts and high finance, and his strongest electoral support came from voters in the South and West who resented the rule of big-money men from the urban Northeast. He rarely spoke about the emerging Jim Crow order, a silence that bothered few of his fellow Democrats. Meanwhile, his biblical moralism, which some critics viewed as childishly sentimental, sounded like common sense to millions of Protestant churchgoers. And while Bryan had never highlighted the cause of trade unions, neither had he said anything to estrange them. After all, they shared the same enemies in corporate offices throughout the land.

Not every reform-minded Democrat was a Bryan man. Some resented him for equating civic virtue with his own positions of the moment. Others bridled at giving a two-time loser another chance at the White House. But it was difficult to reject outright the leadership of a figure who elicited such fury from conservatives and the love of so many grassroots progressives. For every critical editorial in the eastern press, there were testimonies from the likes of Jeff Davis, the governor and senator dubbed "a Karl Marx for hillbillies." Davis, according to his closest aide, "carefully read everything that he could get his hands on that Bryan ever wrote," heard him speak whenever possible, and "believed that everything Bryan said or did was right."[23]

The heroic glow couldn't obscure the difficulties that lay ahead. In the midterm elections of 1906, the Republicans, despite their divisions, lost only twenty-eight seats in the House and increased their majority in the Senate. Samuel Gompers and his fellow AFL chieftains ran an unprecedented campaign that year to depose several of the most anti-union chairmen of House committees. But, despite the work of forty full-time organizers and thousands of local volunteers, the "strike at the ballot box" failed to unseat a single object of labor's wrath. Most voters in the targeted districts in Maine and Illinois were too grateful for the benefits of high tariffs and Civil War pensions to unseat GOP incumbents just because they opposed the eight-hour day and the right of wage earners to picket and boycott.[24]

Democrats also had to contend with an enormously popular lame-duck president. After his landslide win in 1904, Roosevelt had made a noble, if foolish, promise not to run for reelection. His bow to the two-term tradition did free TR to challenge the pro-corporate forces in his own party. It also enabled him to anoint the GOP's next nominee. In the summer of 1907, Roosevelt accused "malefactors of great wealth" of manipulating the stock market, just before a sharp panic on Wall Street sent shares plummeting. That fall, he declared that flagrant violators of the Sherman Anti-Trust Act belonged in prison. A few months later, he endorsed accident compensation and lower hours for workers—and blasted the federal courts for standing in the way of economic reform. Then he named a would-be successor: William Howard Taft, the highly capable, if rather conservative, secretary of war.

TR's rhetorical offensive forced Bryan into a position more ambivalent than he was accustomed to taking toward a political opponent. Although the president lambasted only "bad" trusts and bankers, not corporate power per se, he was endorsing measures Bryan had long advocated, and was doing so with a zealous conviction his fellow orator could appreciate. "I find it very difficult to be partisan now," joked Bryan, "for if I make a straight-out democratic speech, the first thing I know the president makes one of the same kind and then the subject immediately becomes nonpartisan." He did point out that GOP standpatters in Congress prevented the president from being able to enact most of his grand promises into law. But this was not an argument that Bryan, a prophet without office, could rely upon to persuade

Americans who admired Roosevelt for taking such forthright stands. The Democrat refrained from attacking Taft until the secretary of war had the Republican nomination well in hand.[25]

There was nothing Bryan could do to weaken Roosevelt's grip on the popular imagination. Both men were celebrities with a knack for striking poses, verbal and visual, that fascinated the public and won them a loyal following. But only one of them was president.

Roosevelt was the first occupant of the White House to be as adored for his personality as he was respected for his principles. He invited journalists to follow him on horseback rides in Rock Creek Park, on hunting trips into the West, and to drop in on his residential quarters to report on the antics of four boys and a daughter as vigorously unpredictable as he. TR salted his interviews with memorable one-liners and let photographers snap his toothy grin and pugnacious jaw. After rivaling Bryan on the stump during the 1900 campaign, Roosevelt became the first chief executive to travel routinely around the country to address his public. His "rhetorical presidency" depended on nurturing the same amiable, anti-corporate image that the Commoner had pioneered.[26]

As THE ELECTION year of 1908 began, Bryan adopted a three-part strategy he hoped would appeal to a voting public that surely would have reelected Roosevelt if given the opportunity. With his brother's aid, he took command of the Democratic Party before any competitor could mount a serious campaign. Then he put together a bundle of reform proposals Taft was unlikely to favor, evidence the Commoner was a surer bet to carry out the mission of state-sponsored reform that Roosevelt had begun. Finally, Bryan created an alliance with organized labor prefiguring the one that would do much to keep TR's cousin Franklin Delano Roosevelt in the White House for twelve years.

Securing the nomination was the easiest task, although the Bryan brothers left little to chance. During the winter and early spring, Charles sent out as many as six hundred thousand notes to *Commoner* subscribers and other loyalists "to see that no one attended the precinct, city, county, state and national conventions who were not known to be friendly" to his brother's positions. Return letters poured into the Lincoln post office. Will spoke at Democratic banquets in a number of big cities, urging his fellow partisans to embrace the president's agenda but also to go beyond it. One by one, state party conventions endorsed Bryan for president, many reaffirming a gesture they had made when he returned from his trip around the world.[27]

Still, Democratic grandees who once believed Alton Parker would make a splendid candidate had not entirely given up the fight. From his editorial perch in Louisville, Henry Watterson hailed the virtues of John A. Johnson, the young governor of Minnesota, who might enable Democrats to rally once again around a tariff for revenue only. Grover Cleveland soberly lamented the "radical takeover" of the party, while Woodrow Wilson, the esteemed president of Princeton University, longed for someone who could finally break the spell of Bryanism over the rank and file. From his yacht, Joseph Pulitzer instructed his editors at the *World* to float the names of sixteen different individuals, any one of whom he thought could lead the party better than the prairie helmsman.[28]

But Bryan was no longer calling for government to take over the railroads, and most of his critics in the big eastern and midwestern states realized it was too late to organize a boom for anyone else. At the end of 1907, Thomas Taggart, chair of the national committee as well as the wily boss of the Indiana party, urged all Democrats to unite behind a strong, simple platform that would condemn the trusts. The decision to hold the next nominating convention in Denver, a city Bryan had twice carried by wide margins, was further evidence that no serious alternative existed. "To be suspected of disloyalty to Bryan in those days," a journalist later recalled, "was almost like buying a ticket to private life."[29]

Few of the Democrats who gathered that July in the metropolis of the Rockies were willing to take the risk. As in 1900, the leading man stayed back home in Lincoln, but Charles Bryan and James Dahlman came to Denver to make sure the convention generated no embarrassing headlines. The only spontaneous public event worth noting occurred on the second day when, during a routine address, Senator Thomas Gore casually mentioned Bryan's name. The fifteen thousand delegates and spectators burst into an impromptu demonstration and kept it up for some eighty-seven minutes, almost twice the length of the eruption that had followed the Cross of Gold speech. Only the delegates from New York stayed in their seats, as their counterparts had in Chicago a dozen years before.

Early on the morning of July 11, Bryan was nominated on the first ballot with nearly 90 percent of the votes. A day later, delegates unanimously named Senator John Kern from the critical swing state of Indiana to join him on the ticket. Kern was well liked by white unionists in his state and had defended Bryan's views on railroad ownership. Aside from the editors of certain New York dailies, every faction of the party was at least nominally on board. Even Henry Watterson crawled onto the bandwagon and agreed to help smooth relations with his many friends in the press. Mr. Dooley must have been pleased; in a marked change from 1904, "th' dimmycratic party" was again "on speakin' terms with itsilf."[30]

It was more difficult for Bryan to show how his election might benefit the nation in ways the GOP incumbents had not considered. The Democratic platform, every line of which he approved in advance, thundered against "private monopoly," the "sins" of Wall Street "speculators," and "the partnership which has existed between corporations of the country and the Republican party." But its main remedies seemed to differ only slightly from those Roosevelt and Taft were advocating.

Bryan had focused each of his two previous campaigns on an issue of great emotional salience. But in 1908, there would be no analogue to free silver or resistance to empire. In contrast to the crusading language of the recent past, the two parties now seemed to be quibbling over small distinctions. Democrats demanded the publication *before* Election Day of the names of those who had made campaign donations over $100; the GOP preferred to issue such a report *after* the voters had spoken. Only Taft favored a full account of how both parties spent their cash. A year before, Congress, at TR's urging, had deflated some of the public's concern by banning direct contributions by corporations. Of course, individual businessmen could keep donating as much as they liked.

The Denver platform did advocate one proposal that most Republicans despised: a requirement that national banks insure the funds of their depositors. Bryan and other populist-minded Democrats had been talking up the idea since the 1890s; a year before, he had helped write a law for the new state of Oklahoma that taxed each bank there in a similar fashion. In late August, Bryan traveled to Topeka, where he outlined his plan in detail. "There are only 20,000 banks, while there are 15,000,000 depositors, and I do not hesitate to declare that in a conflict between the two, the depositors have a prior claim to consideration." But such a federal mandate had not been widely debated, and his familiar jibes at high finance were unlikely to persuade Republican bank customers to abandon their party allegiance.[31]

"Shall the People Rule?" asked the Democrats' campaign slogan. The abstract, plaintive nature of the question suggested Bryan's great weakness. No one in America could rival his eloquent outrage, grounded in Scripture, against the corrupting influence of big business on public life. "I am willing to go down on my knees and ask my heavenly father: 'Give us this day our daily bread,' " he told a big crowd in Roanoke, Virginia. "I am not willing to make millions of my countrymen get down on their knees and say to some trust magnate: 'Give us this day our daily bread,' and have him reply: 'I will, if you vote the ticket I want you to vote.' "[32] Yet his two losses to McKinley showed that it was not enough to tell voters a gripping story about the people versus the plutocrats. Could Bryan, the architect of moral protest, now be trusted to manage the nation's business?

For the first time in his career, the Democratic nominee courted respectability. That was why he had stopped talking about the need for the government to own and operate the railroads. His tactical retreat helped unite the party; Bryan even gained the endorsement of the five living members of Grover Cleveland's last cabinet. But he had no grand solution to corporate malfeasance distinct from that espoused by TR and Taft. Each man would intervene, with the help of Congress and the courts, to force big business to heed the public's desire for a marketplace governed by rules of fairness and equity. None would attempt to destroy the oligopolies on which increasing numbers of Americans depended for goods, services, and jobs. Audiences cheered when Bryan vowed to humble the trusts and restore an economy where the little man could thrive. But neither he nor his allies had more than the vaguest idea of how to bring that about.

Bryan didn't believe he had signed on to an unwritten pact drafted by his adversaries. He charged that "predators" in expensive suits still bankrolled the GOP because they knew Republicans would never sabotage their vital interests. Democrats distributed a cartoon showing a lean Bryan shoveling hay for exercise while the corpulent Taft awkwardly swung a golf club as part of a twosome with John D. Rockefeller.[33]

Yet Democrats seemed confused about how to challenge that unholy alliance. The Denver platform still had one foot planted nostalgically in the Jeffersonian past, while the other stretched forward to a regulatory state. Democrats scored the Roosevelt administration for "wasting" money on hiring new federal bureaucrats and called the fiscal deficit (of $60 million) "a crime against the millions of working men and women, from whose earnings ... these colossal sums must be extorted" through high tariffs. Taft pinpointed the contradiction at the heart of such statements. Bryan, he regretted, wanted to punish the rich and help the poor. But neither aim could be achieved so long as many Democrats wanted "to reduce the government to a mere town meeting."[34]

On one big issue, Bryan departed emphatically from the incumbents' version of reform. In 1908, he campaigned explicitly as the champion of the American labor movement. The Denver platform vigorously opposed court injunctions against striking unions, declaring that "there should be no abridgement of the rights of wage earners and producers to organize for the protection of wages and the improvement of labor conditions." AFL leaders reviewed the language in advance, and Samuel Gompers personally drafted most of the materials the Bryan campaign passed out in working-class neighborhoods and union halls. It was the first time the two-million-member labor federation had ever endorsed a presidential candidate. AFL leaders had always viewed such a step as a surrender to "party slavery," sure to cause internal strife—although Gompers himself had twice voted for Bryan. But now the nation's largest interest group was immersed in partisan politics to stay.[35]

Each partner desperately needed the other. That February, the Supreme Court had ruled, in a case concerning hat makers from Danbury, Connecticut, that union boycotts were a violation of the Sherman Anti-Trust Law. Gompers complained that workers faced "the most grave and momentous crisis" in American history. No matter how much power a union had built up in a given workplace or industry, the federal government could snatch it away with a simple writ from unelected men in black robes. Notwithstanding TR's occasional pro-labor statements, nearly every open-shop industrialist was a loyal Republican. As a state and federal judge, Taft had ruled that most strikes and all boycotts were criminal conspiracies. During the 1894 national railroad strike, he fumed, "They have killed only six of the mob as yet. This is hardly enough to make an impression." For the AFL, a Democratic president offered the only chance for deliverance.[36]

Labor's active support gave Bryan hope of winning several of the industrial states that had always eluded his grasp. The AFL's tactical embrace required no change in his own position. Although he had never been labor's dream candidate, Bryan had always spoken warmly about the rights of unionists and welcomed endorsements from their locals. One staff writer at *The Commoner* was Will Maupin, a union printer who helped form the Nebraska AFL and was close to the Bryan family. In Bryan's previous runs for the White House, the vaunted bond between rural and urban "producers" had been merely rhetorical. Now, perhaps, a new coalition between wage earners in the North, whites in the South, and true foes of monopoly from any region or calling could lift him into power.[37]

For a change, his own party seemed eager and able to advance his cause. Norman Mack, its new national chairman, was the longtime editor of Buffalo's Democratic daily and understood the need for a publicity apparatus greater than the candidate's own voice. Josephus Daniels, Richard Metcalfe, and Willis Abbot—all experienced journalists and Bryan disciples—issued a slogan-rich *Campaign Textbook* and kept sympathetic papers supplied with copy and cartoons attacking Taft as a toady of the trusts. Pitching in were Herman Ridder, editor of the nation's most popular German-language paper, and Henry Watterson, influential men who had opposed Bryan in the past.

The Democrats also organized a local campaign apparatus and began to raise funds. By Labor Day, over five thousand Bryan-Kern clubs were busy handing out literature and registering voters. In place of the haphazard fund-raising of previous campaigns, a finance committee, headed by a tobacco manufacturer, cast about for donations. By Election Day, the Democrats had attracted some seventy-five thousand contributors, five times more than the GOP. But most wealthy Americans still viewed Bryan as their enemy. His finance committee was able to raise only a third as much cash as the opposition.[38]

The candidate did exploit a novel and inexpensive way to reach the public. That July, Bryan recorded ten brief speeches while at home in Lincoln. The technology, invented by Thomas Edison two decades before, was still quite primitive. Sitting in his library at Fairview, Bryan had to speak loudly and slowly into the massive horn of a phonograph, which transferred the sounds onto a thick slab of vinyl or a wax cylinder six inches high. Recordings could last no more than four minutes, and extraneous noises marred the results.[39]

But no listener could mistake his oratorical skill. Bryan's voice rang out clearly from each recording, forcing key words to attention without apparent strain to his larynx. "The wage earners comprise so *large* a proportion of our population that *every* public question concerns them," began a talk titled "The Labor Question." The tone was that of a man as comfortable speaking from his living room as inside a humid arena. Bryan sounded warmly professorial as he detailed, with mild flourishes, what the Democrats promised to do for workers. His pitch would have been perfect for radio. Alas, broadcasting was still more than a decade in the future.

At the end of one recorded speech about campaign funding, Bryan revived, for a few moments, the spirit of '96. He first offered a calm exegesis of the Democrats' stand on the issue. Then the prophetic voice returned, in Manichean counterpoint. The dark forces of privilege, Bryan warned, must be exposed lest they corrupt the civic order. "Let there be light," he declared, paraphrasing John 3. "If there are any who love darkness, the excuse must be found in Holy Writ, it is because their deeds are evil."[40]

Absent sales totals, it is impossible to tell how the recordings affected the campaign, if they did at all. Taft, somewhat reluctantly, made a few of his own—although his leisurely pace and imperfect diction may have diminished their power to persuade. One phonograph company issued large print

ads announcing, "Mr. William Jennings Bryan Wants to Talk to You Personally." A competing firm appealed to Democratic clubs with the promise
that, machine in hand, they could deliver "daily renditions" of their man's
opinions.[41]

Live or on wax, Bryan's speeches indicated a strong desire to reassure.
Carefully explaining his proposals, he no longer seemed the "Popocrat"
bogeyman depicted in the urban press who had twice scared many voters in
the East and Midwest into choosing McKinley. The 1908 Democratic campaign book quoted the *New York Herald:* "No one now fears that Mr. Bryan's
election would provoke an industrial, commercial, and financial cataclysm."
The nominee helped two Republican journalists from Lincoln prepare a
campaign biography that described his congenial personality and pleasant
home life, while saying almost nothing about his politics.[42]

Such apparent moderation drew the wrath and competition of two former allies. Tom Watson ran for president under the banner of the near-dead
People's Party and mingled salvos at "millionaire plunderers" with the boast
that he was the only candidate "standing squarely for *White Supremacy.*"
William Randolph Hearst, still incensed at Bryan's perfidy in 1904, founded
the Independence Party at a midsummer convention in Chicago. Calling
his former hero "a trickster, a trimmer, and a traitor" for retreating on government ownership, the publisher spent much of the campaign trying to
peel away Democratic voters. The new party's nominees—a kerosene
dealer and a Hearst editor—merely gave the publisher an excuse to make
news.[43]

Bryan seldom felt the need to attack these radical splinters. He may even
have regarded them as a sign that he was truly in the mainstream of a large
and growing progressive movement. His acceptance speech, given in Lincoln in mid-August, quoted Roosevelt's own indictment of "predatory
wealth" and then accused the GOP of doing nothing concrete to curb its
abuses or to help the many citizens it had injured. "The Democratic party
seeks not revolution but reformation," Bryan explained, "and I need hardly
remind the student of history that cures are mildest when applied at once;
that remedies increase in severity as their application is postponed."[44] That
fall, the new Bryan stuck to issues such as guaranteed deposits and the tariff
and largely eschewed the sweeping, messianic rhetoric that had marked his
earlier campaigns.

His opponents didn't buy it. James W. Van Cleave, president of the
National Association of Manufacturers, told his members, "regardless of
party," that it was their duty "to bury Bryan and Bryanism under such an

avalanche of votes" that neither man nor movement could rise again. Taft called the deposit guarantee "wrong in principle and impossible in practice" because it would give bankers an excuse to foist their problems on the government. William Allen White dismissed the notion that Bryan had grown any wiser or more cautious with the years: "His life's business has been to protest, to pronounce, to proclaim, to cry out, but not to adjudge." The party he'd ruled for over a decade, charged White inaccurately, "is a Democracy advocating Federal control of everything that is out of joint." It had "all the childish courage of the mob." Who could trust such a man to grasp the complexities of governing modern America?[45]

To counter this familiar line of attack, Bryan relied on a familiar style of campaigning. On August 20, he departed on the first of several tours that kept him on the road almost constantly until election eve. Bryan hewed, for the most part, to an appeal heavy with detailed prescriptions. But as in his previous races, crowds seemed to prize the man as much as his message. "A stamping, shouting, laughing multitude that seemed frantic with joy" greeted him in Poseyville, the seat of a county in southern Indiana that Bryan had narrowly lost in 1900. In Brooklyn, near the end of the campaign, a boisterous ovation lasting some ten minutes almost prevented him from speaking at all. At night, crowds surrounded his railroad car, demanding that he get out of bed and speak to them.[46]

Bryan also received a small mountain of fan mail. Almost none of it survives, but the reported total of two thousand letters and telegrams a day rivaled that of 1896. Again, admirers dwelled on the candidate's stalwart character and crusading faith. His recitals of "The Prince of Peace" and other moral sermons had clearly left their mark. "Your magnificent stand on all occasions for the advancement of God's Kingdom," wrote a YMCA official from New York, "has won a very warm place in the hearts of Christian men, regardless of political affiliations."[47]

Such mass affection might have made a difference if Bryan had been running against an opponent with an unattractive personality. Two years before, Taft had told his wife, "Politics, when I am in it, makes me sick." At a private dinner in Lincoln, Bryan lampooned his opponent's reticence to speak up on any issue that TR hadn't tutored him about. Indeed, Taft would have preferred to issue statements about his record and leave the oratory to others. But when GOP leaders fretted that Bryan's late-summer charge may have pulled him ahead in the Midwest and New York, Taft changed his mind. Roosevelt urged his protégé to offer voters not an "etching" of his views but a "poster" with "streaks of blue, yellow, and red to catch the eye."

So, starting in mid-September, the large man with a winning laugh and a pleasing voice stumped from Indiana to the Rockies. Taft read out most of his speeches and said nothing worth remembering. Still, he kept a smile on his face and assured everyone he would continue the reforms Roosevelt had begun. It would be almost like reelecting the president after all.[48]

Bryan's only real chance for victory lay in mobilizing a fresh coalition of the discontented from the humbler precincts of eastern and midwestern cities. Aside from his own campaign rhetoric, that task fell primarily to union labor. In 1908, most AFL political operatives received paychecks from the Democratic Party and passed out over five million pieces of literature prepared by Bryan's campaign. Their message was simple populism. As Gompers put it, "The Republican party...lines up with the corporate interests of the country and defies the people to help themselves." In contrast, the Democrats vigorously defended the right to organize and could be counted on to reward their union allies if they gained power. John Kern's pro-labor record in his own key state helped sweeten the promise.[49]

But the AFL proved to be a vulnerable ally. Outside the South, a large number of skilled unionists were Republicans, and many bridled at their leaders' desertion of labor's nonpartisan tradition. "When were you told to tell me how to vote?" an anonymous West Virginian wrote across a pro-Bryan leaflet. "I'll vote to suit meself. Hurrah for TAFT!"

The GOP quickly seized on such resentments. Sounding a theme their party would exploit for decades to come, Roosevelt and Taft accused Gompers of ordering his members to vote against their will, of acting despotically in the name of protecting democratic rights. Hearst and Eugene Debs added their own words of censure to boost their own tickets. Just one of every ten wage earners belonged to a union, and the strife in the AFL made it dubious whether Gompers and his cohorts could deliver even half of the labor vote to Bryan.[50]

While the Democrats were attempting to leap into the political future with labor, they were rejecting a possible alliance across the color line. Theodore Roosevelt had angered African Americans in 1906 when he ordered dishonorable discharges for an entire battalion of black soldiers after a handful of them may have "shot up" the border town of Brownsville, Texas. Taft fully backed the president's decision. During the 1908 campaign, he refused to criticize a rash of new lynchings or Dixie legislators for disenfranchising black citizens. "The greatest hope that the Negro has," Taft smugly advised, "is the friendship and the sympathy of the white man with whom he lives" in the South. GOP leaders no longer thought it either prudent or necessary to uphold the legacy of Reconstruction. Archie Butt, one of Roosevelt's top aides and the son of a Confederate veteran, exulted, "The North is getting very tired of the Negro, and Mr. Taft is the only man at present who can unload him."[51]

For W. E. B. Du Bois, it was time to make a change. His fledgling Niagara movement, founded in 1905 on the Canadian side of the falls, vowed to gain equal rights at the polls, in the economy, in every sphere of society. "The Negro race," Du Bois and his fellow activists complained, "needs protection and is given mob-violence, needs justice and is given charity, needs leadership and is given cowardice and apology, needs bread and is given a stone." They raised the vision of a future alliance with "the white laboring classes," perhaps within the Socialist Party.

Niagara activists knew most blacks still able to vote—at least half a million in the North alone—would stand by the party of Lincoln, even if it seemed to be deserting them. But why not punish such "false friends" by aiding its opponents? In April, a paltry forty delegates attended a Philadelphia convention called to denounce TR and Taft. In July, Du Bois wrote in *The Guardian,* New England's leading voice of black protest: "If between the two parties who stand on identically the same platform you can prefer the party who perpetuated Brownsville, well and good! But I shall vote for Bryan."[52]

The Democratic nominee had not always spurned black support. In 1896, he welcomed the endorsement of Cyrus Bell, an Omaha Republican who edited the only black newspaper in his state. In 1900, Bryan assailed the GOP for giving ex-slaves and their children no more than "janitorships" in return for their decades of loyal support. That year, his campaign even distributed a statement by the small Negro National Democratic League, blasting imperialism in the name of "an oppressed people" who understood the pain of "subjugation" Filipinos were enduring. After Bryan's defeat in 1900, a black attorney from Kansas urged him to speak out against lynchings and expressed confidence that the practice would have stopped if the Democrat had been elected.[53]

But eight years later, the courting of the white South by Taft and Tom Watson scared Bryan into reasserting his commitment to Jim Crow. He wrote that TR "was justified in doing whatever he had power to do" in the Brownsville case and denied the rumor, floated by Watson, that he had ever served lunch at Fairview to "colored men" (he admitted blacks would "call" at his home from time to time). At Democratic headquarters, Josephus Daniels, an arch-segregationist and Bryan's close friend, helped inoculate him against charges that he was soft on racial equality. Meanwhile, pro-GOP black papers reprinted a blast John Kern had made, after losing an earlier race, that "the ignorant nigger vote" defeated him.[54]

Bryan's anxiety to guard his racist reputation seemed pragmatic at the time. The eleven states of the former Confederacy accounted for 120 electoral votes, almost half the total needed for victory. Add border states such as Kentucky, Missouri, and Oklahoma (the last of these voting for the first time), and the Democrat would need only a few big industrial states to push him over the top. But proof that he had broken bread with a delegation of black Americans would have angered and splintered his white base. The disenfranchisement crusade had been well under way during the 1900 campaign; by 1908, it had triumphed nearly everywhere in the South. Nowhere in Dixie did black voters still pose a potential threat to the power of the white majority. Even if Bryan had begun to rethink his racial views, there was nothing to be gained from accepting the endorsement of W. E. B. Du Bois and a great deal to lose.[55]

It took a rare Democrat to grasp that such reasoning spoiled the party's image, not to speak of crippling its soul. One who did was James Manahan, a young lawyer from Minnesota. In 1908, Manahan was in charge of scheduling speakers for Bryan's campaign. Even the most eloquent orators from the South, he learned, were ineffective outside their own region. They insisted on mentioning white supremacy "in the solution of every economic question," and this left northern audiences cold. According to Manahan, the party's "overpowering, localized, negro problem" gave the lie to Bryan's attacks on the haughty, selfish policies of the GOP—a flaw the candidate himself never understood. The Democrats continually pledged their fealty to beliefs that confirmed their underdog status.[56]

Despite multiple handicaps, Bryan thought he would probably win. Not since Grover Cleveland's last campaign had Democrats been so united, and they were running on a tough, anti-corporate platform that seemed in sync with the reformist mood of the nation. Bryan spent most of his time stumping in New York and the industrial Midwest, and the size and passion of the crowds always buoyed his confidence.

In mid-September, Hearst tried to hijack the race. The publisher released purloined correspondence from 1905 disclosing that mighty Standard Oil had traded cash for favors from several leading politicians, including Charles Haskell, governor of Oklahoma and treasurer of the Democratic National Committee. The documents grabbed the headlines, but they also tarred prominent Republicans, and Haskell quickly resigned from his post in the party. "The tide seems to be running in our favor still, and I do not know how they are going to stop it," Bryan wrote to Josephus Daniels on October 19. "With a large slush fund on election day, they can, of course, do something, but... it looks to me like our chances are good."[57]

It was the worst prediction of his career. Taft's victory on November 3 did not equal TR's drubbing of Parker, but it was decisive enough. The first-time candidate who loathed the political fray bested his more seasoned opponent by over 1.2 million votes, about half the GOP's margin in 1904. Once again, the Republicans swept every state in the Northeast and along the Great Lakes. Of the most fiercely contested prizes, Bryan came close only in Kern's Indiana. Outside the Old South, the Democrat managed to capture only Kentucky, Nevada, Colorado, Oklahoma, and his own Nebraska. He gained a hundred thousand fewer popular votes than in 1896 and just 43 percent of the total. "We have beaten them to a frazzle," gloated Roosevelt.[58]

Bryan was particularly disappointed that he did so poorly in the cities. With the exception of Denver, Kansas City, and New Orleans, every metropolis went Republican—even New York City, which Democrats had carried in the previous two campaigns. After his dalliance with Boss Croker in 1900, Bryan routinely accused Tammany Hall and other urban machines of being tools of the trusts; not surprisingly, they returned his animosity. Expecting little patronage from a Bryan presidency and not wishing to alienate local businessmen, these pillars of the Democratic Party gave the crusader from the Plains few precinct workers and scant rhetorical aid.[59]

But why did Gompers and his AFL fail to rally urban workers to Bryan's side? The candidate's own answer revealed both his altruistic spirit and his reluctance to face unpleasant political facts. "It is easy enough to say that a laboring man ought to stand by his convictions," read a postmortem analysis in *The Commoner*. Yet "human nature must always be considered in passing judgment upon human beings."

Bryan did not blame union leaders, who had focused too narrowly on the evils of court injunctions and believed that armfuls of literature could make up for the lack of a true grassroots campaign. Instead, he and fellow progressive Democrats stirred up the still pungent memory of 1896. Coercive employers and their political henchmen had, once again, scared millions of workers into voting Republican. "The election comes... just at the beginning of winter," explained *The Commoner*, "with fuel to pay and warmer clothes to provide for the children." Don't judge wage earners too harshly, the paper counseled. "Let us rather be thankful that there were as many heroes among the laboring men as there were—even if there were not enough."[60]

Indeed, the loss of one's job was often a calamity in a nation that still left relief almost entirely in the hands of families and private charities. But Bryan's problem in the industrial heartland was more personal than that. In key midwestern states, 1908 was a fairly good year to be a Democrat, unless you were running for president. The party took the governorships of Indiana, Minnesota, and Taft's own Ohio, and its candidates for governor ran ahead of Bryan in New York and Illinois. Democrats also gained ten seats in the House and one in the Senate. Observers noted that Bryan's alliance with labor had frightened many small businessmen into voting for Taft, which offset any gains he made among union members.

Bryan had campaigned diligently on his issues, believing voters would view him, not a cautious former judge, as the authentic spokesman for antitrust sentiment in all classes and for the welfare of working Americans. But, at a time of general prosperity, Republicans had a better grasp of what moved and alarmed the northern electorate. They were led by a brilliant president with an insurgent, mildly pro-labor reputation, and this muddied policy distinctions between the parties. TR's lusty cheers for the "melting pot" also weakened the virus of nativism that had previously sapped the GOP's strength in immigrant precincts. Equally important, Republican campaigners persuaded voters not to trust a Democrat who had once advocated inflation, opposed a war in Asia that the United States was winning, and now had taken a side in a class conflict most Americans were not fighting. "Get After Bryan; Forget Platforms," read a newspaper headline about GOP strategy.[61]

Bryan's loyalists were no less numerous or passionate than in his previous campaigns. Their ardor undoubtedly helped boost the total electorate by 1.4 million—and Bryan bested Alton Parker's poor showing by almost the same margin. But the majority of Americans remained wary and unsmitten. In Indianapolis, a Democratic daily summed up the problem. "Much as they admired his personality..., the men who work for wages or salaries had doubts about the wisdom of making a change." Perhaps it was time for someone else to lead the party down the path he had blazed. The results only proved "that Mr. Bryan, though a great campaigner, is a weak candidate."[62]

"HOW DID IT HAPPEN?" *The Commoner* asked in its first postelection issue. Bryan and his closest allies were rather baffled by what they termed the "Mystery of 1908." The candidate knew he had been the underdog in a battle with a wealthier opponent backed by most of the big-city press. He wrote to a loyalist from San Francisco, "When you take into account the power of the corporations to coerce their employes, and the power of the trusts to intimidate business men, you will see what an enormous advantage the republicans had."[63] Still, he seemed to have vanquished the demon of a radical reputation and was a more skillful orator and beloved personality than the man who had defeated him.

So Bryan asked his admirers for help, urging that they send *The Commoner* their solutions to the "mystery" (though they should be "brief" and keep their answers "plain," their tone "respectful," and their language "non-libelous and free from epithet"). Bryan's request showed more than just his continued faith in the good sense of the people, at least of *his* people. By seeking the cooperation of his followers, he also meant to strengthen their bond with him, one he might bequeath to a fellow Democrat who shared his principles and hoped to inherit his constituency.[64]

The letters duly arrived, a generous selection of which appeared in the paper over the next two months. Inevitably, most correspondents echoed Bryan's wail against the corporate Goliath and its well-endowed friends in the press and the opposition party. "The whole force of the federal government was transformed into a political machine," charged A. J. Hunter from Paris, Illinois, "the president at its head while the people's treasury was paying the salaries." Others hinted that Bryan had been fooled by TR's reformist rhetoric and failed to realize that "the money trust controls this government" and would stir up a panic against any man who threatened to expose that fact.[65]

Not every published response alleged a plutocratic conspiracy. Some readers jeered that the voters were too ignorant to see past Republican "humbug." A few pointed out that the GOP had cleverly adopted some of Bryan's main ideas while continuing to tar him as the radical exponent of free silver. L. J. Mason of Kansas City, Kansas, penned a little sermon about the grim trio of "avarice," "prejudice," and "fear" that had lured a majority to choose "special privilege" over "good for mankind." The moral tone familiar from Bryan's Chautauqua speeches thus mingled with a sourness born of yet another defeat, less anticipated than the previous two.[66]

That bitterness also helped persuade a sizeable minority of his followers that there was a more sinister explanation for Taft's victory, one the *Commoner*'s editor did *not* think fit to print: "The cause of your defeat is very plain. It was the Catholic Church aided by the Jews." The libel appeared on a crude, hand-typed form letter sent by a handful of individuals from Philadelphia and its neighbor city of Camden, New Jersey. The message advocated creating a "NATIVE AMERICAN PARTY" that, "in a short time," would convince "fully one-half of the Republican Party" to join up.[67]

Many correspondents repeated the anti-Catholic charge; few fingered

Jews for abetting the Church or favored a new nativist party. These Bryanites snarled an accusation that liberals and radicals on both sides of the Atlantic had been making since the French Revolution: the Catholic Church was a fount of privilege, ignorance, and reaction. "Romanism is always on the side of the enemies of the common people," asserted a Civil War veteran from Virginia, while a Bryanite from Colorado described the contest as "Mr. Roosevelt and the Pope for the rich, and Tolstoy and yourself for the people." Several correspondents cited articles in *The Appeal to Reason*, a Socialist weekly with a large circulation, that shared their view. Indeed, Eugene Debs, the radical party's perennial candidate for president, later called on his comrades to "expose" the Roman hierarchy "as the rottenest political machine that ever stole the livery of heaven."[68]

Bryan had never trafficked in such slurs himself. Despite his evangelical beliefs, he was always ecumenical toward his fellow Christians, whether native-born or immigrant. In his races for Congress and the presidency, he had benefited from his party's reputation for religious tolerance. He knew it would be foolish to alienate Catholics, the only denomination outside the white South that reliably voted Democratic. In 1908, Bryan took pains to see that an Irish Catholic attorney gave his main nominating speech, and he was disappointed to learn that Norman Mack, the DNC's new chairman, was not a member of the Church, as he had thought.

There was a good reason why Catholics who followed world affairs in 1908 felt grateful to Taft. Five years before, when he was governor-general of the Philippines, he had traveled to Rome to successfully negotiate the sale to the U.S. government of 410,000 acres of land owned by various monastic orders. The Vatican was clearly pleased that the new imperial overlord had resolved an issue that had inflamed some American evangelicals as well as advocates of Filipino independence.

At a White House dinner in 1904, the apostolic delegate praised Taft's "admirable equity and prudence" and predicted that "under the wings of the American eagle" the Church would thrive.[69]

During the campaign, Bryan worried that the GOP would use this episode to strip away urban votes he badly needed. He also had to deny charges that his praise of Protestant missionaries in Asia slighted their Catholic counterparts. In early September, Bryan distributed a public letter citing the names of prominent Catholics active in his campaign and included a warm address he had recently given to the Hibernian Society of Washington, D.C. Diocesan papers printed the letter in full and gave no indication that they preferred Taft over the candidate of the party Catholics had traditionally supported. If anything, Church-sponsored publications leaned slightly toward Bryan while training their fire on Debs and his allies for their "vile attacks on the Catholic hierarchy."[70]

Such facts made no impression on angry Bryanites. "The Pope of Rome is the man who caused your defeat, and the downfall of Democracy," John Hamilton from Philadelphia stated flatly. "How can it be said that our elections are free when one man in Rome can dictate the choice of more than 2000000 voters in this country?" asked Lewis Hite of Cambridge, Massachusetts. Cranks unveiled their urgent fantasies: "Recently it has been discovered," wrote Frederick Horton from Chicago, "that the headquarters of the Political Secret Office for Propaganda for all America north of Mexico of the RC Church is and has for nearly 10 year been in Detroit, Michigan (We had supposed it at Washington)." Several correspondents passed on vague stories of Catholic friends whose priests had been ordered to glorify Taft or even to command their parishioners to pull the Republican lever. But in contrast to the detailed charges of employer coercion made after the 1896 contest, no one supplied more than a secondhand rumor that clerical muscle had in fact been applied.[71]

As in nearly every case of mass bigotry, the ostensible issue was not really the issue. In 1908, the more anguished supporters of Bryan tended to be fiercely partisan about both their religion and their politics. Whereas their hero, the optimistic nominee of a mass party, struggled to avoid antagonizing any group of believers, his followers felt no reason to censor themselves, particularly in a personal message. "You may be defeated at the polls but you are still in the minds and always will be in the hearts of the American people," assured Rufus Riggsbie, of Tampa, Florida. Then the bookkeeper with the Dickensian name turned savage: "I believe the time is coming, and that soon, when Protestant America will have to rise as one and place its foot upon the hydra-headed monster of Roman Catholicism. My blood boils at the thought of her, the mother of harlots."[72]

Such venom did not, at the time, flow through a grassroots movement. In the early 1890s, the American Protective Association had been able to sway elections in some parts of the Midwest. But a decade later, the APA had few members and no national presence. So those who sought to pin Taft's victory on the Pope and his minions were only confessing their impotence before a rising tide of "foreigners" (by birth or creed) that threatened to destroy the dominion of clean-living, hardworking Protestants over American culture. In the 1920s, a reborn Ku Klux Klan would add fire and numbers to that doomsday prophecy and almost split the Democratic Party in two.[73]

Glimpsing the bile spilling out of his postelection mailbags may have caused Bryan to fret about his political future. After leading the Democrats for a dozen years and through three bruising presidential campaigns, he was no closer to gaining victory for himself or his party. In their pietist dread, his followers only affirmed his failure.

But Bryan had not traveled, orated, editorialized, and mobilized in vain. Progressives of nearly all stripes—excepting only the most sober of social researchers—used an idiom, at once vengeful toward "the interests" and sanguine about a democratic future, he had done much to pioneer. And no Democrat could be nominated without adhering, sincerely or not, to the principle of shifting power and wealth to the producing classes. That had been party gospel ever since the night Bryan stood up in a hot Chicago convention hall and proclaimed it as such.

But he had achieved his greatest success as a Christian moralist who could rise above partisanship and maneuver. Whenever Bryan quoted Scripture on the campaign trail, the rancor toward him seemed to fade away. In the fall of 1908, he stumped in Tama, Iowa, a town he never managed to carry. According to the journalist Edward Lowry:

> He said that he had been called a dreamer, and went on to compare himself with that other dreamer, Joseph, who was sold into captivity by his brothers. "And when the seven lean years came," concluded Mr. Bryan, "Joseph's brethren had to go down into Egypt for corn, and there they found the dreamer and—Joseph had the corn."
>
> Mr. Bryan made the point with telling emphasis upon his hearers. They had followed his thought closely because they knew the story as well as he, and had caught its application almost before the words were out of his mouth. You can believe they cheered and applauded.[74]

In a sense, the "Prince of Peace" was the most compelling answer to "Shall the People Rule?" Bryan the politician would never win the trust of most Americans. But with the right issue and a favorable context, Bryan the romantic evangelist might yet help transform the nation.

The many public Bryans, c. 1908. NSHS

Left: Mariah Bryan; *right:* Silas Bryan. Both photos c. 1865. NSHS

The house on Broadway Street in Salem, Illinois, where Bryan
was born and lived until the age of six. Author's photo

Bryan, c. 1865. NSHS

Bryan, c. 1880. NSHS

Bryan, mid-1890s. NSHS

Mary Baird Bryan, c. 1890. NSHS

Inside the Chicago Coliseum at the 1896 Democratic Convention. NSHS

Bryan the blasphemer. Drawing by Grant Hamilton, 1896. LC

Fairview, the Bryan family mansion, completed in 1902. From *Bryan the Man*
(St. Louis, 1908)

Bryan with employees of *The Commoner* at the paper's annual picnic,
Crete, Nebraska, c. 1905. NSHS

Above: Bryan relaxes at Camp Cuba Libre in Florida, 1898. To his right is General Fitzhugh Lee, a former officer in the Confederate army. Neither man saw action in the war against Spain.

Left: Bryan; his son, William Jennings Bryan Jr.; and Leo Tolstoy at Yasnaya Polyana, 1903. From *Under Other Flags* (Lincoln, 1905)

Below: Having just returned to the United States after a year abroad, Bryan speaks from his ship anchored in New York harbor, August 1906. NSHS

Bryan, perpetual headliner on
the tent circuit. NSHS

En route to another performance, c. 1912. NSHS

During the 1908 campaign. NSHS

Speaking in Nebraska, c. 1906. From *Bryan the Man* (St. Louis, 1908)

Bryan and Woodrow Wilson at Fairview, October 1912. NSHS

The Wilson cabinet, 1913. NSHS

Bryan signs the official ratification of the Seventeenth Amendment,
providing for the popular election of senators, March 1913. NSHS

Official portrait by Irving R. Wiles of Bryan
as secretary of state. NSHS

Bryan as populist demagogue, 1896. Drawing by J. S. Pughe. LC

Imperialism, according to the GOP. McKinley, the dignified
world leader vs. Bryan, the unpatriotic rebel. Drawing by Victor Gillam. LC

Bryan resurrected after the Democratic debacle of 1904.
Drawing by John T. McCutcheon. NSHS

Back from his world tour, Bryan brings home bricks for the trusts.
September 1906. Artist unknown. NSHS

The hardworking producer vs. the friend of plutocrats:
a pro-Bryan cartoon from the 1908 campaign. Artist unknown. NSHS

Bryan as self-promoter; he even sells recordings of his speeches.
A pro-Taft cartoon from 1908. Drawing by Felix Mahony. LC

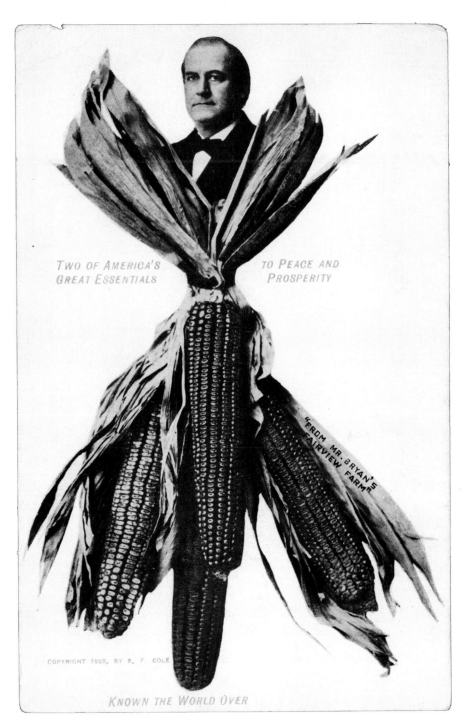

TWO OF AMERICA'S
GREAT ESSENTIALS

TO PEACE AND
PROSPERITY

"FROM MR. BRYAN'S
FAIRVIEW FARM"

COPYRIGHT 1908, BY B. F. COLE.

KNOWN THE WORLD OVER

A postcard from the 1908 campaign—boosting Nebraska's economy
and its sometime favorite son. Collage by B. F. Cole. NSHS

Bryan outmaneuvers Tammany Hall at the 1912 Democratic Convention.
Drawing by Charles Lewis Bartholomew. NSHS

THE PEERLESS PACIFICATOR, AND THEREBY HANGS A TAIL.

Bryan, as Secretary of State, tries to cool revolutionary Mexico with peaceful rhetoric—
while concealing a military option—1913. Drawing by Fred Morgan. LC

CHUCKING THE JONAH.

Wilson throws Bryan overboard, along with his beverage of choice.
Drawing by Sidney Greene. LC

Mary, dressed for a diplomatic dinner, c. 1914. NSHS

The Bryan daughters at Fairview, c. 1912
(Grace on the left, Ruth on the right). NSHS

Old friend and ally Josephus Daniels greets Bryan. Probably 1913. NSHS

A case of dual personality? As Charles Bryan is nominated for vice president, he smiles ambitiously into the mirror. Summer 1924. Drawing by Clifford K. Berryman. LC

Bryan the evangelist, with his flock in Miami, c. 1921

Bryan the rich celebrity turns his back on the people, March 1925.
Drawing by Daniel Robert Fitzpatrick

LEADING FIGURES AT THE "TRIAL OF THE CENTURY"

Bryan

John Scopes

Clarence Darrow

On hand for the spectacle: a scene from downtown Dayton during the Scopes trial.
Special Collections, University of Tennessee Library

Swearing in the jury at the trial, July 10, 1925.
Special Collections, University of Tennessee Library

Bryan's body begins its voyage from Dayton to Washington, D.C., July 1925.
Special Collections, University of Tennessee Library

Bryan as sculpted by Gutzon Borglum, 1934.
The statue now sits in a city park in Salem, Illinois. Author's photo

Ruth Bryan Owen with Eleanor Roosevelt, in Washington, D.C., October 1934.
Franklin D. Roosevelt Library

๛✝๛

Conscience of the Party,

1909–1912

Mr. Wilson is the best modern example of Saul of Tarsus. . . . He has been soundly converted.

—William Jennings Bryan, January 1912[1]

All I know and all I want to know is that Bryan is on one side, and Wall Street is on the other.

—Cone Johnson, delegate from Texas to the 1912 Democratic convention[2]

ON OCTOBER 1, 1909, the Bryans celebrated their silver wedding anniversary at Fairview together with six hundred relatives, neighbors, friends, and admirers. Dolph Talbot, Will's onetime law partner, acted as greeter and master of ceremonies. The couple forswore gifts, but they had neglected to rule out flowers. So the big stone house was stuffed with bouquets as well as visitors. On the veranda, a bulletin board displayed a tiny sample of the many telegrams dispatched to the Bryans from around the globe. Newspaper reporters were as welcome as anyone else to a slice of the mammoth cake, decorated, as in "olden times," with candied peppermint hearts. "Despite its simplicity," reported the *Omaha World-Herald*, straining to preserve Bryan's common-man image, the occasion "took on the character of a world-wide event."[3]

The party took place as Will and Mary were edging into a life absent the joys and anxieties of running for president. The Bryans had always been fond of making important decisions, performing rituals of transition, on their anniversary. Will had arrived in Lincoln to practice law—and politics—on October 1, 1887. The couple broke ground at Fairview on the same day in 1901.

So it was fitting that their twenty-fifth anniversary coincided with Will's transformation from a pioneering, if unsuccessful, candidate into what he and his loyalists believed would be the enduring conscience of his party and nation. From the start of his career, Bryan had portrayed himself as a man who stuck by his principles, even if doing so prevented him from gaining power. Yet he had taken two major steps—endorsing the peace treaty with Spain and backing away from his support for nationalizing the railroads—with his mind fixed on the next presidential campaign.

Now, with little apparent regret, Bryan was free to become a full-time moral scourge and perhaps statesman, while still reigning as the most popular orator in America. A new act was beginning in the longest-running personal melodrama in American politics. In defeat, Bryan, encouraged by his most dedicated followers, could pose as a more authentic exponent of Jefferson and Jesus than any other public figure in the nation. Newspapers reported that Tolstoy, nearing death, kept no other image on his bedroom wall in Yasnaya Polyana than a portrait of his soul mate from Nebraska. Closer to home, an adoring journalist hailed Bryan as "the one only earnest, sincere man, who for twelve years has patiently done his work amid a world of vilification and abuse" and was now "the dominating mind" in the progressive insurgency. The climax of this act would occur in 1912, at the next Democratic national convention.[4]

Mary Bryan was undergoing a different sort of transition. Motherhood was no longer the consuming task it had been through most of her marriage. But she was beginning to suffer from arthritis, which made winters in Nebraska increasingly intolerable. So in 1909, the couple bought a 240-acre farm near the Rio Grande in Mission, Texas. There Will, sporting a large black sombrero and a buckskin coat, took daily horseback rides and hunted ducks, while Mary got accustomed to the dry heat and mountain air. The Bryans' three children were now grown, living away from home and embarking on their own families and careers. Not all their choices were fortunate ones, although Mary and Will never publicly hinted at any difficulties.[5]

Ruth, the eldest, turned twenty-four the day after her parents' silver anniversary party. As a child, she had been something of a rebel. Several times, her father smacked her with a belt after she committed a mild transgression, such as drinking soda pop and lying about it. But the discipline did nothing to dampen her self-confidence or her energy. The lovely girl with a ringing voice vowed to return in triumph to the Capitol, where her father had first gained national renown. After graduating from high school, she threw herself into reform issues, even working briefly at Hull House in Chicago, perhaps under the charismatic guidance of Jane Addams.[6]

In 1903, Ruth married an artist, William Homer Leavitt, who had come to Fairview to paint her father's portrait. Escape as much as love motivated her choice. Her parents utterly disapproved of Leavitt, a rather bohemian gentleman in his late thirties. Mary was so unhappy she refused to attend the ceremony. Will did show up but, atypically, held his tongue.

A chastened Ruth soon came to share her parents' judgment. Leavitt, she recalled, "would have married the daughter of William Jennings Bryan if she had been a yellow dog and I would have married any man in the world to get away from home." In 1909, she sued her husband for divorce on grounds of "incompatibility of temper and non-support." Leavitt did not contest it.[7]

By this time, Ruth had already moved on to other passions. In 1910, she married a handsome British army officer, Reginald Owen, whom she'd met on an earlier trip to Europe when she appeared, at least outwardly, to be a contented wife. Meanwhile, she was trying her hand at the family business: Ruth filled several Chautauqua engagements for her father, spoke on his behalf during the 1908 campaign, and even considered running for Congress in Colorado, where she lived for several months. But her parents did not trust her maternal skills and took charge of raising her son, John, who lived at Fairview and took the name of Bryan. Aside from her temperament and love life, Ruth was determined to emulate her father.[8]

The Bryans' other offspring did not enter adulthood in such tumultuous or ambitious ways. William Junior attended the state university, where he met a fellow student, Helen Berger, whom he married in June 1909. He planned to become a lawyer like his father and grandfather. William Junior soon transferred to the University of Arizona in Tucson. There, in perhaps his first public debate, he argued that the initiative and referendum were needed to curb the "danger of corporate influence" from mining companies and agribusinesses.[9]

Grace, the youngest child, was also the least outspoken one and the most helpful to her parents. Stricken early in life by chronic pneumonia, she often accompanied her father to political events and was the only one of his offspring to attempt to write his biography. In 1911, Grace wed a hometown boy named Richard Hargreaves, an unhappy match that nevertheless produced four children.[10]

BECOMING A GRANDFATHER and losing his third race for president inevitably turned Bryan's thoughts to his legacy. No major party had ever handed out a fourth nomination to the same man. In a letter to a childhood friend, he worried that "my family history does not promise a long life" (his father had died at fifty-seven, his mother at sixty-two). A physician who examined him warned Mary her husband would suffer "a breakdown involving brain, kidney, or heart" if he didn't conserve his energies. Bryan planned to do "a good deal of writing" and take another family tour of the world. Clearly, there was little time to waste on routine political maneuvers.[11]

In and out of Chautauqua season, Bryan now devoted most of his speeches to religious themes and was glad to hear that "The Prince of Peace" and similar talks were hitting their mark. During the winter of 1909, a Chicago foreman known to "scoff" at religion went to hear him speak and emerged, in tears, a follower of Christ. Other correspondents praised Bryan's larger mission, often in the most grandiose terms. "This nation believes that Bryan is chosen of God for this work," wrote a female admirer from Evanston, Illinois, that fall; "therefore let his enemies fear and his friends love him."[12]

Such sentiments no doubt helped persuade Bryan to take a side in what, since the Civil War, had been one of the most fiercely contested issues in American politics. In the spring of 1909, he came out for prohibition, in a limited but decisive way. After Lincoln voted to ban all liquor sales within city limits, *The Commoner* applauded the result in a front-page editorial head-lined "Let the People Rule": "The moral awakening upon which the nation is entering is making both the individual and the public conscience more sensitive." What is more, "the officious and offensive interference of the liquor interests" made it imperative to stand up "for popular government."[13]

During his two decades as an active or potential candidate, Bryan had abstained from either denouncing the legalized "traffic" in alcoholic beverages or apologizing for it. As a lifelong teetotaler from a family of teetotalers, he had no sympathy for saloonkeepers or the manufacturers of hard drink. But since the advent of the prohibition movement in the 1850s, most soldiers in the "dry army" had come from Republican ranks, and their moralistic barbs only stiffened Democrats in their defense of "personal liberty." They really had little choice if they wished to secure the votes of Irish Catholics and of the many immigrants from central Europe who prized communal tippling as one of the few pleasures a workingman could afford. Previously, Bryan had either opposed state prohibition laws or pronounced himself an agnostic on the matter. During the 1908 campaign, with most labor officials in his corner, Bryan denied that prohibition was a "national question" at all.[14] Now he repudiated that dodge, without bothering to explain his change of heart.

In 1910, Bryan came out for county option in Nebraska, siding with the Republican governor and breaking with most Democrats in his state. After several months of internecine squabbles, that stand led him to commit a cardinal political sin: Bryan refused to endorse his party's candidate for governor—who happened to be James Dahlman, his old friend and ally but an ebullient "wet."

At the state Democratic convention that summer, Bryan waved his new standard with the same zeal he had once trained on goldbugs and imperialists. "We never espoused a more righteous cause than that which now appeals to us," he told the skeptical delegates. "If a retreat is to be sounded, it must be sounded by another. I shall never do it, never, never, never!" The response was a storm of boos—for the first time in his public life. Dahlman cracked that the home-state hero had grabbed hold of the "wrong end of a red-hot poker," and he vowed to pass out free beer at his inauguration party. But in the general election, Bryan's snub helped defeat the poker-playing cowboy from Omaha, in what was otherwise an excellent year for Democrats in Nebraska and the nation.[15]

To his followers, the motivation for Bryan's reversal was simple: he had long resented the political influence of the "liquor trust" but had held his tongue for opportunistic reasons. His loss in 1908 freed him to join the battle against the distillers, brewers, and saloon syndicates he branded as "selfish, mercenary, and conscienceless." Bryan thus joined most Protestant reformers of the day, who were determined to purify the nation both in body and soul. During his last campaign, his young aide, James Manahan, had come to Bryan with a lobbyist's request that he "give the liquor business a square deal if elected." The candidate tightened his "big jaw" and replied, "No, Jim, no. The saloons can't use me. I am against them." Now he had decided to prove it.[16]

Bryan's opponents suspected a baser purpose. Several Nebraska Democrats cursed his "treachery" and accused him of trying to position himself for another White House run; with a dry stand, he might appeal to pietistic southerners and northerners alike. President Taft predicted that his erstwhile adversary would "organize a mammoth lecture tour" against the liquor interests before the next election and might even accept the nomination of the declining Prohibition Party. The attorney Clarence Darrow, who had campaigned for Bryan in 1900, came to Omaha's city auditorium in 1910 to denounce the attack on an American's right to buy any kind of drink that pleased him.[17] Everyone conceded that Bryan was a moral man. But he was also a self-righteous one, convinced yet again that only he was capable of guiding the nation along the path of private and public virtue.

His critics were, however, almost certainly wrong to suspect the worm of electoral ambition. Bryan was too shrewd a politician to launch a fresh candidacy by alienating his own state party, which he had dominated since the 1890s. Over the next two years, he would repeatedly deny he was seeking a fourth nomination. Despite his apostasy in the governor's race, he remained a faithful Democrat, eager to convert the brethren to his new cause.[18]

Bryan did enjoy basking in the aura of a soul-cleansing, human-saving endeavor. The first prohibitionists had sprung from the anti-slavery movement and quaffed deeply from the same brew of evangelism and moral stewardship. During the Gilded Age, most of its stalwarts could still be found on the left wing of American politics. The Woman's Christian Temperance Union supported trade unions, woman suffrage, and the municipal ownership of utilities. Frances Willard, the WCTU's charismatic leader until her death in 1898, was a Christian socialist and a founder of the People's Party. Most rank-and-file Populists favored a ban on alcohol, but the national party declined to endorse it, fearing a backlash from urban labor.

While progressive intellectuals often considered it a diversion from more pressing ills, prohibition seemed, to most Protestant insurgents, a rational cure for the inner man and a way to close some of the rawest wounds of industrial society. Saloons, they believed, were sinkholes of depravity: many stayed open all night, sold their wares to children as well as adults, provided a haven for prostitutes, gamblers, and pickpockets, and spent some of their profits on bribes to policemen and municipal officeholders. In the "liquor traffic," Christian reformers saw the apotheosis of all they feared about the immorality of unregulated capitalism—its threat to families, health, and the body politic. In 1909, a veteran prohibitionist from Illinois advised Bryan, "You had better spend that fine talent that God has given you in helping to put down the greatest evil in the world."[19]

Even radical Social Gospelers enlisted in the temperance cause. In *The Jungle,* the best-selling novel of 1906, Upton Sinclair depicted the saloon as a conspiracy to rob workers of their wages and their character. Sinclair saw no contradiction between his socialism, heavily inflected with Christian metaphors, and his desire for a dry America. Neither did Jack London, who battled alcoholism all his life and toward the end of it considered running for office on the Prohibition ticket. Walter Rauschenbusch stated flatly that the liquor business was "a big section of the capitalistic interests of the country.... When it collides with the moral determination of our people to put a stop to its ravages, it fights."[20]

By the time Bryan joined the movement, it was faring better than ever. In 1907, Oklahoma voters passed a prohibition referendum, and legislators in the South were rapidly following suit. Congress had recently passed the Knox Amendment, which effectively outlawed the sale of liquor through the mail.

The organizational dynamo driving such victories was the Anti-Saloon

League, a machine staffed by evangelical ministers and financed by over twenty-five thousand individual Protestant congregations. Unlike the Prohibition Party, which had never gained more than 2 percent of the national vote or bested the liquor lobby in legislative combat, the League rallied behind any politician who endorsed its objectives. League activists were ferociously skillful at propaganda. They assaulted their target from every angle—medical, criminal, economic, moral, populist, and sometimes nativist; they did make an effort to separate foreign-born barkeeps and brewers from the mass of immigrants. The very name of their group promoted the idea that the evils of drink could be traced to an urban elite—whose public face was the corner tavern—that used its profits and power to crush the health and independence of ordinary Americans. In 1913, the League felt confident enough to mount a march of thousands to the Capitol, where a congressman had just proposed a constitutional amendment to abolish the liquor traffic for good.[21]

Bryan appreciated the cleverness of the League's multipronged assault, but he made his own argument in the romantic pitch of Christian humanitarianism. The liquor problem, he insisted, was too serious to be allowed to fester any longer. Saloons were multiplying across the land, and the liquor lobby threw its money and influence against any measure that might disrupt its cozy relationship with urban bosses. To the Nebraska Democrats who howled him down, he protested, "If I have any apologies to offer, I shall not offer them to the liquor interests for speaking now; I shall offer them to the fathers and mothers of this state for not speaking sooner."[22] True Christians, Bryan insisted, must stop ignoring this menacing predator. Yet by embracing prohibition, he was implicitly turning his back on many of the urban wage earners whose votes he'd wooed in 1908.

As an instant general of the dry army, Bryan was characteristically sanguine about its prospects and welcomed everyone to join, regardless of creed. In a long interview with the *New York Times* in 1911, he beamed about "the world-wide religious awakening" he claimed was fueling "signs of uplift all along the line." Bypassing mention of the Anti-Saloon League and the WCTU, he hailed the mass memberships of youth groups such as Christian Endeavor and the YMCA, as well as of the Knights of Columbus. The year before, Bryan had addressed two thousand members of the Catholic Total Abstinence Union. Unlike some of his bigoted followers, he preferred to fight evil with a broad, ecumenical force behind him.[23]

"Without the churches and the religious impulse which they stand for," Bryan acknowledged, "this movement would immediately cease." But the "increasing tendency toward purer government and toward cleaner politics" would triumph so long as Americans remained people of faith. Wasn't the Bible "the great textbook of the moral life"? A large photo of the evangelist cradling two of his baby grandchildren on his lap completed the homiletic tableau.[24]

These were hardly novel sentiments. But in uttering them, Bryan made clear he would intensify the "applied Christianity" he'd promoted throughout his career. His stand for prohibition might also help solve the problem that faces any popular politician after he or she decides to drop out of the chase for high office. How would Bryan retain mass support now that other aspirants for the White House would be grabbing the headlines?

"Men should be redeemers and benefactors—noble clay in the hands of the Almighty, this will bring success and reform always," Mrs. John F. Park wrote from Little Rock in the spring of 1909. Two years later, W. Williamson from Pasadena, California, affirmed that Bryan was that man— "a wise leader, far-sighted as to the needs of the people and unwavering in his efforts to make politics better and cleaner."[25] Thousands of others echoed their sentiments. In 1909, *The Commoner* inaugurated a regular mail column, ennobling it with such titles as "Letters from the People," "Democratic Opinion Freely Expressed," and "If the People Rule."

Women, while a minority of Bryan's correspondents who made it into print, tended to state their allegiance to him in particularly dramatic and sweeping terms. "The questions of the last campaign have not been settled according to the standards of righteousness," wrote Mrs. M. L. Hollingsworth from the hamlet of De Queen, Arkansas, "and it is the duty of every American citizen to press on toward higher moral and political standards." She singled out "the great problem of the saloon and its attendant evils."

Bryan had always appealed to white religious women from every social class. During the 1900 campaign, a wealthy woman had bought thousands of copies of his picture and sent them out to schools, both public and Sunday, all over the country. "Everywhere the female mind was at this orator's service," wrote a hyperbolic observer.[26]

Now his espousal of a dry nation brought him closer to churchgoers of both genders who were eager to lure men back to the pews. By the dawn of the twentieth century, it was common knowledge that women were mainstays of the largest evangelical denominations. A Baptist preacher declared male apathy to be "one of the burning questions of the hour," while the editor of a leading Methodist journal estimated that women were twice as likely to serve the church as were men. The male strategists of the Anti-Saloon League masked the true nature of grassroots prohibitionism. Everywhere, women shouldered the bulk of the petitioning, the writing and editing of didactic literature, and the counseling of families brought low by strong drink. A growing number also argued that equal suffrage was the surest way to destroy the liquor traffic. The hatchet-wielding Carry A. Nation was merely the most colorful and self-promoting member of this female juggernaut.[27]

In their alarm, some male leaders sought to "revirilize" society, as one historian puts it. Teddy Roosevelt famously called for men to lead a "strenuous life" of service to the nation and relished the idea of doing so through war. The evangelist Billy Sunday punched chairs and used tough, slangy language to dramatize his hatred for booze and the devil. Lay preachers from the Men and Religion Forward movement staged urban revivals that urged men to act responsibly as fathers and citizens.[28]

Bryan sometimes shared a platform with such speakers, but he usually took a warmer, even maternal approach to moral reform. He frequently acknowledged his reliance on Mary's advice, abhorred any use of force, and endorsed woman suffrage in 1910—years in advance of most men in his party. *The Commoner* also hailed the "new women" who were helping educate the public about pressing social problems. By framing both his political battles and his religious beliefs in sentimental terms, Bryan demonstrated the resilience and attractiveness of the Victorian ideal, updated to include women as political actors, that TR's toughness aimed to transform, if not destroy. If "love" was "the law of life" and "forgiveness, the test of love," as Bryan declared in a 1910 speech, then only men who behaved altruistically were doing God's work.[29]

There could be no doubt, of course, about who was the altruist in chief. Bryan knew it would be unseemly to go around the country praising himself. But *The Commoner* unfailingly described him as a towering guardian of virtue, both in the United States and the wider world. When he toured Latin America in the late winter and early spring of 1910, the weekly hailed him for stirring a "moral awakening" and cited reports in the local press lauding his brilliance as an orator. "Saul among the prophets!" a journalist called Bryan after hearing him speak that summer in Scotland, and *The Commoner* duly shared the piece with its readers.[30]

As acting editor, Charles Bryan reprinted dispatches from other papers to refute the charge that his brother was no longer a central figure in American life. Often these stories testified to the personality cult that Will refreshed through frequent travel. "Say, colonel, please let me have your fan," a "sweet young lady" from Georgetown, Ohio, asked him in 1911. "So is added another Bryan relic," noted a reporter, "to the collection of Bryan coats and Bryan hats and Bryan trousers and Bryan shirts that are treasured by lucky democrats in various sections of the country." Thousands of parents still named their children after the itinerant hero. William Jennings Bryan Herman—born in New Albany, Indiana, in 1909—grew up to star in the National League; as Billy Herman, he is enshrined in the Baseball Hall of Fame.[31]

Bryan's well-burnished self-image differed sharply from that of the most thoroughgoing insurgent in the rival party. Robert La Follette spoke in a hortative and humorless style; he worried, sometimes with reason, that audiences didn't warm to him. But as governor of and then senator from Wisconsin, La Follette built a record of practical successes that dwarfed Bryan's, and his regard among progressive intellectuals rivaled that of Theodore Roosevelt. "Fighting Bob" battled for direct primaries, the income tax, and a ban on corporate giving to campaigns long before his party's cautious leaders acquiesced to them. He also spoke out for the conservation of natural resources and woman suffrage several years before Bryan did, and he continued to denounce Jim Crow after top GOP officials had ceased to protest lynching and other racial outrages. And La Follette very much wanted to be president.[32]

Yet the publication he launched in 1909 was curiously unequipped to further that end. *La Follette's Weekly Magazine* featured a galaxy of reform thinker-activists that *The Commoner* never could have attracted, even if Bryan had tried. Lincoln Steffens raked the muck of urban corruption, labor economist John Commons advocated improved trade schools, and Jane Addams and the sociologist Edward Ross contributed pieces of their forthcoming books. But La Follette seldom made an appearance, even though he handled most of the editing. While his magazine preached the same progressive gospel as did *The Commoner,* albeit with a greater emphasis on urban problems, it eschewed the devotion to one man's views and his call-and-response routine with a far-flung congregation. *La Follette's* reached a circulation of over thirty thousand. But the periodical gave its editor little assistance in 1912, when he competed with Theodore Roosevelt for the affections of a growing number of Republicans who wanted to unseat a president from their own party.[33]

A CIVIL WAR had broken out inside the GOP only months after Taft's inauguration. La Follette and TR were only the most prominent figures among a cabal of Republican officeholders and journalists whose opinion of the president had moved rapidly from frustration to anger and then to open rebellion. The insurgency was strongest in states west of the Mississippi, where even the GOP was influenced by the demands of Bryanite farmers and trade unionists.

Taft incurred such animus more because of what he failed to do than because of anything he accomplished. In 1908, he had campaigned as a trustworthy reformer, but as president, he was effectively allowing standpatters in his party—led by House Speaker Joseph Cannon and Senator Nelson Aldrich—to call the tune. During his first two years in the White House, Taft blocked an attempt to curb Cannon's dictatorial control over legislation, refused to endorse serious cuts in the tariff, and fired Gifford Pinchot, the leading conservationist in the Interior Department, after he protested the exploitation of public lands by private firms. The president refused to defend himself to reporters who depicted him as the servant of those Republicans who judged friend and foe by the crassest of standards. "Oh, he's all right," Aldrich told colleagues in 1909 about a new lawmaker to whom he had given a plum committee assignment. "I have had him looked up. He is the attorney for seven different corporations."[34]

Soon the igneous rhetoric coming out of both camps made reconciliation impossible. In August 1910, before a big crowd of Civil War veterans in Kansas, TR scolded officials who did not keep their campaign promises and called for a new nationalism that would favor "human welfare" over the interests of property owners. For their part, GOP conservatives vowed to rob the insurgents and their "populistic principles" of influence and power.[35]

For Democrats who had followed Bryan into the wilderness at the end of the last century, whether in joy or sorrow, this nasty split was their best opportunity to return to power. As the minority in Congress, they voted rather solidly against positions that Taft favored and resisted the impulse to bite back when GOP insurgents spurned their embrace. "I hope the Lord will increase the tribe of the progressive Republicans," said Senator Thomas Gore of Oklahoma. In the House, Democrats were led by James "Champ" Clark of Missouri, a folksy speaker and cautious career politician who hoped his advocacy of anti-corporate reform would show him to be Bryan's most logical successor. The rise in both unemployment and farm prices was making it hard for Republicans to claim that they were still the party of the "full dinner pail."[36]

In the spring of 1910, Bryan took time out from evangelizing for prohibition to observe that "the Republican party is passing through the same crisis that the Democratic Party went through in 1896."[37] That fall, it was the GOP's turn to suffer the consequences of internal strife. Democrats gained control of the House by sixty-seven seats, winning dozens of races outside their southern stronghold and capturing a share of national power for the first time since Bryan's whirlwind crusade for free silver. The big swing states of Ohio, Indiana, and New York all elected Democratic governors. New Jersey's new chief executive was Woodrow Wilson—the political scientist and Princeton president who had transformed his university from a glorified gentlemen's club into one of the best schools in the nation. A first-time candidate in his early fifties, Wilson had also recently changed his political outlook: the admirer of Grover Cleveland turned into an energetic progressive eager to take on the bosses of his own state party.

Bryan's reaction to all this good news was remarkably guarded. Labeling it "harvest time" for the patient labors of the past fourteen years, he warned Democrats to beware of GOP "bunco" artists and their friends in "the plutocratic press." After the new House majority unanimously chose Champ Clark to lead them, the Speaker wrote a front-page article in *The Commoner* in which he swore to "religiously fulfill every promise that we made in order to win." He also traveled to Fairview to sing Bryan's praises at his host's fifty-first birthday party. But soon after Congress met in April, Clark's sometime patron began to scold him and other Democratic chieftains for failing to meet that lofty standard.[38]

Bryan grumbled loudest about the tariff, the perpetual obsession of American politics. Almost twenty years before, he'd made his maiden leap onto the national stage with a speech in the House blasting the high duty on wool and accusing the GOP of coddling its wealthy beneficiaries. Now he attacked Representative Oscar W. Underwood of Alabama, chairman of the Ways and Means Committee, for seeking to cut the tariff on wool only in half (to 20 percent) instead of eliminating it altogether. "Without free wool," Bryan moaned, "tariff reform would not amount to much." He also suspected Underwood of trying to scuttle a downward revision of the taxes on imported iron and steel. Bryan announced that opponents of his stand were making a fateful pact with "the predatory interests." He warned Clark that "the fight over wool will prove a crisis in your life as well as in the party's prospects." "A leader must *lead*," even at the risk of losing. The most popular Democrat in the nation had thus made the price of a sheep's coat the supreme test of loyalty to his ideals and status within the party.[39]

Bryan always covered such inflexible postures in haughty moral phrases, and his true reasons for drawing this particular line in the sand are unclear. Perhaps he really did suspect Underwood, a quiet tactician married to a steel heiress from Birmingham, of beginning the betrayal of anti-trust principles with a rather unremarkable compromise. Perhaps he was seeking a rallying point for his own loyalists, in and out of Congress, against conservative Democrats who were hoping to select the next presidential nominee. Bryan came to Washington to argue his case on the tariff and other issues; he made a grand entrance into a packed House chamber, upstaging Clark's formal election as Speaker. *The Commoner* filled up with letters cheering him on. Presaging a future battle, one correspondent from northern Minnesota compared "stand-pat democrats and the interests" seeking to "eliminate Mr. Bryan" from political influence to "those great scientists...who are trying to eliminate God from the creation." Or perhaps he simply could not bear to see his beloved party being steered by other men poised to win victories on "his" issues.[40]

In any case, Bryan's attempt to bully his fellow Democrats proved, at least in the short run, an embarrassing failure. Underwood took the floor of the House in early August to deny, with a rare show of anger, that he had gone back on his word or the beliefs of his party. The speech elicited grins from Speaker Clark and received a five-minute-long ovation. After Underwood sat down, no congressman felt brave enough to defend the man some called the Peerless Leader. Bryan, out on the Chautauqua circuit, joked to an audience in Iowa that he'd been "read out of the Democratic Party...so often that I am used to it." Two weeks later, House Democrats had to swallow a compromise tariff bill written by the Republican-controlled Senate that cut wool duties only slightly. Then they failed to override Taft's veto of the entire package.[41]

Beware the wounded hero with saber still in hand. For Bryan, the end of the tariff debate was the beginning of the 1912 campaign. Having forgone another run, he was all the more determined to use his celebrity in the press and his popularity among rank-and-file Democrats to ensure that the party's next nominee would be faithful to his "radical" principles. For Bryan, the terms of internal conflict had changed little since he'd first donned the armor of a righteous cause. He remained close to Samuel Gompers and other labor leaders and warned that the "Wall Street crowd" that had bolted in 1896 and foisted Parker on the party in 1904 was scheming to hijack it again.[42]

But the electoral prospects were certainly more favorable for 1912. The civil war in the GOP gave Democrats their best chance in two decades to win back the presidency. Taft's ineptness put conservatives on the defensive, afraid of being branded apologists for big business and enemies of all that was ethical and humane. In this environment, Democrats could not risk choosing a nominee whom Bryan did not approve. He was going to enjoy the battle ahead.[43]

In the summer of 1911, *The Commoner* printed a series of nineteen questions it urged readers to ask any man who wanted to be president. The list was unsurprising; it began, "Do you favor tariff for revenue only?" and moved from the income tax to Filipino independence to railroad regulation to guaranteed bank deposits. Still, the idea of ordinary citizens, rather than parties, demanding that candidates pledge themselves to a given program was rather controversial. The California legislature had earlier banned the practice after labor unions initiated it there. But Bryan knew his following was large and fervent enough to entice the ambitious. Joseph Folk, the former governor of Missouri, responded enthusiastically to the query, while Woodrow Wilson and several other aspirants submitted friendly if diffident replies.[44]

Meanwhile, Bryan was judging the Democratic field on political strength and ideological rigor. He quickly wrote off Underwood, whose base in the Deep South and marital connections likely would have eliminated him even if he hadn't tangled with Bryan over taxes. As the twice-elected governor of Ohio, Judson Harmon might be able to win a vital region the party hadn't carried since Cleveland's heyday. But Harmon, a former railroad attorney and Gold Democrat, opposed the income tax as well as the initiative and referendum. That résumé allowed Bryan to write him off as a Wall Street pawn. Folk had been a loyal Bryanite since 1896 and, unlike most Democratic insiders, was also an ardent prohibitionist who wore his Christianity on his sleeve. But he had lost a Senate race in 1908 and had the misfortune of hailing from the same state as the Speaker of the House.[45]

Therefore, as the election year began, Bryan's choice was essentially between Clark and Wilson. To superficial observers, the Speaker appeared, in the parlance of the day, to be the most "available" man. He was the only Democrat in charge of a branch of the federal government, hailed from a critical state that straddled the South and West, and had persuaded both Gompers and William Randolph Hearst (back in his old party again) that he was a stalwart foe of big business. Under his leadership, the House had passed and the Senate had agreed to constitutional amendments on two of the party's perennial demands: an income tax and the popular election of senators. What is more, the influential *New York World,* now under the editorial direction of longtime Bryan-hater Frank Cobb, warned against nominating someone so close in spirit and manner to the three-time loser from Nebraska.

On the other hand, Wilson, before he entered politics, had routinely vented his distaste for Bryan, whom he considered no more than a populist demagogue. "Would that we could do something at once dignified and effective to knock Mr. Bryan once and for all into a cocked hat!" the Princeton president had written in 1907 to Adrian Joline, an attorney who often worked for major railroad firms. A year later, Wilson refused to speak at a Jefferson Day dinner after learning that the putative Democratic nominee was also on the program. How could the Commoner endorse a man who had treated him in such a smug and hostile manner?[46]

That logic overlooked Bryan's deep mistrust of Clark—a former loyalist he believed had strayed from the path of virtue. Since the battle in Congress the previous summer, Bryan had made his disappointment with the Speaker quite clear in an exchange of letters and in several articles and speeches. When Clark claimed he was only seeking to unite Democrats behind low tariffs and an income tax, Bryan shot back, "You seem to ignore the fundamental difference between those who have three times defeated the party and those who have supported it. The getting together is possible on one condition only, namely, surrender to Wall Street." Bryan suspected that Clark would make a deal with the devil if that would gain him the nomination. Didn't he cooperate with Harmon's allies in Missouri in order to turn back a challenge by Folk?[47]

Wilson, on the other hand, was behaving like a repentant sinner. During his first weeks as governor, he goaded the legislature into electing to the U.S. Senate the leading Bryanite in New Jersey, a perennial candidate named James Martine, who had unexpectedly won a nonbinding primary. Then Wilson oversaw passage of an impressive list of reforms—on public utility regulation, workmen's compensation, food inspection, and urban corruption—that New Jersey insurgents had been promoting for over a decade. Meanwhile, he found time to praise Bryan's "stout heart" and put together a campaign team that include Josephus Daniels and a few other aides from Bryan's 1908 campaign. On a speaking tour of the West in the spring of 1911, Wilson spent an amiable afternoon at Fairview, browsing through a clutter of campaign bric-a-brac and gifts from Bryan's followers. After leaving the crowded manse, Wilson acknowledged to a reporter that he still disdained his host. But, to Bryan, the governor's redemption seemed quite genuine.[48]

That preparation enabled Wilson to survive a crisis that could easily have destroyed his chance for the nomination. On January 6, 1912, the *New York Sun* published the text of the Joline letter. Bryan quickly grasped that the paper, a savage opponent since the 1890s, was hoping to destroy the governor for echoing his views. He assured two Wilson allies that "the big financial interests" would not be able to use "such tactics" to divide "Progressive ranks." Two days later, all the would-be nominees, plus Bryan, turned out for a party banquet in a Washington hotel. At the end of his speech, Wilson, with studied grace, turned to Bryan and announced, "If anyone has said anything about any of the other candidates, for which he is sorry, now is the time to apologize." Then he bowed to him and smiled.[49]

The governor continued to try to erase any doubt that he had seen the light on the road to his personal Damascus. In February, before a thousand Democrats at a dinner in Kansas, he lauded Bryan in terms he knew the moralist would appreciate. "No man can displace him," Wilson told the audience; "men love him and trust him because he has kept his own life untainted by improper influences and his own heart absolutely true to Democratic interests." Thus did his fellow Presbyterian elder strum romantic chords Bryan would never have a chance to play in the White House.[50]

As the season of national conventions approached, journalists and politicians traded rumors and guesses about what Bryan would do. Despite his repeated denials, most observers assumed he still expected that his party—if deadlocked between untested competitors—might turn to him. In letters to *The Commoner*, numerous readers pleaded for their hero to run; in May, a group of admirers opened offices in Pittsburgh and a few midwestern cities to "create such a demonstration" that delegates would "be forced" to nominate Bryan again. Both his wife and brother privately hoped the prediction would come true. "I wanted him to take the nomination; I wanted him to be President; I wanted him to conquer his enemies," Mary wrote in the *Memoirs*. Given the animus between Taft and Roosevelt, displayed before the public in a bruising set of GOP primaries (the most extensive ones in history), whomever the Democrats chose would be the early favorite.[51]

But Bryan appeared quite sincere about his desire to lead without running. He told a magazine reporter that he had a single goal: "protection of the people from exploitation at the hands of predatory corporations." Ultimately, the Democrat who most faithfully waved that standard would gain his support. In April, "en route" between speaking engagements, Will instructed his "Dear Bro." to be sure that *The Commoner* remained strictly neutral between Wilson and Clark: "Don't allow either to criticize the other." Having temporarily muted his attacks on the liquor traffic, Bryan won a place in Nebraska's delegation to the Democratic convention. Although Clark had carried the state's primary, Will shrewdly declined to pledge his support to anyone. Meanwhile, he disclosed to Ignatius Dunn, a fellow delegate and old friend, that he had a plan to defeat "the Reactionary forces" in the party and to gain the nomination for a true progressive.[52]

Bryan also accepted a rather unorthodox offer to report the news while making it. *The World*, always willing to separate its desire for higher circulation from its editorial opinions, invited him to write daily dispatches from the Republican convention in Chicago and the Democratic gathering in Baltimore. The prospect was clearly delightful, and not just because his fee would total, by one account, $1,000 a day. After years on the stump and at *The Commoner*, Bryan was an old hand at meeting deadlines. He had always enjoyed the company of the reporters and cartoonists who traveled with him during campaigns, whatever the editorial slant of their publishers. Now, thanks to the *World's* far-reaching syndicate, inhabitants of every major city would be able to pore over his lengthy reflections about the quadrennial dramas he had first witnessed as a teenager and which became mileposts of his career.[53]

The wearing of two hats—well-paid observer and titular leader of his party—did raise a troubling question: how could one tell if Bryan was out to make history or was merely seeking to draw attention to himself in print? The *New York Times*, a longtime critic, inevitably charged him with striking political poses that would "lend a sensational color to his newspaper work." To combine the two roles smelled of insincerity and potential corruption.[54]

Yet Bryan had always been the most prominent and one of the more dramatic narrators of his own life. *The Commoner*, books and articles about his campaigns and foreign travels, and most of his speeches and interviews were transparent attempts to create an image for millions to admire. To be sure, the *World* had handed him an untraditional task. But one does not remain a celebrity without occasionally staging a novel performance. Few journalists in 1912 viewed Bryan as either an interloper or an imposter. Fascinated with the personalities of politicians, they could hardly object when a campaigner who'd supplied them with years of good copy decided to profit from the enterprise himself.

Bryan began his new assignment at the Republican convention, which met from June 18 to 22. There he provided a bit of comic relief for the supporters of Taft and TR who were busily tearing their party in two. "Three cheers for the man who led us to victory three times," a delegate cried as Bryan took his seat in the press section of the Chicago Coliseum, the same hall he had captivated on a hot July day sixteen years before. A bit chagrined, he quickly recovered by teasing the Republicans for not knowing their Bible very well. He also criticized the performance style of several orators while saluting the civility of the combatants: "It is remarkable that so much intensity of speech, so much tenacity of purpose, so much depth of conviction can be brought together on opposite sides with so little display of anger and such an absence of rudeness." When Bryan left the hall for the last time, he received an ovation from the galleries. By that time, Roosevelt and his delegates had already marched out of the convention to form the Progressive Party.[55]

A week later in Baltimore, Bryan neither expected nor obtained so blithe a reception. Most Democrats could taste victory in November and were determined to name a new leader who could transcend the divisions—of region and ideology—that had hamstrung their campaigns for almost two decades. To prevent an emotional stampede for any candidate, convention managers had ordered all state standards to be nailed to the floor so they could not be paraded around the hall. But Bryan, who brought along Mary and Grace, was in no mood to relax his moral rigor. He was sure that the "predatory corporations" and their political cronies were ready to gorge themselves on the vulnerable and the innocent; left unchecked, they would flaunt the progressive will both of rank-and-file Democrats and of the voters. It was the same conflict he had waged at the 1896 convention, albeit with a different set of enemies. This time, Americans would be able to read his reflections on the drama while they ate their breakfast.

Bryan opened his offensive on the eve of the convention with a telegram of protest to all four of the declared candidates (Wilson, Clark, Underwood, and Harmon). In a divided vote, a party committee had proposed that none other than Alton Parker, the tragic pride of New York conservatives, should deliver the keynote address. "I took it for granted," wrote Bryan, "that no committee interested in Democratic success would desire to offend the members of a convention overwhelmingly Progressive by naming a reactionary to sound the keynote of the campaign." This was the first of three controversial steps he would take in Baltimore; each one instantly became the talk not just of the convention but of the country at large.[56]

As Bryan intended, his telegram touched off something of a panic among the contenders. The Underwood and Harmon camps, with little hope of winning the nomination, steeled themselves to defeat the man who had already sworn his enmity to them. Clark's managers arrived at the Baltimore Armory with 60 percent of the votes he needed. Ever a practical man, the Speaker grumbled about the "discord" Bryan's telegram had caused, told his delegates to make up their own minds, but privately instructed his aides to drum up votes for Parker. He feared alienating leaders from any important state, particularly New York, who might block him from gaining the necessary two-thirds margin. Only Wilson, whose defiance of veteran pols in his own state had already incurred the mistrust of Tammany, told Bryan, "You are quite right . . . . No one will doubt where my sympathies lie."[57]

There ensued a number of maneuvers on the floor of the convention to decide who would give the keynote address. To loud applause, Bryan nominated John Kern for the task, but the speech he gave on behalf of his old running mate lasted too long and was constantly interrupted. From the gallery, a perceptive observer noted that Bryan was no longer the commanding figure of his early campaigns: "The fine, strong features that made him so handsome sixteen years ago have hardened and grown coarse.... His neck is thick and his jaw has an iron rigidity." Age and self-righteousness had taken their toll. In a close vote, Parker was chosen and then delivered a spirited but completely forgettable address.[58]

Although defeated, Bryan had achieved his purpose. He had tested the convictions of the two leading candidates and proved he was still the star of his party, whether its lesser lights respected or despised him. Retiring to his hotel room, he wrote that if "the plain every day citizen, who earns his bread in the sweat of his brow, could understand the influences that operate at a convention like this," he would agree that only men "whose hearts are right... and who have the moral courage to stand for the silent masses" ought to be chosen as delegates. Americans quickly wired more than a hundred thousand telegrams to Baltimore, most applauding Bryan's stand. As during the conventions of 1896 and 1904, ordinary Democrats found their voice only after he had defined the terms of battle.[59]

The torrent of support convinced him to make a second gesture that was bolder, as rhetorical theater, than any performance of his life. On the evening of June 27, officials were about to embark on the main business of the convention—the marathon of presidential nominations and balloting. At that moment, Bryan hurried up to the stage to ask a favor from the chairman, Representative Ollie James of Kentucky. Could he offer an impromptu resolution? James, a longtime ally he had earlier proposed as a substitute keynoter, agreed. Bryan began, innocently enough, with a pledge "to the people... that the party of Jefferson and Jackson" still stood for "popular government and equality before the law." Some delegates may have mused that he meant to show, at this key point in the proceedings, that he desired harmony after all.

Then came the assault. "As proof of our fidelity to the people we hereby declare ourselves opposed to the nomination of any candidate for President who is a representative of, or under any obligation to J. Pierpont Morgan, Thomas F. Ryan, August Belmont, or any other member of the privilege-hunting and favor-seeking class." As shouts and curses mounted, Bryan added a second demand—the "withdrawal" of any delegates "constituting or representing the above-named interests." He concluded with a line from the Sermon on the Mount: " 'If thy right hand offend thee, cut it off.' The party needs to cut off those corrupting influences to save itself."[60]

Even to some of his friends in the hall, this seemed an act of pure demagoguery. Ollie James exclaimed to Josephus Daniels, "My God,... what is the matter with Bryan? Does he want to destroy the Democratic party?" Only a few hours before, a committee had approved a platform Bryan had mostly drafted; it was the fifth consecutive time he had written much of the party's core document, which enjoyed a status in the golden age of print journalism it has since lost. And none of the individuals Bryan named—powerful and wealthy financiers—was known to control more than a handful of delegate votes. J. P. Morgan wasn't even a Democrat.[61]

But there was some substance to his bravado. The men Bryan named had worked together in the past to manipulate politicians and make gargantuan profits. During the depression of the 1890s, Belmont and Morgan had cleared as much as $16 million selling government bonds. Ryan had become one of the richest men in America by bribing city officials and issuing watered stock for street railways in New York City. He bought Equitable Life Assurance after a corporate scandal had lowered its value, and then, under shady circumstances, sold his stock to Morgan for a good deal more than it was worth. In May, a House committee chaired by Representative Arsène Pujo of Louisiana began extensive hearings into the operations of a "money trust" in which all three men played an integral part. Now Belmont and Ryan both sat in the armory as delegates, from New York and Virginia respectively. Several journalists accused them of working with Tammany's boss, Charles Murphy, to defeat Wilson and humble Bryan as well.[62]

"Pandemonium does not describe the scene that followed this move on the part of the peerless leader," the *New York Times* reported helplessly. A Virginia associate of Ryan's rushed up to Bryan and loudly accused him of sabotaging the party's chances that fall. The speaker's platform filled up with unruly, gesticulating men. It was, wrote Bryan later that day, "a confusion that I never witnessed before in a convention." After several hours of furious debate, he agreed to drop the unenforceable demand that friends of the "interests" withdraw from the hall. The delegates then voted, by a margin of more than four to one, for the purely rhetorical part of his resolution. To avoid the taint of Wall Street, even the delegation from New York answered aye. With a grin, Charles Murphy turned to Belmont and said, "Now Auggie, listen to yourself vote yourself out of the convention."[63]

Politics is, among other things, the art of seizing a symbolic occasion, and Bryan had again showed himself to be master of the moment. Once he had thrown down his challenge, the delegates could not reject it "and still pretend to be on the side of progressive liberalism," a Wilson confidant wrote later. To a cartoonist from the local Hearst paper, Bryan suggested what he thought would be a fitting image of the drama he'd just incited. The resulting illustration depicts Ryan, his sleeves rolled up and jaw at a brutal thrust, lashing a topless young woman, labeled "Democratic Party." A cat-o'-nine-tails represents Murphy and his fellow urban bosses. Even newspapers that despised Bryan had to quote his statement that the Democrats had officially routed "the Plunderbund" that had tried to throttle their anti-corporate resolve. A second avalanche of supportive telegrams soon crashed down on the conventioneers.[64]

Bryan still had one last shock to administer to his querulous brethren. With Clark and Wilson closely matched, the process of choosing a nominee stretched on for two days and thirteen ballots. New York, led by Tammany, declared for Clark, and this gave the Speaker just over a majority of the delegates. Wilson drafted a note to Bryan denouncing the New York contingent as "controlled by a single group of men" whose backing no gallant candidate should accept. But his campaign manager refused to send it. When the roll call on the fourteenth ballot reached Nebraska, Bryan rose to "explain my vote," which, until then, had gone to Clark. It was as if he had read Wilson's mind. Or perhaps it was the other way around.

"As long as Mr. Ryan's agents—as long as New York's ninety votes are recorded for Mr. Clark," began Bryan, "I withold my vote from him." He could "not be a party to the nomination of any man . . . who will not, when elected, be absolutely free to carry out the anti-Morgan-Ryan-Belmont resolution." Bryan announced he was switching his vote to Wilson, but only so long as the governor received no support from New York, that den of corruption and ill-gotten wealth.[65]

Fistfights broke out between partisans of the two major contenders. A labor attorney from Oklahoma got so furious at his former hero, whom he dubbed "the Niagaric Nebraskan," that he announced he was switching his vote to Clark. James Gerard, later U.S. ambassador to Germany, reportedly muttered, "By God, somebody ought to assassinate him." Bryan had to take refuge behind the forty-man Texas delegation, beefy gentlemen loyal both to his cause and to Wilson's. Even though his vote switch came with a condition attached, Clark's managers realized Bryan had made an unalterable decision to oppose them. As soon as he heard the news, the Speaker took a night train to Baltimore to denounce the "absolutely and wickedly false" charge of a man he had once considered his leader and had still believed was his friend.[66]

Democrats had often charged Bryan with disloyalty before. He'd enraged his Nebraska mentor, J. Sterling Morton, by collaborating with the Populists, soured most Democratic senators when he endorsed the peace treaty with Spain, and risked ostracism from home-state partisans when he bashed the liquor lobby. Bryan's claim that he always chose principle over party, while not strictly accurate, almost guaranteed that such episodes would happen and gain him new enemies with each recurrence.

But Clark should not have been so surprised at the switch on the fourteenth ballot. For the past year, Bryan had spoken with growing warmth about Wilson, while complaining that the Speaker was acting timidly in the face of reaction. For the rest of his life, Clark cursed Bryan for "violating his instructions" as a delegate and believed the "betrayal" had cost him the nomination. But Bryan had never promised to stick by the Speaker on every ballot, and it was naive to expect that an oft-proclaimed "prophet" would feel bound by a primary held months before. At any rate, many other delegates had to switch their allegiance before Wilson was able to capture the nomination—on a record forty-sixth ballot. Bryan had cleverly begun the shift away from Clark, but other Democrats grasped the weakness of a candidate yoked, in the popular mind, to the two-headed albatross of Tammany and Wall Street.[67]

In Baltimore, Bryan achieved all he could have desired. Newspapers of every editorial stripe credited him with securing Wilson's victory; an aide to the nominee told him an "intimate" relationship between the two was now "of the utmost importance." Progressive voices, inside and outside his party, praised Bryan for fighting for his ideals rather than for himself. "From the very first moment," saluted the *American Magazine,* a muckraking journal, "he towered over his enemies, was their superior in boldness, in force of character and in political finesse." *La Follette's Magazine* called him "a towering figure of moral power and patriotic devotion" in contrast with TR, whose actions in Chicago had served only "unworthy ambition." Walter Rauschenbusch wrote that the Baltimore convention "will stand out in our memory chiefly for the dramatic power of a single personality, strong in his sincerity and the trust of his countrymen, to wrest the control of his party at least for a time from evil hands."[68]

Similar sentiments came from mugwumpish Republicans who had not said a kind word in public about Bryan since the campaign of 1900. "Of all men in public life," wrote Erving Winslow of the Anti-Imperialist League, "you have most clearly foreseen the menace to our institutions from the aggregation of wealth, and its corrupting influences." A YMCA secretary from Massachusetts who'd never voted for a Democrat told the Nebraskan, "You were fighting for God and the people." Such plaudits only strengthened Bryan's hold on his traditional followers, particularly those who preferred he be "the finest individual/moral force in the nation," as a Baptist minister called him, rather than take the risk of running for president again and losing. Since the Democrats roared into power with Franklin D. Roosevelt, they have never invested a failed nominee with such authority again.[69]

The ensuing campaign was the most momentous one since 1896, although due to the rupture of the GOP, the outcome was never really in doubt. Wilson and TR quickly emerged as the leading contenders, and reformers through the rest of the twentieth century would echo their sweeping prescriptions for balancing economic growth and social welfare. Wilson's "New Freedom" translated the Bryanite rage against monopoly power into an optimistic brief for a stronger anti-trust act, lower tariffs, and a more elastic currency. TR countered with a forthright defense of regulating big businesses instead of breaking them up—and tacked on his support for such items on the wish list of left-wing unionists as a minimum wage and health insurance. Eugene Debs told big crowds that only working-class control of industry would make the United States a truly democratic nation. Taft gave a few speeches attacking Roosevelt but spent more time playing golf and anticipating a return to private life.[70]

For Bryan, the exciting race was something of an anticlimax. As Wilson prepared to wage his campaign, the previous Democratic standard-bearer peppered him with strategic advice, then spent the summer entertaining Chautauqua audiences with talk of Jesus and altruism. That fall, while Wilson spoke eloquently, if rather coldly, about the "New Freedom," Bryan barnstormed through the Plains and the West, where he needled TR for borrowing all his best ideas and phrases from Democrats. He all but ignored Taft, the man who'd humbled him four years before. In fact, the incumbent was so unpopular that in seven states he even got outpolled by Eugene Debs.

The predictability of the result was no less thrilling for Democrats who had despaired of ever occupying the White House again. Wilson won over four hundred electoral votes, with less than 42 percent of the popular tally. His party took more than two-thirds of the seats in the House and held its own in the Senate. But, absent a close contest, turnout of the electorate dipped below 60 percent—the first time that had occurred since before the Civil War.[71]

In four years, Bryan had shed his image as a habitual, if valiant, loser and emerged as the president-elect's most indispensable ally. The journalist Ray Stannard Baker, a Wilson devotee, later wrote about Bryan's actions in Bal-

timore, "Great Leadership consists in making issues so clear, so simple that
common men who do not think may vote as they feel."[72] Bryan would have
rejected the condescension in that statement. But about the primacy of sentiment, he most emphatically agreed.

Yet he'd established himself as the conscience of the party with behavior
that skirted the unethical. Bryan rejected Champ Clark for failing to echo
his hostility toward a delegation the Missourian felt he needed to gain victory. The Speaker was no reactionary. He endorsed most of the same
reforms as Wilson did and had already showed he could move some of them
through Congress. If Clark had been quicker to recognize the game Bryan
was playing in Baltimore, he would have won the nomination and probably
been elected president.

In this case, perhaps, the end did justify the means. Champ Clark was an
intelligent, if too trusting, politician who'd never expressed a vision beyond
the shibboleths of his partisan heritage. More than a party hack, he was
much less than a statesman. Wilson, in contrast, had a mind that took in the
whole world; with the aid of Bryan and his followers, his administration
would become the most progressive one in the Progressive era. To have
made that achievement possible was one of Bryan's more uncommon gifts to
the future.

CHAPTER NINE

Bryan's People

Hail to the fundamental man
Who brings a unifying plan
Not easily misunderstood
Chanting men toward brotherhood.

— Vachel Lindsay[1]

Certainly all historical experience confirms the truth that man would not
have attained the possible unless time and again he had reached out for the
impossible. But to do that a man must be a leader, and not only a leader but
a hero as well, in a very sober sense of the word.

— Max Weber[2]

ONE SPRING DAY in 1900, Philo S. Bennett, a tea and coffee wholesaler from New Haven, Connecticut, informed his wife that he was bequeathing $50,000 to William Jennings Bryan. "I am earnestly devoted to the political principles which Mr. Bryan advocates," he wrote to her, "and believe the welfare of the nation depends upon the triumph of those principles. As I am not as able as he to defend those principles with tongue and pen, and as his political work prevents the application of his time and talents to money making, I consider it a duty, as I find it a pleasure, to make this provision for his financial aid." Bennett would let Bryan decide whether to spend the money on himself and his family or to donate it "among educational and charitable institutions" of his choice.[3]

Like countless other Americans, the wealthy merchant had fallen for Bryan during the campaign of 1896. A Democratic elector from Connecticut, he briefly rode on the candidate's train and, after the defeat, advised him to mollify "part of the business element" in the East before facing the voters again. Bennett also gave him $3,000, a gift he repeated each year on Bryan's birthday. The two men corresponded frequently and dined together whenever possible. While he never came close to winning Connecticut's electoral votes, Bryan's ability to attract a man such as Bennett indicates his

circle of renown was not limited to the southern farmers and western miners who shared his grievances against the plutocrats of the urban East.[4]

Yet the admiration of a rich man was not free of peril. In 1903, after Bennett died in a stagecoach accident, his widow refused to honor the will.
Grace Bennett had learned that Bryan, with Mary's aide, had prepared at
Fairview the very document that left him a sizeable inheritance. Discover-
ing that her husband had also bequeathed $20,000 to his mistress in Man-
hattan only added to the widow's anger and resolve.

Bryan took her to court. He neither wanted nor needed the money, he
said, and intended to give it away. But Grace Bennett was defying the
explicit wishes of his good friend and benefactor, who had sat beside him
while he drew up the will.

After two years of trials and appeals, Bryan ended up with $30,000,
which he duly passed out to sixty-three different colleges to be used for
scholarships and prizes in public speaking. Despite its conclusion, the
drawn-out case convinced many critics that he was a sanctimonious fraud.
"A man who would rob a widow is not fit for any position," one man grumbled to Woodrow Wilson after the 1912 election.[5]

It is fitting that the only scandal in Bryan's career concerned the generosity of a follower. More than any other politician of his era, he depended
upon the wooing, care, and mobilization of his admirers. Tens of thousands
of them volunteered in his campaigns, convinced their friends and relatives
to subscribe to his newspaper, swelled the size of his audiences, argued with
his opponents, and fed a continual stream of tributes, advice, and consolation—in prose, poetry, and Scripture.

Any successful politician has to cultivate a durable band of supporters.
But Bryan, with his diligence and sunny nature, recruited a virtual army of
them. His brother Charles made sure that every letter received an answer,
even if just a pro forma one. And Bryan worked out a system to recall nearly
everyone "interesting or important" whom he met on his travels. "By
degrees, I have constructed within my memory a special storehouse for
names and faces," he told a reporter. "I concentrate my mind on him for an
instant at our first meeting, and thus get a tag with which I label my recollection of him...for future reference." As a result, many admirers considered themselves to be his friends. After his death, a political scientist mused,
"On a platform of amiability alone Bryan would perhaps have been elected
President."[6]

The mass of followers made it possible to sustain his image as a figure of
probity and independence through all the defeats, controversies, and steady
attacks that came from inside as well as outside his own party. Yet the qual-

ity of their devotion also helped Bryan's enemies to brand him the ringleader of yahoos, an irrational mob instead of a thoughtful following. Of course, they reciprocated the contempt. "Bryan's followers have to be fanatics to off-set the insane hatred of his opponents," observed Ellen Maury Slayden during the 1912 Democratic convention. A sober hero was a hard thing to be.[7]

How big was his peaceful army and who were its troops? It is impossible to give anything close to a precise answer. Bryan, according to a fellow politician, "had a personal acquaintance with more people...than any other man in the United States." The size of his correspondence and audiences seem to confirm that judgment. But no sociologist was handing out questionnaires to Chautauqua crowds on Bryan Day or to the knots of people who greeted his train at nearly every stop.[8]

Most of his correspondents did list their residence, however, and these tidbits of data suggest that, as a follower, Philo Bennett may not have been atypical at all. The bulk of Bryan's surviving mail was not dispatched from the redoubts of a vanishing, agrarian America. During the final days of the 1896 and 1900 campaigns, almost 70 percent of the letters and telegrams came from states that McKinley carried, most in the industrial East and upper Midwest, rather than from Bryan's electoral base in the South and the Rockies. What is more, inhabitants of big cities wrote as often to their hero as did those from the kind of small towns where he lectured inside the tents of summer. New Yorkers were the most numerous, followed by writers from Illinois and Pennsylvania. Due to their large populations, this trio of states naturally gave Bryan some of his largest vote totals, albeit in a losing cause. But it is remarkable how few admirers wrote to him from Texas and Georgia, the most populous states in a region where he received solid support from white voters and their local newspapers.[9]

Neither did Bryan's more articulate fans resemble the hard-bitten farmers and wage earners of populist lore. At the climax of the 1896 campaign, when praise of "the producing classes" sluiced through his rhetoric, those correspondents who mentioned their occupation were mostly small employers or professionals. Lawyers, doctors, teachers, and local merchants predominated. The definition of a "producer" was quite flexible: anyone who earned his or her living in a way that benefited society could qualify, while stockbrokers and other, less reputable, gamblers were among the few who did not. Outside the South, Bryan probably drew most of his electoral support from men who earned their bread with tools in hand or behind a plow. But the admirers who wrote to him most frequently spoke out for "the people" from the relatively advantaged perch of the propertied white middle class.[10]

The politics of this class has long been one of the fuzzier topics in the history of the Progressive Era. Decades ago, George Mowry and Richard Hofstadter argued that the reform impulse was most prevalent among middling Americans who feared that aggressive industrialists were destroying the old republic of small businesses and ethical individuals. "Progress," in their ironic reading, was the faith of an older middle class anxious to reestablish its social status. In contrast, later historians from Robert Wiebe to Michael McGerr emphasized the desire of progressives to apply scientific methods to their cities, workplaces, and governments; the old individualism posed an obstacle to this public-spirited quest.[11]

The dizzying variety of reformers and reforms makes it impossible to resolve the debate. The prohibitionist movement alone included priggish ministers, alcoholic socialists, efficiency-minded employers, altruistic feminists such as Jane Addams, and anti-corporate crusaders such as Bryan. To know that all these people identified themselves as members of a middle class eager for change is to know very little about them indeed.

Two compelling facts do, however, stand out from the views of those middling Americans who adopted Bryan as their leader. First, they felt a community of interest with fellow citizens who had fewer resources and less political influence. "I believe the people will appreciate the difference between the rich man's prosperity and the prosperity of the whole people," an editor from Detroit wrote to Bryan after the election of 1900. "If we are true to ourselves we shall win in the end."[12] Middle-class conservatives of the era longed to emulate the likes of Rockefeller and Morgan; the ability to rise ever higher in the new corporate order was what defined "progress" for them. But Bryanites, as that midwestern journalist's "we" suggested, shared with others on the left wing of progressivism what the Cross of Gold speech called "the Democratic idea," a politics that aimed to unite the working and middle classes against the irresponsible men at the top. "One of the primary tests of the mood of a society," Hofstadter observed, is "whether its comfortable people tend to identify, psychologically, with the power and achievements of the very successful or with the needs and sufferings of the underprivileged. In a large and striking measure, the Progressive agitations turned the human sympathies of the people downward rather than upward in the social scale."[13]

Of course, a democratic vision does not alone explain the personal motivations of the myriad individuals who wrote to Bryan. Most were, like him, Christians who held to a fervently pragmatic faith; it led them to judge politicians by their character and the moral content of their positions. Only a minority of correspondents stated which church they attended, if any. But their habit of quoting at length and with passion from the King James Bible left little doubt that most adhered to one or more of the evangelical Protestant bodies that dominated the religious landscape. His Catholic followers frequently identified themselves as such, perhaps to stress that all Americans who loved God were or, at least, should be equal members of Bryan's flock. "You and you alone," wrote an Irish American attorney from St. Paul, "have taught that our duty to the Republic comes next to our duty to the Almighty, and that it should be rendered just as sincerely, loyally and conscientiously."[14]

For grassroots loyalists from "enemy" states, support for Bryan often entailed a solidarity of loneliness. They wrote to give themselves, as well as him, the courage to fight on. Robert E. Campbell, the New Jersey minister who assured Bryan after the 1900 election, "You are a prophet-statesman, and you lost the presidency because you are," lived in a county where Bryan had twice failed to gain even 40 percent of the vote and where most Protestant clergy probably backed McKinley. For Campbell, the latest loss only underscored the secular power of evildoers; it would make the eventual triumph of Bryan's demands and principles all the sweeter. Campbell confessed, "I have almost been afraid to preach the Gospel ... during these past few months—the gospel of liberty, equality, and fraternity—lest some Church Pharisee sh'd accuse me of making a 'campaign argument in pulpit.' " Isolated in his region and profession, the minister took solace from his steady faith in "the servant of the People."[15]

In one significant way, Bryan's devotees did belong to the majority, albeit a diminishing one. Most were white Christians from "old stock" European roots: British, German, and Irish, with a sprinkling of Scandinavians. Arranged alphabetically, their surnames ring with a homogeneity that would have sounded quite "American" to citizens a century ago, even as it jarred with the polyglot masses who crowded into the neighborhoods and factories of New York, Chicago, and other metropolises. To recite a random sample of Bryanites from the middle of the alphabet: Hall, Hansen, Happel, Harding, Harvey, Havens, Hawkins, Hayes, Hazelwood, Higgs, Higginsbotham, Hilderbrandt, Hildreth, and Hitchcock.[16] Despite their ethnic origins, few followers mentioned the tide of new immigrants from eastern and southern Europe that began arriving in the 1880s. Even the anti-Catholic animus some Bryanites spewed out after his third defeat was directed more at the Irish, who had dominated the Church since antebellum days.

We will never know enough about the social history of Bryan's people, but the sheer repetitiveness of their devotion reveals something vital about why they chose him as their leader. Rather than a band of howling rebels, they portrayed themselves as reverent, law-abiding men and women who believed big business and venal public officials were staging a revolution against their democratic traditions, their livelihoods, and all that was moral and holy. In their romantic view, Bryan was the sole man of courage and principle left in American politics. Even William Howard Taft called him "the least of a liar I know in public life."[17]

Few admirers had any personal link to Bryan other than a handshake, a passing word, a memory of a speech, or a yellowing reply to an old letter. But most stayed loyal because he forcefully defended their common faith— in God and in the type of nation they wanted America to be. Even when he made political compromises, he was able to argue that they were necessary to realize higher goals. As with a fine preacher, it was the consistency of his ideals that mattered, not their originality. As long as Bryan's eloquence could command national attention, that was enough.

LETTERS TO BRYAN can offer only snapshots of his followers—a few emotional phrases and a current address, perhaps a job title, and then the individual vanishes. But a shifting corps of better-known figures, nearly all of them men, aided him in more practical ways. They publicized and echoed his opinions, defended him inside government and on the stump, looked out for his interests in their own states, or spun their esteem into art. Most had the independence of mind to challenge Bryan when they thought him fool-ish or mistaken. Still, he was able to count on them to propagate his views and uphold his reputation in the political world and the enveloping culture.

At the core of this group were Nebraskans who worked on *The Commoner*. Over its twenty-two years of publication, the paper had a remarkably low turnover of regular contributors. Part of the reason was that Bryan offered better wages than any other printer or publisher in the Lincoln area. His entire nonunion staff of about fifty also enjoyed paid holidays and a lavish summer picnic topped off by a baseball game, in which the boss usually played center field with great energy and occasional skill. But the editors and columnists on the paper had more ideological and personal reasons to stay on.[18]

First among them was Charles Wayland Bryan. Seven years younger than Will and his only surviving brother, Charles played a part equal to Mary's in handling his career and a more significant role in boosting his image. Campaign manager, lecture organizer, personal treasurer, and the man responsible for assembling every issue of the paper—Charles was a "dear brother" indeed. He began running for office himself in 1915 and was twice elected mayor of Lincoln and three times governor of Nebraska; in 1924, he ran for vice president on the Democratic ticket. Yet as long as Will was alive, Charles subordinated his ambition and outlook to his brother's and seems to have evinced no resentment at doing so.[19]

The younger sibling probably sensed that he could not have achieved so much on his own. An organizational dynamo, Charles almost completely lacked the qualities of personality that lifted his brother to fame and influence. He spoke too quickly and was often insensitive to listeners. He had little patience with assistants who didn't match his appetite for work, yet he often took credit for *their* good ideas. Charles shared with Will an "insistence that he was always right." But, unmixed with his elder brother's empathetic sweetness, his firmness just appeared as egotism. It didn't help that, due to a neurological ailment, Charles habitually covered his bald pate with a thick black skullcap. In photographs, unsmiling, he looks like an accountant who can't wait to get back to his ledgers.

Meanwhile, Charles tended to regard the moralism so vital to his brother's public image with the skepticism of a political operator. He frequently cursed, bet on horse races, and seldom attended religious services, although his wife was active in Lincoln's First Baptist Church. In the 1920s, he declined to endorse Will's crusade against the teaching of evolution. A good friend even told an interviewer that he believed Charles was an agnostic.[20]

No other major contributor to the Bryan family newspaper skimped on moral rigor. Richard L. Metcalfe first served as Will's ghostwriter during the politician's short stint as editor of the *Omaha World-Herald* in the mid-1890s. For much of the next quarter-century, Metcalfe edited and wrote for *The Commoner,* specializing in didactic stories about adherents to and violators of the Golden Rule, both public and private. "Men obtain the best from life when they cultivate those tender sentiments which cluster around the eternal truth: 'I am my brother's keeper,' " he wrote in a typical homily. A dedicated Social Gospeler, Metcalfe opposed capital punishment and was an ardent prohibitionist. Like nearly all of Bryan's associates who outlived him, he also became a reliable supporter of the New Deal.[21]

Superficially, a gentle piety also distinguished Helen Watts-McVey, the *Commoner*'s sole female columnist. Belonging to what a fellow staff member called "the grand army of useful women," she filled the "Home Department" with the same blend of the quotidian and the inspirational found in similar columns in daily and weekly papers all over America. A cake recipe and a method for dissolving spots followed a poem about Thanksgiving, which followed a bit of advice on how to discipline toddlers. On occasion, Watts-McVey included a dash of feminism—her salute to the surviving participants of the first Woman's Rights Convention, for example.[22]

But she was no happy homemaker just dabbling in journalism. By the time Watts-McVey joined *The Commoner* in 1902, she had already worked for forty years as a typesetter, proofreader, columnist, and devotional poet all over the Mississippi Valley—from a print shop near her birthplace in rural Wisconsin to a religious publishing house in St. Louis. Necessity as well as aptitude drove her peripatetic labors. All but one of Watts-McVey's brothers died in the Civil War, her husband went blind, and two of her children died of illness before they reached adulthood. Out of such painful experiences came verses whose tone was quite distinct from Bryan's boundless optimism: "Grieving and worn, discouraged / Sick of the day-long strife / Bruised by the restless tossing / Over the sea of life; / Hurt by the hands I trusted, / Yearning for rest and home, / Famishing, faint and doubting, / Unto the Book I come."[23]

A cliché-addled writer for *The Commoner* praised Watts-McVey for a "life of self-sacrifice ... filled with the joy that can only come through doing good for others." At least in late middle age her talents had finally earned her a decent wage and the attention of thousands of female readers. Bryan had good reason to be grateful to Watts-McVey as well. Her lengthy columns helped make his paper seem the creation of a like-minded community and not simply that of a crusading politician and his disciples.[24]

Equally vital to that community was the class-conscious viewpoint of Will Maupin, a former Republican who switched parties during the campaign of 1896. Into a weekly column entitled "Whether Common or Not," the typographer and journalist threw anything he thought would make plebeian Democrats look good and their many opponents—particularly the pompous, "trustified" ones—look silly. He made room for doggerel about Rockefeller and J. P. Morgan, contemporary lyrics to old nursery rhymes ("Mary had a little lamb; / Its fleece was white as snow, / And worth a very pretty price— / The tariff made it so"), dialect satires of standpat politicians, and general musings about the foibles of the rich.[25]

Maupin also found time to become a leader in Nebraska's bourgeoning labor movement. From his base in the printer's union, he published *The Wageworker,* a weekly digest of news about strikes, organizing, and politics. In 1909, he helped form the Nebraska Federation of Labor and served as its first president. Maupin clearly viewed himself as the local voice of the workingman, and this often lent his critiques in *The Commoner* a more acerbic tone than Bryan allowed himself. Soon after the Democratic sweep of 1910, the union columnist offered Champ Clark a sharp lesson in the inequities of class:

> If I should be compelled to swipe a side of bacon and a sack of flour to keep my wife and babies from starving, I'd get about three years at hard labor in the penitentiary. In a county jail in my state are three millionaries serving six months each for stealing thirty or forty thousand acres of the public domain, and they have telephones and soft carpets and books and floor in their cells, and a Jap chef cooks and serves their meals. Doggone it, Mr. Clark, that sort o' thing don't strike me as being on the level, and I'm hoping you'll find some way of fixing it up.[26]

Such bitterness didn't prevent Maupin from feeling comfortable with his boss's evangelical convictions. The son of a minister in the Disciples of Christ, he sprinkled his columns with one-liners such as "Satan works overtime when he sees a church closed for the summer vacation" and "Some people become so interested in theology that they lose sight of salvation." The same Christian publishing house where Watts-McVey had worked issued a collection of his writings. Maupin criticized Bryan for dividing Nebraska Democrats over the issue of prohibition; the dispute jeopardized the labor leader's chances for state office. But he defended Bryan's switch to Wilson at the Baltimore convention and stayed loyal to the man he called "the biggest single force in America."[27] For Maupin, as for the other members of the *Commoner* circle, Will Bryan was too kind an employer and too indispensable a leader to exchange for uncertain substitutes.

PROGRESSIVE DEMOCRATS elsewhere in the nation had a more complicated relationship to the godly hero. They admired his courage in the 1896 race and again in 1900 and took his side in duels within the party and in the country as a whole. Not since Abraham Lincoln had so many politicians showed such devotion to a fellow practitioner; Bryan seemed the savior of the Democracy after the debacle into which Grover Cleveland had steered it, with his stubborn eyes wide open.

After the Nebraskan's third defeat, however, a distinction arose between Democratic pols whose support for Bryan was more strategic and those who kept echoing the reverence found in the letters from ordinary citizens. The practical sort deserted to other leaders—particularly Champ Clark and Woodrow Wilson—who had a chance to win. In contrast, the true believers, although capable of tacking with the political winds, were a more pious bunch, anxious that any compromise not be undertaken for the sake of electoral victory alone. Like Bryan, they consistently spoke a language of personal as well as collective morality—and earnestly advocated prohibition and woman suffrage, even though a majority of Democrats opposed them.

"We don't want any politics in our religion," Joseph Folk told a Chautauqua audience in 1906, when he was the governor of Missouri, "but we want all the religion we can get in our politics." That messianic creed alienated many Democrats in St. Louis, his state's largest city, where Catholics were both numerous and politically powerful. For enforcing Sunday closing laws against bars and closing gambling houses, Folk got ridiculed as "Holy Joe." He never won another political office. But Folk and other loyal Bryanites were part of a Protestant left that helped to bury the old Democracy of laissez-faire Bourbons and urban bosses and joined the coalition that rode to victory with Woodrow Wilson.[28]

Such pietistic Democrats didn't challenge *all* their party's inherited beliefs. Whether from North or South, most clung to a faith in the supremacy of both white people and Protestantism. As the reactions of some Bryanites after the election of 1908 showed, such views could lead to bitterness and paranoia. But few other Democrats directly challenged their cultural intolerance, so most stayed within the party long enough to celebrate its return to power in 1912.

Among the most loyal of Bryan's supporters were refugees from the Populist movement, whose meteoric history had done much to shape his early career. The third party splintered after the campaign of 1896 and was never again a serious factor in national elections. In southwestern and mountain states, thousands of "Pops" followed erstwhile Bryan campaigner Eugene Debs into the new Socialist Party. Meanwhile, a rump of stalwarts, dreaming of resurrection, kept the People's Party alive behind Tom Watson and Ignatius Donnelly. But to most activists who had followed the Populist standard, it was Bryan who now embodied the battle against "the money power" and its political vassals. Putting their faith in a live leader rather than a moribund movement, they became Democrats without abandoning their old dream of class equality.

The most prominent member of this group was James Baird Weaver, who had drawn over a million votes as the Populist candidate for president in 1892. Weaver, a strikingly handsome man with the soul of an evangelist, had zigzagged nomadically through the mayhem of nineteenth-century politics. He switched parties several times and helped create two new ones in a restless search for a producers' democracy. Born in 1833, he was first a teenage Jacksonian; then a hatred of slavery drew him to the newly minted Republicans. During the Civil War, he fought bravely in an Iowa company and advanced in rank from lieutenant to brigadier general. When the killing stopped, Weaver, like many other retired Union officers, went into politics. But his harsh attacks on Iowa's railroads and liquor dealers failed to win him the GOP nomination for governor in 1875; his opponents also spread the rumor that he detested immigrants.

The defeat seemed to liberate Weaver's political imagination. Soon, he was condemning both major parties as captives of plutocracy. In 1878, he won a seat in Congress on the Greenback-Labor ticket. "We have reached a juncture in the history of the country," he told his fellow radicals. "The people must decide, must decide quickly, whether this is to degenerate into a European aristocracy." In 1880, Weaver stumped from Arkansas to Maine as the Greenback-Labor candidate for president and won a respectable total of 350,000 votes. In the South, he campaigned among both black and white workers, risking racist assaults at many stops. When the People's Party emerged a decade later, the seasoned veteran of two kinds of civil conflicts was a natural choice to lead it into battle.[29]

But the urgency of saving the nation mattered more to Weaver than organizational purity. He worried, with good reason, that the Populists might divide the anti-corporate armies and hand power back to the GOP. "Synthesis—not division—is the order of God and of common sense," he wrote to Bryan in 1894. Two years later, Weaver helped convince the People's Party to nominate his new Democratic friend for president, and he never looked back.[30]

After half a century in politics, the Iowa warrior had finally found a leader to replace Old Hickory. Weaver thrilled to hear the younger man eloquently defend issues he'd long championed, such as free silver and anti-imperialism. More than that, the old insurgent, a fervent Methodist and prohibitionist, felt a divine hand was guiding Bryan's work. "Since 1896 I have believed that you are commissioned of Heaven to lead in the herculean task to which you are devoting your life," he wrote after the loss in 1900. Weaver despaired that his nation could be delivered from "an elective monarchy" that "ravage[d] and devastate[d]" the Philippines. But until his death in 1912, he routinely dispatched notes of advice and encouragement to "the loftiest democratic leader that ever lived," the only man he believed might be up to the job.[31]

The aging radical was not always content to follow Bryan's lead. After the election of 1908, Weaver, having lost so many battles on which he thought the nation's future depended, let spill the religious bigotry that may always have curdled inside his faith. In a letter to Bryan, he named the members of the vicious cabal he believed had beaten the Democrat yet again. One would have thought the concert of "Liquor forces," "trust and monopoly magnates," and "practically the entire press" sufficient to explain the outcome of the race. But Weaver also fingered a minority group he called "a mighty factor especially in New York." In his troubled fantasy, Jews had given nearly all their votes to Taft because the Republican candidate, a Unitarian, also denied "the Divinity of Our Lord." In so doing, wrote Weaver, "they crucified Him afresh." Thus did one of Bryan's oldest supporters voice the ugliest flaw of populists throughout the Western world.[32]

Weaver's Iowa was a bastion of the GOP, which probably added to his crankiness and despair. But down South, Bryanism was a popular persuasion. Most whites resented and envied the power and wealth of the urban-industrial establishment, and Bryan played to such sentiments whenever he visited the region. Political moderates such as Oscar Underwood disliked Bryan's taste for self-aggrandizing class rhetoric; after 1908, Dixie Democrats also hungered for a candidate who could not just flay their enemies but could win. But the hero of outsiders never lost the esteem of the many southerners able to juggle their grievances—economic, racial, and cultural—with their optimism about the future of that fragile entity known as the New South.

Bryan's key ally and oldest friend in the region was Josephus Daniels of North Carolina. During his sixty years in politics, Daniels stretched the definition of "southern Democrat" almost to the breaking point. He began, in the 1880s, as a sympathizer of the Farmers' Alliance, then served in Grover Cleveland's Interior Department, returned to North Carolina to run a pro-Bryan daily newspaper, abetted a vicious drive to terrorize black voters, became a key aide in the 1908 and 1912 presidential campaigns, was a reform-minded navy secretary in Wilson's cabinet (with the young FDR as his deputy), and was a vocal anti-imperialist as ambassador to Mexico during the New Deal. Finally, at the 1944 Democratic convention, Daniels defended Vice President Henry Wallace against urban bosses who got the pro-Soviet liberal kicked off the ticket. It was a career that defied conventional notions of "right" and "left" while making the North Carolinian useful to every successive leader of his party.[33]

Through all these changes, Daniels remained loyal to his first political hero, who had "stirred . . . the fountains in the hearts of men." Like everyone else, he was initially struck by the power of Bryan's oratory, first in Congress and then at the 1896 convention. Almost half a century later, Daniels could still evoke the thrill of hearing this "young David with his sling, who had come to slay the giants that oppressed the people." Bryan's character seemed as virtuous as his politics: "Clean of limb, clean of heart, and clean of mind, he was a vital figure." Daniels always felt the loss in 1896 was due to "every method known to political chicanery," rather than to a shortage of votes.[34]

If Weaver adored Bryan as a son, Daniels came to love him as a brother. Born just two years apart, they disagreed about certain issues, from the peace treaty with Spain to the fight against teaching Darwinism in public schools. But they trusted each other's judgment about fellow politicians, and their families were close. Bryan and Daniels even dressed alike; they often wore the same string ties, pleated linen shirts, and old-fashioned frock coats. In the early 1890s, each was sometimes mistaken for the other. As Daniels aged, he grew into the very image of a populist Democrat, with a crinkly grin, graying mop of strawlike consistency, ungainly nose, and grizzled chin.[35]

A romantic temperament matched his look. Like Bryan, Daniels believed himself to be locked in perpetual battle with a "moneyed aristocracy" whose predatory ways mocked the ideals both of Jefferson and the Bible. He also tried to lead an exemplary personal life. Daniels taught Sunday school and preached sermons at his Methodist church; at official dinners both in Washington and Mexico City, he served grape juice and mineral water instead of wine. These traits contrasted sharply with the behavior of the irreligious elite. "He kept an almost mystic faith in the people themselves," recalled Daniels's son. "Strength was in them even when their stirring was imperceptible."[36]

In one critical episode of his career, Daniels deployed that "strength" to advance a repugnant cause that Bryan tried to evade. In the fall of 1898, he used his *Raleigh News and Observer*, which he owned and edited, to make propaganda for a race war. "The Negroes Shall Not Longer Rule North Carolina," declared the paper, which had the highest circulation in the state. Black voters were still quite numerous, particularly in eastern counties along the Atlantic. Democrats feared they might tip the upcoming election to a Populist-Republican alliance. Daniels and his fellow party leaders considered this an outrage that called for decisive action. The *News and Observer* accordingly circulated tales of black beasts pushing themselves on white ladies and challenged white men to protect the honor of their womenfolk and the "great Anglo-Saxon" race. In November, the Democrats easily swept to victory.[37]

But that was not enough for their more fanatical partisans in the city of Wilmington, two-thirds of whose residents were black. A few days after their victory, hundreds of white men stormed through the streets, burning down black-owned businesses and attacking any black man unable to hide or escape. The rioters killed at least twenty-five people and destroyed black political influence in the city for generations to come. Daniels, in his retrospective account of the "white supremacy" campaign, blamed the violence on Alex Manley, a black newspaper editor who had the temerity to suggest that some white women actually sought out sexual partners across the color line. Writing in 1966, Daniels's biographer awkwardly tried to explain it away: "Negroes were far less advanced then they were later to become."[38]

For Daniels and many of his readers, the erotic anxieties that burst into violence intermingled with a class-conscious dread similar to that which Bryan stoked. In the summer of 1898, the *News and Observer* ran a series of cartoons that depicted the growing black middle class of urban North Carolina as the symbolic ally of Mark Hanna. In one illustration, a brawny fist labeled "honest white man" thrusts toward a black man in fancy clothes and diamond jewelry. In another, a black man in spats walks over a white figure dressed in overalls. The caption asks, "A Serious Question—How long will this last?" The answer for Daniels, as for many southern populists, would be measured in decades.[39]

Yet their virulent and persistent racism cannot be reduced to a simple matter of sexual jealousy any more than it can be explained away as a consequence of economic competition. The same Josephus Daniels who claimed upstart black Republicans were a threat to ordinary white Americans would later blast corporations for profiteering during World War I, cheer Franklin D. Roosevelt's court-packing plan in the late 1930s, and condemn "warmongers" in the 1940s who thought conflict with the USSR was inevitable. Daniels's image of "the people" as white, hardworking, and exploited allowed him to demonize anyone who bruised their sensibilities or deprived them of the power they deserved. In his old age, those same beliefs were capable of fueling left-wing sympathies that largely ignored the multi-ethnic nature of the new people who underpinned FDR's new liberal coalition. Daniels's unbending faith could be remarkably supple when time altered the nature of both his friends and his enemies.[40]

POLITICIANS HELPED give Bryan the opportunity to run for president, but his appeal was most enduring among moralistic, middle-class Protestants who hoped to free normal politics from the grip of opportunists, liars, and thieves. The Lincoln post office filled up with tributes from clerks and grocers, ministers and doctors; at first, they praised the young orator because he was unafraid to take on the big money men who held interest rates and prices in their firm, if somewhat mysterious, grip. But soon these small businessmen and independent professionals were attributing to Bryan qualities beyond those of a mere silver-tongued protestor.

Here was a self-made hero who cared as much about upholding the Ten Commandments and the Sermon on the Mount as about exposing the crimes of bankers or the perils of empire. In fact, he believed each task essential to the other. Bryan's small-town, pietist background was similar to theirs; in their passion for him, they imagined a better future—of economic independence and collective morality—for Americans like themselves. They were, in a word, egalitarian modernizers with little use for the culture of modernism.

Take Charles N. Davis, who was born in 1849 to a cursing, saloon-crawling boatman on the Erie Canal who nevertheless raised his child to be a "Christian gentleman." His father's dual spirit guided Charles's life in the small towns of eastern Nebraska and the middle-sized county seat of Chillicothe, Missouri, where he made his money and raised a family. The worldly Davis parlayed a shrewd grasp of markets and horseflesh into several successful businesses, including a box factory and a string of prize thoroughbreds. He became a big man in a thoroughly provincial setting. Meanwhile, the reverent Davis prayed at least four times a day and published, with his own money, a series of Anti-Saloon League weeklies that few people read. Davis allowed himself just one vice forbidden by his church—betting on horse races. Unlike cigars or Sunday baseball, he considered wagering at the track "simply a matter of using your knowledge and judgment to direct a business investment."[41]

Davis met Bryan in 1888, when they toiled together in the futile effort to elect J. Sterling Morton to Congress. After hearing "a dozen words" of Bryan's rhetoric, Davis was convinced that God had chosen the young attorney to be a future president. While that prophecy gradually faded, his hero worship continued to bloom. "Only one greater and purer man ever lived on the face of this earth," Davis was fond of saying, "and *He* never trod American soil."[42]

His son recalled Bryan's visit to Chillicothe during the campaign of 1900. It was almost as if the Messiah had gotten off his train to find an audience and a bed for the night. Clyde Brion Davis, who was just six at the time, remembered his mother and sister scrubbing their house to a perfect sheen and preparing a banquet of unprecedented size and quality. The boy understood nothing of Bryan's speech but was "swept along on the waves of that caressing, crooning, booming, mellifluous voice." Writing fifty years later,

Clyde disdained his father's mania for free silver and Christian fundamentals. Yet the presence of Bryan still cast a spell: "There was a godlike dignity about him and you could tell just by looking at him that he wasn't made of ordinary flesh and blood. Anyone could have told that if he only saw Mr. Bryan in a grocery store buying a pound of salt pork to cook with beans and didn't know who he was."[43]

Chillicothe was not a hotbed of populist insurgency. The manufacturing town of twenty thousand residents, most of them native-born Protestants, anchored a swing district in a state Democrats had traditionally carried. Bryan took the county easily in 1896 but barely carried it in 1900 and lost it narrowly eight years later. Alton Parker did only slightly worse.[44]

But the closeness of the results may only have intensified Charles Davis's determination to spread the gospel of the Great Commoner to his business associates and neighbors. Davis's creedal passion rivaled Bryan's, yet it gained him no tangible rewards. His journalistic advocacy of a dry America ate up his profits, and he spent the remainder of his life in a region that had entered a gentle but certain decline. Davis grew despondent about the fate of a nation filled with consumers of frivolous novels and lager beer. Late in middle age, he evidently thought about writing a book "presenting to the world his philosophy of life and giving mankind the key to a harmonious, Christian existence without sin, crime, or poverty." But it never happened.[45]

The zealot of Chillicothe belonged to a rural middle class whose confidence and fortunes were waning, but Bryan boosters could also thrive in more dynamic locations. The Dallas surgeon Charles McDaniel Rosser is a case in point. Rosser met Bryan in 1895 and helped him gain the support of Texas Democrats at the Chicago convention the following year. A day before the election, Rosser brashly predicted, "No matter what may be the result tomorrow you will be greater than any other man since Christ." After Bryan's death, he published an adoring biography, *The Crusading Commoner*, with a foreword by Josephus Daniels. Showing a poor grasp of military tactics, Rosser compared Bryan to a "great general" who "in the march of human progress was much in advance of the more slowly moving multitude."[46]

Fortunately, Rosser's medical and organizational skills were superior to his literary ones. At the start of his career in the 1890s, he conducted operations in his own home, using only the barest rudiments of antiseptic technique. Rosser then helped shove his profession into the modern, standardized era as Dallas grew into the Southwest's biggest city. While building a lucrative practice and conducting research, he established the first medical school in town. He also served as president of the Texas Medical Association, where he led a drive to expose the errors of chiropractors and other "medical cults." When the hospital unveiled Rosser's oil portrait in 1937, a colleague lauded him in terms not often associated with medical science: "He is a man of uncompromising integrity, and if necessary, would become a martyr for his ideals." The temperament of a Bryanite had served the doctor well.[47]

In Denver, a young lawyer also began nearly half a century of civic activism by hitching his star to a Bryan campaign. Wayne C. Williams attended the 1908 Democratic convention, held in his hometown, and that fall helped the nominee win Colorado's electoral votes. Then Williams, an active Methodist, entered local politics. He led a losing effort by the Anti-Saloon League to limit liquor licenses in town. In 1912, he won a county judgeship, the first of many judicial offices he would hold almost continually in his fast-growing state through the end of World War II. A staunch Social Gospeler, Williams saw no contradiction between fighting both for prohibition and the rights of labor unions. A "truly self-conscious nation," he wrote, would "react in universal sympathy to any wrong done to any citizen anywhere." Williams also found time to write *two* hagiographic biographies of his hero, one published before and one after Bryan's death.[48]

In this admirer from the Rockies, one can glimpse what Bryan may have become if he'd lacked a talent for fine oratory and a keen grasp of the political moment. As he prepared to run for the U.S. Senate in 1923, Williams assured his mentor that "the Drys and Labor are almost united behind me." It was time, thought the idealistic lawyer, to rise beyond his local setting. But Williams failed to win the nomination and had to be satisfied with the post of state attorney general. Still, he was a delegate to every Democratic convention from Bryan to Truman and was a respected figure in Denver politics until his death in 1953. Without such careers of service to church, party, and region, liberalism could not have bridged the transition from the crusade for free silver to the battle for the free world. Most of Bryan's followers—for all their big, entrepreneurial dreams—had to make the best of staying close to home.[49]

THE ROMANCE of Bryanism attracted few serious novelists or poets to his cause. *The Leader,* Mary Dillon's pat fable, quickly fell into oblivion. So did the many rough satires about his enemies and tributes to his greatness that Bryan received from disciples.

After the 1912 Democratic convention, a school superintendent from Ohio hailed "The Commoner in Battle": "Alone he stands, and with courageous step / He beards the money lions in their den; / With herculean strength, he flings to earth / The power of greed and gold." These were merely acts of propaganda set to verse, and even *The Commoner* seldom published them.[50]

Bryan's own taste ran to social and spiritual melodrama, to writers whose "work has aided in the upbuilding of a people's nation and contributed to the general welfare." His favorite novelists were Dickens and Hugo. Other than the Bible, the piece of writing he quoted most frequently was an 1815 poem, "To a Waterfowl," by William Cullen Bryant, which his father also loved. In alternating rhymes, the eight stanzas compare a migrating bird to a soul's ascent to Heaven: "He who, from zone to zone, / Guides through the boundless sky thy certain flight, / In the long way that I must tread alone, / Will lead my steps aright."[51]

Millions of Americans knew the poem from their McGuffey's Readers, but its cozy romanticism clashed with the creators of a new realism in prose and verse. Hamlin Garland, Theodore Dreiser, Jack London, Carl Sandburg, Willa Cather, and Edgar Lee Masters increasingly regarded Bryan's faith in a virtuous people and their inerrant Book as naive and quaint. He seemed to embody a time, a place, and system of beliefs that had been appreciated too much and dissected too little. As Cather wrote in 1900, Bryan was much like the Middle West in "its newness and vigor, its magnitude and monotony, its richness and lack of variety,... its high seriousness and self-confidence, its egotism and its nobility."[52]

One event in Bryan's career transcended such ambiguities. For many realists, the campaign of 1896 had been a galvanic event, particularly in the memory of budding artists raised in his own region. For several unrepeatable months that year, the melodramatic seemed quite real. It poured from the crowds who gathered to jeer goldbugs or "Popocrats" and screamed from headlines about "anarchy" or "the money power." Masters hailed Bryan, a fellow son of Illinois, for having "loosened a current of morality which has flowed to the refreshment of a nation; and is one of the curatives of that awful canker of the soul." In his novel *The Titan*, Dreiser, who grew up in a series of Indiana towns, described financiers repulsed by "the vast mass, writing in ignorance and poverty," which had "turned with pathetic fury to the cure-all of a political leader in the West." Willa Cather wrote a story about two prosperous businessmen in a "little wooden town" on the Plains whose political differences, before 1896, had not kept them from being close friends. But after "the most exciting presidential campaign people could remember," they had a vicious quarrel and never spoke again. A few days after the election itself, an eleven-year-old boy from a Philadelphia suburb penned a wistful limerick and got it published, anonymously, in his small-town weekly. Wrote Ezra Pound:

> *There was a young man from the West,*
> *He did what he could, for what he thought best;*
> *But election came round;*
> *He found himself downed,*
> *And the papers will tell you the rest.*[53]

But such writers, being natural skeptics, could not long remain sympathetic to any politician. Most were "village rebels" who escaped to big cities, where they wrote bitter elegies for the places they had left behind, which a bustling modern nation increasingly devalued. In his *Spoon River Anthology,* Masters used a metaphorical graveyard to depict the range of characters who made the small towns of central Illinois venal, squalid, prey to utopian visions as well as spasms of violence, and impossible to rip from memory. "The cooper should know about tubs. / But I learned about life as well," declares a Spoon River craftsman from inside his tomb. "Taboos and rules and appearances are the staves of your tub. / Break them and dispel the witchcraft of thinking your tub is life!" In 1892, the future poet fled north from his own village of Lewistown to practice law in Chicago.[54]

Masters remained a Bryan admirer longer than did most of his fellow realists, in part because the two men became friends. Thanks to his father, a delegate, he heard the Cross of Gold speech from a seat in the gallery of the Coliseum; it evoked for Masters the utopian visions of Milton, of Thomas More, and of Shelley. "A new life had come to me as well as to the Democracy," he later wrote. Masters spent the fall of 1896 campaigning for Bryan and repeated the exercise four years later. Then he organized the Jefferson Club to make sure his chosen leader's opinions would gain a hearing among Chicago reformers. In 1906, Masters and his wife sailed home with the Bryans from Europe at the end of the latter's well-publicized trip around the world.[55]

Disenchantment, however, was slowly replacing adoration. After the 1908 election, Masters gently scolded Bryan for giving high-minded speeches. "I hold that . . . the mere impulse of righteousness never has carried a party to power in this country," wrote the attorney, who had entered a legal partnership with the blunt-speaking Clarence Darrow. "Back of every political victory has stood a hungry or a greedy stomach." Four years later, the two men quarreled over Bryan's endorsement of Woodrow Wilson, whom Masters considered an elitist Hamiltonian in populist disguise. "If I were a Presbyterian, I would understand that a man can have a change of heart," Bryan told his friend. " 'Not at fifty-six,' I retorted." When Bryan failed to secure for Masters a coveted federal judgeship or even to congratulate him on the appearance of *Spoon River,* the poet curtly ended their friendship.[56]

In 1916, Masters issued a final verdict, in blank verse, about his former hero. "The Cocked Hat" begins as a satire of Woodrow Wilson's infamous letter to Joline but soon ambles into an attack on Bryan's godly self-image. Public piety, the poet suggests, was the last refuge of a loser. Assuming the voice of a worker in debt, one of the "six millions" who rallied to Bryan in 1896, Masters snaps that the candidate "got the money that he went after, / And he has a place in history, perhaps—Because we took the blow and fell down / When the ripping ball went wild on the alley." Bryan's Chautauqua sermons were, for Masters, craven retreats from the electoral barricades, an attempt to prove he was "24-carat religious" and bore no trace of anarchism in his soul. So "he wasn't a radical" after all, Masters decided. "Why, a radical stands for freedom, / And for truth—which he never finds / But always looks for. / A radical is not a moralist."[57]

Just one major American writer kept refreshing his memories of 1896 and never rejected their creator. As a teenager during that campaign, Vachel Lindsay, standing "by my best girl ... with wise and laughing eyes," heard Bryan address a crowd in his hometown of Springfield, Illinois. Almost a quarter-century later, he wrote one of his best poems—an affair of 250 lines—that glorifies the speaker, describes the terms of the battle, and mourns a loss that saddened the poet as much as it did the politician:

> *I brag and chant of Bryan, Bryan, Bryan*
> *Candidate for president who sketched a silver Zion,*
> *The one American Poet who could sing outdoors,*
> *He brought in tides of wonder, of unprecedented splendor,*
> *Wild roses from the plains, that made hearts tender ...*
> *Election night at midnight:*
> *Boy Bryan's defeat.*
> *Defeat of western silver.*
> *Defeat of the wheat.*
> *Victory of letterfiles*
> *And plutocrats in miles*
> *With dollar signs upon their coats,*
> *Diamond watchchains on their vests*
> *And spats on their feet ...*

Defeat of tornadoes by the poison vats supreme.
Defeat of my boyhood, defeat of my dream.[58]

Lindsay did not remain a follower. As an adult, he turned to socialism and voted for Eugene Debs in 1908 instead of his childhood idol. He wrote other poems that placed Lincoln, Altgeld, Theodore Roosevelt, Jane Addams, and Tolstoy on adjoining pedestals. And although Lindsay never repudiated his evangelical Protestant background, his only novel, published in 1920, glimmers with pagan dreams about amaranth trees that magically prepare one for the afterlife.[59]

Still, the poet stayed attracted to the one politician whose lyrical impulse and extroverted style resembled his own. Unlike many of his artistic contemporaries, Lindsay was a flamboyant romantic. For six full years, he made a living on the roads of middle America preaching his "Gospel of Beauty." With eyes closed in rapture and one hand tracing the air, Lindsay performed his poems for Chautauqua audiences and at both vaudeville shows and revival meetings. He walked from town to town, accepting food from strangers but refusing alcohol; he was a supporter of the Anti-Saloon League. One evening in 1915, Lindsay saluted Bryan at a party they both attended in Washington, D.C. The politician read a poem about peace, and Lindsay followed with another tribute in verse, entitled "When Bryan Speaks." Unfortunately, the man with "the strange composite voice" that could chase away "the ancient tyrant powers" had to take a telephone call and missed all or most of Lindsay's performance.[60]

THESE INDIVIDUAL sketches suggest that Bryan's people led quite dissimilar lives—unless one puts too much weight on the ethnic and religious heritage they shared, at the time, with most Americans. A wealthy, adulterous merchant such as Philo Bennett and an evangelical unionist such as Will Maupin, a frustrated rural crusader such as Charles Davis and an adaptable southern pol such as Josephus Daniels, a clutch of writers dazzled by the moral drama of a great campaign, and tens of thousands of citizens who wrote to Bryan as if to their best friend or minister: it is hard to find one shared meaning in their collective regard for the Commoner. Some admired him for adhering, under fire, to what they defined as Democratic principles, others for expressing a piety that went beyond politics, others for performing so well in a role he had invented for himself and would never relinquish to others.

An emotional bond of such tenacity seldom has a single explanation. It is striking that Bryan's middle-class followers spent little time railing against the trusts; their letters and memoirs include few specific protests against a big business that injured their dignity or threatened their economic independence. Far more salient was their desire for a moral alternative to the corporate order as a whole. Bryan was the symbol in flesh of that quixotic possibility. His critics scored him as the anti-intellectual chieftain of a rabble of know-nothing followers. But Bryan's people didn't lack ideas; they simply preferred they be wrapped in passionate conviction. To expect the citizens of a mass democracy to choose a leader as if they were electing the president of a learned society is to make a serious and rather undemocratic mistake. As the political scientist Charles Edward Merriam wrote in 1924, "What [Bryan's] enemies could not understand was that the people are as much interested in knowing about their leader's heart as in knowing about his head, and that sympathy no less than intelligence plays its part in the great process of popular control."[61]

CHAPTER TEN

Moralist at State, 1913–1915

I believe there will be no war while I am Secretary of State, and I believe there will be no war so long as I live. I hope we have seen the last great war.

—William Jennings Bryan, May 1913[1]

The wilderness is becoming populated in the Bad Lands of dead men who don't know they are dead. They talked themselves into greatness and, not knowing when to stop, also talked themselves out of it.

—Walter Hines Page, U.S. ambassador to Great Britain, June 1915[2]

IT WAS A FINE DAY to be a Democrat. On an uncommonly mild fourth of March in 1913, Woodrow Wilson took the oath of office before over a hundred thousand spectators massed around the north side of the Capitol. The largest crowd in the history of presidential inaugurations was on hand to witness a political sea change. For the first time in two decades, Wilson's party controlled both elected branches of the federal government. In contrast to the Cleveland era, most Democrats seemed eager to use their power to rein in big business and aid the white wage earners and small property owners who had elected them. "Men's hearts wait upon us; men's lives hang in the balance; men's hopes call upon us to say what we will do," declared the new president, confident in his eloquence even though, without loudspeakers, most of the audience could not make out what he was saying.[3]

Bryan gloried in the occasion. The last time a Democrat sat in the White House, he'd been a young congressman at odds with the leader of his own party. Now, nearing his fifty-third birthday, he had returned to Washington as the designated secretary of state and was sitting directly behind Wilson on the speaker's platform. Mary shared his enthusiasm; after years of keeping house in Nebraska for an absentee celebrity, she could now become one of the premier hostesses in the land. The couple had just rented Calumet

Place, a mansion on Thirteenth Street, NW, with Doric columns and a huge sunporch. It was about the size of Fairview and ideal for entertaining.[4]

When the new president finished his brief address, clusters of Democrats called out, "Bryan! Bryan!" urging the three-time nominee to make a speech of his own. But the object of their affection got up from his seat and, according to his daughter Grace, "wave[d] the crowd into silence." Wilson quickly turned around to clasp Bryan's hand and that of Taft, his predecessor. For a few moments, the three men stood together in the pale sunlight, a tableau of conservative prudence giving way to the evangelism of reform.[5]

It may seem surprising that Wilson chose Bryan to be his secretary of state, a position demanding restraint in speech and self-discipline in action. Few officeholders or journalists thought it odd at the time. Bryan had traveled the world more widely and more recently than Wilson. Precedent was also in his favor. The job had often gone to party leaders, men experienced at running a convention instead of negotiating with foreign officials. Henry Clay and Martin Van Buren, Daniel Webster and William Seward, James Blaine and Elihu Root: each was a renowned, fiercely partisan politician before he became America's chief diplomat. Soon after the 1912 election, scores of Bryan's loyalists clamored for him to be appointed, and most Democratic newspaper editors and Wilson advisers agreed. When he took office, even Grace Bennett cast off her bitterness to congratulate him.[6]

The post certainly did not require an extraordinary administrator. On the eve of World War I, the State Department resembled a bustling campaign office more than a modern bureaucracy. Bryan supervised only 157 employees in Washington and an additional 400 in embassies and consulates abroad. The department's annual budget was a little over $5 million, less than 1 percent of all federal expenditures. The modest size enabled the secretary to apply his well-honed personal touch. Whenever possible, he sought to hire "deserving Democrats," many of whom were longtime supporters—although Wilson insisted on naming most of his key subordinates and ambassadors to all the major European nations. In addition to his other duties, Bryan was able to read most messages that came into his department from elsewhere in the government and from diplomatic posts around the world. He even found time to keep an eighty-three-year-old watchman at the department, who was frequently absent, from losing his job.[7]

The appointment served Wilson's political needs. For the first time in his national career, Bryan would have to do another man's bidding. A run for the White House in 1916 was thus out of the question. At the same time, he would play a large part in deciding what Wilson could achieve as president. Bryan was expected to use his influence with the Democratic majority in

Congress to help convert the New Freedom from rhetoric into law. His attacks on opponents would now become defenses of the administration. As Mr. Dooley remarked, "Beyond all his other charms, with a brick in his hand he's as expert as a rifleman. An' I'd rather have him close to me bosom thin on me back."[8]

Beyond such practical matters, Bryan and Wilson shared a broad view of how the United States should act in the world. Both men were devout Presbyterians with a fondness for messianic gestures. Both abhorred Taft's "dollar diplomacy"—which deemed U.S. overseas investment essential to prosperity and stable government. Instead, Wilson and Bryan preached that only self-governing republics imbued with Christian ethics could avoid war and become dependable allies.

The president did take a stern, Calvinist approach to religion and politics that contrasted with Bryan's sunny, romantic one. Wilson stressed the need to do one's "duty" before God, seldom doubted that millions were on the road to hell, and disliked emotional preaching—whether from the pulpit or the stump. Confident that "God ordained that I should be the next President of the United States," he had to hide his scorn for men who didn't match his intellect or share his mission.[9]

But when Wilson stated his purposes abroad, it was often difficult to tell which of the two men had written the text. "It is a spiritual union which we seek," the president told an audience in Alabama about his policy toward Latin America. He added, "It is a very perilous thing to determine the foreign policy of a nation in the terms of material interest. It not only is unfair to those with whom you are dealing, but it is degrading on the part of your own actions."[10]

Ideological affinity helps explain why Wilson so readily accepted Bryan's two conditions for taking the job. The apostle of Tolstoy first asked for an endorsement of his ambitious plan to prevent war. Bryan proposed that the United States sign bilateral treaties with other nations in which each side would agreed to submit any quarrel to an investigative tribunal and begin no conflict for at least a full year after doing so.

He had conceived of the idea soon after meeting the Russian sage in 1903 and had been talking it up since then, at gatherings both in the United States and in Europe. Several peace activists since the late nineteenth century had floated similar plans for a "cooling-off period," but Bryan was the first to advocate putting *all* disputes on the table—including ones concerning vital national interests. In 1907, at an Arbitration and Peace Congress attended by prominent businessmen, ministers, and politicians, Bryan declared, to loud applause, "I am glad that [this meeting] has the courage to record itself on this proposition, that the killing of human beings shall not be commenced by any nation until the world knows what crime has been committed that requires so high a penalty."[11]

The treaties bespoke his abundant confidence that well-meaning Christians could transform the world into a polite, even brotherly place. In the sunset of Victorian optimism, in matters of the spirit as well as science, Bryan was among the most sanguine of all. Emerson once mused that "the power of love, as the basis of a State, has never been tried." Bryan, at least, would make a start. He told his brother the peace treaties would be "my monument. It is worth being Secretary to get a chance to negotiate them."[12]

A month after taking office, the plan won Senate approval. That summer, the first treaty was signed, with tiny El Salvador; twenty-nine others soon followed. The signers included every major nation in Europe except, ominously, Germany and Austria-Hungary. The grateful secretary presented each partner with a miniature plowshare of his own design. On it was inscribed the familiar quote from Isaiah 2:4 and the motto "Nothing is final between friends."[13]

Bryan's second request of Wilson proved more controversial, although it entailed just a slight change in diplomatic convention. The lifelong teetotaler asked if the president "would regard the exclusion of intoxicating liquors from our table as an insurmountable objection to my assuming the duties of the office." Wilson replied that he and Mary could do as they wished. Bryan did not bring up the issue of prohibition, which he knew Wilson opposed. This was merely a personal preference, not part of the anti-liquor movement. At the first State Department function the Bryans hosted, a farewell luncheon for British envoy (and author) James Bryce, the only libations served were grape juice and spring water. According to Mary, the Russian ambassador confessed "he had not tasted water for years" but "had taken his claret before he came and so all was well."[14]

But as the Bryans surely expected, dry activists from all over the globe made the political connection themselves. Thousands wrote to praise what one South African called "a great step of assistance to the Temperance Cause...on an occasion so auspicious." In fact, Will received so many similar messages that his private secretary had to draft a form letter of thanks to those who applauded what his boss insisted was "merely maintaining a family custom." If nothing else, the crush of mail demonstrated that Bryan was off to a good start in an office he'd never expected to hold.[15]

The honeymoon was brief. By the summer of 1913, Bryan's old antagonists in the eastern press were attacking nearly everything he did that drew public notice: his style of entertaining, his hiring preferences, and his off-the-job speeches. Only his dealings with Congress on domestic matters, most of which he conducted in private, escaped censure. Soon Bryan's troubles expanded into the realm of foreign policy. Blundering U.S. interventions in Mexico and the Caribbean violated his quasi-pacifist convictions. Then the onset of World War I made his peace treaties seem irrelevant, even ridiculous. Opposed to favoring any side in the mounting slaughter, Bryan faced a dilemma he could resolve only by leaving his post.

His twenty-seven months in Wilson's cabinet marked a decisive turn downward in Bryan's career. After his defeat in 1908, he still retained a huge following, one he deployed to humble old enemies within the party and to help lift a new friend into the White House. But when he became secretary of state, a Republican daily predicted that Bryan had "made a greater mistake in so far as [his] comfort and political power are concerned" than had the man who appointed him. Executive power placed a number of land mines before his heroic self-image, and several would explode in his face.[16]

Bryan attempted to hold the moral high ground while serving as secretary of state. He gave up none of his prior commitments—to evangelism, to prohibition, to economic reform, or to world peace. But he was no longer a free or independent agent, and his attempt to merge crusading with governing probably confused and irritated more Americans than it pleased. Bryan's tenure in the highest appointive office in the land, which presented a great opportunity to do good in the world, instead began his political decline.

HIS TROUBLES STARTED with the challenge he posed, inadvertently, to the capital's upper class. During the preceding two decades of GOP rule, Americans with inherited wealth had built lavish second or third homes in the District and nearby suburbs, where they walled off their country clubs and salons from all but about a thousand other families. As the federal government took on new powers, at home and in its overseas empire, Washington became a prime location for those whose riches and status could buy them influence. An English journalist who visited the city during Theodore Roosevelt's administration commented that D.C.'s high society was like a small patch of "exquisite embroidery overweighted by a fringe that is neither small nor exquisite." The inner circle was so select it left nine-tenths of the senators and their wives out in the cold. A similar hauteur led First Lady Nellie Taft to outfit White House footmen in livery, lest her guests confuse one another for servants.[17]

Woodrow Wilson signaled his distaste for such customs in a few undramatic ways. He held no inaugural ball and refused to golf at the Chevy

Chase Club, where nearly all the bluebloods played. Yet the president did not stock his cabinet with controversial figures. Aside from Bryan, its most prominent member was William Gibbs McAdoo at Treasury. McAdoo had made a fortune in New York when he directed the herculean task of building tunnels under the Hudson River between New Jersey and Manhattan. Although Georgia-born, he was on familiar terms with Wall Street investors and others of their class. Most of the other new department heads were provincial men of whom Washington high society knew little and cared less. William B. Wilson, the first secretary of labor, was also the first unionist to sit in a cabinet. But he seldom made policy or headlines.

Only Josephus Daniels at Navy, with his prohibitionist views and strident anti-corporate rhetoric, seemed eager to ruffle the established order. "I faced suddenly the Plutocracy about which my father and Bryan talked," his eleven-year-old son, Jonathan, thought as he gazed at the private "palaces" that stretched along the broad avenues north of the Capitol. To his father, Washington was a "Babylon which needed to be cleansed and chastened."[18]

But it was the secretary of state who most riled the sensibilities of the local gentry and their allies in the GOP, the press, and the diplomatic corps. Although a true foreign policy establishment had yet to congeal, Bryan's immediate predecessors—John Hay, Elihu Root, and Philander Knox— were elegant men with close ties to large corporations and a reputation for cultured discretion. It was disagreeable to gaze instead on the Commoner, with his relentless piety and folksy manner. "W. J. Bryan," scolded a London paper after the first grape juice dinner, "not only suffers for his principles and mortifies his flesh ... but he insists that others should suffer and be mortified." Other dailies scoffed that the secretary didn't always shave before coming to work and, on humid days, took off his jacket and fanned himself at his desk.[19]

Fresh mockery spewed forth after stories that Bryan spent most of his time finding diplomatic jobs for longtime followers from the South and West. The secretary had a great many other responsibilities. But he wanted to reward faithful Democrats, not all of whom were loyal to him, in hopes of bolstering the party's future prospects. "We have been quite short of prefixes ... Secretary so-and-so; Ambassador so-and-so, and Minister so-and-so," he reminded Wilson, suggesting the appointment of at least one man from every state the Democrats had carried in 1912. Bryan did manage to offer a minor consulate in Central America to Charles N. Davis, his aging disciple from rural Missouri. Ill at sixty-four, the struggling businessman looked up the dusty location in an atlas, then turned the post down.[20]

Civil service, for all its merits, had upper-class origins. It had been pressed by mugwumps in the Gilded Age who disdained the calculus of loyalty on which strong parties relied. They and their progeny viewed Bryan—with his baggy pants, his growing paunch, and his heavy perspiration—as the worst kind of hack, one who clothed his greed for power in virtuous intentions. This line of attack continued throughout his time in the cabinet, although fellow Democrats pointed out that patronage, even in the foreign service, was hardly a novel idea.

But that first spring in office, Bryan made a serious error. In late May, he announced that he would soon be taking off on the Chautauqua circuit. This irked Americans beyond the ranks of the GOP and Washington's monied elite. The problem was not solely the secretary's desire to resume his accustomed place alongside brass bands, jugglers, and comedians as if he were still a private citizen. It was Bryan's claim that he *needed* the lecture fees; he simply could not entertain foreign diplomats in an appropriate manner on a salary of $12,000 a year. Official banquets were indeed an onerous expense, one reason why wealth had usually been a qualification for the top post at state. However, compared to the earnings of most Americans, Bryan's pay was quite lavish, and regular newspaper readers knew he had made a comfortable living before joining the cabinet.

His return to the tents thus elicited a large and negative response, much of it tongue-in-cheek. Republican lawmakers and most of the eastern press smothered him in loud, if predictable, scorn. Expecting more respect for his office, Bryan refused to answer most queries from reporters—a marked change for one of the more loquacious of public men—and this only goaded his critics further. George Harvey, a former Wilson enthusiast who had deserted to the GOP, told readers of his *North American Review* that Bryan was absent from the capital for almost one of every four days he'd been in office. "It is a happy circumstance," needled Harvey, "that attention to official duties has not impaired a pleasure which had become habitual."[21]

Some Democrats made fun of Bryan too. One party loyalist sent Wilson a dollar bill with the hope that others might emulate him and keep the good secretary off the road. The ubiquitous Mr. Dooley—who often voiced opinions shared by his fellow Irish Catholics—commented that Bryan needed a long rest after "a fine season." "He's goin' to change his act nex' year an' play his lecture on a piccolo while suspinded from a thrapeze. Th' British Minister called on him th' other day an' discovered him practicin' a handspring."[22]

Throughout his career, Bryan had drawn ridicule from those who considered his public speaking an exercise in bathos and demagoguery. The disrespect seldom damaged his standing as a candidate or performer; rank-and-file Democrats and many others thrilled to hear his resonant baritone spinning out bracing, if familiar, sentiments against plutocrats and for Christ. Moreover, Harvey's specific charge was unfair; his count of absences included Bryan's many unpaid speeches in 1913 as well as his Chautauqua appearances. Harvey also ignored the fact that the secretary had skipped only seven working days during the entire year. If Bryan had taken the one-month vacation that federal rules allowed, he would have been away much longer.[23]

It was a painful irony. The kind of speeches that had made Bryan a hero to millions of Americans now left him vulnerable and defensive. Writing in *The Commoner,* he likened himself to Antaeus, the wrestler in Greek mythology who renewed his prowess whenever he touched the ground: "So the man in public life must keep in contact with the people if he would be strong; only when he allowed himself to be separated from them can he be overcome." If, in the service of democracy, one appeared on the same stage trod by vaudevillians, so be it. Bryan failed to grasp that most citizens expected a top cabinet official to conduct himself in a more dignified fashion—to treat his membership in the republic's inner court as all the compensation one needed. The Olympian first president had struck that pose, and most of George Washington's successors and top aides had emulated him. Bryan broke with the tradition, and he never lived it down.[24]

Wilson did not join the chorus of critics. The president was no admirer of Bryan's mind or executive abilities. But he knew that most of the detractors sided with the GOP and were out to discredit the entire administration as a mess of "spoilsmen." Wilson was not going to abandon a subordinate who had so many allies in Congress and around the nation. So he lauded Bryan's "character, his justice, his sincerity, his transparent integrity," and "his Christian principle." Despite his chilly demeanor, Wilson knew how to flatter a man whose personality was almost the opposite of his own.[25]

THE HARM DONE to Bryan's image did not prevent him from doing his job, and part of that job was helping to make policy at home. Many Democrats in Congress, particularly those from the agrarian South and West, had begun their careers as his disciples. In the spring of 1913, they celebrated with him the ratification of constitutional changes Bryan had been advocating since the 1890s—the Sixteenth Amendment, providing for an income tax, and the Seventeenth, for the popular election of senators. In his joy, Bryan proposed a new amendment that would make it easier to enact others in the future. Why not alter Article Five to allow a simple majority in Congress and of state legislatures to change the Constitution?[26]

But his immediate task was to flesh out the assault on corporate wealth, to turn the Democrats' new power into a boon for the majority of American voters who either earned wages or owned a farm or other small business. What ensued was the greatest rush of reform legislation in U.S. history until the New Deal, one inspired by Bryan's speeches and the party platforms he'd been drafting since 1896.

During his first year in office, he worked, mostly behind the scenes, to help craft new laws on taxes, banking, and trusts. These matters—vital to any developing economy—had been at the heart of his politics since he'd thrilled Congress with speeches against high tariffs and for coining silver. Twenty years later, Bryan hadn't given up his ideal of a republic liberated from the rule of big money. But as a pillar of the administration, he was willing to compromise with men who had once been his intraparty enemies. In the summer of 1913, Bryan and Charles scaled *The Commoner* down from a weekly into a monthly publication and filled its columns with long defenses of government policy, often signed by cabinet officers themselves. The message was clear: his kind of Democrats needed to back up their fulsome rhetoric of protest with results, if they hoped to retain the mantle of progress and keep governing the nation.

They first resolved to lift the tax burden off ordinary consumers and begin to place it on the backs of the richest Americans. The activist president, with a disciplined party caucus behind him, vowed to slash tariffs, the one goal leading Democrats had shared since Grover Cleveland ran for president a quarter-century before. By the time Wilson took office, reformers in both parties viewed high rates as a hidden subsidy to large manufacturers, "class legislation" for a class that neither deserved nor needed the extra help. So Congress was able to pass a historic cut of 26 percent in tariffs on finished goods and, despite the grumblings of some farmers, to eliminate the duties on wool and many other raw materials.[27]

But there was no agreement that a progressive tax on incomes and corporations should make up the difference. Following Jefferson, Democrats had traditionally viewed government as a necessary evil and sought to starve it of revenue. Wilson, despite having moved left on some issues, still subscribed to that part of the old credo. Bryan and his allies in Congress believed the state did more for the wealthy than anyone else—eminent domain for railroads and an army to police the Filipinos being prime examples—and should pay for their privileges. But eastern Republicans were appalled that "these people want to . . . take away the money of the rich and then to pass laws distributing it among their people at home," as Elihu Root, now a senator from New York, complained. Meanwhile, GOP progressives tried to split Democratic ranks by proposing much higher levies than a majority of Congress could support.[28]

So Bryanite Democrats who favored a real tax had to settle for a largely symbolic one. Cordell Hull, a young congressman from Tennessee who would later become FDR's secretary of state, crafted a bill that set the highest rate at a mere 7 percent for individuals and a flat 1 percent for corporations. Firms could also deduct a long list of expenses. No tax would be collected on the first $3,000 of personal income, which meant that most American families would pay nothing at all. Unhappy radical Democrats crowded into Calumet Place, "eager for a sign" of Bryan's opinion. After making sure the president would back him up, Bryan urged his brethren to vote for the measure. A modest redress of economic grievances did result. Andrew Carnegie and John D. Rockefeller each had to dole out a sum in the six figures, while thriving residents of the big industrial states from New York to Illinois supplied most of the revenues.[29]

If Bryan declined to take a hard line on taxes, he did not hesitate to pressure Wilson about how to transform the American banking system. Unlike the income tax, prominent lawmakers from both parties recognized the need to overhaul the laissez-faire, crazy-quilt way that money was created and interest rates determined. Private "national" banks were still in charge of issuing currency and loaning it out, in blithe disregard of the panics that resulted every few years—the latest in 1907—from such unpredictability. Everyone familiar with the problem favored some kind of regulated coordination between banks. A National Monetary Commission, led by Senator Nelson Aldrich, had recently published an exhaustive study in twenty-three volumes. But who would drive the engine of monetary stability—financiers or the state?

The president opposed placing all power in the hands of a central bank, as Aldrich desired, although he would allow bankers essentially to police themselves. Soon after taking office, Wilson supported the idea of creating as many as twenty reserve banks around the country, with a board sitting in Washington to supervise the system. Hoping to avoid rekindling the monetary passions of the 1890s, the president kept his plan from leaking out beyond his closest advisers, while Congress preoccupied itself with lowering the tariff. True to his conservative background, Wilson assumed that the concentration of financial power rather than private control was his fellow

Democrats' main fear, as it had been when Jefferson fought the First Bank of the United States and Jackson vetoed renewal of the Second.

But the party platform on which Wilson had run declared, "Banks exist for the accommodation of the public, and not for the control of business." To Bryan and the Democrats who had supported him through years of strife, the meaning of those words was clear. The administration might not be able to drive the money changers of Wall Street completely out of the temple of the republic. But it should *never* allow them to retain control of the currency. "The government alone should issue money," Bryan told Wilson when they met in the White House in mid-May. If the president did not change his mind, the secretary would lose his "only political asset"—trust in his word and his character. Then resignation, Bryan hinted, would be his only option.[30]

It was a clever move, based on a deep-seated conviction. Bryan had always insisted that only federal power could humble the "money trust"; while he no longer championed free silver, he still suspected that big creditors boosted their profits by keeping small businesses in debt. His challenge to Wilson was made in private. But as with the denunciations of Wall Street that headlined the Baltimore convention, Bryan correctly judged that the balance of political forces was tilting in his favor.

In mid-June, Louis Brandeis backed up his hunch. The brilliant lawyer, who had stiffened Wilson's attitude toward trusts during the 1912 campaign, came to Washington to warn the president that "concessions to the big business interests must in the end prove futile." McAdoo at Treasury and a slew of Democratic lawmakers agreed. Less than two weeks later, Wilson sent to Congress the Federal Reserve Act, largely written by Senator Robert Owen of Oklahoma, which put the U.S. government in charge of issuing money and regulating the banks. The president, not private financiers, would appoint governors to run the system.[31]

Bryan had achieved his main goal, but, as with most significant pieces of legislation, the devil lurked in the details. As the bill moved slowly through Congress, leading bankers and their conservative allies in the Senate labored to weaken or defeat what the *New York Sun* called "this preposterous offspring of ignorance and unreason...covered all over with the slime of Bryanism." At the same time, a group of insurgent House Democrats from the South and West, supported by Brandeis and the American Federation of Labor, saw a chance to free the financial system once and for all from the grip of the "money trust." Infused with the spirit of 1896, they demanded that the Federal Reserve Board include farmers and workers, loan money to states for public works, and forbid executives from serving as directors of multiple banks. As a consequence of what one historian calls "insanely complicated struggles" that lasted almost six months, the entire bill was in jeopardy.[32]

In the midst of it all, Bryan decided to act like a statesman. In late August, he wrote a public letter declaring his support for the president's bank bill and opposing every radical amendment. He even had to swallow a provision sustaining the gold standard, lest wavering lawmakers think government control of the currency would signal a resumption of the old battle. His stance pleased neither plutocrats nor populists. The latter screamed betrayal, while Aldrich accused the administration of seeking "to revive the greenback heresy" and complained that the bill was "certainly a great triumph for Mr. Bryan." But the Democrats held their discipline. In December, Congress passed the most sweeping change in financial policy since the demise of the Second Bank of the United States, eighty years before.[33]

With the advantage of hindsight, one can see that Bryan was more naive than his radical critics. His sunny moralism led him to assume that bankers and standpat politicians would retreat before the new order; now that the government controlled the money supply, a vigilant citizenry would never let the "money trust" grab it back.

But democratic form does not dictate executive function. During House debate on the bill, Oscar Callaway—an obscure congressman from Nip-and-Tuck, Texas—foresaw the future better than the Commoner he'd once revered. "You may have such faith and confidence" in a reform-minded Democratic president, warned Callaway, "that you are willing to put such power in his hands, with an absolute faith that he will never abuse or misuse it." But, "When he is gone the control of the board becomes the greatest prize.... You can safely count on the bankers not overlooking anything that is to their interest." What seemed like a historic victory for "the people" ended up giving legitimacy to figures such as Paul Volcker and Alan Greenspan, who tended to believe that what was good for Wall Street was good for America.[34]

Bryan played a smaller role in crafting a tough new law to regulate the trusts. In 1914, when Congress was debating the measure that became the Clayton Anti-Trust Act, he was preoccupied with a civil war in Mexico and the outbreak of hostilities in Europe. He did, however, find time to encourage the southern Democrats, led by Henry Clayton of Alabama, who wrote the bill and spearheaded its passage. Every party platform Bryan had helped to write promised to rid the nation of monopoly power vested in interlocking directorates, the manipulation of stock markets, and injunctions against union activity. But Wilson and some northern Democrats balked at punitive measures they feared would injure commerce. So Bryan helped persuade his followers to accept language that seemed to protect labor's right to strike and boycott peacefully. Shelving his mistrust for bureaucratic remedies, he also supported the creation of the Federal Trade Commission, to be a watchdog over the trusts instead of a club to destroy them.[35]

Bryan played no direct part in the most shameful decision the administration made during its first year in office, segregating most of the federal government. In 1912, W. E. B. Du Bois and fellow black activists in the North had supported Wilson, hoping his vague promises of "absolute fair dealing," even "sympathy" with their cause might lead him to challenge the bigoted legacy of his party. Instead, the president, whose beloved father had been a stalwart Confederate, behaved like a typical Democrat from Dixie. He allowed his postmaster general and secretary of the Treasury, both raised in the South, to restrict the numerous black workers in their employ to menial jobs or to fire them altogether. To avoid future "race-mixing," each federal job seeker was required to submit a photograph with their application. Bryan's own department had few if any black employees, but he sat in cabinet meetings where the policy was discussed and apparently raised no objection. Jim Crow measures had never bothered him before, and despite rising black protests, he saw no good reason—political or moral—to question them now.[36]

In one small way, Bryan did hint at a certain discomfort with white supremacy. Buried in a miscellaneous section of his papers is a handwritten "Poem on Colored Man" that he roughed out while secretary of state and may never have completed. Awkward and sentimental, the forty-six lines strain to reconcile the fact of Jim Crow with the purposes of a loving God. The most remarkable thing about the poem is that it is written in the voice of a black man: "Father, tis not my fault that I am black," begins the confessional verse. Bryan continues with a reference to the "curse of Ham," the tale from Genesis about Noah's disrespectful son that generations of racists used to justify holding Africans in bondage: "If this dark robe is but the stain / That sin has left upon my race / It was a sin remote / And I have paid the penalty in full / With toil and tears."[37]

The poem does not applaud segregation, but the poet seems to accept it as divine will. Since "Thou didst adorn with different hue / the violet the lily and the rose / Instead of mingling all the colors / In a rainbow flower," there must be a similar reason why "Thou madst the races separate and distinct." How can the humble narrator question His motives? One must instead develop "the strength within." "Teach me to love my brother as myself / To feel that growing for his betterment that proves a kinship with the Father of us all." After "a life of willing service," the black man "may win" his place in heaven.

With this mawkish verse, Bryan may have been attempting to still a mind troubled by hypocrisy. Forced segregation posed a blatant contradiction between his vision of social equality and the assault on black rights he abetted by ignoring it. To tell an oppressed people to find solace in helping others was not as patronizing as it sounds. Bryan thought "service" the highest calling for every Christian, regardless of race. But, nestled within a surrender to Jim Crow, his advice was an unwitting display of bad faith.

A SIMILAR MYOPIA afflicted how Wilson and Bryan treated the nations of the Caribbean basin. Both men rejected any desire to take colonies or seek material plunder. They sincerely hoped to guide America's southern neighbors to a peaceful, democratic, and Christian future. "We must show ourselves friends by comprehending their interest whether it squares with our interest or not," said the president. Today, this style of foreign policy is simply dubbed "Wilsonian." But Bryan, in his post at State and with his knack for giving sermons, voiced its messianic tones more frequently than did Wilson himself. "National ethics cannot differ from individual ethics," he preached. "As it is impossible for an individual to gain permanent advantage by doing injury to his fellows, so it is impossible for a nation to so isolate itself as to profit by another's downfall."[38]

On the wings of the Golden Rule, Bryan hoped to replace the region's violent past with a new order marked by amiability and self-determination. Thus, he persuaded most Latin countries to sign peace treaties with the United States and floated the idea of a hemispheric nonaggression pact. He also recommended, unsuccessfully, that his government give direct loans to cash-poor regimes so that they would no longer be in thrall to foreign investors. Such debts had often provoked European countries to threaten force in order to collect what their banks were owed. Bryan's "new gospel for the nations," as one American diplomat (and old political ally) called it, promised to rescue the peoples of warmer climes from their benighted pasts.[39]

But the grand mission turned into a series of embarrassing failures, in part because neither the president nor the secretary was able to curb the arrogance that lay behind it. They believed the United States had a duty to share the blessings of self-government with its neighbors. But altruistic motives did not make their creed less overbearing or more effective than the realpolitik they disdained. Architects of what one historian has called "the imperialism of idealism," they had little patience with the messy details of local politics or cultural distinctions. In their clumsy efforts to heal a sinful world, they shaped a mold for future disasters.[40]

Bryan assumed people who needed outside help would welcome American advice. When they resisted it, he reluctantly prescribed a dose of military force to change their minds. But violence, as Bryan had often pointed out, rarely solved deep-seated problems. In the Caribbean, U.S. arms only increased distrust of the Yankee overlord who spoke as a brother but behaved with the caprice of a tyrant.

Events in the Dominican Republic and Haiti, which share the same island, demonstrated the folly of his approach. In the fall of 1913, Bryan came to the defense of a Dominican president, José Bordas Valdez, whose efforts to stay in office beyond his provisional, single-year term had touched off a growing rebellion. The secretary got Wilson's approval to dispatch several navy vessels to the harbor of Santo Domingo, "for moral effect." Supplying Bryan with vital information was U.S. envoy James Sullivan, an erstwhile promoter of boxing matches with splendid political connections. Sullivan often told lies to boost the fortunes of Santo Domingo's biggest bank, whose directors were close to Bordas. Bryan gradually learned that he'd been fooled, and Sullivan had to resign in disgrace.

But, with U.S. artillery ready offshore, Bryan kept trying to convince Dominicans to lay down their guns and machetes and choose a "responsible and representative" government. Inevitably, every political faction tried to curry favor with him by promising to hold free elections. Inevitably, the secretary tacked from one leader to another, restating the virtues of democracy and warning that "no more revolutions will be permitted." After Bryan left office, Wilson abandoned the gentler approach altogether. U.S. Marines occupied the country in 1916 and ran it under a military command.[41]

The course of the American mission in Haiti resembled that in its island neighbor. For decades after black revolutionaries wrested their independence from France in 1803, southern slaveholders had persuaded a series of presidents to treat the tiny nation as a bad example that should be left to rot in squalor and anarchy. After the Civil War, U.S. policy began to change; diplomats urged the Haitian government to allow the United States to use the strategic port of Môle Saint-Nicolas for a naval base. But French and German investors were still more active in the chronically unstable nation than were their counterparts in the big republic to the North.

During Bryan's tenure, he repeated in Haiti the same mistakes he'd made on the other side of the island. This time, he put his trust not in the American minister but in Roger Farnham, a local railway and bank president who, despite his corporate ties, seemed to grasp the Haitians' psychology and to have their best interests at heart. Bryan also intervened sporadically, with bold statements and a show of naval power, to assist one would-be native leader after another. As in the Dominican Republic, he denied any intent to favor Mammon over man. "We shall give all legitimate assistance to American investors," he told the Haitians late in 1914, "but we are under obligation just as binding to protect Haiti, as far as our influence goes, from injustice and exploitation at the hands of Americans." "Protection," in the form of a U.S. military regime, arrived in July 1915. It lasted for almost twenty brutal years. "The Americans are enemies of despotism," observed a Haitian journalist, "and to prevent its return, they invaded the country."[42]

Bryan's statements about the mess in Haiti contained little of the syrupy idealism he had vainly sprinkled on the Dominicans. He doubted that the people of the largely unchurched black nation would do much to save themselves. The Haitian authorities, he advised Wilson, would "respect" a white American envoy more than one of their own race. After the marines took over, Bryan grumbled, "The Government of the United States is a better friend to them than the native chiefs, who have been little better than bandits in uniform."[43]

Yet he almost certainly did *not* utter an ignorant line about Haitians that an American banker later attributed to him: "Dear me, think of it! Niggers speaking French." Nowhere in his papers, it seems, did Bryan use the notorious epithet. On the rare occasions when he talked about race, he favored paternalism over the coarser mode of stereotyping—as his "Poem on Colored Man" illustrated. And it is quite unlikely that Bryan didn't know that the official language of Haiti was French. Before joining the cabinet, he had traveled to the Caribbean several times and written detailed articles about the culture of nearly every land he visited. In the end, one suspects he simply tired of the effort to reform such a poor and "backward" nation. Haiti was simply not important enough to U.S. interests, however defined, to sustain the uplifting enterprise, either in rhetoric or action.[44]

Mexico was quite a different matter. The first great revolution of the twentieth century had broken out there in 1910, and several armies were contesting for power in nearly every region between the Rio Grande and the jungles of Chiapas. Bryan's tenure at the State Department coincided with the most perilous and, ultimately, decisive period in the struggle. From the spring of 1913 to the summer of 1915, no legitimate state existed in Mexico. Every warring faction declared it would gain social justice for the impoverished majority; those led by the charismatic Emiliano Zapata in the south and the wily Pancho Villa in the north promised to break up big estates and distribute fields to the peasants. U.S. newspapers reported extensively on every turn in the conflict. With American private investments in the country reaching $600 million (compared with barely $4 million in Haiti) and refugees streaming north across the border, the Wilson administration inevitably played the role of a stern father plagued by bickering children.[45]

The faction that eventually triumphed—the Constitutionalists, led by the prosperous landowner Venustiano Carranza—was the least radical one; it made no move to expropriate American holdings. But in the meantime, Wilson and Bryan had stirred up a whirlwind of mistrust by trying, with diplomatic pressure and troops, to force the Mexican rebels to behave like good American progressives. In April 1914, they landed soldiers in the port of Veracruz to punish a leader who had killed his rival and insulted the Stars and Stripes; more than a hundred Mexicans and nineteen Americans died in the fighting. Later that year, they scolded Zapata for threatening to seize properties belonging to the Catholic Church. As a pillar of the old order, the Church was an inevitable target for an insurgency of the landless poor.[46]

Bryan strived to square this erratic policy with his larger ideals of reform. In mid-1913, he angered a group of wealthy Americans whose mines, ranches, and several family members had been placed in harm's way by the revolution. "You seem to be afraid that one of your steers will be killed and eaten by the Mexicans," he told them. The U.S. Army would not come to their aid. Later, Bryan made clear he preferred Villa over Carranza. Although the bandit-turned-general was barely literate and did not flinch from slaughtering his enemies, he was, in his way, a true Commoner. "His soldiers idolize him and he claims to have no ambition whatever except to see [land] reforms carried out," Bryan wrote to Wilson in August 1914. He was also glad to learn that Villa was a "teetotaler" and that the women in his family regularly attended church.[47]

None of this rescued U.S. policy makers from a frustrating denouement. Carranza's forces took Mexico City in the winter of 1915 and decimated Villa's army that spring. The victors were, to use the bloodless term, consolidating the revolution. But the United States refused to recognize their government. The unruly child still had a good deal to learn from his older neighbor to the north. "The Mexican leaders will certainly know," Bryan wrote to an American priest, "that in order to gain sympathy and moral support of America, Mexico must have . . . just land tenure, free schools, and true freedom of conscience and worship."[48] He thought his own country, with God-fearing progressives at the helm, was rapidly becoming a model of economic justice and ethical behavior. Yet neither sermons nor troops could persuade the rest of the world to follow its example.

IN THE SPRING of 1913, a photographer snapped a revealing image of Woodrow Wilson and his cabinet seated around a polished table in the White House. At the head of the table, the president looks off to the right, as if oblivious to the presence of the camera. All his appointees, save one, either face the lens or glance sideways toward their elected leader. The exception is Bryan. He occupies the center of the photo, taking up more space in the image than does Wilson himself. The secretary of state has swiveled his leather chair toward the president, on whom he fixes a level, solemn gaze.[49]

Such scrutiny was seldom in evidence during Bryan's first year in office. The two men rarely disagreed about what policies to follow abroad, and the secretary fought loyally for the legislative compromises Wilson asked of Democrats in Congress. In the fall of 1914, Bryan took a month's leave from his official duties to travel the rails, exhorting voters in the midterm election to keep his party in power.

Of course, the personal attacks never ceased. One Republican paper claimed, based on hostile hearsay, that Bryan demanded cash for his campaign speeches. "A great many Washingtonians," reported *Collier's*, "have practiced disapproving of Bryan until any little thing he may do causes them the most exquisite pain." The steady abuse was diminishing his status in the country at large. In mid-1914, readers of Hearst's *American Magazine*, asked to name "the Greatest Man in the United States," ranked Bryan only fifth, with fewer than half the votes cast for Wilson. Theodore Roosevelt finished first. But few imagined that the president would welcome a break with the man who was still the most popular and influential member of his official family.[50]

Wars have a way of upsetting the conventional wisdom. Bryan's shock and revulsion at the great bloodletting that commenced with the assassination of Archduke Francis Ferdinand in Sarajevo at the end of June 1914 made it impossible for him to remain a loyal subordinate. The "world-wide moral awakening" he'd hailed at Chautauquas the previous year had literally gone up in smoke. In sharp contrast to his stance in the Caribbean, Bryan stuck to his anti-militarist principles. There could be just one response, he believed, to a war he described a month after it began as "so horrible that no one can afford to take responsibility for continuing it a single hour." Americans must remain absolutely neutral, avoiding any step, even private loans, that would favor one belligerent power over its enemies. Armed with only its scruples, the administration would then be able to mediate an end to the killing.[51]

Woodrow Wilson was equally troubled by the mounting slaughter in Europe. In mid-August, at Bryan's urging, he asked Americans to be "impartial in thought as well as action." Reading history as a moral tale taught the president, according to his best biographer, that "nations as well as men transgressed the divine ordinances at their peril." Neutrality was the only sane option.[52]

But Wilson did not consistently take his own advice. He also thought it immoral to stifle commerce on the seas and to target civilian ships as if they were vessels of war. Nations, like individuals, had to preserve their honor. "There is such a thing as a man being too proud to fight," the president declared in May 1915. But Wilson regarded the German tactic of submarine warfare as a devious, dishonorable mode of combat. With the aid of his U-boats, the kaiser might also win the war. For Wilson, a great admirer of England's laws and institutions, that would be a great calamity. The only member of the cabinet who dissented from his view was the secretary of state.[53]

If he had not been in power, Bryan's hatred of the war might have aligned him with the American radicals who were waging a vigorous campaign to keep the United States from intervening. But he did not share the Marxian left's analysis or solution. For socialists and anarchists, the Great War was the natural spawn of materialist greed. Emma Goldman toured the nation, reviling the "international war supply trust who cares not a hang for patriotism, or for love of the people, but who uses both to incite war and to pocket millions...out of the terrible bargain." Eugene Debs scoffed, "Let the capitalists do their own fighting and furnish their corpses and there never will be another war on the face of the earth." Both looked forward to a proletarian uprising that would demolish the engines of death.[54]

Bryan also attacked businessmen who sought to profit from the bloodshed; he pleaded with Wilson to "make money a contraband of war." Yet his outrage was inspired by Jesus and Tolstoy, not Marx. Violence of any kind, he believed, was a sickness of the heart and soul. Thus, capital punishment was wrong because it "violate[d] the sacredness of human life," and armed conflict was immeasurably worse. Governments should teach citizens that "there is as much inspiration in a noble life as in an heroic death," he told a Baltimore audience gathered to mark the centennial of the "Star-Spangled

Banner." "Both sides," he wrote to Wilson, "seem to entertain the old idea that fear is the only basis upon which peace can rest." By offering to mediate peace, the president would prove himself to be the leader of a truly Christian nation. "If you will not consider it irreverent," he told his chief, "the Lord never had a better opportunity or reason than now to show His power."[55]

The perfect solution was ready at hand. Bryan proposed that the United States ask all the belligerents in this "causeless war" to sign one of his arbitration treaties and abide by it. Doggedly, he pressed his lofty plan on the president, on U.S. ambassadors to the warring nations, and on lecture audiences. Repeatedly, Wilson brushed him off, saying the time wasn't ripe or that the treaties were "impractical."

But Bryan kept up the struggle. A better prophet than diplomat, he argued that the awesome toll on peoples and nations eclipsed debates about the virtue of one side or the other. The world would enter a dark and dangerous era if the conflict didn't end soon. But his holy passion to turn dreadnoughts into plowshares could not persuade the mightiest military forces in history from attempting to annihilate each other. No sermon, however perceptive, could accomplish its end without a canny political strategy.

Bryan's defeat was a drama in three acts. The first and only hopeful act began with the onset of war and lasted through September 1914. As armies deployed across the Continent in early August, Bryan, by default, took charge of American foreign policy. On August 6, First Lady Ellen Axson Wilson died of kidney disease with her husband of almost three decades clutching her hand. The president slept little in the nights before her death; then he left the capital for a week of solitary mourning. In his absence, Bryan pressed to stop J. P. Morgan and Co. from loaning millions to Britain and France. He also refrained from denouncing either the German invasion of Belgium or the kaiser's charge that his enemies were using dumdum bullets, unusually destructive weapons outlawed by treaty in 1899. The United States, argued Bryan, had to remain agnostic on smaller matters in order to remain an honest broker for peace.[56]

For a short time, his wishes were in harmony with the president's designs. In September, Bryan pursued a hint dropped by the German ambassador, Count Johann von Bernstorff, that his government was open to a mediated peace. The kaiser's armies were surging forward on both the western and eastern fronts and might have ended the war largely on their own terms. On the fifteenth of the month, Bryan hosted a lavish ceremony at which he signed arbitration treaties with Britain, France, Spain, and China. He invited Mary to sit alongside the foreign envoys and made up the luncheon menus himself. The meal began with Neutrality Soup and ended with American Ice Cream, because "Diplomacy is the Art of Keeping Cool." Although Colonel Edward House, the president's closest adviser, warned against letting the "absolutely visionary" Bryan approach the crafty Europeans, Wilson saw no harm in trying.[57]

But such hopes rested on quicksand. Von Bernstorff had never cleared the peace feeler with his superiors in Berlin, and neither the British nor the French were willing to negotiate from weakness. In any case, matters of economy and allegiance were rapidly undermining Bryan's vow of strict neutrality. With no embargo in place, U.S. factories were churning out bullets, barbed wire, boots, and military vehicles for the Allies, who, thanks to the Royal Navy, dominated the North Atlantic. Flush with new jobs and higher wages, AFL unionists downplayed the anti-militarism that had long been part of labor's gospel. In October, when Bryan was away on the stump, Wilson suggested that American bankers might offer commercial credits rather than outright loans to the governments at war. The distinction fooled nobody, but Bryan lacked a legal basis to protest it. In February, he was delighted to accept a peace petition signed by 350,000 American children. But the pleasant ceremony on the steps of the State Department was his best moment all winter.[58]

Inside the administration, Bryan was increasingly becoming a party of one. Josephus Daniels sympathized with his good friend's views but had worked too hard and long to elect a Democratic president to risk a break with Wilson. The war news in U.S. papers came largely from British sources, convincing most readers that the Germans fought like savages, particularly when they invaded "brave little" Belgium. In London, U.S. ambassador Walter Hines Page, who despised Bryan, openly sided with the "struggle" to defend "English civilization" against "Prussian military autocracy" and privately mocked his superior's efforts to stay above the battle.[59]

Wilson told several friends that he hoped Bryan would soon resign. His old contempt for the man resurfaced in conversations about the political future. "If I run again for the Presidency," Wilson told a visitor early in January, "it will be only to keep Bryan out.... He would be ruinous to the country, ruinous to his own reputation." Behind his secretary's back, the president sent House to talk with ambassadors from the belligerent powers and vowed he'd force Bryan to step down if he insisted on going to Europe to wage peace. But House's sympathy for Great Britain was notorious, and he failed utterly.[60]

The erosion in Bryan's status prepared the way for the last act in his role as the diplomat who hated war. On March 28, exactly nine months after the assassination of Archduke Ferdinand, a U-boat patrolling the Irish Sea sank the *Falaba*, a small British steamer. Among the III dead was an American citizen, Leon Thrasher, a young mining engineer en route to a job on the Gold Coast of West Africa. It was the first time a submarine had torpedoed a passenger ship. The fact that Thrasher and others were on deck at the time seemed to confirm Allied propaganda about the shameful tactics of "the Huns." The American press reprinted outraged editorials from British newspapers, and Undersecretary Robert Lansing drafted a note damning the Germans for sinking ships without giving those on board a chance to escape.[61]

Bryan feared that U.S. neutrality might soon expire as well. So he took a stand he suspected that Wilson and perhaps even a majority of Americans would not support. Thrasher's death was a tragedy, Bryan acknowledged. But wasn't any American at fault "who takes passage upon a British vessel knowing that this method of warfare will be employed"? It was so urgent to preserve the chance to make peace that the secretary of state was willing to apologize for a heinous act of war. Echoing German charges, he added that the Royal Navy's blockade of enemy ports was an evil equal to, if not more serious than, U-boat attacks on passenger ships: "Why be shocked at the drowning of a few people if there is no objection to starving a nation?" Bryan urged Wilson to invite the belligerents to attend a peace conference under American auspices.[62]

At the end of April, the president thanked the secretary for voicing his passionate opinions—and soundly rejected them. He did, however, delay sending a protest to Germany. Then on May 7, a U-boat torpedoed the *Lusitania*, a huge British-owned passenger liner, just off the coast of Ireland. One hundred twenty-eight of the victims were American citizens.

Bryan's first response to this calamity was as heretical as ever: he blamed the British government. "I wonder if that ship carried munitions of war," he told Mary. "If she did carry them, it puts a different phase [*sic*] on the whole matter!" Later, it was revealed that six million rounds of ammunition in the ship's hold had sharply increased the death toll. But hardly anyone in the United States at the time, aside from German Americans, was in a mood to muckrake. Theodore Roosevelt fumed about this "act of piracy." The entire cabinet, save Bryan, agreed, as did all but two English-language dailies in the nation. Colonel House and Ambassador Page predicted the United States would be at war by summer.[63]

As in a Greek tragedy, Bryan embraced his own doom. Wilson was not ready to call the nation to arms; he knew most Americans had not yet translated their anger into a hunger for revenge. But to side with Bryan's position would have sparked a political rebellion, even if the president's heart had not been with Great Britain. So all that remained for the secretary of state was to accept defeat.

The final act began with a dispute about the proper language of protest. On May 11, Wilson read to the cabinet his draft of a harsh note to Germany demanding that it protect the lives and property of neutrals or abandon submarine warfare altogether. Bryan signed and transmitted the message, as requested. But he did so "with a heavy heart," telling the president it would please "the jingo element," unless equally strong words were hurled at Britain's blockade. He also suggested that Wilson warn Americans not to travel on the ships of warring nations. The president called that idea "both weak and futile." Within the administration, the only support for evenhand-edness came from Cone Johnson, the solicitor of the State Department and a veteran Bryanite from Texas.[64]

Bryan spent the rest of May seeking to halt what, to him, seemed a steady march to war. Hoping to spark a compromise, he fired off cables to the American embassy in Germany and met with Constantine Dumba, Aus-tria-Hungary's envoy to Washington. As a cabinet officer, Bryan could not publicly air his differences with Wilson. But they were no secret to reporters, and each day his influence over policy waned further.

The meeting with Dumba backfired in a pernicious way. German offi-cials reported, inaccurately, that Bryan had told their ally, "The *Lusitania* note ... is only intended as a sop to public opinion." The secretary protested the error. But his hunger for peace on almost any terms made it difficult to believe him. At the end of the month, the kaiser's government responded to Wilson's note: its submarine had acted "in self defense" by "destroying ammunition destined for the enemy." Surely the American authorities would agree once they were able to investigate the matter for themselves. The Germans regretted the loss of civilian lives, but U-boats would con-tinue to prowl the depths of the Atlantic. Speaking for most of the Ameri-can press, the *New York World* called the note "the answer of an outlaw who assumes no obligation toward society."[65]

Bryan realized that his chance to advance the cause of peace from within the government had failed. Full of anguish and unable to sleep, he made up his mind to quit. When the cabinet met on June 1, he "seemed to be labour-ing under a great strain," according to Agriculture Secretary David Hous-ton. Bryan "sat back in his chair most of the time with his eyes closed."

But he was quite awake when his colleagues objected to the idea of send-ing a protest to England for interfering "with our trade." Bryan snapped that they had always taken the side of the Allies. Wilson, in a rare show of temper, "sharply rebuked Bryan, saying that his remarks were unfair and unjust.... Each one was merely trying to be a good American." But this was no time, he said, to shift the subject away from Germany's awful deed. When the meeting adjourned, Bryan turned to Wilson and, in a voice others could not hear, told him he was planning to resign. The president exclaimed, "You must not do that! Stay and help keep us out of war!"[66]

As usual in his relations with Bryan, Wilson spoke from political necessity rather than conviction. To his fiancée, Edith Galt, the president confessed he feared "that strange man" could afflict the country with his "singular sort of moral blindness." Bryan's resignation must appear to be a rash decision made against the earnest objection of his chief. So, for the next week, Wilson made a show of consulting him about what he should say in a second note to Germany and listened politely as Bryan begged him to avoid phrases that would jeopardize neutrality. On June 5, Wilson sent the State Department the draft of another strong protest, appending his "hope" that "you will think a little better of it," along with his "warmest regard." Bryan was unmoved. On June 7, he met with Wilson for an hour and accused him of treating House as the true secretary of state. "I have never had your full confidence," he moaned. Early the next morning, June 8, a courier delivered Bryan's letter of resignation to the White House.[67]

His tone was remarkably cordial, even affectionate. Bryan wrote that both he and Wilson were "desirous of reaching a peaceful solution of the problems arising out of the use of submarines against merchantmen" but "find ourselves differing irreconcilably as to the methods which should be employed." They were quarreling about tactics, not principles. "It falls to your lot," the letter continued, "to speak officially for the nation; I consider it to be none the less my duty to endeavor as a private citizen to promote the end which you have in view by means which you do not feel at liberty to use." Bryan regretted having to break off "the intimate and pleasant relations, which have existed between us during the past two years." The president was clearly no Grover Cleveland, a turncoat from Democratic ideals. He was merely mistaken, albeit about the most urgent of issues. Now Bryan would be free to explain why.[68]

THE RESIGNATION upset those he loved and depended on. Mary, usually a politician's model wife, gave in to her rage and disappointment. Instantly, she had lost a position of prominence and ease, as well as a lovely mansion. On the evening of June 8, she sprang up from the dinner table and locked herself in her bedroom. "For the only time in her life," Grace recalled, "she gave way to loud hysterical sobbing." Josephus Daniels scolded Bryan for not "talking to me about" the decision first. The navy secretary, who knew Wilson well, guessed correctly that the United States was not really on the verge of war. Edith Newlands, wife of a Nevada senator who'd been Bryan's ally since the silver crusade, reported after a cross-country voyage that "the trainmen, the passengers, and people at the stations" all regretted that "the exponent of morality in politics" had left his post. Joe Eagle, a Democratic congressman from Texas and a former Populist, described Bryan as "the most useful citizen of the Republic" since Jefferson but could not endorse his reason for leaving.[69]

In fact, he was not compelled to resign. Other cabinet officials, before and since, had fallen out with their president but stayed on, seeking opportunities to soften or alter a policy they abhorred. The *Washington Bee,* an African American weekly in the capital, scoffed that Bryan should have left the cabinet much earlier—to protest the segregation of the federal government and "the democratic south [that] continues to disfranchise the Colored Americans and burns them without a cause."[70]

Bryan believed, as did his nemeses Page and House, that war with Germany was inevitable if U-boat attacks didn't cease. Once he framed a question in stark moral terms, no retreat was possible. But he muddled the motives of his departure. Why had he signed the first protest note to Germany if he disagreed with it? The very warmth of his resignation letter blunted his moral argument with the president. Daniels knew his friend had been "going through a Gethsemane" of conscience but doubted that most Americans understood the decision that had created such an uproar.[71]

Bryan's enemies leaped into the breach with savage abandon. Since the sinking of the *Lusitania,* most big-city papers, whether Democratic or Republican, had been demanding a forceful response just short of war. Now their least favorite cabinet member wanted to divide a nation still in mourning—and to let a nation of undersea criminals off the hook. "Unspeakable treachery," roared the *World.* Henry Watterson contended that "men have been shot and beheaded, even hanged, drawn and quartered, for treason less heinous." George Harvey and other political insiders assumed Bryan had acted partly out of jealousy; now he would certainly run for the nomination in 1916. Walter Hines Page cursed "the yellow streak of a sheer fool" who longed to return to "the applauding multitude." The ambassador called Bryan a "dead" man who hadn't yet read his obituary. But all the vitriol suggested a fear that the corpse was still capable of rallying that "multitude" for his nefarious ends.[72]

Moments after the press learned about the resignation, Bryan's antiwar campaign began, in a solipsistic fashion. He attended one more cabinet meeting and then invited his colleagues to a final lunch. Near the end of the meal, he gave a short speech. "I believe I can do more on the outside to prevent war than I can on the inside," he said. "I can work to control popular opinion so that it will not exert pressure for extreme action which the President does not want." Interior Secretary Franklin Lane declared, "You are the most real Christian that I know." This brought Bryan to the verge of tears. "I go out into the dark," he rasped. "The President has the Prestige and the Power on his side." After a short silence, he concluded, "I have many friends who would die for me."[73]

His admirers did respond, although none seems to have volunteered for martyrdom. The hundreds of supportive telegrams and letters that survive form a less coherent portrait than during earlier crises in Bryan's career. Editors of German American papers sent unwelcome praise of his "dignified and courageous" stand. A Socialist from industrial Pennsylvania assured him that "the men of the factories and the shops" were solidly anti-war. The popular mood looked quite different to a pacifist from Manhattan's wealthy East Side; she damned the press for stirring up "suspicion and hatred among the masses." Several longtime followers swore that, whatever the issue, Bryan would always be their leader. "For 20 years when asked what I thot of anything you have done," wrote a traveling salesman from Minneapolis, "my reply has always been, The King can do no wrong, you are my King." Representing the hopes of the evangelical left, one Baptist minister called him "an inspired prophet" showing the way "toward a Christ-future."[74]

Rarely did Bryan or his correspondents voice the kind of sentiment that historians have dubbed "isolationist"—a reluctance to jump into the Old World's endless, bloody quarrels. On returning home to Lincoln, Bryan did salute a crowd for living behind the "dyke" of the Allegheny Mountains, which protected them from "that portion of the eastern press which affects a foreign accent." But he was referring to the papers' "intolerance" toward his Christian, neutral views rather than to the ethnic background of their publishers or staff members. Since war erupted in Europe, he'd played the chorus of mediation and compromise so often that one editorial cartoonist depicted him strumming a harp. Many of his followers, like their hero, had strong views about world affairs and an equally strong desire to see virtue triumph over evil. Rather than staying above the battle, they strongly disagreed about how the president was waging it.[75]

At the same time, some loyalists mingled their fears of racial outsiders with their hatred of the war. A few days after leaving office, Bryan received a petition from 206 residents of Weatherford, Oklahoma, seat of a county where Debs had drawn almost one-seventh of the vote in the last presidential election. Almost all "of our voters is opposed to war over any thing that has so far taken place," wrote George W. Cornell in an accompanying letter. Many residents, he claimed, sympathized with Germany, "a people already struggling for their existence." Echoing Bryan's own views, Cornell accused the "New York Press" of aching for intervention and attacked politicians who "pray for peace" but let U.S. factories produce munitions. Then Cornell added, "The people of this Country are not willing to fight the English battles alongside the dagoes and Japanees."[76]

Bryan had not consciously stirred up such tribal sentiments. But, as with the spurt of anti-Catholicism that followed his loss in 1908, neither had he warned against them. Admirers such as Cornell heard him voice a growing alarm that the government was moving away from strict neutrality and toward an alliance with foreign empires. Bryan wanted the United States, in a spirit of Christian forbearance, to persuade the belligerents to cease the killing. But he had nothing to propose aside from his pet treaties. Like a schoolteacher who primly instructs his class that fighting is wrong, the nostrum gained less respect the more he repeated it. Not surprisingly, Cornell and his neighbors applauded his anti-jingoism and made up their own minds about the rest.

So Bryan exchanged the only powerful office he had ever held for a return to the lecture halls and Chautauquas. His personal failure became a minor national tragedy. Alone in the administration, Bryan had tried to speak for the large, if inchoate, mass of Americans who opposed the drift to war. He refused to shift his ground as submarine attacks, a boom in manufacturing, and sympathy for Britain made Wilson and his closest advisers tacit supporters of the Allies. But, as secretary of state, Bryan could not be the leader of a movement, and the organized left was too weak and dogmatic to play that role. When he did resign, he chose a poor occasion: a protest note against the murder of civilians. Used to battling for a moral cause and losing, Bryan seemed not to realize that this time his defeat was largely self-inflicted.

One wonders what he might have accomplished if he had remained in the cabinet, as an irritating conscience. Perhaps he would have trained his eloquence on matters of human suffering that more "practical" men brushed aside. On July 8, exactly one month after his resignation, Bryan was lecturing in San Francisco against the world war. At his hotel, he received an urgent note from an Armenian resident of the city who had heard him speak. "Tens of thousands of [my] people have been massacred in wholesale," testified Vabar Cardarbian; "hundreds of villages and towns have been converted into ashes; women in thousands have been violated; men in large numbers have been collected on the pretense of enlistment only to be shot and hanged." Cardarbian pleaded, "Will Civilization tolerate the perpetration of a crime so ghastly and so sweeping as the obliteration of a whole race?" That April, Bryan had tried to secure funds for American missionaries helping Armenians, nearly all of whom were Christians, to avoid starvation. Now he immediately sent Cardarbian's letter on to his successor, Robert Lansing.[77]

Two days later, Henry Morgenthau, the U.S. ambassador to Turkey, cabled the State Department, citing the same horrors and urging a "public protest" against them. But Lansing, unlike Bryan, believed in following the protocols of diplomacy. He allowed Morgenthau to send only a mild, private note of concern to the Ottoman regime and forwarded Cardarbian's letter to the German embassy in Washington. Perhaps Turkey's most powerful ally might inquire into the "purported persecution of the Armenians"? A century of genocide had begun.[78]

※✝※

CHAPTER ELEVEN

Moralist in Retreat, 1916–1919

I claim no right to tell anybody else what to do, but I believe in the Christian doctrine that brethren should commune with each other and they they should seek to help each other.

—William Jennings Bryan, 1916[1]

Have I missed the mark, or, like a true archer, do I strike my quarry? Or am I prophet of lies, a babbler from door to door?

—Cassandra, in Aeschylus's *Agamemnon*[2]

ONE WINTRY DAY in 1916, John Reed left his Greenwich Village apartment to travel down to the swamps of northern Florida. *Collier's Weekly* had assigned him to interview William Jennings Bryan. The Commoner invited the journalist to join him, Mary, and their grandson John on a slow boat trip along the lush Ocklawaha River, stopping at small towns along the way for Bryan to emit a few bursts of oratory.

Reed's vivid dispatches from revolutionary Mexico had already made him something of a celebrity while still in his mid-twenties. The romantic leftist saluted Bryan for "talking popular government twenty years ago and getting called 'anarchist' for it" and shared his revulsion for the ongoing war in Europe. But in every other respect, the portrait Reed drew confirmed the worst fear of any politician. He reduced Bryan to little more than a sideshow for yokels and Bible-thumpers, a man whose time had decisively passed.[3]

For Reed, the setting was ideal for satire. In his eyes, the rural crowds belonged to a more predictable species than did the alligators or giant turtles who slithered past the boat. One local colonel declared himself a Bryan "convert" and promised his entourage a glimpse of "two million gallons of God's crystal beverage ... pouring out from a thousand bubbling fountains." His fellow Floridians chortled, as if on key, when Bryan made fun of "jingoes" who, if war came, "would be too busy...loaning money at high rates of interest, to reach the front." And they nodded solemnly when he intoned, "We Americans should make the Sermon on the Mount real in the law of nations." Reed did pick up a few discordant notes along the way. A traveling salesman refused to pay the fifty-cent fee to hear the famous orator, and a black Republican, sitting in the colored seats, laughed at inappropriate moments.

Back on the boat, Bryan told Reed he had no desire to run for office again and was content to spend the rest of his days taking care of his wife and lecturing about the moral truths of Christianity. To the cosmopolitan journalist, the whole scene was quite droll, if rather sad: "Through that... wild anarchy of tropical nature, moved William Jennings Bryan on a gasoline yacht, in black statesmanlike cutaway, white clerical tie, light gray fedora hat, his hands clasped across his stomach, benevolently bringing love and order into his simple world."[4]

Reed's article, published in one of the nation's most popular and progressive magazines, illustrated a key transition in the history of the American left. That both Bryan and he were great idealists who agreed on most political issues mattered less than did the cultural gulf between them. A month after conducting the interview, the journalist sent his subject a letter that Mary, who read it in Bryan's absence, described as "full of bitterness" toward the YMCA and similar institutions. "He is perfectly impossible," she told her husband, "and I shudder to think of the thing he will write about you.... I think the less we say to him the better. He cannot understand our point of view."[5]

As prairie Victorians, Will and Mary recoiled at John Reed and the qualities that had turned him into a modernist hero. Son of a rich Republican merchant from Oregon, Reed had attended an eastern prep school and then Harvard, where he blossomed as a writer and socialist. He then moved to Greenwich Village and quickly became an avatar of the new bohemianism—literary, philosophical, and sexual. One can only imagine what Mary Bryan would have thought about the famous 1916 photo of Louise Bryant, Reed's lover and political comrade, nude on a beach in Provincetown, her breasts arched back and her long hair plunging toward the sand. John Reed hated monopolists, whose greed he thought made war inevitable, and he placed his formidable talents at the service of striking workers. But he had no use for churches, the temperance movement, or rural America—all of whose virtues Bryan and most of his followers took for granted.

By the time Reed graduated from college in 1910, the left was beginning to drift away from such roots. Sophisticated, secular urbanites seemed

exotic, at best, among radical Democrats and ex-Populists in such states as
Nebraska and Georgia. But Reed and his comrades flocked to Manhattan's
radical salons, adorned the ranks of the local Socialist Party, and were welcomed by Jewish and Italian immigrant unionists during a big strike in the
factory town of Paterson, New Jersey. *The Masses,* the irreverent and witty
magazine of arts and politics that Reed helped to edit, was as dissimilar from
the earnest righteousness of *The Commoner* as was the poetry of William
Carlos Williams (an occasional contributor) from that of William Cullen
Bryant. Dedicated to "free and spirited expressions of every kind," *The
Masses* pointed toward a radicalism that had no place for leaders such as
Bryan. The idea of a Christian left, so vital to his appeal, would soon sound
rather quaint, almost an oxymoron.[6]

Yet Bryan saw no reason to change his views about either politics or religion. After resigning from the cabinet, he opposed U.S. entry into the cataclysm in Europe until the day Congress finally declared war on Germany.
Following the armistice, he criticized Wilson's unyielding stance on making
changes in the Versailles Treaty. Through it all, Bryan remained a loyal
Democrat and endorsed policies to aid the party's urban, working-class
constituents: a minimum wage, an eight-hour day, and the right of labor to
organize and strike. He also denounced corporate "profiteers" at every turn.
But during the war years, Bryan spent much of his time urging Americans
to support prohibition and woman suffrage. He hoped these intertwined
causes would both humanize society and bring it closer to God. The first
goal could never be accomplished if the larger mission did not succeed.

Out of government and with no plans to run for office, Bryan inevitably
suffered a decline both in his following and his influence in the party. Mary
would later refer dismissively to the period from his resignation until the
election of 1920 as "the next five years." Yet in retreat, Bryan managed to
embellish his reputation among people John Reed could never reach. "I
want you to know that I am one of the thousands of young men in this country that you have helped into lofty conceptions of life and its meaning," a
Presbyterian cleric from Michigan wrote to Bryan in the summer of 1916. "I
am a better citizen, and by the grace of God a better minister for having
heard you." Once again, moral celebrity might yield its own rewards.[7]

THE WANING of power coincided with a shift in geography. In 1916, Will
and Mary abandoned the harsh extremes of Nebraska's weather for the
soothing monotony of southern Florida. Mary's arthritis had worsened, and
she had trouble walking without assistance. In 1912, the couple began build-

ing a Spanish-style mansion in Miami they called Villa Serena. They celebrated Christmas in the house the following year. Will continually fretted
about the comfort of his "darling girl," whom he treated with the unstinting
ardor of a fiancé. On their wedding anniversary in 1915, he paused during a
lecture tour in Arkansas to write:

> It is just 31 years ago that we were married and never for a moment have
> I regretted the fate that brought us together and entwined our lives....
> You have been my only real companion for more than three decades—
> the sharer of every secret and the partner of every purpose. If I have
> found favor in the sight of God I pray that He may show it by allowing
> you to be my comfort while I live and then by making us joint tenants of
> the many mansions in the skies.

Mary soon relocated the entire household to Miami. Will stayed there
whenever his peripatetic schedule allowed; until 1921, for voting purposes,
he remained a citizen of Nebraska.[8]

The move could have been difficult for the lifelong midwesterner. It
took Bryan away from his political base in the agrarian North, although, in
Lincoln, Charles Bryan and *The Commoner* kept up a semblance of the family
machine. In Florida, as across the Deep South, the Democratic Party
monopolized every major office. Bryan liked to boast, "I have no more loyal
followers anywhere than in the states of the South." But if he wished to
revive his electoral career, he would have to compete with well-connected
local men who were hungry to lead their booming state to national prominence. Rail connections to the Chautauqua circuit from Miami, which was
incorporated only in 1896, took far longer than those from the urban Plains.
Thus, the spacious house encircled by palm trees and fringed with bougain-
villeas may at first have seemed an island in an alien sea.[9]

But Bryan quickly learned to exploit the new opportunities available to
him. Tourists were crowding into Miami, whose permanent population bal-
looned 600 percent from 1910 to 1920. Building tradesmen, mostly white, and
laborers, mostly black, were busily erecting hotels, skyscrapers, and new
vacation homes for such tycoons as Andrew Carnegie and William K. Van-
derbilt as well as for the wealthy journalist Henry Watterson and the poet
James Whitcomb Riley. As the town's most "distinguished"—that is,
famous—resident, Bryan could promote himself and his beliefs almost any
way he chose. He and Mary opened Villa Serena to the public every Friday
afternoon, and hundreds of people routinely came to chat over tea, fruit
punch, and sandwiches. Bryan praised the city's winter climate and its "phe-

nomenal growth" and made numerous suggestions for developing the tourist trade and starting a local university. Characteristically, he said nothing about the problems of the 40 percent of Miamians who were black. Few could live outside the cramped dwellings of Colored Town, and they were prevented from owning businesses that catered to whites.[10]

In his new hometown, Bryan also cultivated his spiritual garden. Ever the pietist entrepreneur, he revived the Men's Club at the largest Presbyterian church in town and headed a fund-raising drive for the YMCA. He taught an outdoor Bible class in a spacious oceanfront park festooned with royal palms. On winter Sunday mornings, thousands of tourists and locals attended, in the same clothes they would have worn to church. Bryan had always been as comfortable preaching about "eternal truths" as crusading for the latest worldly reform. Now a second, if not quite so prominent, career as an evangelist was dawning.

YET HE STILL gave no thought to abandoning his more worldly calling. After Bryan left the administration, the debate about the nation's slide toward war only grew more intense and bitter. In the fall of 1915, Woodrow Wilson joined the advocates of "preparedness," most of whom were either Republicans from the East or their close allies in industry and banking. The president asked Congress to fund a hundred new warships and to boost the army from one hundred thousand to about four hundred thousand men. Left progressives—from Jane Addams to the suffragist Carrie Chapman Catt to the conservationist Amos Pinchot to a variety of union leaders of Irish and German heritage—accused Wilson of selling out to "militarism." A group of Democrats in Congress, headed by majority leader Claude Kitchin of North Carolina, echoed the charge and gained the support of Robert La Follette's rump of GOP insurgents. Somewhat surprisingly, Henry Ford joined the anti-war camp as well. At the end of 1915, the wealthy carmaker financed a "peace ship" full of American activists who sailed to Europe hoping to talk sense to leaders of the belligerent nations.

Traveling from coast to coast, Bryan lent his oratory to the anti-war effort but didn't attempt to lead it. Neutrality, he told every crowd, whatever its political leanings, was the only response a Christian patriot could make to the "causeless" war and the "scaredness" program. A month after resigning, before a throng of one hundred thousand gathered at the San Francisco World's Fair, he lamented, "Across the seas, our brothers' hands are stained in brothers' blood. The world has run mad. They need a flag that speaks the sentiment of the human heart, a flag that looks toward better things than war." Early the next year, Bryan engaged in a newspaper debate with William Howard Taft over the best way to ensure world peace. The former president, backed by Roosevelt and Senator Henry Cabot Lodge, argued that armies should punish any nation that refused to sign an arbitration treaty. Bryan considered the idea a mockery of his own cherished plan. "Peace is not a thing that can be enforced," he objected.[11]

But the born-again pacifist shied away from proposing any fresh solution of his own. Bryan declined to sail on the "peace ship," although he did see it off from a dock in Hoboken and defended Ford's scheme from the ridicule of the press. He was also gratified in January 1916 when Senator Thomas Gore of Oklahoma and Representative Jeff McLemore of Texas introduced bills that would bar Americans from traveling on the ships of belligerent nations or on any craft that transported munitions. But anti-war legislators were disorganized and failed to parry the president's objection that Congress ought not to make foreign policy ad hoc and on the fly. Far away from the Capitol, Bryan could only send telegrams and make passionate speeches; most urban papers sided with Wilson, and even Democrats who disagreed knew that GOP leaders lacked all sympathy for their position. Bryan kept in close touch with Kitchin but refrained from giving him strategic advice. Bryanism in Congress appeared to be a flickering and frustrated faith.[12]

Bryan faced his own dilemma in coping with Woodrow Wilson. He genuinely enjoyed the president's company and hesitated to break off all personal relations. But in February 1916, he got angry enough to complain to Josephus Daniels that Wilson seemed to want "to drag this nation into this war." Bryan even considered opposing a second term for the only Democrat in a generation to occupy the White House. Yet, at the same time, he applauded the president for signing laws to aid labor, increase the income tax, and rein in the trusts. He admired Wilson's skill as a domestic politician even as he no longer trusted his Christian ethics. What was an idealist who hated war but loved his party to do?[13]

For his part, Wilson was far less ambivalent about the man who had shattered the unity of his cabinet at a time of crisis. One fall day in 1915, he met with Bryan and discovered that the former secretary wanted to reestablish their friendship, which had never been true or close. "He had the air of one who feels himself at home and a member of the family," Wilson wrote to his fiancée, Edith Bolling Galt, about the "amusing and amazing" encounter with a man she called "the Traitor." "We spent a third of the time ... telling stories and discussing matters that had no connection whatever with public affairs.... He looked extraordinarily well and seemed quite happy." The president concluded, "I cannot, I am glad to say, understand such a person."[14]

Indeed, Wilson's low regard for Bryan was akin to that of John Reed, the bohemian Socialist. Politics per se had little to do with it. By the time he took office, Wilson had endorsed most of the specific reforms Bryan had long advocated. But Bryan's emotional makeup—his preference for heart over mind, the grand gesture over the subtle phrase—always violated Wilson's sense of taste and rectitude. Like the well-born young editors of the *New Republic,* Wilson believed Bryan "an unnecessary peril injected into a situation that is already perilous enough." The president wanted to marry noblesse oblige to a practical social vision. His approach was thus closer to that of secular intellectuals such as John Dewey and Walter Lippmann than to his fellow Presbyterian moralist. Reed interviewed Wilson in 1914 and found him a magnetic figure, the first president since Lincoln to care more for "principles" than "policies." No doubt both men would have chuckled at Mary Bryan's preference for her husband's "approachableness" over Wilson's "reserve." Despite his misgivings about the war, Bryan could do little to damage the president's reputation among the best and brightest of his day.[15]

Neither did Bryan attempt to become the cynosure of anti-war sentiment. Several loyalists wrote to assure him that he was waging what a small businessman from Oklahoma called "the fight of light against darkness" because "war is indefensible among Christian peoples." Yet Bryan was under steady attack, both from the pro-administration press and from new, more ominous sources. In March 1916, an anonymous correspondent from Tennessee threatened to assassinate him for advocating "Peace at Any Price"; from Rhode Island, another vowed to kill him for "lower[ing] the standard of the American Flag." In such an environment, no Democrat was willing to run against the incumbent on an anti-war platform. When Bryan returned to Lincoln that month to celebrate his fifty-sixth birthday with a few thousand friends and admirers, he endorsed the president for reelection. "There is no other candidate," he told a local paper. The statement could be read either as praise or acquiescence.[16]

Soon Wilson was able, at least temporarily, to calm the fears of his neutralist critics. Early that spring, a flurry of U-boat attacks on American merchant ships had brought another exchange of truculent, threatening notes between Washington and Berlin. But in May, the kaiser's government backed down, promising that its submarine commanders would visit and search civilian vessels before deciding to destroy them.

That was enough to reawaken hope that Wilson might be able to mediate an end to the fighting. He privately urged the Allies to attend a peace conference in the near future and gave a speech that looked forward to the postwar creation of a "universal association of the nations to maintain the inviolate security of the highway of the seas." It was a harbinger of the League of Nations. But these steps did nothing to slow the pace of slaughter in the trenches and from the skies. With the aid of poison gas, the German army continued to batter the French at Verdun in an exhausting battle that claimed almost a million casualties before it ended. But at least the president was again trying to stop the madness without clearly favoring either side. Not since the beginning of the war had he sounded so much like that dreamer, William Jennings Bryan.[17]

The Democrats could now hold their national convention free of rancor, if virtually without drama. The June gathering in St. Louis was also the first in twenty years at which Bryan played no official role—as either candidate, delegate, or member of the platform committee. He had run for a seat as a delegate at large in Nebraska's April primary. But his frequent absences from the state and the furious opposition of local "wet" Democrats resulted in a humiliating defeat, if not an unexpected one. "Don't lose any sleep and take care of your health," Mary wrote him after the loss. "These next four years are important ones." At any rate, he would attend the convention. A newspaper syndicate hired him to report on it (as well as on the meetings of the GOP and Progressives in Chicago). Bryan's dispatches were briefer and less prominent than in 1912, since hardly anything unpredictable occurred.[18]

He did manage to crown his own party's convention with another memorable speech. Wilson, obeying tradition, was not present at his second nomination. He stayed in the capital where, to protect his right flank, he marched, little flag in hand, at the head of a big preparedness parade and warned against "disloyalty active in the United States." Meanwhile, the delegates in St. Louis were cheering a keynote address that praised Wilson for keeping the nation at peace. Yet they hankered for the rippingly romantic rhetoric that every Democratic convention since 1896 had provided. So on the night of June 15, the rules were unanimously suspended to give the floor to a loquacious nondelegate from the press section.[19]

Bryan did not disappoint. He began with a clever remark that the party "encourages independent thought among its members," even one who had thought his way right out of Wilson's cabinet. Then he quickly turned to domestic achievements every partisan in the hall could cheer. Bryan hailed tariff revision and the income tax, a stronger anti-trust law, and the creation of the Federal Reserve as victories that, just as in the heyday of Andrew

Jackson, a Democratic president and his party had won against "an unholy combination of the powers of high finance." The trio of reform measures demonstrated that the republic was no longer "controlled, as the [GOP's] convention in Chicago was, by the expert representatives of the favor-seeking corporations." The stakes hadn't changed for Bryan since 1896. But ordinary Americans finally had their elite enemies on the run.

Having refreshed the old terms of partisan conflict, Bryan could then call upon a higher authority: "Today Christ and Pilate stand again face to face, and Force and Love are again striving for mastery and dominance." In a messianic chord that would reverberate into the twenty-first century, he identified Europe with the Roman procurator who ordered the Crucifixion and declared that "God, in his providence" expected the United States to apply the Golden Rule, "the moral code that governs individuals," through-out the world. The quest for secular redemption dovetailed with the spiritual kind. "What party is more fit" to bring about world peace, asked Bryan, "than the party that preaches the brotherhood of man as next in importance to the fatherhood of God?" His short address was interrupted forty times by applause. When Bryan left the platform, every delegate lined up to shake his hand.[20]

The performance also drew splendid reviews in the press and made it logical for Wilson to request his aid in the difficult campaign to follow. The Democrats were once again the underdog since Theodore Roosevelt had declined to run on a third-party ticket. TR complained about the GOP's "sordid" convention, with the old bosses in command. But he despised Wilson even more for "being too proud to fight." His decision killed the Progressive Party, which was already in sharp decline. The Democrats would now have to capture a sizeable portion of Roosevelt's constituency. Bryan's popularity among some prominent Social Gospelers—Washington Gladden and Charles Sheldon wrote to praise his St. Louis speech—might aid that strategy. So would his continued appeal west of the Mississippi, where Republicanism remained a distinctly progressive faith.[21]

Bryan leaped into the fight with his customary energy and spirit. He had always loved campaigning, and the prospect that the standpatters of the GOP might return to power behind their nominee—the stolid Justice Charles Evans Hughes—filled him with genuine dismay. "Who nominated Mr. Hughes?" he asked a crowd of sixteen thousand in Kansas City. "The same men who nominated Mr. Taft. And were they repentant? Not a bit of it."[22]

Beginning in mid-September, after the tent Chautauquas closed down for the year, Bryan spent the next six weeks on the road, speaking as often as five times a day. He did most of his stumping west of the Mississippi, where the crowds were as large and boisterous as in his epic campaign twenty years before. Although every American knew his name, many people, particularly in western towns the tent circuit didn't visit, had never heard his voice. So local Democrats—such as those in the small town of Perry, Oklahoma—could exploit his renown as "the world's greatest orator" who for a quarter-century "has defied the power and influence of Mammon and Monopoly." Bryan sometimes criticized his own party's platform for endorsing preparedness and snubbing prohibition. But party chairmen across the swing region hailed his efforts as indispensable.[23]

Indeed, Wilson would have lost in 1916 if he had not carried most of the states where Bryan headlined his campaign. Although the president gained a comfortable majority in the popular vote, his advantage in the electoral college was agonizingly slim—just twenty-three votes. Other factors also nudged Wilson over the top: a powerful labor movement worked diligently for him in California, which he carried by fewer than four thousand ballots; the Socialists ran a surrogate for the ailing Debs, which limited their appeal; and prominent western refugees from the sinking Progressive Party endorsed the Democratic nominee, many doing so for the first time in their lives. But Bryan's stumping helped his party draw a sharp contrast between the camp of anti-corporate reform and peace and the camp of conservatism at home and belligerence abroad. As in 1912, he performed a great service for a man who had never liked or respected him. In victory, all Democrats could brag that they stood alone on top, tribunes of a progressive America.[24]

Their unity dissolved even before Wilson could take his second oath of office. At the start of February 1917, the German government announced that U-boats would no longer restrict their deadly operations. Since winning reelection, the president had labored zealously to head off that step. He asked the warring powers to state publicly their terms for peace, a move Bryan had urged on him two years before. Then on January 22, Wilson gave a special address to the Senate that thrilled altruistic liberals everywhere. Only a "peace without victory" could be a lasting one, he declared. Democratic rule, general disarmament, "a sense of justice, of freedom, and of right" in daily life—these, not massed armies and dreadnoughts, were the true elements of a stable world. But the British rejected Wilson's overture, and the kaiser's government decided it must win the war before the great power across the Atlantic had a chance to join it. On February 3, the United States severed diplomatic relations with Germany. All sides assumed a declaration of war would soon follow.

To Bryan, these events only confirmed the lunacy of intervention. "If we go to war," he wrote in a passionate open letter to Congress, "it should be for a cause which history will justify." For the first time since leaving the cabinet, he joined hands with radical pacifists and Socialists such as John Reed in a final effort to keep the nation at peace. At a packed meeting of the left in Madison Square Garden, Bryan strongly endorsed the demand to hold a national referendum on the ultimate question of whether America should enter the war. Meyer London, New York City's Socialist congressman, praised his "service" as akin to what Tolstoy had done for Russia.[25]

The idea of trumping "jingoistic" politicians with a blast of direct democracy had no basis in the Constitution. But there was no time to wait for his beloved treaty plan to gain universal favor. In late March, a dejected Bryan repeated to his brother a conspiracy theory popular on the left: "Eastern financiers are going to force this country into war in order to make their investments in the war loans of the Allies profitable." Without a revolution in Germany to match the one that had just broken out in Russia, Bryan feared that U.S. soldiers would soon be fighting and dying to balance the books of a privileged few.[26]

His pessimism was fully justified. Most congressmen and senators were ready, if not necessarily eager, to vote for war if the president requested it. Bryan's statements brought down a cascade of criticism, not just from old rivals such as Alton Parker but also from onetime followers who, in the words of a real-estate agent from Washington, D.C., were "chagrined and pained" to watch his "blind" attempt to stop the nation from doing its duty. On February 5, a Republican representative from Minnesota drew cheers in the House when he urged the press to stop reporting on Bryan's "unpatriotic" speeches and even suggested he be jailed for the duration of the crisis. George Huddleston, a progressive Democrat from Birmingham, Alabama, came to Bryan's defense: "In a time like this...it takes a lion-hearted courage for a man to stand up on his feet and dare to speak for peace." But no other members of the party Bryan had campaigned so hard to keep in power took the floor to back him up. In March, two insurgent Republicans—Robert La Follette and George Norris from Nebraska—led an anti-war filibuster that the president denounced and all but five Democrats shunned.[27]

The fateful vote in Congress followed the same pattern. On April 2, Woodrow Wilson asked for a declaration of war against imperial Germany. On April 5, the House did his bidding by a vote of 373 to 50. Only 16 representatives were brave or foolish enough to oppose the president of their own party; George Huddleston was not among them. The only influential Democrat to vote no was House majority leader Claude Kitchin. Just after midnight on the sixth, he took the floor wearing a Bryanite string tie and upheld a stance that his hero would likely have adopted if he'd been eligible to participate in the debate. "[I] have marked out the path of my duty," Kitchin declared, "and I have made up my mind to walk it, if I go barefooted and alone.... Half the civilized world is now a slaughterhouse for human beings. This nation is the last hope of peace on earth ... the only remaining star of hope for Christendom."[28]

The next day, Bryan told both Wilson and the press that he was ready to undertake any task the president might desire. Burned once, Wilson declined to appoint him to another federal job. But he did ask the orator to use his famous talent to help sell the war. Soon the same newspapers that had been indicting Bryan as a virtual traitor were praising his selfless spirit in the nation's cause.

The irony was rich and telling. From the day he joined the administration to the days after Congress declared war, broad acclaim had come to Bryan, the paragon of principle, only when he subordinated his own views to Wilson's. He always spoke with more vigor and authenticity when he challenged the president, whether over private control of banking or the descent into belligerence. But Bryan was unfit by ideology and temperament to work closely with the likes of John Reed, Louise Bryant, Meyer London, and the other anti-war activists who led the campaign for a national referendum and who kept resisting after April 1917, despite the threat of jail and vigilante attacks. In New York and a few other metropolises, "Mr. Wilson's war" was never popular. In August, a worried administration official told a colleague that Bryan could carry New York City if he were running for president.[29]

But Bryan had never been that kind of rebel. He actively resisted a policy only as long as he was convinced that most Americans agreed with him, or might be persuaded to do so without risking a civil war or national chaos. On April 3, he told an anti-war congressman from Colorado that if he were representing a majority of pro-war constituents, "I would resign and leave them to speak through someone in harmony with their views." Now that the United States was officially, unalterably at war, Bryan could not imagine opposing it.[30]

Few of his followers seemed to challenge that reasoning. In June, Bryan did receive an angry letter from a Unitarian minister who wrote that "your peace principles appear to be apllicable [*sic*] only to foreign countries," as well as a scattering of notes from men who reminded him how much the "financial interests" hungered for war. But most Democrats unhappy about intervention seemed to grasp his democratic logic, such as it was. Or perhaps they just understood the risks of dissent at a time when "100 per cent Americanism" was rapidly turning from nativist rhetoric into wartime practice. Even after he'd pledged his loyalty, Bryan lost at least one speaking engagement—from a Presbyterian church, no less—because of his anti-war reputation. Despite such rebuffs, or perhaps because of them, the quasi-pacifist scolded anti-war protestors for "abusing free speech" and did not object when Eugene Debs and hundreds of his comrades were arrested for violating the Espionage Act or Sedition Act. Several members of the audience that had cheered Bryan at Madison Square Garden six months before were probably among them.[31]

Yet when he talked about the war from April 1917 to the armistice nineteen months later, Bryan usually addressed the subject at a slant. His speeches included no alarms about German "butchers" and "autocrats" and few of the militant defenses of liberty that thousands of "Four Minute Men" were making, under government sponsorship, all over the land. Instead, Bryan mingled anodyne pleas for conserving food with more spirited attacks on businessmen who sought to profit from the economic boom. He reserved his true fire for advocating prohibition and woman suffrage. The best thing about going to war, Bryan implied, was that it was hastening the victory of such "moral issues."[32]

IN 1917, the great struggle that had lasted for almost a century seemed to be nearing its climax. Over half the states had enacted some kind of prohibition, from local option to the "bone dry" extreme. In the new Congress, a bipartisan majority favored a constitutional amendment to ban the liquor traffic, and President Wilson, despite his misgivings, was not inclined to stand in the way. The coming of war proved a great boon to the cause. The Anti-Saloon League joyfully publicized the fact that German American *biermeisters* dominated the U.S. Brewers Association; dry activists also wooed lawmakers with the argument that grain should not be fermented at a time of national crisis. In May, Congress established "dry zones" encircling military bases and made it illegal to dispense liquor to anyone in uniform. The *New Republic* wrote, "Crepe is now hanging on the door of every rum shop in the land."[33]

Bryan dedicated himself to driving such concerns out of business forever. He saw himself as a Christian educator, determined to teach the young about the perils drink posed both to their bodies and to the larger social order. While secretary of state, he had occasionally taken time to speak to high school and college students about the virtues of temperance. At one appearance in March 1915, thousands of Philadelphia youngsters staged a "near-riot" when they rushed the stage to ask Bryan to sign their abstinence pledges; he did so for half an hour, which quelled the mob of teetotalers. After resigning, he routinely alternated pleas for peace with ones about the issue he admitted was "nearer his heart."

Not even the imminence of war could alter his priorities. In February 1917, with U-boats free again to prowl the seas, the wife of a Texas congressman was amazed to hear Bryan talk solely about prohibition at a Washington luncheon given in his honor. Dry soldiers in both the South and the North cheered him as "a leader of the moral forces in the country" and suggested he run again for president on that basis alone.[34]

A number of film companies sought to turn his reputation to their mutual profit. From 1916 to 1919, at least three different producers contacted Bryan about making a movie to dramatize his crusade for applied Christianity. One overly ambitious Chicago entrepreneur wanted to use his lecture "The Prince of Peace" as the germ for a production "on the same big scale" as D. W. Griffith's famed *Birth of a Nation*. The other proposals aimed, more modestly, to expose the evils of liquor in a documentary style. All assumed Bryan had great box-office potential and were willing to pay him upward of 20 percent of the proceeds to play a starring role. But due to a shortage of funds and squabbles over contracts, none of these ideas was consummated. It was far easier, the would-be film actor may have mused, to book a hall and give a speech.[35]

Bryan had come fairly late to the prohibition movement, and he made no original arguments for the cause. By the 1910s, Americans were so familiar with the alleged sins of the "liquor interests"—from destruction of the body to corruption of the body politic—that they could recite chapter and verse all by themselves. But Bryan crusaded with an ecumenical openness few veteran propagandists shared. Anti-Saloon League literature was filled with drawings of swarthy, mustachioed men luring fair-haired Americans into their lethal enterprises. Bryan avoided such nativist libels and kept his focus squarely on the capitalists, regardless of ethnicity, who "impoverish the poor and multiply their sufferings" and "increase the death rate among the children."[36]

Neither did his ardor for a dry nation tolerate religious divisions. Social Gospelers such as Charles Sheldon and officials of the Federal Council of Churches viewed Bryan as a natural ally in their effort to link prohibition to a larger vision of reform. Bryan and his wife also became friends with Billy Sunday, the popular evangelist whose graphic "booze sermon" converted tens of thousands of Americans to the cause. That Sunday was a loyal

Republican and mocked Social Gospelers for "trying to make a religion out of social service with Jesus Christ left out" did not prevent Mary from sending him poems to use in his sermons or Will from speaking at his urban revivals. Anyone who saved as many souls as Billy Sunday was clearly exempt from political criticism.[37]

Bryan also welcomed the small number of Catholics willing to endorse prohibition. He exchanged warm letters with George Zurcher, a parish priest from a Buffalo suburb, and published one of his speeches in *The Commoner*. Zurcher cited several bishops who had inveighed against the "hell holes of iniquity" in their midst. At the same time, he confessed to Bryan his frustration with cardinals who warned him against sharing a platform with Protestants. Catholic hierarchs blessed the effort to stop individuals from throwing away their lives on whiskey and beer. But banning the *commerce* in alcohol was quite unpopular in eastern cities where most immigrant Catholics lived. One character in a 1916 vaudeville show, set in New York, joked that he'd imbibed a number of "Bryan cocktails—it's made of grape juice and a nut." Catholic leaders could not support outlawing an industry that brought profits to thousands of their parishioners and pleasure to millions more.[38]

Ever the optimist, Bryan brushed away such objections with a faith in the larger Christian majority. He was certain a cleaner, more honest, more productive nation would arise from the ashes of the saloon and the factories that supplied its noxious wares. Buoying his confidence was the simultaneous progress of woman suffrage, which most prohibitionists had supported since the Gilded Age.

Like most pietist reformers, Bryan had long believed that women were the morally superior gender. At the start of the new century, he had declared, "The world needs the brain of woman as well as the brain of man, and even more does it need the conscience of woman." While in Lincoln, Mary had presided over a women's club that endorsed suffrage, and she no doubt encouraged her husband to do the same before any other major Democrat came to his senses.[39]

In 1916, for the first time Bryan made votes for women a central part of his rhetoric. His party's national platform "recommend[ed]" that states pass equal-suffrage laws, and this helped him rebut white southerners who feared a federal amendment would extend the franchise to black women. Bryan emphasized "the mother argument"—the hand that rocked the cradle had a right to "determine whether her child will realize her hopes or bring her gray hairs in sorrow to the grave." He agreed that American women deserved equal treatment under the law. But the idea that a loving parent made the most responsible citizen appealed to him more than did any constitutional claim; it also enabled him to promote other "righteous causes." No good mother wanted her son to go to war or for saloons to tempt her offspring into a life of depravity and crime. This had been the gospel of the WCTU for four decades, and it was just as well suited to a male evangelist who believed he and his fellow Christians had a duty to purify the world.[40]

As if to confirm that view, Mary became a national figure in her own right. Despite frequent pain, she gave addresses in several states to promote votes for women and prohibition, became an official in the WCTU and the National American Woman Suffrage Association, and lobbied the wives of congressmen to urge their husbands to put both federal amendments over the top. Villa Serena, like Fairview before it, became a headquarters as well as a home. In a 1916 letter to her husband, Mary bragged about how well she was managing the complementary spheres of the domestic and the political. That week, she had answered all the mail, found a new school for their grandson John, attended a WCTU meeting where she "made a little speech on woman's influence in the developement [sic] of temperance sentiment," and finished embroidering "my cross stitch peacocks." Mary could not resist a proud addendum: "Perhaps you had better put this letter away to show what your wife does when you are not here."[41]

The couple could soon raise their glasses of grape juice in triumph. Late in 1917, Congress easily passed the amendment banning the manufacture and sale of alcoholic beverages and sent it on to the states for ratification. Suffragists didn't achieve the required two-thirds margin in both houses until June 1919. Before the United States went to war, women had achieved the vote in fewer states than had banned the liquor traffic, and most southern Democrats were still reluctant to take the risk of upsetting the racial order. But the two causes that the Bryans and many other Americans had always viewed as twins marched together into the Constitution in 1920. At the moment national prohibition became law, Mary sang a temperance hymn she had written, and Will quoted one of his favorite lines from the Gospel of Matthew: "They are dead which sought the young child's life."[42]

CHRISTIAN PERSUASION WAS less effective as a method for shaping the postwar world. Bryan desperately wanted to play an official role in the peace conference alongside the elected leaders of the victorious powers. He realized his treaties were no longer relevant and endorsed the idea of a League of Nations. But he still thought his pacific, benevolent instincts would serve the country well on the global stage. A note of affirmation came from the Nobel Committee, which considered him for a Peace Prize in 1918, before honoring Wilson with it the following year.[43]

Months before the armistice, Bryan wrote to Josephus Daniels, who was still secretary of the navy, and to various friends in Congress, pleading with them to convince the president to give him a seat on the future American delegation to the peace conference. Who better understood the roots of the Great War and had served his nation (and party) longer and more faithfully? "The interests of our country as well as the interests of struggling humanity the world over would have an advocate worthy of the cause," cheered John Baer, a Republican representative and populist cartoonist from North Dakota. Bryan even offered to pay his own expenses abroad and, like an eager schoolboy, assured Wilson he was "devoting all my time this winter to study of European politics of the past century and the more important treaties." The human race was about to pivot toward harmony or greater catastrophe; Bryan could not merely stand aside and watch.[44]

Despite numerous requests, Wilson never considered making the appointment. Five days after the armistice, he wrote to Daniels, "it would be unjustly but certainly taken for granted that he would be too easy and that he would pursue some Eutopian [*sic*] scheme." To advisers who had no love for Bryan, the president undoubtedly dispensed with such courtesies.[45]

The rejection helped turn Bryan into a skeptic toward Wilson's own grand design for the future of the world. The president returned from the Paris conference in 1919 with a visionary peace treaty in hand and the cheers of thousands of ordinary Europeans still ringing in his ears. But many members of the Senate—controlled narrowly by the GOP since the recent midterm election—protested that the convenant of the League of Nations would threaten American sovereignty. Wilson dismissed their worries with contempt. He would not compromise with "isolationists" who had neither a plan nor a commitment to prevent future wars.[46]

Bryan sided with the doubters. He agreed that the United States should have a larger vote in the League than smaller and weaker nations and insisted that Congress alone should decide whether to commit American troops to battle. Still, he avoided an open break with the president. In a rhetorical flourish, Bryan declared the League "the greatest step toward peace in a thousand years" because it proposed "substituting reason for force" in the conduct of disputes between nations.[47]

Increasingly, Bryan was regaining his oppositional voice. "The people do not act through gratitude, but from expectation," he wrote in March 1919, "and now that the war is over we can no longer call upon the people to support the administration as a patriotic duty." All over the industrial world, workers were engaging in mass strikes, and activist-intellectuals were issuing manifestos calling for radical change, if not socialist revolution. Bryan came up with his own "Constructive Program." It included older ideas such as the federal guarantee of bank deposits and arbitration of labor conflicts and added a ringing demand for government ownership of railroads, telephones, and the telegraph. He also wanted to place the constitutional power to declare war in the hands of the voters rather than Congress. It was a daring, if largely unheralded, response both to Republican gains in Congress and to Wilson's obsession with the peace treaty.[48]

Bryan did urge the Senate to ratify Wilson's handiwork, even without amendments. The bad sections of the treaty, he argued, could be altered later. But the president did not trust him, and the sentiment was mutual. Six months after Wilson left office, Bryan even declined to join a committee to honor his deeds. The erstwhile secretary of state accused his former boss of abandoning all vigilance against profiteers after the guns had fallen silent in Europe. But the major charge in Bryan's indictment was Wilson's "refusal to permit ratification with reservations" of the Versailles treaty. The president even declined to consider an amendment that would have allowed the United States to use force without advance approval from the League. That stubbornness had defeated the best chance in decades to construct a just and peaceful world.[49]

Bryan's Cassandra-like posture was fitting for a moralist in retreat. And in retrospect, he was quite correct to oppose American entry into the Great War. It was not a conflict that history has justified. The main consequence of turning Europe into a killing field was a great bitterness from which grew, like poisonous plants, the trio of Fascism, Nazism, and Bolshevism. Bryan also foresaw that Wilson, by rejecting compromise, would lose the fight over the peace treaty and deprive the League of the one powerful nation that might have halted the drift toward a second world war. Disparaged as a pathetic utopian, Bryan proved himself a better prophet and realist than the erstwhile academic he did so much to place and keep in the White House.[50]

At the time, few observers, other than his followers and family members, gave Bryan credit for being right as well as self-righteous. Part of the reason was his style of rhetoric and his hortatory reputation; part was due to the choices he had made. Bryan longed for ordinary citizens and diplomats to regard him as a statesman. But he had resigned the highest post in the cabinet for dubious reasons and had performed unimpressively while there. Speaking from his romantic heart and Christian soul, Bryan could help the movements for prohibition and woman suffrage—profoundly moral matters—win over the nation. "He has been and will continue to be as long as he lives, a great force in our politics," commented Interior Secretary Franklin K. Lane in 1919 after hearing Bryan talk to a group of prominent Democrats about the faltering peace treaty. "People believe that he is honest and know he is sympathetic with the moral aspirations of the plain people." That truth was lost on John Reed and his comrades who rushed to embrace the Bolshevik Revolution and never recovered from the affair.[51]

Yet Bryan was always most effective when he spoke as a preacher. His skills as a negotiator and administrator invited more satire than praise. Chained to the image he had fashioned for himself, he would embark on his last and most controversial mission.

CHAPTER TWELVE

Save the Children,
1920–1925

*Children are a part of God's plan; they come into the world without their
own volition, and every child has as much right to all the advantages which
life can give as has your child or mine.*

—William Jennings Bryan, 1923[1]

*I have always been thinking of the different ways in which Christianity is
taught, and whenever I find one way that makes it a wider blessing than
any other, I cling to that trust—I mean that which takes in the most good of
all kinds and brings in the most people as sharers in it. It is surely better to
pardon too much than to condemn too much.*

—Dorothea in *Middlemarch*[2]

ON CHRISTMAS DAY 1922, several thousand people crowded into
Bryan's weekly Bible class beside the ocean in Miami. Among them was
Amy Howley, a middle-aged British immigrant. Four days later, Howley
rushed up north with her mind fixed on his "beautiful address" and the
refrain of a hymn sung that day—"Just leave it to Him." At a Pennsylvania
hospital, Howley watched her daughter die in childbirth.

Her letter to Bryan contained another horrific revelation. Years before,
Howley's insane husband had tried to murder her before slitting his own
throat. "God only knows why I am telling you all this," Howley concluded.
"But somehow I thought you'd pray for me. I know how very largely our
Pathways are divided here Below. But up there, there will be no distinction
and I hope I shall know you as a Big Brother even though I may never meet
you again on earth."[3] This was not the type of thank-you message most
politicians received. But then Bryan had never been like most politicians.

In the 1920s, he ensured his place in the history of America's religion as
well its politics. Bryan was in his sixties, and his health was declining. But he
mustered the energy to make himself one of the nation's leading evangel-

ists—without bothering to get ordained or to cease his passion for secular reform. He delivered sermons in packed venues from Royal Palm Park to Presbyterian temples in the East to the Church of the Foursquare Gospel in Los Angeles, where the charismatic Aimee Semple McPherson held sway. He wrote popular books of lectures and essays and had his Bible talks published in almost a hundred urban newspapers. He was one of the first preachers to appear on radio. He debated, in person and in print, leading exponents of the modernist creed and fought them for control of the national Presbyterian Church. Most notably, he became chief spokesmen for an inchoate movement of pietists who demanded limits to or an outright ban on the teaching of Darwinian theory in public schools.

This new mission returned Bryan to the national spotlight he had enjoyed and exploited from his first national campaign through his exit from the Wilson administration. Once again, journalists gave his opinions the routine notice, if not always the respect, due a major public figure, and he elicited a fresh outpouring of admiration and derision. In 1922, the *New York Times* even reported that Bryan "got a real hair-cut for the first time in years" while on the road in Nebraska.[4] The climax of all the attention, and of his life, took place three summers later at the trial of *State of Tennessee* v. *John Thomas Scopes.*

His part in that famous trial—and the controversy that still surrounds it—has spurred more debate than anything else in his long career. Latter-day creationists applaud Bryan as a defender of Holy Writ, while contemporary humanists scorn him as an enemy of learning and academic freedom—"the Fundamentalist Pope," as H. L. Mencken called him. *Inherit the Wind,* the fictionalized 1955 play and then 1960 movie about the trial, remains a lightning rod for Bryan's fans and critics half a century after its first performance—although its scriptwriters chose the event as a metaphor for McCarthyism and were not much concerned about the teaching of evolution.

Scholars have increasingly warmed to Bryan's motives, if not his actions, in Dayton, Tennessee, during that hot week in July. Midway through the twentieth century, such liberal historians as Richard Hofstadter and Ray Ginger shuddered at Bryan's religious "bigotry" and his mistrust of intellectuals. In recent years, however, the recognition that most evolutionists in the 1920s were dedicated to "improving" the human race through eugenics has made Bryan seem more sympathetic, even to a secular Darwinist such as Stephen Jay Gould and an unorthodox Catholic such as Garry Wills. For them, Bryan's rejection of modern biology was mitigated somewhat by his revulsion at the prospect of sterilizing the slow-witted and the disadvantaged.[5]

But few commentators appreciate how firmly Bryan had always stuck to a pragmatic view of religion. He spent little time defending the "truth" of the Bible and a good deal hailing its power to correct human flaws and solve social problems. *"Christ went about doing good,"* he emphasized in a 1922 lecture. The emotional relief Bryan brought to Amy Howley, a woman he never met, was a small, individualized piece of that larger mission. To paraphrase Tolstoy, a Christlike society was the name of his desire.[6]

Bryan was thus not a fundamentalist, as we now understand that term. He hardly ever described himself as such, preferring to say simply that he was defending Christianity. Certainly, he wanted ministers to preach the opening chapters of Genesis as a factual narrative rather than an ancient Semitic myth. But that conviction stemmed primarily from a fear that skepticism was the handmaiden of inhumane, aggressive power. Theological debate, in itself, held no interest for him. He may not even have owned or read *The Fundamentals,* the twelve-booklet anthology published between 1910 and 1915 that gave biblical literalism a new name that has stuck. Bryan burned only and always to see religion heal the world.[7]

The waning of that prospect thus seemed a body blow to civilization. "There has not been a reform for twenty-five years that I did not support," Bryan told his fellow Presbyterians in 1923, "and I am now engaged in the biggest reform of my life. I am trying to save the Christian Church from those who are trying to destroy her faith."[8] Protestant modernists increasingly thought of God as little more than a good conscience; Bryan thought of a good conscience as a gift from God, one only a knave or fool would turn down.

Never before had he made a religious question into a political priority. But World War I shredded the ideal of peaceful progress and brotherhood, giving materialist doctrines such as Marxism and Darwinism the benefit of the doubt when it came to explaining why warfare intensified and inequality endured. Unlike political conservatives, Bryan did not think that socialism or communism were gaining in postwar America. But he was alarmed that the "Darwinian doctrine" he had always condemned in a minor way had now become the prime enemy of a just society. Its exponents, he charged, had "plunged the world into the worst of wars, and [are] dividing society into classes that fight each other on a brute basis." A Christian counteroffensive was needed to save the coming generation.[9]

As he donned the armor of this latest righteous cause, Bryan refused to abandon any of the others. He remained a figure to reckon with in his party—a progressive, "dry" leader against what he took to be a resurgence of "wet" reactionaries. Respecting the separation between church and state, he never asked his fellow Democrats to endorse his views on evolution. Yet neither could Bryan imagine retreating on this issue as he had on free silver after 1900 and, later, the independence of the Philippines. "If it be true, as I believe it is, that morality is dependent upon religion," he told an audience of seminarians in 1922, "then religion is not only the most practical thing in the world, but the first essential." If defeated in this battle, every other he had fought would lose its meaning.[10]

BRYAN WORKED SO furiously to defend and apply his faith in postwar America in part because he sensed his death was near. When a reporter asked him why he didn't run for office again, Bryan responded that he was "at the end of life." As he traveled around the nation during the early twenties, he often got tested for diabetes, the same disease that had killed his father at the age of fifty-seven. The results, as one physician put it delicately, "did not look so good." The level of sugar in Bryan's urine consistently topped 1 percent, a sign of danger. Insulin had recently been discovered and had already extended the lives of some notable Americans—including Robert Lansing, his successor at State. Early in 1923, Bryan's doctor in Washington, J. Thomas Kelley, treated him with the new drug for a week. But the patient then returned to the road and gave up the regimen. For the rest of his life, Bryan avoided sweets yet continued to gorge himself on bread and other starches, believing erroneously that they could do him no further harm.[11]

Premonition of death spurred Bryan to earn a fortune large enough to ensure that his wife would have all the care and comfort she needed. His love was mingled with guilt. "I have been absent most of the time for a quarter of a century," he wrote to a minister in Fort Worth. "But it is a continual fight to get any time whatever at home." As she aged, Mary endured a variety of arthritis therapies and spent many weeks in hospitals. At one point in 1924, she even called in a faith healer, a sign of desperation for an orthodox Protestant. "My wife…is entirely helpless, unable to stand or walk or to dress or undress herself," Bryan confided to a friend. He filled their Miami estate with a corps of servants and fretted about Mary's plight and the sizeable expenses it entailed. After the Eighteenth Amendment was ratified, Bryan complained to the Pennsylvania Anti-Saloon League that he had not been paid for several talks on its behalf. He had never asked to be compensated for such efforts before.[12]

One way he swelled his bank account gave his detractors a fresh reason to chuckle. During the winter of 1925, George Merrick, a Florida real estate man infatuated with Mediterrean design, paid Bryan as much as $100,000 in fees and property to tout his new development, Coral Gables. The town featured a massive Venetian pool, a fleet of ocean-worthy gondolas, and a hotel that resembled the Alhambra in Spain. Bryan spoke for an hour each day while sitting under an umbrella and wearing a big white Panama hat. After he finished, an orchestra and "shimmy dancer" entertained the potential customers.

The role of booster suited Bryan's genuine enthusiasm for the region. Since moving down south, he'd given a stream of talks, both paid and unpaid, that predicted Miami and its suburbs would blossom into a metropolis of "clean" middle-class residents who welcomed their neighbors from the Caribbean and Latin America. But now editorial cartoonists portrayed him with wads of cash bulging from his pockets. Defensively, Bryan told the press he was not a wealthy man; more honestly, he pointed out that as a good Christian, he donated 10 percent of his earnings to charity.[13]

At least his children were taking care of themselves—and in ways their parents could approve. William Junior attended law school at Georgetown University while his father served in the cabinet. After graduation, he returned to Arizona as an assistant U.S. attorney and graced the YMCA, the state university's board of regents, and the local Democratic Party with his celebrated name. In 1921, he moved to Los Angeles with his wife and three children. Soon he joined a legal practice and started dabbling in politics. With good reason, Junior worried that he'd never gain the renown of his illustrious namesake. But his father praised him for thinking more about his church and serving "the masses" than about making money. His sister Grace and her unhappy family followed William Junior to southern California. Although never satisfied with her lot, she did some public speaking and took notes for a biography of her father, whom she considered to be "a Christian statesman."[14]

Then there was Ruth. The ordeal of world war and her joy in a second marriage combined to transform the young rebel into a woman of poise and moral substance. In London, she volunteered alongside Lou Hoover (wife of the future president) in a women's relief group that aided injured soldiers, the unemployed, and Belgian refugees. She traveled to Egypt, where her officer-husband, Reginald, was stationed, and nursed the victims of combat in several military hospitals. These experiences made her a pacifist. After the armistice, Ruth and Reggie, partly disabled with kidney disease, moved to Miami and rented a small house across the street from her parents. But she refused to ask them for financial aid.

Ambitious as well as proud, Ruth launched her own career, lecturing about her experiences abroad and the urgent need to prevent another "maelstrom of war." "She has her distinguished father's command of language," reported the *Miami Herald* in 1919, along with a "magnetic and charming personality." Ruth sent the clipping to Papa Bryan, along with the boast that "my voice carries a very long way without effort." In the early 1920s, her talent and name made her a headliner on the Chautauqua circuit, which provided a healthy income. Ruth also found time to produce and direct a feature film based on a tale from the Arabian Nights. Alas, *Scheherazade* never appeared on a commercial screen—whether due to the sexism of Hollywood distributors, as Ruth believed, or because the costume drama, no copy of which survives, simply lacked artistic merit. But the editor of *The Commoner* was happy to reprint an Indiana reporter's comment that his daughter "is truly a Bryan in stature" and in "the strenuous life she lives."[15]

THE PATRIARCH was doing his best to live up to his tireless image. As if to make up for his partial eclipse during the war, Bryan blazed around the nation during three out of the four seasons, stopping in Miami for the winter to comfort Mary and deliver his weekly Bible talks. Not content to save individual souls, he worked to stoke an insurgent spirit among Democrats and the public at large. This led Bryan to take some positions more radical than any he had adopted before.[16]

America's short but contentious role in the world war had given new life to the ideological extremes at home. A reborn Ku Klux Klan gained a vast membership by promoting fear of militant Catholics, blacks, and Jews. The American Legion sounded a similar alarm about "homegrown Bolsheviks," whose ranks included anyone who organized an industrial strike or admired Lenin and Trotsky. Marcus Garvey voiced a message of racial pride and pan-Africanism that appealed to many "New Negroes" fed up with white supremacy. The white left's own ardor for revolution led to a nasty split in the Socialist Party, out of which two different Communist parties were born. Even the cautious leaders of the AFL talked about abandoning the Democrats for a more class-conscious alternative, such as a farmer-labor party.

While Bryan was neither so bold nor reckless, he did promote a number of ideas identified with Socialists and left-wing populists. His "Constructive Program" of 1919 had helped kindle support for nationalized railroads and a government-run telephone and telegraph system. The next year, he added demands that Congress subsidize farm prices and pay an immediate bonus to World War I veterans. He also favored laws that would guarantee a living wage as well as protect collective bargaining and the right to organize unions—but also encourage both sides in an industrial dispute to arbitrate their differences. In 1924, after the Teapot Dome scandal had demonstrated yet again that big business corrupted politics, Bryan proposed a daringly simple remedy: the federal government should pay all "legitimate" campaign expenses, including advertising. "This would put the parties on an equality," he wrote, "and prevent the obligating of parties or candidates to the predatory interests."[17]

Such proposals made clear that Bryan, despite his worship of Jefferson, no longer shared the Virginian's preference for a weak federal state. "The power of the government to protect the people is as complete in time of peace as in time of war," Bryan declared in 1922. "The only question to be decided is whether it is necessary to exercise that power." Authority to outlaw the commerce in alcohol clearly fit that definition, as did measures to protect and uplift wage earners, farmers, women, and the voting public at large. During the 1896 campaign, Bryan accused bankers and industrialists of using the government to enrich themselves. A quarter-century later, he had become an unambiguous advocate of a strong liberal state that would aid the unprivileged majority. New Dealers in the 1930s only had to flesh out this conviction with a profusion of agencies and regulations.[18]

What is more, Bryan wanted the government to advance the cause of sexual equality. In the spring of 1920, he wrote a remarkable article for *Collier's* in which he called for "a single moral standard." Now that women had the vote, Bryan reasoned, all forms of discrimination based on gender could and should be abolished. This included the most intimate terrain of all. Bryan proposed making the age of sexual consent the same for women and men and enforcing antiprostitution laws against male clients as well as against ladies of the night. Champions of women's rights from Elizabeth Cady Stanton to Frances Willard to Emma Goldman had long demanded the same reform. Now the best-known political evangelist in the land was taking their side.

Of course, Bryan had not suddenly become a radical feminist. He wanted the church, not an independent movement of women, to lead this struggle: "While it holds up before the woman the ideal of perfect purity, it will force man to consider the unspeakable selfishness of one who, for a moment's fleeting pleasure, will blast a human life and drag down to the bottomless pit one made in the image of the Creator." He thus echoed the spiritual protest lodged earlier by the WCTU (led by Willard) against the sexual double standard. Every evangelical American condemned prostitution, at least publicly. But it was quite rare for a Christian man to hold his own gender responsible for what Goldman excoriated as the "traffic in women."[19]

Moral rigor ranked far ahead of electability for Bryan as the 1920 campaign season began. Everyone knew the Democrats were unlikely to retain the White House. Wilson still refused to consider amendments to the unpopular Versailles treaty; neither, despite his recent stroke, would he rule out running for a third term. Massive strikes in nearly every major industry and race riots in Chicago and other northern cities kindled fears of social upheaval and a prolonged recession. With revolution rampant in Europe and Asia, the world seemed much less safe for democracy after the Great War than before it.

Amid the global turmoil, the issue that most engaged Bryan's party was the merit of legalized prohibition. Urban immigrants and their offspring so resented the Volstead Act that the Democratic governors of New York and New Jersey, Alfred E. Smith and Edward Edwards, urged their legislatures to amend it by legalizing wine and beer. But to the drys' relief, the U.S. Supreme Court confirmed that the law had to be enforced, even in states where most people despised it. The likelihood of electoral defeat in 1920 encouraged Bryan to stick to all his positions, whether or not they were popular. "Is it 1904 Over Again?" asked *The Commoner* in February. Once again, he urged Democrats to preach a sweeping vision of moral and economic reform if they ever hoped to recapture the nation's trust.[20]

Inevitably, a number of followers hoped Bryan would lead the chorus by running for the presidency himself. "Brother Wilson and the other administration leaders have gotten things in a devil of shape," wrote an admirer from Wyoming. "Our party seems up against it, and you are again needed at the helm." Bryan Clubs sprang up in Washington, D.C., and a few other cities, while leaders of the Prohibition Party let the dry crusader know their nomination was his for the asking. "Two very prominent clergymen have volunteered to stump their respective states [for you] in [the] coming election," announced one club organizer. That March, *The Commoner* printed a cartoon by a fourteen-year-old reader from East Texas who depicted Smith and Edwards leading a "motley crew" to the upcoming Democratic national convention in San Francisco: tycoons in top hats, hoboes (both black and white) in patches, and ward bosses in checkered vests. Who but the godly hero could stop them?[21]

The temptation to run was stronger than at any time since 1908, but Bryan could not convince himself to do it. From Miami, he wrote to his brother, who was keen to oil up the personal campaign engine, "I would not accept a nomination unless it seemed a duty." That condition would be met only *if* the Republicans again split in two, *if* "the labor people and the pro-hibitionists" got behind him, and *if* Democratic delegates expressed "a need for me" in San Francisco. Bryan realized any of these occurrences was a long shot and the combination of all three a virtual impossibility.[22]

So he thanked his "friends" for their "loyalty and confidence" and planned, as in 1904 and 1912, to dominate the convention without running for office. "If I can help this world to banish alcohol, and after that to banish war...no office, no Presidency, can offer the honors that will be mine." To advance his ends, Bryan gained a seat in the Nebraska delegation—and a syndicate's agreement to pay him $12,000 to report, once again, on both major party conventions. A *Literary Digest* poll completed in mid-June ranked him fourth among potential Democratic candidates, even though he'd taken himself out of the running months before.[23]

But Bryan failed to recognize how few allies he still had within the inner councils of his party. Democratic bosses in the big industrial states viewed the Eighteenth Amendment as a direct assault on the very people who kept them in power, few of whom worshiped at evangelical churches. While open to any measures that would boost the incomes of their constituents, the bosses had no patience with nationalization schemes that had little chance of success. Bryan seemed to them a self-proud grandstander, "the Beerless leader" whose rigid principles had never produced victory.

At the same time, his ongoing squabble with the ailing Wilson made him anathema to keepers of the incumbent's flame. To call the president a sick man who "has been denied the information essential to sound judgment and safe leadership" appeared to insult the cause for which over a hundred thousand Americans had died. Bryan still had many admirers, particularly in from the South and West. But few were eager to undertake the rhetorical purging he thought necessary.[24]

As a result, his effort to save the Democrats from opportunism was an utter failure. At the rostrum in San Francisco, Bryan delivered a long, elo-quent plea for prohibition and rapid disarmament: "Some day I shall stand before His judgment bar; and when I appear there, there shall not be upon my hands the blood of people slaughtered while I talked politics." Admirers staged a twenty-minute-long demonstration, which brought Bryan to tears. But he disdained to use one of the microphones that were, for the first time in convention history, available to speakers. The new technology broke Bryan's unique spell over the far galleries; now even the thinnest voices could be heard throughout the hall.

On the forty-fourth ballot, the tired and dispirited delegates settled on Governor James Cox of Ohio as their nominee. Bryan floated the names of a dozen dark-horse figures and then declined to vote on the final ballots. Cox had a mildly reformist record, particularly on labor issues, and hailed from a pivotal state, where he owned several newspapers. Opposed to making "the population 'moral by statute,'" Cox did pledge that if elected, he would dutifully enforce the Volstead Act. The nomination of young Franklin D. Roosevelt for vice president, mostly on the strength of his surname, signaled that the Democrats were still a progressive party.[25]

Bryan refused to believe it. Before coming to San Francisco, he warned that choosing Cox "would make the Democratic Party the leader of the lawless element of the country." Now he had to mull over a platform that said nothing about prohibition and applauded Wilson's doomed posture on the League of Nations. In his elegant suite at the St. Francis Hotel, he treated his fellow journalists to a cocktail of self-pity and despair. "My heart is in the grave with our cause. It must pause until it comes back to me." A month later, he rejected the Democratic National Committee's plea for help with the excuse that any speeches he gave "would alienate the elements to which [Cox] is making his appeal." He also declined to head the Prohibition ticket, after the drys nominated him without a single dissenting vote.[26]

That fall, Bryan broke a habit of four decades: he tended to his own concerns instead of stumping for his party. The Cox-Roosevelt ticket got buried in a GOP landslide, winning only 34 percent of the popular vote and taking dozens of congressmen down with it. Never had the Democrats performed so abysmally in a presidential contest.

In 1904, Bryan had responded to a similar debacle by vowing to take his party back, inspiring an effort that led to his third nomination. After Cox's defeat, he couldn't resist gloating, "The day is past when the liquor machines and Wall Street interests of the large cities can successfully dictate to the great moral majority of the nation." Early in 1921, Will and brother Charles issued a legislative wish list for "progressive Democrats" that reiterated proposals Bryan had been advocating since the end of the war. Later, he added a more radical one: a farmer, a wage earner, and a small businessman should immediately be added to the Federal Reserve Board—to bring true democracy to the powerful agency he'd helped create. There would be no surrender to the wet *or* the greedy.[27]

BUT BRYAN'S EFFORT to reverse the erosion of religious faith eclipsed every other cause. A newspaper syndicate run by evangelical Protestants began distributing his Bible talks in 1921. These homilies soon became his most popular mode of expression; both *The Commoner* and the tent Chautauquas were undergoing gradual but irreversible declines. Pioneering radio stations in Pittsburgh, Los Angeles, Miami, and elsewhere broadcast some of Bryan's sermons, making him one of the first evangelists to exploit the new medium. He also recorded the Lord's Prayer and Bible verses for a fledgling firm in the Midwest. As a string quartet warbled behind him, Bryan preached in the ponderous, sentimental style one can still hear on Christian radio stations across much of America.[28]

These activities had the desired effect. More correspondents hailed him for "bringing tardy-minded Christians" to embrace "their inheritance in the Word of God," as one Chicagoan put it, than for upholding the gospel of reform. Not that Bryan ever missed a chance to underline the contemporary relevance of Scripture. In one typical Bible talk, he construed Belshazzar's besotted feast—which ends with the writing on a wall that predicts the king's death—as "a lesson against drink in any form."[29]

Bryan would surely have preferred to apply his faith in such familiar ways and to avoid a break with his fellow Christians. But the pious optimism of old was no longer appropriate. Inside major Protestant denominations, self-assured modernists were preaching a doctrine every biblical literalist found not just abhorrent but a clear sign that the nation was sick at its soul. Articulate urban ministers and college professors were doubting the Virgin Birth and dismissing the idea that the Bible was directly inspired by God. A 1919 survey found that evolution was taught in three-quarters of the colleges in the Midwest, Bryan's home region. The acceptance of Darwinism stemmed from the desire to repudiate what a leading modernist called "wild anachronisms," to revitalize Christianity as a faith for rational people eager to leave all superstitions behind. For Bryan, this kind of thinking tore at the very heart of his faith: its capacity to inspire ordinary men and women to devote themselves to the common good.[30]

In retrospect, his anxiety seems irrational. Churchgoing actually rose during the 1920s. At mid-decade, the Census Bureau reported that close to 60 percent of Americans belonged to a congregation, a historic high. "Questioning the truth or adequacy of their religious beliefs is not within the conversational area of most people," reported Robert and Helen Lynd in their landmark study of everyday life in Muncie, Indiana. The sociologists did suspect, however, that "doubts and uneasiness among individuals" about their faith were on the rise in the mostly white and Protestant city.[31]

A growing number of Americans prayed to a Catholic, Eastern Orthodox, or Jewish God. But religious diversity had never bothered Bryan before, and he didn't protest it now. In fact, he frequently condemned the sin of religious prejudice. Supporters got scolded for alleging a Papist conspiracy, and Bryan attacked Henry Ford for reprinting the anti-Semitic fraud *The Protocols of the Elders of Zion* in his Dearborn newspaper. He also accepted several invitations to speak at synagogues. After one such talk, at a Miami temple, Libbie Friedlander, a "true daughter of Israel," praised his sermon on King David as far superior to the insincere prattle of her own rabbi back in Brooklyn.[32]

Bryan's only quarrel was with his fellow Protestants who questioned the veracity of the Bible. He assumed that his coreligionists would form the American majority for some time to come. That made him all the more determined to expose the modernist heresy that had wormed its way into citadels of learning where the gospel his parents had taught him in the cottage on Broadway Street had once reigned supreme.[33]

Higher education had been utterly transformed since the days when Bryan attended Illinois College, where some students read Darwin but all were drilled in rhetoric, the classics, and moral philosophy. Science—both hard and social—now dominated the curriculum in institutions that socialized thrice the percentage of young people who had attended during the Gilded Age. Professors who enjoyed the hard-won right of academic freedom encouraged students to question the authority of churches, past and present. Educators, often trained in Europe, had replaced ministers at the helm of the more prestigious private colleges, and public universities did away with required chapel and theology courses altogether.

The products of applied science thrilled Bryan as much as they did other Americans living at the dawn of the age of radio and film, automobiles and air travel. In 1924, he even joined the American Association for the Advancement of Science to rebut the notion that he was an enemy of the profession. But he recoiled at any research in biology or geology that denied the supernatural. The acceptance of such work, he believed, opened the door to every manner of immoral behavior, from defiance of the Volstead Act to a lust for war.[34]

Surprisingly, he could cite two influential disciples of Darwin to back up his fears. Early in the Great War, Vernon Kellogg, a Stanford professor who wrote widely about evolution, spent several weeks with German scientists who had become officers on the kaiser's general staff. In a 1917 book, he reported alarmingly that, to these men, natural selection meant "a violent and competitive struggle" that could end only with "the most advanced" nation dominating or destroying the others. In 1918, Benjamin Kidd, a popular British author, published a repudiation of his earlier defenses of applied Darwinism. Theorists of evolution, Kidd now maintained, sought to replace Christian ethics with a philosophy "resting on inequality.... If in the struggle for existence A was able to kill B before B killed A, then the [human] race became a race of A's inheriting A's qualities."[35] Bryan hated war and militarism as much as any political figure in America. In the writings of Kellogg and Kidd, he found an explanation for these evils that might convince Christians to trust in the gospel of brotherhood against a science that made brutality seem inevitable and thus legitimate.

In the spring of 1922, Bryan delivered a series of lectures that presented his case with great passion and clarity. The setting was a friendly one—a Presbyterian seminary in Richmond, Virginia, that was known for its orthodox views. Aware that every previous speaker in the school's annual Sprunt lectureship held a divinity degree and that most were ministers, Bryan identified himself as a mere "journalist" who hoped "to repay" his late parents for "having brought into my life the Christian principles upon which their own lives were builded." Perhaps he could help persuade contemporary students that they needed God and his Book to follow the moral path, just as he had at their age.[36]

That bland, if heartfelt, sentiment prefaced a sustained defense both of the Social Gospel and of the biblical account of creation. On one hand, Bryan declared that laws that "put human rights before property rights"— such as curbs on child labor and trusts—had "put the teachings of the Saviour into modern language and appl[ied] them to present-day conditions." He criticized the notion that anyone could be independent from the labor and troubles of others. Bryan cited Tolstoy's conviction that religion was a practical faith because it taught men how to love and live in harmony with those of different classes and beliefs. At a time when many of his co-religionists were returning to the comfort of a private faith, Bryan reasserted the need for a crusading Christianity dedicated to improving the lot of ordinary people.

His longest lecture, "The Origin of Man," used that populist conviction to blast the teaching of Darwinism. What made the theories of the late naturalist so dangerous, Bryan argued, was their influence on the young. Darwinism, he claimed, opened the door wide to immoral behavior. If human beings were created not in the image of God but as brute mammals, "how can one feel God's presence in his daily life?"[37]

Bryan insisted he was opposed neither to scientific research nor to the academic institutions that cultivated it: "There is nothing *unreasonable* about Christianity, and there is nothing *unscientific* about Christianity." The problem was that Darwinists were substituting "guesses" for observable facts— and indoctrinating boys and girls with their anti-religious twaddle.

The consequences of that were appalling, he thought. Students who learned that humans were nothing but animals and that animals survived only through violence and hatred had little reason to care for "the weak and the helpless" among them. They rapidly lost faith in a God "ready to give at any moment the aid that is needed." A society run by Darwinists could justify a law barring the feebleminded and poor from having babies and could engage in endless wars of conquest. It was time to call a halt to the propagation of this malignant philosophy.[38]

Bryan considered his cure to be the epitome of democracy. Taxpayers should prevent the public schools they financed from teaching "atheism, agnosticism, Darwinism, or any other hypothesis that links man in blood relationship with the brutes." Nonbelievers were free, of course, to say whatever they liked in their own private schools, just as Christians did in their sectarian institutions. But the public schools, free and open to any child, should refrain from promoting either a single faith or none at all. Wasn't that the American way?[39]

As Walter Lippmann later observed, Bryan's logic was the mirror image of what Jefferson, his political hero, had employed 150 years earlier in the Virginia Statute for Religious Freedom. "If it is wrong to compel people to support a creed they disbelieve," asked Lippmann, how can one "compel them to support teaching which impugns the creed in which they do believe?" The journalist labeled Bryan an "American inquisitor," but he granted his point.[40]

The Richmond lectures, entitled *In His Image,* were an instant hit. The book sold over a hundred thousand copies within a few months of publication and gained support for Bryan from several prominent figures in the world of reform. Charles Sheldon, who was editing a leading religious journal, applauded his stand and thanked Bryan for his help in bringing *In His Steps* to the movie screen. While most national political figures avoided the issue, Bryan received supportive notes from Senator Robert Owen, the populist Democrat from Oklahoma; Raymond Robins, a former leader of the Progressive Party and Red Cross official in revolutionary Russia; and New York City mayor John F. Hylan, an anti-Tammany Democrat. "Between the animal and the man...there is an impassable gulf," agreed Louis Post, a friend and veteran Single Taxer who'd recently held a top post in Wilson's Labor Department.[41]

Equally significant to Bryan were the numerous letters he received from ministers, parents, and college students who confirmed his warning about the peril Darwinism posed to children. "A young girl came home from school last year and was telling me what she had learned as to her monkey ancestorship," wrote an admirer from a town near Palm Beach. "I asked her if she believed God was a monkey and she was horrified." A freshman at Columbia University, who was also a pastor, reported that nearly all his instructors were atheists and that the school passed out pamphlets espousing Darwinism, while discouraging contrary views. What is more, he told Bryan, "your name is used as the very symbol of narrowness and bigotry and intollerance [*sic*]."[42] Audiences at elite eastern colleges had never warmed up to the Commoner. Now he could fight back, with evidence that the virus that had driven Europeans to mass slaughter was infecting America's intellectual elite as well.

Into the lion's den of academia he charged, brandishing the saber of correction. At Middlebury College, Bryan defended the veracity of certain passages in Scripture. At the University of Rochester, he angered some professors by "exposing" the theory of evolution. At a public meeting in Madison, he challenged the president of the University of Wisconsin, E. A. Birge, to explain why so many students who entered his school as believers graduated as atheists. When a local minister informed Bryan that Birge was an elder of his church, the crusader was unmoved. "If he does not agree with what is being taught, it is his duty to try to purge the institution of any false doctrine. The drawing of a large salary . . . carries with it responsibility."[43]

The fact that the university president was a churchgoer only made him a more dangerous foe. As Christians, Birge and his peers had a legitimacy that rebels who dismissed the Bible as a pack of lies would never enjoy. Such "theistic evolutionists," Bryan wrote to a follower, ". . . claim to believe in God the Creator although they put Him so far away that He is likely to exert a decreasing influence over their lives. The atheist shocks us into resistance while the theistic evolutionist is more apt to mislead us." Like many a true believer, Bryan dreaded nothing so much as the enemy within.[44]

This conviction spurred him into a battle to control the doctrine of his own denomination. Before the 1920s, Bryan had never paid much heed to the internal business of the Presbyterian Church in the U.S. He certainly felt comfortable belonging to a body that boasted seven presidents—Jackson and Wilson among them—and a tradition of strict pietism dating back to its origins in sixteenth-century Scotland. Yet he often attended Methodist services and, in keeping with his ecumenical outlook, never claimed that one denomination was superior to any other.

But leading modernists in church heaped scorn on his views, goading him to counterattack. In March 1922, Harry Emerson Fosdick, a Baptist serving as "guest preacher" at the venerable First Presbyterian Church in Manhattan, lambasted the fundamentalists and their unofficial leader. "The real enemies of the Christian faith," he announced in the *New York Times*, "are not the evolutionary biologists, but folk like Mr. Bryan who insist on setting up artificial adhesions between Christianity and outgrown scientific opinions." Fosdick compared Bryan's "sincere but appalling obscurantism" to the Catholic Church's squelching of Galileo and to Martin Luther's rejection of Copernicus's discovery that the earth moved around the sun. Two months later, Fosdick delivered a sermon at First Presbyterian that called fundamentalists "essentially illiberal and intolerant" and accused them of dividing Christians at a time when "colossal problems" in the world demanded their attention. Widely reprinted, the address lost Fosdick his New York pulpit but established him as a leading voice of liberal Protestants. His fame for coining quaint moralisms—such as "A person wrapped up in himself makes a small package"—lay off in the future.[45]

The Fosdick affair galvanized orthodox Presbyterians to drive heresy from their midst. What better instrument could they find but Bryan, the modernists' most aggressive and popular foe? In 1923, he ran for the post of moderator of the Presbyterian Assembly, the titular head of the church. Fittingly, his main opponent was the president of a denominational college in Wooster, Ohio, where biology students studied *The Origin of Species*.

The result was no different from Bryan's other national campaigns. He lost, although by a closer margin than in any of his presidential races. He did manage to push through the assembly a warning to Presbyterians who educated the young: "official approval" would be withcld from any school "which seeks to establish a materialistic evolutionary philosophy of life."[46]

Such a sanction sounds chilling today, when even the most dedicated creationists ask only that their version of human origins receive equal time. But Bryan thought he was only asserting the principle of majority rule. As he wrote to the editor of the *Christian Herald,* who fretted about a Protestant schism, "It is deplorable that there should be a division upon matters that seem so plain, but…the believers in evolution number less than ten per cent of the professing Christians…we cannot make a religion to suit only those who have a college education." Bryan reminded his correspondent that "Christ selected His followers from the common people—fishermen, tent makers, etc.… He himself worked in a carpenter shop."[47]

BRYAN WOULD NEVER extend that lifelong faith in "the people" to black Americans, most of whom worked at decidedly common jobs. In the memoir he began to draft in the early 1920s but never completed, Bryan paid tribute to his "good fortune." This included being "born in the greatest of all ages" when the "opportunity for large service" was abundant and as "a member of the greatest of all the races, the Caucasian race" and "a citizen of the greatest of all lands" instead of among "the most backward of earth's peoples."[48] Since relocating to the South, Bryan seemed to have grown more convinced that the region's white majority, to protect the civic order, had to hold a whip hand over the minority race.

In February 1923, he gave a brief talk to the Southern Society of Washington, D.C., explicitly endorsing segregation and suffrage restriction in any state with large numbers of black residents. Bryan also praised the superiority of laws made by whites, "the advanced race," to those black Americans might help make for themselves. Ironically, the great foe of Darwinism invoked "the right of self-preservation" to justify what he acknowledged was a departure from his egalitarian principles.[49]

A few days later, Bryan heard from a Washington patent attorney, one of the "New Negroes" who had found his militant voice during the turmoil of the Great War. "You call yourself a Christian, a believer in God," protested W. Thomas Soders, "and yet you do not believe that the Black man as a race is equally as good as the White man as a race. Pray tell me what kind of Christianity is this you profess?" Soders blasted the "democrats and Southern hypocrites" who lynched black men for miscegenation while "seduc[ing] his sister, his daughter" and conceiving "four and a half million mulattos." Bryan responded, in a chillier tone than he normally used with white critics, "Your letter... confirms my views and I shall be glad to preserve it as evidence of what the colored race would do if they had the power to legislate for the whites, although I think it would be an injustice to attribute to the average colored man the malignant spirit which your letter manifests."[50]

Bryan's passion for democracy had always cooled at the color line. He made an exception for the Japanese, whom he considered quaint but virtual equals, and regarded Mexicans and other Latinos with the eye of an amiable paternalist. But he spurned the idea of wooing any sizeable group of black voters away from the GOP and didn't object when allies such as Josephus Daniels stomped on the rights of their fellow citizens.

When Bryan was running for president, his racism was a moral failing rather than a flaw in electoral strategy; the white South surely would have rejected him if he'd welcomed the support of such figures as W. E. B. Du Bois. But the demography of politics is ever changing. Bryan never understood that his stance would put him and his party at a disadvantage when blacks and other ethnic minorities began to exert the power to match their numbers.

In the 1920s, the racial mote threatened to blot out Bryan's vision of brotherhood triumphing over the "brutishness" of Social Darwinism. Throughout his career, he had railed against conservatives and denied prejudice against Americans who didn't share his faith or ethnic background. But in battling for the Lord, he showed a fresh wariness toward newcomers who, as a Democratic nominee, he had always coveted and courted. One reason he moved to Florida, Will told his brother, was that "the large foreign element" in Nebraska "may not be only against prohibition but other moral issues which are coming." Few of that sort lived and voted in the Deep South.[51]

But Bryan would need a broad coalition to win his fight against the amoral, intellectual elite. In the 1923 race for moderator, black delegates to the Presbyterian Assembly, angered by his racist views, provided the votes that narrowly elected his opponent. Many urban Catholics may have agreed with his views on evolution, but few sided with Bryan on prohibition, an issue that was fueling attacks on them and the Church by the KKK and likeminded bigots.[52]

Increasingly, Bryan found secure allies only among those of his fellow white evangelicals who resisted the advance of an urban, polyglot culture. The teenage cartoonist from Texas who drew immigrant bosses and black vagrants as members of the same cabal illustrated that view. So did correspondents who praised Bryan for defending the Bible but didn't share his support for public enterprise and labor unions. Among the latter was Governor R. A. Nestos of North Dakota, a Republican who had just gained office in a controversial recall election. The man he ousted was a leader of the Non-Partisan League, a quasi-socialist group with whom Bryan agreed on nearly every secular issue.[53]

For numerous Americans, Bryan remained a figure of unflagging principles, a "vessel of the Lord" whose enemies, like Goliath, could humble but never defeat him. But their current admiration stemmed less from a hunger for democratic change than from a dread of moral decline. To repel that threat, he had nothing specific to offer but restraints on individual freedoms—enforcing the increasingly unenforceable Volstead Act and banning textbooks written by leading scientists. Not surprisingly, few of his admirers still called him a prophet, the scourge of economic overlords and their ideology of war and empire. Instead, like Evangeline Booth, leader of the Salvation Army, they simply cheered Bryan for upholding "the Old Truths."[54]

He did provide anti-Darwinists with a proven leader and guaranteed them a shower of publicity. For several years, small groups with grandiose names—the Bible League of North America and the World's Christian Fundamentals Association—had put out pamphlets and held meetings to sound the alarm. They were a mere sideshow in the national press until Bryan made their cause his own and defined it as a crusade to save the young. But the fervor of his new orthodox flock could not make up for the narrowness of its creed. For the first time in his career, Bryan was fighting to preserve the religious past against a future in which a multitude of faiths would coexist and thrive.[55]

That reactionary image had an ominous consequence for his campaign against Darwinism. In the 1920s, anti-evolution laws passed only where Bryan's kind of Christianity had few competitors. A score of states considered such legislation, and he showed up in most of their capitals to make his case. But only five states actually restricted the teaching of evolution in some way, either by banning it altogether or by condemning it as "improper and subversive." Four of these, Tennessee, Mississippi, Arkansas, and Florida, were in the Deep South, while the other, Oklahoma, was home to large numbers of white migrants from Dixie who swore by both segregation and the inerrancy of Scripture.[56]

As he aided these efforts, Bryan strained to avoid the image of intolerance he knew would sully his mission. He urged lawmakers in Florida and Tennessee to attach no criminal penalty to their bills. Only prohibit teaching the theory of evolution "as true," he counseled. There was no harm in describing Darwinism to students as a mere "hypothesis," albeit a wretched one. "We are dealing with an educated class that is supposed to respect the law"; legislators should not let them "divert attention" from the evil of materialist indoctrination.[57]

But some local culture warriors could not keep their animus in check. J. T. Stroder, one of the representatives who introduced an anti-evolution bill in the Texas legislature, also demanded that professors at the state university be fired for assigning such "immoral" authors as Nietzsche and Flaubert and a strange volume he misspelled as "Frouds Neurosis." Stroder added the charge that "several communists or bolshevists from Europe" had spoken on the Austin campus. In Oklahoma, the bill to prohibit the teaching of Darwinism passed by a single vote in 1923. "But for the influence of the K.K.K.," the state's governor told Bryan, "I doubt if it could have carried in either House."[58]

However unwittingly, the great apostle of "brotherhood" and bottom-up reform had found a key ally in the most hate-filled, repressive corner of Protestant America. The Klan boasted as many as four million members in the early 1920s and wielded formidable clout in states such as Oregon, Indiana, and Colorado, as well as through most of the South. Despite their vio-

lent reputation, most local Klaverns immersed themselves in lawful struggles to enforce prohibition and finance public schools. Yet everywhere, they
accused a conspiracy of Catholics, Jews, and recent immigrants of plotting
to destroy the order that "100 per cent Americans" such as themselves had
built. During and just after World War I, this sentiment had helped inspire
state laws to ban the teaching of German and to outlaw radical groups that
allegedly harbored "foreign spies." Now it was rallying some of the fearful
to join the fundamentalist crusade.[59]

Bryan made clear in a letter to Senator Thomas Walsh, a Catholic and a
dry, that he deplored the Klan's hostility to other faiths, as well as its
secrecy. But he was still a politician. Obeying the instinct of the species, he
hated to condemn any group of activists who could further his purposes.
There would, after all, soon be another difficult election campaign to
wage.[60]

IN 1924, Bryan shifted temporarily from battling for the Lord to attempting, once again, to save the soul of his party. He believed the Democrats
were still vulnerable to capture by the wizards of Wall Street, "predatory"
corporations, and pols who did their bidding. The forces of darkness, he
charged, were bankrolling the campaigns of tractable men and turning
major newspapers into attack dogs against their populist critics. Since abandoning the chimera of a fourth run for president, Bryan had become the
unofficial moralist of his party. He took the podium at every national convention to remind delegates—and, through the press, every rank-and-file
Democrat—to adhere to the standard he had planted in 1896. That rhetorical stance had worked splendidly in 1912 and regained the party's affections
for him in 1916. But it had flopped in 1920, as his zeal for a dry America
turned off more delegates than it attracted.

As a new campaign year began, Bryan thought he had a chance to deliver
another brilliant, righteous performance. The political environment seemed
more promising than at any time since the end of the Great War. The
Democrats gained over seventy House seats in the 1922 midterm election,
the kind of boost that usually translated into victory in the next presidential
contest. Voter disgust at corruption in Warren Harding's administration
revived hope that progressives in both parties who favored relief for small
farmers and wage earners could again dominate the legislative agenda.
Franklin D. Roosevelt, recovering from polio in Hyde Park, wrote Bryan a
warm letter in which he disparaged "the hopeful idiots who think the demo-

cratic platform will advocate a repeal of the 18th amendment." FDR agreed that "certain reactionary forces" would try to stop a dry progressive from gaining the next presidential nod.[61]

Among the Democrats swept into office in 1922 was Charles Bryan, the new governor of Nebraska. As soon as he moved into the executive mansion in Lincoln, Charles vowed to "let the people know" about overcharges by oil companies and other private contractors that allegedly had caused the state's budget to soar. Only nationalizing the energy industry, he remarked, could halt such gouging. His views contrasted sharply with those of President Calvin Coolidge, who took office when Harding died of a heart attack in the summer of 1923. The taciturn New Englander had first gained national prominence by breaking a Boston police strike. Although Coolidge's honesty was unquestioned, he took the same hands-off policy toward big business that had entangled his late predecessor in scandal. Just before Christmas in 1923, Will predicted to his brother that a "Coolidge nomination will compel the selection of a Democratic candidate from the South or the West." Why not another Bryan? "Keep up the fight on the profiteers," Will advised his favorite governor.[62]

Early the next spring, he made his own intentions clear. In Florida's Democratic primary, Bryan was easily elected a delegate at large on the promise that he would support only a nominee "who is both progressive and dry." *The Commoner* had ceased publication after Charles took office in Lincoln, but Will hoped his followers would find his weekly Bible talks an acceptable substitute for the monthly catalogue of his opinions. The same firm that syndicated the talks also hired him to write about the Democratic convention, in which he hoped to play a leading role.[63]

But for all his lifelong optimism, Bryan was helpless to understand, much less solve, the internal crisis of his party. From his more strident Protestant followers, he heard calls to deport foreign-born bootleggers and pleas to vanquish the Tammany-led "gang who wrecked" the Democrats in the last campaign. Few mentioned the KKK, but neither did they condemn it, unlike the scattering of Catholics who wrote to him asking for help. William Gibbs McAdoo was eager to inherit Bryan's evangelical base in the South and West, but the faithful were suspicious of the slick attorney who was Wilson's son-in-law and had played a minor role in Teapot Dome. Bryan endorsed no one, which inevitably stirred rumors that he hoped to be nominated himself.[64]

Meanwhile, powerful Democrats from the urban East and Midwest were no longer willing to defer to their provincial brethren. The image of big-city bosses as venal thugs that Bryan had used against Champ Clark at the

1912 convention now seemed out of style. The metropolises of the 1920s were booming, thrilling places to live. Broadcasts of blues, jazz, and polka music, packed ethnic theaters, and prosperous immigrant banks all signaled that a new culture dominated by white Catholics, Jews, and African Americans had come of age. Such Democratic kingpins as Charles Murphy from Tammany Hall and George Brennan in Chicago eagerly defended their working-class constituents against their self-righteous enemies—whether nativists in Congress, the KKK, or drys who cringed to think of anyone buying a shot of bourbon or a stein of lager.[65]

Northern Democrats were also rallying around a presidential candidate whom the "reactionary" label didn't fit. Governor Alfred E. Smith of New York had come up through the ranks of Tammany, the most promising young man in the century-old machine. But he gained the affection of voters statewide by building highways and schools, mediating labor disputes, and still managing to cut their taxes. Smith also made clear that as long as he was in power, New York officials would do as little as possible to enforce the hated Volstead Act. The 1924 convention was going to be held right in the middle of his hometown, where Bryanites were convinced that anyone weaned by the Tammany Tiger was incapable of changing his spots. It was an invitation to disaster.[66]

What the Democrats did to themselves that summer in Madison Square Garden remains the most embarrassing public display in the history of American political conventions. For sixteen long, humid days, delegates impugned one another's religion and region and accused one another of being outright bigots or the lapdogs of plutocrats. The convention had opened to great excitement; Democrats hopeful about their fall prospects were willing to pay up to $100 for a ticket in the gallery. But it took a record 103 ballots to choose a nominee for president, exhausting delegates and spectators alike. By the time John W. Davis, a brilliant Wall Street lawyer and former envoy to Great Britain, agreed to head the ticket, the galleries were almost empty, and even political reporters were sick of the whole affair. Nearly every ugly session was broadcast over a national radio network, and newsreel cameras were present for part of the time as well. The unprecedented nature of the coverage, added to its ridiculous length, ensured that Americans would be laughing at the Democrats long after every delegate had fled for home.[67]

Bryan moved through the ordeal at the Garden like a veteran actor performing an old-fashioned play for precisely the wrong audience. On his arrival in New York, he unveiled a progressive platform of his own design and announced that it had McAdoo's full support. Then four days into the convention, Bryan joined a scorching debate about whether to denounce the Ku Klux Klan by name—and poured gasoline on the coals. Why, he asked, should "the Catholic Church, with its legacy of martyr's blood and...its long line of missionaries," or the Jews, who "have Moses...and Elijah...[,] need a great party to protect [them] from a million Klansmen"? Bryan had severely undercounted the size of the KKK and dismissed the ire it aroused in Gotham. "It requires more courage to fight the Republican party," he continued to mounting jeers from the galleries, "than to fight the KKK—more courage to save a nation than to throw a brick." Bryan's side won the day, and the Klan appeared nowhere in the platform.[68]

But the winning margin of just one vote out of more than a thousand cast—and the howling that followed the result—presaged the long deadlock that lay ahead. In trying to change the subject from bigotry to "gigantic combinations of capital," Bryan had managed only to incite his foes against both him and McAdoo, who, with the two-thirds rule in place, had no votes to spare.

Four days later, Bryan rose to praise his former cabinet colleague and got into a shouting match with the partisans of Al Smith. "Every line of his face, and there were many, stood forth pitilessly in that white glare" of the camera lights, wrote a reporter for the *New York Times*. "Mr. Bryan, his customary suavity entirely gone, appeared almost distraught with anger and bitterness. The crowd—his own crowd—was not with him, and he knew it." In his syndicated column, Will Rogers dripped a bit of comedic acid humor into the wound. "If I could have only gotten Bryan to have just made one speech against me I would be having my picture taken for the campaign buttons."[69]

The face of a politician named Bryan did soon appear on the lapels of loyal Democrats. But it was the round, balding image of Charles Wayland Bryan, who had been nominated for vice president on the first ballot after a quick conference among party leaders. As a progressive from the West, he balanced the ticket headed by Davis, who had recently called the income tax an assault on "human liberty." The need for a leftward feint was rather urgent. Senator Robert La Follette was running an aggressive independent campaign for president and had won the support of both the AFL and the Socialist Party. At sixty-nine, "Fighting Bob" was as brash as ever. He offered voters a full-strength version of the anti-corporate, pro-government-ownership, farmer-labor gospel Bryan had been preaching since the end of the war. If unchecked, La Follette would split the opposition, handing Coolidge an easy victory.[70]

Will was overjoyed at his brother's nomination; it was a just reward for

Charles's long labors in the shadows of his own career. But it only slightly softened his opinion of Davis, whom he had earlier called "a man of high character," adding, "So is Mr. Coolidge. There is no difference between them." At least the Democratic platform included such planks as a curb on large donations to campaigns, a vow to increase income taxes on the rich (which Davis ignored), and a promise to enforce prohibition.[71]

That fall, Will actually gave more campaign speeches than did Charles, who had a state to run and more sympathy with La Follette's views than with those of his own running mate. The governor may also have bet that inactivity would make him acceptable to Congress as a compromise president if no party won a majority of electoral votes in the three-way contest. Charles knew there was no chance the Democrats could win an outright victory. But the result in November was worse than any partisan had imagined. Davis and Bryan gained just 29 percent of the popular vote and carried the eleven states of the Old Confederacy plus Oklahoma—and nothing else. The party's second crushing loss in a row may have inspired Will Rogers to quip, "I don't belong to any organized Political faith, I am a democrat."[72]

The debacle of 1924 left Will Bryan with no clear road to reclaiming political influence. Half of active Democrats considered him a sworn enemy, and his capacity to rally loyalists to take back "their" party seemed all but spent. Back in Florida for the winter, he received many letters asking for spiritual advice or cheering his views on modernist theology but few about the perpetual conflict between the noble people and the vexatious special interests. When an offer came that spring to join prosecutors in upholding Tennessee's new law against the teaching of evolution, Bryan immediately agreed. He persuaded William Junior to come from Los Angeles to work alongside him, predicting this would "become one of the greatest trials in history."[73]

IN FACT, *State of Tennessee v. John Thomas Scopes* lacked nearly all the elements of a classic courtroom drama. Both sides agreed that the defendant was guilty as charged. Scopes had violated the statute unintentionally one day while substituting for the regular biology instructor. Knowing little about the subject, the twenty-four-year-old teacher did not even take the stand in his own defense. Although convicted, he suffered in no way for his "crime." In fact, Scopes, who had been hired more to coach the Dayton High football team than to teach science, basked in the renown of the case for the rest of his life.[74]

Yet his trial drew over a hundred reporters, a national radio audience, and became the touchstone for a debate that continues to rage. As Bryan commented at the end of the eight-day event, "Here has been fought out a little case of little consequence as a case, but the world is interested because it raises an issue and that issue will some day be settled right, whether it is settled on our side or the other side."[75]

The issue was not just whether one could reconcile the Bible with the writings of Charles Darwin. The Tennessee law also raised the question of whether a teacher in a public school was free to teach the truth as he saw it or "whether the people...have the right to control the educational system which they have created and which they tax themselves to support," as Bryan wrote to local supporters. Clarence Darrow agreed to head Scopes's defense only after learning that Bryan was joining the other side. Once an ally of the politician, the great attorney now reviled him as a foe of intellectual liberty and a symbol of "despair and bigotry." The six-year-old American Civil Liberties Union financed the defense to protect free speech, not to pit science against Christianity. In fact, of the four lawyers who represented John Scopes, only Darrow, a proud agnostic, was willing to mock the authority of Scripture.[76]

The spectacle of a divided nation also stirred the popular imagination. H. L. Mencken regaled his big-city, northern readers with descriptions of Bryan's "peculiar imbecilities" and "theologic bilge." Darrow later called Bryan "the idol of all Morondom." Modernist skeptics had grown in stature and confidence since John Reed had made fun of the Commoner cruising through the Florida swamps. After the United States failed to save democracy abroad and prohibition didn't stop Americans from drinking, how could anyone take Bryan's bloviated piety seriously? But to millions of evangelical Christians, the defeat of political altruism only increased the need to stand by the one text that would never fail them. In the smirking Darrow and his admirers in the press, they saw proof of Bryan's warnings about the perils of amoral education.[77]

Ironically, the site of the trial had as much in common with the new urban America as with its rural past. Located in the foothills of East Tennessee, Dayton was settled only in the late nineteenth century and soon became the seat of agrarian Rhea County. Its railroad line, iron and coal mines, and hosiery mill were all financed by moneymen from the North. The industries lured hundreds of immigrant Scots as well as local farmers seeking a steady wage. To show off their prosperity, Daytonites built a huge, three-story county courthouse, one of the largest in the South. The KKK had few if any members in the reverent yet tolerant community.

But by the 1920s, Dayton's economy was faltering, and its population sank below two thousand. So its leading citizens were receptive when George Rappleyea, a Ph.D. engineer from New York who managed the local mines, suggested that the first test of the anti-evolution law be held in their very own courthouse. Rappleyea himself was a confirmed modernist. He regularly attended Methodist services but hoped the ban on teaching evolution would be judged a violation of the state constitution. During a friendly meeting at a corner drugstore, Scopes gladly agreed to stand trial for the good of the local economy.[78]

The young defendant's biography illustrated the tensions of recent religious history. Scopes's father, a British immigrant machinist, had served as an elder in the Cumberland Presbyterian Church of Paducah, Kentucky—the same denomination Bryan had joined in his youth. But he soured on "the myths and miracles of Christian dogma" and left the church when his fellow congregants drove local prostitutes out of town instead of helping them reform their lives. The elder Scopes also voted the Socialist ticket. His father's dissent aside, young John faithfully attended Sunday school and weekly services until his senior year in high school. He spent his teenage years in Salem, Illinois.

In one of those occasions that history inserts for comic relief, the main speaker at Scopes's graduation from Salem High School in 1919 was Bryan, the hometown hero. As the great orator began his address, the boy and some friends started giggling from the front row at a whistling sound he was accidentally making. Bryan "stared hard at us," Scopes recalled, and kept watch on the miscreants even "after he had his speech flowing evenly again." After moving to Dayton, the new teacher joined a local church. But, like his father, he still doubted that the Gospels were based on fact.[79]

Darrow and his colleagues built their defense around just such ambivalences. "I know there are millions of people in the world who look on [the Bible] as being a divine book, and I have not the slightest objection to it," declared the agnostic, rather disingenuously. But he added, "It is not a book of science. Never was and was never meant to be." In using the Bible to curb the teaching of biology, the legislature had violated logic, as well as the First Amendment. The ACLU was thus funding an elaborate brief for theistic evolution.[80]

To make its case, the defense brought to Dayton a number of honored scientists from elite universities. The prosecution had begun the trial by proving the obvious: several of Scopes's students told the court he had indeed reviewed a lesson about evolution in class. The textbook used was a standard in the field: *A Civic Biology* by George William Hunter, a high

school biology teacher from New York City. Darrow and his colleagues—
Dudley Field Malone and Arthur Garfield Hays—hoped to impress the
jury and the outside world by placing on the stand men of learning who
were also practicing Christians. The prosecution objected that such testimony was irrelevant to the question of whether a state law had been violated. But on the fourth day of the trial, Judge John T. Raulston allowed one
expert witness to testify—Maynard Metcalf, a zoologist from Johns Hopkins University and a Sunday-school teacher. The judge had not yet
decided whether such evidence was admissible, so he ordered the jury to
leave the courtroom. Metcalf then spent an hour lucidly explaining the
rudiments of evolution.

The next morning, the prosecutors asked Raulston to halt the biology
lectures. Such testimony, argued William Bryan Jr. in his only extended
speech of the trial, took power away from jurors and gave it to supposed
experts. To allow it would be "to announce to the world your honor's belief
that this jury is too stupid to determine a simple question of fact." His argument touched off a day of provocative speeches, which frequently strayed
from the question at hand. With savage wit, Hays, a secular Jew from New
York who was the ACLU's lead attorney, asked, "Is there anything in Anglo-
Saxon law that insists that the determination of either court or jury must be
made in ignorance?" Two of the local prosecutors shot back that the men on
the jury knew their Bible better than "these experts" and hadn't signed up
for a science class. At a quarter before twelve, as the attorneys continued to
snipe at one another, the judge announced a long recess to enable mechan-
ics to install fans in the ceiling of the overstuffed, stifling courthouse.[81]

That afternoon, July 16, occurred the most dramatic confrontation of the
trial to date. For the first time, William Jennings Bryan took center stage.
The room was so crowded, with disappointed spectators lined up in the
halls, that Judge Raulston had to warn everyone against making noise and
venting "emotion," lest the floor give way. Bryan began by rephrasing his
son's argument that the wisdom of the anti-evolution law was not at issue.
"This is not the place to try to prove that the law ought never to have been
passed. The place to prove that, or teach that, was to the legislature."[82]

Given the magnitude of the cause, he could hardly rest there. For almost
an hour, Bryan summarized, with occasional humor, the case he'd been
making for half a decade. He defended the right of parents to control what
their children learned in school. He claimed that Darwinism was a mere
"hypothesis" because "never have [scientists] traced one single species to
any other." He bewailed the loss of faith among intellectuals and accused

Darrow's team of trying to take from the people of Tennessee "every moral standard that the Bible gives us."

Midway through his speech, Bryan held aloft the best-selling text that Scopes reviewed with his class. *A Civic Biology* depicted a rather crudely drawn "evolutionary tree" that named, in circles of different sizes, every class of animals, from protozoa at the bottom to mammals on the highest branch. The author had rounded off the totals in each group. Bryan joked, "I don't think all of these animals breed in round numbers.... I am satisfied from some I have seen that there must be more than 35,000 sponges." Human beings went unmentioned, subsumed within the mammalian bubble: "How dared those scientists possibly think of shutting man up in a little circle like that with all these animals, that have an odor, that extends beyond the circumference of this circle, my friends." The "extended laughter" that erupted after his statement underlined Bryan's point. Why, he implied, would one substitute such foolery for the Word of God?

Strangely, he neglected to say anything about Hunter's use of *social* Darwinism. Almost seventy pages after the "tree"—which the author urged students to copy in their notebooks—appeared a vigorous endorsement of eugenics. Clearly, the "civic" in the title of the text was no accident. Hunter believed the same principles of breeding that produced healthier, stronger horses could and should improve "the future generations of men and women on the earth." He described two families, the Jokeks and Kallikaks, plagued for generations by "immorality and feeble-mindedness." People like these, wrote Hunter, "are true parasites...if such people were lower animals, we would probably kill them off to prevent them from spreading." But all we can do with degenerate humans is to put them in asylums so they will have no contact with the opposite sex. Perhaps Bryan hadn't read these pages in *A Civic Biology* or thought Hunter's point would take too much time to describe and refute. But absent such an effort, his address came off sounding careless, demagogic, and evasive. He seemed to be opposing science to religion, instead of objecting to the nefarious uses to which science could be put.[83]

The defense attorney who spoke next did a far better job. Nothing in the career of Dudley Field Malone should have allowed him to best a great orator in an unfriendly environment. The handsome forty-three-year-old was a partner in Hays's New York firm and an able divorce lawyer; a Democrat, he had served under Bryan for nine months as an assistant secretary of state. But on this July afternoon, Malone delivered a stirring tribute to free thought that was the most effective speech of the entire trial. Malone began by scolding Bryan for attacking teachers, "the poorest paid profession in America." He then praised his former boss for "his enthusiasm, his vigor, his courage, his fighting ability these long years for the things he thought were right." Having put aside any personal animosities, Malone could focus on the "conflict of ideas."[84]

Why, he asked, should Bryan or anyone else dictate theological correctness? Muslim invaders had burned the great library of Alexandria, Malone reminded the court, because their commander thought "the Koran contains all the truth." The Bible is a wonderful book, the attorney admitted, but it is not a work of science. "Keep it as your consolation, keep it as your guide, but keep it where it belongs, in the world of your own conscience, in the world of your individual judgment, in the world of the Protestant conscience that I heard so much about when I was a boy." Malone challenged Bryan's claim that only his side was protecting the young. Shouldn't students learn every view and make their own decisions? "The truth is no coward," declared Malone. Then, imitating the cadence of a pivotal passage from the Cross of Gold speech, he concluded:

> We feel we stand with fundamental freedom in America. We are not afraid. Where is the fear? We meet it, where is the fear? We defy it, we ask your honor to admit the evidence as a matter of correct law, as a matter of sound procedure and as a matter of justice to the defense in this case.[85]

The courtroom, filled with anti-Darwinists, exploded into applause that lasted for several minutes. Bryan, chagrined yet magnanimous, walked over to Malone and said, "Although we differ, I have never heard a better speech." The defense attorney replied, "I am terribly sorry I had to do it."[86]

But the oratorical drama failed to sway the judge. Raulston opened the next morning of the trial, a Friday, by ruling in favor of the prosecution. He announced, "It is not within the province of the court to decide and determine what is true, the story of divine creation as taught in the Bible, or the story of the creation of man as taught by evolution." Darrow complained bitterly and sarcastically, which earned him a citation for contempt of court. Tom Stewart, the chief prosecutor, rejoiced that "the aspect of novelty" that had dominated the case would now fade away. After court adjourned for the weekend, H. L. Mencken and William Jennings Bryan Jr. both departed for home, confident that nothing remained except closing arguments and a certain verdict of guilty.[87]

But neither of the main protagonists was satisfied. The cause of Darrow's discontent was obvious: his attempt to show the world that scientific reason was superior to religious superstition had essentially been thrown out of court. Bryan also nursed a frustrated ambition. He had not joined the prosecution to preserve a single law in a single state but to defend the word of God as the sole guide most Americans had for behaving in moral, selfless ways. In the months before Dayton, he had struggled to present his goal as a broadly ecumenical, even tolerant one. But the drafters of the Tennessee bill rejected his advice that they prohibit only the teaching of Darwinism "as true" and waive any penalty for violating the law. Bryan also failed to convince a Jewish attorney, his friend Samuel Untermyer, and a Catholic one, Senator Thomas Walsh, to join the prosecution. Many African American ministers, whose guiding metaphor was the covenant between the slaves of ancient Israel and their God, preached support for Bryan's stand. But this was not the kind of united front he sought or desired. So Darrow and Bryan both felt they were missing an opportunity to alter the public's opinion of their respective causes.[88]

Mary Bryan would have been happier if her husband had stayed away from this battle altogether. While in Dayton, she dispatched weekly "bulletins" to her absent daughters, Ruth and Grace. Mary's sharp comments about the proceedings included none of the verbal charity her husband could dispense by the bucketful. The "mountain people" who flocked to Dayton for the spectacle were, she wrote, "both interresting [*sic*] and pathetic. They do not shave every day and the proper costume is a blue shirt, generally worn open at the neck, and a pair of blue overalls." The wife of America's leading foe of Darwinism thought so little of the crowd, most of whom admired her husband, that she scribbled a phrase any eugenicist could applaud. How, she wondered, could "this mass of people ... have no real part in American life; marry and intermarry until the stock is very much weakened."[89]

Mary also wrote cholerically about nearly every member of the defense. Scopes was "a long-jawed, mountain product" who "carries himself wretchedly," while Darrow wore "a weary hopeless expression, which might well prove his lack of faith." Arthur Hays agitated her the most, and his ethnicity was the main reason. He "is as forward and self-asserting as the New York Jews can be," she wrote, adding that he "reeks of East End impertinence" and "his eyes are full of shrewdness." Mary viewed the trial through the scrim of her chronic pain and concern that Will's exertions would further damage his own health. But to dump contempt on both the devout men of Rhea County and the modernists who challenged their beliefs was very much in character. Although she seldom revealed such bigotry, Mary had always cared far less about her husband's many causes than about whether he could win.[90]

The next, penultimate day of the trial fully justified her concern. On Monday afternoon, July 20, Darrow apologized to the court and, in a bit of disarming rhetoric, charmed the judge and spectators by saying he had "been treated, kindlier and more hospitably than I fancied would have been the case in the north," despite his unorthodox views about religion. Raulston, clearly moved, forgave the attorney with a little speech about Christian redemption. The judge then announced that the proceedings would move to the lawn outside the courthouse, where a speaker's platform and wooden seats stood ready. He was still afraid that the floor inside might collapse and also wanted to allow as many people as possible to hear the closing arguments. Stepping down from the bench, Raulston smiled at Darrow and warmly shook his hand.[91]

Soon after court reconvened in the open air, Arthur Hays shocked and delighted the throng of about three thousand with a single sentence: "The defense desires to call Mr. Bryan as a witness." It was quite unusual for a prosecutor to take the stand, but Bryan eagerly accepted the challenge. Before doing so, however, he asked the judge to allow him to grill all three defense attorneys after they had finished with him. Now the trial could finally become the great contest of faith for which Bryan had hoped and prepared and that the press had expected. Darrow, the most experienced trial lawyer on his team, would conduct the cross-examination.[92]

"You have given considerable study to the Bible, haven't you, Mr. Bryan?" "Yes, sir, I have tried to," was how it began. For the next two hours, the celebrated attorney kept his foe on edge with a cascade of short queries about the trustworthiness of Scripture: "Do you believe a whale swallowed Jonah?" "Do you believe Joshua made the sun stand still?" Do you take "the story of the flood to be a literal interpretation?" "Do you think the earth was made in six days?"

Bryan avoided giving an unqualified yes to any of Darrow's questions. The whale, he supposed, was only "a large fish," and perhaps God had not specifically directed it to ingest a man. Neither did Bryan speculate about how the Lord had suspended the laws of physics long enough to stop the rotation of the earth. And he flatly rejected the notion that each day of creation mentioned in Genesis referred to a period of twenty-four hours. Like many pious critics of Darwin, Bryan had long assumed that a biblical "day" referred to an eon of time. An exponent of common sense in worldly affairs, he could not easily abandon it when discussing the loftiest text of all.[93]

But this attitude forced him to evade direct questions with answers that seemed merely thoughtless and dogmatic. When Darrow asked for the date of the Flood, Bryan responded that he'd "never made a calculation." The skeptic pressed on, "What do you think?" Bryan bristled and said, "I do not think about things I don't think about." The door to ridicule was wide open: "Do you think about things you do think about?" "Well, sometimes." "Laughter in the courtyard," noted the court reporter, in the laconic custom of his trade.[94]

After several minutes of this, Tom Stewart frantically asked the judge to stop the cross-examination. Darrow, he claimed, was straying too far "from the origin of the case." Raulston reminded the chief prosecutor that Bryan "wants to ask the other gentlemen questions along the same line," and the witness himself was still keen to continue. "They came here to try revealed religion," Bryan declared; he would never back down from such a fight. But the only weapon he could muster against Darrow was a vow to protect the Bible against its defamers. "I want the Christian world to know," he said near the end of his time on the stand, "that any atheist, agnostic, unbeliever, can question me any time as to my belief in God, and I will answer him." It was the seventh day of the trial, and Bryan should have rested.[95]

The cause of his failure lay in the resolute worldliness of his faith. On the platform, the printed page, and the radio, Bryan moved people by describing how those who believed in Scripture could transform humanity into a just and peaceful race. Such blissful evangelism bolstered the hopes of millions and provided comfort to poor souls such as Amy Howley.

But if Bryan knew most of the words of the Bible by heart, he had not studied them as would a theologian out to correct errors of logic and judgment by scientists or anyone else. When Darrow grilled him about the age of the human race, the politician-evangelist could only sputter, ungrammatically, that he was too busy to "speculate on what our remote ancestors were and what our remote descendants have been. . . . I have been more interested in Christians going on right now, to make it much more important than speculation on either the past or the future." Bryan's uncharacteristic clumsiness betrayed his frustration. Unwilling to debate the details of either biology or Scripture, he was no match for a shrewd opponent who asked sharp questions and would not let up.[96]

The day ended with a merciless exchange between the two titans. Bryan shouted that Darrow's "only purpose" was "to slur at the Bible." Coldly, Darrow objected to the charge and snapped, "I am exempting you on your fool ideas that no intelligent Christian on earth believes."[97]

The next morning, the judge ordered Bryan's testimony expunged from the official record. Like the unheard evidence from noted scientists, it could "shed no light upon any issues that will be pending before the higher courts." This spared Bryan further embarrassment, but it also prevented him from cross-examining any defense attorney. Then Darrow made sure that the last meaningful words uttered in the trial would be his. He quickly asked the judge to instruct the jury to bring in a guilty verdict, making any closing arguments unnecessary. After huddling briefly in the hall, the twelve stalwarts of Rhea County did their duty. Judge Raulston fined Scopes the minimum of $100, which Mencken's paper, the *Baltimore Evening Sun*, immediately offered to pay.[98]

Despite the verdict, most of the press, in the United States and abroad, concluded that Bryan and his allies had lost. The *New York Times* called the confrontation on the lawn "an absurdly pathetic performance, with a famous American the chief creator and butt of a crowd's rude laughter." Other northern papers, many of which had lampooned him throughout his career, happily joined the chorus. Bryan, in their view, had confirmed that his mind was a good deal weaker than his voice. Even most dailies in the Democratic, evangelical South had critical things to say about their erstwhile hero. "Darrow succeeded in showing that Bryan knows little about the science of the world," reported the Memphis *Commercial Appeal*. "Bryan succeeded in bearing witness bravely to the faith which he believes transcends all the learning of men." Meanwhile, opinion in the homeland of Darwin was almost uniformly hostile. In all of Great Britain, the *Times* could find just one county paper, the *Hemel Hempstead Gazette* in Hertfordshire, willing to take Bryan's side.[99]

But the man himself appeared cheerful and unbowed. He and Mary stayed on in Tennessee, where he saw a doctor about his diabetes and gave several well-attended speeches and interviews to defend his performance. Darrow had unfairly quizzed him about "technical knowledge" that only five hundred scientists possess, he told a reporter. If allowed to cross-examine his opponent, he would have exposed the fact that evolution "substitutes the law of force for the law of love" and dispelled the cloud of ignorance around him. When Americans read the closing argument he did not get to give at the trial, they would understand.[100]

On Sunday morning, July 26, Bryan attended a local church in Dayton and offered a prayer. Then he had lunch with Mary and arranged for the publication of his undelivered address. To conserve his strength for an evening sermon, Bryan went to his bedroom for an afternoon nap. He never woke up.[101]

With a timing that had escaped him on the stand, Bryan's closing argument became his final oration. Detailed and polished, it raised the doubts about evolutionary theory and its application to human affairs he had failed to convey during the trial. He pointed to reservations and inconsistencies in Darwin's work and quoted passages in *The Descent of Man* that appeared to endorse the elimination of "the weak members of civilized society." It was the type of writing Bryan did best—a political homily instead of a scientific treatise or a theological defense: "Science is a magnificent material force, but it is not a teacher of morals. It can perfect machinery, but it adds no moral restraints to protect society from the misuse of the machine."[102]

In the concluding paragraphs, Bryan returned to the Crucifixion—the master image of his faith and the metaphor spoken in a hot Chicago hall twenty-nine years before that had gained him the affection of millions and the attention of the world. The romance of faith and democracy had come full circle since he vowed to rescue mankind from a cross of gold.

One last time, Bryan made personal defeat sound almost like victory. "Again force and love meet face to face," he declared, "and the question, 'What shall I do with Jesus?' must be answered. A bloody, brutal doctrine—Evolution—demands, as the rabble did nineteen hundred years ago, that He be crucified." With nullification of this law, Bryan predicted, "there will be a rejoicing wherever God is repudiated, the Savior scoffed at and the Bible ridiculed." But if upheld, "millions of Christians will call you blessed and, with hearts full of gratitude to God, will sing again that grand old song of triumph:

> 'Faith of our fathers, living still,
> In spite of dungeon, fire and sword;
> O how our hearts beat high with joy
> Whene'er we hear that glorious word—
> Faith of our fathers—holy faith:
> We will be true to thee till death!' "[103]

Epilogue:
The Fate of a Christian Liberal

Woe to the political leader who preaches a new doctrine of deliverance, and who, out of tenderness of heart, offers a panacea for human ills. His truly shall be a crown of thorns.

—Theodore Dreiser[1]

THREE DAYS AFTER his death, Bryan made a final tour of rural and small-town America. A special Southern Railways train picked up his bronze coffin in Dayton, carried it to Chattanooga, and then rolled it slowly up the foothills of the Alleghenies through Virginia and into the nation's capital. The conductor was a longtime admirer; he had taken Bryan along a similar route during the campaign of 1896. Mary, anticipating popular demand, arranged for the back door of the car to be left open at each stop so that the casket would be visible to all.

"Everywhere, at every station," wrote a reporter, there were "men in shirt-sleeves and overalls, women in gingham and barefoot children." At most towns along the route, work was suspended to allow laborers, clerks, and factory hands, both black and white, to visit the train. At Jefferson City, Tennessee, a male quartet stood beside the railroad car and sang one of Bryan's favorite hymns; at a tiny village in Virginia, an entire congregation came down to the tracks to pray as the train passed by. When the coffin arrived in downtown Washington, an estimated twenty thousand people viewed it inside the New York Avenue Presbyterian Church, three blocks from the White House. The reception would certainly have pleased Bryan, who believed that he had never lost the love of his fellow commoners.[2]

Yet he was always a man caught between two contradictory impulses. As a moralizing populist, Bryan courted both applause and hostility. "When reform comes in this country," he declared, "it starts with the masses. Reforms do not come from the brains of scholars."[3] But he also longed for the respect that Theodore Roosevelt, an upper-class reformer comfortable with both aspects of his identity, gained from both the erudite and the plebeian. Bryan's optimism and warmth—and his unceasing lecture tours and stints as a journalist—were methods, unconscious or not, of attaining that status. He thus drew as much satisfaction from Tolstoy's praise and the practiced amity of foreign diplomats as from the cheers of dirt farmers and factory hands. No American politician in the Progressive Era had more loyal friends or more dedicated enemies. But it would have been difficult for Bryan to retain the former if he had found a way to mollify the latter. He never understood that a rebel who becomes an icon of legitimacy loses the ability to speak truth to power.

Perhaps this confusion explains why he chose to be buried at Arlington National Cemetery. The decision puzzled many observers, and neither he nor his widow bothered to explain it. Writing a few days after his death, a journalist recalled that when Bryan had visited Westminster Abbey twenty years before, he called its "stately tombs...monuments to blood" and disdained "the glorification" of men "whose fame rested on their feats of arms." It is also curious that the near-pacifist wanted to be remembered for his short, prosaic service in a war whose imperial consequences he abhorred.[4]

Perhaps the Bryans wanted to avoid having to choose between graveyards in Illinois, Nebraska, and Miami. Perhaps they considered Arlington the most fitting location for a "statesman" not universally acknowledged as such. Or perhaps, as he aged, Bryan thought better of his part in the popular, if squalid, conflict of 1898. At least the bones of this battler for many causes, including an end to war, now lay near those of other national heroes.[5]

Whatever the reason, several hundred friends and relatives crossed the Potomac in a steady rain on July 31 to climb to one of the highest spots inside the sprawling grounds filled with veterans' graves. There they interred Colonel Bryan, late of the Third Nebraska Volunteers, under a wild cherry tree. Mary later added a granite headstone no larger than those of other former officers buried nearby. Below her husband's military rank and his dates of birth and death, stonemasons chiseled a line from Alexander Pope's *Moral Essays:* "Statesman, yet friend to truth! of soul sincere, in action faithful, and in honor clear." In 1931, Mary joined him there.[6]

IF NOTHING ELSE, the choice of cemetery demonstrated that Bryan's knack for breeding controversy lived on after his voice was still. Near the end of the *Memoirs,* Mary Bryan asked, "What is it that has caused this man to be so widely known, so greatly loved, and so ardently hated?"[7] She never addressed the last, distasteful part of the question. But a legion of commentators eagerly took up the task.

Obituary writers began the debate over Bryan's legacy, and its terms have changed remarkably little since then. His many opponents attempted to bury his historical significance along with his remains. An editorial writer for the *New York World* rapidly dispensed with mild praise for Bryan's speaking style to focus on the many defeats he had hung on the once proud Democratic Party. The *New Republic* considered him no more than a "platform fundamentalist" whose amiable sincerity could not make up for his lack of legislative accomplishments. The same theme, familiar since the 1890s, appeared in nearly every negative postmortem: Bryan's gifts as an orator and his undeniable love for his followers could not mask the shallowness of his politics. Several critics took the short step from deprecating the leader to maligning his "people" themselves.[8]

The most memorable of such writers was H. L. Mencken. The great iconoclast had little respect for politicians, particularly those who professed their undying ardor for the common folk. Yet until reporting on the Scopes trial, he had not thought Bryan any worse than the other performers, authentic or humbug, who strutted across the electoral stage. On occasion, Mencken had even paid tribute to Bryan for enlivening a Democratic convention.

But two weeks in Dayton changed his mind. It was the first time the sophisticate from Baltimore had witnessed the raw enthusiasm of a religious revival and met so many people who preferred their Bibles to the cold reason of science and the law. "I had never been on close terms with country people before," Mencken told a friend. "I set out laughing and returned shivering." The experience hardened his conviction that democracy was simply a way to fire the hatred of the lower orders against their mental superiors. And Bryan was ringleader of the mob.[9]

"He seemed only a poor clod like those around him," wrote Mencken, "deluded by a childish theology, full of an almost pathological hatred of all learning, all human dignity, all beauty, all fine and noble things. He was a peasant come home to the barnyard." Mencken refused to play any grace notes. Bryan was only ambitious, not sincere; he looked "like a dog with rabies" in the Dayton courtroom; he "liked people who sweated freely, and were not debauched by the refinements of the toilet."[10]

Mencken's loathing was driven by fear. He predicted that Bryan would quickly become a saint to millions of "yokels" outside the big cities who were intent on turning America over to the KKK and like-minded regiments of Bible-spouting youths. The specter of a theocratic state run by idiots has haunted secular intellectuals ever since. Mencken did find one cause for cheer: Bryan's noxious legacy might help "break up the demo-cratic delusion, now already showing weakness, and so hasten its own end."[11]

This vicious portrait struck many young American intellectuals as the unvarnished truth. Like Mencken, they scorned sentimental piety, trusted in science, and gloried in the culture of big cities. For authors and scholars on the left who came of age during the Great Depression, the true Bryan would always be the one whom Darrow had exposed on the stand. In 1948, Richard Hofstadter wrote that Bryan "was never a rebel at all." His torpid mind lacked "a sense of alienation," and "he never felt the excitement of intellectual discovery." Hofstadter was as eloquent as Mencken, if more restrained, and a generation of liberal thinkers—many Jewish and the chil-dren of immigrants—echoed his opinion. Some also spied a close resem-blance between Bryan's native-born populist throng and the grassroots conservatives of their own day, screaming for the heads of "pinko" profes-sors and cursing anyone who opposed prayer and Bible reading in public schools. The authors of *Inherit the Wind* modeled the character of Matthew Harrison Brady—in all his vainglorious rigidity—on Bryan as Mencken had depicted him.[12]

Few noted the irony. As his correspondence makes clear, Mencken was a lifelong anti-Semite with a reverence for German culture so strong it blinded him to the menace of Nazism. He also hurled acid opinions at Franklin D. Roosevelt throughout the 1930s. Thus, the writer most responsi-ble for shaping Bryan's postmortem image for liberals hated the president they adored and only reluctantly backed a world war against their mortal enemy. Yet progressive intellectuals continue to repeat Mencken's great slur. In 2000, the historian Ronald Steel marveled that Bryan, "who today would be considered a windbag fit only for a career as a TV evangelist, mes-merized crowds for hours with his mellifluous prose."[13]

Bryan's admirers were equally quick to enshrine him in their small pan-theon of democratic heroes. In his popular column, Will Rogers wrote: "Bryan was just a plain citizen, holding no office. Yet this country holds hun-dreds and thousands of people who feel that they haven't got a Soul now who will conscientiously fight for them, the plain people. Bryan had no Vice President." Down in Dallas, Dr. Charles Rosser hailed "the friend of the American masses and the illustrious tribune of the people." For many Bryan followers, the Scopes trial was simply another example of how he "stood for his convictions and for them he'd always fight," as the country singer Vernon Dalhart put it.[14]

At first, his defenders saw no reason to separate Bryan the orthodox Christian from Bryan the fearless reformer. "He loved the laboring man and they loved him," claimed Robert Henry, a former congressman who had opposed intervention in World War I. The Texan also hailed Bryan for besting those who "challenged...the Christian faith of the greatest army the Commoner ever led." Bluegrass musician Charlie Oakes warbled a similar tune: "He fought the evolutionists, and infidels, and fools / Who were trying to ruin the minds of children in the schools / Three times he ran for president, but capitalists wouldn't let him win / Because he was a friend to the poor and to the working man."[15]

Neither jazz crooners nor the pop stars of Tin Pan Alley would have sung those words. By his death, the core of Bryan's appeal had shrunk to what Americans were calling the Bible Belt. Until World War I, his followers had been numerous nearly everywhere, scarce only in the upper reaches of New England. But in the era of Republican "normalcy," his battle to save the young from Darwinism placed him on the defensive outside the most pietist, Democratic, and impoverished region in the land.

When bad times hit the entire nation in the 1930s, Bryan's economic populism did seem vital again. In the pit of the Great Depression, both Father Charles Coughlin and Huey Long mined parts of his legacy: free silver for the radio priest and the slogan "Every Man a King" for the jocular tyrant from Louisiana. Most politicians who had been close to Bryan transferred their loyalties to the New Deal. The Democrats who ruled Congress enacted numerous measures he certainly would have applauded, from guaranteed bank deposits to progressive tax reform to protection for labor organizers. And Josephus Daniels kept Bryan's name alive at commemorative breakfasts held during Democratic national conventions through 1944.[16]

Bryan's children also stayed faithful to his party as it became the unchallenged standard-bearer of modern liberalism. Characteristically, Ruth took the lead. In 1928, she won a seat in Congress from a Florida district that stretched from the Keys to Jacksonville. In the House, she worked to protect the Everglades and proposed a new cabinet department, Home and Child, that would take responsibility for education and social welfare. Although defeated by a wet candidate in the 1932 primary, Ruth remained a force among Democratic women and strengthened her friendship with Eleanor Roosevelt. With the help of the new First Lady, she was appointed minister to Denmark in 1933. Ruth was the first woman in U.S. history to hold so high a diplomatic post, which was equivalent to an ambassadorship. Meanwhile, William Junior became a pillar of the Democratic establishment in Los Angeles, where he held several federal jobs; Grace gamely lectured about social issues to any audience that would have her but failed to secure a government job. So Bryan's political legacy was handed down, unbroken, to the next generation.[17]

Yet the public revival of his memory was short-lived. Bryan's crusading moralism held little more attraction for the white ethnic workers who became the linchpin of the new Democratic coalition than for the cosmopolitan policy makers they brought to power with their votes. In 1934, FDR dedicated a twelve-foot statue of Bryan by Gutzon Borglum, the creator of Mt. Rushmore. "We are building today," said Roosevelt, on the "sincerity which served him so well in his life-long fight against sham and privilege and wrong." But it was a perfunctory tribute, soon forgotten, and the sculpture was relegated to a park on the fringe of the capital city.[18]

During most of his career, Bryan's admirers had followed his rhetorical lead, cursing the monied eastern elite for being both godless and plutocratic. If their hero had died after one of his presidential campaigns, they might have continued to rail against the money power that defeated him. But his demise days after the Scopes trial inevitably made him a martyr to people whose conservative faith burned brighter than did any zeal for economic and social change.

In the late 1920s, most fundamentalists and other conservative evangelicals retreated from political life to build an empire of their own. The preachers and laypeople who broadcast over Christian radio stations, taught at Bible institutes, and took off on foreign missions occasionally invoked Bryan's example, but few mentioned that his lifelong purpose had been to place "the heart of the masses against the pocketbooks of a few." The curriculum at the small college named after him that opened in Dayton in 1930 was heavy on Bible studies, foreign languages, and business courses. But William Jennings Bryan University offered just one class in American history and none at all about contemporary issues. All this marked a decisive break from the century-long tradition of prophetic reform movements that Christian agitators, lay and ordained, had first created in Jacksonian America.[19]

For a time, Catholic liberals picked up the activist baton. In 1919, the American bishops issued a Program for Social Reconstruction whose core ideas, such as insurance for the jobless and the elderly and the construction of public housing, would be enacted by the New Deal. During the Great Depression, parish priests aided union drives and established schools that taught a brand of class solidarity in line with papal teachings. "A victory for labor in its struggles for decent conditions is a victory for Americanism and for Christianity," declared Father Charles Owen Rice in the benediction he gave at the first convention of the Congress of Industrial Organizations. But the Cold War blunted and then largely reversed this leftward thrust in the Church. Amid the decline of organized labor and the persistence of the great abortion controversy, it all but disappeared from view.[20]

In the late 1970s, when large numbers of white evangelical Protestants again threw themselves into electoral politics, they did so largely for pro-corporate Republicans whom Bryan would have loathed. In 1994, Ralph Reed hailed him as "the most consequential evangelical politician of the twentieth century," as significant a force for civic virtue in his era as Martin Luther King Jr. was in his. But Reed was then lead organizer of the Christian Coalition, the strong right arm of Newt Gingrich's GOP. In the early twenty-first century, it is the promoters of "creation science" who most frequently yoke Bryan's memory to their cause—which enjoys the sympathy of tens of millions of Americans and a large number of state and local officials.[21]

The demands of postmortem celebrity leave scant room for paradox. As some members of the Christian right lionized Bryan, the left largely ignored how central he had been to many of the issues for which it continued to struggle—the rights of labor and women, the regulation of big business, the reform of campaign finance, progressive taxation, anti-militarism, and more. By the 1940s, the conventional wisdom among radicals and liberals echoed Eugene Debs's remark upon hearing of Bryan's death: he began his career as a progressive, yet "grew more and more conservative until finally he stood before the country as a champion of everything reactionary in our political and social life."[22]

In the long shadow of the Scopes trial, other memories of Bryan gradually faded from public consciousness. By the 1960s, distaste among liberals for evangelicals and their beliefs helped make *Inherit the Wind* a favorite of high school drama teachers, and most textbooks repeated the opinion of Mencken and Hofstadter. A handful of Bryan biographers did point out that a rigorously Christian liberalism was not a contradiction in terms. In 1965, Lawrence Levine cogently warned against "the misguided effort to characterize him at various stages of his career as *either* a progressive or a reactionary, without understanding that a liberal in one area may be a conservative in another not only at the same time but also for the same reasons." But hardly anyone in the academy—whether secular or devout—was listening.[23]

The decline of the Social Gospel among white evangelicals contributed mightily to the silence. Although, as president, FDR called on church leaders to "return to the religion as exemplified in the Sermon on the Mount," his eagerness to repeal prohibition alienated many Protestant clergy. A number of ministers did work with the ACLU, the labor movement, and other progressive causes. But their faith increasingly seemed ancillary to their politics, and the notoriety of a pro-Soviet figure such as Harry F. Ward, a Methodist minister active in the Popular Front, served to warn others about the perils of adopting too worldly a doctrine. After prosperity returned in the 1940s, conservative churches grew rapidly, while their liberal counterparts barely held their own. Most white progressives either ignored religious devotion or thought it an impediment to genuine social change.[24]

That was certainly not the case for most Americans of African or Latino heritage. Martin Luther King Jr. heard himself introduced to the 1963 March on Washington as "America's moral leader," and in the South the freedom movement was akin to a religious revival. But even the militant faith of the black insurgency and of the California farm workers who, in the same era, marched for union rights under the image of the Virgin of Guadalupe failed to alter the dominant image of a left that hoped to quarantine the sacred from the realm of politics. If liberal icons such as King and César Chávez couldn't revive the Social Gospel, a fresh look at Bryan, with his hostility to evolution and his retrograde views on race, didn't stand a chance.[25]

The obvious problem for liberals is that most Americans don't share their mistrust of public piety. Time and again, secular reformers defeat themselves by assuming that this difference doesn't matter, that they can appeal solely to the economic self-interest of working-class Americans and ignore moral issues grounded in religious conviction. But more than 80 percent of Americans believe in a God and an afterlife. Like Bryan, millions derive their political views from their faith and prefer that others do the same. As Mario Cuomo, a Catholic liberal, writes, "I do desperately want to believe in something better than I am. If all there is is me in this society, then I have wasted an awful lot of time, because I am not worth it." Any revival of a religious left must begin from the premise that one's fellow Americans of the lower and middle classes are brothers and sisters whose well-being ought to be the main goal of political activism.[26]

THE RHETORIC of shared responsibility sounds rather hollow today, except when it is tethered to a war of self-defense against terrorists. Yet a century ago, those who spoke about collective sin and collective redemption occupied the political mainstream. They took their place in a long narrative of reform that included the abolitionists, early temperance agitators (who battled poverty as much as saloons), the Knights of Labor, and the Populist insurgency—all led by men and women whose faith motivated their activism. From William Lloyd Garrison and Sojourner Truth to Frances Willard and

Edward Bellamy, nineteenth-century progressives never advanced without a moral awakening entangled with notions about what the Lord would have them do.

To inspire another such upheaval was Bryan's fondest desire. His record was impressive, particularly for someone who held no office during most of his career. Starting with the campaign of 1896, the Democrats ceased being the more conservative of the two major parties—with the fateful exception of their support for Jim Crow. Bryan was the leading proponent of three constitutional amendments—for the income tax, the popular election of senators, and prohibition. He also did much to place on the national agenda a variety of other significant reforms: insured bank deposits, government-owned railroads, publicly financed campaigns, and a reliable method for preventing war. None of these became law during his lifetime—he had better luck with statewide curbs on the teaching of Darwinism. But it was certainly not for lack of promotion or resolve. "With the exception of the men who have occupied the White House," wrote William Gibbs McAdoo in 1931, "Bryan...had more to do with the shaping of the public policies of the last forty years than any other American citizen."[27]

It is probably fortunate that he was never elected president. As Bryan demonstrated while secretary of state, he relished confrontations over principle and abhorred compromise. If he had captured the White House, that trait would have made it difficult for him to rally an enduring majority in what would have been a nation rent by angry divisions of class, region, and party.

But neither was he a classic demagogue, burning to seize power and vengeful toward anyone who opposed him. Unlike Tom Watson, Huey Long, George Wallace, and others of their ilk, Bryan never appealed to the violent or authoritarian impulses of his fellow citizens. He was satisfied to feed a grassroots hunger for changes in the American social order, which he believed would have profound moral implications. Bryan's oratory infused the idea of a welfare state with passionate intensity. If the Golden Rule was too simple a prescription, it was certainly superior to impersonal bureaucracy or strong-man rule.

Whatever he achieved depended on the power and durability of his voice and the romantic tenor of his words. Every other progressive giant—TR, Woodrow Wilson, Robert La Follette, Jane Addams, Booker T. Washington, and the radical Eugene Debs—was a gifted orator. But each had to worry about operating an institution—whether a local one such as Hull House or Tuskegee Institute, a state, or the entire federal government. But

Bryan could devote decades to honing the art of preaching both for God and for the welfare of the common white American.

That rhetoric and the new style of politics it helped to create may be his most enduring legacy. " 'Um, um, um. Look at all those folks—you'd think William Jennings Bryan was speakin',' " jokes a character in *To Kill a Mockingbird* as her Alabama town fills up for a dramatic trial. After the stirring contest of 1896, most presidential candidates learned to engage in an aggressively affable, go-to-the-people campaign to demonstrate that theirs was a cause of and for the common people. For over half a century, every subsequent Democratic nominee, with the exception of the hapless Alton Parker and John W. Davis, played the happy populist warrior—cracking jokes, beaming for the cameras, flaying the corporate rich before audiences of the insecure. Even after its party's candidates stopped bashing "economic royalists," Democrats tried their best to appear friendly, optimistic, and visionary. John Scopes, of all people, regretted that Bryan hadn't survived into the age of television, when "he could have projected his personality to millions" and had a good chance of being elected president. For Americans with a sense of history, Bryan remains a paragon of eloquence for "a lazy-tongued people." And unlike contemporary candidates for high office, he wrote every word that he spoke, except when he was quoting someone else.[28]

The triumph of the ever accessible, always loquacious political style helps reassure ordinary citizens as well as to mobilize partisan crowds. As the federal government grew in size and complexity, Americans hankered for leaders who could make the enterprise of governing seem more personal and comprehensible. The electorate struck an implicit bargain with the political class: "If we can no longer understand or control much of what you do, at least give us men and women at the top who can comfort us and, on occasion, provide a thrill." This was as true for Ronald Reagan and George W. Bush as it was for Franklin Roosevelt and John Kennedy.

Yet Bryan was a great Christian liberal, and to neglect the content of his prophecies sells both his career and American political history short. Vachel Lindsay wrote in 1915:

> *When Bryan speaks, the sky is ours,*
> *The wheat, the forests, and the flowers.*
> *And who is here to say us nay?*
> *Fled are the ancient tyrant powers.*
> *When Bryan speaks, then I rejoice.*
> *His is the strange composite voice*

Of many million singing souls
Who make world-brotherhood their choice.[29]

Critics from Mencken onward failed to appreciate what drew millions of Americans to Bryan and that our own era of nonstop satire and twenty-four-hour commerce manifestly lacks: the yearning for a society run by and for ordinary people who lead virtuous lives. As everyone who heard him could attest, Bryan made significant public issues sound urgent, dramatic, and clear, and he encouraged citizens to challenge the motives and interests of the most powerful people in the land. That is a quality absent among our recent leaders, for all their promises to leave no man, woman, or child behind. Bryan's sincerity, warmth, and passion for a better world won the hearts of people who cared for no other public figure in his day. We should take their reasons seriously before we decide to mistrust them.

NOTES

ABBREVIATIONS FOR NOTES

BPLC William Jennings Bryan Papers, Manuscript Room, Library of Congress, Washington, DC

BPNSHS William Jennings Bryan Papers, Nebraska State Historical Society, Lincoln

BPOXY William Jennings Bryan Papers, Occidental College, Los Angeles, CA

BSB-NSHS Bryan Scrapbooks, Nebraska State Historical Society, Lincoln

Coletta, *Bryan* Paolo Coletta, *William Jennings Bryan*, volume 1: *Political Evangelist, 1860–1908* (Lincoln, NE, 1964); volume 2: *Progressive Politician and Moral Statesman, 1909–1915* (Lincoln, NE, 1969); volume 3: *Political Puritan, 1915–1925* (Lincoln, NE, 1969)

Comm. *The Commoner*, 1901–23

CR *Congressional Record*

CWB Charles Wayland Bryan

GBH Bio Grace Bryan Hargreaves, unpublished biography of WJB, c. 1941, Bryan Papers, Library of Congress, Boxes 64 and 65

Koenig, *Bryan* Louis W. Koenig, *Bryan: A Political Biography of William Jennings Bryan* (New York, 1971)

Levine, DF Lawrence W. Levine, *Defender of the Faith: William Jennings Bryan: The Last Decade, 1915–1925* (Cambridge, MA, 1987 [1965])

MBB Mary Baird Bryan

Memoirs *The Memoirs of William Jennings Bryan by Himself and His Wife, Mary Baird Bryan* (Chicago, 1925)

NH *Nebraska History*

NYT *New York Times*

Transcript *The World's Most Famous Court Trial: Tennessee Evolution Case: A Complete Stenographic Report of the Famous Court Test of the Tennessee Anti-Evolution Act, at Dayton, July 10 to 21, 1925, Including Speeches and Arguments of Attorneys* (Cincinnati, 1925)

WJB William Jennings Bryan

WW Woodrow Wilson

INTRODUCTION: THE ROMANCE OF JEFFERSON AND JESUS

1. Tocqueville, *Democracy in America,* translated and edited by Harvey C. Mansfield and Delba Winthrop (Chicago, 2000), 275.

2. WJB, "A Conquering Nation," in *Under Other Flags: Travels, Lectures, Speeches* (Lincoln, NE, 1905), 261.

3. W. G. Comerford and wife, et al. to WJB, 11/2/1896, BPLC, Box 5.

4. Quoted in Ferenc Szasz, "William Jennings Bryan, Evolution, and the Fundamentalist-Modernist Controversy," NH 56 (Summer 1975), 275.

5. Richard Hofstadter, *The American Political Tradition and the Men Who Made It* (New York, 1948), 187.

6. Mark A. Noll, *A History of Christianity in the United States and Canada* (Grand Rapids, MI, 1992), 166–70; Noll, *America's God: From Jonathan Edward to Abraham Lincoln* (New York, 2002), 9–11; Nathan Hatch, *The Democratization of American Christianity* (New York, 1989).

7. WJB to Mrs. Mary R. Foy, Los Angeles, 6/5/1912, File 5, BPOXY. In reality, the modern Democratic Party was not established until the mid-1820s, when Martin Van Buren converted his New York Regency into a machine of political professionals to elect Andrew Jackson president. The Democratic-Republicans whom Jefferson had led a generation before were little more than a faction of notable citizens.

8. Jefferson quotes from *Bartlett's Familiar Quotations,* 15th ed. (Boston, 1980), 388, and *The Jefferson Cyclopedia,* ed. "J.P.F." (New York, 1900), 144. Notes of thanks for Bryan's gift include Henry Ford to WJB, 1/3/1917, BPLC, Box 31; J. Chinda [Japanese ambassador to the United States] to WJB, ibid. Bryan often referred to the book as the *Jefferson Encyclopedia.* The list, dated 1923, can be found in BPLC, Box 38.

9. Of course, many evangelical Christians resisted such worldly uses of their faith. On the political quietism of one growing segment of Protestant America, see Grant Wacker, *Heaven Below: Early Pentecostals and American Culture* (Cambridge, 2001), 220–23. The quotes from the Knights and WCTU are borrowed from my *The Populist Persuasion: An American History,* rev. ed. (Ithaca, 1998), 32–33, 83, where the original citations can be found. The Alliance and Populist statements are from Robert C. McMath Jr., *Populist Vanguard: A History of the Southern Farmers' Alliance* (Chapel Hill, 1975), 68; Joseph W. Creech Jr., "Righteous Indignation: Religion and Populism in North Carolina, 1886–1906," Ph.D. diss., University of Notre Dame, 2000, 230–31.

10. Henry George, *Progress and Poverty* (New York, 1962 [1879]), 552.

11. Quoted in John L. Thomas, *Alternative America: Henry George, Edward Bellamy, Henry Demarest Lloyd and the Adversary Tradition* (Cambridge, 1983), 276. Also see the obituary by John Clark Ridpath, "Is the Prophet Dead?" *Edward Bellamy Speaks Again!* (Kansas City, MO, 1937), 241–48.

12. The phrase comes from Sydney E. Ahlstrom, *A Religious History of the American People* (New Haven, 1972), 738.

13. Quoted in William McLoughlin, *The Meaning of Henry Ward Beecher: An Essay on the Shifting Values of Mid-Victorian America, 1840–1870* (New York, 1970), 251.

14. James Parton, quoted in Lyman Abbott, *Henry Ward Beecher: A Sketch of His Career…* (Hartford, 1887), 269–70.

15. Quotes from Kathleen Minnix, *Laughter in the Amen Corner: The Life of Evangelist Sam Jones* (Athens, GA, 1993), 51, 35, 76.

16. Quotes from the best biography of the man, James F. Findlay, *Dwight L. Moody: American Evangelist, 1837–1899* (Chicago, 1969), 244; Marsden, *Fundamentalism and American Culture* (New York, 1980), 35. The lyrics are quoted in Anthony Fels's unpublished manuscript on Masonry in Gilded Age San Francisco, in author's possession.

17. On the ecumenism of the era, see the perceptive article by Grant Wacker, "The Holy Spirit and the Spirit of the Age in American Protestantism, 1880–1910," *Journal of American History* 72 (June 1985), 45–62.

18. Gladden in 1885, quoted in a fine essay by Richard Wightman Fox, "The Discipline of Amusement," in *Inventing Times Square: Commerce and Culture at the Crossroads of the World,* ed. William R. Taylor (New York, 1991), 94–95. As Fox points out, some preachers and denominations (the Methodists, most prominently) recoiled from this departure. They formally admonished members for attending theaters, horse races, and dancing parties, and sometimes held "heresy trials" for miscreants. But this did little to stop the backsliding. Ibid., 90.

19. D. H. Meyer, "American Intellectuals and the Victorian Crisis of Faith," in *Victorian America,* ed. Daniel Walker Howe (Philadelphia, 1976), 76.

20. William James, "The Will to Believe" (1896), in *The Will to Believe and Other Essays in Popular Philosophy* (Cambridge, 1979), 19.

21. E. P. Thompson, *The Making of the English Working Class* (New York, 1963), 12.

22. Ernest R. May, *The World War and American Isolation, 1914–1917* (Cambridge, 1959), 461. May might be excused from the charge of sexism. No woman, other than his daughter Grace, has ever written a biography of Bryan, and hers was neither completed nor published. Several largely sympathetic biographies have appeared in recent decades. Major works include Coletta, *Bryan;* Levine, DF; and Koenig, *Bryan.* Two excellent shorter treatments are Robert W. Cherny, *A Righteous Cause: The Life of William Jennings Bryan* (Boston, 1985), and LeRoy Ashby, *William Jennings Bryan: Champion of Democracy* (Boston, 1987).

23. Sometime in the early 1950s, the Bryans' daughter Ruth, who was living in Ossining, New York, allowed Paolo Coletta to read a number of letters her parents had sent to each other that were "stuffed into a suitcase." But Coletta quotes sparingly from them in his three-volume biography of Bryan, and I have been unable to discover if they still exist. Author interview with Coletta, Annapolis, MD, 3/4/2000.

24. Levine, DF, 236.

25. See Lawrence W. Levine, "The Historian and the Culture Gap," in Levine, *The Unpredictable Past: Explorations in American Cultural History* (New York, 1993), 14–31.

26. Moses Hadas, "Introduction," *Greek Drama,* ed. Hadas (New York, 1965), 4.

CHAPTER ONE: EDUCATION OF A HERO, 1860–1890

1. "Oratory," unsigned essay found in his mother's papers, BPOXY, File #5.

2. My observations are based on a visit in July 2004. For statistics from the 2000 Census, see censtats.census.gov/data/il/05017121.

3. *Salem Advocate,* 6/15/1854, 2; Continental Historical Bureau of Mt. Vernon, IL, "History of Salem, Illinois and Surrounding Territory," c. 1961. A typescript of this pamphlet can be found in the Marion County Genealogical and Historical Society in Salem.

4. On the low status of nomadic male teachers in the mid-nineteenth century, see David J. Russo, *American Towns: An Interpretive History* (Chicago, 2001), 196.

5. On the context, see Timothy R. Mahoney, *Provincial Lives: Middle-Class Experience in the Antebellum Middle West* (New York, 1999), 168–212.

6. Jean H. Baker, *Affairs of Party: The Political Culture of Northern Democrats in the Mid-Nineteenth Century* (New York, 1998 [1983]), 255. On the culture of minstrelsy, see Eric Lott, *Love and Theft: Blackface Minstrelsy and the American Working Class* (New York, 1993), and David Roediger, *The Wages of Whiteness: Race and the Making of the American Working Class* (London, 1991), 95–131.

7. James Buchanan, during the 1840 campaign, quoted in John Gerring, *Party Ideologies in America, 1828–1996* (New York, 1998), 173. In keeping with this view, party propaganda tended to disparage advocates for women's rights as insufferable moralists. As one historian writes, "The ideal Democrat... was an independent white man, master of his home, quick to defend his interests, and vigilant for signs of corrupt government power." Rebecca Edwards, *Angels in the Machinery: Gender in American Party Politics from the Civil War to the Progressive Era* (New York, 1997), 26.

8. On the racial populism of the Democrats, see Alexander Saxton, *The Indispensable Enemy: Labor and the Anti-Chinese Movement in California* (Berkeley, 1971), 21–30. On the place of Andrew Jackson in this ideology, see my *The Populist Persuasion: An American History*, rev. ed. (Ithaca, 1998), 19–22.

9. Koenig, *Bryan*, 18–19; Robert Cherny, *A Righteous Cause: The Life of William Jennings Bryan* (Boston, 1985), 15; *Columbia Herald* (Missouri), 8/23/1901. Douglas quoted in Gerring, *Party Ideologies in America*, 163.

10. In 1872, Bryan also received the support of the fledgling Greenback Party. On his politics, see *Salem Advocate*, 10/9/1856, 2; 10/23/1856, 2 (quote); Coletta, *Bryan*, vol. 1, 6–7.

11. "Presentation of Portrait of Judge Bryan," *Comm.*, July 1915, 21; Koenig, *Bryan*, 36–37; *Salem County Herald*, 4/2/1880. For a succinct summary of the intellectual history of the concept, see James Davison Hunter, *The Death of Character: Moral Education in an Age Without Good or Evil* (New York, 2000), 15–24, 32–53.

12. WJB, *The First Battle* (Chicago, 1896), 44.

13. Koenig, *Bryan*, 39.

14. Bryan wrote of his father's legacy, "I have credited him with a definite influence in the shaping of my religious views; I am also indebted to him for the trend of my views on some fundamental questions of government, and have seen no reason to depart from the line he laid out." *Memoirs*, 25.

15. In 1870, Salem's population was 1,182; no figure was reported in 1860 (*The Illinois Fact Book and Historical Almanac, 1673–1968*, ed. John Clayton [Carbondale, 1970]). There is no authoritative number for either those who served or those who died. In the official Union muster rolls, 360 soldiers reported their residence as Salem in Marion County. But there were, at the time, six different towns in Illinois with the same name, and the muster rolls double-counted men who reenlisted. The numbers given here are derived from contemporary histories of Marion County, which had just over 8,000 residents in 1860. I derived the mortality count from the names listed in *History of Marion and Clinton Counties, Illinois* (Philadelphia, 1881), and the number of enlistees from J. H. G. Brinkerhoff, *Brinkerhoff's History of Marion County, Illinois*

(Indianapolis, 1909), 67–68. I am indebted to Karl Moore of the Illinois State Archives for helping to gather these statistics.

16. For details, see Robert W. Cherny, *A Righteous Cause: The Life of William Jennings Bryan* (Boston, 1985), 1, 3–5.

17. Leon F. Litwack, *North of Slavery: The Negro in the Free States, 1790–1860* (Chicago, 1961), 69–71; U.S. Census of 1860 for Marion County, accessed at http://fisher.lib.virginia .edu/census/.

18. *Salem County Herald,* 10/13/1876, 1.

19. *Memoirs,* 27.

20. Ibid., 35.

21. *Salem Herald-Advocate,* 7/3/1896, 1; *Marion County Republican,* 7/2/1896, 3.

22. Coletta, *Bryan,* vol. 1, 16. One tale, recounted by her son, was about a woman unable to "have anybody criticized in her presence." Her children tested her by condemning the devil himself. "They had not proceeded far when the mother interrupted them with the admonition, 'Well, children, if we were all as industrious as the devil is, we should all accomplish more.' " *Memoirs,* 30–31.

23. See the insightful discussion in Bradley J. Longfield, *The Presbyterian Controversy: Fundamentalists, Modernists, and Moderates* (New York, 1991), 60–62.

24. Coletta, *Bryan,* vol. 1, 4.

25. Most of these details are taken from the superb monograph by Don Harrison Doyle, *The Social Order of a Frontier Community: Jacksonville, Illinois, 1825–70* (Urbana, IL, 1978).

26. Dr. Henry E. Storrs, quoted in George R. Poage, "College Career of William Jennings Bryan," *Mississippi Valley Historical Review* 15 (September 1928), 173.

27. Jones is largely forgotten today, but a short portrait will be included in *A Dictionary of Modern American Philosophers* (Bristol, UK, in preparation).

28. Julian M. Sturtevant, *Economics or the Science of Wealth* (New York, 1878), 274. This was a popular textbook, brimming with such opinions about free trade, money, concentrations of capital, and other subjects. On Bryan's crisis of faith, see LeRoy Ashby, *William Jennings Bryan: Champion of Democracy* (Boston, 1987), 14.

29. WJB to "Tommie," 12/8/1879, BPLC, Box 1. In his later career, Bryan certainly took to heart Phillips's view that "college bred men should be agitators to tear a question open and riddle it with light and to educate the moral sense of the masses." Quoted in Richard Hofstadter, *The American Political Tradition* (New York, 1948), 137.

30. W. B. Morey to MBB, 6/27/1912, BPLC, Box 28.

31. Quoted in Koenig, *Bryan,* 33.

32. Poage, "College Career," 171.

33. Taken from the fragment of an 1896 newspaper article in BSB-NSHS, Reel 2. Neither the author nor the name of the source is given. Mary Bryan mentions his "first recorded efforts of declamation" at the age of seven or eight in *Memoirs,* 241.

34. Peter Cherches, "Star Course: Popular Lectures and the Marketing of Celebrity in Nineteenth Century America," Ph.D. diss., New York University, 1997, 304–11.

35. Kazin, *Populist Persuasion,* 56.

36. Finley Peter Dunne, *Dissertations by Mr. Dooley* (New York, 1906), 19.

37. See the excellent summary of these developments in Paul Starr, *The Creation of the Media: Political Origins of Mass Communication* (New York, 2004), 250–66.

38. Some historians see the very ubiquity of public speaking in the Gilded Age as a

symptom of its decline. Applying a kind of Gresham's law, they contrast the studied eloquence of such antebellum stalwarts as Henry Clay and Daniel Webster with the florid utterances audible at nearly any public gathering in the last decades of the century. "American oratory," writes one scholar, "became more identified with the 'elocution' of schoolboys than with shaping the national destiny." Daniel Walker Howe, "Victorian Culture in America," *Victorian America,* ed. Howe (Philadelphia, 1976), 25. Professors at Harvard and other elite universities were instructing students to employ a "plain" style and to quarantine practical prose from the virus of useless ornamentation.

Yet some respect should be paid to familiarity. Oratory in the Gilded Age was not merely popular, it was strikingly egalitarian. In the era of Clay and Webster, it was still rare for a black man to give a public address, and controversial for a woman of any race to do so. But the abolition of slavery (whose fiercest advocates included notable orators such as Sojourner Truth and Frederick Douglass, who themselves had once been property), together with the expanded market for entertaining talk, did away with such restrictions. Such female reformers as Susan B. Anthony, Frances Willard, and Jane Addams routinely took to the road to publicize their causes. Black journalist Ida B. Wells made lynching visible, for the first time, to large numbers of whites outside the South when she went on a speaking tour of the United States and England.

Henry Clay certainly had a melodic voice and a gift for argument. But he was frequently verbose and, according to a biographer, "simply could not excite the majority's attention and interest in his vision of the nation's future." Robert V. Remini, *Henry Clay: Statesman for the Union* (New York, 1991), 410.

39. Dunne, *Dissertations,* 23.

40. One popular volume advised, "The orator who would persuade must feel deeply," while another recommended ending each speech with an appeal "full of feeling." Quoted in Nan Johnson, *Nineteenth-Century Rhetoric in North America* (Carbondale, IL, 1991), 127.

41. *Memoirs,* 58, 85–86. Ingersoll spoke about Shakespeare. Bryan didn't mention Beecher's topic. WJB, "Why I Lecture," *The Ladies' Home Journal,* April 1915, 9.

42. *Memoirs,* 85–89. The memory of WJB's renown as a young orator led Jane Addams, who attended Rockford College at the same time, to claim, erroneously, in her autobiography that he had bested her in an 1881 speaking contest in Jacksonville. Bryan, she wrote, displayed "a moral earnestness which we had mistakenly assumed would be the unique possession of the feminine orator." In fact, neither had competed there. Victoria Bissell Brown, *The Education of Jane Addams* (Philadelphia, 2004), 66–67.

43. WJB, *First Battle,* 45; *Memoirs,* 246.

44. WJB, "Oratory," a handwritten essay written in either 1877 or 1878. BPOXY, File #5.

45. *Memoirs,* 222.

46. 1 Kings 11:3. The tale was told to Paolo Coletta by Bryan's daughter Ruth. Coletta, *Bryan,* vol. 1, 22–23.

47. Willa Cather, "Two Women the World Is Watching," *Home Monthly,* September 1896, in *The World and the Parish: Willa Cather's Articles and Reviews, 1893–1902,* vol. 1, ed. William M. Curtin (Lincoln, 1970), 311.

48. Mrs. McGuirk [*sic*], "Next President's Lady," *New York World*, reprinted in *Afro-American Sentinel* (Omaha), 7/25/1896; *The Autobiography of William Allen White* (New York, 1946), 328. "Mrs. Bryan to *The Globe* [St. Louis?]," 7/19/1896, BSB-NSHS, Reel 2.

49. *Memoirs*, 215; GBH Bio, 183. Mary was proud that her maternal great-grandfather, the Reverend Gregory Dexter, was a prominent British colonist in New England, and she displayed an engraving of his coat of arms in her home. *Omaha World-Herald*, 10/2/1909, 1.

50. *Memoirs*, 227.

51. Ibid., 228–30; Coletta, *Bryan*, vol. 1, 25.

52. Clarence Darrow, *The Story of My Life* (New York, 1996 [1932]), 42.

53. See Paul Avrich, *The Haymarket Tragedy* (Princeton, 1984), 85–87 and passim; Richard Schneirov, *Labor and Urban Politics: Class Conflict and the Origins of Modern Liberalism in Chicago, 1864–97* (Urbana, 1998), 120–23, 145–52.

54. See Horace White, *The Life of Lyman Trumbull* (Boston, 1913). Bryan also befriended Lyman's son, Henry, who had enrolled at Union College after drinking and gambling his way through several years at Yale. Paxton Hibben, *The Peerless Leader: William Jennings Bryan* (New York, 1929), 94–95.

55. Coletta, *Bryan*, vol. 1, 27.

56. *Memoirs*, 63–64.

57. Ibid., 74–75.

58. Willa Cather, "Nebraska: The End of the First Cycle," *The Nation*, 9/5/1923, 237.

59. See the list at www.rootsweb.com/~nerailrd/byrr.html. The biggest, most extensive state networks were those of the Burlington and Missouri and the Union Pacific. The Missouri Pacific also served six counties in the eastern part of Nebraska.

60. *Memoirs*, 78; Andrew B. Koszewski, "William Jennings Bryan, Attorney Before the Nebraska Supreme Court," *Law and the Great Plains: Essays on the Legal History of the Heartland*, ed. John R. Wunder (Westport, CT, 1996), 115–34.

61. Ibid., 118–19.

62. Alexander Keyssar, *The Right to Vote: The Contested History of Democracy in the United States* (New York, 2000), 117–71.

63. Ibid., 239.

64. Quoted in Edward L. Ayers, *The Promise of the New South: Life After Reconstruction* (New York, 1992), 36. For an incomparable overview of southern politics in this period, see J. Morgan Kousser's *The Shaping of Southern Politics: Suffrage Restriction and the Establishment of the One-Party South* (New Haven, 1974), 11–44. For good descriptions of campaign events elsewhere, see Michael E. McGerr, *The Decline of Popular Politics: The American North, 1865–1928* (New York, 1986), 3–41.

65. *Memoirs*, 97. During the rest of his lifetime, Bryan missed only three Democratic conventions: that of 1880, when he was busy at home after his father's death, and those of 1900 and 1908, when, sure of nomination, he obeyed the custom of the time and stayed in touch only by telegraph.

66. Quoted in Koenig, *Bryan*, 63. There is no record of a Cleveland reply.

67. On Whitney, see Horace S. Merrill, *Bourbon Leader: Grover Cleveland and the Democratic Party* (Boston, 1957), 73–74 and passim; John R. Lambert, *Arthur Pue Gorman* (Baton Rouge, 1953); Isaac F. Marcosson, *"Marse Henry": A Biography of Henry Watterson* (New York, 1951).

68. See the scores of illustrations of representatives and senators in Chandos Fulton, *The History of the Democratic Party from Thomas Jefferson to Grover Cleveland* (New York, 1892). Fulton, a native Virginian who had made his career in New York City, insisted on glorifying every prominent figure once identified with the party. This included John Calhoun and Roger Taney, whose opinion in the Dred Scott case Fulton defended. The author also inserted heroic portraits of Jefferson Davis and Stonewall Jackson.

69. Quoted in Elizabeth Sanders, *Roots of Reform: Farmers, Workers, and the American State, 1877–1917* (Chicago, 1999), 189.

70. He also joined eight different fraternal societies and, as in Jacksonville, played a leading role in the local YMCA. The groups, many of which retained Bryan as an inactive member for decades, were the Knights of Pythias, Elks, Masons, Odd Fellows, Moose, Royal Highlanders, Modern Woodmen, and Rotarians. He also joined the Chamber of Commerce. Mary Bryan founded a local chapter of Sorosis, a women's club. Paolo Coletta, "William Jennings Bryan's First Nebraska Years," NH 33 (June 1952), 88.

71. Morton quoted in Coletta, *Bryan*, vol. 1, 35. The only full biography of the man is James C. Olson's *J. Sterling Morton* (Lincoln, 1942).

72. Morton to WJB, 5/23/1888, BPLC, Box 1.

73. For succinct accounts of these events and their relationship to the growth of the state, see James C. Olson and Ronald C. Naugle, *History of Nebraska*, 3rd ed. (Lincoln, 1997).

74. For rich accounts of these charges, see Lawrence Goodwyn, *Democratic Promise: The Populist Moment in America* (New York, 1976), and Robert McMath, *American Populism: A Social History* (New York, 1993).

75. Quoted by a woman who remembered the song from her childhood on a farm in Lancaster County. Mary Louise Jeffery, "Young Radicals of the Nineties," NH 38 (March 1957), 31. On the Nebraska Farmers' Alliance, see Olson and Naugle, *History*, 221–25.

76. Quoted in Robert W. Cherny, *Populism, Progressivism, and the Transformation of Nebraska Politics, 1885–1915* (Lincoln, 1981), 10. This is the most sophisticated treatment of its subject.

77. Coletta, "Bryan's First Nebraska Years," 78. The image was borrowed from a popular editorial cartoon.

78. On the confusion of names, see W. H. Beekman to WJB, 11/13/1890, BPLC, Box 2; Coletta, "Bryan's First Nebraska Years," 92.

79. Joseph Edwin McGovern, quoted in Jon Gjerde, *The Minds of the West: Ethnocultural Evolution in the Rural Middle West, 1830–1917* (Chapel Hill, 1997), 391.

80. Undated, unattributed clipping, c. 1888–1890 in BSB-NSHS; Thomas Colfer to WJB, 10/8/1888 and 9/21/1888, BPLC, Box 1.

81. *Memoirs*, 248–49; Koenig, *Bryan*, 62–63.

82. G. P. Putnam's responded that such a volume would not be "a wise business investment for ourselves." Putnam's to WJB, 9/13/1889, BPLC, Box 1. A month before Bryan failed to persuade Walter Hines Page of the *New York Post* to sponsor the project. Page to WJB, 8/16/1889 and 8/27/1889, ibid.

83. Cherny, *Populism, Progressivism*, 32–34 (quote, 32); Olson, *History*, 224–30.

84. Platform adopted, 7/30/1890, BPLC, Box 37. Speech the same day, quoted in Koenig, *Bryan*, 73.

85. Paolo E. Coletta, "The Morning Star of the Reformation: William Jennings Bryan's First Congressional Campaign," NH 37 (June 1956), 112–14; Lawrence H. Larsen and Barbara J. Cottrell, *The Gate City: A History of Omaha*, enlarged ed. (Lincoln, 1997), 96–97. Foreign-born residents made up 21.2 percent of the First District; 9.8 percent of the residents were Catholic. Stanley B. Parsons et al., *United States Congressional Districts, 1883–1913* (Westport, CT, 1990), 76.

86. Quote in Koenig, *Bryan*, 77; cartoons by "Goodall," no date or source (but clearly 1890), BSB-NSHS, Reel 1. Bryan's only misstep came late in the campaign when, referring to the tariff, he said, "I am tired of hearing about laws made for the benefit of the men who work in the shops." The state leader of the declining Knights of Labor urged his members to vote for Connell. Coletta, "Morning Star," 112–13. Bryan's memorandum book listed expenses of only $34.85, but a close associate estimated he'd spent about $200. "Expenses in Congressional Campaign 1890," BPLC, Box 51; Coletta, *Bryan*, vol. 1, 48. In either case, Connell clearly outspent him.

87. Sheehan also reminded Bryan of "the first collection you made for me ($1.30)." Sheehan to WJB, 11/6/1890, BPLC, Box 2. The only other Democratic congressman was John McShane, an Irish Catholic from Omaha, who was elected in 1886 but served only a single term.

88. It proved to be a Pyrrhic victory. For the next year, John Thayer, the incumbent Republican governor, held on to office by challenging the legality of Boyd's citizenship papers. See Olson, *Nebraska*, 231–32.

89. For a cogent summary, see Robert W. Cherny, *American Politics in the Gilded Age, 1868–1900* (Wheeling, IL, 1997), 104–8.

90. James Reed to WJB, 10/7/1890, BPLC, Box 2; S. Hulfish, Annie Hulfish, and W. H. Dunning to WJB, 11/6/1890, ibid.; T. H. Gillan to WJB, 11/6/1890, ibid.

91. W. R. Kelly to WJB, 11/7/1890, ibid.

92. "Bryan on the Stump," *Omaha World-Telegram*, 10/16/1890, BSB-NSHS, 15.

CHAPTER TWO: SPEAKER IN THE HOUSE, 1891–1894

1. "A Song for Mr. Bryan (by One Who May Not Vote)," *Omaha World-Herald*, 6/21/1892, quoted in GBH Bio.

2. Charles M. Pepper, *Every-Day Life in Washington with Pen and Camera* (New York, 1900), 184.

3. The average term was increasing, however. In the 1870s, over half of House members had been first-termers; this figure fell to 30 percent by 1900. Roger H. Davidson, "Congressional Leaders, Parties, and Committees, 1900 and 2000," paper given at the Woodrow Wilson International Center for Scholars, 1999, 5 (in author's possession). In 1890, 67 percent of congressmen were lawyers. George B. Galloway, *History of the House of Representatives*, 2nd ed. (New York, 1976), 37. The lame-duck session didn't end until ratification of the Twentieth Amendment, in 1933.

4. For a detailed account, see Randall Strahan, "Thomas Brackett Reed and the Rise of Party Government," *Masters of the House: Congressional Leadership over Two Centuries*, ed. Roger H. Davidson et al. (Boulder, CO, 1998), 33–62.

5. Bride had nothing but scorn for any politician, including both Theodore Roosevelt and Woodrow Wilson, who had ever crossed his hero. Bride to unknown recipient, 11/15/1920, BPLC, Box 33; Koenig, *Bryan*, 87. On Bryan's relationship with his uncle, "Cotter T. Bride," *Comm.*, January 1919, 8.

6. On work and social life in D.C., see Constance McLaughlin Green, *Washington: Capital City, 1879–1950* (Princeton, 1963), 77–86 and passim; James Borchert, *Alley Life in Washington: Family, Community, Religion and Folklife in the City, 1850–1970* (Urbana, 1980).

7. Quoted in M. R. Werner, *Bryan* (New York, 1929), 30. For details on his early days in Congress, see Coletta, *Bryan*, vol. 1, 50–52; clippings from Nebraska papers in BSB-NSHS, Reel 1.

8. CR, 52nd Congress, 1st session (1892), 160–61.

9. Undated and unattributed newspaper stories entitled "Governor Thayer Scores Bryan" and "Bryan Roasts the Usurper" are included in BSB-NSHS, Reel 1. All through his statement, Thayer referred to his adversary as "O'Bryan." Thayer convinced the state supreme court that Boyd's father, an Irish immigrant, had never completed his citizenship papers. But just two weeks after Bryan's speech, the U.S. Supreme Court reversed the judgment, putting Boyd back in the governor's office. See www.rootsweb.com/~neresour/OLLibrary/SCHofNE/pages/schno120.htm.

10. Edward Stanwood, *American Tariff Controversies in the Nineteenth Century*, vol. 2 (New York, 1904), 306–11.

11. CR, March 16, 1892, 52nd Congress, 1st session, 2115–23.

12. All quotes in this section are drawn from ibid., 2124–36.

13. Burrows quoted in Koenig, *Bryan*, 95. Jefferson's statement is from his First Inaugural Address, delivered in 1801.

14. "Tariff-Reform Champion," NYT, 3/17/1892, 5; *Lincoln Sun*, no date but clearly March 1892, BSB-NSHS, Reel 1. At least one paper, the *New York Recorder*, dismissed his talk as "long-winded" and imitative of ones Democrats gave during the 1890 campaign. Ibid.

15. For the Randall parallel, see *New York World*, 3/17/1892; *Boston Herald*, 4/1/1892; and an undated and unattributed clipping on p. 71 of BSB-NSHS, Reel 1. For the McKinley one, *Pittsburgh Dispatch*, 3/17/1892, ibid.

16. Cameron, quoted in Kazin, *Populist Persuasion*, 31–32. For a good recent history of this arcane controversy, see Gretchen Ritter, *Goldbugs and Greenbacks: The Antimonopoly Tradition and the Politics of Finance in America, 1865–1896* (New York, 1997). For a brilliant critique of the free-silver position, see Richard Hofstadter, "Free Silver and the Mind of 'Coin' Harvey," *The Paranoid Style in American Politics and Other Essays* (New York, 1967), 238–315.

17. Bryan quoted in Koenig, *Bryan*, 84; D. C. Deaver to WJB, 6/14/1891, BPLC, Box 2; Senator William M. Stewart to WJB, 7/23/1891, ibid.; Thomas Kilpatrick to WJB, 7/13/1891, ibid.

18. For details of their falling out, see Paolo E. Coletta, "The Nebraska Democratic State Convention of April 13–14, 1892," NH 39 (December 1958), 317–34.

19. In the new first district, only 14.6 percent of residents were foreign-born, lowest of any district in the state. Stanley B. Parsons et al., *United States Congressional Districts, 1883–1913* (Westport, CT, 1990), 236.

20. The manager, Jefferson Broady, collected about $4,000. Coletta, *Bryan*, vol. 1, 73.

Bryan, however, declined a Wall Street broker's offer to join a mining syndicate, writing, "I do not care to invest in ores so long as legislation is likely to enrich the value." William Spilman, New York City, to WJB, 5/14/1892; WJB to Spilman, 5/16/1892, BPLC, Box 2.

21. For the fullest account of the 1892 campaign in Nebraska, see Koenig, *Bryan*, 98–114.

22. Other historians have emphasized the "educational" element of the 1892 canvass, contrasting it with earlier Gilded Age ones in which emotional displays of partisanship were virtually the entire campaign. But the passivity of the nominees, the issues at stake, and the challenge of an anti-monopoly party were all common features of campaigns during the prior two decades.

23. The regional discrepancy was extreme. Weaver won a majority of the votes in three Rocky Mountain states and Kansas, but his New York score of 1.2 percent was the highest of any state in the Northeast. Walter Dean Burnham, *Presidential Ballots, 1836–1892* (Baltimore, 1955), table 4.

24. Quoted in the excellent study by Douglas Steeples and David O. Whitten, *Democracy in Desperation: The Depression of 1893* (Wesport, CT, 1998), 33.

25. Quoted in John Gerring, *Party Ideologies in America, 1828–1996* (New York, 1998), 169.

26. Quoted in H. Wayne Morgan, *From Hayes to McKinley: National Party Politics, 1877–1896* (Syracuse, 1969), 451.

27. J. Alexander Fulton, Dover, Delaware, to WJB, 2/10/1893, BPLC, Box 2; William J. Hammonds, Hastings, Nebraska, et al. to WJB, 2/10/1893, ibid.

28. *The Education of Henry Adams* (Boston, 1918), 344.

29. Quoted in Coletta, *Bryan*, vol. 1, 83.

30. CR, 53rd Congress, 1st session, 8/16/1893, 400. The entire speech can be found on pp. 400–11.

31. Ibid., 401, 404, 405.

32. Ibid., 409, 411.

33. Quotes from BSB-NSHS, Reel 1, 47; Coletta, *Bryan*, vol. 1, 86; BSB-NSHS, Reel 1, 39.

34. Unauthored, unattributed newspaper clippings in BSB-NSHS, Reel 1, 118, 49.

35. Koenig, *Bryan*, 148–49.

36. Its average daily circulation from 1894 to 1896 was 18,256. *World-Herald*, 7/4/1896, 4.

37. Bryan also purchased $2,400 worth of stock in the paper. Paul V. Peterson, "William Jennings Bryan: World-Herald Editor," NH 49 (1968), 349–71; Coletta, *Bryan*, vol. 1, 101.

38. Daniels to WJB, 9/19/1894, BPLC, Box 3; James Weaver to WJB, 9/30/1894, ibid. Also see, from Chicago, Carter Harrison to WJB, 8/8/1894; from North Carolina, Carr to WJB, 8/22/1894; and from a silver Republican in Missouri, F. N. Dyer to WJB, 9/24/1894, ibid.

39. C. J. Smyth to WJB, 10/13/1894, ibid. Koenig mentions the "barrage of threats" from bank and loan companies but gives no evidence, and no other biographer makes the same charge. *Bryan*, 153. For a long report of the last Bryan-Thurston debate, see "Battle of the Giants," *Omaha Weekly World-Herald*, 10/26/1894.

40. A shrewd analysis of the election in a key region is Richard Jensen's *The Winning of the Midwest: Social and Political Conflict, 1888–1896* (Chicago, 1971), 209–37. Clark is quoted in Morton Keller, *Affairs of State: Public Life in Nineteenth Century America* (Cambridge, 1977), 570–71.

41. Editorial, *Omaha World-Herald*, 11/9/1894, 4.

42. Dahlman to WJB, 11/15/1894, BPLC, Box 3.

43. J. C. Mattern to WJB, 11/9/1894, BPLC, Box 3.

44. Bride statement, 11/15/1920, BPLC, Box 33. Bryan had made a similar statement at the Nebraska Democratic convention earlier that year when he told allies of the Cleveland administration that if they held on to control of the party, "I will go out and serve my country and my God under some other name, even if I must go alone." Quoted in Stanley L. Jones, *The Presidential Election of 1896* (Madison, 1964), 41.

CHAPTER THREE:
IN THE ARMOR OF A RIGHTEOUS CAUSE, 1895–1896

1. From a speech given in Baltimore. WJB, *The First Battle: A Story of the Campaign of 1896* (Chicago, 1896), 463.

2. Quoted in *Literary Digest*, 7/25/1896, 386.

3. Quoted in Coletta, *Bryan*, vol. 1, 94 (CR, 53rd Congress, 2nd session, 27: 785–89).

4. C. Selden Smart (of *The Arena*) to WJB, 2/8/1895; 2/18/1895, BPLC, Box 3.

5. *Memoirs*, 102; M. W. Meagher, Chicago, to WJB, 5/2/1895, BPLC, Box 3; W. E. Ludwick to WJB, 3/12/1895, BPLC, Box 3; J. D. Newton to WJB, 4/26/1895, ibid.; WJB to L. W. Hubbell (Aurora, MO), 5/9/1895, ibid.

6. The Library of Congress lists cylinders of two Bryan speeches recorded in New York during the 1900 campaign but has no copies of them. See Chapter 7 for discussion of the 1908 recordings, which give a poor rendition of Bryan's oratorical powers.

7. Boyce House, "Bryan the Orator," *Journal of the Illinois Historical Society* 53 (Autumn 1960), 279; "Dan Quin's Letter," January 1892, source unknown, BSB-NSHS, Reel 1; William Allen White, *Masks in a Pageant* (Westport, CT, 1971 [1928]), 248; NYT, 7/11/1896, 1; Willis J. Abbot, *Watching the World Go By* (Boston, 1933), 163; Clarence E. Macartney, *Six Kings of the American Pulpit* (Philadelphia, 1942), 187.

8. Republican kingmaker Mark Hanna once remarked that "he would like to see Bryan play Hamlet." House, "Bryan the Orator," 279.

9. *Memoirs*, 253.

10. Julian Hawthorne, *New York Journal*, 8/11/1896. Reproductions of Hamilton's color cartoons can be found in NH 77 (Fall/Winter 1996), 138–39.

11. White, *Masks in a Pageant*, 244; Ira R. T. Smith with Joe Alex Morris, *"Dear Mr. President...": The Story of Fifty Years in the White House Mail Room* (New York, 1949), 92. For an admiring description of Bryan's "magnetism," see John S. Ogilvie, *Life and Speeches of William J. Bryan* (New York, 1896), 14–16.

12. Thomas Carlyle, *On Heroes, Hero-Worship, and the Heroic in History* (London, 1968 [1841]), 59. On "magnetic" personality, see Casey Blake, "The Young Intellectuals and the Culture of Personality," *American Literary History* 1 (Fall 1989), 511–12.

13. WJB, *First Battle*, 156–57. On its authorship, see Coletta, *Bryan*, vol. 1, 96–97.

14. See the sympathetic analysis in Milton Friedman and Anna Jacobson Schwartz, *A Monetary History of the United States, 1867–1960* (Princeton, 1963), 89–134.

15. From *Coin's Financial School*, quoted in Richard Hofstadter, "Free Silver and the Mind of 'Coin' Harvey," *The Paranoid Style in American Politics and Other Essays* (New York, 1967), 267; *The Nation* quoted in Koenig, *Bryan*, 175.

16. Quoted in Gretchen Ritter, *Goldbugs and Greenbacks: The Antimonopoly Tradition and the Politics of Finance in America, 1865–1896* (New York, 1997), 172, 161.

17. Bryan in CR, 53rd Congress, 2nd session, January 30, 1894, 1658; Associate Justice Stephen Field, quoted in David E. Kyvig, *Explicit and Authentic Acts: Amending the U.S. Constitution, 1776–1995* (Lawrence, KS, 1996), 198.

18. Fuller was also concerned that federal regulations would override the prerogatives of the states that had granted the corporate charters. Naomi Lamoureaux, *The Great Merger Movement in American Business, 1895–1904* (New York, 1985), 164–66.

19. WJB, *First Battle*, 126.

20. For example, see J. Burrows, Tilley, Nebraska, to James Weaver, 5/23/1896, BPLC, Box 4; J. B. Weaver to WJB, 1/3/1896, BPLC, Box 3; John Lind to WJB, 5/11/1895, ibid.; Josephus Daniels to WJB, 6/1/1895, ibid.; L. C. Harris to WJB, 10/21/1895, ibid.; Davis Waite [former Populist governor of Colorado] to WJB, 11/26/1895, ibid; *Memoirs*, 101.

21. *Salem Herald-Advocate*, 7/3/1896, 1; *Marion County Republican*, 7/2/1896, 3.

22. *Chicago Tribune*, 7/7/1896, 3; *St. Louis Post-Dispatch*, 7/8/1896, 4; Stanley L. Jones, *The Presidential Election of 1896* (Madison, 1964), 218–19.

23. Quoted in Koenig, *Bryan*, 175.

24. Jones, *Presidential Election*, 213. The Chinese activist was a newspaper editor from St. Louis named Wong Chin Foo who vowed that if he was not allowed to speak at the convention, he would rent his own hall "and rally the humanitarians around me and make a new platform." *Chicago Tribune*, 7/9/1896, 11.

25. Quoted in Gilbert C. Fite, "Election of 1896," *History of American Presidential Elections, 1789–1968*, vol. 5, ed. Arthur M. Schlesinger Jr. (New York, 1985), 1806. Conservative Democratic newspapers routinely referred to Altgeld, the governor of a major state, as "an anarchist." See, for example, "Governor Altgeld Raves," NYT, 4/16/1895, 2.

26. Quoted in Koenig, *Bryan*, 186.

27. The platform can be found in *History of American Presidential Elections*, vol. 5, ed. Schlesinger, 1827–31. Its primary author was Charles H. Jones, editor of the *St. Louis Post-Dispatch*, a lifelong Democrat who had turned sharply against Cleveland's policies earlier in the decade. Thomas Graham, *Charles H. Jones: Journalist and Politician of the Gilded Age* (Tallahassee, 1990), 144–45. For a somewhat inflated claim of Bryan's role in its composition, see Coletta, *Bryan*, vol. 1, 130.

28. The platform also contained a few planks on which nearly all Democrats agreed, such as a demand to stop "the importation of foreign pauper labor" and a statement of "sympathy to the people of Cuba in their heroic struggle for liberty and independence."

29. *Chicago Tribune*, 7/4/1896, 3.

30. On the size and history of the Coliseum, see *Chicago Tribune*, 7/4/1896, 3; *New York World*, 7/10/1896, 2; Web site of Chicago Historical Society.

31. For these observations, I am indebted to the expert help of Jack E. Randorff, an acoustical engineer in Ransom Canyon, Texas, who has helped the Republican Party plan its recent national conventions. Randorff to author, 6/12/2002, in author's possession.

32. Francis Butler Simkins, *Pitchfork Ben Tillman: South Carolinian* (Gloucester, MA, 1964 [1944]), 335. For a colorful, if unfriendly, description of the speech, see *New York World*, 7/10/96, 2.

33. *Official Proceedings of the Democratic National Convention, 1896* (Logansport, IN, 1896), 209–10.

34. *New York World*, 7/9/1896, 1; *Official Proceedings*, 210, 211. On Hill's pragmatic conservatism, see Herbert J. Bass, *"I Am a Democrat": The Political Career of David Bennett Hill* (Syracuse, 1961). The only exception to the New York rule was James Buchanan, in 1856.

35. *Constitution*, 7/11/1896, quoted in Coletta, *Bryan*, vol. 1, 136.

36. *Memoirs*, 113. On Bryan's status, compare *Chicago Tribune*, 7/5/1896, 1, with ibid., 7/9/1896, 1. On the morning of July 9, the *Wall Street Journal* predicted that Bryan would be nominated. William D. Harpine, "Bryan's 'A Cross of Gold': The Rhetoric of Polarization at the 1896 Democratic Convention," *Quarterly Journal of Speech* 87 (August 2001), 296.

37. *Proceedings*, 225–26; Koenig, *Bryan*, 194.

38. *Memoirs*, 114–15.

39. The speech has, of course, been reprinted in countless places, often abridged. For the complete version, see WJB, *First Battle*, 190–200, 203–6.

40. *Memoirs*, 115.

41. Ibid., 114.

42. *Chicago Tribune*, 7/10/1896, 9.

43. See the description in Coletta, *Bryan*, vol. 1, 141.

44. *New York World*, 7/10/1896, 2.

45. The irony in Altgeld's statement was that, as a German immigrant, he was constitutionally barred from holding the office. Abbot, *Watching the World*, 165; Edgar Howard, in "The Cross of Gold Reburnished: A Contemporary Account of the 1896 Democratic Convention," NH 77 (Fall/Winter 1996), 120; Charles M. Rosser, *The Crusading Commoner: A Close-up of William Jennings Bryan and His Times* (Dallas, 1937), 48–49; Coletta, *Bryan*, vol. 1, 142.

46. On the morning he gave his speech, even Bryan's own newspaper failed to name him one of the ten principal figures at the convention. *Omaha World-Herald*, 7/9/1896, 1.

47. Clarence Darrow, *The Story of My Life* (New York, 1996 [1932]), 92.

48. "Hysteria in Politics," *New York World*, 7/12/1896, 6; NYT, 7/10/1896, 1; Cleveland quoted in Allan Nevins, *Grover Cleveland: A Study in Courage* (New York, 1932), 708.

49. *Chicago Tribune*, 7/10/1896, 1, 6; 7/11/1896, 2; 7/12/1896, 3, 5; *New York World*, 7/12/1896, 6. McKinley was endorsed by 503 of the 581 German-language papers. Robert W. Cherny, *American Politics in the Gilded Age, 1868–1900* (Wheeling, IL, 1997), 124.

50. Jerome Kearby, quoted in Lawrence Goodwyn, *Democratic Promise: The Populist Moment in America* (New York, 1976), 478–79.

51. J. Swan et al., Helena, MT, to WJB, 7/20/1896, BPLC, Box 4; Debs to WJB, 7/27/1896, ibid.

52. Weaver quoted in Jones, *Presidential Election*, 260–61; unnamed delegate in ibid., 261.

53. Quoted in WJB, *First Battle*, 294–95. A National Silver Party, composed mostly of former Republicans from the West, met at the same time in St. Louis and nominated Bryan and Sewall, but it had no local membership and little impact on the subsequent campaign.

54. Quoted in Gil Troy, *See How They Ran: The Changing Role of the Presidential Candidate*, rev. ed. (Cambridge, MA, 1996), 105.

55. See the smart, sympathetic biography by Kevin Phillips, *William McKinley* (New York, 2003).

56. Quoted in Jones, *Presidential Election*, 277.

57. McKinley may have spoken to as many as 750,000 people. Walter Dean Burnham, *Critical Elections and the Mainsprings of American Politics* (New York, 1970), 73.

58. The best sources on Hanna are still two sympathetic biographies written by men who knew him: Herbert Croly, *Marcus Alonzo Hanna: His Life and Work* (New York, 1912) and Thomas Beer, *Hanna* (New York, 1929).

59. Jonathan Auerbach, "McKinley at Home: How Early American Cinema Made News," *American Quarterly* 51 (Fall 1999), 797–832.

60. Quote from Margaret Leech, *In the Days of McKinley* (New York, 1959), 66. At the time, some critics of Hanna wrote that the national GOP had raised as much as $16.5 million, but congressional hearings in 1912–13 discredited those claims. No one, to my knowledge, has tried to count the amount raised by local and state parties. See Croly, *Hanna*, 218–23; Louise Overacker, *Money in Elections* (New York, 1974 [1932]), 71, 73.

61. Unfriendly newspapers alleged that Bryan received funds from silver mine owners, but there is no hard evidence of that. See Jones, *Presidential Election*, 301–2; Coletta, *Bryan*, vol. 1, 198. The Democrats did distribute some ten million copies of pro-silver speeches.

62. Coletta, *Bryan*, 152.

63. See Mark A. Lause, *The Civil War's Last Campaign: James B. Weaver, the Greenback-Labor Party and the Politics of Race and Section* (Lanham, MD, 2001); Troy, *See How They Ran*, 82–107 and passim.

64. Remarkably, Bryan had to travel on regularly scheduled trains until October 7, when the Democratic Committee secured him a private car. For the miles, see WJB, *First Battle*, 604; *New York World*, 11/3/1896, 2. This includes the 830 miles traveled in July between the Chicago convention and his home in Lincoln. On Jones' performance, see Coletta, *Bryan*, vol. 1, 204.

65. Bryan in Philadelphia, *First Battle*, 477.

66. Ibid., 360. A paper friendly to Bryan reported that he spoke to three-fifths of all the voters in Michigan. *New York Journal*, 10/18/1896, 1.

67. From the 1892 Omaha Platform of the People's Party. *Populism: The Critical Issues*, ed. Sheldon Hackney (Boston, 1971), 4.

68. Richard Schneirov, *Labor and Urban Politics: Class Conflict and the Origins of Modern Liberalism in Chicago, 1864–97* (Urbana, 1998), 343–53; Chester M. Destler, *American Radicalism* (New London, 1946), 162–254. Gompers did, however, give a few speeches for Bryan that fall and he voted for him.

69. WJB, *First Battle*, 378.

70. Ervin Wardman of the *New York Press*, cited by William M. Osborne in letter to William McKinley, 8/11/1896, McKinley Papers, Series 1, Reel 1, Library of Congress; Croly, *Hanna*, 209–11. On union support, see Gwendolyn Mink, *Old Labor and New Immigrants in American Political Development: Union, Party, and State, 1875–1920* (Ithaca, 1986), 145–48.

71. C. H. Bosworth, "To the Employes of the Chicago, Peoria, and St. Louis Railroad," 9/1/9/1896, McKinley Papers, Series 1, Reel 1; WJB, *First Battle*, 617–18; Jones, *Presidential Election*, 289–90.

72. WJB, *First Battle,* 523.

73. Ibid., 355, 581, 560–61. For other examples of Bryan's revivalistic style, see Richard Jensen, *The Winning of the Midwest: Social and Political Conflict, 1888–1896* (Chicago, 1971), 275–77.

74. Quoted in ibid., 473. For the opinions of censorious ministers, see *New York World,* 10/19/1896, 1, 3; Jones, *Presidential Election,* 337–38.

75. WJB, *First Battle,* 469; Joseph Creech, "Righteous Indignation: Religion and Populism in North Carolina, 1886–1906," Ph.D. diss., University of Notre Dame, 2000, 159 and passim; Laura A. Weeks, Jamestown, NY, to WJB, 10/27/1896, BPLC, Box 4.

76. 1 Corinthians 14:3; Coletta, *Bryan,* vol. 1, 178; WJB, *First Battle,* 458. After Moody's death, his son told Bryan, "As a Republican he was not in accord with your political views but was a very great admirer of your power with men. He often used to say that he wished he could convince men of his message as you did with yours." W. R. Moody to WJB, 3/21/1900, BPLC, Box 24.

77. *St. Louis Post-Dispatch,* 8/8/1896; *New York World,* 9/1/1896, 9/25/1896, 10/26/1896, 9/29/1896. Thanks to Siobhan O'Neil's close reading of the *World;* WJB, *First Battle,* 612–14. The Yale students chanted "Ho-ax, ho-ax" in an attempt to drown out Bryan's speech. The university president later apologized to him.

78. For examples, see *St. Louis Post-Dispatch,* 11/1/1896; *Rocky Mountain News,* 7/12/1896, 7/19/1896, 8/29/1896. *New York Journal,* 8/2/1896, 9; 8/8/1896, 2; 8/14/1896 (on Mary Bryan); 9/13/1896 (on pumas).

79. White quoted in his *Autobiography,* 278; *Arena,* April 1897, quoted in James A. Barnes, "Myths of the Bryan Campaign," *Mississippi Valley Historical Review* 35 (December 1947), 395.

80. Lindsay, "When Bryan Speaks," 1915, at http://oldpoetry.com/poetry/22452.

81. The sender of the broom was Max Glas of Oakland, CA. Glas to WJB, 9/21/1896, BPLC, Box 4. The other gifts are all mentioned in letters contained in the same box.

82. Form letter, 8/4/1896, BPLC, Box 4. MBB to Charles Moore (chief of Manuscript Division, Library of Congress), 10/24/1925, WJB administrative case file, Manuscript Division, Library of Congress. Thanks to John Earl Haynes for locating this depressing letter. I arrived at the total of 250,000 by multiplying 2,000 pieces by the 120 days between July 10 and November 10. Although this includes Sundays, when no mail was delivered, it is probably a low estimate, given the days when the Bryans received far more than two thousand letters and telegrams. It is impossible to account for repeat writers, but in the surviving correspondence, the number of these is small. Paolo Coletta, author of the fullest biography of Bryan, gave a total of "186,000 letters and telegrams" received but supplied no source. Coletta, *Bryan,* vol. 1, 188. Bryan himself wrote that he received "as many as 2500 letters a day" after the election but gave no figure for the entire campaign. *Memoirs,* 145.

83. Smith, *"Dear Mr. President . . . ,"* 12, 46; *Down and Out in the Great Depression: Letters from the "Forgotten Man,"* ed. Robert S. McElvaine (Chapel Hill, 1983); Cornelia R. Levine and Lawrence Levine, *The People and the President: America's Conversation with FDR* (Boston, 2002); Grover Cleveland Papers, William McKinley Papers, Theodore Roosevelt Papers, all in Library of Congress. The largest number of letters to TR can be found in Series 1, Reel 49 of his papers. As with Bryan's papers, the preservation of correspondence to all these men is incomplete, but their biographers do not

mention that letters from hundreds of thousands of ordinary citizens were discarded. In comparison, leaders of social movements received far less mail. In 1886, Terence Powderly was the nationally prominent leader of the Knights of Labor, which had a million members. But that spring and summer, he received an average of only 118 letters a month. Thanks to Timothy Meagher, archivist of the Catholic University of America, for that information.

84. The correspondence from July 10 to November 10 can be found in BPLC, Boxes 4–13 and Box 45. There are some 800 pieces up to November 3 and about 4,200 in the following week.

85. Willis N. Shaw to WJB, 11/1/1896, BPLC, Box 5; W. H. Holford, Bloomington, WI, to WJB, 10/16/1896, ibid., Box 4.

86. W. J. Thurmond to WJB, 10/28/1896, ibid; Joe Morris to WJB, 11/2/1896, ibid, Box 5; L. S. T. (?) Farnham, Spirit Lake, IA, to WJB, 11/1/1896, ibid. One tea merchant in San Francisco wrote, "As I have ruined my business … to work for your election, I hope you will not forget me after you are elected." William Emmons to WJB, 10/31/1896, ibid.

87. J. F. King, Marshfield, MO, to WJB, 11/1/1896, ibid.

88. D. D. Hatfield, Monarch P.O., to WJB, 10/26/1896, BPLC, Box 4; Mary Martin to MB; 10/19/1896, ibid.; W. B. McCormick to WJB, 10/29/1896, ibid.

89. Gertrude Sauteren et al., Guerneville, CA, to WJB, 11/8/1896, BPLC, Box 5; Sister Bryan Farrow et al. to WJB, 11/6/1896, ibid.; Caesar A. Roberts, Denver, to WJB, 11/4/1896, ibid; Baby Baker, Escanaba, MI, to WJB, 10/8/1896, ibid., Box 4.

90. *St. Louis Republic*, 11/3/1896, 6 (ginger ale); *Christian Herald*, 11/4/1896, 821 (self-exile); Edytha N. Gregg, Cleveland, to WJB, 11/5/1896, BPLC, Box 5. Thirty years later, Willa Cather wrote a story about two leading businessman and close friends in a small Nebraska town who backed different candidates in 1896 and never spoke again. "Two Friends," in Willa Cather, *Collected Stories* (New York, 1992), 315–31.

91. Dr. Ernest G. Epler, Fort Smith, AR, to WJB, 10/31/1896, BPLC, Box 5.

92. See the list in William Diamond, "Urban and Rural Voting in 1896," *American Historical Review* 46 (January 1941), 297–98. Bryan lost just three of the twenty-five states west of Minnesota and south of the Ohio River: North Dakota, Oregon, and California. McKinley's *combined* plurality in this trio of states was just 9,489 votes.

93. A sophisticated recent statement of this view is Richard Franklin Bensel, *The Political Economy of American Industrialization, 1877–1900* (Cambridge, 2000), 253–72 and passim. Older discussions include Diamond, "Urban and Rural Voting," and Walter Dean Burnham, "The System of 1896: An Analysis," in Paul Kleppner et al., *The Evolution of American Electoral Systems* (Westport, CT, 1981), 147–202.

94. *New York Staats-Zeitung*, quoted in Jensen, *Winning of the Midwest*, 292. Besides Jensen, the leading exponent of this view is Paul Kleppner, *The Cross of Culture: A Social Analysis of Midwestern Politics, 1850–1900* (New York, 1970).

95. On Tammany Hall's "suspicious lack of energy," see Robert Slayton, "Enemy's Country: William Jennings Bryan and the Forces of Organized Democracy in New York City in 1896," honors thesis, State University of New York at Buffalo, 1973. On the Irish vote, see Jensen, *Winning of the Midwest*, 296–300.

96. Richard Hofstader, *The American Political Tradition* (New York, 1948), 137. For a intelligent analysis of the failure of the farmer-labor alliance, see Elizabeth Sanders,

Roots of Reform: Farmers, Workers, and the American State, 1877–1917 (Chicago, 1999), 138–47; and Bensel, *Political Economy,* 260, 264.

97. Ezekial Altshul, Jersey City, NJ, to WJB, 11/4/1896, BPLC, Box 6; J. F. Brazier, Anderson, IN, to WJB, ibid.

98. On employer coercion, see Jones, *Presidential Election,* 339; on GOP fraud, see Coletta, *Bryan,* vol. 1, 192–94. The latter essentially accepts the charges of Bryan's allies, some of which are clearly not credible. For example, Coletta writes, "Bryan's loss of Minnesota may be ascribed in large degree to fraud" (193). But McKinley won the state by almost 54,000 votes, 56.6 percent to Bryan's 40.9 percent. Corruption that massive, in a state not hitherto notorious for it, would certainly have drawn tremendous attention. On the varied forms of fraud practiced during the period, see Peter H. Argersinger, "New Perspectives on Election Fraud in the Gilded Age," *Political Science Quarterly* 100 (Winter 1985–86), 669–87.

99. On the emerging GOP coalition, see Phillips, *McKinley,* 57–85.

100. WJB, *First Battle,* 605, 630.

CHAPTER FOUR: A REPUBLIC, NOT AN EMPIRE, 1897–1900

1. Bryan, "Naboth's Vineyard," given in Denver, January 17, 1899, reprinted in *Speeches of William Jennings Bryan,* vol. 2 (New York, 1909), 8.

2. James to Francis Boott, a composer, 9/15/1900. *The Correspondence of William James,* vol. 9, ed. Ignas K. Skrupskelis and Elizabeth M. Berkeley (Charlottesville, 2001), 303.

3. W. R. Alexander to WJB, 11/8/1896, Box 10, BPLC. It seems that at least one of the couple's prayers was answered. According to the Des Moines City Directory, they continued to live at the same address, 1431 Linden St., through 1901. But Alexander stopped working as a printer and became a clerk at a local tobacco store. R. L. Polk and Co., City Directory, Des Moines, IA, 1896–97/1900–01. Thanks for the research assistance of Kate Delimitros.

4. J. H. Sauers to WJB, 11/6/1896, BPLC, Box 9.

5. A. E. Randall to WJB, ibid.

6. Jones quoted in Ralph M. Goldman, *The National Party Chairmen and Committees: Factionalism at the Top* (Armonk, NY, 1990), 159.

7. *Memoirs,* 119.

8. Mary quoted in ibid., 334. On the two files, see Larry Gene Osnes, "Charles W. Bryan: Latter-Day Populist and Rural Progressive," Ph.D. diss., University of Cincinnati, 1970, 95–99. Alas, neither, it seems, has survived.

9. Henry F. Graff, "The Soul of Integrity," *New Leader,* 9/10/2000, 34.

10. At least one boy was named after WJB as early as 1893. See freepages.genealogy. rootsweb.com/~rhio/Bryan.htm. Quotes from Marshall Stone to WJB, February 1897 [no day], BPLC, Box 44; Noah Scott, 2/11/1897, ibid.; Lewis H. Thompson to WJB, 10/30/1896, ibid.; Permealia Sisson, 2/13/1897, ibid. Just over a thousand namesake letters, dating from late 1896 and early 1897, are catalogued separately in BPLC, Boxes 44 and 45; others are scattered throughout Bryan's correspondence for these and later years. Given the couple's penchant for discarding mail, there were surely thousands more. Celebrities in business and popular entertainment—the Du Ponts, John D. Rockefeller, Mark Twain, Jenny Lind—routinely received "begging letters."

See the fascinating article by Scott A. Sandage, "The Gaze of Success: Failed Men and the Sentimental Marketplace, 1873–1893," in *Sentimental Men: Masculinity and the Politics of Affect in American Culture,* ed. Mary Chapman and Glenn Hendler (Berkeley, 1999), 181–201.

11. Sallie E. Miller, Hamburg, IA, to MBB, 3/20/1897, BPLC, Box 44.

12. Sales up to August 31, 1897, were 199,443, worth $35,643.60. W. B. Conkey Co. to WJB, no date but probably misfiled with letters from August 1898. BPLC, Box 22. No audited best-seller lists yet existed, but the sales figure was comparable to those of hugely popular tracts such as *Looking Backward* and *Progress and Poverty.* See Frank Luther Mott, *Golden Multitudes: The Story of Best Sellers in the United States* (New York, 1947).

13. Bradford Merrill (managing editor of *New York World*) to WJB, 9/11/1897, ibid., Box 20. R. Hal Williams, *The Democratic Party and California Politics, 1880–1896* (Stanford, 1973), 259. On intraparty struggles in 1897–98, see Koenig, *Bryan,* 256–71; Goldman, *National Party Chairmen,* 158–64. In the spring of 1897, Bryan did serve as associate counsel before the Supreme Court in *Smyth v. Ames,* a case in which he favored upholding a Nebraska law setting maximum railroad rates. But he took no pay, and the Court ruled against his position. Letters from college officials thanking Bryan for his donations can be found in BPLC, Box 20.

14. *New York Journal,* 9/10/97, 1; NYT, 9/9/1897, 1. A day after the accident, Bryan inquired if all the families of the dead railway workers were receiving aid. Frank J. Dale, Emporia, KS, to WJB, 9/11/1898, BPLC, Box 20.

15. The price of a bushel of corn rose from 25 cents in 1895 to 35 cents in 1900; cotton went from $7.62 a pound in 1895 to $9.15 in 1900; wheat boomed from 51 cents a bushel in 1895 to 81 cents in 1897 before declining to 58 cents in 1898 and then rising to 62 cents in 1900. *Historical Statistics of the United States* (Washington, DC, 1975), 512, 518.

16. For congressional votes on the gold standard after 1896, see Richard F. Bensel, *The Political Economy of American Industrialization, 1877–1900* (Cambridge, 2000), 426–33. For the supply of gold, see ibid., 409.

17. Willis J. Abbot to WJB, 11/20/1897, BPLC, Box 19.

18. WJB to Willis Abbott [*sic*], 3/16/1898, BPLC, Box 20. The previous fall, Abbot had advised Bryan, "Don't press the silver issue too much." Abbot to WJB, 11/20/1897, ibid.

19. See, for example, Adella Schoettler, Philadelphia, to WJB, 11/6/1896, ibid., Box 9; H. C. Read, Big Springs, TX, to WJB, 11/8/1896, ibid.

20. Starr Lasher, Plainwell, MI, to WJB, 12/18/1897, ibid.

21. On Jones's role, see Goldman, *National Party Chairmen,* 160–61.

22. For judicious summaries of these events, which give due credit to McKinley's political and diplomatic acumen, see Robert L. Beisner, *From the Old Diplomacy to the New, 1865–1900,* 2nd ed. (Arlington Heights, IL, 1986), 115–29; and Kevin Phillips, *McKinley* (New York, 2003), 90–96.

23. Bryan statement, late March 1898, quoted in Coletta, *Bryan,* vol. 1, 222. WJB to McKinley, 4/25/1898, BPLC, Box 20.

24. Merle E. Curti, *Bryan and World Peace* (Northampton, MA, 1931), 118.

25. William V. Allen to WJB, 5/18/1898, BPLC, Box 21; J. D. Botkin to WJB, ibid.; Coletta, *Bryan,* vol. 1, 223. Botkin's definition of the paramount conflict was "the war in which

we are engaged with a certain jew and his cohorts." Such overt anti-Semitism, an apparent reference to one of the Rothschilds, was quite rare among Bryan's followers. More prosaically, Bryan's Florida cousin, W. S. Jennings, advised him against entering military service, commenting that the weather in Cuba was horrible during the summer. Jennings to WJB, 5/26/1898, BPLC, Box 21.

26. Thomas O'Toole, Arcadia, KS, to WJB, 5/29/1898, ibid.; J. H. Cobb, Friend, NE, to WJB, 5/18/1898, ibid. Men (?) Mayhall, Vandalia, MO, to WJB, 6/6/1898, ibid. Box 20 of BPLC is filled with such letters.

27. GBH Bio, Box 64, 140. Muster rolls for the regiment are contained in BPLC, Box 48. On the military's recruitment policy—and the preference of Democrats and Populists for the all-volunteer National Guard over the regular army—see Graham A. Cosmas, *An Army for Empire: The United States Army in the Spanish-American War* (Shippensburg, PA, 1994 [1971]), 80–93.

28. Coletta, *Bryan*, vol. 1, 224. None of these charges cited any hard evidence.

29. On Dixie: Mrs. R. C. Alexander, Jacksonville, to WJB, 8/14/1898, Box 22. Bryan mollified her, and she wrote back two weeks later that it must have been a false rumor, planted by goldbugs. Alexander to WJB, 9/1/1898, ibid. The horoscope report was attached to a letter from WJB to MBB, 7/29/1898, ibid.

30. Vifquain was a Belgian immigrant who ran unsuccessfully for Congress from Nebraska in 1892. On Bryan's brief military career, see C. F. Beck, "Bryan as a Soldier," *The Arena*, October 1900, 393–96; Coletta, *Bryan*, vol. 1, 223–32; Koenig, *Bryan*, 271–87.

31. Quoted in J. R. Johnson, "Imperialism in Nebraska, 1898–1904," NH 44 (September 1963), 145.

32. "Mr. Bryan on the War," NYT, 6/15/1898, 3.

33. Quoted in Paolo E. Coletta, "Bryan, McKinley, and the Treaty of Paris," *Pacific Historical Review* 26 (May 1957), 132–33. This article is the fullest study of the episode. Also see Merle E. Curti, *Bryan and World Peace* (New York, 1969 [1931]), 121–32; Koenig, *Bryan*, 121–32, 288–93; Margaret Leech, *In the Days of McKinley* (New York, 1959), 353–60.

34. WJB to Carnegie, 1/13/1899, BPLC, Box 22.

35. Curti, *Bryan and World Peace*, 125. Teller's position was similar to Bryan's; he feared the silver forces would take the blame if the treaty went down to defeat, emboldening Filipino insurgents to attack U.S. troops. Elmer Ellis, *Henry Moore Teller: Defender of the West* (Caldwell, ID, 1941), 316–19. The only letters opposing Bryan's position that are preserved in BPLC are from politicians and prominent figures such as Carnegie.

36. Curti, *Bryan and World Peace*, 127.

37. John R. Lambert, *Arthur Pue Gorman* (Baton Rouge, 1953); on Hoar, see Robert L. Beisner, *Twelve Against Empire: The Anti-Imperialists, 1898–1900* (New York, 1968), 139–64.

38. Stuart Creighton Miller, *"Benevolent Assimilation": The American Conquest of the Philippines, 1899–1903* (New Haven, 1982), 29.

39. Bryan, "America's Mission," BPLC, Box 50.

40. Grayson quoted in Daniel B. Schirmer, *Republic or Empire: American Resistance to the Philippine War* (Cambridge, MA, 1972), 129.

41. For the military history of the war, see two careful works by Brian McAllister Linn,

The U.S. Army and Counterinsurgency in the Philippine War, 1899–1902 (Chapel Hill, 1989) and *The Philippine War, 1899–1902* (Lawrence, KS, 2000). At the age of eighty-eight, Aguinaldo was still angry at Bryan for backing the peace treaty with Spain for what he believed were nakedly political reasons. General Emilio Aguinaldo with Vincente Albano Pacis, *A Second Look at America* (New York, 1957), 88–89, 161–62.

42. Quote from Matthew Frye Jacobson, *Special Sorrows: The Diasporic Imagination of Irish, Polish, and Jewish Immigrants in the United States* (Cambridge, 1995), 181. On the racial ambiguities of these immigrants' views toward U.S. imperialism, see ibid., 177–216. Hoar quoted in Beisner, *Twelve Against Empire*, 160.

43. Sen. George Vest, "Objections to Annexing the Philippines," *North American Review* 168 (January 1899), 112; Tillman quoted in Stephen Kantrowitz, *Ben Tillman and the Reconstruction of White Supremacy* (Chapel Hill, 2000), 263. This was not just a southern viewpoint. In 1895, Rep. "Honey Fitz" Fitzgerald opposed annexation of Hawaii and asked rhetorically, "Are we to have a Mongolian state in this union?" Quoted in Miller, "*Benevolent Assimilation*," 15.

44. Bryan, "America's Mission." See the incisive comments on this speech in Paul A. Kramer, "Empires, Exceptions, and Anglo-Saxons: Race and Rule Between the British and United States Empires, 1880–1910," *Journal of American History* 88 (March 2002), 1340.

45. On Louisiana in 1898, see Michael Perman, *Struggle for Mastery: Disenfranchisement in the South, 1888–1908* (Chapel Hill, 2001), 143; on North Carolina in 1900, see Josephus Daniels, *Editor in Politics* (Chapel Hill, 1941), 354–55. On Bryan's general view, "The Negro Question," *Comm.*, 11/1/1901. In Chicago, Julius F. Taylor edited a paper, the *Broad Ax*, which in 1900 urged his fellow blacks to vote for Bryan, as a way of defying the man Taylor called "the Great Beggar of Tuskegee." *The Booker T. Washington Papers*, vol. 8, ed. Louis Harlan (Urbana, IL, 1979), 514; "Address to the Public" by the Negro National Democratic League, *Chicago Broad Ax*, 7/21/1900 at www.boondock-snet.com/ai/ailtexts/nndl0700.html.

46. "The Negro Question," *Comm.*, 11/1/1901. As one biographer puts it, "Bryan was a more appealing figure when he entertained no reservations than when he did." Paul W. Glad, *The Trumpet Soundeth: William Jennings Bryan and His Democracy, 1896–1912* (Lincoln, 1960), 107.

47. Letter from Jones to WJB, 7/23/1900, BPLC, Box 25; Kantrowitz, *Ben Tillman*.

48. Quoted in Coletta, *Bryan*, vol. 1, 221. On the size of the crowds, see, for example, *Houston Daily Post*, 3/10/1899, 1, and *Denver Evening Post*, 1/17/1899.

49. "A Busy One from His Arrival," *Denver Post*, 1/16/1899, 2. P. J. Quigley, no address, to WJB, 4/20/1899, BPLC, Box 22.

50. Gardner to WJB, 3/20/1899, ibid. Hobson had commanded an unsuccessful effort to block the harbor of Santiago de Cuba and was one of the highest-ranking Americans taken prisoner. Patrick McSherry, "Constructor Richmond Pearson Hobson, 1870–1937," www.spanam.simplenet.com/hobson/htm.

51. Gardner closed with a plea that Bryan answer her "unimportant letter ... saying that you do not condemn my very hasty action and that you understand it was only intended as a joke." Gardner to WJB, 3/20/1899, BPLC, Box 22.

52. *Brenham Daily Banner*, 1/26/1899 (Tammany), 1/29/1899 (imperialism), 11/5/1899 (prosperity). For a capsule description of the town in this period, when it had about

six thousand inhabitants, see *A Complete Pronouncing Gazeteer and Geographical Dictionary of the World,* ed. A. L. Helprin (Philadelphia, 1906), 266–67.

53. In January, a Wall Street lawyer who had worked in the Cleveland administration but backed Bryan in 1896 told him, "Your complete command of the party machinery in every state of the Union is everywhere conceded." But after this exaggerated assessment, John S. Seymour asked Bryan not to run because every Democratic leader agreed he would lose. Seymour to WJB, 1/23/1900, BPLC, Box 24.

54. George Fred Williams, 4/24/1900 to WJB, ibid.

55. Martin J. Sklar, *The Corporate Reconstruction of American Capitalism, 1890–1916: The Market, the Law, and Politics* (Cambridge, 1988), 46–47; Naomi Lamoreaux, *The Great Merger Movement in American Business, 1895–1904* (Cambridge, 1985). Bryan quoted in Koenig, *Bryan,* 297. Even in Florida, state Democrats labeled imperialism and "the enormous growth and influence of the power of the trusts" the primary issues of the campaign and relegated silver coinage below tariff reduction. See the 1900 state platform, in William T. Cash, *History of the Democratic Party in Florida* (Tallahassee, 1936), 174–76.

56. A classic study of this literature is Frederic Cople Jaher, *Doubters and Dissenters* (London, 1964).

57. McKinley, 1899 Message to Congress, quoted in Sklar, *Corporate Reconstruction,* 341; George Cortelyou quoted in Margaret Leech, *In the Days of McKinley* (New York, 1959), 547.

58. Eugene W. Brewster to WJB, 3/17/1900, BPLC, Box 24.

59. William James to Henry James III, 3/18/1900, in *The Correspondence of William James,* vol. 9, 167. For a sample of James's views, see Beisner, *Twelve Against Empire,* 35–52.

60. On the survey, which questioned local postmasters (key political appointees at the time) of both parties, see Goran Rystad, *Ambiguous Imperialism: American Foreign Policy and Domestic Politics at the Turn of the Century* (Lund, Sweden, 1975), 95–98.

61. Loomis, "The Political Horizon," *Atlantic Monthly,* April 1900, 560, 562.

62. WJB, "The Issue in the Presidential Campaign," *North American Review,* 753, 771.

63. Henry F. Pringle, *Theodore Roosevelt: A Biography* (New York, 1931), 224.

64. Dewey, quoted by John J. Miller, "Summer *Olympia,*" *National Review Online,* August 8, 2000.

65. According to political custom, nominees were supposed to wait at home to be "notified" of the convention's choice. Bryan's attendance at the 1896 convention in Chicago didn't violate tradition because he was not, at the outset, a favorite and didn't speak after being nominated there. On the opening of the gathering in Kansas City, see *The Second Battle, or The New Declaration of Independence, 1776–1900: An Account of the Struggle of 1900 as Discussed in Selections from the Writings of the Hon. William J. Bryan and Others* (Chicago, 1901), 9 and passim.

66. Ibid., 21–27. Oldham's granddaughter is Joyce Appleby, a prominent historian of the American Revolution and the early republic.

67. On Bryan's contact with the convention, "To Manage It from Lincoln," *Kansas City Star,* 7/1/1900; on dictatorial conduct, "Bryan's Own Words," ibid., 7/4/1900; on the committee vote, *New York World,* 7/6/1900, 2. For the close relationship between Towne and Bryan, see the former's letters, 7/18/1900 and 7/23/1900, in BPLC, Box 24.

68. *Anamosa Journal,* 7/12/1900, 1. In the inaugural issue of the *Chicago American,* Bryan wrote an open letter praising Hearst's support for him in 1896. David Nasaw, *The Chief* (New York, 2000), 153.

69. Editor's note to William Allen White, "Bryan," *McClure's,* July 1900, 232.

70. Ibid., 232–37.

71. Ibid. On White's career and politics, see Sally Foreman Griffith, *Home Town News: William Allen White and the* Emporia Gazette (New York, 1989).

72. Willa Cather, "The Personal Side of William Jennings Bryan," *Home Monthly,* 7/14/1900, reprinted in *The World and the Parish: Willa Cather's Articles and Reviews, 1893–1902,* vol. 2, ed. William M. Curtin (Lincoln, 1970), 782–89. Cather wrote the piece under the pseudonym "Henry Nickelmann."

73. Ibid.

74. Ibid.

75. Jones quoted in Walter LaFeber, "Election of 1900," *History of American Presidential Elections, 1789–1968,* vol. 5, ed. Arthur M. Schlesinger Jr. (New York, 1985), 1893. For a typical report of disinterest, in this case from Ohio, see *Washington Evening Star,* 8/8/1900, 3.

76. Franklin D. Roosevelt, in 1932, was the first nominee of either major party to deliver his acceptance speech at the convention that nominated him. On changes in the ritual, see David B. Valley, *A History and Analysis of Democratic Presidential Nomination Acceptance Speeches to 1968* (Lanham, MD, 1988).

77. NYT, August 9, 1900, 1.

78. The speech is available online at www.boondocksnet.com/ai/ailtexts/bryanimp.html. My citations are to the copy included as an appendix to LaFeber, "Election of 1900," 1943–56. Bryan included the address, titled "Imperialism," in *Speeches of William Jennings Bryan, Revised and Arranged by Himself,* vol. 2 (New York, 1909), 17–50.

79. Republican Platform of 1900, appendix to LaFeber, "Election of 1900," 1928.

80. On Long's rhetoric, see T. Harry Williams, *Huey Long* (New York, 1969), and Alan Brinkley, *Voices of Protest* (New York, 1982). Walter LaFeber offers an insightful analysis of the speech in "Election of 1900," 1893–4.

81. Charles R. Wendling, Charles Town, WV, to WJB, 8/12/1900, BPLC, Box 24; J. F. Jones, from Cebu, Philippines, to WJB, 9/8/1900, ibid. Also see Joe Lee Jameson, Austin, TX, to WJB, 4/1900 [no day] and 5/2/1900; Sherman Leonard, Balanga, Philippines, to WJB, 7/24/1900, ibid. On anti-imperialists warming to Bryan, see Schirmer, *Republic or Empire,* 200–1.

82. Leech, *In the Days of McKinley,* 549–51; William James to Frances Rollins Morse (a friend and social worker), 9/19/1900, *Correspondence of William James,* vol. 9, 313. Standard Oil gave the largest amount, $250,000 (the same sum as in 1896), but received $50,000 of it back from the Republican National Committee after the election. Herbert Croly, *Marcus Alonzo Hanna: His Life and Work* (New York, 1912), 325.

83. Hill and Croker battled almost every election season over which candidates to promote for governor and lesser state offices. See Rystad, *Ambiguous Imperialism,* 287–90; Coletta, *Bryan,* vol. 1, 274. Just before the election, a Boston magazine opposed to imperialism published an article by Croker that predicted most young voters would cast their ballots for Bryan. Croker, "The Interest of the First Voter," *North American Review,* October 1900, 455–60. For a detailed, if not always accurate, description of

the Tammany boss's decision to back Bryan, see Lothrop Stoddard, *Master of Manhattan: The Life of Richard Croker* (New York, 1931), 216–26. Two decades later, Bryan was still grateful to Croker. *Memoirs,* 126–27.

84. Quotes from Paolo E. Coletta, "Will the Real Progressive Stand Up? William Jennings Bryan and Theodore Roosevelt to 1909," NH 65 (Winter 1984), 16–17; Kathleen Dalton, *Theodore Roosevelt: A Strenuous Life* (New York, 2002), 161; LeRoy Ashby, *William Jennings Bryan: Champion of Democracy* (Boston, 1987), 91; Henry F. Pringle, *Theodore Roosevelt: A Biography* (New York, 1931), 225.

85. TR, from a 1902 speech, quoted in Stephen Skowronek, *The Politics Presidents Make: Leadership from John Adams to George Bush* (Cambridge, 1993), 235.

86. Mr. Dooley quoted in Dalton, *Theodore Roosevelt,* 192; TR speech in Grand Rapids, MI, quoted in Rystad, *Ambiguous Imperialism,* 276. On the masculine cast of rhetoric in this period, see Kristin L. Hoganson, *Fighting for American Manhood: How Gender Politics Provoked the Spanish-American and Philippine-American Wars* (New Haven, 1998). On the precedent set by TR and Bryan, see Gil Troy, *See How They Ran: The Changing Role of the Presidential Candidate,* rev. and exp. ed. (Cambridge, MA, 1996), 108–12.

87. Bryan speech in New York City, October 16, 1900, quoted in LaFeber, "Election of 1900," 1903.

88. Ben Procter, *William Randolph Hearst: The Early Years, 1863–1910* (New York, 1998), 157. Hearst did accompany the candidate when he came to New York City in mid-October. Of course, his flagship paper gave lavish attention to that.

89. J. G. Kremblebine to WJB, 10/19/1900, BPLC, Box 25; unnamed farmer quoted by A. J. Dowling, New York City, to WJB, 11/3/1900, ibid. Also see the religious references in Charles Banks, New York City, to WJB, 10/26/1900; Henry Ilawizi, Philadelphia, to WJB, 10/29/1900; Leo Cokelair, Chicago, to WJB, 11/2/1900. Gravestone photo in miscellaneous folder, BPLC, Box 52. No one kept a record of the mail received in either election year. But there are about 75 percent fewer letters archived in the BPLC. My estimate is based on a count of all letters received in the three days before each election, when the amount of preserved correspondence is heaviest. As in 1896, McKinley's correspondents were almost exclusively government and campaign officials. See Series 1, Reels 11 and 12, McKinley Papers, Library of Congress.

90. Rystad, *Ambiguous Imperialism,* 260–61; Hanna quoted in Koenig, *Bryan,* 341.

91. Congressional Quarterly, *Presidential Elections Since 1789,* 4th ed. (Washington, DC, 1987), 110–11; Eugene E. Robinson, *The Presidential Vote, 1896–1932* (Stanford, CA, 1934), 4–9; Rystad, *Ambiguous Imperialism,* 291–311.

92. See the tables and analysis in Mark Lawrence Kornbluh, *Why America Stopped Voting: The Decline of Participatory Democracy and the Emergence of Modern American Politics* (New York, 2000), 89–99.

CHAPTER FIVE: I HAVE KEPT THE FAITH, 1901–1904

1. Article by Harrydele Hallmark, in BSB-NSHS, Reel 1.

2. E. V. Dollars, president of Hiram College (one of whose predecessors was James A. Garfield), to WJB, BPLC, Box 25; T. W. C. Cheesman, Ashland, NE, to WJB, ibid.; Thomas B. Gregory, 11/8/1900 to WJB, ibid., Altgeld to WJB, 11/7/1900, ibid. Bryan

wrote later, "After 1900 I received very few letters that expressed hope for the future of the Democratic Party. Most of my correspondents were disappointed; they did not see how we could win after the defeats we had suffered." *Memoirs,* 146.

3. Robert E. Campbell, Bordentown, NJ, to WJB, 11/12/1900, BPLC, Box 25.

4. The eighth stanza of Lowell's *The Present Crisis,* John Bartlett, *Familiar Quotations,* 15th ed. (Boston, 1980), 567. Quoted by Samuel "Golden Rule" Jones, mayor of Toledo, to WJB, 11/8/1900, BPLC, Box 25.

5. TR to Lodge, 10/14/1900, quoted in Coletta, "Will the Real Progressive Stand Up?" 22.

6. Clinton Babbitt, Beloit, MI, to WJB, 11/8/1900, BPLC, Box 25.

7. Peter Brooks, *The Melodramatic Imagination: Balzac, Henry James, Melodrama, and the Mode of Excess* (New Haven, 1976), 12.

8. Ibid., 206.

9. Samuel G. Blythe, "Great Men and Their Neighbors," *Saturday Evening Post,* 6/29/1907, 12. In sharp contrast to *The First Battle,* which is ubiquitous, few contemporary libraries own a copy of *The Second Battle.* Even the Library of Congress possesses only a facsimile of it on microfilm.

10. T. A. Kiesselbach, who attended Bryan's class sometime after 1900, recalled that the politician was not as content with his electoral fate as he seemed to be in public. The children were discussing "Success," and Kiesselbach, flattering his instructor, "took the position that one's success should be judged by the effort put forth, rather than by actual attainment of the objective. But Mr. Bryan thought otherwise. He believed that to be considered successful, one must succeed in accomplishing a meritorious objective." Kiesselbach, "What's in a Life?" unpublished autobiography, 58–59. Thanks to Julie Greene, who sent me this anecdote from her grandfather's manuscript.

11. *Comm.,* 1/23/1901, 1; Philip Kief, Murdock, MN, to WJB, 2/17/1902, BPLC, Box 27. These articles, like most in the paper, were unsigned. On plans for the paper, see Bryan's form letter to editors, 12/20/1900, Louis Post Papers, Manuscript Division, Library of Congress, Box 1; "William Jennings Bryan, Orlando Jay Smith, and the Founding of *The Commoner:* Some New Bryan Letters," ed. Robert F. Himmelberg and Raymond J. Cunningham, NH 48 (1967), 69–79. In 1875, the black historian George Fred Williams published, in Washington, DC, eight issues of a newspaper also named *The Commoner.* David W. Blight, *Race and Reunion: The Civil War in American Memory* (Cambridge, MA, 2001), 169.

12. The regional guess was Bryan's, WJB to CWB, 6/8/1914, BPOXY, File 13–14. I was unable to find any list of subscribers.

13. *Comm.,* 1/23/1903, 2. The paper's circulation in 1906 was 145,528, according to *Rowell's American Newspaper Directory* (New York, 1906). Also see N. W. Ayer and Son's *American Newspaper Annual* (Philadelphia, 1902), 518; ibid. (1903), 523; ibid., (1905), 520. On Bryan as employer, see Thomas H. Tibbles, "Bryan as a Man," *Polk County Democrat,* Osceola, NE, 5/16/1907, in Clippings File, BPNSHS. For a good portrait of the paper and its staff, see Koenig, *Bryan,* 351–54.

14. "Fairview," *Comm.,* 2/06/1903. Also see "Docent Manual," Fairview. Thanks to Gina Brophy of Volunteer Services at BryanLGH Medical Center (built on the grounds of Fairview) for allowing me to read these materials.

15. See W. A. Swanberg, *Pulitzer* (New York, 1967), 352–56; Gorman quoted in William H. Harbaugh, "Election of 1904," *History of American Presidential Elections, 1789–1968,* ed. Arthur M. Schlesinger Jr. (New York, 1971), 1974.

16. A fine analysis of TR's love affair with the press is George Juergens, *News from the White House: The Presidential-Press Relationship in the Progressive Era* (Chicago, 1981), 1–62 and passim.

17. *Comm.,* 8/8/1902, 1; "The Negro Question," ibid., 10/30/1903, 16 (an editorial cartoon backing La Follette against "Republican politicians").

18. "Discusses Party Politics," in Finley Peter Dunne, *Mr. Dooley's Opinions* (New York, 1901), 93.

19. Ben Procter, *William Randolph Hearst: The Early Years, 1863–1910* (New York, 1998), 163–92.

20. For a good thumbnail biography of Parker, see Harbaugh, "Election of 1904," 1975–76. Edmund Morris describes him as "drably decent, colorlessly correct... Even the heart of Alton B. Parker was a gray area." Morris, *Theodore Rex* (New York, 2001), 339–40.

21. James Creelman, "Bryan Arrives and Meets a Frost," *New York World,* 7/4/1904, 2; "Bryan," *Louisville Courier-Journal* (Henry Watterson's paper), 7/7/1904, 2; Samuel J. Blythe, "Pathetic Position of Mr. Bryan," *St. Louis Post-Dispatch* (flagship of the Pulitzer chain), 7/6/1902, 6.

22. Quotes from Koenig, *Bryan,* 377.

23. Coletta, *Bryan,* vol. 1, 329–30. "Mr. Bryan Has Not 'Passed,'" *New York World,* 7/9/1904. The 1904 platform is appended to Harbaugh, "Election of 1904," 1995–2002.

24. Coletta, *Bryan,* vol. 1, 337. Bryan's speech is reprinted as "The St. Louis Convention," in *Speeches of William Jennings Bryan,* vol. 2 (New York, 1909), 50–62. On Hearst's reaction, which led him to mistrust all career politicians, see David Nasaw, *The Chief: The Life of William Randolph Hearst* (Boston, 2000), 187.

25. 2 Timothy 4:7, 2.

26. WJB, "St. Louis Convention," *Speeches,* 52, 53, 60.

27. William Allen White in *Collier's Weekly,* 7/16/1904, BSB-NSHS, Reel 1, 2nd series.

28. Charles Willis Thompson, *Presidents I've Known and Two Near Presidents* (Freeport, NY, 1970 [1929]), 59–60; Coletta, *Bryan,* vol. 1, 328; *Louisville Courier-Journal,* 7/10/1904, 3; Belmont quoted in Coletta, *Bryan,* vol. 1, 339.

29. H. L. Mencken, "Beaters of Breasts [1936]," in Mencken, *Heathen Days, 1890–1936* (Baltimore, 1996), 283–84.

30. On Parker's telegram and the hostile reaction to it (including an impromptu speech by Bryan, who was still quite ill), see Coletta, *Bryan,* vol. 1, 340–44. On Davis, see ibid. and Thomas Richard Ross, *Henry Gassaway Davis: An Old-Fashioned Biography* (Parsons, WV, 1994).

31. Alton Parker to WJB, 7/23/1904, BPLC, Box 27.

32. The participation rate was 65.2 percent, fourteen points lower than in 1896.

33. *Comm.,* 11/18/1904, 16. Debs's total in 1904 was five times higher than in 1900, and his percentage of the vote was particularly impressive in states in the Rockies and on the Pacific Coast that Bryan had either carried or come close to taking in the two previous elections. Congressional Quarterly, *Guide to U.S. Elections,* 282.

CHAPTER SIX: PROPHET ON THE ROAD

1. *Comm.,* 10/28/1904, 1.
2. "At the New York Reception," delivered on 8/30/1906, *Speeches of William Jennings Bryan,* vol. 2 (New York, 1909), 65.
3. Bryan's writings en route are collected, with additional commentary, in his *The Old World and Its Ways* (St. Louis, 1907). Also see Mary's recollections of the trip in *Memoirs,* 308–19.
4. Unfortunately, neither WJB nor either monarch disclosed the content of their discussions.
5. On the Mexico trips, see Boyd Carter, "William Jennings Bryan in Mexico," NH 41 (March 1960), 53–64. On his travels in Europe (accompanied by his son) in the fall and winter of 1903–04, see WJB, *Under Other Flags* (Lincoln, NE, 1905).
6. Quote from the *Times of Bombay,* reprinted in *Comm.,* 5/4/1906, 6.
7. Edward G. Lowry, *Washington Close-ups: Intimate Views of Some Public Figures* (Boston, 1921), 39–40.
8. In response to a 1924 query from the journalist Mark Sullivan, Bryan estimated that he had given an average of two hundred "lectures" a year since 1894. Bryan judged this to be a total of about five thousand, but obviously his multiplication was flawed. WJB to Sullivan, 3/11/1924, BPLC, Box 39.
9. WJB to Transportation Club of Indianapolis, 2/5/1915, BPLC, Box 30. For a healthy sample of his humor, see the chapter "Bryan Stories" in GBH Bio, BPLC, Box 57.
10. The *Times of Bombay,* 3/27/1906, in *Comm.,* 5/4/1906, 6.
11. Bryan, "The Next Awakening," *Public Opinion,* reprinted in *Comm.,* 6/16/1905, 1.
12. Charles Sheldon, *In His Steps* (Philadelphia, 1936 [1896]). Most white Social Gospelers also shared Bryan's blindness to racial injustice. As W. E. B. Du Bois wrote, "The one great moral issue of America upon which the Church of Christ comes nearest to being dumb is the question as to the application of the golden rule between White and Black folk." Quoted in Ralph E. Luker, *The Social Gospel in Black and White: American Racial Reform, 1885–1912* (Chapel Hill, 1991), 312.
13. WJB, "The Larger Life," speech given 4/21/1912 at Calvary Methodist Church, New York City, *Comm.* 6/7/1912, 4; Matthews, from an essay published in 1921, quoted in Ronald C. White Jr. and C. Howard Hopkins, *The Social Gospel: Religion and Reform in Changing America* (Philadelphia, 1976), xi; Richard Hofstadter, *The Age of Reform* (New York, 1955), 205. For an extensive discussion of Bryan's religious views, see Willard H. Smith, *The Social and Religious Thought of William Jennings Bryan* (Lawrence, KS, 1975), 17–40, an article originally published in *The Journal of American History* in 1966.
14. Smith, *Social and Religious Thought,* 33–34; *Comm.,* 6/19/1903, 3.
15. Bryan to the Alumni Association of Syracuse University, *Comm.,* 2/17/1905, 3.
16. Clarence Truc Wilson to WJB, 11/3/1923, BPLC, Box 38. Quoted in Smith, *Social and Religious Thought,* 35. Bryan in 1906, quoted in Coletta, *Bryan,* vol. 1, 385. James H. Moorhead comments that the great debate about millennialism probably failed to grip rank-and-file Protestants at the time: "Most persons probably had not sorted out their views clearly but lived with a mental hodgepodge of images of the last things, which they had not ordered into a distinct or coherent theory." Moorhead,

World Without End: Mainstream Protestant Visions of the Last Things, 1880–1925 (Bloomington, 1999), 17.

17. *Comm.*, 1/23/1901, 5/3/1901; Tolstoy, "Introduction to a Short Biography of William Lloyd Garrison," *The Kingdom of God and Peace Essays* (London, 1935), 579; Kenneth C. Wenzer, "Tolstoy and Bryan," NH 77 (Fall/Winter 1996), 140–48.

18. Compare Tolstoy's recollection of this exchange in "Introduction to a Short Biography," 579, with Bryan's noncommittal one in *Under Other Flags*, 101–2.

19. Jane Addams, *Twenty Years at Hull House*, ed. Victoria Bissell Brown (Boston, 1999), 147–152. Henri Troyat, *Tolstoy* (New York, 1967), 667. For an excellent survey of Tolstoy's international following, see Steven G. Marks, *How Russia Shaped the Modern World: From Art to Anti-Semitism, Ballet to Bolshevism* (Princeton, 2003), 102–39.

20. Isaiah Berlin, "The Hedgehog and the Fox: An Essay on Tolstoy's View of History," in Berlin, *The Proper Study of Mankind: An Anthology of Essays*, ed. Henry Hardy and Roger Hausheer (New York, 1997), 436. Bryan also explained that Tolstoy had only "lived under the dark shadow of Russian absolutism and despotism" and thus could be excused for thinking that governments couldn't reform themselves. *Comm.*, 4/7/1905, 2.

21. Charles Willis Thompson, *Presidents I've Known and Two Near Presidents* (Freeport, NY, 1970 [1929]), 91.

22. WJB, *Under Other Flags*, 73.

23. WJB, *Old World*, 444, 419–20; Daniel Rodgers, *Atlantic Crossings: Social Politics in a Progressive Age* (Cambridge, MA, 1998), 504. Rodgers's book is a wonderful study of such discoveries by American reformers in Europe.

24. Ibid., 28–31, 69, 79, 86, 83, 56–58; *Comm.*, 11/24/1905, 13.

25. TR quoted in Walter LaFeber, *The Clash: U.S.-Japanese Relations Throughout History* (New York, 1997), 82. For opinion, see Eleanor Tupper and George E. McReynolds, *Japan in American Public Opinion* (New York, 1937).

26. The house was in Saitama prefecture. William Jennings Bryan Jr., "My Japanese Brother," *Reader's Digest* (June 1955), 17–21; David Hesselgrave, "The Church That God Grew," *Trinity Magazine* (Winter 2000), at www.tiu.edu/trinitymagazine/TIU-Winter/churchgodgrew.htm. In 1939, Yamashita traveled to the United States "for the purpose of paying tribute to [Bryan's] memory"; Yamashita to Mr. and Mrs. Daniel[s], 2/20/1939, Josephus Daniels Papers, Library of Congress, Reel 44.

27. WJB, *Old World*, 156; Clements, *Bryan*, 70–75.

28. *Comm.*, 11/19/1909, 3.

29. WJB, *Old World*, 156, 158, 193, 299, 221; *Comm.*, 2/16/1906, 11–12. Pro-British newspapers in India harshly criticized Bryan's remarks; one asked him how long it would be before "a negro will become President of the United States," NYT, 8/31/1906, 2. Mary Bryan did not seem to share her husband's loathing for colonialism. She remembered Java only as a "charming island" where the Dutch "had a system of forced native labor which produced wonderful results." *Memoirs*, 314.

30. Bryan wrote a more extended defense of democracy and Christianity, American style, in *Letters to a Chinese Official: Being a Western View of Eastern Civilization* (New York, 1906).

31. WJB, *Old World*, 79, 261, 380, 374, 330.

32. Ibid., 374–75.

33. Victoria Case and Robert Ormond Case, *We Called It Culture: The Story of Chautauqua* (Garden City, NY, 1948), 87, 95; *Memoirs*, 284–85. The Sioux Falls date appears on a schedule for Bryan in BPLC, Box 41, which contains days and locations but no year. Judging from correspondence in the Redpath Collection, University of Iowa Libraries (hereafter Redpath Coll.), it was probably 1919.

34. On Churchill, Case and Case, *We Called it Culture*, 85. On politicians and evangelists, see Harry P. Harrison and Karl Detzer, *Culture Under Canvas: The Story of Tent Chautauqua* (New York, 1958), 116–55.

35. Harrison and Detzer, *Culture Under Canvas*, 156; James Paul Eckman, "Regeneration Through Culture: Chautauqua in Nebraska, 1882–1925," Ph.D. diss., University of Nebraska–Lincoln, 1989, 233 and passim; "Chautauqua Engagement Contract," 4/9/1912, Redpath Coll. On salaries, I am grateful to historian Susan Glenn, e-mail message to author, 5/22/2003, and to her *Female Spectacle: The Theatrical Roots of Modern Feminism* (Cambridge, 2000); Coletta, *Bryan*, vol. 1, 388.

36. Richard Wightman Fox, *Reinhold Niebuhr: A Biography* (New York, 1982), 1–3, 14.

37. See the itinerary in BPLC, Box 51, #2.

38. In advance, Harrison had promised that the trip "will be comparatively easy and will be mostly by streetcar." Harrison to CWB, 5/8/1912, Redpath Coll.

39. I have used the relevant data from 1910 in www.census.gov/population/www/censusdata/hiscendata.html.

40. Harrison and Detzer, *Culture Under Canvas*, 92–93; *Flint Daily Journal*, 7/18/1912; *Mt. Clemens Monitor*, 7/19/1912; *Niles Daily Sun*, 7/1/1912; *South Bend Tribune*, 7/22/1912, 7. Only in Mt. Clemens was attendance below organizers' expectations, but the local newspaper blamed that on the novelty of the affair for the town and not on its lead speaker. In 1896, Bryan had narrowly won three of the eight counties, all located in Michigan. Edgar Eugene Robinson, *The Presidential Vote, 1896–1932* (Stanford, 1934), 185–92, 228–34.

41. *Marinette Eagle*, 8/4 and 8/5/1899; *Marinette Eagle-Star*, 4/20/1922. Thanks to Professor Sidney Bremer for these references.

42. *Marinette Eagle-Star*, 4/20/1922; Harrison and Detzer, *Culture Under Canvas*, 158.

43. Harrison and Detzer, *Culture Under Canvas*, 163, 161 (extra talks).

44. *Memoirs*, 287. Examples of historical interpretation are Case and Case, *We Called It Culture*, 87–94; Paul W. Glad, *The Trumpet Soundeth: William Jennings Bryan and His Democracy, 1896–1912* (Lincoln, NE, 1960), 14–20.

45. I have borrowed these details from the two fullest studies of the institution: Theodore Morrison, *Chautauqua: A Center for Education, Religion, and the Arts in America* (Chicago, 1974), which quotes James, 83, and Andrew C. Rieser, *The Chautauqua Moment: Protestants, Progressives, and the Culture of Modern Liberalism* (New York, 2003).

46. Vincent quoted in Morrison, *Chautauqua*, 57. According to Rieser, "about one in four [of the local assemblies] failed or moved within a few seasons." *Moment*, 81.

47. Program for Beatrice Chautauqua Assembly, July 6–18, 1905, in NSHS. The assembly had been founded in 1888 by five local businessmen who convinced the Methodist bishop of Omaha to serve as its president. Rieser, *Moment*, 60–61.

48. The figure comes from a 1921 report directed by circuit manager Charles F. Horner and is probably inflated. But no independent survey exists. Morrison, *Chautauqua*, 181.

49. Jones quoted in Rieser, *Moment,* 266.
50. Morrison, *Chautauqua,* 182.
51. Quote in *Goshen Daily News,* 7/22/1912, 1; Harrison and Detzer, *Culture Under Canvas,* 92, 162; Richard W. Fox, "The Discipline of Amusement," *Inventing Times Square: Commerce and Culture at the Crossroads of the World,* ed. William R. Taylor (New York, 1991).
52. WJB, "The Value of an Ideal," *Speeches of William Jennings Bryan, Revised and Arranged by Himself* (New York, 1909), vol. 2, 236. The speech was frequently reprinted in *Comm.* and other periodicals.
53. Ibid., 237–39.
54. Ibid., 239–40.
55. Ibid., 241–43.
56. Ibid., 245–46, 251.
57. Ibid., 252, 253.
58. Ibid., 258–59.
59. "The Prince of Peace," *Speeches,* 261, 272.
60. Ibid., 274, 266; Alan Hajek, "Pascal's Wager," *The Stanford Encyclopedia of Philosophy* (Winter 2001 edition), plato.stanford.edu/archives/win2001/entries/pascal-wager/.
61. "Prince of Peace," *Speeches,* 264–65, 274; Jefferson quoted by F. Forrester Church in his introduction to *The Jefferson Bible: The Life and Morals of Jesus of Nazareth* (Boston, 1989), 12.
62. "Prince of Peace," *Speeches,* 263, 269, 286. In 1905, the sociologist Edward A. Ross encountered Bryan reading Darwin's *The Descent of Man* on the campus of the University of Nebraska. Later, Ross quoted him as fearing that Darwinism would "weaken the cause of democracy and strengthen class pride and the power of wealth." Quoted in Lawrence G. Buckley, "William Jennings Bryan in American Memory," Ph.D. diss., University of Hawaii, 1998, 267.
63. Ibid., 288. On the centrality of the Social Gospel to early-twentieth-century reform, see Eldon J. Eisenach, *The Lost Promise of Progressivism* (Lawrence, KS, 1994) and Robert M. Crunden, *Ministers of Reform: The Progressives' Achievement in American Civilization, 1889–1920* (New York, 1982).
64. NYT, 1/8/1908, 2; Bryan, "Why I Lecture," *Ladies' Home Journal,* April 1915, 9.
65. "A Visit to the East," *Comm.,* 1/31/1902, 3.

CHAPTER SEVEN: THE ORDEAL OF REFORM, 1906–1908

1. Speaker unnamed, NYT, 8/28/1906, 1.
2. Quoted in John J. Whitacre, "What Dreamers Have Done," *Comm.,* 3/24/1911, 5.
3. See the splendid summary and analysis by Richard L. McCormick, "The Discovery That Business Corrupts Politics: A Reappraisal of the Origins of Progressivism," *American Historical Review* 86 (April 1981), 247–74; Cockran quoted in David Sarasohn, *The Party of Reform: Democrats in the Progressive Era* (Jackson, MS, 1989), 10.
4. William Hoge, Commercial Travelers Anti-Trust League, to WJB (in Cairo, Egypt), 4/28/1906, BPNSHS.
5. See, for example, *Comm.,* 6/19/1908, 13. In 1909, according to a reminiscence by

Buehler Metcalfe (who had played on the varsity team at the University of Nebraska), Bryan made "a shoe string" catch of a pop fly to end an inning. Then "he ran all the way in to home plate. He was collarless, hatless and his great baggy unpressed trousers were held by one suspender strap, the other having dropped down to his throwing arm." BPLC, Box 50, #16.

6. N. W. Ayer and Sons, *American Newspaper Annual* (Philadelphia, 1905), 520; *Rowell's American Newspaper Directory* (New York, 1906); Larry G. Osnes, "Charles W. Bryan: 'His Brother's Keeper,' " NH 48 (January 1967), 55–56, 59; Sarasohn, *Party of Reform*, 37.

7. The latest count was published in *Comm.*, 1/19/1906, 6. Quotes from Merritt Moore, Northfield, MN, *Comm.*, 3/31/1905, 5; Banks P. Turner, Newbern, TN, *Comm.*, 5/26/1905, 8. The "primary pledge" campaign was announced in March 1905, and the paper continued to print letters of support until autumn of the following year.

8. NYT, 8/31/1906, 1.

9. Mary Dillon, *The Leader* (New York, 1906), 20–21.

10. Ibid., 255.

11. Ibid., 325.

12. Quotes from *New York World*, 8/30/1906, 1 ("browned"); NYT, 8/31/1906, 3 (hotel scene). *The New Encyclopedia of Social Reform*, ed. W. D. P. Bliss (New York, 1970 [1910]), 134.

13. "At the New York Reception," *Speeches of William Jennings Bryan*, vol. 2 (New York, 1909), 84.

14. Ibid., 85, 86.

15. Quote, undated, from Arthur Wallace Dunn, *From Harrison to Harding* (Port Washington, NY, 1971 [1922]), vol. 2, 48; *New York World*, 8/31/1906, 6; NYT, 8/31/1906, 4; Coletta, *Bryan*, vol. 1, 378–79.

16. NYT, 8/30/1906, 1; Ken Hubbard, quoted in Seymour Smith, "Personal Recollections of William Jennings Bryan," BP-NSHS, Box 1.

17. "Government Ownership," *Speeches*, 99.

18. For the membership of Debs's party in 1906, see Ira Kipnis, *The American Socialist Movement, 1897–1912* (New York, 1952), 174.

19. Michael McGerr, *A Fierce Discontent: The Rise and Fall of the Progressive Movement in America, 1870–1920* (New York, 2003), xvi. Other influential works on the subject include Daniel Rodgers, *Atlantic Crossings*, and Arthur Link and Richard L. McCormick, *Progressivism* (Arlington Heights, IL, 1982). For a summary of the conventional wisdom, see Alonzo Hamby, "Progressivism: A Century of Change and Rebirth," in *Progressivism and the New Democracy*, ed. Sidney Milkis and Jerome M. Mileur (Amherst, MA, 1999), 40–80.

20. For examples and analysis, see Elizabeth Sanders, *Roots of Reform: Farmers, Workers, and the American State* (Chicago, 1999); Sarasohn, *Party of Reform*; Ann Firor Scott, "A Progressive Wind from the South, 1906–1913," *Journal of Southern History* 29 (February 1963), 53–70; Robert C. McMath Jr., "C. Vann Woodward and the Burden of Southern Populism," *Journal of Southern History* 67 (November 2001), 741–68.

21. Tom Johnson, *My Story* (Seattle, 1970 [1911]); Stephen L. Piott, *Holy Joe: Joseph W. Folk and the Missouri Idea* (Columbia, MO, 1997); John D. Buenker, *Urban Liberalism and Progressive Reform* (New York, 1973).

22. Monroe Lee Billington, *Thomas P. Gore: The Blind Senator from Oklahoma* (Lawrence, KS, 1967), quote, 11. On the rise of the Farmers' Union, see Sanders, *Roots of Reform*, 149–53.

23. Charles Jacobson, quoted in Raymond Arsenault, *The Wild Ass of the Ozarks: Jeff Davis and the Social Bases of Southern Politics* (Philadelphia, 1984), 49. On Bryan's image among most reporters, see Charles L. Ponce de Leon, *Self-Exposure: Human-Interest Journalism and the Emergence of Celebrity in America, 1890–1940* (Chapel Hill, 2002), 181.

24. Julie Greene, *Pure and Simple Politics: The American Federation of Labor and Political Activism, 1881–1917* (Cambridge, 1998), 107–41.

25. WJB address to the People's Lobby in Newark, NJ, 5/1/1907, *Comm.*, 5/24/1906, 1; *Comm.*, 10/25/1907, 2. On the relationship between the two men, see Paolo E. Coletta, "Will the Real Progressive Stand Up? William Jennings Bryan and Theodore Roosevelt to 1909," NH 44 (January 1984), 15–57.

26. See David C. Roller, "Theodore Roosevelt," *Popular Images of American Presidents*, ed. William C. Spragens (Westport, CT, 1988), 185–209; Theodore P. Greene, *America's Heroes: The Changing Models of Success in American Magazines* (New York, 1970), 232–37.

27. CWB to WJB, 6/28/1909, BPOXY, Files 19/20. The number was probably inflated, but few copies of these letters have survived. Bryan's banquet talks in *Comm.*, 12/20/1907, 1, 3.

28. On the feeble opposition, see Coletta, *Bryan*, vol. 1, 396–98; Sarasohn, *Party of Reform*, 36–37; W. A. Swanberg, *Pulitzer* (New York, 1967), 391.

29. Arthur Wallace Dunn, quoted in Sarasohn, *Party of Reform*, 38. On Taggart's role, see Ralph M. Goldman, *The National Party Chairmen and Committees: Factionalism at the Top* (Armonk, NY, 1990), 215, and James Philip Fadely, *Thomas Taggart: Public Servant, Political Boss, 1856–1929* (Bloomington, IN, 1997).

30. *Rocky Mountain News*, 7/9/1908, 1–2; Coletta, *Bryan*, vol. 1, 403–8; Claude G. Bowers, *The Life of John Worth Kern* (Indianapolis, 1918), 95–96, 156–87; "John W. Kern on Government Ownership," *Comm.*, 11/2/1906, 16.

31. *History of American Presidential Elections, 1789–1968*, vol. 5, ed. Arthur M. Schlesinger Jr. (New York, 1985), 2091–101; Federal Deposit Insurance Corporation, *A Brief History of Deposit Insurance in the United States* (Washington, DC, 1998), 16–23; Bryan, "Guaranteed Deposits," *Speeches*, vol. 2, 159.

32. Quoted in *Atlanta Journal*, 9/16/1906, 1.

33. The cartoon, evidently from a Democratic campaign book, was copied for me by Harry Rubenstein of the National Museum of American History.

34. *History of Elections*, 2091–92; Taft quoted in Donald F. Anderson, *William Howard Taft: A Conservative's Conception of the Presidency* (Ithaca, 1973), 54.

35. *History of Elections*, 2096–97. The authoritative history of this aspect of the 1908 campaign is Greene's *Pure and Simple Politics*, 142–214.

36. Gompers quoted in Greene, *Pure and Simple Politics*, 142. On Taft's labor rulings, see William E. Forbath, *Law and the Shaping of the American Labor Movement* (Cambridge, MA, 1991), 74–75 (quote), 88–89.

37. Patricia Gaster, "Nebraska Newspaperman Will M. Maupin," NH 69 (Winter 1988), 182–92.

38. *The Campaign Textbook of the Democratic Party of the United States* (Chicago, 1908); Isaac F. Marcosson, *"Marse Henry": A Biography of Henry Watterson* (New York, 1951), 177–79;

Washington Evening Star, 9/9/1908, 9; Louise Overacker, *Money in Elections* (New York, 1974 [1932]), 73, 136.

39. On the technology of and commerce in early phonographs, see Andre Millard, *America on Record: A History of Recorded Sound* (Cambridge, 1995), 37–64.

40. "The Labor Question," Victor 5540, and "Publication of Campaign Contributions," Victor 5537, Recorded Sound Division, Library of Congress.

41. *Comm.,* 8/21/1908, 14; 9/11/1908, 16.

42. *Campaign Textbook, 1908,* 301. For a similar quote from the pro-GOP *New York Post,* see *Comm.,* 8/14/1908, 4. Albert L. Gale and George W. Kline, *Bryan the Man: The Great Commoner at Close Range* (St. Louis, 1908); the book was subtitled *An Appreciation From a Republican Viewpoint.*

43. On Watson's campaign, see C. Vann Woodward, *Tom Watson: Agrarian Rebel* (New York, 1938), 398–400; on the Independence Party, see Ben Procter, *William Randolph Hearst: The Early Years, 1863–1910* (New York, 1998), 246–53.

44. "Shall the People Rule?" 8/12/1908, *Speeches,* vol. 2, 103, 117.

45. Quotes from Henry F. Pringle, *The Life and Times of William Howard Taft,* vol. 1 (New York, 1939), 363 (Van Cleave); Coletta, "Election of 1908," 2085 (Taft); William Allen White, "Twelve Years of Mr. Bryan," *Collier's,* 10/17/1908, 12–13.

46. Quote from *Indianapolis News,* 9/10/1908, 1, 3. The *News* was a Democratic paper, which made its failure to report the content of Bryan's speech particularly suggestive. On nocturnal fans, see *Washington Evening Star,* 9/10/1908, 12. The most complete account of the campaign tours is Edgar A. Hornig, "The Indefatigable Mr. Bryan in 1908," NH 37 (September 1956), 183–99. He recounts the Brooklyn story on p. 193.

47. Remarkably, this is one of only *four* letters written during the ten months before Election Day archived in BPLC. On the volume of mail, see NYT, 9/6/1908, Sect. 5, 5.

48. Quotes from Donald F. Anderson, *William Howard Taft: A Conservative's Conception of the Presidency* (Ithaca, 1973), 27 (Taft); Pringle, *Life and Times,* vol. 1, 359 (Roosevelt). For Bryan's imitation of Taft, see Lawrence Glen Buckley, "William Jennings Bryan in American Memory," Ph.D. diss., University of Hawaii, 1998, 66–67.

49. Gompers quoted in Greene, *Pure and Simple Politics,* 160. On Kern's record, see Claude G. Bowers, *The Life of John Worth Kern* (Indianapolis, 1918), 95–96; Sarasohn, *Party of Reform,* 44.

50. Quote from Greene, *Pure and Simple Politics,* 189. Democrats accused the few national labor officials who backed Taft, such as Daniel J. Keefe of the longshoremen's union, of having received federal job offers in return. But patronage was hardly a cause for scandal. See the reports reprinted in *Comm.,* 3/7/1913, 6.

51. Taft quoted in Paolo E. Coletta, *The Presidency of William Howard Taft* (Lawrence, KS, 1973), 30; Archie Butt to Clara Butt, in *The Letters of Archie Butt: Personal Aide to President Roosevelt,* ed. Lawrence F. Abbott (Garden City, NY, 1924), 59.

52. Quotes from "Third Annual Meeting of the Niagara Movement, Aug. 26–29, 1907," in *Pamphlets and Leaflets of W. E. B. Du Bois,* ed. Herbert Aptheker (White Plains, NY, 1986), 76; David Levering Lewis, *W. E. B. Du Bois: Biography of a Race, 1868–1919* (New York, 1993). On the political furor and its consequences, see Emma Lou Thornbrough, "The Brownsville Episode and the Negro Vote," *Mississippi Valley Historical Review* 44 (December 1957), 469–93.

53. Koenig, *Bryan,* 334; "Address to the Public," *Chicago Broad-Ax,* 7/21/1900, at www.

boondocksnet.com/ai/ailtexts. Bell's paper was *The Afro-American Sentinel.* Scattered copies exist in the LC Newspaper Room. G. W. Jones to WJB, 11/15/1901, BPLC, Box 27. Bryan also received several letters from E. George Biddle, a black minister and newspaper editor in Troy, New York, who had supported him in 1896 and 1900, though "it has cost me considerable to take a stand for you as against McKinleyism." Biddle to WJB, 10/26/1901, BPLC, Box 27.

54. WJB to Josephus Daniels, no day, 1908, in Daniels Papers, Library of Congress, Box 69. Kern quoted in Julie Greene, "Dinner-Pail Politics: Employers, Workers, and Partisan Culture in the Progressive Era," in *Labor Histories: Class, Politics, and the Working-Class Experience,* ed. Eric Arnesen et al. (Urbana, IL, 1998), 87.

55. On the chronology of disenfranchisement, see J. Morgan Kousser, *The Shaping of Southern Politics: Suffrage Restriction and the Establishment of the One-Party South, 1880–1910* (New Haven, 1974), 239; Alexander Keyssar, *The Right to Vote: The Contested History of Democracy in the United States* (New York, 2000), 111–16.

56. James Manahan, *Trials of a Lawyer: Autobiography* (Minneapolis, 1933), 110–11.

57. WJB to Daniels, 10/19/1908, Daniels Papers, Box 69. On the Archbold letters, see Nasaw, *The Chief,* 221–23; Sarasohn, *Party of Reform,* 50–51.

58. TR quoted in Coletta, "Election of 1908," 2087. Third parties did poorly and had only a marginal impact on the result. Thomas Hisgen, of the Independence League, drew 82,600 votes, and Tom Watson only 28,400, most of it in his home state of Georgia. Eugene Debs drew 420,000 for the Socialists, less than 3 percent of the total. In Indiana, his vote was larger than the plurality for Taft, but the prohibitionist candidate did better there. Congressional Quarterly, *Presidential Elections Since 1789,* 4th ed. (Washington, DC, 1987), 113, 135.

59. For one scathing critique of the performance of the Chicago machine under Roger Sullivan, see Louis F. Post to WJB, Louis Post Papers, Library of Congress, Box 1. On Tammany's coolness to Bryan and hope that a third defeat would eliminate him from leading the party, see Coletta, *Bryan,* vol. 1, 432.

60. *Comm.,* 11/20/1908, 1.

61. *Indianapolis News,* 9/1/1908, 1. It's not clear how much Roosevelt feared a Bryan victory. His aide Archie Butt quoted TR's belief that Bryan was "a wonderful man and would make a strong, able President." But the editor of Butt's letters had gained a more negative impression after corresponding with Roosevelt during the 1908 campaign. *The Letters of Archie Butt,* 91, 46–47.

62. *Indianapolis News,* 11/4/1908, 2, 6. Bryan received just over 1.3 million votes more than Parker had.

63. WJB to Thomas F. Hayden, 1/2/1909, BPLC, Carton 27.

64. *Comm.,* 11/13/1908, 1.

65. Quotes from Hunter, *Comm.,* 1/8/1909, 6; Thomas F. Hynes, Phillipsburg, MT, *Comm.,* 12/18/1908, 7. For an example of criticism, see A. B. Evenden, Herkimer, NY, *Comm.,* 12/18/1908, 7.

66. Quotes from J. W. Biard, Sulphur, OK, *Comm.,* 12/18/1908, 7 (also see W. S. Byram, Harrisonville, MO, 12/25/08, 7); L. J. Mason, Kansas City, MO, 1/1/1909, 8.

67. J. K. Mason, Philadelphia, to WJB, 11/9/1908, BPLC, Box 27. An identical letter, signed by John K. Essler, Camden, NJ, was dated the same day.

68. James E. Irvine, Whitehall, VA, to WJB, 11/5/1908, and W. H. Wallick to WJB, Edge-

water, CO, 11/11/1908, BPLC, Box 27. On articles, Frank H. Packard, Ceylon, MN, to WJB, 11/08/1908, ibid. Debs to Fred D. Warren (editor of *The Appeal*), 12/12/1912, in *Letters of Eugene V. Debs*, vol. 1, *1874–1912*, ed. J. Robert Constantine (Urbana, IL, 1990), 560. For the history of anti-Catholicism in the United States, see John T. McGreevy, *Catholicism and American Freedom: A History* (New York, 2003), especially 91–165.

69. Frank T. Reuter, *Catholic Influence on American Colonial Policies, 1898–1904* (Austin, 1967), 159 and passim; Wilson D. Miscamble, "Catholics and American Foreign Policy from McKinley to McCarthy: A Historiographical Survey," *Diplomatic History* 4 (1980), 225–26. When Taft first arrived in the Philippines in the fall of 1899 as the head of an investigating commission, the small Dominican order complained that he was hostile to the Church. "The Taft Commission and the Catholic Church," ed. Jose S. Arcilla, S.J., *Philippiniana Sacra* (1973), 458ff. On Bryan's fears, see Josephus Daniels, *Editor in Politics* (Chapel Hill, 1941), 540; Charles Weidler, South Bend, IN, to WJB, 11/5/1908, BPLC, Box 27.

One layman, E. L. Scharf of Washington, DC, did employ the Catholic News Agency, a tiny outfit he owned, to accuse Bryan of having voted to defund Catholic schools for Indians when he was in Congress. But Scharf only mentioned Taft's disposal of Church properties in passing. Scharf, "William Jennings Bryan and the Littl [*sic*] Plot of 1894," BPNSHS, Box 3, Folder 57. Three years later, two Catholic Democrats in Congress were able to get Scharf expelled from the Knights of Columbus for mixing his "religion with politics." *Comm.*, 11/3/1911, 3.

70. Quote from *The Tablet*, newspaper of the Brooklyn diocese, 10/3/1908, 7. For comments by Catholic papers on the campaign, see *The Tablet*, 10/17/1908, 9; *Catholic Columbian-Record* (Indianapolis), 8/22/1908, 1, and 10/3/1908, 1; *Catholic Telegraph* (Cincinnati), 11/5/1908, 4.

71. John Hamilton to WJB, 11/5/1908; Lewis Hite to WJB, 11/9/1908; Frederick S. Horton to WJB, 12/3/1908, all BPLC, Box 27. For allegations of orders to vote for Taft, see George L. Banks, Camden, NJ, to WJB, 11/6/1908; Charles Weidler to WJB, 11/5/1908, BPLC, Box 27.

72. Rufus Riggsbie to WJB, 11/3/1908, BPLC, Box 27. Riggsbie had been employed at the same furniture dealer for eighteen years.

73. Donald L. Kinzer, *An Episode in Anti-Catholicism: The American Protective Association* (Seattle, 1964), 213–41. One Bryan correspondent did enclose an issue of *The American Citizen*, a Boston paper affiliated with the APA.

74. Edward G. Lowry, "Troubadour Bryan," *Collier's*, 2/28/1914, 30.

CHAPTER EIGHT: CONSCIENCE OF THE PARTY, 1909–1912

1. NYT, 1/31/1912, 4.
2. Johnson was an attorney blessed with a voice as loud "as a human fog-horn." He later became the solicitor general at the State Department under Bryan. Quoted in Coletta, *Bryan*, vol. 2, 64.
3. *Omaha World-Herald*, 10/2/1909, 1; *Comm.*, 10/8/1909, 7; Koenig, *Bryan*, 462.
4. Tolstoy did take issue with Bryan's support for curbs on liquor sales. NYT, 9/11/1910, C3; John J. Whitacre, "What Dreamers Have Done," *Comm.*, 3/24/1911, 5.

5. For Bryan's irenic portrait of his children, see *Memoirs,* 190–97. The Bryans sold their Texas farm in 1913 after several cold snaps that killed some of their fruit trees. Spencer C. Scott, "William Jennings Bryan and Texas," 1995, self published, copy in BPNSHS. When they owned property in Mission, *The Commoner* ran several ads touting the bright future of farming there. See *Comm.,* 2/26/1909, 12, 14, and the Bryan's for-sale notice in *Comm.,* 2/14/1913, 14.

6. On Ruth's upbringing, I am indebted to the unpublished memoir by Rudd Brown, her youngest daughter, and an interview with Ms. Brown in April 2004. A few newspapers mentioned Ruth's sojourn at Hull House, but Jane Addams's most recent and quite thorough biographer, Victoria Bissell Brown, did not come across any mention of it while researching *The Education of Jane Addams* (Philadelphia, 2004); communication with author.

7. Sarah Pauline Vickers, "The Life of Ruth Bryan Owen: Florida's First Congresswoman and America's First Woman Diplomat," Ph.D. diss., Florida State University, 1994, 23–28; NYT, 8/24/1903, 1. Quote from Rudd Brown memoir, iv, 3, in author's possession.

8. Vickers, "Life of Ruth Bryan Owen," 29–30, 33.

9. *Comm.,* 3/3/1911, 16.

10. Hargreaves abandoned his family, which forced Grace to rely on the kindness of her parents. She died in 1945, in her mid-fifties. See her unpublished biographical manuscript, dated 12/10/1941, in BPLC, Box 64. For her rage at her husband and desire for a political job, see her letter to Josephus Daniels, 7/6/1933, in Daniels Papers, Reel 44. Also see Koenig, *Bryan,* 423–24.

11. WJB to Judge S. L. Dwight, 11/9/1911, BPOXY, File 5/6; George P. Ikirt, MD, to MBB, 4/21/1912, BPLC, Box 28; Coletta, *Bryan,* vol. 2, 37.

12. William S. Young, 2/18/1909, BPLC, Box 28; *Comm.,* 10/1/1909, 15.

13. *Comm.,* 5/14/1909, 1. Six months later, Bryan made clear that he did not yet favor making prohibition a "paramount" issue in politics; *Comm.,* 12/10/1909, 1. Mary Bryan later wrote that her husband began supporting local option in 1904, but I could find no evidence of that in *The Commoner* or in his more prominent speeches; *Memoirs,* 290. In 1910, as he began to separate himself from Taft, Theodore Roosevelt also said the nation needed a "moral awakening." Quoted in James Chace, *1912: Wilson, Roosevelt, Taft and Debs: The Election That Changed the Country* (New York, 2004), 113.

14. *Rocky Mountain News,* 6/12/1908, 3.

15. Dahlman quoted in Coletta, *Bryan,* vol. 2, 15.

16. Bryan quoted in NYT, 2/13/1910, 1. James Manahan, *Trials of a Lawyer* (n.p., 1933), 112–13. For one perceptive biographer's view, see LeRoy Ashby, *William Jennings Bryan: Champion of Democracy* (Boston, 1987), 127–33.

17. Arthur Mullen, *Western Democrat* (New York, 1940), 135–45; Taft, in 1910, quoted in Coletta, *Bryan,* vol. 2, 10; Koenig, *Bryan,* 472. For the context of state politics, see Robert W. Cherny, *Populism, Progressivism, and the Transformation of Nebraska Politics, 1885–1915* (Lincoln, 1981), 109–48.

18. For example, see NYT, 8/4/1911, 2; Coletta, *Bryan,* vol. 2, 25.

19. J. T. Killiam, Tower Hill, IL, *Comm,* 7/23/1909, 15. Killiam had been active in the cause for two decades.

20. Rauschenbusch, *Christianizing the Social Order* (New York, 1913), 240.

21. On these aspects of prohibition, see Gaines M. Foster, *Moral Reconstruction: Christian Lobbyists and the Federal Legislation of Morality, 1865–1920* (Chapel Hill, 2002), 176–82; K. Austin Kerr, *Organized for Prohibition: A New History of the Anti-Saloon League* (New Haven, 1985); "Prohibition," *The New Encyclopedia of Social Reform,* ed. William D. P. Bliss (New York, 1910), 966–72; Richard F. Hamm, *Shaping the 18th Amendment: Temperance Reform, Legal Culture, and the Polity, 1880–1920* (Chapel Hill, 1995), 23–24, 123–26. The best single study of the rise and fall of the cause is Norman H. Clark, *Deliver Us from Evil: An Interpretation of American Prohibition* (New York, 1976).

22. Quoted in Cherny, *Righteous Cause,* 121.

23. Edward Marshall, "A Talk with William Jennings Bryan, Evangelist," NYT 9/10/1911, SM9; *Comm.,* 6/3/1910, 3. For a longer argument for the link between Christianity and prohibition, see Bryan's speech to the Presbyterian General Assembly, reprinted in *Comm.,* 7/28/1911, 7.

24. Marshall, "A Talk."

25. Park letter, *Comm.,* 4/2/1909, 6; Williamson letter, *Comm.,* 3/3/1911, 16. I am indebted to Laura Wacker for collecting and summarizing this and other correspondence to the newspaper during this period.

26. *Comm.,* 5/21/1909, 15; Thomas Beer, *Hanna* (New York, 1929), 228–29.

27. Margaret Lamberts Bendroth, *Fundamentalism and Gender, 1875 to the Present* (New Haven, 1993), 14–19. Quote by Cortland Myers, 17.

28. Gail Bederman, *Manliness and Civilization: A Cultural History of Gender and Race in the United States, 1880–1917* (Chicago, 1996), 16. For a summary of this viewpoint, see Arnaldo Testi, "The Gender of Reform Politics: Theodore Roosevelt and the Culture of Masculinity," *Journal of American History* 81 (March 1995), 1509–33.

29. Bryan apparently supported votes for women in 1890 but only began to advocate the issue publicly after 1910. LeRoy Ashby, *William Jennings Bryan: Champion of Democracy* (Boston, 1987), 171; WJB to Charles W. Bryan, 12/12/1912, BPOXY, File 13/14. Quotes from *Comm.,* 3/29/1901, 2; *Comm.,* 8/19/1910, 3.

30. *Comm.,* 4/13/1910, 3; *Comm.,* 6/24/1910, 10.

31. Reprinted from the *Cincinnati Post, Comm.,* 9/1/1911, 4. *The Commoner* occasionally revealed a pricklier side of the Bryan cult. In late 1910, the leaders of the Oklahoma legislature wrote to the Associated Press to object to a story the AP had run alleging that a portrait of Bryan that hung in the chamber of the state house of representatives "had been turned to the wall, covered with maps, or otherwise discredited." In fact, a map of Oklahoma City and its suburbs had "covered all the pictures at that end of the hall" for perhaps an hour. *Comm.,* 1/20/1911, 3.

32. For details, see the most recent and fullest biography, Nancy C. Unger, *Fighting Bob La Follette: The Righteous Reformer* (Chapel Hill, 2000).

33. Bound copies of the magazine are included in Box 270, La Follette Family Papers, Library of Congress. Also see Unger, *Fighting Bob,* 184–85.

34. The senator in question was William E. Borah of Idaho, who, ironically, soon became a leading GOP insurgent. Arthur Wallace Dunn, *From Harrison to Harding* (Port Washington, NY, 1971 [1922]), vol. 2, 107.

35. Quotes from Kathleen Dalton, *Theodore Roosevelt: A Strenuous Life* (New York, 2002),

366; Brett Flehinger, *The 1912 Election and the Power of Progressivism* (Boston, 2003), 69. The best study of the GOP revolt remains James Holt, *Congressional Insurgents and the Party System, 1909–1916* (Cambridge, MA, 1967).

36. Gore quoted in David Sarasohn, *The Party of Reform: Democrats in the Progressive Years* (Jackson, MS, 1989), 67. On economic statistics, see Paul Kleppner, *Continuity and Change in Electoral Politics, 1893–1928* (Westport, CT, 1987), 138–39.

37. *Comm.,* 5/20/1910, 1.

38. Ibid., 11/25/1910, 1; 1/6/1911, 1; 2/17/1911, 1; 3/31/1911, 2.

39. The 5/30/1911 letter to Clark is reprinted in *Memoirs,* 163.

40. H. H. Osterhout, Aitkin, MN, letter to *Comm.,* 7/28/1911, 12. For discussion of this conflict, see Sarasohn, *Party of Reform,* 103–6; Coletta, *Bryan,* vol. 2, 21–24.

41. Koenig, *Bryan,* 475–76; NYT, 8/4/1911, 2; Paolo E. Coletta, *The Presidency of William Howard Taft* (Lawrence, KS, 1973), 149–50.

42. Gompers to WJB, 8/11/1911; Gompers to Frank Morrison (AFL secretary), 8/12/1911, *The Samuel Gompers Papers,* ed. Peter J. Albert and Grace Palladino (Urbana, 2001), vol. 8, 255–57.

43. "It was practically impossible to nominate or elect a man that Mr. Bryan would oppose," Colonel Edward House, soon to be Wilson's closest confidant, told James Creelman of the *New York World.* Quoted in Coletta, *Bryan,* vol. 2, 26. Also see Sarasohn, *Party of Reform,* 126; Dunn, *Harrison to Harding,* vol. 2, 183.

44. *Comm.,* 7/21/1911, 4; 7/28/1911, 1; 8/4/1911, 1. Elisabeth S. Clemens, *The People's Lobby: Organizational Innovation and the Rise of Interest Group Politics in the United States, 1890–1925* (Chicago, 1997), 122, 316.

45. *The Commoner* gleefully printed a letter from an official of the Union Pacific boosting Harmon's candidacy, 2/2/1912, 2. Also see the interview with Bryan, reprinted from *The Outlook,* in *Comm.,* 1/12/1912, 1. On Harmon's conservatism, see the biographical sketch at www.ohiohistory.org/onlinedoc/ohgovernment. On Folk, see Steven L. Piott, *Holy Joe: Joseph W. Folk and the Missouri Idea* (Columbia, MO, 1997).

46. Wilson to Adrian F. Joline, 4/29/1907, as quoted in Arthur S. Link, *Wilson: The Road to the White House* (Princeton, 1947), 353. Cobb, who took the reins of the influential daily after Pulitzer's death in the fall of 1911, had supported Taft over Bryan in the previous campaign. Sarasohn, *Party of Reform,* 129–30.

47. Clark to Bryan, 8/26/1911; Bryan to Clark, 9/5/1911, in BPOXY, Section 10; Estal E. Sparlin, "Bryan and the 1912 Democratic Convention," *Mississippi Valley Historical Review* 22 (March 1936), 537–46.

48. For details of the events in New Jersey, see Link, *Wilson,* 205–75. For Bryan's acclaim of Wilson's performance, see *Comm.,* 2/3/1911, 1. Wilson also assured Bryan he'd voted for him in both 1900 and 1908. Wilson to WJB, 4/3/1912, BPLC, Box 28. The reporter, Frank P. Stockbridge, later wrote that soon after leaving Fairview, Wilson asked his opinion of the house. "A cross-section of Bryan's mind," Stockbridge quipped. "Just what I was thinking of," replied Wilson. Coletta, *Bryan,* vol. 2, 31.

49. Coletta, *Bryan,* vol. 2, 39–43; Link, *Wilson,* 353–57.

50. *The Papers of Woodrow Wilson,* ed. Arthur S. Link (Princeton, 1977), vol. 24, 188–89.

51. "Booming Bryan," NYT, 5/21/1912; Coletta, *Bryan,* vol. 2, 25; *Memoirs,* 335. In the early runup to the campaign, Bryan had led in some opinion polls conducted by newspapers. For example, see *Comm.,* 5/6/1910, 2.

52. Interview in *The Outlook,* reprinted in *Comm.,* 1/12/1912, 1; WJB to CWB, no date but clearly April, BPOXY, File #5. "Statement of I. J. Dunn... with Reference to the Democratic National Convention... in 1912," written in 1945, BPNSHS, #464.

53. The amount of the fee appeared in a competing daily. "Bryan Finds Profit in Political Game," NYT, 6/30/1912. His reports, supplemented by various speeches and editorial cartoons, were published later that year as *A Tale of Two Conventions* (New York, 1912). On his playful informality with journalists, see *Comm.,* 8/28/1903, 11; Homer Davenport (Hearst's leading cartoonist) to WJB, 5/12/1899, BPLC, Box 23; WJB to William Allen White, 3/22/1911, in BPOXY, File #7–8.

54. "Bryan Finds Profit."

55. WJB, *Tale,* 29, 67, 86. When a fellow journalist in Chicago asked him if he were a candidate himself, Bryan replied, "My boy, do you think I am going to run for President just to get the Republican party out of a hole?" Quoted in Coletta, *Bryan,* vol. 2, 53.

56. Quoted in *Memoirs,* 164. For a shrewd evaluation of the context, see William G. McAdoo, *Crowded Years* (Port Washington, NY, 1971 [1931]), 137–42.

57. Wilson quoted in McAdoo, *Crowded Years,* 140.

58. NYT, 5/26/1912, 1–3; *Washington Wife: Journal of Ellen Maury Slayden from 1897–1919* (New York, 1963), 179. Slayden's husband was a longtime congressman from Texas.

59. WJB, *Tale,* 121–22; Link, *Road to White House,* 436; Ralph M. Goldman, *The National Party Chairmen and Committees: Factionalism at the Top* (Armonk, NY, 1990), 227; Coletta, *Bryan,* vol. 2, 60.

60. For Bryan's resolution and his speech justifying it, see WJB, *Tale,* 172–75.

61. James quoted in Coletta, *Bryan,* vol. 2, 62. The platform, described by Arthur Link as "a progressive document, in the best Bryan tradition," vowed to destroy the trusts, opposed Aldrich's plan for banks to regulate themselves, called for exempting unions from anti-trust laws and for establishing a Department of Labor, pledged the nominee to serve only a single term, and declared that Filipinos should get their independence as soon as they had a stable government. Link, *Wilson,* 463.

62. Link, *Wilson,* 441–43; Gustavus Myers, *History of the Great American Fortunes* (New York, 1936), 380–83, 613–15; Steve Fraser, *Every Man a Speculator: A History of Wall Street in American Life* (New York, 2005), 176, 315. Some critics of Belmont, a German Jew, lapsed into anti-Semitic stereotyping. But I could find no trace of that in Bryan's denunciations of the man.

63. The vote was 883 to 201½. NYT, 6/29/1912, 1; WJB, *Tale,* 169; Link, *Wilson,* 445.

64. To embody the party as a seductively helpless woman was the cartoonist's idea, not Bryan's. But *The Commoner* did reprint the illustration from the *Baltimore American* on 7/12/1912, 10. McAdoo, *Crowded Years,* 149. Several papers compared Bryan's conduct in Baltimore to Roosevelt's bolt from the GOP convention in Chicago. For example, see *Niles Daily Sun* (Michigan), 6/28/1912, 1.

65. Quoted in Coletta, *Bryan,* vol. 2, 69.

66. Champ Clark, *My Quarter Century of American Politics* (New York, 1920), vol. 2, 417, 420. The Gerard quote was reported to Bryan, secondhand, in a 1921 letter. H. C. Bell to WJB, 6/15/1921, BPLC, Box 34.

67. For Clark's passionate indictment, see his *My Quarter Century,* 392–428. The most complete and reliable account of how Wilson finally won the nomination remains Arthur Link's in *Wilson,* 454–65. After the convention, a small Democratic weekly in

Iowa that routinely backed the party's national candidates editorialized, "The scoring of such politicians as Murphy…, whose sole interest was self-interest…and winning a clean fight without catering to their influence, will, without question clarify the situation in succeeding conventions." *Anamosa Journal,* 7/4/1912, 4.

68. Luke Lea to WW, 7/13/1912, *Wilson Papers,* vol. 24, 547; no author, "Chicago and Baltimore: With the Political Scene Shifters," *American Magazine,* September 1912, 520; *La Follette's Magazine,* 7/13/1912, 3; Rauschenbusch, *Christianizing the Social Order,* 461.

69. Winslow to WJB, 7/4/1912, BPLC, Box 28; Benjamin Pierce, Brockton, MA, to WJB, 7/3/1912, ibid. Also see David Starr Jordan to WJB, 7/4/1912, ibid.; W. R. L. Smith, Chapel Hill, NC, to Mrs. Bryan, 7/16/1912, ibid.

70. On the campaign, see Chace, *1912: Wilson, Roosevelt, Taft and Debs;* Dalton, *Theodore Roosevelt,* 392–407; Nick Salvatore, *Eugene V. Debs: Citizen and Socialist* (Urbana, IL, 1982), 263–64.

71. On Bryan's nonstop campaigning for Wilson, see Coletta, *Bryan,* vol. 2, 78–83. For a sample of his attack on TR, see "Mr. Roosevelt as a Borrower," *Comm.,* 10/4/1912, 1. The seven states were Arizona, California, Nevada, Florida, Louisiana, Mississippi, and South Dakota (where the president wasn't even on the ballot). *Presidential Elections Since 1789,* 4th ed. (Washington, DC, 1987), 114.

72. Quoted in Paul W. Glad, *The Trumpet Soundeth: William Jennings Bryan and His Democracy, 1896–1912* (Lincoln, NE, 1960), 171.

CHAPTER NINE: BRYAN'S PEOPLE

1. Lindsay, "When Bryan Speaks," BPLC, Box 51. The poem was written in 1915.

2. Weber, "Politics as a Vocation," *From Max Weber: Essays in Sociology,* ed. H. H. Gerth and C. Wright Mills (New York, 1946), 128.

3. Philo Bennett to his wife and to WJB, 5/22/1900, BPLC, Box 46.

4. The annual gifts were reported in the probate court proceedings in New Haven in October 1903, BPLC, Box 46. For examples of meals together, see NYT, 10/28/1900, 2, and 10/29/1900, 1. Bennett was not uncritical. Soon after the *Commoner* began publishing, he sent letters to both Bryan and Mary, urging them to hire "skilled writers" who could produce "aggressive" copy with "more snap and ring in them." Bennett to MBB, 2/18/1901, and Bennett to WJB, 2/27/1901, BPLC, Box 26.

5. Quote, Coletta, *Bryan,* vol. 1, 316. For Bryan's summation of the case, see "The Bennett Case Settled," *Comm.,* 9/8/1905, 2; *Memoirs,* 129–44.

6. "An Old Friend of Bryan," undated clipping, BPNSHS, Box 2, Folder 27; Charles Edward Merriam, *Four American Party Leaders* (Freeport, NY, 1971 [1926]), 75.

7. *Washington Wife: Journal of Ellen Maury Slayden from 1897–1919* (New York, 1963), 179.

8. William Gibbs McAdoo quoted in Robert Cherny, *A Righteous Cause* (Boston, 1985), 128.

9. These totals are based on a sample from the two days of heaviest mail during and just after the 1896 election and from the first ten days of November 1900. The pattern continued in 1908, although the number of surviving letters is much smaller than in the previous two elections.

10. The roster of occupations is drawn from 258 letters written to Bryan in November 1896, by people with surnames beginning with *G* through *R.* One hundred four men-

tioned their job, business, and/or profession. Of those, 38.5 percent were employers or merchants, 42 percent members of a profession. Hardly any were professional politicians. Thanks to Sarah Snyder for her research assistance.

11. Richard Hofstadter, *The Age of Reform* (New York, 1955); Robert Wiebe, *The Search for Order* (New York, 1967); Michael McGerr, *A Fierce Discontent* (New York, 2003).

12. V. W. Richardson to WJB, 11/7/1900, BPLC, Box 25.

13. Hofstadter, *The Age of Reform* (New York, 1955), 243–44. For an often brilliant study inspired by this idea, see Robert D. Johnston, *The Radical Middle Class: Populist Democracy and the Question of Capitalism in Progressive Era Portland, Oregon* (Princeton, 2003).

14. C. D. O'Brien to WJB, 11/11/1908, BPLC, Box 27.

15. Robert Campbell, rector of Christ Church in Bordentown, Burlington County, to WJB, 11/12/1900, BPLC, Box 24; Edgar Eugene Robinson, *The Presidential Vote, 1896–1932* (Stanford, 1934), 271.

16. The names are taken from letters in BPLC, Box 11.

17. Taft to Archie Butt, after Bryan made a visit to the White House on 4/7/1910. Archie Butt, *Taft and Roosevelt: The Intimate Letters of Archie Butt, Military Aide* (New York, 1930), vol. 2, 610.

18. Thomas Tibbles, "Bryan as a Man," *Polk County Democrat* (Nebraska), 5/16/1907, in clipping files of BPNSHS; Buehler Metcalfe, untitled and undated reminiscence, BPLC, Box 50, #16; *Comm.*, 6/19/1908, 13.

19. For an excellent summary of their relationship, see Larry G. Osnes, "Charles W. Bryan: 'His Brother's Keeper,'" NH (1967), 45–67. Also see Osnes, "Charles W. Bryan, Latter-Day Populist and Rural Progressive," Ph.D. diss., University of Cincinnati, 1970.

20. Osnes, "Latter-Day Populist," 121; Osnes, "'His Brother's Keeper,'" 52.

21. Metcalfe, *Of Such Is the Kingdom and Other Stories from Life* (Lincoln, 1908). Most of the selections in this book were published earlier in *The Commoner*.

22. "The Story of a Talented Woman," *Comm.*, 12/22/1905, 6; *Comm.*, 8/8/1902, 9.

23. Watts-McVey, "Healing for Broken Hearts," *Zion's Watchtower*, December 1, 1893, 359.

24. *Comm.*, 12/22/1905, 6.

25. Maupin wrote the column regularly from 1901 to 1913 and left *The Commoner* only because he wanted to augment his income. For a biographical sketch, see Patricia Gaster, "Nebraska Newspaperman Will M. Maupin," NH 69 (Winter 1988), 182–92.

26. *Comm.*, 12/16/1910, 13.

27. Ibid., 5/3/1912, 15; 1/14/1910, 10.

28. Quoted in Steven L. Piott, *Holy Joe: Joseph W. Folk and the Missouri Idea* (Columbia, MO, 1997), 113.

29. Mark A. Lause, *The Civil War's Last Campaign: James B. Weaver, the Greenback-Labor Party and the Politics of Race and Section* (Lanham, MD, 2001), 82, 97; Fred Emory Haynes, *James Baird Weaver* (Iowa City, 1919), 111; *The National Cyclopedia of American Biography* (New York, 1937), vol. 16, 146.

30. Weaver to WJB, 9/1/1894, BPLC, Box 3.

31. Weaver to WJB, 11/10/1900, BPLC, Box 25; Weaver to WJB, 3/15/1901, BPLC, Box 26; Haynes, *Weaver*, 398.

32. Weaver to WJB, 11/13/1908, BPLC, Box 28.

33. For a consistently sympathetic view, see Joseph L. Morrison, *Josephus Daniels: The*

Small-d Democrat (Chapel Hill, 1966). On Daniels and Wallace, see John C. Culver and John Hyde, *American Dreamer: A Life of Henry A. Wallace* (New York, 2000), 249, 358, 365. On his long and warm relationship with FDR, see *Roosevelt and Daniels: A Friendship in Politics,* ed. Carroll Kilpatrick (Chapel Hill, 1952).

34. Josephus Daniels, *Editor in Politics* (Chapel Hill, 1941), 164–65.

35. On Daniels's appearance, see his son's memoir, Jonathan Daniels, *The End of Innocence* (Philadelphia, 1954), 34, and the photos in Morrison, *Daniels.*

36. Daniels, *End of Innocence,* 17.

37. For his unapologetic account, see Daniels, *Editor in Politics,* 283–312. On the sexual politics of the offensive, see Glenda Gilmore, *Gender and Jim Crow: Women and the Politics of White Supremacy in North Carolina, 1896–1920* (Chapel Hill, 1996), 61–89.

38. Daniels, *Editor in Politics,* 307–9; Morrison, *Daniels,* 35.

39. Dolores Janiewski, "The Reign of Passion: White Supremacy and the Clash Between Passionate and Progressive Emotional Styles in the New South," *An Emotional History of the United States,* ed. Peter N. Stearns and Jan Lewis (New York, 1998), 130.

40. For his later career, see Kilpatrick, ed., *Roosevelt and Daniels,* and Morrison, *Daniels.*

41. Clyde Brion Davis, *The Age of Indiscretion* (Philadelphia, 1950), 36, 39; e-mail from David Brion Davis to author, 1/10/2000.

42. Quoted in Davis, *Age of Indiscretion,* 38.

43. Ibid., 201.

44. Robinson, *Presidential Vote,* 252. Descriptions of the economy and demography of the town appear in Davis, *Age of Indiscretion,* 24–25, as well as in Clyde Davis's autobiographical novel, *Follow the Leader* (New York, 1942), 69–70. In the 1900 census, fewer than 4 percent of Livingston County residents were counted as foreign-born, and roughly the same number were "colored."

45. Clyde Davis, *Follow the Leader,* 93. Livingston County lost almost 35 percent of its population from 1900 to 2000. Ravindra Amonker and Ryan Burson, "Population Change of Missouri During the 20th Century," *Missouri Electronic Journal of Sociology* 2 (2001), 44. On their Web site, Chillicothe officials proudly claim the town as "the Home of Sliced Bread" because the product was first offered for sale there in 1928 (www.chillocothethecity.org/bread.html).

    Charles's grandson, David Brion Davis, became a prolific author and world-famous historian of slavery and abolition at Yale. In his sixties, Professor Davis converted to Judaism.

46. Rosser to WJB, 11/2/1896, BPLC, Box 5; Rosser, *The Crusading Commoner: A Close-up of William Jennings Bryan and His Times* (Dallas, 1937), 320.

47. John S. Fordtran, MD, "Medicine in Dallas 100 Years Ago," *Baylor University Medical Center Proceedings* 13 (2000), 34–44; Rosser obituary in *Texas State Journal of Medicine* 40 (April 1945), 671–72.

48. Quote from Wayne C. Williams, *American Tomorrows* (New York, 1939), 25. For biographical details, see *National Cyclopedia* (New York, 1962), vol. 44, 319; NYT, 6/3/1910. Williams's biographies are *William Jennings Bryan: A Study in Political Vindication* (New York, 1923) and *William Jennings Bryan* (New York, 1936).

49. Williams to WJB, 3/24/1923, BPLC, Box 37. Bryan told him that, due to undetailed family commitments, he had to support another candidate for the Senate. Williams obituary in *Denver Post,* 8/16/1953, 19A.

50. E. W. Howey, superintendent of public schools in Defiance, Ohio, to WJB, no date but internal evidence suggests July 1912, BPLC, Box 51.

51. *Comm.,* 7/19/1901, 3; Bryant, "To a Waterfowl," reprinted in the first issue of *Comm.,* 1/23/1901, 6, and frequently thereafter. Silas Bryan often had his son read the poem to him. Bryan, *In His Image* (New York, 1922), 27.

52. Quoted in Hermione Lee, *Willa Cather: Double Lives* (New York, 1989), 44; *The McGuffey Readers: Selections from the 1879 Edition,* ed. Elliott J. Gorn (Boston, 1998), 191–92.

53. Masters, *The New Star Chamber and Other Essays* (Chicago, 1904) at www.boondock-snet.com/ai/masters/star/elm_bryan.html; Dreiser, *The Titan* (New York, 1914), 388; Cather, "Two Friends," in Willa Cather, *Collected Stories* (New York, 1992), quote from p. 329. The story was written sometime between 1924 and 1932. Pound, "On the Defeat of William Jennings Bryan," originally published in *Times-Chronicle* of Jenkintown, PA. Although unsigned, Pound later claimed it as his first published poem. Jonathan Peter Gill, "The Law of the Modernist Letter: Anti-Semitism and the Technology of Representation in the Poetry of Ezra Pound," Ph.D. diss., Columbia University, 1999, 33–41.

54. Richard Lingeman, *Small Town America: A Narrative History, 1620–the Present* (New York, 1980), 364–91 (the term is borrowed from Carl Van Doren's "The Revolt of the Village"); Masters, *Spoon River Anthology* (New York, 1915).

55. Edgar Lee Masters, *Across Spoon River: An Autobiography* (Urbana, IL, 1991 [1936]), 209.

56. Masters to WJB, 11/11/1908, BPLC, Box 27; Masters, *Across Spoon River,* 325.

57. "The Cocked Hat," in Edgar Lee Masters, *Selected Poems* (New York, 1925 [1916]), 84–89. Masters later wrote, "His [Bryan's] wealth went to a family that would have been better off without it." Masters, *Vachel Lindsay: A Poet in America* (New York, 1935), 321.

58. "Bryan, Bryan, Bryan, Bryan," in Vachel Lindsay, *Collected Poems* (New York, 1925), 96–105.

59. Ann Massa, *Vachel Lindsay: Fieldworker for the American Dream* (Bloomington, IN, 1970), 83; Vachel Lindsay, *The Golden Book of Springfield* (New York, 1920), 320 and passim.

60. About Lindsay, H. L. Mencken wrote, "The yokels welcomed him, not because they were interested in his poetry, but because it struck them as an amazing and perhaps even a fascinatingly obscene thing for a sane man to go about the country on any such bizarre and undemocratic business." Quoted in Massa, *Lindsay,* 237. For Lindsay's reminscences of the road, see www.english.uiuc.edu/maps/poets/g_l/lindsay; on his meeting with Jonathan Daniels, *End of Innocence,* 161; *The Cabinet Diaries of Josephus Daniels, 1913–1921,* ed. E. David Cronon (Lincoln, NE, 1963), 96.

61. Charles Edward Merriam, *Four American Party Leaders* (Freeport, NY, 1971 [1926]), 83–4.

CHAPTER TEN: MORALIST AT STATE, 1913–1915

1. Speech to visiting delegates from Britain, Canada, and Australia to the centennial celebration of the Treaty of Ghent, NYT, 5/13/1913, 1.

2. Page to Edward House, 6/10/1915, *The Intimate Papers of Colonel House,* ed. Charles

Seymour (Boston, 1926–8), vol. 2, 9. Page, as editor of the *Atlantic Monthly* and then *World's Work*, had been a longtime Bryan critic.

3. Thanks to the first movie cameras to cover such an event, many Americans did later see him delivering the speech. Wilson quoted in NYT, 3/5/1913, 1.

4. For a description, see James M. Goode, *Capital Losses: A Cultural History of Washington's Destroyed Buildings* (Washington, DC, 1979), 36–37.

5. Ibid., 2; *Chicago Tribune*, 3/5/1913, 1; *Washington Post*, 3/5/1913, 1; GBH Bio, vol. 2, ch. 6, 1–2, BPLC, Box 65.

6. Arthur S. Link, *Wilson: The New Freedom* (Princeton, 1956), 7–8; Coletta, *Bryan*, vol. 2, 86–89. The widow added, "Mr. Bennett would be so happy to join me in these good wishes." Grace Bennett to WJB, 3/8/1913, BPLC, Box 29.

7. Coletta, *Bryan*, vol. 2, 111; *Statistical Abstract of the United States* (Washington, DC, 1976), 1141; *Encyclopedia of U.S. Foreign Relations*, eds. Bruce W. Jentleson and Thomas G. Paterson (New York, 1997), vol. 4, 123; Ernest R. May, "Bryan and the World War, 1914–1915," Ph.D. diss., UCLA, 1951, 39; WJB to Colonel William R. Harts (superintendent of the State, War, and Navy Building), 4/12/1915; Harts to WJB, 4/22/1915; WW to WJB, May 6, 1915, all in BPLC, Box 59.

8. Finley Peter Dunne, NYT, 2/2/1913, quoted in Link, *New Freedom*, 8.

9. Quoted in Marie D. Natoli, "Woodrow Wilson," *Popular Images of American Presidents*, ed. William C. Spragens (New York, 1988), 247.

10. Wilson quoted in NYT, 10/28/1913, 5. For a careful examination of Wilson's religious beliefs and their bearing on his politics, see John W. Mulder, *Woodrow Wilson: The Years of Preparation* (Princeton, 1978). For a provocative, if somewhat exaggerated, argument about how his and Bryan's Presbyterianism affected their foreign policy, see Robert Crunden, *Ministers of Reform: The Progressives Achievement in American Civilization, 1889–1920* (New York, 1982), 225–73.

11. Bryan, "The Power That Is Greater Than Force," *Proceedings of the National Arbitration and Peace Congress: New York, April 14th to 17th, 1907* (New York, 1907), 358; for precursors see Merle E. Curti, *Bryan and World Peace* (Northampton, MA, 1931), 143–44; David S. Patterson, *Toward a Warless World: The Travail of the American Peace Movement, 1887–1914* (Bloomington, IN, 1976), 196–97.

12. WJB to CWB, no date but clearly written in 1913, BPOXY, File 5/6. Emerson quoted in Curti, *Bryan and World Peace*, 116.

13. One of the metal objects is displayed at the Department of State building in Washington. For a photo, see Coletta, *Bryan*, vol. 2, following 180. Bryan also sent them as gifts to selected peace activists, including Andrew Carnegie. Carnegie to WJB, 1/13/1915, BPLC, Box 30.

14. *Memoirs*, 188, 351.

15. D. F. Stevens, Pretoria, to WJB, 5/13/1913, BPLC, Box 29; Morton Wyvell to "My dear sir," undated but in 1913 letters, BPLC, Box 29. George Bernard Shaw also commended Bryan but urged him to cut all meat products out of his menus as well. *Comm.*, 5/9/1913, 3.

16. *Philadelphia Public Ledger*, quoted in *Comm.*, 3/14/1913, 3.

17. Anonymous writer in *Harper's Weekly*, quoted in Constance McLaughlin Green, *Washington: Capital City, 1879–1950* (Princeton, 1963), 190; George Fitch, "Bryan—Democracy's Goat," *Collier's*, reprinted in *Comm.*, May 1915, 30. On the emergence of a

national elite in these years, see Alan Dawley, "The Abortive Rule of Big Money," *Ruling America: Wealth and Power in a Democracy*, ed. Steve Fraser and Gary Gerstle (Cambridge, 2005), 149–180.

18. Jonathan Daniels, *The End of Innocence* (Philadelphia, 1954), 35. On Wilson's cabinet, the best summary remains that in Link, *New Freedom*, 93–144.

19. Coletta, *Bryan*, vol. 2, 99; Crunden, *Ministers of Reform*, 226–27.

20. WJB to WW, 5/24/1913, Bryan-Wilson Correspondence, National Archives, Microfilm T-841; Clyde Brion Davis, *The Age of Indiscretion* (Philadelphia, 1950), 207–8; Link, *New Freedom*, 111, 103; Fitch, "Bryan," 31. Bryan was the first secretary of state from west of the Mississippi River.

21. "Mr. Bryan Rides Behind," editorial, *North American Review*, March 1914, 328–30.

22. "Mr. Dooley Comments on Current Politics," NYT, 12/21/1913, SM6.

23. Coletta, *Bryan*, vol. 2, 106.

24. Bryan, "Why I Lecture," *Ladies' Home Journal*, April 1915, 9.

25. This included the "insurgent" lawmakers who had opposed Taft in Congress and then backed Roosevelt in 1912. See James Holt, *Congressional Insurgents and the Party System, 1909–1916* (Cambridge, MA, 1967), 86–87; Wilson quoted in "Mr. Bryan Rides Behind," 323. On Wilson's persistent contempt for Bryan, see Link, *New Freedom*, 112–13.

26. *Comm.*, 1/31/1913, 1. In his official position, Bryan had the pleasant task of signing the ratification papers, exercises which he turned into public ceremonies. *Comm.*, 6/6/1913, 1.

27. The literature on this subject is vast. For insightful narratives, see the recent works by Sanders, *Roots of Reform*, 217–32; Steven R. Weisman, *The Great Tax Wars: Lincoln to Wilson* (New York, 2002), 237–88.

28. Root quoted in Weisman, *The Great Tax Wars*, 280; Holt, *Congressional Insurgents*, 92–93.

29. Sanders, *Roots of Reform*, 230; Edward G. Lowry, *Washington Close-ups* (Boston, 1921), 45–46. Until Congress altered the law on the eve of U.S. entry into World War I, fewer than half a million Americans filed tax returns. *Statistical Abstract of the U.S.* (Washington, DC, 1976), 1110.

30. Paolo E. Coletta, "William Jennings Bryan and Currency and Banking Reform," NH 45 (1964), 47 and passim.

31. Brandeis quoted in Melvin I. Urofsky, "Introduction," Louis D. Brandeis, *Other People's Money and How the Bankers Use It*, ed. Urofsky (Boston, 1995 [1914]), 27. For the complex process of forging and passing the legislation, see Link, *New Freedom*, 199–240.

32. *Sun* quoted in Sanders, *Roots of Reform*, 249; James Livingston, *Origins of the Federal Reserve System: Money, Class, and Corporate Capitalism, 1890–1913* (Ithaca, 1986), 215.

33. Aldrich quoted in Coletta, "Bryan and Currency and Banking Reform," 55.

34. Callaway quoted in Sanders, *Roots of Reform*, 259. See William Greider's scathing study, *Secrets of the Temple: How the Federal Reserve Runs the Country* (New York, 1987).

35. On passage of the Clayton Act, the labor plank of which was gutted by the Supreme Court in the 1920s, see Coletta, *Bryan*, vol. 2, 139–43; Sanders, *Roots of Reform*, 282–97.

36. Quotes from Kenneth O'Reilly, *Nixon's Piano: Presidents and Racial Politics from Washington to Clinton* (New York, 1995), 83. On this policy, see ibid., 82–95; Link, *New Freedom*, 243–54.

37. The poem, written on seven pieces of unlined notebook paper, is not dated. But it is enclosed in an official State Department envelope, which Bryan used only when he served in the administration. BPLC, Box 41.

38. WJB, April 1913, quoted in Coletta, *Bryan*, vol. 2, 183; speech to the American-Asiatic Association in New York City, 1/26/1914, *Comm.*, February 1914, 6; Wilson, 1913, quoted in Sumner Welles, *Naboth's Vineyard: The Dominican Republic, 1844–1924* (New York, 1928), vol. 2, 739. A recent statement is Walter Russell Mead's *Special Providence: American Foreign Policy and How It Changed the World* (New York, 2002), 132–73. Mead erroneously classifies Bryan as a Jeffersonian, because he opposed the use of force. But Bryan was not consistent in this position, as his service in the war of 1898 and his conduct in the Caribbean demonstrated. During Bryan's tenure, he also helped to make policy toward Asia—particularly Japan and the new Chinese Republic. But he was most intimately involved with conflicts in Mexico, the Caribbean, and the world war in Europe, and I have decided to focus on those.

39. George Fred Williams, U.S. minister to Greece, to WJB, 4/1/1914, BPLC, Box 29.

40. William Appleman Williams, *The Tragedy of American Diplomacy* (New York, 1962).

41. The clearest narratives of Bryan's role in this country are Kendrick Clements, *William Jennings Bryan: Missionary Isolationist* (Knoxville, TN, 1982), 63–64, 83–87; Coletta, *Bryan*, vol. 2, 194–200.

42. WJB quoted in Hans Schmidt, *The United States Occupation of Haiti, 1915–1934* (New Brunswick, NJ, 1971), 55. Editor Charles Moravia in August 1915, quoted in Alan McPherson, "Americanism Against American Empire," *Americanism: New Perspectives on the History of an Ideal*, ed. Michael Kazin and Joseph McCartin (Chapel Hill, 2006). On the occupation, see Mary Renda, *Taking Haiti: Military Occupation and the Culture of U.S. Imperialism, 1915–1940* (Chapel Hill, 2001).

43. WJB to WW, 3/8/1915, BPLC, Box 59; WJB, quoted in Coletta, *Bryan*, vol. 2, 207.

44. The alleged statement was cited by John H. Allen, "An Inside View of Revolutions in Haiti," *Current History* 32 (May 1930), 325. Aside from such personal factors, Allen's claim is factually shoddy. In the first two paragraphs of the article, the only ones that mention Bryan, he makes two significant mistakes. First, he claims he was "invited" to Washington in 1912 to tell Secretary of State Bryan "all about Haiti." But Republicans were still in power that year. Second, he quotes Bryan informing him, the same day, that "approximately 400 Haitians had been killed" in an explosion, including President Cincinnatus Leconte. The event, an accident, did occur on August 8, 1912, but Bryan was on the Chautauqua circuit at the time. In a 1915 note to Wilson, Bryan referred in passing to the advantage of having a U.S. ambassador to Haiti who could speak French. WJB to WW, 4/3/1915, BPLC, Box 59.

45. Schmidt, *Occupation of Haiti*, 54; Mira Wilkins, *The Emergence of Multinational Enterprise: American Business Abroad from the Colonial Era to 1914* (Cambridge, 1981), 113–34. For an excellent summary of this period, see John Tutino, "Revolutionary Confrontation, 1913–1917: Regional Factions, Class Conflicts, and the New National State," *Provinces of the Revolution: Essays on Regional Mexican History, 1910–1929*, ed. Thomas Benjamin and Mark Wasserman (Albuquerque, 1990), 41–70.

46. For the complex narrative of U.S. policy during these years, see Coletta, *Bryan*, vol. 2, 147–81; Robert E. Hannigan, *The New World Power: American Foreign Policy, 1898–1917* (Philadelphia, 2002), 157–83.

47. "Say Bryan Snubbed Them," NYT, 6/18/1913, 1; WJB to WW, 8/2/1914, National Archives, Microfilm T-841.

48. WJB quoted in Coletta, *Bryan*, vol. 2, 177.

49. *Memoirs*, following 396.

50. George Fitch, "Bryan—Democracy's Goat," reprinted in *Comm.*, May 1915, 30–31; WJB to editor of *Des Moines Register and Leader*, 11/14/1914, BPLC, Box 30. Thomas Edison finished second and Wilson third; "Mr. Ordinary Citizen" came in a close fourth. The only other politician in the top ten was Robert La Follette, who tied for seventh place. "The Greatest Man in the United States," *American Magazine*, October 1914, 63.

51. WJB quotes from NYT, 8/31/1913, SM6; May, "Bryan and World War," 159. May's youthful work is still the fullest and shrewdest account of its subject. Also see his broader study, *The World War and American Isolation, 1914–1917* (Cambridge, 1959).

52. Link, *New Freedom*, 64.

53. May, "Bryan and World War," 151.

54. Emma Goldman, "Preparedness, the Road to Universal Slaughter," originally published in December 1915, reprinted at sunsite.berkeley.edu/Goldman; Debs quoted in Ray Ginger, *Eugene V. Debs: The Making of an American Radical* (New York, 1962), 346.

55. WJB to governor of Georgia (praising him for commuting Leo Frank's sentence), 6/21/1915, BPLC, Box 30; *Comm.*, October 1914, 3; *Memoirs*, 390.

56. On Bryan as "the principal guide" of U.S. policy, see May, "Bryan and World War," 124ff. The following section is based primarily on May's work; Coletta, *Bryan*, vol. 2, 239–361; and Arthur S. Link, *Wilson: The Struggle for Neutrality, 1914–1915* (Princeton, 1960), 349–455.

57. May, "Bryan and World War," 161, 180. After the war, both Von Bernstorff and the Austro-Hungarian ambassador, Constantine Dumba, wrote that they regretted not signing a treaty with the United States and that doing so might have pressured them to accept a mediated peace. Ibid., 181.

58. *Comm.*, March 1915, 19.

59. John Milton Cooper Jr., *Walter Hines Page: The Southerner as American, 1855–1918* (Chapel Hill, 1977), 291 and passim; Burton J. Hendrick, *The Life and Letters of Walter H. Page* (Garden City, NY, 1924), vol. 1, 327, 362, 400. Neither man seems to have brought up Page's snub in 1889 of Bryan's attempt to get his speeches published.

60. Wilson quoted in Link, *New Freedom*, 113; May, "Bryan and World War," 384.

61. For example, see the front-page story in NYT, 3/31/1915, which reprints several British dispatches, including one that accuses Germany of being a lawless state whose "people have repudiated alike Christianity and civilization."

62. Quotes from May, "Bryan and World War," 393; Coletta, *Bryan*, vol. 2, 306.

63. WJB quoted in MBB's lost journal; Coletta, *Bryan*, vol. 2, 311; May, "Bryan and World War," 407–8.

64. May, "Bryan and World War," 412–15; Coletta, *Bryan*, vol. 2, 323.

65. Link, *Struggle for Neutrality*, 403–5, 410; Coletta, *Bryan*, vol. 2, 322–26.

66. Houston disliked Bryan, but his account of the meeting is the only detailed one. David F. Houston, *Eight Years with Wilson's Cabinet* (Garden City, NY, 1926), vol. 1, 132–37; Coletta, *Bryan*, vol. 2, 331.

67. WW to Edith Galt, 6/8/1915, *The Papers of Woodrow Wilson*, ed. Arthur S. Link (Princeton, 1980), vol. 34, 366; Link, *Struggle for Neutrality*, 421–22.

68. For the text of the letter and Wilson's friendly reply of the same day, see Link, ed., *Papers of Woodrow Wilson*, vol. 34, 422–23.

69. GBH Bio, vol. 2, ch. 6, 5–6; Josephus Daniels, *The Wilson Era: Years of Peace—1910–1917* (Chapel Hill, 1944), 427; Edith Newlands to MBB, 6/20/1915, BPLC, Box 30; Rep. Joe H. Eagle to WJB, 6/10/1915, BPLC, Box 30. Eagle ran for Congress as a Populist in 1896.

70. *Washington Bee*, quoted in *Cleveland Advocate*, 6/19/1915, 4. Other black papers cited in the same article accused Bryan of being jealous of Wilson's leadership.

71. Daniels, *Wilson Era*, 432. Also see Coletta, *Bryan*, vol. 2, 353–55.

72. Quotes from Levine, DF, 18; Link, *Struggle for Neutrality*, 426–27. Also see Daniels, *Wilson Era*, 434.

73. Houston, *Eight Years*, 146; Daniels, *Wilson Era*, 431–32. Both men were present, but, unsurprisingly, Daniels's account is more favorable to WJB than is Houston's.

74. Benedict Prieth to WJB, 6/9/1915; John Hecker to WJB, 6/10/1915; Robert V. Ringler to WJB, 6/12/1915; Juliet Barrett Rublee to WJB, 6/9/1915; T. J. Hickey to WJB, 6/12/1915; Rev. H. O. Rowlands to WJB, 6/10/1915, all in BPLC, Box 30. Fewer than a hundred messages of this type are stored in BPLC, but Mary wrote on June 30 that "we were deluged with letters and telegrams." *Memoirs*, 426.

75. For a counterargument, see Clements, *Bryan*, 110–11.

76. Cornell et al. to WJB, 6/14/1915, BPLC, Box 30. Debs's total in Custer County was twice as much as his national percentage but three points less than in the state as a whole, which Wilson carried. Edgar Eugene Robinson, *The Presidential Vote, 1896–1932* (Stanford, CA, 1934), 300.

77. Cardarbian to WJB, 7/8/1915, Miscellaneous Records of Secretary and Undersecretary of State, 1911–1918, RG 59, Entry 662, National Archives; Suzanne E. Moranian, "The Armenian Genocide and American Missionary Relief Efforts," *America and the Armenian Genocide of 1915*, ed. Jay Winter (Cambridge, 2003), 192.

78. Morgenthau quoted in Samantha Power's indispensable study, *"A Problem from Hell": America and the Age of Genocide* (New York, 2002), 6. For reproductions of Lansing's and Cardarbian's letters, see www.armenocide.net.

CHAPTER ELEVEN: MORALIST IN RETREAT, 1916–1919

1. From a speech given at the General Assembly of the Presbyterian Church, May 21, 1916. Quoted in Levine, DF, 106.

2. Lines 1194–5. See courses.dce.harvard.edu/~clase116/txt-agamemnon.

3. John Reed, "Bryan on Tour," *Collier's*, 5/20/1916, 11–12, 40–41, 44–47, quote 47; Robert A. Rosenstone, *Romantic Revolutionary: A Biography of John Reed* (New York, 1975).

4. Reed, "Bryan on Tour," 12, 41. On Reed's milieu, see Christine Stansell, *American Moderns: Bohemian New York and the Creation of a New Century* (New York, 2000).

5. MBB to WJB, 3/12/1916, BPLC, Box 31.

6. Quoted in Rosenstone, *Romantic Revolutionary*, 107.

7. *Memoirs*, 429–49; Rev. H. H. Pitzer, Lansing, MI, to WJB, 8/4/1916, BPLC, Box 31.

8. WJB to MBB, from Hot Springs, AR, 10/1/1915, BPLC, Box 30. For the following sec-

tion, I have drawn on Howard Glenn McKenzie, "William Jennings Bryan in Miami, 1915–1925," M.A. thesis, University of Miami, 1956. For sending me a copy of the thesis, along with selected clippings from Miami newspapers of the period, I am indebted to Arva Parks, who chronicles the history of her city.

9. Quote from May 1912, in McKenzie, "Bryan in Miami."

10. Paul S. George, "Miami: One Hundred Years of History," *South Florida History Magazine* 24 (Summer 1996); "Miami," *Comm.*, December 1920, 15; *Memoirs*, 435–36; Marvin Dunn, *Black Miami in the Twentieth Century* (Gainesville, FL, 1997), 51–78.

11. *San Francisco Examiner*, 7/6/1915; WJB to German ambassador, quoted in Levine, DF, 62; *Comm.*, February 1916, 5.

12. In defending Ford, Bryan drew upon his favorite source of metaphors: "If any of the people on the ark had been making money out of the flood, they would probably have ridiculed Noah for sending out the dove." "The Peace Mission," *Comm.*, December 1915, 2. Also see WJB to CWB, 12/25/1915, BPOXY, File 5. On the Gore-McLemore resolutions, see Ernest R. May, *The World War and American Isolation, 1914–1917* (Cambridge, 1959), 182–89; Alex M. Arnett, *Claude Kitchin and the Wilson War Policies* (Boston, 1937), 116.

13. WJB to Daniels, 2/4/1916, BPLC, Box 69. Also see WJB to Daniels, 2/22/1916, on Wilson's unchristian behavior.

14. WW to Edith Bolling Galt, 9/23/1915, *The Papers of Woodrow Wilson* (Princeton, 1980), vol. 34, 510–11.

15. *New Republic*, March 1915, quoted in Arthur S. Link, *Wilson: The New Freedom* (Princeton, 1956), 112; Reed quoted in Rosenstone, *Romantic Revolutionary*, 175–76; *Memoirs*, 329–30.

16. John E. White, Chickasha, OK, to WJB, 4/21/1916, Anonymous, Providence, RI, to WJB, 3/8/1916, "A Committee of S.E.N.," Johnson City, TN, to WJB, March 1916 (no day), all BPLC, Box 31. The latter warned, "Now don't consider this as an idle threat—where ever you are—in Hotels, trains, RR or trolleys, from this time to July 1st you will be under the strictest surveilance [*sic*]." *Comm.*, April 1916, 1, 15.

17. Wilson speech of 5/27/1916, quoted in Robert E. Hannigan, *The New World Power: American Foreign Policy, 1898–1917* (Philadelphia, 2002), 252.

18. MBB quoted in Coletta, *Bryan*, vol. 3, 34. For examples of Bryan's reporting, see *Comm.*, June 1916, 12ff.

19. Wilson quoted in Coletta, *Bryan*, vol. 3, 37.

20. Quotes from *Official Proceedings of the Democratic National Convention, 1916* (n.p., 1917), 94–100. Also see "Bryan Extols President," NYT, 6/16/1916, 1–2.

21. TR quoted in Kathleen Dalton, *Theodore Roosevelt: A Strenuous Life* (New York, 2002), 466; Gladden to WJB, 7/4/1916, BPLC, Box 31; Sheldon to WJB, 7/7/1916, BPLC, Box 31. Sheldon did say that he could vote for neither major party candidate "as long as their parties keep silent on the great moral and spiritual issues you were brave enough to mention in your speech." However, he endorsed Wilson late that fall.

22. Quoted in an article by David Lawrence of the *New York Evening Post*, reprinted in *Comm.*, December 1916, 20. Hughes was not as conservative as Taft, but Bryan paid no attention to the nuances of his views.

23. Democratic leaflet from Perry, OK, 10/7/1916, BPLC, Box 31. For quotes from party activists, see Levine, DF, 79–80.

24. See the sophisticated analysis of the 1916 campaign and results in David Sarasohn, *The Party of Reform: Democrats in the Progressive Era* (Jackson, MS, 1989), 192–238.

25. WJB letter to the members of the U.S. Senate and House of Representatives, 3/28/1917, BPLC, Box 31; London cited by Louis Lochner to WJB, 3/10/1917, BPLC, Box 31.

26. WJB to CWB, 3/26/1917, quoted in Coletta, *Bryan,* vol. 3, 53.

27. Parker telegram to WJB, 3/4/1917, BPLC, Box 31; Elijah Knott to WJB, 2/6/1917, BPLC, Box 31; CR, 64th Congress, 2nd session, 2/5/1917, 2648, 2650. Thanks to George Packer, Huddleston's grandson, for sending me a copy of this interchange. On his grandfather's political odyssey, see Packer's eloquent *Blood of the Liberals* (New York, 2000).

28. NYT, 4/6/1917, 1. Thirty-two Republicans, most from the Midwest, opposed the declaration of war, as did Meyer London, the lone Socialist in the House, and a Prohibitionist from California. London was the only easterner to vote no. Kitchin quoted in Arnett, *Claude Kitchin,* 227–35. Like most Bryanites from the South, Kitchin had taken part in the campaign to disenfranchise black voters; Arnett, *Claude Kitchin,* 23. Three of the six senators who voted against going to war were Democrats. Only one, the race-baiting populist James Vardaman of Mississippi, was a longtime Bryan supporter.

29. Ralph Easley to George Creel, 8/10/1917, American Federation of Labor Papers, Reel 87, George Meany Memorial Archives, Silver Spring, MD. Thanks to Grace Palladino for this reference.

30. WJB to Rep. B. C. Hilliard (D-Colo.), 4/3/1917, BPLC, Box 31.

31. Henry Pinkham, Melrose, MA, to WJB, 6/12/1917, and F. M. Collord, Waterloo, IA, to MBB, 4/11/17, both BPLC, Box 31. Supportive mail came, for example, from the left-wing philanthropist George Foster Peabody, Saratoga Springs, NY, to WJB, 4/23/1917; a Western mining executive, Fred Emerson Brooks, San Francisco, to WJB, 5/18/1917; and a lawyer from Anderson, South Carolina, Samuel M. Wolfe to WJB, 6/30/1917, all BPLC, Box 31. See also *Comm.,* August 1917, 1.

32. On Bryan's wartime speeches, see "Col. Bryan in Lewiston," *Comm.,* January 1918, 10; "The War," *Comm.,* June 1918, 3; Levine, DF, 93–102.

33. Quoted in K. Austin Kerr, *Organized for Prohibition: A New History of the Anti-Saloon League* (New Haven, 1985), 193.

34. Clipping from an unnamed Philadelphia newspaper, 3/16/1915 in BSB-NSHS, Reel 1; *Washington Wife: Journal of Ellen Maury Slayden from 1897–1919* (New York, 1962), 292; Horace Hood to WJB, 1/3/1917, BPLC, Box 31. Also see Arthur Barton (of Texas ASL) to WJB, 1/25/1917; Thomas B. Felder (Atlanta) to WJB, 1/22/1917; J. A. White (of Ohio ASL) to WJB, 1/23/1917, all in BPLC, Box 31.

35. Samuel Quinn to WJB, 12/7/1916, BPLC, Box 31; William Anthony McGuire to WJB, 2/7/1917 and 2/24/1917, BPLC, Box 31; Richard Gradwell to WJB, 9/25/1919, BPLC, Box 32; NYT, 6/3/1920, 18; 6/4/1920, 10; 6/14/1920, 10; Kevin Brownlow, *Behind the Mask of Innocence* (New York, 1990), 128–30.

36. Bryan, "Prohibition," *Comm.,* January 1916, 13.

37. Sheldon to WJB, 7/7/1916, BPLC, Box 31; Shailer Matthews (president of Federal Council of Churches) to WJB, 10/11/1915, BPLC, Box 30; Sunday quoted in Robert F. Martin, *Hero of the Heartland: Billy Sunday and the Transformation of American Society,*

1862–1935 (Bloomington, 2002), 105–6. On Sunday's relationship with the Bryans, see Roger A. Bruns, *Preacher: Billy Sunday and Big-Time American Evangelism* (New York, 1992), 111, 174; Sunday to MBB, 1/15/1915, BPLC, Box 30. The 1915 meeting in Philadelphia where Bryan got mobbed by adoring students was part of a Sunday campaign.

38. Zurcher also hailed Bryan's anti-war stand. Zurcher, North Evans, NY, to WJB, 2/20/1917, BPLC, Box 31; Zurcher, "The Catholic Mind on Prohibition," *Comm.*, March 1918, 7. Quote from W. E. Colby's skit "The Rube and the Ragamuffin," American Memory Collection, Library of Congress, 2.

39. In 1912, both the Progressives and Socialists endorsed woman suffrage, but neither major party did. Soon after that election, Will asked his brother, "Can't prohibition be delayed until the women get a vote?" WJB to CWB, 12/12/1912, BPOXY, File 13/14. For the views of the Sorosis Club that MBB led, I am indebted to Barbara Sommer's research and her unpublished lecture, "Mary Baird Bryan, Helpmate." In author's possession.

40. The GOP took a similar stand that year. *National Party Platforms, 1840–1972*, compiled by Donald Bruce Johnson and Kirk H. Porter (Chicago, 1973), 199, 207. On Democrats, see Marjorie Spruill Wheeler, *New Women of the New South: The Leaders of the Woman Suffrage Movement in the Southern States* (New York, 1993), 19–20, 147. See Bryan's developing arguments about suffrage in *Comm.*, July 1914, 3; November 1914, 2; March 1916, 10–11; and August 1916, 1; Levine, DF, 128–30.

41. MBB to WJB, 3/23/1916, BPLC, Box 31. Also see Carrie Chapman Catt to MBB, 8/26/1916, and Anna Gordon to MBB, 4/13/1917, both BPLC, Box 31.

42. *Comm.*, January 1920, 1.

43. S. K. Huntsman to WJB, 7/17/1918, BPLC, Box 31. The following section is based on Levine, DF, 132–47; Coletta, *Bryan*, vol. 3, 83–102; Kendrick A. Clements, *William Jennings Bryan: Missionary Isolationist* (Knoxville, 1982), 127–35.

44. J. M. Baer to WJB, 1/16/1918, BPLC, Box 31; WJB to WW, 1/15/1918, quoted in Coletta, *Bryan*, vol. 3, 84. Also see Coletta, *Bryan*, vol. 3, 83–85, and WJB to Josephus Daniels, 12/13/1917, Daniels Papers, Box 69.

45. WW to Daniels, 11/16/1918, Daniels Papers, Box 110.

46. The most complete and recent study is John Milton Cooper Jr., *Breaking the Heart of the World: Woodrow Wilson and the Fight for the League of Nations* (Cambridge, UK, 2001).

47. *Comm.*, March 1919, 1.

48. Ibid., 2; the program is printed in *Comm.*, January 1919, 5. The *Times* mentioned only Bryan's plan for the nationalization of railroads, essentially the same one he had proposed in 1906, and not his larger program. NYT, 2/7/1919, 4.

49. WJB to Hamilton Holt, 9/17/1921, BPLC, Box 34. This had been Bryan's position on the League since Wilson returned from Paris more than two years before. See Coletta, *Bryan*, vol. 3, 96–98.

50. On this irony, see Coletta, *Bryan*, vol. 3, 85.

51. Quoted in Coletta, *Bryan*, vol. 3, 96.

CHAPTER TWELVE: SAVE THE CHILDREN, 1920–1925

1. WJB, *Orthodox Christianity Versus Modernism* (New York, 1923), 29.

2. George Eliot, *Middlemarch* (New York, 1964 [1872]), 481.

3. Amy Howley to WJB, 1/18/1923, BPLC, Box 36.

4. NYT, 8/8/1922, 7.

5. For an excellent discussion of *Inherit's* text and context, see Edward J. Larson, *Summer for the Gods: The Scopes Trial and America's Continuing Debate over Science and Evolution* (Cambridge, MA, 1997), 239–45. For the scholarly debate, see Richard Hofstadter, *Anti-Intellectualism in American Life* (New York, 1963), 127–29; Ray Ginger, *Six Days or Forever? Tennessee v. John Thomas Scopes* (New York, 1974); Stephen Jay Gould, "William Jennings Bryan's Last Campaign," NH 77 (Fall/Winter 1996), 177–83, originally published in *Natural History*, November 1987; Garry Wills, *Under God: Religion and American Politics* (New York, 1990), 97–107; James Gilbert, *Redeeming Culture: American Religion in an Age of Science* (Chicago, 1997), 23–35. Alan Dershowitz writes empathetically about Bryan's position in his introduction to a reprint of Clarence Darrow's *The Story of My Life* (Chicago, 1996 [1932]), vii–xi. Also see Constance Areson Clark, "Evolution for John Doe: Pictures, the Public, and the Scopes Trial Debate," *Journal of American History* 87 (March 2001), 1275–303, and Ronald L. Numbers, *Darwinism Comes to America* (Cambridge, MA, 1998), 76–91.

6. WJB, *In His Image* (New York, 1922), 136.

7. *The Fundamentals* was not listed in an inventory done in the early 1920s of the books at Bryan's home in Miami, and I have found no evidence that he quoted from it. "Book Inventory—Villa Serena," BPLC, Box 51, #1.

8. Quoted in Bradley J. Longfield, *The Presbyterian Controversy: Fundamentalists, Modernists, and Moderates* (New York, 1991), 74. Lawrence Levine did take this approach in DF, 269–70, as did Willard H. Smith in *The Social and Religious Thought of William Jennings Bryan* (Lawrence, KS, 1975), 167–218.

9. WJB, "The Bible and Its Enemies," pamphlet of speech delivered at Moody Bible Institute (Chicago, 1921), 43.

10. WJB, "The Origin of Man," in *In His Image* (New York, 1922), 86. This address was widely distributed as a pamphlet with the title "The Menace of Darwinism." Bryan told a supporter in 1924 that he didn't "regard" the teaching of Darwinism "as a political issue and do not discuss it in my campaign speeches, although I believe that nine tenths of the Christian people reject the idea that man is a descendent of the brutes." WJB to W. A. McRae (of Palm Beach), 4/5/1924, BPLC, Box 39.

11. Dr. J. Thomas Kelley Jr. to WJB, 2/7/1922, BPLC, Box 35; Dr. C. P. Fall to WJB, 8/5/1922, BPLC, Box 35; urinalysis report from unnamed laboratory in Chicago, 1/17/1923, BPLC, Box 36; WJB to J. Fred Essery, *Baltimore Sun*, 2/15/1922, BPLC, Box 35; Charles Morrow Wilson, *The Commoner: William Jennings Bryan* (Garden City, NY, 1970), 397–98. On early administrations of the drug, see Chris Feudtner, *Bittersweet: Diabetes, Insulin, and the Transformation of Illness* (Chapel Hill, 2003), 6–9.

12. WJB to Rev. J. Frank Norris, 5/1/1923, BPLC, Box 37; WJB to Mrs. R. L. Goss, 4/15/1925, BPLC, Box 40; WJB to "my dear grandchildren," 4/17/1925, BPLC, Box 40; WJB to Superintendent Swift, Harrisburg, PA, 3/5/1919, BPLC, Box 32; Coletta, *Bryan*, vol. 3, 119.

13. Howard Glenn McKenzie, "William Jennings Bryan in Miami, 1915–1925," M.A. thesis, University of Miami, 1956, 97–100; Levine, DF, 237–40; *Miami Herald*, 11/25/1920, 1; *Comm.*, December 1920, 15; WJB to Rotary Club of Miami, 11/16/1913, BPLC, Box 38.

As with most other aspects of Bryan's financial history, there appear to be no records of exactly how much he was paid to boost Coral Gables.

14. GBH Bio, unpaginated preface; WJB to WJB Jr., 6/17/1922, BPOXY, File 21/22.

15. Ruth Bryan Owen to WJB, 11/23/1919, BPLC, Box 32; Sarah Pauline Vickers, "The Life of Ruth Bryan Owen: Florida's First Congresswoman and America's First Woman Diplomat," Ph.D. diss., Florida State University, 1994, 42–55; author interview with Rudd Brown, 4/17/2004, Pasadena, CA; *Comm.*, August 1921, 15.

16. This point was first made by Lawrence Levine in DF.

17. Bryan gave Theodore Roosevelt credit for proposing the latter reform "in one of his later messages." "Statement by WJB," 4/1/1924, BPLC, Box 39.

18. WJB, "The Farmers Aroused," *Comm.*, February 1922, 2.

19. Bryan article, reprinted in *Comm.*, April 1920, 10. On the anti-prostitution efforts of Christian activists, see Gaines M. Foster, *Moral Reconstruction: Christian Lobbyists and the Federal Legislation of Morality, 1865–1920* (Chapel Hill, 2002), 140–46; Ruth Rosen, *The Lost Sisterhood* (Baltimore, 1982).

20. *Comm.*, February 1920, 1.

21. Ibid., October 1919, 5; February 1920, 1; March 1920, 5; George H. Boyd, Washington, DC, to WJB, 2/11/1920, BPLC, Box 33.

22. WJB to CWB, 1/3/1920, BPOXY, #13–14; WJB to CWB, undated but probably written in February 1920, BPOXY, #5.

23. *Comm.*, March 1920, 1, quoted in Coletta, *Bryan*, vol. 3, 125; *Literary Digest*, 6/12/1920, 20. The top three vote-getters, in order, were William G. McAdoo, Woodrow Wilson, and Edward Edwards.

24. WJB quoted in *Literary Digest*, 6/12/1920, 18. On the lineup of forces at the convention, see Coletta, *Bryan*, vol. 3, 122–24; Douglas B. Craig, *After Wilson: The Struggle for the Democratic Party, 1920–1934* (Chapel Hill, 1992), 15–18.

25. WJB quoted in Coletta, *Bryan*, vol. 3, 129; Cox quoted in Craig, *After Wilson*, 21. Also see James E. Cebula, *James M. Cox: Journalist and Politician* (New York, 1985).

26. WJB quotes from Cebula, *James M. Cox*, 104; NYT, 7/7/1920, 1; WJB to Pat Harrison, 8/9/1920, BPLC, Box 33.

27. *Comm.*, January 1921, 1; February 1921, 1; and July 1921, 1.

28. Bryan recordings, 1921, on Gennett label, in Recorded Sound Division, Library of Congress.

29. One of Bryan's talks in Pittsburgh was heard as far away as Arkansas, Cuba, and Canada. W. O. Green to WJB, 3/12/1922, BPLC, Box 35; P. H. Barker to WJB, 3/18/1922, BPLC, Box 35. On his talk in Los Angeles, see *Bridal Call*, October 1924, 32. Bryan, accompanied by a string quartet, recorded for the Gennett label in Richmond, Indiana; Lyell Rader to WJB, 1/18/1922, BPLC, Box 35; "Mr. Bryan's Bible Talks," *Comm.*, August 1922, 7. In 1924, a Miami company offered to arrange regular broadcasts of Bryan's Sunday lessons. But he declined, citing the problem of competition with the printed version, which he claimed reached at least ten million people. Fred Mizer to WJB, 3/5/1924, and WJB to Mizer, 3/8/1924, both BPLC, Box 39. On the avidity with which Protestant preachers took to the air, see Tona J. Hangen, *Redeeming the Dial: Radio, Religion and Popular Culture in America* (Chapel Hill, 2002), 21–25.

30. Harry Emerson Fosdick, "A Reply to Mr. Bryan in the Name of Religion," NYT, 3/12/1922; Ronald Numbers, *The Creationists* (New York, 1992), 40.

31. Robert S. Lynd and Helen Merrell Lynd, *Middletown: A Study in Modern Culture* (New York, 1929), 317, 331.

32. Friedlander to WJB, 3/16/1924, BPLC, Box 39. Also see Miami YMHA to WJB, 3/29/1921, BPLC, Box 33; Charles Beaver, Los Angeles, to WJB, 9/19/1923, BPLC, Box 37; "Libelling the Jews," *Comm.*, December 1920, 2; WJB to anonymous "friend," c. 1924, BPLC, Box 41. On anti-Catholicism, see the letters from Robert R. Hull, associate editor of *Our Sunday Visitor,* to WJB, 6/27/1923 and 8/25/1923, BPLC, Box 41. Father George Zurcher also supported Bryan's views on evolution. Zurcher to WJB, 12/15/1922, BPLC, Box 34.

33. The following section is indebted to Mark A. Noll, *A History of Christianity in the United States and Canada* (Grand Rapids, 1992), 360–89; George M. Marsden, *Fundamentalism and American Culture: The Shaping of Twentieth-Century Evangelicalism, 1870–1925* (New York, 1980), 141–84.

34. His membership certificate is in BPLC, Box 40. Of course, his affiliation didn't prevent attacks on him by speakers at annual meetings of the AAAS, before and after he joined. See "A New Oligarchy," *Comm.*, January 1923, 3; *Science,* 2/6/1925, 148–49; NYT, 12/31/1924, 15.

35. Kellogg, *Headquarters Nights,* quoted in Gould, "Bryan's Last Campaign," 180; Kidd, *The Science of Power* (London, 1918), 102. The latter went through nine different editions by 1920.

36. WJB, *In His Image* (New York, 1922), 7. The invitation specifically asked Bryan to counter "those who in our time have been disturbed and confused by current skepticism and who are none too ready to listen to professional teachers of religion." W. W. Moore, president of the seminary, to WJB, 5/21/1921, BPLC, Box 34.

37. WJB, *In His Image,* 112.

38. Ibid., 119, 110, 27.

39. Ibid., 121–22.

40. Lippmann, *American Inquisitors: A Commentary on Dayton and Chicago* (New York, 1928), 14.

41. For sales figures, see Guy T. Viskniskki to WJB, 12/11/1922, BPLC, Box 36; Sheldon to WJB, 2/28/1921, BPLC, Box 34; Sheldon to WJB, 12/29/1922, BPLC, Box 36; Owen to WJB, 3/9/1921, BPLC, Box 34; Robins to WJB, 8/25/1921, BPLC, Box 34; Hylan to WJB, 6/21/1923, BPLC, Box 37; Post to WJB, 3/23/22, Post Papers, Library of Congress, Box 1. Also see Mark Edwards, "Rethinking the Failure of Fundamentalist Political Antievolutionism After 1925," *Fides et Historia* 32 (Summer/Fall 2000), 96–99. The leading figure in the Mormon Church also endorsed Bryan's views. Heber Grant to WJB, 2/26/1921, BPLC, Box 33.

42. Ransom, Canal Point, FL, to WJB, 3/3/1923, BPLC, Box 37; Rev. T. M. Tankersley, Brooklyn, to WJB, 4/14/1923, BPLC, Box 37. For a similar view from an alienated student at the University of Chicago, see Frank H. Nelson to WJB, 2/23/1923, BPLC, Box 37.

43. D. Hayden Parry, Middlebury, to WJB, 11/9/1921; A. G. Slaught, Rochester, to WJB, 12/1/1921; Edward S. Worcester, Madison, to WJB, 10/2/1921, and WJB to Worcester, 10/4/1921, all BPLC, Box 34.

44. WJB to Annette Parkman Smith, Los Angeles, 1/31/1923, BPLC, Box 36. Bryan engaged in several debates through the mail with other Christian evolutionists. For example, he had a lengthy correspondence with William Keen, an eminent surgeon in his eighties who wrote the book *I Believe in God and Evolution*. WJB to Keen, 6/24/1922 and 7/29/1922; Keen to WJB, 7/18/1922, all BPLC, Box 35.

45. Fosdick in NYT, 3/12/1922; Fosdick, "Shall the Fundamentalists Win?" reprinted in *Christian Work* 102 (June 10, 1922). Both texts are widely available on the Internet. The fullest study of the intradenominational conflict is Bradley J. Longfield, *The Presbyterian Controversy: Fundamentalists, Modernists and Moderates* (New York, 1991).

46. Coletta, *Bryan*, vol. 3, 224. The motion is quoted in Longfield, *Presbyterian Controversy*, 74.

47. WJB to Graham Patterson, 6/10/1922, BPLC, Box 35.

48. *Memoirs*, 10.

49. WJB summarized and defended his speech in "Bryan Says North Would Act as South on Negro Question," NYT 3/18/1923, Sect. 8, 1. He favored no restrictions based on race "where the percentage of blacks is small compared with the total population."

50. W. Thomas Soders to WJB, 2/25/1923, BPLC, Box 36; WJB to Soders, 3/3/1923, BPLC, Box 37. During the Great Depression, Soders moved to Chicago and founded a grassroots group, John Brown Organization of Cook County, which protested the lack of jobs for black residents; see xroads.virginia.edu/~UG00/30n1/worldfair/plantsho.htm. A month after his interchange with Soders, Bryan received an admiring letter from a black man in Chicago who denied that most of his people wanted to mix with whites, although he concluded, "You must pardon my liberty and don't crush the poor defenseless negro." William Fennick to WJB, 4/3/1923, BPLC, Box 37.

51. Undated letter but probably late 1919, quoted in Coletta, *Bryan*, vol. 3, 116.

52. According to Bryan, black delegates voted for his opponent by a 23–8 margin. WJB to Rev. D. S. Kennedy, 6/12/1923, BPLC, Box 37.

53. R. A. Nestos to WJB, BPLC, Box 36. On the league, see Robert L. Morlan, *Political Prairie Fire: The Nonpartisan League, 1915–1922* (Minneapolis, 1952).

54. Evangeline Booth to WJB, 6/19/1923, BPLC, Box 37.

55. On these groups, see Norman F. Furniss, *The Fundamentalist Controversy, 1918–1931* (New Haven, 1954), 49–75.

56. See the accounts in Numbers, *Creationists*, 41–44; Levine, DF, 270–71.

57. WJB to Senator W. J. Singleterry, 4/11/1923, BPLC, Box 37; WJB to Senator John A. Shelton, 2/9/1925, BPLC, Box 40.

58. Stroder to WJB, 1/30/1924, BPLC, Box 39; Walton to WJB, 5/26/1923, BPLC, Box 37.

59. R. M. Whitney, *Reds in America* (New York, 1924); Christopher Capozzola, "The Only Badge Needed Is Your Patriotic Fervor: Vigilance, Coercion, and the Law in World War I America," *Journal of American History* (March 2002). The Klan, whose state affiliates acted autonomously, was far from united about the need to fight Darwinism. See Furniss, *Controversy*, 37–38.

60. Walsh to WJB, 12/20/1922 and WJB to Walsh, 12/30/1922, both BPLC, Box 36. On the cultural politics of the KKK, see Stanley Coben, *Rebellion Against Victorianism: The Impetus for Cultural Change in 1920s America* (New York, 1991), 136–56; Kathleen Blee,

Women of the Klan: Racism and Gender in the 1920s (Berkeley, 1991); Leonard Moore, *Citizen Klansmen: The Ku Klux Klan in Indiana, 1921–1928* (Chapel Hill, 1991).

61. FDR to WJB, 6/20/1923, BPLC, Box 37.

62. Larry G. Osnes, "Charles W. Bryan: Latter-Day Populist and Rural Progressive," Ph.D. diss., University of Cincinnati, 1970, 284–88, 336; WJB to CWB, 12/21/1923, BPOXY, #5–6.

63. WJB official statement for the 1924 Florida primary, in BPLC, Box 56. "A Word of Farewell," *Comm.*, 4/1923, 1.

64. Anonymous "common laborer" from Wenatchee, WA, to WJB, 6/29/1924, BPLC, Box 39; S. M. Partridge, Los Angeles, to WJB, 6/19/1924, BPLC, Box 39.

65. For fine, if quite different, analyses of urban culture in the 1920s, see Lizabeth Cohen, *Making a New Deal* (Cambridge, 1991) on Chicago, and Ann Douglas, *Terrible Honesty: Mongrel Manhattan in the 1920s* (New York, 1995).

66. Robert A. Slayton, *Empire Statesman: The Rise and Redemption of Al Smith* (New York, 2001), 171–88.

67. Robert K. Murray, *The 103rd Ballot: Democrats and the Disaster in Madison Square Garden* (New York, 1976), 115 and passim.

68. Bryan's speech in the June 28 debate was reprinted as "Religious Liberty" (Miami, 1924), copy in BPLC, Box 49. On the debate, see Murray, *103rd Ballot*, 148–62. The KKK also went unmentioned that year in the 1924 platforms of the Republican and Progressive parties.

69. NYT, 7/3/1924, 3. Rogers, who hailed from Oklahoma, was actually quite fond of Bryan; the two men were under contract for the same syndicate and often worked alongside each other. *Convention Articles of Will Rogers*, ed. Joseph A. Stout Jr. (Stillwater, OK, 1976), 87 (quote), 79.

70. Davis quoted in Craig, *After Wilson*, 57.

71. WJB quoted in Craig, *After Wilson*, 59; Johnson and Porter, *Party Platforms*, 243–52.

72. Rogers spoke the line in a short talk he delivered in 1930, but he may have used a version of it earlier. Thanks to Steven K. Gragert, editor of the papers of Will Rogers, for tracking it down. Gragert e-mails to author, 8/11/2004, 12/29/2004.

   According to his biographer, CWB's kind words for La Follette "raised speculation" that he hoped the House of Representatives would be too divided to choose a president from the three nominees, leaving the progressive majority in the Senate to elect him over Charles Dawes, the conservative Republican nominee for vice president (who, ironically, was also a resident of Lincoln). CWB, of course, denied the rumor. Osnes, "Latter-Day Populist," 334–35.

73. Letters on religious topics include Charles Keppel to WJB, 1/18 and 4/15/1925, and George Zurcher to WJB, 3/23/1925, all BPLC, Box 40. The invitation from attorney Sue K. Hicks is reprinted in *Memoirs*, 483. WJB to WJB Jr., 6/17/1925, BPOXY, file #21–22.

74. Scopes usually taught only math and physics. John T. Scopes and James Presley, *Center of the Storm: Memoirs of John T. Scopes* (New York, 1967), 33, 60.

75. Transcript, 316.

76. WJB to Fundamentalist Convention, Memphis, TN, no date but c. June 1925, BPLC, Box 40; Clarence Darrow, *The Story of My Life* (New York, 1996 [1932]), 277.

77. Mencken, column of 7/16/1925, excerpted in www.law.umkc.edu/faculty/projects/ftrials/scopes/menk.htm; Darrow, *My Life*, 249.

78. Larson, *Summer*, 87–92; Charles Reagan Wilson, "The South, Religion, and the Scopes Trial," www.vanderbilt.edu/rpw_center/scope/htm. On social changes in the eastern part of the state more generally, see Jeanette Keith, *Country People in the New South: Tennessee's Upper Cumberland* (Chapel Hill, 1995).

79. Scopes and Presley, *Center of the Storm*, 26–27.

80. Transcript, 78.

81. Ibid., 153, 154, 164.

82. For Bryan's address, see ibid., 170–82; George William Hunter, *A Civic Biology: Presented in Problems* (New York, 1914), 194–95.

83. Hunter, *Civic Biology*, 261–63. At the end of the chapter, the author did briefly recommend cleaning up slum districts to help produce "a stronger race," but his emphasis was clearly on eugenics. Ibid., 264–65. Stephen Jay Gould first drew attention to these passages in "Bryan's Last Campaign," 182–83.

84. Transcript, 183–84.

85. Ibid., 185, 187, 188.

86. Bryan quoted in Coletta, *Bryan*, vol. 3, 253.

87. Transcript, 202, 205; Larson, *Summer*, 182–83.

88. WJB to Sue Hicks, 6/10/1925; Hicks to WJB, 6/12/1925 and 6/13/1925, all BPLC, Box 47; Jeffrey P. Moran, "The Scopes Trial and Southern Fundamentalism in Black and White: Race, Region, and Religion," *Journal of Southern History* 70 (February 2004), 95–120.

89. The only member of the jury she respected was a man "who looked exactly like a Kentucky colonel." He dressed "quite like a natty gentleman—like a rose among humble thistles." MBB, "First Bulletin," 7/11/1925, in GBH Bio., chapter IX.

90. MBB, "Bulletin No. 2," 7/20/1925, in GBH Bio. In 1940, Grace wrote to former prosecutor Sue Hicks, "Mother was greatly opposed to father's activities in assisting the passage of the anti-evolution laws in several States. Mother did all she could to prevent father from taking part in the Scopes trial." Quoted in Larson, *Summer*, 199. Nothing in her bulletins, however, was that explicit.

91. Transcript, 225–26.

92. For the entire cross-examination, see ibid., 284–304.

93. On the age-day thesis of many anti-evolutionists, see Numbers, *Creationists*, 11.

94. Transcript, 287.

95. Ibid., 288, 301.

96. Ibid., 290. One religious historian comments, "As Bryan's testimony at Dayton revealed, his grasp of Hebrew narratives in the Old Testament was less keen than his sense of democratic politics and the interests of ordinary citizens." D. G. Hart, *The Lost Soul of American Protestantism* (Lanham, MD, 2002), 103.

97. Transcript, 304. Mary Bryan wrote to her children that the judge called an adjournment at this point because he feared for Darrow's life: "the gunmen in the audience thought Darrow was about to lay hold of Papa in the heat of the debate and one of them had his hand on his gun, saying afterwards that if Darrow had taken hold of Papa Darrow would never have left the platform alive." MBB, 7/25/1925, quoted in

Coletta, *Bryan*, vol. 3, 270. But Larson's *Summer*, the most complete study of the trial, does not mention this allegation, which at one stroke confirmed Mary's low opinion of the "mountain people" and mitigated her husband's poor performance on the stand.

98. Transcript, 305.

99. NYT, 7/21/1925, 2; Larson, *Summer*, 190–91; NYT, 7/23/1925, 9; Donald F. Brod, "The Scopes Trial: A Look at Press Coverage After Forty Years," *Journalism Quarterly* 42 (1965), 219–26.

100. Interview with Associated Press, NYT, 7/25/1925, 10.

101. According to Bryan's physician in Washington, DC, he died, like his father, of diabetes, with "the immediate cause being the fatigue incident to the heat and his extraordinary exertions due to the Scopes Trial." But the doctor, J. Thomas Kelley Jr., was not present in Dayton, and no autopsy was conducted. Kelley to Grace Bryan Hargreaves, 6/25/1931, BPLC, Box 40.

102. Transcript, 338.

103. Ibid., 338–39.

EPILOGUE: THE FATE OF A CHRISTIAN LIBERAL

1. Dreiser was referring to Bryan in 1896. Dreiser, *The Titan*, Trilogy of Desire, vol. 2 (New York, 1974 [1914]), 400.

2. NYT, 7/30/1925, 1–4; *Memoirs*, 488–90. Also see shorter reports in *New York World*, 7/30/1925, 2, and the Associated Press report published in numerous papers that day.

3. Undated quote, Garry Wills, *Under God: Religion and American Politics* (New York, 1990), 102.

4. *New York World*, 7/29/1925, 1.

5. None of his previous biographers sheds light on the decision, and I have found no documents by either Mary or Will that discuss it.

6. *Bartlett's Familiar Quotations*, 15th ed. (Boston, 1980), 336.

7. *Memoirs*, 493.

8. *New York World*, 7/28/1925, 10; "William Jennings Bryan," *New Republic* 8/12/1925, reprinted in *The Faces of Five Decades: Selections from Fifty Years of* The New Republic, *1914–1964*, ed. Robert B. Luce (New York, 1964), 129–32.

9. Quoted in Terry Teachout, *The Skeptic: A Life of H. L. Mencken* (New York, 2002), 220.

10. Mencken, "In Memoriam: W.J.B.," *Prejudices: Fifth Series* (New York, 1926), 68, 71, 64.

11. Ibid., 74. Mencken mentioned the Christian Endeavor Society and the Epworth League.

12. Richard Hofstadter, *The American Political Tradition* (New York, 1948), 193–94; Teachout, *The Skeptic*, 221. Hofstadter acknowledged a debt to the condescending biography by Paxton Hibben, *The Peerless Leader: William Jennings Bryan* (New York, 1929). Bryan also plays a nefarious role in Hofstadter's *Anti-Intellectualism in America* (New York, 1963). For the anti-populist views of this cohort of thinkers, see *The Radical Right*, ed. Daniel Bell (New York, 1963) and my *The Populist Persuasion: An American History*, rev. ed. (Ithaca, 1998), 190–93.

13. Teachout, *The Skeptic*, 276–97; Ronald Steel, "Mr. Fix-It," *New York Review of Books*, 10/5/2000, 19.

14. Will Rogers, "Bryan Missed the White House, but Not Hearts of the Plain People," *Sioux City Sunday Journal*, 8/9/1925, 13, in BPOXY, Scrapbooks, Reel 2, Item 12; Charles Rosser, *The Crusading Commoner* (Dallas, 1937), 317; Vernon Dalhart, "William Jennings Bryan's Last Fight," Columbia Records #15039. Thanks to Stephen Wade, master singer and folklorist, who made a tape of this and other country songs about WJB.

15. Henry was the great-great-great-grandson of Patrick Henry. Robert Henry address to Bryan Memorial Service, Houston, 8/2/1925, BPLC, Box 40; Charlie Oakes, "The Death of William Jennings Bryan," Vocalion 15094.

16. "Address Made by Ambassador Josephus Daniels," Philadelphia, 6/24/1936, BPNSHS.

17. On Ruth, see Sarah Pauline Vickers, "The Life of Ruth Bryan Owen: Florida's First Congresswoman and American's First Woman Diplomat," Ph.D. diss., Florida State University, 1994, 66–127; Blanche Wiesen Cook, *Eleanor Roosevelt*, vol. 2: *1933–1938* (New York, 1999), 68–69, 377–78. On William Junior, see his address in Lincoln on the centennial of his father's birth in 1960, in Bryan, *The Credo of the Commoner*, ed. Franklin Modisett (Los Angeles, 1968), 126–31; Greg Mitchell, *The Campaign of the Century: Upton Sinclair's Race for Governor of California and the Birth of Media Politics* (New York, 1992), 214, 447–48; on Grace, see her letters to Josephus Daniels in Daniels Papers, Library of Congress, Reel 44. Ruth's daughter, Helen Rudd, also became a liberal Democratic activist in California during the 1950s and ran, unsuccessfully, for Congress.

18. "Address made by Ambassador Josephus Daniels at the William Jennings Bryan Breakfast…, June 24, 1936," BPNSHS, #464; "Roosevelt's Bryan Tribute," NYT, 5/4/1934, 2. The Borglum statue resided in a park near the Potomac River until the late 1950s, when it was shipped back to Salem. FDR had been privately critical of Bryan when they both served in the Wilson administration. But, chastened by the consequences of the Great War, he wrote to Daniels in the mid-1930s, "Would that W.J.B. had stayed on as Secretary of State—the country would have been better off." Quoted in Warren I. Cohen, *The American Revisionists: The Lessons of Intervention in World War I* (Chicago, 1967), 161.

19. On the flowering of this current after the Scopes trial, see Joel A. Carpenter, *Revive Us Again: The Reawakening of American Fundamentalism* (New York, 1997); annual catalogue, William Jennings Bryan University, 1930–31 through 1937–38. Thanks to Professor Travis Ricketts of Bryan University for sending me copies of these bulletins. In the 1930s, several fundamentalists did build followings on a combination of chiliastic anti-Semitism and accusations of elite conspiracies against ordinary white Protestants. But their politics was more akin to that of the Ku Klux Klan than to the tradition to which Bryan belonged. See Leo P. Ribuffo, *The Old Christian Right: The Protestant Far Right from the Great Depression to the Cold War* (Philadelphia, 1983).

20. Rice quoted in Kazin, *Populist Persuasion*, 152. Also see E. J. Dionne, "Faith Full," *The New Republic*, 2/28/2005, 12–14.

21. Ralph Reed, *Politically Incorrect: The Emerging Faith Factor in American Politics* (Dallas, 1994), 150–55. To avoid the controversy over Darwinism and "intelligent design" (an updated form of creationism), science teachers in many areas have circumvented the topic. Cornelia Dean, "Evolution Takes a Back Seat in U.S. Classes," NYT,

2/1/2005, D1; Peter Slevin, "Battle on Teaching Evolution Sharpens," *Washington Post*, 3/14/2005, A1.

22. Debs quoted in *New York World*, 7/28/1925, 2.

23. Levine, DF, 363.

24. FDR quoted in James A. Morone, *Hellfire Nation: The Politics of Sin in American History* (New Haven, 2003), 354; Doug Rossinow, " 'The Model of a Model Fellow Traveler': Harry F. Ward, the American League for Peace and Democracy, and the 'Russian Question' in American Politics, 1933–1956," *Peace and Change* 29 (April 2004), 177–220.

25. One can hear the introduction on numerous documentaries. For the southern civil rights movement as a revival, see David L. Chappell, *A Stone of Hope: Prophetic Religion and the Death of Jim Crow* (Chapel Hill, 2004).

26. Mario Cuomo, "In the American Catholic Tradition of Realism," *One Electorate Under God? A Dialogue on Religion and American Politics*, ed. E. J. Dionne Jr., Jean Bethke Elshtain, and Kayla M. Drogosz (Washington, DC, 2004), 17–18.

27. *Crowded Years: The Reminiscences of William Gibbs McAdoo* (Port Washington, NY, 1971 [1931]), 337. For a similar judgment by a respected political scientist, see Charles Edward Merriam, *Four American Party Leaders* (New York, 1926), 63.

28. Harper Lee, *To Kill a Mockingbird* (New York, 1960), 162. Thanks to Danny Kazin for noticing this line. See also John T. Scopes and James Presley, *Center of the Storm: Memoirs of John T. Scopes* (New York, 1967), 26–27; Bob Sheppard (a speech professor and the public address announcer in Yankee Stadium), quoted in "Yan-kee Ac-cent," *New Yorker*, 10/4/1993, 69.

29. Vachel Lindsay, "When Bryan Speaks," at www.worldwideschool.org/library/books/lit/poetry/ChineseNightingaleetal/chap3.html.

INDEX

A NOTE ABOUT THE AUTHOR

Michael Kazin is a professor of history at Georgetown University. He is the author of three previous books: *Barons of Labor: The San Francisco Building Trades and Union Power in the Progressive Era,* which won the Herbert Gutman Prize; *The Populist Persuasion: An American History;* and, with Maurice Isserman, *America Divided: The Civil War of the 1960s.* He is a frequent contributor to the *New York Times,* the *Washington Post,* the *Nation, Mother Jones,* the *American Prospect, Dissent,* and other periodicals. Kazin has received fellowships from the John Simon Guggenheim Memorial Foundation, the National Endowment for the Humanities, and the Woodrow Wilson Center, and has been a Fulbright fellow in the Netherlands and Japan. He lives near Washington, D.C., with his wife, Beth Horowitz, his two teenage children, Danny and Maia, and a dog named Zoe.

A NOTE ON THE TYPE

This book was set in Janson, a typeface long thought to have been made by the Dutchman Anton Janson, who was a practicing typefounder in Leipzig during the years 1668–1687. However, it has been conclusively demonstrated that these types are actually the work of Nicholas Kis (1650–1702), a Hungarian, who most probably learned his trade from the master Dutch typefounder Dirk Voskens. The type is an excellent example of the influential and sturdy Dutch types that prevailed in England up to the time William Caslon (1692–1766) developed his own incomparable designs from them.

Composed by North Market Street Graphics, Lancaster, Pennsylvania

Designed by Robert C. Olsson